A FRAMEWORK FOR CRITICAL THINKING

Understand that thinking critically is vital to your success in college and in the workplace. Critical thinking means asking questions, analyzing results, evaluating sources of information, and coming up with creative solutions to problems. *Keys for Writers* shows you how to apply critical thinking to your college writing, reading, research, and project design and presentation. When you see this small icon take some time to consider purpose, audience, voice, and medium, referring to this page for more help with each element.

PURPOSE	AUDIENCE
• What is/was the text meant to accomplish? Is that purpose explicit or implied? • What possibilities are there for creating a text that could meet that purpose? • Are there specific expectations the text must meet to achieve its intended purpose? If so, what are they?	• Who is the audience for this piece of writing? Is there more than one audience? If so, are their interests similar or competing? • What does the audience expect in terms of content, language use, tone, style, format, and delivery method? • If expectations are not met, what is the impact on the audience?
VOICE	**MEDIUM**
• What unique perspective does the author bring to this piece of writing? How is that unique perspective communicated? • How explicitly does/should the author make reference to his or her perspective? Does the author use I, and if so, when and why? • What is the author's tone in the piece of writing? For example, is it playful, serious, accusing, encouraging, hopeful, factual? What effect does that tone have on the piece of writing?	• How could the writing be delivered to its intended audience to meet its purpose? Via a blog posting? A printed essay? A Web site? A newspaper article? An academic journal article? An MP3 file? A YouTube video? • What formatting rules should the text follow in that medium? • What would the impact be of delivering the text in another medium?

 See the "KEY TO FEATURED CONTENT" on pages 651-653 for a quick reference guide to critical thinking, writing, reading, researching, and using media.

Thinking Critically About

DESIGN & MEDIA

PROCESSES FOR DESIGNING YOUR PROJECT

Plan a format and design for your finished project.

❶ Plan.

PURPOSE AUDIEN
VOICE MEDIUM

Use the Critical Thinking Framework to consider your context.

❷ Experiment.

Take time to try more than one medium. In any medium, try to get feedback from a classmate or colleague about your design elements (such as typeface and layout in a written document). If you're unfamiliar with the medium you think would best suit your context, find someone who can help you and consu a user's guide.

❸ Consider standard design principles.

Think about how to help your audience focus on what's most important: Which colors, what amount of white space, what size type, for example, wi make your message clear? If you're preparing audio or video, what type of file will your audience be most comfortable accessing?

❹ Be consistent.

Once you've experimented with different media and design elements within those media, you'll want to bring consistency to the design. For example, main headings might be blue and use 16-point font throughout a Web site, whereas subheadings might always be italicize and in 12-point font.

❺ Always give credit.

Finally, as with any medium, provide a credit line or attribution for any illustrations, music, video, or other features from another publication, just as you would give credit for text sources.

See the "KEY TO FEATURED CONTENT" on pages 651-653 for a quick reference guide to critical thinking, writing, reading, researching, and using media.

SEVENTH EDITION

KEYS FOR WRITERS

**TRIO-SSS San Marcos
Inventory #236**

Ann Raimes

Susan K. Miller-Cochran
North Carolina State University

WADSWORTH
CENGAGE Learning

Australia • Brazil • Japan • Korea • Mexico • Singapore • Spain
United Kingdom • United States

WADSWORTH
CENGAGE Learning

Keys for Writers,
Seventh Edition
Ann Raimes,
Susan K. Miller-Cochran
Publisher: Lyn Uhl
Publisher: Monica Eckman
Acquiring Sponsoring Editor:
  Kate Derrick
Senior Development Editor:
  Leslie Taggart
Senior Development Editor:
  Judith Fifer
Development Editor:
  Stephanie P. Carpenter
Assistant Editor:
  Danielle Warchol
Editorial Assistant:
  Marjorie Cross
Managing Media Editor:
  Cara Douglass-Graf
Brand Manager: Lydia LeStar
Senior Marketing
  Communications
  Manager: Linda Yip
Senior Content Project
  Manager: Rosemary Winfield
Art Director: Marissa Falco
Manufacturing Planner:
  Betsy Donaghey
Rights Acquisition Specialist:
  Alexandra Ricciardi
Production Service: Aaron
  Downey, Cenveo Publisher
  Services
Text Designer: Alisha Webber,
  Cenveo Publisher Services
Cover Designer: Emily
  Chionchio, Roycroft Design
Cover Image: Alisha Webber,
  Cenveo Publisher Services
Compositor: Cenveo Publisher
  Services

For product information and technology assistance, contact us at **Cengage Learning Customer & Sales Support, 1-800-354-9706.**

For permission to use material from this text or product, submit all requests online at **www.cengage.com/ permissions**. Further permissions questions can be emailed to **permissionrequest@cengage.com**.

Library of Congress Control Number: 2012950525

ISBN-13: 978-1-111-84175-1

ISBN-10: 1-111-84175-6

Wadsworth
20 Channel Center Street
Boston, MA 02210
USA

Cengage Learning is a leading provider of customized learning solutions with office locations around the globe, including Singapore, the United Kingdom, Australia, Mexico, Brazil and Japan. Locate your local office at **international.cengage.com/region**.

Cengage Learning products are represented in Canada by Nelson Education, Ltd.

For your course and learning solutions, visit **www.cengage.com**.

Purchase any of our products at your local college store or at our preferred online store **www.cengagebrain.com**.

Instructors: Please visit **login.cengage.com** and log in to access instructor-specific resources.

Printed in China
1 2 3 4 5 6 7 16 15 14 13 12

The seventh edition of *Keys for Writers* welcomes the substantial contributions of Susan Miller-Cochran as a coauthor. Susan is an Associate Professor of English and Director of the First-Year Writing Program at North Carolina State University. She earned a master's degree in teaching English as a Second Language and a doctoral degree in rhetoric and composition at Arizona State University. In addition to her writing program administration experience, she has also taught writing and ESL courses at a community college, in adult education programs, and abroad. She is also a coauthor of the *Wadsworth Guide to Research*. We are delighted to be working together and pooling our experience and expertise for this new edition.

In these days of texting, tweeting, blogging, e-mailing, and posting to Facebook, we are all writing more than ever before. Now, for most of us, daily writing is brief, purposeful, and informal, so much so that students facing an important writing task raise all kinds of questions of what is expected and what to do to meet expectations. Recent technological changes and our present-day culture of rapid written communications have certainly made writing less of an unfamiliar and scary enterprise than it was once, but when much is at stake—such as a grade or a promotion at work—the specter of what instructors and bosses expect still looms large.

This new edition of *Keys for Writers* preserves the aim of helping student writers bridge the gap between what they already know and do in their everyday writing and what academic readers and readers in the workplace expect. This handbook still helps students plan and edit their writing and make it fit into academia. There are still many examples that show how to construct effective sentences, paragraphs, and essays. And to follow the tradition of earlier editions, the needs of multilingual writers are taken into account both in Part 9, Writing across Languages and Cultures, and throughout the text in the many Notes for Multilingual Writers.

An important and timely new emphasis of this edition is a sharper focus on critical thinking, anchored by a "Critical Thinking Framework" in Part 1 that helps students consider the context of their writing at all points in the writing process. New activities, checklists, and discussion questions in Part 1 prompt students to consider critically the purpose, audience, voice, and medium of their writing. Critical thinking icons throughout the text remind students of the need to think critically when researching, reading, and considering how to present their projects.

Also new to this edition are exercises at the ends of all of the writing, research, and grammar sections of the text (including Writing across

Languages and Cultures) that allow students to practice important concepts. Answers to these exercises are found on the Instructor's Resource Manual, located online. Additional exercises are also found in many of the supplements, both print and online, described below.

In addition, this new edition pays increased attention to showing how to search online for academic sources, how to cite them accurately, and how to select and use visuals that enliven and dramatize written work. The fifteen Source Shots in Parts 3 and 4 display what sources look like when students access them on a page or screen and show how to use the information in a citation list in a paper. The use of technology in academic writing is also highlighted, notably in dozens of updated and revised Tech Notes.

Feedback from users has indicated how useful samples of student writing are, so this edition includes many new samples of student writing from various stages throughout the process—annotated drafts, brainstorming lists, and outlines; a passage annotated and revised for style; a working bibliography—as well as full researched essays in different documentation styles. Full student papers in MLA style include a new argument essay, a literary analysis, a new rhetorical analysis of academic essays in three disciplines, and a new essay on the effects of the profit motive on the world of theatre. In addition, there are complete APA and *Chicago* papers, as well as excerpts from a CSE paper. All of the student samples are highlighted in the tab contents pages. Many of these papers include visuals, a way of communication familiar to many students who will find guidance in Part 5 on how to evaluate, incorporate, and document visuals.

The success of the previous editions of *Keys for Writers* tells us to keep this handbook's distinctive navigation and its two (yes, only two) color-coded, numbered, and descriptively labeled rows of tabs; the coaching tone that students see as lively but respectful; and the concise explanations and examples of grammar and style that have guided and delighted many users. Yet *Keys for Writers* has also changed because both teachers and students have conveyed in person, mailed, and e-mailed invaluable suggestions to help the book keep pace with current trends in writing and be as accurate and timely as a handbook should be. We are grateful for those shared ideas and are happy to incorporate them.

So you are reading a handbook that provides solid instruction and lively examples in an updated design, keeps up with change, guides you through the critical thinking process, insists on authentic examples of student writing, and conveys the challenges of writing for multiple audiences in multiple settings and sometimes in multiple media. We'd like to hear your reactions. You can write to us in care of (c/o) Kate Derrick at Cengage Learning, 20 Channel Center Street, Boston, MA 02210.

Cengage Learning has prepared the following expanded summary of what's new to the seventh edition, a summary of the features that have been hallmarks of this book and that continue in the new edition, and a guide to its comprehensive supplements package, which includes several exciting additions and is described in this Preface beginning on page viii.

New to the Seventh Edition

In addition to a dynamic new design, this edition of *Keys for Writers* offers the following new coverage and features:

Completely revised Part 1, The Writing Process

- New Critical Thinking Framework that supports all stages of the writing process
- New sample student argument essay, annotated with student strategies
- Expanded coverage of writing in academic disciplines, including a new sample student rhetorical analysis of writing in different academic disciplines
- Exercises on analyzing the audience for a piece of writing, exploring a topic, evaluating thesis statements, and more

Revised and updated Part 2, Research/Sources/Documentation

- New focus on critical thinking in the research process
- New approach to finding sources, taking into account the wide variety of sources now found via databases and other online sources
- New tips from the perspective of an often untapped resource—the reference librarian
- Expanded support for critically evaluating sources, based on the Critical Thinking Framework
- Exercises on finding and evaluating Web sources as well as paraphrasing, quoting, and incorporating sources, and appropriate citing of sources to avoid plagiarism

Revised Parts 3 and 4, MLA, APA, CSE, and *Chicago* Documentation

- MLA section completely revised to reflect the 2009 MLA updates, including a revised order of entries and more on citing online sources
- In the MLA section, seven Source Shots (five of them new) show students where to find documentation information on sources ranging from print books and scholarly articles to transcripts of television interviews
- APA documentation revised to reflect 2010 revisions, including additional online citation formats

- Five new APA Source Shots show students where to find citation information on sources from journals to online sources (including visuals)
- Expanded coverage of *Chicago* style, including a full student paper, and three new Source Shots

Revised Part 5, Design, Media, and Presentation

- New attention to choosing an appropriate medium and considering audience expectations, based on the Critical Thinking Framework
- New coverage of the latest technologies for presentations, including *Prezi* and *Google Docs,* as well as helpful guidelines for working with *PowerPoint*
- New student examples include an e-portfolio, résumé, and cover letter
- Concise new table outlining commands for formatting academic writing in various versions of *Microsoft Word*
- Exercises that help students practice formatting academic writing, locate and incorporate visuals, and plan oral presentations or e-portfolios

Revised, updated, and expanded coverage of many topics, including annotated bibliographies (9e); scratch and formal outlines (1h); how to use, integrate, and document sources (new chapter 10 in Part 2); and tips for multilingual writers (Part 9).

New Key Points boxes appear throughout the handbook, including one titled "A Critical Thinking Framework," prompting students to consider purpose, audience, voice, and medium in their writing.

More Source Shots, the majority of them new Part 3 (MLA) now includes seven of the text's popular Source Shots, five of them new, including several that feature government publications and Web sites, and Part 4 (APA, CSE, and Chicago) now includes eight Source Shots, all of them new.

Continuing Proven Features

This text's intuitive, color-coded two-part organization, laminated tabbed part dividers, quick reference features such as Key Points boxes, abundant examples and models, friendly writing style, and uncluttered design continue in this new edition, making information easy for student writers to find, understand, and apply.

Two rows of color-coded divider tabs The unusual simplicity and clarity of only two rows of tabs make it easy to find information quickly. The first row is red, for writing and research issues; the second row is gold, for sentence-level issues.

Practical "Key Points" boxes   These handy boxes open or appear within most major sections of the handbook to provide quick-reference summaries of essential information. Seventh edition Key Points boxes include Using the Critical Thinking Framework for Brainstorming (Part 1); What Every Librarian Wishes You Knew (Part 2); Guidelines for the MLA List of Works Cited (Part 3); Working with DOIs and URLs (Part 4); Guidelines for College Essay Format (Part 5); Checklist for Word Choice (Part 6); Forms of Personal Pronouns (Part 7); Titles: Quotation Marks or Italics/Underlining (Part 8); and Articles at a Glance: Four Basic Questions about a Noun (Part 9).

Bracketed labels on selected sample citations in all styles These clearly labeled models show at a glance what types of information students need to include and how to format, arrange, and punctuate that information when documenting sources in all covered styles.

Thorough coverage of style   *Keys for Writers* continues to devote a full part (Part 6, Style: The Five C's) to the important area of style, covering sentence- and word-related style issues in a unified presentation. The popular coverage advises students in straightforward, memorable fashion to Cut, Check for Action, Connect, Commit, and Choose the Best Words.

Thorough, consolidated, and clear coverage of grammar   Part 7, Common Sentence Problems, gives students one central place to turn to when they have grammar questions. Grammar coverage is not divided confusingly over several parts, as in other handbooks. A section on students' frequently asked grammar questions begins Part 7.

Distinctive approach to English as a new language, Englishes, and vernaculars Superior coverage for multilingual writers takes a "difference, not deficit" approach presented within Language and Culture boxes, an extensive Editing Guide to Multilingual Transfer Patterns, an Editing Guide to Vernacular Englishes, and Notes for Multilingual Writers integrated throughout the text.

Helpful tips for using technology   Tech Note boxes provide useful ideas and resources for writing, using the Web, and researching with technology. Tech Notes in the seventh edition include "Tips for Using Search Engines," "Using Social Bookmarking to Annotate Texts Online," and "Multimedia Presentation Design."

Coverage of writing and communicating throughout and beyond college   *Keys for Writers* prepares students for a range of writing and communicating tasks they may encounter in college as well as in the community and the workplace. Part 1 supports students' writing in different academic disciplines, and Part 5 provides model documents, Web pages, presentations, and other resources for writing, communicating, and document design in a range of media for diverse audiences.

A Complete Support Package

The seventh edition of *Keys for Writers* is accompanied by a wide array of supplemental resources developed to create the best teaching and learning experience inside as well as outside the classroom, whether that classroom is on campus or online.

Supplemental Resources for Instructors

Instructor's Resource Manual

ISBN: 9781133352020

The online **Instructor's Resource Manual** provides an overview of the handbook and ideas on how to use it, a section on teaching composition to multilingual students, advice on using the Internet both within the composition classroom and throughout the course, diagnostic test handouts on five main areas of grammar, and answers to the in-text exercises as well as numbered items in the print exercises booklet. It can be located on the free faculty companion Web site under a password-protected link, accessed at *login.cengage.com*.

Exercises to accompany *Keys for Writers*   A print exercise workbook is available with additional exercises on grammar, punctuation, usage, and style, with clear directions and examples. Answers to half of the exercises are provided in the back of the booklet so students can check their own work; or the booklet can be used for quizzing.

 Enhanced InSite™ for *Keys for Writers*, Seventh Edition

Printed Access Card (1 semester) (ISBN: 9781285172125)
Instant Access Card (1 semester) (ISBN: 9781285172149)
Printed Access Card (2 semester) (ISBN: 9781285171500)
Instant Access Card (2 semester) (ISBN: 9781285171524)
Printed Access Card (4 semester) (ISBN: 9781285172187)
Instant Access Card (4 semester) (ISBN: 9781285172194)

With Enhanced InSite™ for *Keys for Writers*, Seventh Edition, instructors and students can manage the flow of papers online, check for originality, and conduct peer reviews. Students can access the multimedia e-book for a text-specific workbook, private tutoring options, and resources for writers that include anti-plagiarism tutorials and down-loadable grammar podcasts. Enhanced Insite™ provides the tools and resources instructors and students need, plus the training and support they want. Learn more at *www.cengage.com/insite.* *(Access card/code is required.)*

 English CourseMate

Printed Access Card (**ISBN:** 9781285171920)
Instant Access Code (**ISBN:** 9781285171937)

Keys for Writers includes English CourseMate, a complement to your textbook. English CourseMate includes:

- an interactive e-book
- interactive teaching and learning tools including:
  - Quizzes
  - Flashcards
  - Videos
  - and more
- Engagement Tracker, a first-of-its-kind tool that monitors student engagement in the course

Go to *login.cengage.com* to access these resources, and look for this icon, ᴾCourseMate which denotes a resource available within CourseMate.

 Aplia for *Keys for Writers*, Seventh Edition

Printed Access Card (1 semester) (ISBN: 9781285186535)
Instant Access Code (1 semester) (ISBN: 9781285186504)
Printed Access Card (2 semester) (ISBN: 9781285186443)
Instant Access Code (2 semester) (ISBN; 9781285186429)
Printed Access Card with e-book (1 semester) (ISBN: 9781285186405)
Instant Access Code with e-book (1 semester) (ISBN: 9781285186399)
Printed Access Card with e-book (2 semester) (ISBN: 9781285186337)
Instant Access Code with e-book (2 semester) (ISBN; 9781285186320)

Aplia™ is dedicated to improving learning by increasing student effort and engagement. Aplia with e-book for *Keys For Writers* is an online, auto-graded homework solution that keeps your students engaged and prepared for class and has been used by almost two million students at over 1,700 institutions. Visit *www.cengage.com/aplia* for more details. **(Available for the Fall 2013 semester)**

writ⊜xperience **Write Experience**

Printed Access Card (ISBN: 9781285186597)
Instant Access Code (ISBN: 9781285186559)

Cengage Learning's Write Experience is a technology product that allows you to assess written communication skills without adding to your workload. This new product utilizes artificial intelligence to not only score student writing instantly and accurately, but also provide students with detailed revision goals and feedback on their writing to help them improve. Write Experience is the first product designed and created specifically for the higher education market through an exclusive agreement with McCann Associates, and powered by e-Write IntelliMetric Within™. IntelliMetric is the gold standard for automated scoring of writing and is used to score the Graduate Management Admissions Test® (GMAT®) analytical writing assessment. Better Writing. Better Outcomes. Write Experience. Visit www .cengage.com/writeexperience to learn more.

q u e s t ⓘ a **Questia**
Trusted online research

Instant Access Code 12 Month Subscription (ISBN: 9781285079202)
Instant Access Code 6 Month Subscription (ISBN: 9781428277434)

Questia is the online library that provides 24/7 access to the Web's premier collection of full textbooks and academic journal and periodical articles in the humanities and social sciences. And, it is more than a vast collection of online sources. Questia can help your students in the entire research process, from topic selection and research to organization of their notes and proper citations. Questia will help your students write better papers, providing a wider array of scholarly sources, and enabling them to organize what they've learned into a better thought-out paper.

Resources for Writers

Instant Access Code (ISBN: 9781133044383)

Resources for Writers offers a variety of activities for students to practice and refine their understanding of key concepts via interactive grammar and proofreading exercises, anti-plagiarism tutorials, writing and research modules, multimedia activities, and downloadable grammar podcasts.

Supplemental Resources for Students

Interactive e-book for *Keys for Writers,* Seventh Edition
Printed Access Card (ISBN: 9781285171487)
Instant Access Code (ISBN: 9781285171531)

This interactive, multimedia e-book includes interactive exercises, an integrated text-specific workbook, a highlighting and note-taking tool, a printing option, and a search tool.

Infotrac® College Edition with InfoMarks™

ISBN: 9780534558536

InfoTrac® College Edition, an online research and learning center, offers over 20 million full-text articles from nearly 6,000 scholarly and popular periodicals. The articles cover a broad spectrum of disciplines and topics—ideal for every type of researcher.

Turnitin®

Printed Access Card 1-Semester User Guide (ISBN: 9781413030181)
Instant Access Card 2-Semester User Guide (ISBN: 9781413030198)

This proven online plagiarism-prevention software promotes fairness in the classroom by helping students learn to correctly cite sources and allowing instructors to check for originality before reading and grading papers. Visit www.cengage.com/turnitin to view a demonstration.

Personal Tutor

Printed Access Card (ISBN: 9781285171906)
Instant Access Code (ISBN: 9781285171784)

Access to Personal Tutor's private tutoring resources provides your students with additional assistance and review as they write their papers. With this valuable resource, students will gain access to multiple sessions to be used either as tutoring services or paper submissions—whichever they need the most.

Merriam-Webster's Collegiate® Dictionary, e-Book

Instant Access Code (ISBN: 9781285054360)

America's best-selling dictionary delivers accurate, up-to-date information while working on writing assignments, composing e-mail, and designing spreadsheets—you name it. This eleventh edition of Merriam-Webster's Collegiate Dictionary and Thesaurus contains thousands of new words and meanings from all areas of human endeavor, including electronic technology, the sciences, and popular culture. This indispensable tool will give your students fast and easy access to the words they need to know today.

Ordering options for student supplements are flexible. Please consult your local Cengage Learning sales representative or visit us at **www.cengage.com** for more information, including ISBNs; to receive examination copies of any of these instructor or student resources; or for product demonstrations. Print and e-book versions of this text and many of its supplements are available for students to purchase at a discount at **www.cengagebrain.com**.

Acknowledgments

The *Keys* handbooks have always made a point of using authentic student writing. For giving permission to use their work, we offer many thanks to the following, all of whom were responsive, helpful, and a pleasure to work with:

Tiffany Brattina, Charles Bentley Brooks, Jr., Andrew Dillon, Brian Cortijo, Yulanda Croasdale, Daniel Familia, Ashley Hanson, Bibi Bhani K. Khalsa, Maria Saparauskaite, Daniel Sauve, Patricia Suchan, Catherine Turnbull, Jared Whittemore, and Natasha Williams.

The following composition instructors were instrumental in suggesting changes in this new edition. We are grateful to them for sharing their wisdom and experience in detailed reviews:

Craig Bartholomaus, *Metropolitan Community College–Penn Valley;* Kristin Bivens, *Harold Washington College;* Barbara Blackburn, *Erie Community College;* Candace Boeck, *San Diego State University;* Laura Bowles, *University of Central Arkansas;* Janice Brantley, *University of Arkansas at Pine Bluff;* Suzane Bricker, *University of Maryland University College;* Michel Briggs, *East Tennessee State University;*

Sandra Burgess, *St. Louis Community College;* Stephen Byars, *University of South Carolina;* Stephen Calatrello, *Calhoun Community College;* Gary Cale, *Jackson Community College;* Amber Carini, *San Diego State University;* William Carney, *Cameron University;* Marjorie Church, *High Point University;* Frank Cioffi, *Baruch College–CUNY;* Nicole Clyncke, *South Piedmont Community College;* Gertrude Coleman, *Middlesex County College;* Marianne Conley-Ramsey, *University of Hawaii at Hilo;* Sally Cooperman, *California State University–East Bay;* F. Brett Cox, *Norwich University;* Kennette Crockett, *Harold Washington College;* Anthony Daniels, *Wayne County Community College;* Christine Denecker, *University of Findlay;* Michael Dubson, *Bunker Hill Community College;* Michael Duffy, *Moorpark Community College;* Daniel Fitzstephens, *University of Colorado;* Kathy Ford, *Lakeland Community College;* Gayle Fornataro, *Los Angeles Valley College;* Carol Fox, *Middlesex County College;* Judith Funston, *State University of New York at Potsdam;* Janet Gerstner, *San Juan College;* Christine Geyer, *Cazenovia College;* Karen Gibson, *State University of New York at Potsdam;* Steve Goldberg, *Wayne County Community College;* Carey Goyette, *Clinton Community College;* Joshua Grasso, *East Central University;* Sue Greenberg, *San Diego State University;* Kim Haywood, *Medtech College;* Michael Held, *Richard J. Daley College;* Philip Hutcheon, *San Joaquin Delta College;* John Hyman, *American University;* Shereen Inayatulla, *York College, CUNY;* Melanie Jenkins, *Snow College;* Jason Kahler, *Saginaw Valley State University;* Timothy Kenyon, *Saginaw Valley State University;* Marshall Kitchens, *Oakland University;* Helene Krauthamer, *University of the District of Columbia;* Roba Kribs, *Ancilla College;* Leslie Leitch, *Wayne County Community College;* Richard Levesque, *Fullerton College;* Anna Maheshwari, *Schoolcraft College;* Barbara Masten, *Lourdes College;* Diane Matza, *Utica College;* Sheila McAvey, *Becker College;* Mahli Xuan Mechenbier, *Kent State University at Geauga;* Robert Mellin, *Purdue North Central;* Paul Minifee, *San Diego State University;* Mary Nagler, *Oakland Community College;* Lonetta Oliver, *St. Louis Community College–Florissant Valley;* Shelley Palmer, *Rowan-Cabarrus Community College;* Miguel Powers, *Fullerton College;* Jonathan Purkiss, *Pulaski Technical College;* Jennifer Richardson, *State University of New York at Potsdam;* Gabrielle Rose, *Hamline University;* Kiki Rydell, *Montana State University;* Ruth Salter, *Boise State University;* Diane Saylor, *Saginaw Valley State University;* Dixie Shaw-Tillmon, *University of Texas at San Antonio;* Andrew Smith, *Piedmont Virginia Community College;* Donna Smith-Raymond, *State University of New York at Potsdam;* James Sodon, *St. Louis Community College–Florissant Valley;*

Rachel Strickland, *Appalachian State University;* Isera Tyson, *State College of Florida;* Paul Walker, *Murray State University;* Matt Willen, *Elizabethtown College;* Terry Williams, *San Diego State University;* Lee Wright, *Saginaw Valley State University;* Pam Wright, *University of California, San Diego*

We are also grateful to the following dedicated instructors who completed a helpful survey:

Lorri Barrier, *Stanley Community College;* Tara Blaser, *Lakeland College;* Diane Boehm, *Saginaw Valley State University;* Joel Boehner, *Bethel College;* Donald Brasted-Maki, *Lane Community College;* Sydney Brown, *Grossmont College;* Nancy Cheeks, *California State University;* Cynthia Denham, *Snead State Community College;* Nichole Diederich, *University of Findlay;* Kathy Dillon, *Harding University;* Kathrynn Ditommaso, *Bronx Community College of The City University of New York;* Rose Mary Foncree, *Belhaven University;* Carol Fox, *Middlesex Community College;* Chris Geyer, *Cazenovia College;* Elaine Hays, *College of the Holy Cross;* Shana Hirsch, *Tech College of the Low Country;* Suzanna Holmes, *Columbia State Community College;* Elizabeth Imafuji, *Anderson University;* Aaron Jason, *California State University–East Bay;* Travis Jensen, *Nebraska Wesleyan University;* Suzanne Labadie, *Oakland Community College–Southfield;* Teresa LaRocco, *University of Findlay;* Sharynn Etheridge Logan, *Claflin University;* Jimmy McClure, *Oakland University;* Vince Moore, *Tiffin University;* Lonetta Oliver, *St. Louis Community College–Florissant Valley;* Gwen Schwartz, *University of Mount Union;* Johnie Scott, *California State University–Northridge;* Timothy Sedore, *Bronx Community College of The City University of New York;* John Singleton, *Harding University;* Ben Sloan, *Piedmont Virginia Community College;* James R. Sodon, *St. Louis Community College–Florissant Valley;* Jill Sumstad, *California State University–East Bay;* MaryAnn Sullivan, *Hesser College*

In addition we extend grateful thanks to the following, who helped at earlier stages of composition:

Joseph A. Alvarez, *Central Piedmont Community College;* Akua Duku Anokye, *University of Toledo;* Jennie Ariail, *University of South Carolina;* Janet Badia, *Marshall University;* Pamela J. Balluck, *University of Utah;* Jennifer Banning, *Illinois State University;* Lona Bassett, *Jones County Junior College;* Jennifer Beech, *Pacific Lutheran University;* Richard Beighey, *Community College of Allegheny County–North Campus;* B. Cole Bennett, *Abilene Christian University;* Robin A. Benny, *Chicago State University;* Linda Bergman, *Illinois Institute of Technology;* Clair Berry, *State Technical Institute at Memphis;* Christina Pinkston Betts, *Hampton University;* Curtis W. Bobbit, *College of Great Falls;* Candace A. Boeck,

San Diego State University; Darsie Bowden, *Western Washington University;* Laurie Bower, *University of Nevada, Reno;* Linda Brender, *Macomb Community College;* Fahamisha Patricia Brown, *Metropolitan College of New York;* Terry Brown, *University of Wisconsin, River Falls;* Vincent Bruckert, *Wright College;* Stephen M. Byars, *University of Southern California;* Jeffrey P. Cain, *Sacred Heart University;* Bettina Caluori, *DeVry Institute, New Brunswick;* Karen A. Carlton, *Humboldt State University;* Laura B. Carroll, *Abilene Christian University;* Sherry Cisler, *Arizona State University;* Gina Claywell, *Murray State University;* Linda Clegg, *Cerritos College;* Robert Cousins, *Utah Valley State College;* Gene Crutsinger, *Tiffin University;* Ned Cummings, *Bryant and Stratton College;* Lisa Davidson, *Passaic County Community College;* Ben Davis, *Cuyahoga Community College;* Judith Davis, *Old Dominion University;* Virginia B. DeMers, *Ringling School of Art and Design;* Rob Dornsife, *Creighton University;* Amie Doughty, *State University of New York, Oneonta;* David A. Dzaka, *Messiah College;* Darlynn R. Fink, *Clarion University of Pennsylvania;* Murray A. Fortner, *Tarrant County College;* Katherine Frank, *University of Southern Colorado;* Muriel Fuqua, *Daytona Beach Community College;* David W. Furniss, *University of Wisconsin, River Falls;* Lynée Lewis Gaillet, *Georgia State University;* Philip Gaines, *Montana State University;* Bart Ganzert, *Forsyth Technical Community College;* Dennis Gartner, *Frostburg State University;* Dorothy Gilbert, *California State University, Haywood;* Thomas Goodman, *University of Miami;* Katherine Green, *Albuquerque Technical-Vocational Institute;* John Gregorian, *Contra Costa Community College;* Claudia Gresham-Shelton, *Stanly Community College;* Patricia Griffin, *Saint Joseph's University;* Elizabeth Grubgeld, *Oklahoma State University;* Keith Gumery, *Temple University;* Jane E. Hardy, *Cornell University;* D. Alexis Hart, *University of Georgia;* Leean Hawkins, *National Park Community College;* Beth L. Hewett, *Community College of Baltimore County, Essex;* Karen Heywood, *Stephens College;* Christopher Z. Hobson, *State University of New York, College at Old Westbury;* Franklin E. Horowitz, *Columbia University;* Michael Hricik, *Westmoreland City Community College;* Margaret Hughes, *Butte College;* Mary L. Hurst, *Cuyahoga Community College;* John Hyman, *American University;* Clark Iverson, *Macomb Community College–Center Campus;* Ernest H. Johansson, *Ohio University;* Ted E. Johnston, *El Paso Community College;* Karen Jones, *St. Charles Community College;* Mary Kaye Jordan, *Ohio University;* Ann Judd, *Seward County Community College;* Lewis J. Kahler, *Mohawk Valley Community College;* Susan Kincaid, *Lakeland Community College;* Noel Kinnamon, *Mars Hill College;* Martha Kruse, *University of Nebraska, Kearney;* Sally Kurtzman, *Arapahoe Community*

College; Joseph LaBriola, *Sinclair Community College;* Victoria Lannen, *Southwestern College;* Lindsay Lewan, *Arapahoe Community College;* Chad Littleton, *University of Tennessee at Chattanooga;* Daniel Lowe, *Community College of Allegheny County;* Kelly Lowe, *Mount Union College;* Dianne Luce, *Midlands Technical Community College;* Mike MacKey, *Community College of Denver;* Mary Sue MacNealy, *The University of Memphis;* Gina Maranto, *University of Miami;* Louis Martin, *Elizabethtown College;* JoAnne Liebman Matson, *University of Arkansas, Little Rock;* Ann Maxham-Kastrinos, *Washington State University;* Nancy McTaggart, *Northern Virginia Community College;* Michael G. Moran, *University of Georgia;* Marie Nigro, *Lincoln University, Pennsylvania;* Carolyn O'Hearn, *Pittsburgh State University;* Liz Parker, *Nashville State Technical Institute;* Sally Parr, *Ithaca College;* Kathy Parrish, *Southwestern College;* Jane Peterson, *Richland College;* Lillian Polak, *Nassau Community College;* Orit Rabkin, *University of Oklahoma;* Susan Richardson, *Macomb Community College;* Jeffrey Rice, *Wayne State University;* Nelljean M. Rice, *Coastal Carolina University;* Kenneth Risdon, *University of Minnesota at Duluth;* Mark Rollins, *Ohio University;* Julia Ruengert, *Pensacola Junior College;* Cheryl W. Ruggiero, *Virginia Polytechnic Institute;* Michael E. Smith, *Western Carolina University;* Kristin L. Snoddy, *Indiana University at Kokomo;* James R. Sodon, *St. Louis Community College at Florissant Valley;* Ellen Sostarich, *Hocking College;* Eleanor Swanson, *Regis University;* Jami M. Taylor, *ECPI College of Technology;* Michael R. Underwood, *San Diego State University;* Amy Ulmer, *Pasadena City College;* Jane Mueller Ungari, *Robert Morris College;* Margaret Urie, *University of Nevada;* Sandra Van Pelt, *Belhaven College;* Catherine Vedder, *Kentucky State University;* Thomas Villano, *Boston University;* Brian K. Walker, *Pulaski Technical College;* Colleen Weldele, *Palomar College;* Barbara Whitehead, *Hampton University;* Stephen Wilhoit, *University of Dayton;* Debbie J. Williams, *Abilene Christian University;* James D. Williams, *University of North Carolina, Chapel Hill;* James Wilson, *LaGuardia Community College, City University of New York;* Sallie Wolf, *Arapahoe Community College;* Randell Wolff, *Murray State;* Martin Wood, *University of Wisconsin, Eau Claire;* Randal Woodland, *University of Michigan, Dearborn;* Pamela S. Wright, *University of California, San Diego;* Pavel Zemliansky, *James Madison University;* Laura W. Zlogar, *University of Wisconsin, River Falls.*

The publisher plays a large role in the development and publication of a new edition. Thanks go to Lyn Uhl and Monica Eckman, Publishers, and Kate Derrick, Acquiring Sponsoring Editor, for their support and encouragement throughout the process; to Leslie Taggart and Judy Fifer, Senior Development Editors, Stephanie P. Carpenter, Development Editor, and

Kathy Smith, Copy Editor, for their contributions to the manuscript; and to both Rosemary Winfield, Senior Content Project Manager, and Aaron Downey, Project Manager at Cenveo Publisher Services, for coping so ably with production details, snags, and deadlines. Grateful acknowledgments are also due to others on the *Keys* team for their help and expertise: at Cengage Learning, Marjorie Cross and Danielle Warchol, and all at Cenveo Publisher Services, especially Jerilyn Bockorick and Alisha Webber.

The authors would also like to include additional words of personal thanks. First, we offer appreciation to the students we have been privileged to work with over the years. We hope those students who use this book find it comprehensive and useful in their college courses.

Ann Raimes: I have written thanks to my friends and family for the past six editions. By now, they all know the importance of their role. Now I add thanks to Susan Miller-Cochran for her innovative contributions and hard work on this new edition. It has been a pleasure to work with her.

Susan Miller-Cochran: A special thank you is due to my husband, Stacey Cochran, and my children, Sam and Harper, who have been extraordinarily generous in their support of my work on this edition. I also have deep gratitude for Ann Raimes, whose work I have read, cited, and respected for many years. It has been an honor to work with such a gracious collaborator and mentor.

questa

Need to find a topic for your research paper?
Need a library at 2 a.m.?
Want to create accurate citations in a snap?

Write better research papers faster—with Questia℠.

Questia℠ is a research tool that provides 24/7 access to the Web's premier online collection of books, academic journals, newspapers, and magazines. Read titles cover to cover or simply find passages to support your thesis. Whether you're doing research, or just interested in topics that touch on the humanities and social sciences, you'll find relevant titles. You'll also find help in all aspects of the research process.

With Questia, you can

- **Develop a deeper understanding of the research process** through tutorials (including videos).

- **Quote and cite reliable materials** with confidence, using auto-citation and bibliography generators.

- **Access an online library** of 70,000+ full-text books and more than 6 million academic journal and periodical articles.

- **Use books and articles** no matter how many others are reading the same materials.

- **Select** from thousands of paper-worthy topics.

- **Save time** with intuitive research tools for organizing, managing, and storing your work.

1 The Writing Process

CREATE

To obtain study resources for this section, visit the English CourseMate for this text at **www.cengagebrain.com**

1 The Writing Process

Critical Thinking, Reading, and Writing

1a Getting started

Starting on a writing project can be hard if you think of a piece of writing only as a permanent document that others will judge. A blank page or an empty screen can be daunting, but the act of writing generally offers an advantage over speaking: You can go back and make changes. You are not locked into what you have written until you decide to turn your finished work over to readers, whether by printing a document, sending an e-mail, or posting a message. You can also present whatever image of yourself you choose. You have the freedom to invent yourself anew. As journalist Adam Gopnik says fondly of writing, "It's you there, but not quite you." One of the pleasures of writing is taking advantage of that freedom.

As you get started on a writing project, it can help to remember that writing is a conversation. When you write, you write for someone. With some writing tasks, you might write only for yourself, and other times you might write for another individual (a teacher, a supervisor, a friend) or for a group of people (a class, a work group, an admissions committee). How and what you write are influenced by your knowledge, by your reading and thinking about a subject, and also by the expectations of the audience you are writing for. Keeping that audience in mind, along with your purpose for writing, can help you get started in the writing process.

1b Understanding context: Purpose, audience, voice, and medium

A helpful way to think about your writing is to understand your writing context. There are four elements to keep in mind for understanding the context of a writing project: purpose, audience, voice, and medium.

Your purpose   Ask yourself: What is your main purpose for writing in a particular situation, beyond aiming for an A in the course? Here are some possibilities common in academic writing:

- to explain an idea or theory or to explore a question (expository writing)
- to analyze the structure or content of a text (analytical writing)

- to report on a process, an experiment, or lab results (technical or scientific writing)
- to provide a status update on a project at work (business writing)
- to persuade readers to understand your point of view, change their minds, or take action (persuasive or argumentative writing)
- to record and reflect on your own experiences and feelings (expressive writing)
- to tell a story, whether imaginative or real (narrative writing)

The purpose of your writing will determine your options for presenting your final text.

KEY POINTS
Four Questions about Context

Your answers to the following four questions shape the writing you do in significant ways.

- What is your purpose?
- Who is your audience?
- What is unique about your voice on this subject?
- What medium of delivery will you use?

Your audience   A good writer keeps readers in mind at all times. Achieving this connection, however, often proves challenging because not all readers have the same characteristics. Readers come from different regions, communities, ethnic groups, organizations, and academic disciplines, all with their own linguistic and rhetorical conventions.

This means that you as a writer have several shifting selves depending on your audience. In other words, you write differently when you text a friend, post a message on Facebook, post a blog, write an essay for a college instructor, or apply for a grant, an internship, or a job.

Your voice   Academic writing, as well as business writing and news reporting, is characterized by an unobtrusive voice. The writer is obviously there, having confronted ideas and sources and having decided what to say about them, but the person behind the writing needs to come across as someone who knows what he or she is writing about and expresses the ideas with an authority that impresses the reader. The content takes precedence.

Your voice in writing is the way you come across to readers. What impression do you want them to form of you as a person, of your values and opinions? One of the first considerations is whether you want to draw attention to your opinions as the writer by using the first person pronoun *I* or whether you will try the seemingly more neutral approach of keeping that *I* at a distance. Many academic disciplines have specific expectations for when and how you use *I*. Even if you try to remain neutral by not using *I*, though, as is often recommended for academic and especially for scientific writing, readers will still see you behind your words. Professor Glen McClish at San Diego State University has pointed out how the voice—and consequently, the effect—of a text such as the one below changes significantly when the first fourteen words, including the first person pronouns, are omitted:

> *In the first section of my paper, I want to make the point that* the spread of technology is damaging personal relationships.

The *I* phrases may be removed to make the sentence seemingly more neutral and less wordy. However, the voice also changes: What remains becomes more forceful, proffered confidently as fact rather than as personal opinion.

Regardless of whether you use the word *I* in a particular piece of writing, beware of the leaden effect of using *I*-avoiding phrases such as "it would seem" or "it is to be expected that" and of overusing the pronoun *one*. William Zinsser in *On Writing Well* points out that "good writers are visible just behind their words," conveying as they write "a sense of I-ness." He advises at least thinking of *I* as you write your first draft, maybe even writing it, and then editing it out later. It's worth a try.

LANGUAGE AND CULTURE

Using "I" in Academic Writing

When readers read for information, it is generally the information that appeals to them, not the personality of the writer. Views differ on whether *I* should be used in academic writing, and if so, how much it should be used. Scholarly journals in the humanities several decades ago used to edit out uses of *I*. Not any more. In the sciences and social sciences, however, a neutral voice is still preferred unless there is a reason to give specific information about the writer. To be safe, always ask your instructor whether you can use *I*.

Your use of media   What are you working toward? A print document? A document with embedded images or other media? A multimedia presentation? An online document with hyperlinks, images, sound, or video? As you work through the process of choosing and developing a topic for a defined purpose and audience, consider simultaneously the communication means available to you, especially if you are presenting your work online or with the help of presentation software. Always bear in mind how you can enhance your ideas with the design of your document and the use of images, graphs, or multimedia tools.

● TECH **NOTE**

Taking Accessibility Issues and Disabilities into Account

For documents you prepare for online viewers or for oral and multimedia presentations, thinking about audience means considering issues of accessibility.

- Consider whether readers have reliable high-speed connections before you post large image files online.
- For any viewers with vision impairments, increase type size, provide a zoom function, and either limit the number of visuals or describe them in words.
- Pay attention to color in visuals. Colors with high contrast work better for some viewers.
- Use online sites such as AChecker, WAVE, or Webagogo to test your documents for accessibility.

1c **Reading and writing in context: A framework for critical thinking**

Texts in academic, personal, and professional settings all have contexts that influence how we interpret, respond to, use, or ignore them. Understanding that context, both when you're reading and when you're writing, is a key to critical thinking. The word *critical* isn't negative and does not indicate that you are finding fault with something. Instead, *critical thinking* refers to the careful, reflective consideration that writers give to a text when they are reading closely and writing deliberately. In this sense, the ability to understand the context of a piece of writing (either one that you're reading or one that you're writing) and to consider the ways in which the purpose, audience, voice, and medium shape the text is a key component of critical thinking.

KEY POINTS
A Framework for Critical Thinking

As you read and write, especially for academic purposes, you might find the following framework useful for critically considering the relationship between context and writing:

PURPOSE	AUDIENCE
• What is/was the text meant to accomplish? Is that purpose explicit or implied? • What possibilities are there for creating a text that could meet that purpose? • Are there specific expectations the text must meet to achieve its intended purpose? If so, what are they?	• Who is the audience for this piece of writing? Is there more than one audience? If so, are their interests similar or competing? • What does the audience expect in terms of content, language use, tone, style, format, and delivery method? • If expectations are not met, what is the impact on the audience?
VOICE	**MEDIUM**
• What unique perspective does the author bring to this piece of writing? How is that unique perspective communicated? • How explicitly does/should the author make reference to his or her perspective? Does the author use *I*, and if so, when and why? • What is the author's tone in the piece of writing? For example, is it playful, serious, accusing, encouraging, hopeful, factual? What effect does that tone have on the piece of writing?	• How could the writing be delivered to its intended audience to meet its purpose? A blog posting? A printed essay? Via a Web site? A newspaper article? An academic journal article? An MP3 file? A YouTube video? • What formatting rules should the text follow in that medium? • What would the impact be of delivering the text in another medium?

As you read, you could use these questions as a guide for understanding and interpreting the text. When you write, you can use these questions to help you make decisions at important points in the writing process. These questions can be useful for writing that you do in many contexts, including professional settings and college courses.

1d Reading and writing in college

Academic writing such as reports, essays, and research papers, and everyday writing such as letters, lists, and online messages are *genres*, or types, of writing. Other genres include creative writing (novels, poems, plays) and business writing (memos, résumés, proposals, presentations). An awareness of the genre in which you are writing and reading is important because it is tightly tied to all elements of context: the purpose for writing, an understanding of the audience for the writing, the voice or tone used, and the medium through which the writing is presented. It puts your writing and reading tasks into perspective, which may make the task seem more manageable and even save you time.

When reading, for example, an understanding of genre can help you determine which of three common reading strategies would be best to use in different contexts:

Skimming	Reading for Information	Close Reading
Find what's relevant. **Key question:** Should I read this more closely?	Understand important facts. **Key question:** What do I need to understand and remember?	Examine how the context of a piece of writing impacts how it is written and understood. **Key question:** What is the relationship between the context of the reading and how it is written?

When reading genres such as online messages or personal letters, you might not go beyond skimming or reading for information. If you're reading an academic text, however, you might start with skimming, and then you might move to one or both of the other reading strategies depending on your reason for reading the text. If you're preparing for an exam, you might stick to reading for information as a study strategy. If you're reading a novel or a literary analysis for an English class, however, a close reading would be more appropriate.

How does understanding genres help with your writing tasks? By paying attention to *conventions*—the writing practices associated with a genre—you do a better job of meeting your readers' expectations and thus stand a better chance of achieving your intended purpose. If you ignore conventions, readers might be distracted and they might miss the message you are trying to convey. In a text message, direct message, or tweet, for example, writers use abbreviations, cultural references, shortcuts, and code words that are conventions online:

Smiley 123: hey sup?

Nicagalxoxo: hey did u c colbert last night?

Smiley 123: no, need 2 hulu

Nicagalxoxo: i was rotfl

Many students know this code from using it in daily life. If that same exchange were written in academic language, it would sound faintly ridiculous. Similarly, there is a code for academic writing, which leads to very different and more formal texts. The later chapters in this book will help you become familiar with these conventions for academic writing.

KEY POINTS

How to Be a Close Reader of Text and Images

❶ Do multiple readings.

Read more than once; examine a text or an image slowly and carefully, immersing yourself in the work and annotating to record your reactions. Start by skimming, and then go back and examine the text more closely, paying attention to context.

❷ Look for common ground.

Note where you nod in approval at points made in the text or image.

❸ Question and challenge.

Take on the role of a debater in your head. Ask yourself: Where does this idea come from? What biases does the writer reveal? What interesting information does the writer or creator provide—and is it convincing? Does the writer use sound logic? Is the writer fair to opposing views? Does the writer even take opposing views into account?

❹ Write as you read.

Write comments and questions in the margins of a page, between the lines in an online document saved to your word processor, on a blog, or on self-stick notes. In this way, you start a conversation with anything you read. If you have made the text you are reading look messy, that's a good sign.

❺ Remember that readers will read critically what you write.

It is not enough just to *read* critically. Be aware that your own writing has to stand up to readers' careful scrutiny and challenge, too.

Critical reading in action: A "conversation" with a text   While reading the following passage about the effects of drinking milk on children and young adults, a student annotates the passage as she reads it. Her comments, questions, and challenges establish her role in the conversation.

Over the past 20 years, the National Institutes of Health, the National Academy of Sciences, and the US Department of Agriculture have made recommendations for calcium intake for children and adults for the intended purpose of osteoporosis prevention. Recommended intakes have escalated gradually, and dairy products have been promoted often in federal nutrition policy documents as a "preferred" calcium source.

Should I be suspicious? This raises red flags.

Is there some way the government benefits?

However, because the level of dairy product consumption in the United States is among the highest in the world, accounting for 72% of dietary calcium intake, and osteoporosis and fracture rates are simultaneously high, numerous researchers have called into question the effectiveness of nutrition policies aimed at osteoporosis prevention through dairy consumption. Findings from recent epidemiologic and prospective studies in women, children, and adolescents also have raised questions about the efficacy of the use of dairy products and other calcium-containing foods for the promotion of bone health.

Uh-oh. This looks really suspicious.

Look up

So, is drinking milk harmful to me? Or is there just not evidence that it's necessary?

—Amy Joy Lanou, Susan E. Berkow, and Neal D. Barnard, "Calcium, Dairy Products, and Bone Health in Children and Young Adults: A Reevaluation of the Evidence"

● **TECH** NOTE

Using Social Bookmarking to Annotate Texts Online

If you are reading a text online, you can use a social bookmarking application such as *Diigo* to both save the link so that you can find the resource later and to annotate the reading. *Diigo* will allow you to save the link and your annotations and also to share them with others, making the application "social."

---

2 Drafting in Stages

Writing itself helps you develop ideas, make connections, and raise questions. That is, in writing, you do not just *display* what you know; you also *discover* what you know and think. How is that possible? It's possible because writing is not a linear or step-by-step procedure but a frequently messy *process*—a sort of adventure, one that you control but that often surprises you with your own insights as you progress through a sequence of several overlapping and recurring activities that comprise the writing process:

2a Using critical thinking to find a topic

Whether you have to choose your own idea for a topic or have had a topic assigned, you need strategies other than staring at the ceiling or waiting for inspiration to fly in through the window. Professional writers use a variety of prewriting techniques to generate ideas at various stages of the process. In her article "Oh Muse! You Do Make Things Difficult!" Diane Ackerman reports that the poet Dame Edith Sitwell used to lie in an open coffin, French novelist Colette picked fleas from her cat, states- man Benjamin Franklin soaked in the bathtub, and German dramatist Friedrich Schiller sniffed rotten apples stored in his desk.

Extreme methods aside, perhaps you have devel- oped your own original approach for generating the ideas that will help you choose and develop a topic. If what you do now does not seem to produce good results, though, or if you are ready for a change, try

See the full model on page 7.

starting by thinking about the context of your writing. Focusing on your purpose, your audience, your voice, and your medium can help narrow the options to make them feel more manageable.

If you have not had a topic assigned to you, think about the things that matter to you most when choosing a topic. This is a way of consid- ering your voice as part of the context for your writing. Writers do their best work when they write about things they care about. Reflect on is- sues raised in your college courses; read newspapers and magazines for current issues; consider campus, community, city, state, and nationwide issues; and look at the Library of Congress Subject Headings to get ideas. If you can, begin with an idea that has caught your interest and has some connection to your life. Think about why you are interested in it, what unique perspective you have on the subject, and whether you will be able to sustain your interest to complete the project.

In addition to thinking about what will spark your interest most, read the prompt for your writing assignment very carefully. What guidelines

does your instructor give for topic selection? Are there specific requirements that might limit what you could write about? Look for key words
about what your instructor is asking you to do. Look for words such as the
following, each of which asks the writer to do something slightly different:

- Define
- Describe
- Compare
- Contrast
- Provide an example
- Analyze
- Annotate
- Summarize

● TECH NOTE

Web Sites for Generating Ideas and Planning

Web directories assembled by librarians and academic institutions provide reli-
able sources for finding good academic subjects. The *Librarians' Index to the
Internet, Academic Info,* and *Voice of the Shuttle,* a University of California at
Santa Barbara directory for humanities research, are among the best.

The Purdue University Online Writing Lab and other online resources also
include information on generating ideas and planning.

Adapting to an assigned topic that does not interest you   This can
happen, but don't panic. If you spend time reading as much as you can
on the topic, something is bound to capture your interest. Ask yourself,
Is there an angle I could take on the issue or a part of the topic I could
focus on to make it more interesting to me? You may have to go beyond
the obvious approaches to a topic. Imagine, for instance, a biology student who is assigned to write a literary analysis of Nathaniel Hawthorne's
The Scarlet Letter. She notices that there are many references to medici-
nal herbs and poisons in the novel, and she decides to explore how they
are used as metaphors in the narrative. Suddenly she can do a close reading of the novel from the perspective of a scientist.

You might try challenging the point of view of one of your sources,
taking the opposite position. Or you can set yourself the task of showing
readers exactly why the topic has not grabbed people's interest—maybe
the literature and the research have been just too technical or inaccessi-
ble? If you can, find a human angle.

For more on topics, see 4c.

Drawing from journals, blogs, and online conversations   *Your own daily journal* can be far more than a personal diary. Many writers carry a notebook, either paper or electronic, and write in it every day, jotting down observations, references, quotations, questions, notes on events, and ideas about assigned texts or topics, as well as specific pieces of writing in progress. Your journal can also serve as a review for final examinations or essay tests, reminding you of areas of special interest or subjects you did not understand.

The *double-entry journal* provides a formalized way for you to think critically about readings and lectures. Two pages or two columns or open windows in your word processor provide the space for interaction. On the left side, write summaries, quotations, and accounts of readings, lectures, and class discussions. The left side, in short, is devoted to what you read or hear. On the right side, record your own comments, reactions, and questions about the material. Doing so gives you a way to visualize the conversation between you and your sources.

A *blog* gives you the opportunity to think aloud in public. Not only can others read your posting, but they can respond to it as well. Other than this social element, a blog can be similar to a writer's journal. The unedited blog entitled "The *Life* of a Salesman" (p. 14) was posted on a writing course blog site by Tiffany Brattina, a student at Seton Hill University in Greensburg, Pennsylvania. Here she works out a personal, original, and critical point of view as, after missing a class, she considers an interpretation of the character Willy Loman in Arthur Miller's play *Death of a Salesman*. Notice how Brattina takes advantage of the conventions of the genre (that is, of the blog posting) to engage her classmates and build a topic.

2b Getting started

If you have difficulty getting started with your writing once you have narrowed down a possible topic, try some of these strategies.

Freewriting   If you do not know what to write about or how to approach a broad subject, try doing five to ten minutes of *freewriting* either on paper or on the computer. When you freewrite, you let one idea lead to another in free association without concern for correctness. The important thing is to keep writing. If you cannot think of a word or phrase while you are freewriting, simply write a note to yourself inside square brackets, or put in a symbol such as #. On a computer, use the Search command to find your symbol later, when you can spend more time thinking about the word.

A student's blog on a course site

March 16

The *Life* of a Salesman

Ok. So, I'm sure during class today everyone talked about how crazy Willy was, and I am the first to agree. Willy was insane, in the end. However, what about his life?

In *Death of a Salesman* we see the end of Willy's life as a salesman. He went through his entire life working on the road selling things to buyers, he didn't know how to do anything else. Don't you think that would make you go crazy? If a company you worked for your entire life took you off of salary and put you on commission like you were just starting out wouldn't you feel like you were unworthy? Then there is the fact that Willy and his family didn't really have any money to their names at all. Willy kept borrowing money from Charley so that Linda wouldn't know that he wasn't getting paid anymore. Then the company he worked for fired him! I feel bad for Willy, I really do. His kids thought that he was insane and wanted nothing to do with him. The people he worked for his entire life turned him away. Willy was old, tired, and worn out and people including his family turned their backs on him.

Let me make this personal for a minute. My dad recently went through something very similar at his place of work. The company he worked for came into new management and they tried to put my dad on commission. My dad has major tenure where he works considering he is now 56 and has been working there for 40 years making him the longest member still working at the company. He took the new management to court and won his case. I know that while my dad was going through that time he was a total mess,so seeing my dad I can understand what Willy was going through.

What do you guys think? Do you feel bad for Willy or do you think he was just a jerk? Why or why not?

Posted by Tiffany Brattina at March 16, 06:49 PM

Comments

Do you remember Greek Tragedy? I do, and let me say that Willy is the tragic hero. I kept wanting him to succeed, and he didn't. I really felt that there was a chance for him to make something of himself, and couldn't. I had the feeling that Willy was going to kill himself,but something kept telling me that he was going to get out of the severe skid that he was in.

Posted by The Gentle Giant at March 16, 08:58 PM

Never thought of that Jay ... you are right though. I did feel like he was going to succeed, especially there at the end ... Oh well.
Tiff

Posted by Tiffany at March 16, 09:57 PM

Jimmy Wong did some freewriting on the topic of uniforms (an excerpt from a classmate's paper appears in 3d):

> When I think of uniforms I think of Derek Jeter and A-Rod and how cool they look as they leap for a baseball, spin around and throw it straight to first to get someone out. But does the uniform add anything to the skill? I'd say not, but it probably adds a lot of other stuff. Baseball is a team game so a uniform can work as a reminder that the game is about the team winning, not just one player scoring well and earning a place in the Hall of Fame.

Just this short piece, done very quickly, gave Wong an indication that he could develop a piece of writing focused on the unity-building effect that uniforms can have on those wearing them and on outsiders.

● TECH **NOTE**

Using a Word Processor for Freewriting

If you find that you're focusing too much on grammar, spelling, or phrasing when freewriting, try turning off the monitor (if you're using a desktop computer) or changing your font to white so that you can't see what you're typing. You might feel uncomfortable at first, but this strategy can help you take your focus off surface features when you're in the important stage of generating content and ideas. Once you are finished freewriting, you can turn the monitor back on, or Select All and change the font back to black.

Looping   One way to expand on the ideas you develop as you freewrite is to try *looping*. After a few minutes of freewriting, go back and underline or highlight the one idea that you think is the most important. Then try freewriting on that idea for a few minutes. You might try this activity several times to narrow down a broad topic and figure out what is most interesting to you or what might be the most promising focus for your writing.

Brainstorming   Another way to generate ideas is by *brainstorming*—making a list of ideas as you think of them. Brainstorming is enhanced if you do it collaboratively in a group, discussing and then listing your ideas (see also 2i, Writing with others). You can then, by yourself or with the group, scrutinize the ideas, arrange them, reorganize them, and add to or eliminate them.

Before they were assigned a chapter from *Uniforms: Why We Are What We Wear* by Paul Fussell, a group of students working collaboratively made the following brainstorming list on the topic of what uniforms signify:

Pink for girls, blue for boys—perpetuating stereotypes

Uniforms in parochial schools and in many British schools

Men's suits and ties

Uniforms for prisoners and wardens

Team uniforms; nurse uniforms

Municipal employee uniforms

The uniform of fashion—ripped jeans fashionable

Official vs. nonofficial uniforms

Advantages of uniforms—but for whom?

Keep them in line. Keep them recognizable.

Armed services

How do we treat uniforms—respect, contempt, pity, indifference?

Once the students had made the list, they reviewed it, rejected some items, expanded on others, and grouped items. Thus, they developed subcategories that led them to possibilities for further exploration and essay organization:

Uniforms for spectators

Uniforms that command respect

Uniforms that mark occupations

Fashion as a uniform of social markers—part of an "in-group"

KEY POINTS
Using the Critical Thinking Framework for Brainstorming

Try writing about your purpose, audience, voice, and medium as a way to brainstorm ideas for your draft:

PURPOSE	AUDIENCE
• What does your writing need to accomplish? How could writing about this topic fulfill that purpose? Is there something specific you need to do to accomplish that purpose?	• What expectations will your audience have for this piece of writing? Will they have specific expectations or opinions related to your topic? How might that influence your writing?
VOICE	MEDIUM
• What is your unique perspective on this topic? How can you bring your voice into the writing?	• What options do you have for the medium of delivery, given the purpose and audience for your writing? How does the medium influence what you write and how you write about it?

Mapping *Mapping*, also called *clustering*, is a visual way of generating and connecting ideas. It can be done individually or in a group. Write your topic in a circle at the center of a page, think of ideas related to the topic, and write those ideas on the page around the central topic. Draw lines to make connections. For a writing assignment that asked for a response to a chapter in Paul Fussell's book *Uniforms* (see Source Shot 2, pp. 190–191), a student created the following map. She saw that it indicated several possibilities for topics, such as the increasing casualness of American society and the power of uniforms to both camouflage and identify their wearers. You can see an excerpt from her draft in 3d.

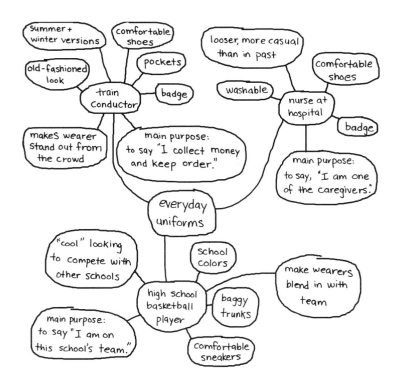

● TECH **NOTE**

Using Mind Mapping Software

Web-based applications such as *MindMeister* can be useful for doing clustering activities, mapping out your ideas, and even embedding links to resources that you think you might want to use in your writing. An online mind map can serve as a way to organize your thoughts and also to track your research.

Using journalists' questions   Journalists check for thorough coverage of their stories by making sure they answer six questions—though not in any set order: Who did it? What happened? When did it happen? Where did it occur? Why did it happen? How did it turn out? If you are telling the story of an event, either as a complete essay or as an example in an essay, asking the journalists' six questions will help you think comprehensively about your topic.

Including descriptions   Whatever your topic, ask questions about color, light, location, movement, size, shape, sound, taste, and smell. Doing so can help you discover an interesting angle on your topic. Putting these details in writing can also eventually help your reader "see" your topic—whether it is a person, place, object, or scientific experiment—exactly as you see it.

Making comparisons   You can better understand a topic—and help your audience understand it too—by describing what it might be similar to and different from. For example, how is learning to write like learning to ride a bike—or not?

Assessing cause and effect   Try approaching your topic by asking what causes or produces it and what effects or results emerge from it. For example, what are the causes and effects of dyslexia? inflation? acid rain? hurricanes? salmonella? asthma?

Responding to what you read   If you are assigned a response to something you have read, the following types of statements can be good starting points for exploring possible responses:

▶ When I read X, I think of my own experience...

▶ When X says..., I don't agree because...

▶ Generally, X makes good points but misses the fact that...

▶ When X tells us that..., I immediately think of a very different example:...

Thesis is statement of many nts for her views could be interpreted
unless writing connection than
you suggested, stand on response ....ncing because...

2c   Finding focus and a main idea (thesis statement)

Your main idea is your statement of opinion or message that unifies your piece of writing, makes a connection between you and the subject area, lets your reader know where you stand in relation to the topic, and responds to the question posed, if appropriate. In some essays, readers may expect to see your main idea formulated as what is called a *thesis statement*. A thesis statement is a sentence that makes a specific claim that is subsequently supported with clear reasons and evidence. Formal essays that are stating a claim will often have a thesis statement, but essays that don't have a persuasive purpose might just have a main idea but not an identifiable thesis statement. See 4c for help in understanding the difference between effective and ineffective thesis statements.

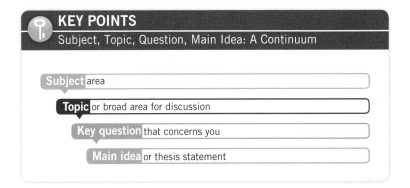

From subject to topic to main idea   After analyzing some readings on social networking, discussing Web sites, and making notes, students were given the task of working together in groups to formulate a progression from subject to question to main idea based on what they had read about social networking and issues of privacy. This is what one group produced:

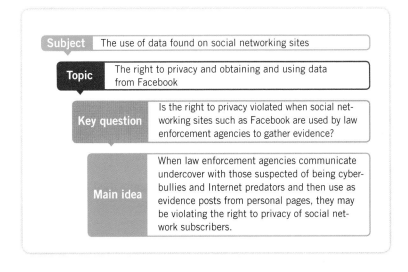

If you choose a topic and a question that are too broad, you will find it difficult to generate a main idea (or thesis) with focused ideas and examples. Whenever you find yourself thinking, for instance, "There's so much to say about social life online that I don't know where to start," narrow your topic. If you begin by choosing a topic and a question that are too narrow, you probably will not find enough material and will end up being repetitive. Above all, stay flexible. You may want to revise your topic or your question as you discover more information.

Progressing from topic to main idea   It is not enough to say, "I am writing about Facebook," although that may be what you start with. This simply names your topic. It does *not* indicate what you might explore about Facebook. Are you going to address the hazards teens need to be aware of when they enter a social networking site? The way teens can gain friends but also expose themselves? The places where predators lurk? Are you going to analyze Facebook postings? Its effects on predatory behavior? The ethics of using postings to catch predators? In short, work toward considering the most important point you want to make about the right to privacy and social networking sites. Maybe you will compare Facebook with another social networking site such as LinkedIn, or perhaps you will interview parents to get their reactions to their children's participation. Or you could explore how the networks provide outlets for students who need an alternative to parental authority. Whichever road you take, play with your first general idea until it gels more for you and you find something that makes a point you know you can describe, explain, and support.

Start drafting the point you want to make, or start with three or four statements that you would like to explore more.

2d Using outlines and other drafting aids

Outlining often supports drafting. Alternatively, in the initial stages of a research project, a purpose statement or a proposal may work better for you than a scratch outline.

The following table is a guide to two frequently used types of outlines, *scratch* and *formal,* with samples following.

Using Outlines while Drafting

	Scratch Outline	Formal Outline
What it is	a rough list of numbered points that you intend to cover in your essay	spells out, in order, what points and supportive details you will use to develop your main idea or thesis and arranges them to show the overall form and structure of the essay
What it helps you do	lets you see what ideas you already have, how they connect, what you can do to support and develop them, and what further planning or research you still need to do	serves as a check on the logic and completeness of what you have written, revealing any gaps, repetition, or illogical steps in the development of your essay
When you use it	early in the process and at midpoints if integrating major revisions	early in the process, but you are likely to find that making an outline with a high level of detail is more feasible after you have written a draft
Starting point	chosen topic	thesis statement or main idea

Scratch outline   One student in a class discussing social networking sites made the following scratch outline:

Subject: The use of data found on social networking sites

Topic: The right to privacy and obtaining and using data from Facebook

Question: Is the right to privacy violated when social networking sites such as Facebook are used by law enforcement agencies to gather evidence?

Possible main idea: Law enforcement agencies that use social networking sites to pursue cyberbullies and Internet predators might be violating a citizen's right to privacy.

Points:

1. Information stored on home computers and private servers may be protected by privacy law.

2. Information stored on external servers such as Facebook may not be considered private.

3. Social networking sites such as Facebook have guidelines and privacy policies.

4. Evidence from updates, tweets, IP addresses, uploaded photographs, and Web sites that track relationships is currently being used by law enforcement agencies.

5. Law enforcement agencies that engage in analytical or undercover operations using social networking sites and similar media avoid violations of privacy when pursuing crimes against sexual predators and cyberbullies.

Possible directions: Ways law enforcement can use social networking sites; visibility of sites' privacy policies; ethics of using false identities online; ways to prevent youth from sharing too much online; legal risks for minors?

Formal outline   When the same student began to work on a new draft, however, he developed a more nuanced and more focused thesis. Note how to structure an outline:

Main points: I, II, III, etc.

2nd level: A, B, C, etc.

3rd level: 1, 2, 3, etc.

4th level: a, b, c, etc.

The following shows an outline of just one main point, with complete sentences for the first two levels. When you create your own outline, be sure you have at least two items in each of the levels: if you have an "a," then you must have a "b," for example.

Thesis: Law enforcement agencies that use social networking sites to pursue cyberbullies and Internet predators might be violating a citizen's right to privacy.

I. Facebook has historically cooperated with law enforcement agencies by providing user-generated information that has been used in criminal investigations.

A. Personal profiles have provided contact and employment information.

B. Status updates and blog entries have provided insight into an individual's whereabouts and activities.

C. Photographs have been used to establish location information, personal relationships, and even character.

1. The use of dated photographs to establish or refute alibis
2. Joshua Lipton drunk driving case

D. Messaging and status updates can be linked to a device and the time and place it was used.
1. Rodney Bradford's avoidance of robbery charges because he updated his status from his father's computer at the time of the crime
2. How Jonathan G. Parker checked his Facebook status at the scene of the crime

Other strategies for drafting   Writing offers opportunities that speech can never provide: the ability to revise your ideas and the way you present them. Writing drafts allows you to work on a piece of writing until it meets your goals. Try the following ideas for drafting:

- **Plan the steps and set a schedule.** Work backward from the deadline, and assign time in days or hours for each of the following tasks: deciding on a topic, generating ideas, making a scratch outline, writing a draft, getting feedback, analyzing the draft, making large-scale revisions, finding additional material, editing, proofreading, formatting, and printing. Be certain to include additional time for revisiting any of these stages if needed.

- **Manage writer's block.** If you feel yourself suffering from what is called *writer's block*, try to ignore any self-imposed rigid rules that hinder you, such as "Always stick with a complete outline" or "Check everything and edit as you write." Editing too early may prevent you from thinking about ideas and moving forward.

- **Don't start at the beginning.** Don't automatically begin by writing the introduction. Begin by writing the essay parts for which you already have some specific material. Then you will know what you need to introduce.

- **Pace yourself.** Write in increments of twenty to thirty minutes to take advantage of momentum. When you take a break, have a set time that you will get back to writing and a specific place that you will begin writing again in the document.

- **Put your first draft to work.** Write your first draft as quickly and fluently as you can and print it double-spaced. Write notes to yourself in capitals or surrounded by asterisks to remind yourself to add or change something or to do further research. Sometimes seeing your writing in print can help you identify possibilities for revision or expansion that you cannot see on the screen.

- **Be specific.** Avoid obvious, vague, or empty generalizations (such as "All people have feelings"). Be specific, and include interesting supporting details. Keep in mind that claims always need evidence.

- **Use Comment and AutoCorrect.** Word processing programs have a Comment function that allows you to type notes that appear only on the screen, not in a printout, provided you set the Print options to ignore them. These notes are easily deleted from later drafts. In addition, if you use a term frequently (for example, the phrase "bilingual education"), abbreviate it (as "b.e.") and use a tool like AutoCorrect and Replace to substitute the whole phrase throughout your draft as you type.

- **Resist the lure of Copy and Paste.** Copying a passage from an online site and pasting it into your own document may seem like a good solution when you are facing a looming deadline and surfing for good Web sources. However, the penalties for plagiarism are far worse than those for lateness (see 9a). So the bottom line here is ***don't do it***.

2e Paragraph and topic sentences

Paragraphs   A good paragraph makes a clear point, supports your main idea, and focuses on one topic. Some paragraphs, however, may have more to do with function than with content. They serve to take readers from one point to another, making a connection and offering a smooth transition from one idea to the next. These transitional paragraphs are often short.

To indicate a new paragraph, indent the first line a half-inch from the left margin or, in business and online documents, begin it at the left margin after a blank line.

KEY POINTS
When to Begin a New Paragraph

1. To introduce a new point (one that supports the claim or main idea of your essay)

2. To expand on a point already made by offering new examples or evidence

3. To break up a long discussion or description into manageable chunks that are easier to read

   Both logic and aesthetics dictate when it is time to begin a new paragraph. Think of a paragraph as something that gathers together in one place ideas that connect to each other and to the main purpose of the piece of writing.

Topic sentences   A *topic sentence* in a body paragraph lets readers know explicitly what the main idea of the paragraph is. Readers should notice a logical flow of ideas as they read through a paragraph and as they move from one paragraph to another through an essay.

When you write a paragraph, imagine a reader saying, "Look, I don't have time to read all this. Just tell me in one sentence (or two) what point you are making here." Your reply would express your main point. Each paragraph in an academic essay generally contains a controlling idea expressed in a sentence (called a *topic sentence*) and does not digress or switch topics in midstream. Its content is unified. A *unified paragraph*, in academic writing, includes one main idea that the rest of the paragraph explains, supports, and develops.

The following paragraph is devoted to one broad topic—tennis— but does not follow through on the topic of the *trouble* that the *backhand* causes *average* players (key terms highlighted in yellow). The unity of the paragraph could be improved. What is Grand Slam winner Serena Williams doing in a paragraph about average players? What relevance does her powerful serve have to the average player's problems with a backhand? The writer would do well to revise by cutting out the two sentences about Serena Williams (sentences highlighted in blue).

> The backhand in tennis causes average weekend players more trouble than other strokes. Even though the swing is natural and free flowing, many players feel intimidated and try to avoid it. Serena Williams, however, has a great backhand, and she often wins difficult points with it. Her serve is a powerful weapon, too. When faced by a backhand coming at them across the net, midlevel players can't seem to get their feet and body in the best position. They tend to run around the ball or forget the swing and give the ball a little poke, praying that it will not only reach but also go over the net.

When placed first, as it is in the paragraph on the troublesome backhand, a topic sentence makes a generalization and serves as a reference point for the rest of the information in the paragraph. When placed after one or two other sentences, the topic sentence focuses the details and directs readers' attention to the main idea. When placed at the end of the paragraph, the topic sentence serves to summarize or draw conclusions from the details that precede it.

Some paragraphs, such as the short ones typical of newspaper writing or the one-sentence paragraphs that make a quick transition, do not always contain a topic sentence. Sometimes, too, a paragraph contains such clear details that the point is obvious and does not need to be explicitly stated. However, in academic essays, a paragraph in support of your essay's claim or thesis (main point) will usually be unified and focused on one clear topic, regardless of whether you state it in a topic sentence.

2f Using transitions and links for coherence

However you develop your individual paragraphs, readers expect to move with ease from one sentence to the next and from one paragraph to the next, following a clear flow of argument and logic. When you construct an essay or paragraph, do not force readers to grapple with "grasshopper prose," which jumps suddenly from one idea to another without obvious connections. Instead, make your writing *coherent*, with all the parts connecting clearly to one another with transitional expressions, context links, parallel structures, and word links.

Transitional words and expressions Make clear connections between sentences and between paragraphs either by using explicit connecting words like *this, that, these,* and *those* to refer to something mentioned at the end of the previous sentence or paragraph or by using transitional expressions.

KEY POINTS
Transitional Expressions

Adding an idea also, in addition, further, furthermore, moreover

Contrasting however, nevertheless, nonetheless, on the other hand, in contrast, still, on the contrary, rather, conversely

Providing an alternative instead, alternatively, otherwise

Showing similarity similarly, likewise

Showing order of time or order of ideas first, second, third (and so on), then, next, later, subsequently, meanwhile, previously, finally

Showing result as a result, consequently, therefore, thus, hence, accordingly, for this reason

Affirming of course, in fact, certainly, obviously, to be sure, undoubtedly, indeed

Giving examples for example, for instance

Explaining in other words, that is

Adding an aside incidentally, by the way, besides

Summarizing in short, generally, overall, all in all, in conclusion

For punctuation with transitional expressions, see 45e.

Although transitional expressions are useful to connect one sentence to another or one paragraph to another, do not overuse these expressions. Too many of them, used too often, make writing seem heavy and mechanical.

Context links   A new paragraph introduces a new topic, but that topic should not be entirely separate from what has gone before. Let readers know the context of the big picture. If you are writing about the expense of exploring Mars and then switch abruptly to the hazards of climbing Everest, readers will be puzzled. You need to state clearly the connection with your main idea: "Exploration on our own planet can be as hazardous and as financially risky as space exploration."

Word links   You can also provide coherence by using repeated words or connected words, such as pronouns linked to nouns; words with the same, similar, or opposite meanings; or words linked by context. Note how Deborah Tannen maintains coherence not only by using transitional expressions (*for example, furthermore*) but also by repeating words and phrases (blue) and by using certain pronouns (red)—*she* and *her* to refer to *wife*, and *they* to refer to *Greeks*.

> Entire cultures operate on elaborate systems of indirectness. For example, I discovered in a small research project that most Greeks assumed that a wife who asked, "Would you like to go to the party?" was hinting that **she** wanted to go. **They** felt that **she** wouldn't bring it up if **she** didn't want to go. Furthermore, **they** felt, **she** would not state **her** preference outright because **that** would sound like a demand. Indirectness was the appropriate means for communicating **her** preference.
>
> —Deborah Tannen, *You Just Don't Understand*

2g Eight examples of paragraph development

Whether you are writing a paragraph or an essay, you will do well to keep in mind the image of a skeptical reader always inclined to say something challenging, such as "Why on earth do you think that?" or "What could possibly lead you to that conclusion?" Show your reader that your opinion is well founded and supported by experience, knowledge, logical arguments, the work of experts, or reasoned examples, and provide vivid, unique details. Here are illustrations of some rhetorical strategies you can use to develop ideas in paragraphs and essays. They may serve as prompts to help you generate ideas.

Give examples   Examples that develop a point make writing interesting and informative. The following paragraph about Harry S. Truman (president of the United States 1945–53) as a young boy follows an account of his happy childhood. It begins with a topic sentence that announces the controlling idea: "Yet life had its troubles and woes." The author then gives examples of some "troubles and woes" that young Harry faced. Beginning with a generalization and supporting it with specific illustrative details is a common method of organizing a paragraph known as *deductive organization*.

> Yet life had its troubles and woes. On the summer day when his Grandfather Truman died, three-year-old Harry had rushed to the bed to pull at the old man's beard, trying desperately to wake him. Climbing on a chair afterward, in an attempt to comb his hair in front of a mirror, he toppled over backward and broke his collarbone. Another time he would have choked to death on a peach stone had his mother not responded in a flash and decisively, pushing the stone down his throat with her finger, instead of trying to pull it out. Later, when Grandpa Young [Harry's mother's father] lay sick in bed and the little boy approached cautiously to inquire how he was feeling, the old pioneer, fixing him with a wintry stare, said, "How are you feeling? You're the one I'm worried about."
>
> —David McCullough, *Truman*

In addition, you may decide to illustrate an idea in your text by using a visual image as an example.

Tell a story   Choose a pattern of organization that readers will easily grasp. Organize the events in a story chronologically so that readers can follow the sequence. In the following paragraph, the writer tells a story that leads to the point that people with disabilities often face ignorance and insensitivity. Note that she uses *inductive organization*, beginning with background information and the specific details of the story in chronological order and ending with a generalization.

> Jonathan is an articulate, intelligent, thirty-five-year-old man who has used a wheelchair since he became a paraplegic when he was twenty years old. He recalls taking an able bodied woman out to dinner at a nice restaurant. When the waitress came to take their order,

she patronizingly asked his date, "And what would he like to eat for dinner?" At the end of the meal, the waitress presented Jonathan's date with the check and thanked her for her patronage. Although it may be hard to believe the insensitivity of the waitress, this incident is not an isolated one. Rather, such an experience is a common one for persons with disabilities.

—Dawn O. Braithwaite, "Viewing Persons with Disabilities as a Culture"

Describe with details appealing to the senses   To help readers see and experience what you feel and experience, describe people, places, scenes, and objects by using sensory details that re-create those people, places, scenes, or objects for your readers. In the following paragraph from a memoir about growing up to love food, Ruth Reichl tells how she spent days working at a summer camp in France and thinking about eating. However, she does much more than say "The food was always delicious" and much more than "I looked forward to the delicious bread, coffee, and morning snacks." Reichl appeals to our senses of sight, smell, touch, and taste. We get a picture of the campers, we smell the baking bread, we see and almost taste the jam, we smell and taste the coffee, and we feel the crustiness of the rolls. We feel that we are there—and we wish we were.

> When we woke up in the morning the smell of baking bread was wafting through the trees. By the time we had gotten our campers out of bed, their faces washed and their shirts tucked in, the aroma had become maddeningly seductive. We walked into the dining room to devour hot bread slathered with country butter and topped with homemade plum jam so filled with fruit it made each slice look like a tart. We stuck our faces into the bowls of café au lait, inhaling the sweet, bitter, peculiarly French fragrance, and Georges or Jean or one of the other male counselors would say, for the hundredth time, "*On mange pas comme ça à Paris.*" Two hours later we had a "*gouter,*" a snack of chocolate bars stuffed into fresh, crusty rolls. And two hours later there was lunch. The eating went on all day.
>
> —Ruth Reichl, *Tender at the Bone: Growing Up at the Table*

Develop a point by providing facts and statistics   The following paragraph supports with facts and statistics the assertion made in its first sentence (the topic sentence) that the North grew more than the South in the years before the Civil War.

> While southerners tended their fields, the North grew. In 1800, half the nation's five million people lived in the South. By 1850, only a

third lived there. Of the nine largest cities, only New Orleans was located in the lower South. Meanwhile, a tenth of the goods manufactured in America came from southern mills and factories. There were one hundred piano makers in New York alone in 1852. In 1846, there was not a single book publisher in New Orleans; even the city guidebook was printed in Manhattan.

—Geoffrey C. Ward, *The Civil War: An Illustrated History*

Here, too, visuals such as tables, charts, and graphs would help present data succinctly and dramatically.

Define key terms   Sometimes, writers clarify and develop a topic by defining a key term, even if it is not an unusual term. Often, they will explain what class something fits into and how it differs from others in its class; for example, "A duckbilled platypus is a mammal that has webbed feet and lays eggs." In his book on diaries, Thomas Mallon begins by providing an extended definition of his basic terms. He does not want readers to misunderstand him because they wonder what the differences between a diary and a journal might be.

The first thing we should try to get straight is what to call them. "What's the difference between a diary and a journal?" is one of the questions people interested in these books ask. The two terms are in fact hopelessly muddled. They're both rooted in the idea of dailiness, but perhaps because of *journal*'s links to the newspaper trade and *diary*'s to *dear*, the latter seems more intimate than the former. (The French blur even this discrepancy by using no word recognizable like *diary*; they just say *journal intime*, which is sexy, but a bit of a mouthful.) One can go back as far as Dr. Johnson's *Dictionary* and find him making the two more or less equal. To him a diary was "an account of the transactions, accidents, and observations of every day; a journal." Well, if synonymity was good enough for Johnson, we'll let it be good enough for us.

—Thomas Mallon, *A Book of One's Own: People and Their Diaries*

Analyze component parts   Large, complex topics sometimes become more manageable to writers (and readers) when they are broken down for analysis. The *Columbia Encyclopedia* online helps readers understand the vast concept of life itself by breaking it down into six component parts:

Although there is no universal agreement as to a definition of *life*, its biological manifestations are generally considered to be organization, metabolism, growth, irritability, adaptation, and reproduction.... Organization is found in the basic living unit, the cell, and in the organized groupings of cells into organs and organisms. Metabolism includes the conversion of nonliving material into cellular components (synthesis) and the decomposition of organic matter (catalysis), producing energy. Growth in living matter is an increase in size of all parts, as distinguished from simple addition of material; it results from a higher rate of synthesis than catalysis. Irritability, or response to stimuli, takes many forms, from the contraction of a unicellular organism when touched to complex reactions involving all the senses of higher animals; in plants response is usually much different than in animals but is nonetheless present. Adaptation, the accommodation of a living organism to its present or to a new environment, is fundamental to the process of evolution and is determined by the individual's heredity. The division of one cell to form two new cells is reproduction; usually the term is applied to the production of a new individual (either asexually, from a single parent organism, or sexually, from two differing parent organisms), although strictly speaking it also describes the production of new cells in the process of growth.

—*Columbia Encyclopedia*, ed. Paul Lagasse, © 2006 Columbia University Press.
Reprinted with the permission of the publisher.

Classify into groups   Dividing people or objects into the classes or groups that make up the whole gives readers a new way to look at the topic. In the following paragraphs, the writer develops her essay on personality by classifying people into two categories and providing back and forth comparisons between the two types of personalities.

Although introverts and extraverts may seem like they come from different planets, introversion and extraversion exist on a continuous dimension that is normally distributed. There are a few extremely extraverted folk, and a few extreme introverts, while most of us share some extravert and some introvert traits.

Although there is no precise dividing line, there are plenty of introverts around. It's just that perceptual biases lead us all to overestimate the number of extraverts among us (they are noisier and hog the spotlight). Often confused with shyness, introversion does not imply social reticence or discomfort. Rather than being averse to social engagement, introverts become overwhelmed by too much of it, which explains why the introvert is ready to leave a party after an hour and the extravert gains steam as the night goes on.

—Laurie Helgoe, "Revenge of the Introvert"

Compare and contrast   When you examine similarities and differences among people, objects, or concepts, block style and point-by-point style achieve different purposes:

Block style	Point-by-point style
You can deal with each subject one at a time, perhaps summarizing the similarities and differences at the end. This organization works well when each section is short and readers can easily remember the points made about each subject.	You can select and organize the important points of similarity or difference, referring within each point to both subjects.

The following example uses the point-by-point approach in comparing John Stuart Mill, a British philosopher and economist, and Harriet Taylor, a woman with whom Mill had a close intellectual relationship. The author, Phyllis Rose, organizes the contrast by points of difference, referring to her subjects' facial features, physical behavior, ways of thinking and speaking, and intellectual style. (A block organization would deal first with the characteristics of Taylor, followed by the characteristics of Mill.)

Library of the London School of Economics

Harriet Taylor

You could see how they complemented each other by the way they looked. What people noticed first about Harriet were her eyes—flashing—and a suggestion in her body of mobility, whereas his features, variously described as chiselled and classical, expressed an inner rigidity. He shook hands from the shoulder. He spoke carefully. Give him facts, and he would sift them, weigh them, articulate possible interpretations, reach a conclusion. Where he was careful, she was daring. Where he was disinterested and balanced, she was intuitive, partial, and sure of herself. She con-

Bettmann/Corbis

John Stuart Mill

cerned herself with goals and assumptions; he concerned himself with arguments. She was quick to judge and to generalize, and because he was not, he valued her intellectual style as bold and vigorous where another person, more like her, might have found her hasty and simplistic.

—Phyllis Rose, *Parallel Lives: Five Victorian Marriages*

2h Writing introductions and conclusions

Introductions   Readers like to know a little about a topic, about why it is even worth discussing, before you pronounce your opinion on it. Think of your introduction as a way to establish your purpose for writing and to make an important connection with your intended audience. If you find it difficult to write an introduction because you are not yet clear about your claim or how you will support it, wait until you have written the body of your essay. You may find it easier to introduce the actual text you have composed than something you have not yet written.

When you write an essay in the humanities, keep the following points in mind. Other disciplines have slightly different ways of introducing writing, depending on the conventions of the genre.

KEY POINTS
How to Write a Good Introduction

Options

- Make sure your first sentence stands alone and does not depend on readers' being aware of the essay title or an assigned question. For instance, avoid beginning with "This story has a complex plot."

- Provide context and background information.

- Indicate what claim you will make in your essay, or at least indicate the issue that your main idea concerns.

- Define any key terms that are pertinent to the discussion.

- Establish the tone of the paper: informative, persuasive, serious, humorous, personal, impersonal, formal, informal.

- Engage the interest of your readers to make them want to explore your topic with you. Tell them something they may not know or something to surprise them, such as an unlikely fact or statistic, a challenging question, a pithy quotation, interesting background details, a joke, an intriguing opinion, a startling verbal image, or a description of a problem.

What to Avoid

- Avoid being overly general and telling readers the obvious, such as "Crime is a big problem" or "In this fast-paced world, TV is a

(Continued)

(Continued)

popular form of entertainment" or "Since the beginning of time, the sexes have been in conflict."

 • Do not refer to your writing intentions, such as "In this essay, I will …"

• Do not make extravagant claims, such as "This essay will prove that bilingual education works for every student."

• Do not restate the assigned essay question.

Consider these attention-grabbing beginnings of books or chapters:

▶ **"You gonna eat that?" The woman is eyeing the tray the flight attendant has just set before me. I can't tell if she wants reassurance that I find it as repellent as she does or if she is simply hungry and hopeful that I will hand my food over. I loosen my seatbelt, swivel in my narrow seat, and see that her face holds a challenge. Is she daring me to eat the food?**

—Ruth Reichl, *Garlic and Sapphires*

▶ **Faced with working-class life in towns such as Winchester, I see only one solution: beer.**

—Joe Bageant, *Deer Hunting with Jesus: Dispatches from America's Class War*

▶ **It is a truth universally acknowledged, that a single man in possession of a good fortune, must be in want of a wife.**

—Jane Austen, *Pride and Prejudice*

▶ **It was a bright cold day in April, and the clocks were striking thirteen.**

—George Orwell, *1984*

▶ **Every day in the United States, roughly 200,000 people are sickened by a foodborne disease, 900 are hospitalized, and fourteen die.**

—Eric Schlosser, *Fast Food Nation*

Brainstorming may help you come up with catchy openings. A brainstorming session, for example, produced the following openers for an essay on fashion:

A description	Everyone stared at him as he walked in. His jeans were torn, his sneakers stained and ripped, his jacket a shapeless rag, his tee shirt sweaty. He was the coolest guy in the room.
A memorable quotation	The flamboyant author Oscar Wilde advises, "One should either be a work of art or wear a work of art."
A startling fact	How far obedience to fashion can be taken was shown in China when for hundreds of years women were truly fashionable when they had undergone the torture and permanent disfigurement of having their feet bound so they could fit into unnaturally tiny shoes.
An anecdote	I keep clothes I have rarely worn for a time when they might come back into fashion and I can maybe wear them again. I still have bright green pants with vast bell bottoms and a purple jacket with football-quarterback shoulders in my closet. The sad thing is that a fashion never returns in exactly the same style or colors. When I put on the pants, my friends just laugh and say "Nice Halloween costume!"
A question	"Who are you wearing?" Such a question, the one most often heard on the red carpet before the Oscars, would have been unintelligible a few decades ago.
An interesting observation	Identical twins can live apart for twenty years without ever having been in touch and yet at any moment can be wearing the same colored dress, shoes of the same make, hair cut in the same style.

Conclusions   Think of your conclusion as completing a circle. You have taken readers on a journey from presentation of the topic in your introduction, to your main point, to supporting evidence and discussion, with specific examples and illustrations. Remind readers of the purpose of the journey. Recall the main idea of the paper, and make a strong statement about it that will stay in their minds. Readers should leave your document feeling satisfied, not turning the page and looking for more.

Each academic discipline has slightly different ways of concluding a piece of writing, depending on the conventions of the genre. When you write an essay in the humanities, keep the following points in mind.

> ## KEY POINTS
> ### How to Write a Good Conclusion
>
> **Options**
>
> - Frame your essay by reminding readers of something you referred to in your introduction and by reminding readers of your main idea. End on a strong note: a quotation, a question, a suggestion, a reference to an anecdote in the introduction, a humorous insightful comment, a call to action, or a look to the future.
>
> - Leave readers with a sense of completion of the point you are making.
>
> **What to Avoid**
>
> - Do not use the obvious "In conclusion."
>
> - Do not apologize for the inadequacy of your argument ("I do not know much about this problem") or for holding your opinions ("I am sorry if you do not agree with me, but …").
>
> - Do not repeat the identical wording you used in your introduction.
>
> - Do not introduce a totally new direction. If you raise a new point at the end, readers might expect more details.
>
> - Do not contradict what you said previously.
>
> - Do not be too sweeping in your conclusions. Do not condemn the whole medical profession, for example, because one person you know had a bad time in one hospital.

2i Writing with others

Writing is not necessarily a solitary process. In the academic or business world, you will often have to work collaboratively with one or more classmates or colleagues. You might be part of a group, team, or committee assigned to draft a proposal or a report. You might be expected to produce a document reflecting the consensus of your section or group. Or you might need to draft and circulate a document and then incorporate into it the comments of many people.

In group settings, you can make sure that every member contributes by assigning each person a set of specific tasks. These tasks might include making lists of ideas, drafting, analyzing the draft, revising, editing, assembling visuals, and preparing the final document. You also might divide a project into parts and assign each person a section to draft. Schedule regular meetings, and expect everyone to come with a completed written assignment. Build on strengths within the group. For example, ask the member skilled in document design and computer graphics to prepare the visual features of the final document.

However, make sure that you work collaboratively only when doing so is expected. An instructor who assigns an essay will not always expect you to work on it with your sister, classmate, or tutor.

● TECH NOTE

Writing Collaboratively on the Computer

Word processing programs and e-mail provide useful tools for collaboration. You can work on a text, make and highlight changes, insert comments, and attach the revised text to an e-mail message to a colleague, who can then accept or reject the changes. *Google Docs* also provides a useful tool for working with others, allowing you to upload a document that others can then access, change, and add to. Group members can even edit the document simultaneously.

3 Revising, Editing, and Proofreading

Revising—making changes to improve a piece of writing—is an essential part of the writing process. It is not a punishment inflicted on inexperienced writers. Even Leo Tolstoy, author of the monumental Russian novel *War and Peace,* commented: "I cannot understand how anyone can write without rewriting everything over and over again."

Take a look at one manuscript page from Chapter 1 of this text. You'll notice that, even though both authors of this text are professional writers and teachers, we worked with our editor to revise and edit a page of this book in significant detail.

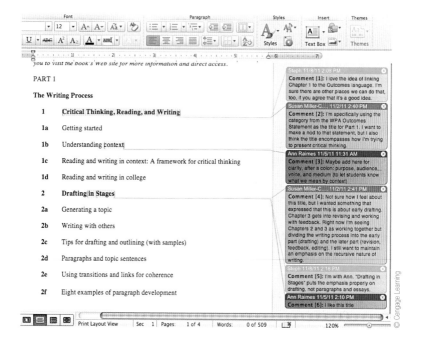

● **TECH NOTE**

Computer Tools for Revising an Essay

- **Copy and paste first sentences.** Select the first sentence of each paragraph, and use the Copy and Paste features to move the sequence of sentences into a new file. Then examine these first sentences to check for logical progression of ideas, repetition, or omission.

- **Use different file names.** Write multiple drafts and save every draft under a separate file name, one that clearly labels the topic and the draft. Some people prefer to save deleted sections in a separate "dump" file so that they can retrieve deleted parts.

- **Use the Find feature.** The Find feature helps you locate words and phrases that you tend to overuse. Use it to look for instances of "there is" or "there are," for example, and you will see if you are using either phrase too often.

- **Use the Insert Comment feature.** The Insert Comment feature allows you to write a note to yourself in the middle of a draft and see it highlighted on your screen. You can then choose to print your document with or without the comments showing.

3a Revising content

It is often tempting just to correct errors in spelling and grammar and see the result as a new draft, but revising entails more than fixing errors. Reworking a draft to reconsider ideas and logic and to add interest is what revision is all about. Use these proven strategies to improve your writing in substantial ways:

- **Wait.** Don't start revising until you have completed a significant part of your draft.
- **Create distance and space.** Put a draft away for at least a few hours or days, and then read it again with fresher, more critical eyes.
- **Make room.** Write a triple-spaced draft so that if you print it out, you can easily write in changes and comments.
- **Consider the context of your writing.** Remind yourself of your intended purpose, your audience's expectations, the elements of your voice that are important to have in the draft, and how the choice of medium might influence the piece of writing.

See the full model on page 7.

- **Highlight key words in the assignment.** Then mark passages in your draft that address those key words. If you fail to find any, that could signal where you need to revise.
- **Read your draft aloud.** Mark any places where you hesitate and have to struggle to understand the point. Go back to them later. Alternatively, ask somebody else to read a copy of the draft aloud to you and note where he or she hesitates or seems confused.
- **Make an outline.** Outlining what you have written will help you to discover gaps or repetitions.
- **Use the "Triggers for Revision" Key Points box.** These points will alert you to things to look for as you read your draft.

 KEY POINTS
Triggers for Revision

Any of the following should alert you to a need for revision:

1. Is the introductory paragraph weak or boring?
2. Do you have a worried frown, a pause, or a thought of "Huh? Something is wrong here" in any spot as you read your draft?
3. Do you find a paragraph that never makes a point?

(Continued)

(Continued)

4. Are there any paragraphs that seem unrelated to the thesis of the essay?

5. Do you read a phrase, sentence, or passage that you cannot immediately understand (if you have trouble grasping your own ideas, readers surely will have trouble, too)?

6. Do you use generalizations excessively—*everyone, most people, all human beings, all students/lawyers/politicians,* and so on (instead use specific examples: *the students in my political science course this semester*)?

7. Do you have a feeling that you would have difficulty summarizing your draft (maybe it is too vague?)?

8. Did you just read the same point earlier in the draft?

9. Do you fail to find a definite conclusion?

3b Giving and getting feedback

Ask a friend, colleague, or tutor to read your draft with a pencil in hand or the Track Changes feature turned on in the word processor, noting passages that work well and placing a question mark next to those that do not. Ask your reader to tell you what main point you made and how you supported and developed it. This process might reveal any lack of clarity or indicate gaps in the logic of your draft. Your reader does not have to be an expert English teacher to give you good feedback. If you notice worried frowns (or worse, yawns) as the person reads, you will know that something in your text is puzzling, disconcerting, or boring. Even that simple level of feedback can be valuable.

If you are asked to give feedback to a classmate or colleague, use the following guidelines.

KEY POINTS
Giving Feedback to Others

1. Don't think of yourself as an English teacher armed with a red pen. Instead, ask the writer who the intended audience is, and try to read the piece from that perspective.

2. Start by providing positive reactions to ideas and clarity. Look for parts that make you think, "I agree," "I like this," or "This is well done."

3. As you read, put a light pencil mark or highlight one or two passages that make you pause and send you back to reread. If you can, write a comment next to those passages that indicates what you would like to have clarified ("I would like to know more about…" or "I wasn't sure what you meant by…").

4. Try to avoid comments that sound like accusations ("You were too vague in paragraph 3"). Instead, ask questions of the writer ("Could you give a specific example in paragraph 3?"). Questions invite a response, and they'll help the writer revise.

Here is a sample peer response form that can be used to provide feedback.

Draft by _____   Date _____

Response by _____   Date _____

1. Who is the audience and what is the purpose for this piece of writing? Consider offering a suggestion if either the audience or purpose is not clearly established.

2. What do you see as the writer's main point in this draft?

3. Which part of the draft interests you the most? Why?

4. Where do you feel you would like more detail or explanation? Where do you need less?

5. Do you find any parts unclear, confusing, or undeveloped? Mark each such spot and write a question in the margin to the writer.

6. Which medium did the author choose for presenting his or her work? Is the medium appropriate, or would you suggest an alternative?

7. Give the writer **one** suggestion about one change that you think would improve the draft the most.

● TECH **NOTE**

Using Track Changes

The Track Changes feature in *Microsoft Word* allows you to see and keep track of changes you make to your own document or one that you receive electronically to work on collaboratively. This feature lets you see clearly on the screen and on the printed page the changes you have made. Settings allow you to choose the color of your text inserts and label your comments with whatever initials or name you specify. The Accept Changes and Reject Changes options allow you to accept or reject the changes either individually or all at once.

3c Editing surface features

Once you have developed a solid draft and revised for issues of content and context, you should turn your attention to editing for surface features. Surface features are smaller-order concerns such as grammar, mechanics, and formatting. Paying attention to these issues will help you polish your draft for presentation to your audience.

Drafting and revising a title   A good title captures the reader's attention, makes the reader want to read on, and lets the reader know what to expect in a piece of writing. You might have a useful working title as you write, but after you finish writing, brainstorm several titles and pick the one you like best.

Working title	**The Benefits of Travel**
Revised title	**From Katmandu to Kuala Lumpur: A Real Education**
Working title	**Effects of the Economic Recession in the United States**
Revised title	**Portraits of Persistence: Two Case Studies of Women Searching for Employment during the Recession**

Correcting grammar, punctuation, and spelling   Examine your draft for grammar, punctuation, and spelling errors. Often, reading your essay aloud will help you find sentences that are tangled, poorly constructed, or not connected. If you pay attention to your own reading, your hesitations and restarts will flag possible problem areas that are not well constructed or gracefully phrased. Looking carefully at every word and its function in a sentence can also alert you to grammatical problem areas. Part 7 will help you with Standard English and methods for correcting common errors.

● TECH **NOTE**

Computer Tools for Editing

- A **spelling checker** will flag any word it does not recognize, and it is very good at catching typographical errors such as *teh* for *the* or *responsability* for *responsibility*. However, it will not consistently identify minor grammatical errors such as missing plural or *-ed* endings. Nor will it flag an omitted word or find a misspelled word that forms another word, such as *then* for *than*, *their* for *there*, or *affect* for *effect*.

- An online **thesaurus** will prompt you with synonyms and words close in meaning to a highlighted word; check suggested words in a dictionary for their connotations to be sure you're choosing the most precise word.

- The **Word Count** feature of word processing programs is handy when you are given a word limit; it provides an immediate, accurate count.

● NOTE **FOR MULTILINGUAL WRITERS**

Beware of Grammar-Check Programs

Never make a change in your draft at the suggestion of a grammar-check program before verifying that the change is really necessary. A student from Ukraine wrote the grammatically acceptable sentence "What he has is pride." Then, at the suggestion of a grammar-check program, he changed the sentence to "What he has been pride." The program had not recognized the sequence "has is."

See 35b for more on the uses and dangers of grammar-check programs.

3d A student's annotated drafts

With her class, student Catherine Turnbull was assigned to read a chapter of Paul Fussell's book *Uniforms: Why We Are What We Wear* and respond to it. After she wrote a first draft, she read it aloud to a group of classmates and took note of their comments. She also received feedback from her instructor in a conference. Turnbull's first draft of her first two paragraphs and her conclusion shows her notes and annotations for revision. Following that is her second draft, in which she moved material from the end to the beginning for a clearer statement of her main idea; fine-tuned her style, sentence structure, and word choice; and cited her source. Her major changes are noted. She did not include full MLA parenthetical references (see 21a) or works-cited information until she was ready to write her final edited draft.

FIRST DRAFT

Shift from self to topic— get readers interested

Think up better title

Reader Response Essay: Nonmilitary Uniforms

I read the wedding gown chapter from Paul Fussell's assigned book. This chapter covered the history of the white tradition, cost, fanciness, and saving the dress afterwards, etc. This chapter and the idea of the book made me look at the uniforms of people around me. While wedding dresses are intended to be incredibly special and are basically heavy, tight, and uncomfortable, many "real" uniforms are intended to be comfortable, casual, and are team- or job-related.

Say how?

Move to end?

Expand this point.

Change this

My first example is my aunt, a nurse at a hospital. She wears colorful, baggy, easy-wash scrubs most days, like pajamas with pockets, badge, and a stethoscope. Her name and credentials (RN) are on her badge. She wears super-comfortable shoes because she has to walk miles in the course of making her rounds, day or night. Her uniform says, I am part of the hospital team and am hear to help you. *sp*

add More details

[Two more paragraphs were included: on her brother's basketball uniform and a train conductor's uniform.]

Move to beginning.

Make Stronger

In sum, Paul Fussell writes on wedding dresses in his uniform book, but they are not really uniforms in the sense most working people mean the term. More commonly, uniforms are functional and comfortable garments, symbolizing an active day-to-day role played for the larger good. They make you one with your team and also stand out from the rest of the general populace. Unlike a wedding dress, an average uniform is not so special that it needs special storage. It is what people do and their roles in society that are special.

thesis

choppy

SECOND DRAFT

Comfortable Shoes: Everyday Uniforms
and the People Who Fill Them

How many people would call a bridal gown a uniform? Paul Fussell makes this somewhat startling claim in a chapter in a recent book in which he examines the so-called uniform of the formal wedding gown, its history, cost, and traditions, particularly the way it is often stored carefully away for future generations (167–69). He may justify his classification of the wedding dress as a uniform, but that is not the way most people mean the term. Surely it is more common to see uniforms as functional and comfortable garments, symbolizing an active day-to-day role played for a larger good.

My aunt, for instance, a nurse at Boston City Hospital, wears colorful, baggy, cotton medical scrubs to work, like pajamas with pockets, a badge, and a stethoscope. She says this outfit is easy to wash, which is important in the hygienic hospital setting. She wears the most comfortable rubber-soled shoes she can find since her job involves a lot of walking in the course of a day, making her rounds. Her name and credentials (RN) are on her badge, letting people know her official status and role as well-trained caregiver. In the past, nurses might have had to dress in white or wear more formal outfits and hats, but today the code is relaxed, with an emphasis on comfort and ease of laundering. Still, no matter how casual, her uniform definitely communicates the message, "I am an experienced member of the hospital team. I am here to help you."

Title revised to include word *everyday*

New intro: third person

Cites author and page

Thesis moved here from last ¶ of first draft

Deletes reference to "my first example"

Has added descriptive details of uniforms

[Turnbull included two more paragraphs.]

Paul Fussell stretches the definition of uniform when he includes wedding gowns. He correctly points out that wedding dresses conform to many set features, but even so they are meant to be as out of the ordinary and beautiful as possible. They are usually expensive, heavy, and snugly fitting, made with impractical fabrics and beads. In contrast, however, most everyday uniforms are loose, comfortable, and inexpensive; they identify wearers as part of a particular team with a particular mission, thus making them stand out from the crowd. Unlike a wedding dress, an average uniform is not so valuable that it needs to be preserved in a special garment bag. It is what people *do* in their uniforms and the roles they have taken on within their larger community that has special value.

Makes a strong point about Fussell

Synthesis of role of uniforms in 3 adjectives

Ends with a strong claim

3e Proofreading

Even after editing carefully with help from computer tools and this handbook, you still need to write a final draft and format it according to the conventions of the discipline you are studying or your instructor's directions. Sections 21a and 21b show how to format a document for page or screen, and chapter 22 shows how to include visuals.

Before you submit or post a paper, give it one more careful proof-reading to make sure no errors remain.

KEY POINTS
Proofreading Tips

All of these tips will help you spot remaining errors.

- Do not try to proofread on the computer screen. Print out a hard copy.

- Make another copy of your manuscript, and read it aloud while a friend examines the original as you read.

- Put a blank piece of paper under the first line of your text. Move it down line by line as you read, focusing your attention on one line at a time.

- Read the last sentence first, and work backward through your text. This strategy will not help you check for meaning, logic, pro-noun reference, fragments, or consistency of verb tenses, but it will focus your attention on the spelling, punctuation, and gram-matical correctness of each individual sentence.

- If possible, put your manuscript away for a few hours or longer after you have finished it. Proofread it when the content is not so familiar.

Chapters 21, 22 and 25–27 show you how to format and design your document for print or online presentation.

4   Writing and Analyzing Arguments

In an argument, your purpose is to persuade. You present your opinions on an issue as clearly and convincingly as you can. A well-formed argument—one that will persuade readers that your point of view is based on solid evidence—presents a carefully chosen and developed claim (a thesis) along with compelling reasons and supporting evidence specifically geared to the intended audience. The best arguments establish common ground as they consider and address opposing views in a manner that allows those who may have been opposed to save face as they change their minds. A good argument is strategically arranged and written in a voice likely to appeal to an audience's logical, ethical, and emotional inclinations. With such tact and strategy, it is no wonder that argument is called the *art* of persuasion.

But it is also a *science* of persuasion when you consider that behind a good argument is a writer who has gone through the rigorous process of considering and weighing his or her own assumptions, biases, and quick conclusions. In his introduction to John Brockman's *What Have You Changed Your Mind About?* Brian Eno points out that as an intellectual invention, science is "a construction designed to neutralize the universal tendency to see what we expected to see and overlook what we didn't expect." Although the brilliance of the human brain, he continues, allows us to discern "complex ideas from insubstantial data," the downside is that it all too easily allows us to reach a familiar but wrong conclusion rather than an unfamiliar but right conclusion.

When you write and analyze arguments, you challenge that tendency in yourself and invite others to do the same through a careful weighing of evidence and reason.

Understanding the process of constructing a well-formulated argument goes beyond writing essays for your composition class. As you become more practiced in the process of writing and analyzing arguments in your courses, you become more aware of the arguments all around you—in magazine articles, advertisements, blogs, visually displayed information, letters to publishers, scientific explanations, political opinions, newsletters, and business reports. Understanding the structures and strategies that form arguments is the very essence of what it means to be a critical thinker, reader, and writer.

4a Using critical thinking to read and write arguments

Whatever your topic, approach it by considering the context of the argument you are developing. Considering your purpose, audience, voice, and use of media will give you a framework for thinking critically as you read, research, and write.

See the full model on page 7.

It is a good habit to step back and read an argument critically, whether it is your own or someone else's, to identify its merits and faults. As you read, develop a system of inquiry. Do not assume that because something is in print, it is accurate. Assume that readers will use the same care when they read an argument that *you* write. So put yourself in a critical reader's shoes when you evaluate your own arguments. Here are questions to ask while analyzing an argument, either your own or someone else's:

1. **What is the writer's purpose?** Is the writer expressing an opinion, arguing for a course of action, making an evaluation, arguing against another claim?

2. **Who is the writer's audience?** Are there choices the writer has made to present the argument most persuasively to the intended audience?

3. **Who is the writer?** What is the writer's background and credentials? What is the writer's bias? Is the writer credible?

4. **How reliable are the writer's statements?** Are the writer's statements measured, accurate, fair, and to the point? Do readers feel the need to interject a challenge, using "but…"?

5. **What assumptions does the writer make?** If a writer argues for a college education for everyone, is the underlying assumption that a college education automatically leads to happiness and success?

6. **Does the writer support claims with evidence?** Is the writer relying on extreme language or name-calling rather than presentation of evidence? Does the writer fail to support any part of the claim?

7. **Where does the evidence come from?** Can the reader trust the sources? Is the evidence persuasive to the writer's intended audience?

8. **What medium has the writer chosen to deliver the argument?** Is the choice of medium appropriate for the argument? Does it constrain the argument in any way? Would another medium be more appropriate or accessible?

4b Developing an effective argument

The goal of argument is to persuade. We often associate the word *argument* with combat and confrontation, but the Latin root of the word *argue* means "to make clear." The Greek word *persuasion* derives from the verb "to believe." So, in the process of formulating and constructing a good argument, your work lies in making your claim so clear to your readers that they may come to believe what you do. Your readers need to recognize that the claim you make about your topic rests on solid, reliable evidence and that you have provided a fair, unbiased approach to this evidence. In reading your argument, your readers will discover that you have good reasons for your position.

> **KEY POINTS**
> The Features of a Good Argument
>
> A good argument
> - deals with a controversial, debatable issue
> - is not based on strong gut reactions or beliefs but on careful analysis of reliable information
> - stands up to a critical reading
> - takes a position on and makes a clear claim about the topic
> - supports that position with detailed and specific evidence (such as reasons, facts, examples, descriptions, and stories)
> - establishes common ground with listeners or readers and avoids confrontation
> - takes opposing views into account and either refutes them or shows why they may be unimportant or irrelevant
> - is engaged and vital, a reflection of the writer's careful, critical thinking rather than just a collection of others' opinions

4c Choosing a topic and developing a claim (thesis)

Choosing a topic   Choose an issue that is fresh. Avoid topics such as the death penalty, drug laws, and abortion, which have been written about so often that original or interesting arguments are hard to develop. Global warming and the environment, the church and morality, or racial prejudice may be issues that mean a great deal to you personally, but you will have difficulty structuring a logical argument around them.

Knowing what a thesis statement looks like—and why you need one   Suppose someone were to ask you, "What is the main point that you want to communicate to your reader in your piece of writing?" The sentence you would give in reply is your *thesis statement*, also known as a *claim*. Your thesis, or claim, tells readers what stand you are going to take on a topic. It won't take you far to say, for instance, "I am interested in writing about sustainable/ethical food sources" if you stop right there and hope that somehow ideas will shoot right out at you. What aspects of sustainable and ethical food practices interest you and what are the issues? Which readers do you regard as your primary audience? Which geographical areas will you discuss? Will you be concerned with the present or the future? What do you intend to propose about food practices—both about producing food and consuming it? In short, what point will you end up making (purpose) and for which readers (audience)? You don't have to know exactly where to put your thesis statement in your essay right now, but having a thesis will focus your thoughts as you read and write.

A good thesis statement may be one or more of the following:

1. a strong, thought-provoking, or controversial statement

   ▸ **Although food costs can be kept low by producing food in large quantities and shipping it long distances, the benefits are outweighed by the risks to the environment.**

2. a call to action

   ▸ **The best way to promote sustainable production of food is to support legislation that encourages the use of locally grown crops.**

3. a generalization needing support

   ▸ **Ethical production of food sources should focus on humane treatment of animals raised for consumption.**

4. an analytical statement that sets up the structure of the essay

   ▸ **Two examples illustrate the complexity of issues surrounding the humane treatment of animals produced for consumption and the importance of supporting humane treatment: the production of veal and the production of foie gras.**

Keep a working thesis in front of you on a self-stick note or an index card as you write your first draft, but be flexible. You are the boss as you write. You can change and narrow your thesis whenever you like. Many readers will expect to discover your point within the introductory paragraphs of your essay, but your thesis may, in fact, not take shape in your mind until you have read, written, and revised a great deal. Sometimes, a clear thesis may not emerge for you until the end of your first draft, pointing the way to the focus and organization of your next draft.

Formulating an arguable claim (thesis)   The position you take on a topic constitutes your thesis or claim. Avoid using any of the following as claims because they are not debatable:

- a neutral statement, which gives no hint of the writer's position
- an announcement of the paper's broad subject
- a fact, which is not arguable
- a truism (statement that is obviously true)
- a personal or religious conviction that cannot be logically debated
- an opinion based only on your own feelings
- a sweeping generalization

Here are some examples of nondebatable claims, each with a revision that makes it more debatable.

Neutral statement	**There are unstated standards of beauty in the workplace.**
Revised	**The way we look affects the way we are treated at work and the size of our paychecks.**
Too broad	**This paper is about violence in video games.**
Revised	**Violence in video games has to take its share of blame for the violence in our society.**
Fact	***Plessy v. Ferguson,*** **an 1896 Supreme Court case that supported racial segregation, was overturned in 1954 by** ***Brown v. Board of Education.***
Revised	**The overturning of** ***Plessy v. Ferguson*** **by** ***Brown v. Board of Education*** **has not led to significant advances in integrated education.**
Truism	**Bilingual education has advantages and disadvantages.**
Revised	**A bilingual program is more effective than an immersion program at helping students grasp the basics of science and mathematics.**

Personal conviction	Racism is the worst kind of prejudice.
Revised	The best weapon against racism is primary and secondary education.
Opinion based only on feeling	I think jet-skiing is a dumb sport.
Revised	Jet-skiing should be banned from public beaches.
Sweeping generalization	Women understand housework.
Revised	The publication of a lengthy guide to housekeeping and its success among both men and women suggest a renewed interest in the domestic arts.

Avoiding loaded terms   In your claim, avoid sweeping and judgmental words—for instance, *bad, good, right, wrong, stupid, ridiculous, moral, immoral, dumb,* and *smart.*

Seeing your thesis as a signpost or indication of where you have been   In much academic writing in the humanities and social sciences, a thesis is stated clearly in the essay, usually near the beginning. View your thesis statement as a signpost—both for you as you write your

KEY POINTS
A Good Working Thesis

- **answers a question** that is guiding your argument and writing
- **narrows your topic** to a single main idea that you want to communicate
- **makes your point** clearly and firmly in one sentence or two
- **states not simply a fact but rather an opinion or a summary conclusion** from your observation
- **makes a generalization that can be supported** by details, facts, and examples within the assigned limitations of time and space
- **stimulates curiosity and interest in readers** and prompts them to wonder, "Why do you think that?"

draft and, later, for readers as they read your essay. A clear thesis prepares readers well for the rest of the essay. If you use key words from your thesis as you write, you will keep readers focused on your main idea.

Sometimes, though, you may choose to imply your thesis and not explicitly state it. In such a case, you make your thesis clear by the examples, details, and information you include. An essay that details all the beneficial—or harmful—changes to a neighborhood may not need a bald statement that, for example, the South Congress area of Austin has made great strides. You may also choose to state your thesis at the end of your essay instead of at the beginning, presenting all the evidence to build a case and then making the thesis act as a climax and logical conclusion about the outcome of the evidence.

On not falling in love with your thesis   Many writers begin with a tentative working thesis and then find that they come to a new conclusion at the end of the first draft. If that happens to you, start your second draft by focusing on the thesis that emerged during the writing of the first draft. Be flexible: It's easier to change a thesis statement to fit new ideas and newly discovered evidence than to find new evidence to fit a new thesis. Note that your final thesis statement should provide a clear answer to a question. Flexibility during the writing process is not the same as indecision in the final product.

LANGUAGE AND CULTURE

Arguments across Cultures: Making a Claim and Staking a Position

Often, writers who have developed their writing skills in one language notice distinct differences in the conventions of writing in another language, particularly with respect to the explicit statement of opinion in the thesis. In 1989, when China was more rural than it is now, a Chinese writer, Fan Shen, presented the opinion that the explicit thesis statement favored in Western writing was "symbolic of the values of a busy people in an industrialized society, rushing to get things done" (*College Composition and Communication* [Dec. 1989]: 462).

The types of arguments described in this section are those common in academic and business settings in North America and the Western world. Writers state their views directly, arguing for their viewpoints. The success of their arguments lies in the credibility and strength of the evidence they produce in support. But such an approach is not universal. Other cultures may prefer a less direct approach, one that begins by exploring and evaluating all options rather than by issuing a direct claim. One of the basic principles of writing well—knowing your audience's expectations—is especially relevant to writing arguments for cultures different from your own.

4d Supporting a claim with reasons and evidence

Supporting your claim means telling your readers what reasons, statistics, facts, examples, and expert testimony bolster and explain your point of view. If a reader asks, "Why do you think that?" about your claim, then the support you offer answers that question in detail.

Reasons Imagine someone saying to you, "OK. I know your position on this issue, but I disagree with you. What led you to your position?" This is asking you to provide the reasons for your conviction. To begin to answer the question, add at least one "because clause" to your claim.

> **Claim:** Colleges should stop using SAT scores to determine admissions.
>
> **Reason:** (because) SAT scores are biased toward certain demographic groups.
>
> **Claim:** Organized hunting of deer is necessary in suburban areas.
>
> **Reason:** (because) With a diminishing natural habitat, deer are becoming an otherwise uncontrollable hazard to people and property.
>
> **Claim:** A large coal-fired cement factory in a rural scenic region could be an ecological disaster.
>
> **Reason:** (because) Its operation would threaten water, wildlife, and the residents' health.

Once you have formulated a tentative claim, make a scratch outline listing the claim and developing and expanding your reasons for supporting it. As you develop your reasons, consider what your audience will find most convincing. After you have determined some tentative reasons, you will then need to find specific and concrete evidence to explain and support each one.

Concrete evidence   You need reasons, but reasons are not enough. You also need to include specific evidence that supports, illustrates, and explains your reasons. Imagine a reader saying, after you give one of your reasons, "Tell me why I should believe that." Your evidence will make your argument more persuasive by supporting your reasons.

Add to the outline any items of concrete evidence you will include to illustrate and explain your reasoning. What counts as evidence? Facts, statistics, stories, examples, and testimony from experts can all be used as evidence in support of your reasons.

LANGUAGE AND CULTURE

Evidence Used to Support an Argument

The way arguments are structured, the concept of *expertise*, and the nature of evidence regarded as convincing may vary from one culture to another. In some cultures, for example, the opinions of religious or political leaders may carry more weight than the opinions of a scholar in the field. Be sure to consider your audience and what evidence they will accept and find persuasive.

4e Four questions for constructing an argument (Toulmin)

The four questions in the Key Points box, derived from Stephen Toulmin's *The Uses of Argument*, will provide you with a systematic way to construct a logical argument.

KEY POINTS
Four Questions to Ask about Your Argument

1. **What is your claim?** (What is the point you want to make?)

2. **What do you have to go on?** (What reasons can you give for your claim, and what evidence supports those reasons?)

3. **What connections hold your argument together?** (What assumptions—Toulmin calls them *warrants*—would your audience have to accept in order to find your argument persuasive?)

4. **What is getting in the way of your argument?** (What qualifications do you need to include, using *but, unless,* or *if* or adding words such as *usually, often, several, mostly,* or *sometimes,* to provide exceptions to your assumptions?)

Here is an example showing how the Toulmin questions can be used to develop the claim and supporting reasons introduced in 4d:

Claim	**Colleges should stop using SAT scores in their admissions process.**
Support	**(because) SAT scores are biased toward certain demographic groups.**
Assumptions	**Colleges use SAT scores to predict success in college.**
	Colleges should not use measures that are demographically biased.
Qualifier	**… unless the colleges use a variety of measures to predict student success.**
Revised claim	**Colleges that use SAT scores to predict college success should consider other measures of student success to balance proven test bias.**

Examine your assumptions   Pay special attention to examining assumptions that link a claim to the reasons and evidence you provide. Consider whether readers will share those assumptions or whether you need to explain, discuss, and defend them. Your audience matters. For example, the claim "Internet pop-up ads should be monitored because they prey on those who are not technologically savvy" operates on the assumption that monitoring will catch and reduce abuses. The claim "Internet pop-up ads should be encouraged because they benefit the economy" operates on the assumption that benefiting the economy is an important goal. These different assumptions will appeal to different readers, and some may need to be persuaded of the assumptions before they attempt to accept your claim or the reasons you give for it.

Note that if your claim is "Internet pop-up ads should be encouraged because they are useful," you are saying little more than "Internet pop-up ads are good because they are good." Your reader is certain to object to such circular reasoning and reject your claim. That is why it is important to ask question 3 from the Key Points box on page 56. That question leads you to examine what assumptions your audience would have to accept in order to find your argument persuasive.

4f Appeals, common ground, and opposing views

You can choose from several approaches to persuade your readers as you develop and support your argument. Appeals, common ground, and refutations of opposing positions can all act as support for your argument.

Ask who your readers are First, consider the readers you are writing for. Assess what they might know, what assumptions they hold, what they need to know, how they can best be convinced to accept your position, and what strategies will persuade them to respect or accept your views.

If you are writing for readers with no specific prior knowledge, biases, or expertise—a *general audience*—remember to include background information: the place, the time, the context, the issues. Do not assume that a general reader knows a great deal more than you do.

See the full model on page 7.

Appeal to readers Aristotle classified the ways that writers appeal to readers in arguments. Your knowledge of your readers will help you decide what types of appeal to use. Within one extended argument, you may find it necessary to use more than one type of appeal to reach all readers' needs. The examples of the appeals that follow, for example, were used by Peggy Orenstein in a *New York Times Magazine* article in which she argued against a trend in US kindergartens toward increased instruction and testing ("Kindergarten Cram: Toss Out the No. 2 Pencils and Let Them Play." 3 May 2009. 13).

Rational appeal (Logos) A rational appeal bases an argument's conclusion on facts, examples, and authoritative evidence. Such an appeal is appropriate for educated readers and useful when readers are uninformed or hostile.

> *Sample rational appeal:* Orenstein presents authoritative evidence that assigning homework and testing young children neither predicts nor improves their academic success. In addition, instruction and testing in reading and math take up the time previously allotted to free play, which has proven instrumental not only in children's intellectual development but also in their emotional, psychological, social, and spiritual development. To underscore just how much of a decline in play there is, Orenstein cites a survey of kindergarten teachers. It found that kindergartners spent less than

30 minutes a day playing in comparison to two to three hours a day being instructed or tested in math and reading. In a visual illustration of survey results, a simple, colorful graph effectively displays the shrinking free play of Los Angeles kindergarten classes. (For more on the use of visual arguments, see 4i. For more on creating and using tables, charts, and graphs, see chapter 22.)

TELLING TIME

Average number of minutes spent daily on **literacy**, **math**, **test prep** and free play in 112 Los Angeles kindergarten classes:

89

47 21

19

SOURCE: "Crisis in the Kindergarten," Alliance for Childhood. March 2009 <http://www.nytimes.com/2009/05/03/magazine/03wwln-lede-t.html>

Appeal to credibility (Ethos)   In an appeal to credibility, you represent yourself or any sources you refer to as reliable, experienced, thoughtful, objective, and fair, even when considering opposing views. Such an appeal is appropriate for formal situations in business and academic worlds. In advertising, too, ethical appeals often include testimony from famous people, regardless of whether they are experts—for example, Ben and Jerry's uses celebrities such as Stephen Colbert and Jimmy Fallon to promote their ice cream.

> *Sample appeal to credibility:* Orenstein presents as experts in early childhood education the Alliance for Childhood, a nonprofit research and advocacy group and draws from their report, "Crisis in the Kindergarten." She cites as a reliable source Daniel Pink, a writer on the changing world of work who argues that without the "imagination economy" fostered by among other things, "playfulness," the United States' continued viability in the twenty-first century is at risk. She addresses and refutes opposing views by invoking Jean Piaget, the twentieth century's groundbreaking child psychologist, who famously challenged the American penchant for speeding up children's development.

Emotional appeal (Pathos)   In an emotional appeal, you try to gain the empathy and sympathy of your readers by assessing their values, and attempt to persuade them by using descriptions, anecdotes, case studies, and visuals to appeal to those values. Such an appeal is less common in academic writing than in journalism and the other media. It is appropriate when readers are regarded as either already favorable to particular ideas or apathetic toward them. Emotional appeals can also be compelling in introductions or conclusions as ways to either grab a reader's attention or leave a reader with a powerful image or thought.

> *Sample emotional appeal:* Orenstein shares personal anecdotes to establish a bond with her readers. She wants for her child what the *New York Times Magazine*'s readers want for their children. Although she and her readers want their children to grow up ethical, thoughtful, and responsible, they are concerned with how their early education will impact their ability to compete in a future job market. She confesses to her readers, "I wonder how far I'm willing to go in my commitment to the cause: would I embrace the example of Finland—whose students consistently come out on top in international assessments—and delay formal reading instruction until age 7?" Orenstein ends her article on a note that will seal her readers' empathy: her daughter, now enrolled in a school that does not assign homework until fourth grade, has complained that she doesn't have homework like "all the other kids."

Within one extended argument, you will probably find it necessary to use all types of argument to reach the maximum number of readers, each with individual expectations, preferences, and quirks.

Establish common ground   Remember that readers who are turned off by exaggerations or extreme language have the ultimate power to stop reading and ignore what you have to say.

KEY POINTS
Ways to Establish Common Ground with Readers

1. **Avoid extreme views or language.** Do not label someone's views as *ridiculous, ignorant, immoral, fascist,* or *crooked,* for example.

2. **Write to convince, not to confront.** Recognize shared concerns, and consider the inclusive use of *we.*

3. **Steer clear of sarcastic remarks** such as, "The mayor's office has come up with the splendid idea of building a gigantic parking garage right in the middle of a popular and historic city park."

4. **Use clear, everyday words** that sound as if you are speaking directly to your readers.

5. **Acknowledge valid arguments from your opponents,** and work to show why the arguments on your side carry more weight.

6. **If possible, propose a solution** with long-term benefits for everyone.

Refute opposing views   It is not enough to present your own reasons and evidence for your claim. When you take into account any opposing arguments and the reasons and evidence that support those arguments, you present yourself as objective and evenhanded, furthering your appeal to credibility. Examine opposing arguments; describe the most common or convincing ones; evaluate their validity, applicability, and limitations; and explain what motivates people to take those positions. Then discuss why you see your reasons and evidence as more pertinent and convincing than those in opposing arguments.

Be careful to argue logically and rationally without insulting your opponents. Take pains to explain rationally why your views differ from theirs. You may choose to do this by following each one of your own points with a discussion of an opposing view. Or you may prefer to devote an entire section of your essay to dealing with opposing views.

4g Structuring an argument

Written arguments are typically structured to follow one of four basic patterns: (1) general to specific, (2) specific to general, (3) problem and solution, and (4) cause and effect.

KEY POINTS
Basic Structure for a General-to-Specific Argument

Introduction	Provide background information on the issue, why it is an issue, and what the controversies are. After you have introduced your readers to the nature and importance of the issue, announce your position in a general statement of your claim or thesis statement, perhaps at the end of the first paragraph or in a prominent position within the second paragraph depending on the length and complexity of your essay.
Body	Provide evidence in the form of supporting points for your thesis, with concrete and specific details. For each new point, start a new paragraph.
Acknowledgment of opposing views	Use evidence and specific details to describe and logically refute any opposing views.
Conclusion	Return to the topic as a whole and your specific claim. Without repeating complete phrases and sentences, remind readers of the point you want to make. End on a strong note.

General to specific   The general-to-specific structure is used frequently in the humanities and arts. It moves from the thesis to support and evidence. Obviously, writers experiment with many variations on this structure, but it is one you can use as a reliable starting point.

Specific to general   Alternatively, you might choose to begin with data and points of evidence and then draw a conclusion from that evidence, provided the evidence is relevant and convincing. A basic specific-to-general argument on the topic of driving while using a cell phone looks like this:

Introduction: background, statement of problem and controversy

Data:

1. Cell phone users admit to being distracted while driving (cite statistics).
2. Many accidents are attributable to cell phone use (cite statistics).
3. Several states have passed laws against using handheld cell phones while driving.
4. The National Safety Council attributes at least 28% of all traffic accidents (1.6 million accidents) to cell phone use and texting while driving (http://www.nsc.org).

Conclusion: Discussion of data and presentation of thesis (generalization formed from analysis of the data): All states should pass laws prohibiting the use of handheld cell phones while driving.

In an argument in the sciences or social sciences (as in sample paper 5 in chapter 16), writers often begin with a hypothesis they can test. They list their findings from experimentation, surveys, facts, and statistics. Then, from the data they have collected, they draw conclusions to support, modify, or reject the hypothesis.

Problem and solution   If your topic offers solutions to a problem, you probably will find it useful to present the details of the problem first and then offer solutions. Think about the strongest position in your paper for placing the solution: at the beginning of your solutions section or at the end? Do you want to make your strong point early, or would you rather lead up to it gradually?

Cause and effect   Writers of arguments in history, art history, and social movements often examine the causes and effects of events and trends to enhance their point of view. The reasoning behind an analysis of causes and effects is far from simple, involving many variables and interpretations. Take care not to reduce your analysis to one simple cause, and avoid the logical fallacy of assuming that one event causes another simply because it precedes it.

4h Logical reasoning, logical fallacies

Reasoning logically As you evaluate the logic of your arguments, assess whether they are valid examples of deductive or inductive reasoning and ensure that they do not fall prey to logical fallacies.

Deductive reasoning The classical Aristotelian method of constructing an argument is based on a reasoning process (a syllogism) that moves from true premises to a certain and valid conclusion.

Major premise	**Coal-fired factories can cause significant damage to the environment.**
Minor premise	**The proposed cement plant will use coal for fuel.**
Conclusion	**The proposed cement plant could cause significant damage to the environment.**

Even if the major premise is not stated, readers must nevertheless accept it as the truth:

Major premise not stated	**Since the new proposed cement plant will be coal-fired, it could cause significant damage to the environment.**

The premises must be true for a conclusion to be valid.

Inductive reasoning An inductive argument begins with details that lead to a *probable* conclusion. Inductive arguments are used often in the sciences and social sciences. Researchers begin with a tentative hypothesis. They conduct studies and perform experiments; they collect and tabulate data; they examine the evidence of other studies. Then they draw a conclusion to support, reject, or modify the hypothesis. The conclusion, however, is only probable and not necessarily certain. It is based on the circumstances of the evidence. Different evidence at a different time could lead to a different conclusion. Conclusions drawn in the medical field change with the experiments and the sophistication of the techniques—eggs are called good for you one year, bad the next. That is because the nature of the evidence changes.

Recognizing logical fallacies   Faulty logic can make readers mistrust you as a writer. Watch out for some common flaws in logic (called *logical fallacies*) as you write and check your drafts.

Sweeping generalization   Generalizations can sometimes be so broad that they fall into stereotyping. Avoid them.

▶ **All British people are stiff and formal.**

▶ **The only thing that concerns students is grades.**

The reader will be right to wonder what evidence has led to these conclusions. Without any explanation or evidence, they will simply be dismissed. Beware, then, of the trap of words like *all*, *every*, *only*, *never*, and *always*.

Hasty conclusion with inadequate support   To convince readers of the validity of a generalization, you need to offer enough evidence—usually more than just one personal observation. Thoughtful readers can easily spot a conclusion that is too hastily drawn from flimsy support.

▶ **My friend Arecelis had a terrible time in a bilingual school. It is clear that bilingual education has failed.**

▶ **Bilingual education is a success story, as the school in Chinatown has clearly shown.**

Non sequitur   *Non sequitur* is Latin for "it does not follow." Supporting a claim with evidence that is illogical or irrelevant causes a non sequitur fallacy.

▶ **Maureen Dowd writes so well that she would make a good teacher.** (The writer does not establish a connection between good writing and good teaching.)

▶ **Studying economics is a waste of time. Money does not make people happy.** (Here the writer does not help us see any relationship between happiness and the study of a subject.)

Causal fallacy   You are guilty of a causal fallacy if you assume that one event causes another merely because the second event happens after the first. (The Latin name for this logical flaw is *post hoc, ergo propter hoc*: "after this, therefore because of this.")

▶ **The economy collapsed because a new president was elected.** (Was the election the reason? Or did it simply occur before the economy collapsed?)

▶ **The number of A's given in college courses has increased. This clearly shows that faculty members are inflating grades.** (But does the number of A's clearly show any such thing? Or could the cause be that students are better prepared in high school?)

Examine carefully any statements you make about cause and effect.

Ad hominem attack *Ad hominem* (Latin for "to the person") refers to unfair ethical appeals to personal considerations rather than to logic or reason. Avoid using arguments that seek to discredit an opinion through criticizing a person's character or lifestyle.

> ▸ **The new curriculum should not be adopted because the adminis-trators who favor it have never even taught a college course.**

> ▸ **The student who is urging the increase in student fees for social events is a partygoer and a big drinker.**

Argue a point by showing either the logic of the argument or the lack of it, not by pointing to flaws in character. However, personal considerations may be valid if they pertain directly to the issue, as in, "The two women who favor the abolition of the bar own property on the same block."

Circular reasoning In an argument based on circular reasoning, the evidence and the conclusion restate each other, thus proving nothing.

> ▸ **Credit card companies should be banned on campus because companies should not be allowed to solicit business from students.**

> ▸ **That rich man is smart because wealthy people are intelligent.**

Neither of these statements moves the argument forward. They both beg the question; that is, they argue in a circular way.

False dichotomy or false dilemma Either/or arguments reduce complex problems to two simplistic alternatives without exploring them in depth or considering other alternatives.

> ▸ **After September 11, 2001, New York could do one of two things: increase airport security or screen immigrants.**

This proposal presents a false dichotomy. These are not the only two options for dealing with potential terrorism. Posing a false dilemma like this will annoy readers.

● TECH NOTE

Logical Fallacies on the Web

Go to the *Logical Fallacies* Web site at <http://www.logicalfallacies.info/> for lists of many more types of logical fallacies (including the "No True Scotsman" Fallacy and the Fallacist's Fallacy) with explanations, examples, and real-world examples.

4i Using and analyzing visual arguments

We commonly think of arguments as spoken or written, but we encounter visual arguments every day. Because of their immediacy and subtle appeals to a viewer's reason, emotions, and morals, visual arguments can be as compellingly persuasive as written

PURPOSE | AUDIENCE
VOICE | MEDIUM
See the full model on page 7.

arguments—if not more so. Whether their purpose is to strengthen an argument or to illustrate an argument in its complexity, writers often choose to supplement their essays with visuals. When you write an argument, consider adding to the impact of your thesis by including visual support.

Using visuals in arguments You can supplement your written arguments with visual arguments: maps, superimposed images, photographs, charts and graphs, political cartoons—vivid images that will say more than many words can to your readers.

An argument essay that argues for the health benefits of milk, for example, would make a strong visual impact if it included an image such as this example of tennis stars Venus and Serena Williams in the "Got Milk?" campaign. The ad implies that milk consumption contributes to their athletic achievements.

Visual arguments make their appeals in ways similar to written arguments by appealing to logic, showcasing the character and credentials of the author, or appealing to viewers' emotions. But unlike written arguments, which present arguments, reasons, and evidence in a linear and logical manner, arguments made in cartoons, advertisements, and works of art can simultaneously pit our logic against our ethics while moving us emotionally.

Image courtesy of The Advertising Archives

Analyzing visual arguments Photographs of hurricane devastation or of starving children in Africa are carefully chosen to appeal for donations and can distract viewers from asking important questions

KEY POINTS
Using Visuals

1. Use visuals in your argument when:
   - the visual serves to strengthen or illustrate your argument
   - your paper focuses on a visual topic (an analysis of an ad, a cartoon, a work of art)
   - your paper relies on visual images for its evidence and support of your argument

2. Choose an appropriate visual in your argument that:
   - has a concrete connection to your argument
   - appeals to your readers' reason, emotions, and/or ethics

3. Integrate the visual into your paper by:
   - connecting the visual to your text with a comment
   - locating the visual close to the text that describes it
   - including a caption with the figure number and title or a brief description
   - providing complete documentation in your works-cited page

like: What exactly will my money be used for? Analyzing a visual for its unspoken argument or point of view is part of the critical thinking process that underlies good reading and writing.

Consider, for example, this 2004 advertisement, also from the popular "Got Milk?" campaign. The ad features Dr. Phil McGraw, a mental health professional and former clinical psychologist who hosts the popular television talk show, *Dr. Phil*. The text to the left of Dr. Phil's image uses his catch-phrase "Get real" to make a claim about milk's potential for helping people lose weight. Dr. Phil says "Get real. About losing weight," above a thumbnail picture in the lower left-hand corner of the ad of Dr. Phil's just-published book, *The Ultimate Weight Solution*. Are the connections among Dr. Phil's credibility, milk, and his book logical ones? Just as written arguments challenge readers to question assumptions and implications, visual arguments push viewers to think critically about the implications and intended effects of images. If a picture is worth a thousand words, it is still up to us to interpret what those words are.

Using visuals as tools for analysis   Visuals can be used as tools for analysis. Using word clouds, for example, the *New York Times* analyzed the language of presidential inaugural addresses by visually depicting word frequency in the inaugural address (indicated by the size of each word) and word frequency compared to other presidential inaugural addresses (indicated in yellow highlight). The word clouds here show George W. Bush's 2005 inaugural address (left) and Barack Obama's 2009 inaugural address (right).

SOURCE: <http://www.nytimes.com/interactive/2009/01/17/washington/20090117_ADDRESSES.html>

● TECH NOTE

Exploring Data Visualization Tools

IBM's *Many Eyes* project <http://manyeyes.alphaworks.ibm.com/manyeyes/> provides a wide range of data visualization examples that allow you to see how you might use visuals to show relationships among data points (plots and network diagrams), comparisons (bar charts), changes over time (line graphs), ratios (pie charts), textual relationships (word clouds and word trees), and maps. You can also use the *Many Eyes* site to create visualizations using your own data.

Creating multimedia arguments   Present-day technology allows for a new way to express ideas. No longer limited to using type on a page, writers now can use screens to present an interaction of words, color, music, sound, images, and movies to tell a story and make a point.

In preparing a multimedia presentation, consider, then, the effectiveness of juxtaposing images and conveying emotion and meaning through colors and pictures as well as through words. If you use media imaginatively, you can do what writing teachers have long advised: Show, don't just tell.

An outstanding example of a multimedia visual argument was created by undergraduates at the University of Southern California for a course in Near Eastern and Mediterranean archeology. The students chose the ancient city of Troy as the subject of their presentation. Using excavation records, archeological findings, and Homer's texts (as well as architectural modeling software, audio, and virtual reality techniques), the students reconstructed "the citadel as it may have appeared at the time of the Trojan War in the 13th century B.C." You can see the story of this fascinating project on YouTube at http://www.youtube.com/watch?v=E0qOzjT2BSY

4j Sample paper 1: A student's argument essay

Here is a draft of Bibi Bhani Khalsa's argument paper on whether the consumption of milk is necessary, or even healthy, for humans.[*] The draft is annotated to point out the strategies in her argument. Note how she presents her thesis, supports it, considers and refutes opposing views, and varies appeals to readers. For her final draft she included her name and page number as a running head on every page.

Does Everybody Need Milk?

We are bombarded with commercials from the dairy industry telling us that milk is one of the best sources of nutrition and is essential for good health. One popular advertising slogan is "Everybody needs milk." Posters and billboards display this slogan with various pictures: a baby, a muscular man, and even Uncle Sam. We have been told cow's milk is a "perfect food" that helps build healthy bodies and strong bones. Commercials and nutritional guidelines have long told us that we should all consume dairy products daily, beginning at birth, as the advertisement in Fig. 1 shows. Is this true or a myth perpetuated by the dairy industry? We need to know the facts about dairy products so we can make informed decisions

Draws in audience with use of "we" and reference to common experiences

---

[*]Used by permission of Bibi Bhani Khalsa.

Fig. 1 Carnation Milk ad from the 1940s. Source: Carnation Milk. Advertisement. *Advertising Archives.* Web. 18 Mar. 2012.

about whether or not to consume them. Through my research I've discovered that many people, including respected physicians, believe that cow's milk products can be harmful to our health and that there are safer ways to get high-quality nutrition. I've also learned that organic and raw milk are superior to conventional dairy products, but they may not be suitable for everyone. I will prove through compelling evidence that, contrary to propaganda from the dairy industry, everybody does not need milk.

Clear statement of thesis

On its Web site the National Dairy Council lists the nine nutrients and their daily values that are contained in an eight-ounce glass of milk and recommends "2 to 3 servings [per] day of milk and milk products (e.g., cheese, yogurt), the specific amount depending on the age group" (McBean, "Dairy Foods' Inclusion"). Citing research conducted by the Dairy Research Institute, the website reminds us that dairy "is a substantial contributor of many nutrients in the U.S. diet that are important for good health, including calcium, potassium, phosphorus, magnesium, zinc, protein, vitamin A, vitamin D, vitamin B_{12}, and riboflavin" (McBean, "Dairy's Unique"). Now consider this statistic cited by Irene Jakobsson and Tor Lindberg in an article in the journal *Pediatrics*: it is estimated that "in one third of breast-fed infants, infantile colic is related to cow's milk consumption by the mother" (270). Further, in a European telephone survey of more than 44,000 contacts, 5 million claimed to be allergic to milk" (Fiocchi et al. 1120). If so many people have problems with milk, is it really good for us or even a natural source of nutrition for humans?

Includes counterargument

If we observe nature, we see that no other animal consumes the milk of another species. The nutritional elements in cow's milk are suited for calves and not humans (Sears, "Milk Allergies"). Dr. Robert Kradjian, former chief of General Surgery at Seton Medical Center in California, notes that cow's milk has three to four times as much protein as human milk, is five to seven times higher in minerals, and has far fewer essential fatty acids than human milk. He explains that biochemists and physiologists have learned that each species' milk contains the specific elements required for the optimal growth and development of that kind of mammal (Kradjian). Dr. William Sears says that the protein in milk "is suited for bovine intestines" and that it can cause irritation and damage to humans' intestinal lining. When these proteins are absorbed into the circulatory system, they are attacked by the immune system as foreign substances. This reaction can lead to symptoms such as runny nose, rashes, and wheezing and can also cause frequent ear infections, colds, and behavioral changes. Sears says it has been estimated that, when tested, about "75 percent of infants under one year of age were allergic to cow's milk" ("Milk Allergies").

Draws on several experts from the medical field to develop ethos.

Another famous pediatrician, Dr. Benjamin Spock, also warns against dairy consumption. In the ninth edition of his book *Dr. Spock's*

Baby and Child Care, he recommends that vegetables, fruits, grains, and beans should make up the bulk of children's diets and that meat, fish, and dairy products should be limited or avoided. Green leafy vegetables and beans, he says, contain calcium that is as easily if not more easily absorbed than the calcium in milk is. Whereas milk generally lacks iron, vitamins, complex carbohydrates, and fiber, vegetables and beans are a good source of these nutrients. Spock gave up dairy products himself at age 88 and within two weeks was cured of chronic bronchitis (380). Similarly, Alisa Fleming, author of *Go Dairy Free*, describes her suffering from numerous health problems until an alternative doctor suggested she give up dairy products. She did so, and within days all her symptoms disappeared (6). In my own experience, I've had fewer colds and illnesses since I began following a vegan diet (no meat, fish, eggs, or dairy).

Uses transitions to provide a roadmap for readers

The list of concerns about milk continues. According to Dr. Spock, dairy products contribute to a number of children's health problems since "cow's milk itself . . . is *not* safe for infants" (*Spock's Baby* 321). He points out that in addition to containing little iron itself, milk can cause iron deficiency by interfering with a child's ability to absorb iron (*Spock's Baby* 376). The proteins in cow's milk, he says, are a common cause of colic (*Spock's Baby* 322). Spock also notes that the American Academy of Pediatrics has confirmed evidence that links cow's milk consumption to "constipation, ear infections, and even (in rare cases) type-1 diabetes" (*Spock's Baby* 385). On his Web site Sears tells his readers that studies show "a statistical correlation between young children drinking milk and the later onset of insulin-dependent diabetes" ("Medical Problems"). Spock recommends that after being weaned from breast milk, children should be given soy or rice milk products (*Spock's Baby* 387). There are many great alternatives to dairy products that are much better for our health.

Includes multiple sources to support argument, although some sources are dated

Another concern about dairy products is the hormones they contain. To stimulate milk production, most cows are injected with bovine growth hormone (BGH), a genetically engineered drug. Fifty years ago the average yearly milk production of a cow was 2,000 pounds while today many cows produce up to 50,000 pounds of milk a year (Kradjian). According to an article in *Science* discussing an FDA review of genetically engineered milk, the presence of BGH in milk increases the concentration of IGF-1, an insulin-like growth factor

(Juskevich and Guyer 875). This is sobering evidence that should give us pause before eating that bowl of ice cream or sinking our teeth into a slice of double-cheese pizza.

Other toxic substances found in cow's milk include antibiotics, chemicals, pesticides, and white blood cells, also known as pus. The FDA does not adequately test for these contaminants. According to Kradjian, "authorities test for only 4 of the 82 drugs in dairy cows." Cows frequently get udder infections, or mastitis, which are treated with antibiotics. "Mastic milk" has been found to contain pus cells, which Kradjian argues is acceptable to the FDA.

In spite of all this, don't we still need milk to build strong bones and prevent osteoporosis? An article published in *Pediatrics* in 2005 that was based on numerous studies states that there is no conclusive evidence to prove daily consumption of dairy products is beneficial to bone health in children and young adults (Lanou et al. 740). In addition, the Harvard Nurses' Health Study of more than 78,000 women over a period of 18 years showed that increasing milk consumption did not result in lower risk of bone fracture (Feskanich et al. 994–95). To decrease the risk of osteoporosis, the Physicians Committee for Responsible Medicine (PCRM) recommends consuming less animal protein and sodium, eating more fruits and vegetables, exercising, and getting calcium from green leafy vegetables and beans ("Health Concerns").

If all this isn't enough to make us reconsider the benefits of milk, there is more. Depending on the cow's feed, milk can be a source of cholesterol, hydrogenated and saturated fats, and trans fatty acids (Sears, "Fat Content"). The high level of cholesterol and saturated fat in many dairy products increases the risk of heart disease ("Health Concerns"). So why not just consume low-fat or non-fat dairy products? First of all, low-fat milk is not really low in fat: 24 to 33% of its calories come from fat (Kradjian). Secondly, I've observed that even those who use skim or low-fat milk or don't drink milk at all usually won't pass up foods such as pizza, Mexican food, macaroni and cheese, butter, and ice cream. Dairy products are ubiquitous.

For those who can't go without dairy, here are some safer options: organic and raw milk products. *Organic* can mean various things; it can mean the cows were not given antibiotics, were not given hormones, or were fed organic grain ("Organic Milk"). Organic milk is better than conventional milk, but organic raw (unpasteurized) milk is better still. Pasteurizing milk means heating it, and "when something is heated enough to kill pathogens, you can assume there will be other effects as well. Milk pasteurization destroys enzymes, promotes unstable blood sugar, damages nutrients, and kills beneficial bacteria" ("Pasteurized Milk"). On his Web site, Dr. William Campbell Douglass II writes:

> There are many indications that raw milk consumption can relieve allergies, asthma, digestive disorders—even autism. That's a lot of power in one glass of milk. So it's no wonder that smart folks everywhere are ignoring the warnings and seeking out the small, organic dairies that sell raw milk ("Raw Milk's").

His book *The Raw Truth about Real Milk* talks about milk in historical terms and connects modern illnesses to pasteurization. Dr. Thomas Cowan, a family practitioner in New Hampshire, also supports the use of raw milk. He harkens back to the "pre-processed food era" in the US before the 1930s when people drank fresh raw milk. He claims there were very few cases of coronary artery disease and prostate or breast cancer then. According to Cowan, the problem with dairy products is pasteurization, not the milk itself ("Raw Milk"). Kradjian, however, warns that raw milk may be contaminated with E. coli, salmonella, and staphylococcus bacteria (Kradjian). And even raw milk is better suited for calves than for human beings. We really don't need milk at all.

Uses counterargument to bring closure to section and provide transition into conclusion

We have been conditioned through advertising and education to believe that dairy products are essential to build strong bones and bodies. But when we examine the facts, we see that this assertion is far from the truth. Everybody does *not* need milk, and many do much better without it. Milk allergies and lactose intolerance are widespread. Heart disease, diabetes, osteoporosis, and several forms of cancer have been linked to dairy consumption ("Health Concerns"). Do we really want to risk our children's health and our own when there are much safer ways to get the nutrition we need? If you do choose to eat dairy products, find a source of uncontaminated, organic raw milk. Better yet, take Dr. Spock's advice and follow a primarily plant-based diet ("Good Nutrition"). And if you want milk on your cereal or in your coffee, use the kind made from soy, whole grains, or nuts.

Works Cited

Cowan, Thomas. "Raw Milk." *AnthroMed Library*. Physicians' Association for Anthroposcopic Medicine (PAAM), 2009. Web. 23 Mar. 2012.

Douglass, William Campbell, II. "Raw Milk's Popularity Growing by Leaps and Bounds." *The Douglass Report*. The Douglass Report, 14 May 2008. Web. 23 Mar. 2012.

---. *The Raw Truth about Real Milk*. Rogers: Rhino, 2007. Print.

Feskanich, Diane, et al. "Milk, Dietary Calcium, and Bone Fractures in Women: A Twelve-Year Prospective Study." *American Journal of Public Health* 87 (1997): 992–97. Print.

Fiocchi, Alessandro, et al. "DRACMA (Diagnosis and Rationale for Action against Cow's Milk Allergy): A Summary Report." *Journal of Allergy Clinical Immunology* 126 (2010): 1119–28. Print.

Fleming, Alisa. *Go Dairy Free: A Guide and Cookbook for Milk Allergies, Lactose Intolerance, and Casein-Free Living*. Henderson: Fleming, 2008. Print.

"Health Concerns about Dairy Products." *PCRM: Physicians Committee for Responsible Medicine*. Physicians Committee for Responsible Medicine, n.d. Web. 31 Mar. 2012.

Jakobsson, Irene, and Tor Lindberg. "Cow's Milk Proteins Cause Infantile Colic in Breast-Fed Infants: A Double-Blind Crossover Study." *Pediatrics* 71 (1983): 268–71. Print.

Juskevich, Judith C., and C. Greg Guyer. "Bovine Growth Hormone: Human Food Safety Evaluation." *Science* 249.4971 (24 Aug. 1990): 875–84. Print.

Kradjian, Robert. "The Milk Letter: A Message to My Patients." *Notmilk*. Robert Cohen, n.d. Web. 29 Mar. 2012.

Lanou, Amy Joy, Susan E. Berkow, and Neal D. Barnard. "Calcium, Dairy Products, and Bone Health in Children and Young Adults: A Reevaluation of the Evidence." *Pediatrics* 115.3 (2005): 736–43. *Pediatrics: Official Journal of the American Academy of Pediatrics*. Web. 29 Mar. 2012.

McBean, Lois D. "Dairy Foods' Inclusion in Dietary Guidance and
Recommendations." *Dairy Council Digest* 82.5 (2011): n. pag.
Dairy Council Digest Archives. National Dairy Council. Web. 21
Mar. 2012.

---. "Dairy's Unique Nutrient Package and Contribution to Americans'
Dairy Intake." *Dairy Council Digest* 82.5 (2011): n. pag. *Dairy
Council Digest Archives*. National Dairy Council. Web. 21 Mar.
2012.

"Organic Milk FAQ." *National Dairy Council*. National Dairy Council,
n.d. Web. 2 Apr. 2012.

"Pasteurized Milk: Killing the Bad and the Good." *HealthyFixx*. David
Hall and Brian Simonis, 24 Feb. 2011.Web. 30 Mar. 2012.

Sears, William. "Fat Content." *Ask Dr. Sears*. William Sears and
Martha Sears, 2011.Web. 29 Mar. 2012.

---. "Medical Problems." *Ask Dr. Sears*. William Sears and Martha
Sears, 2011.Web. 29 Mar. 2012.

---. "Milk Allergies." *Ask Dr. Sears*. William Sears and Martha Sears,
2011. Web. 29 Mar. 2012.

Spock, Benjamin. *Dr. Spock's Baby and Child Care*. 9th ed. New York:
Simon, 2011. Print.

---. "Good Nutrition for Kids." *Good Medicine* 7.2 (1998): n. pag.
Good Medicine Archive. PCRM: Physicians Committee for
Responsible Medicine. Web. 29 Mar. 2012.

5 Writing in Academic Disciplines

Writing is required in many, if not most, college courses. In fact, colleges and universities that emphasize the importance of writing often have initiatives or programs commonly referred to as Writing Across the Curriculum (WAC) or Writing in the Disciplines (WID) that encourage instructors in a broad array of disciplines to require writing in their courses.

5a Writing in all your courses

Writing can be a way to explore what you know, discover new ideas, and assess what you have learned. Instructors in many of your courses in college might use writing for these purposes, to help you learn and master subject matter in the course. You can expect to write both low-stakes (usually ungraded or with a minor amount of credit) and high-stakes (carrying more assessment weight) assignments in your college courses. When you are given a writing assignment in a college course, be sure to determine how much weight is given to the assignment and what the instructor's expectations are.

5b Writing to join academic conversations

One semester you may be writing about *Hamlet*, and the next semester you may move to exploring the census, writing about Chopin's music, discussing geological formations, researching the history of the civil rights movement, or preparing a paper on

See the full model on page 7.

Sigmund Freud and dreams. You may be expected to write scientific laboratory reports or to manipulate complex statistical data and to use a style of documentation different from one you learned in an English course. Find out which style of writing and documenting is expected in each of your courses. Each discipline has specific expectations for the genres that are most common.

> ### KEY POINTS
> #### The Cultures of the Academic Disciplines
>
> When you take a course in a new discipline, you are joining a new academic community with established conventions and ways of thinking and writing. Use the following strategies to get acquainted with the discipline's conventions.
>
> - Listen carefully to lectures and discussions; note the specialized vocabulary used in the discipline. Make lists of new terms and definitions.
> - Read the assigned textbook and note the conventions that apply in writing about the field.
> - Use subject-specific dictionaries and encyclopedias to learn about the field. Examples include *Encyclopedia of Religion* and *Encyclopedia of Sociology.*
> - When given a writing assignment, make sure you read samples of similar types of writing in that discipline.
> - Look at published writing in that field by reading articles from scholarly journals.
> - Talk with your instructor about the field, its literature, and readers' expectations.

● TECH NOTE

Useful Sites for Writing in the Disciplines

Try these Web sites for useful advice on writing in all your courses and for more links to other sites:

- The Dartmouth College site with advice to non-majors on writing in the humanities, sciences, and social sciences
- The George Mason University Writing Center site on writing in public affairs, management, psychology, biology, and history

5c Sample paper 2: A student's analysis of academic essays across disciplines

If you take a look at how publications from different disciplines cover the same event, you'll get a good idea of the ways various disciplines use language and evidence in differing ways. That's exactly what Charles

Brooks does in this essay about the Chernobyl nuclear disaster. He assesses the focus, organization, language use, and tone of academic essays in three disciplines to understand what the expectations are for writing in those disciplines.

Charles Brooks

Professor Shawna Jones

ENG 101

24 April 2012

Differences in Chernobyl Articles

Generally speaking, there are three disciplines into which academic pursuits can fall. Natural sciences concern themselves with the physical world, and include subjects such as biology, physics, or engineering. Social sciences focus their pursuits on humans and how they interact with each other and the world around them. Psychology, anthropology, and economics can all be categorized as social sciences. The third academic discipline encompasses fields such as art, language, and philosophy, and is known as the humanities. The humanities explore the way humans experience the world. Each of these disciplines demands a different style of writing for their audiences.

Introduction provides a basic overview of the differences between the three disciplinary areas

In order to examine the differences between the published research in each of these disciplines, I consider three articles written about the same general topic, but from the perspective of each academic discipline. The natural science article, "Chromosome Alterations in Cleanup Workers Sampled Years after the Chernobyl Accident," written by Elizaveta Neronova, Natalia Slozina and Alexey Nikiforov, was published by *Radiation Research* in 2003. In the December 2007 edition of *Acta Psychiatrica Scandinavica*, a social sciences article entitled "Chernobyl Exposure as Stressor during Pregnancy and Behaviour in Adolescent Offspring" was published and credited to authors Anja C. Huizink, Danielle M. Dick, Elina Sihvola, Lea Pulkkinen, Richard J. Rose, and Jaakko Caprio. Finally, "Lessons of Chernobyl: The Cultural Causes of the Meltdown" is a humanities article written by Sergei P. Kapitza and published in *Foreign Affairs* in 1993. All of these articles are written about some aspect of the Chernobyl accident of 1986, but they differ in their foci, their organization, and the diction used by the authors.

One aspect of an academic article that will always differ between the disciplines is its specific focus. One could even venture to say that an article's focus determines the discipline whose writing style it will follow. "Chromosome Alterations" reports on an experiment which tested chromosome alterations in Chernobyl cleanup workers and found that "different types of unstable chromosomal aberrations were found in Chernobyl cleanup workers many years after their exposure to low-dose radiation" (Neronova, Slozina and Nikiforov 50). This article falls under natural science because it explores how the radioactive environment has physically affected a particular group of people. The article "Chernobyl Exposure" certainly explores Chernobyl's effects on people, but not physically. Instead, this social sciences article looked at "the potential harmful effect of in utero exposure to the Chernobyl disaster in April 1986, and maternal anxiety associated with that exposure, on symptoms of behaviour disorder observed at age 14" (Huizink et al. 439). The focus on emotional response to radiation exposure is typical of research done in the social sciences. The third article, "Lessons of Chernobyl," does not place its focus on the effects of Chernobyl, but rather explores the causes. This is not the main difference, however. The aspect of this article that sets it apart most from its scientific brethren is the lack of experimentation. The article features a thoughtful discussion about whether the Chernobyl disaster was an inevitable outcome produced by the Soviet culture of that time.

While an article's focus directly reflects its discipline, focus is not the only distinguishing feature of an academic article. When reading an academic article, one rarely makes note of the article's organization even though the organization plays an instrumental role in the way the reader experiences the article. All three of these articles are divided into headed sections, but the similarity between the social and natural science articles is more significant. These two articles share the exact same headings: Introduction, Materials and Methods, Results, Discussion, Acknowledgments, and References. This organization and these headings are indicative of lab reports. These articles, as is the case with most social and natural science

Defines how the natural sciences explore questions about the natural world

research, are reporting the procedure and results of experiments that were conducted. It is important that professionals in these disciplines use this standardized format to report their experimental findings, because the objective of these reports is not only exposition, but also confirmation and potential replication. These reports are meant to provide other scientists with a guide to replicate the experiment and possibly the results. There is a slight addition to these headings within "Chernobyl Exposure." Each of the sections mentioned above is further divided into subsections. For instance, the "Material and Methods" section is divided into the following headings: Sample, Procedure, and Statistical Analyses. While these extra subheadings are not necessary, they do present the reader with a more organized, lucid experience with the article.

Explores both the similarities and differences between research in different disciplines

While the humanities article is organized into headed sections, it does not follow the scientific formula. Humanities writers are afforded much more freedom in their organization because they have different objectives than the writers of scientific articles. Instead of presenting data acquired through experiments, humanities articles often explore ideas or present an argument. In the case of "Lessons of Chernobyl," the idea that Soviet culture was responsible for the Chernobyl disaster is explored in depth, but without one referential staple of the science articles: documentation. While Kapitza does include two footnotes, one describing his own qualifications and another providing extra detail, he does not give any sources for his material. This lack of references does not leave the reader doubting the article's credibility, however. Upon further examination, Kapitza's mini-biographical footnote reveals that he is a "Professor of Physics at the Institute for Physical Problems, [of the] Russian Academy of Sciences" (7). This implies that Kapitza was a part of the Soviet culture he describes, and likely involved in the Soviet nuclear program. This would make references a moot point, because the article is a personal account of what he experienced and observed.

Although this particular article is free of sources and a documentation style, one cannot assume that all humanities research is so. Likewise, one cannot assume that all humanities articles share the same tonal and diction attributes. A

Uses clarification of prior point as transition into final section

humanities writer can exercise much more freedom with language. Tone and attitude can be incorporated, and sentence structure can be varied. Kapitza writes, "Apart from disregarding all formal instructions and rules, the engineers and administrators involved displayed a total lack of understanding of nuclear power reactor physics" (Kapitza 9). This sentence demonstrates the subjectivity that can, and often does, present itself in writing in the humanities. Kapitza uses strong language and an almost condescending tone to place blame on the "engineers and administrators." Kapitza is also free to use figurative language, like hyperbole: ". . . every possible safety rule was broken . . ." (9). All of these freedoms of language combine to make humanities articles a generally more enjoyable reading experience, at least to the general public, than literature from the scientific disciplines.

Writers hoping to get their research published in the natural or social sciences can expect much stricter standards for their writing style. Authors in the sciences are expected to be as objective as possible. While science writers are limited to a certain tone, they are free to use as much technical jargon as they see fit. These articles are meant for other professionals in a given field, and thus the reader should not require any further explanation. The article in *Radiation Research* includes this sentence: "To estimate cytogenetic damage from ionizing radiation in Chernobyl cleanup workers, unstable chromosomal aberrations in peripheral blood lymphocytes were studied" (Neronova, Slozina, and Nikiforov 47). If this had been written for the general public, much of the preceding sentence would require explanation. This sentence also exemplifies the passive voice that is used throughout the natural sciences article, especially in the "Materials and Methods" section of the article. Passive voice is often used in natural science articles because it places the emphasis on the object receiving the action instead of the performer of the action, which is insignificant in natural science experiments.

In contrast, an article written in the social sciences will have much more active voice, because nothing in a psychological experiment is insignificant. Seemingly insignificant details, such as the type of chair the participants sit in, can skew the results. The authors of the social science article, "Chernobyl Exposure," write, "Because the distribution of symptom counts was skewed, we used

Poisson regression analyses, yielding an incidence rate ratio (IRR) and its 95% confidence interval (CI)" (Huizink et al. 441). This sentence is a great example of both passive and active voice, but also first person point-of-view and a bit of technical jargon.

First person perspective was barely used in "Chromosome Alterations," and even then only in the "Discussion" section of the article. This is not the case in "Chernobyl Exposure"; while first person is used sparingly, it appears throughout the article. The jargon used in this social science article is not quite as frequent as it was in "Chromosome Alterations," but would still raise questions in readers outside of the field.

Because of the technical jargon, objective tone, standardized organization, and highly specific subject matter, one could label "Chromosome Alterations" and "Chernobyl Exposure" as being "reader unfriendly," while "Lessons of Chernobyl" is more "reader friendly" because of its broad focus, flowing organization, and varied writing style. While this may be the case to the general reader, each of these articles has a specific purpose, and each of these articles fulfills its purpose effectively for their specific audiences.

Works Cited

New page in final MLA draft

Huizink, Anja C., Danielle M. Dick, Elina Sihvola, Lea Pulkkinen, Richard J. Rose, and Jaakko Caprio. "Chernobyl Exposure as Stressor during Pregnancy and Behaviour in Adolescent Offspring." *Acta Psychiatrica Scandinavica* 116.6 (2007): 438–46. Print.

Kapitza, Sergei P. "Lessons of Chernobyl: The Cultural Causes of the Meltdown." *Foreign Affairs* 72.3 (1993): 7–11. Print.

Neronova, Elizaveta, Natalia Slozina, and Alexey Nikiforov. "Chromosome Alterations in Cleanup Workers Sampled Years after the Chernobyl Accident." *Radiation Research* 160.1 (2003): 46–51. Print.

5d Writing and researching in the humanities and arts

Courses in the humanities generally focus on questions about interpretation and understanding the human experience. Classes you might take in the humanities could include literature, history, music, philosophy, and religion, to name a few.

Writing in the humanities is generally driven by a clear thesis or claim, supported by reasons and evidence. The evidence is often drawn from texts such as novels, poems, essays, works of art, or historical artifacts. The following guidelines will help you effectively write papers in your humanities courses.

Guidelines

- Consult primary sources first, such as original works of literature, or attend original performances, such as plays, films, poetry readings, and concerts.

- Form your own interpretations of works. The first person *I* is used in personal and expository writing in the humanities more than in other disciplines.

- Use secondary sources (works of criticism) only after you have formed your own interpretations and established a basis for evaluating the opinions expressed by others. Secondary sources can provide additional support for an interpretation.

- Look for patterns and interpretations supported by evidence, not for one right answer to a problem.

- Use the present tense to refer to what writers have said: *Emerson points out that...*

- Use MLA guidelines (chapters 11–13) or *The Chicago Manual of Style* (chapters 19–20) for documentation style. These documentation styles are most common in the humanities.

5e Writing about literature

In English classes, you are likely to be asked to write about literature. Pay careful attention to the content and form of the work of literature by reading the work more than once and highlighting significant passages. Then use the Key Points box on pages 85–86 to help you analyze the work systematically.

Here are some basic guidelines for writing about literature, followed by more specific guidelines for analyzing fiction, nonfiction, poetry, and drama.

- **Assume a larger audience than your instructor.** Think of your readers as people who have read the work but have not thought of the issues you did.

- **Make sure that you formulate a thesis.** Do not devote a large part of your essay to summary; assume that readers have read the work. Occasionally, though, you may need to include a brief summary of the whole or parts of the work to orient readers. Make sure you tell them not just what is in the work but also how you perceive and interpret important aspects of the work.

- **Turn to the text for evidence, and do so often.** Text references, in the form of paraphrase or quotation, provide convincing evidence to support your thesis. But do not let your essay turn into a string of quotations.

KEY POINTS
Ten Ways to Analyze a Work of Literature

1. **Plot or sequence of events** What happens and in what order? What stands out as important?

2. **Theme** What is the message of the work, the generalization that readers can draw from it? A work may, for example, focus on making a statement about romantic love, jealousy, sexual repression, courage, ambition, revenge, dedication, treachery, honor, lust, greed, envy, social inequality, or generosity.

3. **Characters** Who are the people portrayed? What do you learn about them? Do one or more of them change, and what effect does that have on the plot or theme?

4. **Genre** What type of writing does the work fit into—parody, tragedy, love story, epic, sonnet, haiku, melodrama, comedy of manners, or mystery novel, for example? What do you know about the features of the genre, and what do you need to know? How does this work compare with other works in the same genre? What conventions does the author observe, violate, or creatively vary?

5. **Structure** How is the work organized? What are its major parts? How do the parts relate to each other?

6. **Point of view** Whose voice speaks to the reader and tells the story? Is the speaker or narrator involved in the action or an observer of it? How objective, truthful, and reliable is the speaker or narrator? What would be gained or lost if the point of view were changed? *(Continued)*

(Continued)

7. **Setting** Where does the action take place? How are the details of the setting portrayed? What role, if any, does the setting play? What would happen if the setting were changed?

8. **Tone** From the way the work is written, what can you learn about the way the author feels about the subject matter and the theme? Can you, for example, detect a serious, informative tone, or is there evidence of humor, sarcasm, or irony?

9. **Language** What effects do the following have on the way you read and interpret the work: word choice, style, imagery, symbols, and figurative language?

10. **Author** What do you know, or what can you discover through research, about the author and his or her time and that author's other works? Does what you discover illuminate this work?

Writing about prose   As you read novels, short stories, memoirs, and biographies or autobiographies, consider these basic questions for thinking about what you read: What happened? When and where did it happen? Who did what? How were things done? Why? Then extend your inquiry by considering the ten options for analyzing literature in the preceding Key Points box in addition to the following:

- **Narrator** What is the author's attitude to and depiction of the narrator: omniscient, deceived, observant, truthful, biased, crazy?

- **Style** What do you notice in regard to the author's word choice, sentence length and structure, significant features?

- **Imagery** What effect do the figures of speech, such as similes, metaphors, and others, have on you? (see pp. 87–88 and section 32e)

- **Symbols** Are there objects or events with special significance or with hidden meanings?

- **Narrative devices** How, if at all, does the author use foreshadowing, flashback, leitmotif (a recurring theme), alternating points of view, turning point, and dénouement (outcome of plot)?

Writing about poetry   In addition to using some of the suggestions relating to prose, consider the following factors when you analyze a poem.

stanza: lines set off as a unit of a poem

rhyme scheme: system of end-of-line rhymes that you can identify by assigning letters to similar final sounds—for example, a rhyme scheme for couplets (two-line stanzas), *aa bb cc;* and a rhyme scheme for a sestet (a six-line stanza), *ababcc*

meter: number and pattern of stressed and unstressed syllables (or *metric feet*) in a line. Common meters are trimeter, tetrameter, and pentameter (three, four, and five metric feet). The following line is written in iambic pentameter (five metric feet, each with one unstressed and one stressed syllable):

Bright Stár/wŏuld Í/wĕre stéd-/făst ás/thŏu aŕt   —John Keats

foot: unit (of meter) made up of a specific number of stressed and unstressed syllables

Writing about drama   As you prepare to write about a play, use any of the relevant points listed for prose and poetry, and in addition, focus on the following dramatic conventions:

structure of the play: acts and scenes

plot: episodes, simultaneous events, chronological sequence, causality, climax, turning point

characters: analysis of psychology, social status, relationships

setting: time, place, and description

time: real time depicted (all action takes place in the two hours or so of the play) or passage of time

stage directions: details about clothing, sets, actors' movements, expressions, and voices; information given to actors

scenery, costumes, music, lighting, props, and special effects: purpose and effectiveness

presentation of information: recognition of whether the characters in the play know things that the audience does not or whether the audience is informed of plot developments that are kept from the characters

Figurative language   The writers of literary works often use figures of speech to create images and intensify effects.

metaphor: implied comparison, with no *like* or *as*

The still, sad music of humanity   —William Wordsworth

The quicksand of racial injustice   —Martin Luther King, Jr.

simile: type of metaphor, but with two sides stated

Like as the waves make towards the pebbled shore,
So do our minutes hasten to their end. —William Shakespeare

The weather is like the government, always in the wrong. —Jerome K. Jerome

Playing for teams other than the Yankees is "like having a crush on Cinderella but dating her ugly stepsisters." —David Wells (when Yankees pitcher)

irony: mismatch of words and meaning, meaning the opposite

Yet Brutus says he was ambitious;
And Brutus is an honourable man. —William Shakespeare, *Julius Caesar*

metonymy: substitution of one term for another closely associated with it

Washington has set in motion a huge bailout. (that is, the US government)

The *pen* is mightier than the *sword.*

synecdoche: use of part for whole or whole for part

The ranch owner rode into town with thirty *head* of cattle and two hired *guns.*

oxymoron: contradiction, as in "clean coal"

alliteration: repetition of consonant sounds

He bravely breach'd his boiling bloody breast. —William Shakespeare

assonance: repetition of vowel sounds

And feed deep, deep upon her peerless eyes —John Keats

onomatopoeia: sound of word associated with meaning

murmuring of innumerable bees —Alfred, Lord Tennyson

personification: description of a thing as a person

rosy-fingered dawn —Homer

zeugma: use of a word with two or more other words, forming different and often humorous logical connections

The art dealer departed in anger and a Mercedes.

He came out in a top hat and a rash.

For more on using figurative language, see 32e.

🔑 KEY POINTS
Common Conventions in Writing about Literature

- **Tense** Use the present tense to discuss works of literature even when the author is no longer alive.

- **Authors' Names** Use an author's full name the first time you mention it: *Stephen King.* Thereafter, and always in parenthetical citations, use only the last name: *King,* not *Stephen,* and certainly not *Steve.*

- **Author / Narrator Distinction** Make a clear distinction between author and narrator. The narrator is the person telling a story or serving as the voice of a poem and does not necessarily express the author's views. Often, the author has invented the persona of the narrator. Keep the terms distinct.

- **Titles of Works** Underline or italicize the titles of books, journals, and other works published as an entity and not as part of a larger work. Use quotation marks to enclose the title of a work forming part of a larger published work: short stories, essays, articles, songs, and short poems.

- **Quotations** Integrate quotations into your text, and use them to help make your point. Avoid a mere listing and stringing together: "Walker goes on to say,... Then Walker states,..." When quoting two or three lines of poetry, separate lines with a slash (/). When using long quotations (more than three lines of poetry or four typed lines of prose), indent one inch, but do not add quotation marks; the indentation signals a quotation.

5f Sample paper 3: A student's literature paper

The following essay draft was written by sophomore Brian Cortijo for a course on multicultural American literature. The assignment was to compare and contrast two collections of stories according to the way they present a concept of identity and to focus on the texts themselves without turning to secondary sources. Cortijo was writing for his instructor and classmates, all of whom were familiar with the stories, so summary was unnecessary. He decided to focus on three of the ten areas in the Key Points box on pages 85–86: theme, setting, and language, specifically symbols. The draft is documented according to MLA style; in a later draft, the writer added a paper identification and a page break for the works-cited list. For more on this and MLA format for a final draft, see 21a and chapters 11–13.

Identity and the Individual Self

While distinct in their subject matter, the collections of stories presented in Sherman Alexie's *The Lone Ranger and Tonto Fistfight in Heaven* and Edwidge Danticat's *Krick? Krack!* are strikingly similar in the responses they evoke and in their ability, through detached or seemingly detached narratives, to create a sense of collective selfhood for the peoples represented in those narratives. Through connected stories, repetition of themes and events, shifting of narrative voice and honest, unapologetic discussion of the problems and the beauty of their personal experiences, Danticat and Alexie provide frank, cohesive portrayals of a Haitian and Native American peoplehood, respectively.

While it may not be the intention of these authors to address such a collective identity, it is clear that each is working from some conception of what that identity is, if not what it should be. Each author has symbols and characters that are used to display the identity in all its glory and shame, all its beauty and horror. For Alexie, both characters and objects are used, each for its own purpose. Most notable among these are Thomas Builds-the-Fire, a symbol of spirituality; Norma, who remains uncorrupted by the life imposed on the Indian peoples; and the seemingly ubiquitous drum, a symbol of religion that, if played, "might fill up the whole world" (23). Danticat, by contrast, concentrates more on objects than on characters to embody the ideals and the fears of the identity she is constructing through her narrative. The most prominent among these symbols are the bone soup, braids, and, more generally, hair.

Danticat's use of the bone soup in her last story, "Caroline's Wedding," and of the braids in her "Epilogue: Women Like Us" is of paramount importance to any claim of Haitian peoplehood, or Haitian womanhood, that she might try to make. The use of these elements is indicative of the loving imposition and inclusion of past generations into one's own, as well as the attempt to pass down all that has gone

Margin annotations:

Introduces the works with complete names of authors

States thesis, emphasizing similarity

Refers to setting and theme

Now uses last names only

Points out how theme is addressed

Integrates quotation

Uses present tense

Analyzes symbols

Provides
specific
references to
the text and
the characters

before to those who will one day bear the burden of what that past means. Thus, Hermine's soup is her daughter Gracina's soup as well, not because she eats of it but because those bones—that ancestry—are a part of her and she will one day be responsible for passing them (and it) on. Likewise, Danticat's reader in the epilogue must know her history and her lineage, not only to know how to braid her daughter's hair but for whom those braids are tied.

Returns to
similarities
in theme

Not surprisingly, as both books deal greatly with ancestry, they also deal with the transition and maintenance of an identity over time. Both authors assert that the collective self represented by the past is part and parcel of that embodied by the future—bound to it and inseparable. The one serves to define the other. Likewise, there is a call to make the efforts and struggles of the past worthwhile—to do better, if simply for the sake of one's ancestors.

In *Tonto*, Alexie goes as far as to suggest that time is unimportant, if even existent, with respect to reality. Watches and keeping track of time are of no consequence. One's past will always be present, and the future always ahead, so there is no need to dwell on either, but that does not mean that they do not matter. A person lives in the now, but every "now" was once the future and will become the past (22). Alexie makes extensive use of the period of five hundred years, as though that is a length of time perceptible to the human consciousness, if appreciated more by the Indian.

Gives
specific
references

Focuses on
structure of
work

Danticat's twisting of time is less blatant than Alexie's, but that may be because it is not necessary to speak of things in terms of hundreds of years. A few generations suffice, and the connections between her characters rely so heavily on the similarities between their stories that their relations are obvious. The suicide of the new mother in the first story is mirrored perfectly in the last, though they might take place fifty years apart. The question and answer game played by the sisters forces one to wonder whether Caroline and Grace's mother went through an experience similar to Josephine's mother's. Then there is Marie, who finds and claims the dead baby Rose, who very well may be the daughter of Josephine, who is connected to at least two of the other tales. Beyond the characters themselves, the reuse of the

Provides
specific
details about
characters

Points out relevance of symbols

symbols of hair and the bloody water is striking. The Massacre River, which took the lives of many who attempted to cross it, is named (44), but it is also implied in the bloody stream of Grace's dream with her father, even though the character may know nothing of it. After years, generations, and physical separation, the events at that river seem to pervade the collective consciousness of the Haitian people.

Draws threads together with term "collective identities"

Clearly, these authors make no attempt to glorify the identity that they are helping to define. What is vital to the presentation of these collective identities is that they are transcendent of both time and location and that they are honest, if not visceral, in their telling. As beautifully told as these pieces of fiction are, they aim for truth and are unapologetic in presenting the faults and difficulties inherent in that truth. By telling these tales honestly and without pretense, Alexie and Danticat help to reveal what many may not be willing to admit or acknowledge about others or about themselves—the importance, beauty, and complexity of a collective selfhood.

Ends on a strong note, affirming thes of "peoplehoo

New page in final MLA draft

Works Cited

Follows MLA for citing book (12a, 12d)

Alexie, Sherman. *The Lone Ranger and Tonto Fistfight in Heaven.*
    New York: HarperCollins, 1994. Print.

Danticat, Edwidge. *Krick? Krack!* New York: Vintage-Random, 1996.
    Print.

5g Writing and researching in the natural sciences

Most writing in the natural sciences (such as astronomy, biology, chemistry, and physics) and applied sciences (agriculture, engineering, environmental studies, computer science, and nursing, for example) concerns itself with empirical data—that is, with the explanation and analysis of data gathered from a controlled laboratory experiment or from detailed observation of natural phenomena. Frequently, the study will be a replication of a previous experiment, with the new procedure expected to uphold or refute the hypothesis of that previous experiment.

GUIDELINES

- Be prepared to write according to a set format, using sections with headings such as Abstract, Introduction, Methods, Results, Analysis, Discussion, Conclusion.
- Focus on empirical data.
- Avoid personal anecdotes.
- Report firsthand original experiments and calculations.
- Present a hypothesis.
- Give background information in the introductory section of your paper, a section sometimes called "Review of Literature."
- Use the present perfect tense to introduce a survey of the literature: *Several studies have shown that…*
- Use the past tense for details of specific studies: *Cocchi et al. isolated the protein fraction…*
- Use the passive voice more frequently than in other types of writing, especially to avoid using first person *I*: *The muscle was stimulated…*
- Use APA (chapters 14–16) or CSE (chapter 17) documentation style, or follow specific style manuals in scientific areas.

KEY POINTS

A Model for the Organization of an Experimental Paper in the Sciences

1. **Title page:** running head, title, author's name, institution

2. **Table of contents:** a list of the sections in the paper, necessary for a long paper or for a paper posted online

3. **Abstract:** a summary of your research and your conclusions (about 100 to 175 words)

4. **Introduction:** why the study is necessary, review of other studies, your research questions and hypothesis

5. **Method:** description of the system of inquiry used to answer the research question, with headed subsections on participants, apparatus, procedures

6. **Results:** reporting of statistics, survey data, or observation data collected with tables, charts, and graphs where appropriate

(Continued)

(Continued)

7. **Analysis:** interpretation of the results, explaining what they mean

8. **Discussion:** evaluation of the results from the perspective of your hypothesis

9. **Conclusion and recommendations:** implications of the results of the study and suggestions for further research; might also include discussion of limitations of study

10. **References:** a list of the works cited in the paper

11. **Tables and figures:** a list of any visuals included in the paper, check with your instructor about placing these at the end or within your text.

Abstract   The following abstract from a paper titled "*Longaeva*: The Scientific Significance of the Ancient Bristlecone Pine" was written by Andrew Dillon for a first-year course on "Volcanoes of the Eastern Sierra Nevada" at Indiana University.* You can read excerpts from Dillon's paper in Chapter 18.

More than any other species of tree, the bristlecone pine (*Pinus longaeva*), of the White Mountains in California, helps scientists to understand the environmental conditions of the past. With some living specimens attaining ages nearing 5,000 years, and dead matter persisting for another several thousand, these ancient trees have provided climatologists, geologists, and dendrochronologists with a continuous tree-ring chronology that dates back to the last Ice Age. This paper examines the complex physiology and habitat of the species and considers what scientists have learned from the bristlecone about the earth's history. Research from the past half century illuminates the magnificence of bristlecone pine as living evidence of past millennia.

Excerpt from a student's lab report   The following annotated excerpt is from Natasha Williams's lab report on microbial genetics conjugation, written for a cell biology course.

---

*Used with permission of Andrew Dillon.

Discussion

Conjugation involves transfer by appropriate mating types.

F+ and Hfr are donor cells with respectively low and high rates

of genetic transfer. F- cells are recipients. Contact between

the cell types is made by a conjugation bridge called an F pilus

extending from the Hfr cell. The donor chromosome appears to

be linearly passed through the connecting bridge. Sometimes

this transfer is interrupted. The higher the frequency of

recombination, the closer the gene is to the beginning of the

circular DNA. In this way one can determine the sequence of

genes on the chromosome.

    Table 1 shows consistently that histidine is the last

amino acid coded with the smallest number of recombinants,

and arginine is the second to last coded with the next smallest

number of recombinants. However, the results obtained for

proline and leucine/threonine vary.

Major section heading centered

Passive voice common in lab reports

Use of one for general reference

Discussion of table included in paper

5h Writing and researching in the social sciences

The social sciences (anthropology, business, economics, geography, political science, psychology, and sociology) examine how society and social institutions are constructed, how they work (or don't work), and what the ramifications of structures, organizations, and human behavior are.

    Two types of writing prevail in the social sciences. Some writers use empirical methods similar to those used in the natural sciences to gather, analyze, and report data, with a focus on people, groups, and their behavior. Ethnographic studies are common, for example, in which researchers take detailed notes as they observe a situation they want to analyze—the behavior of fans at a baseball game, for example.

GUIDELINES

- Understand that the research method you choose will determine what kind of writing is necessary and how you should organize the writing.
- Decide whether your purpose is to describe accurately, measure, inform, analyze, or synthesize information.
- Decide what kind of data you will use: figures and statistics from experimental research, surveys, the census, or questionnaires; observational data from case studies, interviews, and on-site observations; or your reading.
- For an observational study, take careful field notes that describe accurately everything you see. Concentrate on the facts rather than interpretations. Save the interpretive possibilities for the sections of your paper devoted to analysis, discussion, and recommendations.
- Examine research studies in the field, evaluate their methodologies, compare and contrast results with those of other studies, and draw conclusions based on the empirical evidence uncovered. Devote a section of the paper to a review of the literature. (If your field is public policy, international relations, or ethnography, however, your writing will examine trends and draw conclusions, an approach closer to the humanities than to the natural sciences.)
- Look for accurate, up-to-date information, and evaluate it systematically against stated criteria.
- Use sections and headings in your paper. See the APA paper in chapter 16 written as the research paper in a first-year composition course.
- Report facts and data. Add comments and expressions such as "I think" only when this is a specific requirement of the task.
- Use the past tense to refer to another researcher's work: *Smith's study (2004) showed that . . .*
- Use the passive voice when it is not important for readers to know the identity of the person performing the action: *The participants were timed . . .*
- Present statistical data in the form of tables, charts, and graphs whenever possible (chapter 22).
- Follow the APA *Publication Manual* or whichever style manual is recommended.

Turn to chapter 16 for an example of a complete documented paper in the social sciences.

5i Writing for community service projects

Service learning projects link a college to the community. For such projects, students volunteer for community service, often related to the content of a discipline or a particular course. They then must demonstrate what they learned from the service experience. You'll probably do three main types of writing for community service projects:

1. You'll work with the site supervisor to outline the goals, activities, and desired outcomes of the service project.

2. During the service work, you'll prepare reports to a supervisor, daily records, summaries of work completed, and documents such as flyers and brochures (22c).

3. In the course, you'll write reflective reports that describe the service objectives and your experiences and that assess the project's success.

To reflect fully on the work you do, keep an ongoing journal of your activities so that you can provide background about the setting and the work, and give specific details about the problems you encounter and their solutions. Link your comments to the goals of the project.

5j Writing under pressure: Essay exams and short-answer tests

One of the highest-stakes and highest-stress writing situations in college is the essay exam. Essay exams and short-answer tests are a challenge because you have to organize your thoughts and write quickly on an assigned topic, and the end result is usually worth a considerable amount of your grade in a course. Having a solid strategy to approach essay exams is important.

For short-answer tests   In short-answer tests, use your time wisely. So that you know how long you should spend on each question, count the number of questions and divide the number of minutes you have for taking the test by the number of questions (add 1 or 2 to the number you divide by, to give yourself time for editing and proofreading). Then, for each answer, decide which points are the most important ones to cover in the time you have available. You cannot afford to ramble or waffle during short-answer tests. Get to the point fast, and show what you know. To increase your confidence, answer the easiest question first.

For essay exams and short-answer tests Always read the questions carefully, and make sure you understand what each question asks you to do. Test writers often use the following verbs when specifying writing tasks:

analyze: divide into parts and discuss each part

argue: make a claim and give your reasons

classify: organize people, objects, or concepts into groups

compare: point out similarities

contrast: point out differences

define: give the meaning of

discuss: state important characteristics and main points

evaluate: define criteria for judgment and examine good and bad points, strengths and weaknesses

explain: give reasons or make clear by analyzing, defining, contrasting, illustrating, and so on

illustrate: give examples from experience and reading

relate: point out and discuss connections

KEY POINTS
Guidelines for Essay Exams

1. **Prepare.** Prior to a content-based essay test, review assigned materials and notes; assemble facts; underline, annotate, and summarize significant information in your textbooks and other assigned materials; predict questions on the basis of the material your instructor has covered in detail in class; and draft some answers.

2. **Highlight or underline key terms in the assigned questions.**

3. **Think positively about what you know.** Work out a way to emphasize the details you know most about. Stretch and relax.

4. **Make a scratch outline to organize your thoughts.** Jot down specific details as evidence for your thesis.

5. **Focus on providing detailed support for your thesis.** In an exam, this is more important than an elaborate introduction or conclusion.

6. **Check your essay for content, logic, and clarity.** Make sure you answered the question.

Exercises on the Writing Process

EXERCISE 1 Write about your own writing process `1a–1b`

Think about your most recent written assignment. Write an account of what the assignment was, how you generated ideas, how you wrote it, where you did your writing, and what technology you used as you were writing (a computer, a pen and paper). How much time was given between the assignment and the due date, and how did you use that time? How did you feel as you wrote the essay? Be thorough and frank in describing your writing process. The point is to examine the way you write. Read your account aloud to a group of classmates. Then discuss any differences between their accounts and yours.

EXERCISE 2 Write for different audiences `1b`

Write three passages on the general topic of "lying"—one for your eyes alone (a diary entry or a freewrite), one for an e-mail message to a close friend (for more on writing e-mail messages, see 23a), and one for a college instructor. Keep each version short—no more than two paragraphs each. How do the versions differ, and why?

EXERCISE 3 Explore a topic in several ways `2a–2b`

Work with a group of students to select a broad topic (such as the environment, heroes, immigration, aging, or fast food). Each person in the group will explore the topic using two of the following methods:

- writing a blog to initiate an online discussion
- freewriting
- brainstorming and grouping ideas
- mapping
- writing answers to the journalists' questions

Read each other's explorations, and discuss which methods generated good ideas.

EXERCISE 4 Revise thesis statements `2c`

The following thesis statements are too narrow, too broad, or too vague, or they are factual statements that are not debatable. Revise each one to make it an appropriate thesis statement for a three- to five-page essay.

1. Legalizing same-sex marriage is a controversial issue.
2. Literacy is an important issue that must be dealt with.
3. Plants enhance the beauty of a home.
4. People with disabilities can face employment discrimination in several ways.

5. Alcoholism affects children.
6. Advertisers of food products use color-enhanced images to entice consumers into purchasing their products.
7. The media are responsible for causing eating disorders, lowering self-esteem, and encouraging unrealistic ideals of beauty.

EXERCISE 5 Write thesis statements 2c

Read the following list of topics and, together with a group of classmates, refine the topics into thesis statements for a three- to four-page argumentative or persuasive essay. Use the four levels outlined in the example below:

Example

Level 1:	Subject	Reality TV shows
Level 2:	Narrowed topic	Reality TV shows such as *The Amazing Race*
Level 3:	Key question	Why did they become popular?
Level 4:	Tentative thesis	Reality TV shows such as *The Amazing Race* enjoy widespread popularity and high ratings because of interest in the contestants, challenging activities, and financial prizes.

1. Level 1: Subject   Your college's registration process
2. Level 1: Subject   America's system of movie ratings

   [Note: G (general audience, all ages admitted); PG (parental guidance suggested); PG-13 (parents strongly cautioned); R (restricted—under 17 requires accompanying parent or adult guardian); NC-17 (no one 17 or under admitted)]

3. Level 1: Subject   Women in combat
4. Level 1: Subject   Alternative energy sources for automobiles

EXERCISE 6 Write a scratch outline and a formal outline 2d

Choose one of the thesis statements you wrote in Exercise 5 and write a scratch outline. Bring your outline to class and, as a group, select one scratch outline to develop together into a formal outline.

EXERCISE 7 Identify topic sentences in paragraphs 2e

Read each of the following paragraphs. Then determine whether the topic sentence is at the beginning, at the end, or implied.

1. Lisa wrote a list of all items they needed. She then went to the store, purchased essentials, and upon returning, packed the overnight bags for the family weekend getaway trip to upstate New York in the Catskills. Her husband, Charlie, confirmed the reservations at the resort and wrote down the directions. Their son Dave, who had recently received his

driver's license, got the car washed and filled the tank with regular unleaded gas. Everyone in the family pitched in. Teamwork is essential in planning a trip.

2. On Wednesday, I ran for a bus and made it. The dentist said I had no cavities. The phone was ringing when I arrived home and even after I dropped my key a couple of times, I answered it and they were still on the line. The Avon lady refused me service saying I didn't need her as I already looked terrific. My husband asked me what kind of a day I had and didn't leave the room when I started to answer.

—Erma Bombeck, *If Life Is a Bowl of Cherries, What Am I Doing in the Pits?*

3. There are only three ways to make money. One is to go out and work for it. However, few among us can work forever, and there will likely come a time in our lives when working for a paycheck may not be an option. The second way to make money is to inherit it or to win the lottery. Again, not something we all can count on. The third way, and the only one that is available to all of us for an unlimited amount of time, is to invest what we earn during our working years wisely, so that the money we work so hard for goes to work for us.

—Suze Orman, *The Courage to Be Rich*

EXERCISE 8 Experiment with different methods of development `2g`

Choose a topic that interests you. First, write a paragraph about some aspect of your topic using one of the following methods of development:

1. one extended illustration
2. facts and statistics
3. an account of a process
4. definition of terms

Then write another paragraph on another aspect of your topic using a second method of development from the preceding list. In groups, discuss how different aspects of your topic worked with the two methods of development that you chose. Did one method of development work better or less well than the other, and if so, why?

EXERCISE 9 Use the Track Changes feature to work collaboratively `3b`

Select one or two paragraphs (about ten to twelve lines) of an assignment you have written for a course, and paste the text into your word processing program. Then e-mail the document to another student. Your partner will open the document in Word, use the Track Changes feature to make changes to the text, and send it back to you. Decide whether to accept or reject each change. Print out the final version and discuss it with your partner.

EXERCISE 10 Evaluate thesis statements 4c

Which of the following statements work well as a thesis statement to focus an essay of three to five pages in length, and which do not? Give reasons for your assessment.

1. Adding a sixth day of classes is more effective in helping students than extending the hours of the present five-day class schedule.
2. Although solar panels and wind farms offer promising energy alternatives, the economic relationships among countries using fuel oil make alternative energy sources highly unlikely to succeed.
3. Although art and music therapies differ in their approaches, there are compelling similarities between these methods.
4. In order to assist the increasing population of young homeless people, new policies are needed to improve the quality of shelters, create back-to-work employment programs, and fund medical and mental health treatment.
5. Although several studies reveal that placebos are effective in healing ill patients, physicians need to conduct more research into how and why placebos work.
6. Understanding personality types provides us with insights into ourselves and the world.
7. "Mindfulness" or "paying attention" to the world around us is a vital skill to develop because it enriches our lives, sharpens our memory skills, keeps us safe, and helps us become more aware eyewitnesses.

EXERCISE 11 Find details to use in support of a thesis 4d

For each of the following thesis statements, discuss with other students which types of supporting details you would choose to support the thesis and provide evidence to make a convincing case to readers (for example, facts and statistics, examples, stories, descriptions, definitions, instructions; see the Key Points box immediately preceding these exercises). Create a list of the types of supporting details that would be effective for each thesis statement, and include any specific details that would illustrate the point.

1. The current adoption systems must be reformed so that couples seeking to adopt a child avoid long delays, unnecessary extensive paperwork, and costly fees.
2. Community centers in ethnic neighborhoods play an important role in helping new immigrants assimilate into America by providing job assistance, English language instruction classes, and interaction with other immigrants who have successfully struck a balance between assimilation and preservation of heritage.
3. "Recycle, Reduce, and Reuse" are three activities citizens can do on a daily basis to help protect our environment from the hazards of pollution and solid waste.
4. Although law enforcement authorities claim that video surveillance of neighborhood streets protects residents from crime, video surveillance infringes on our civil liberties and should not be used.

5. Internships help students explore their intended careers, make important contacts, and gain valuable work experience.

EXERCISE 12 Examine an argument for logic 4h

For each of the following statements, determine whether the argument is logical or contains a logical fallacy. If it contains a logical fallacy, identify the logical fallacy and explain why it is a fallacy.

1. The new vice president of sales is untrustworthy because many years ago he was arrested for civil disobedience while in college.
2. Married couples without children often experience societal pressure to have or adopt children.
3. Mary can either matriculate as a full-time student in the fall or wait until the following fall to attend classes.
4. Keeping a diary is cathartic because writing on a daily basis releases bottled-up emotions.
5. All men like sports.

EXERCISE 13 Experiment with figurative language 5e

In groups of two or three, write five sentences about your favorite food, object, activity, sport, or sports figure using at least four of the following stylistic devices: simile, metaphor, alliteration, personification, and irony.

EXERCISE 14 Identify key terms in essay questions 5j

Underline key terms that writers should address when they respond to the following essay exam questions from various courses.

1. In Chapter 10, we explored the controversial issues surrounding the death penalty. Write a 350-word essay arguing for or against the death penalty, making reference to some or all of these issues. You have the entire class period.
2. Define *coup d'état*.
3. Compare and/or contrast the major characteristics of the Romantic period in Britain with the Augustan period in Britain. Be sure to refer to at least two writers whom you believe are representative of each period.
4. What are the various ways rocks can be classified?
5. Discuss the key issues presented by both candidates during the last mayoral election.
6. Evaluate the significance of Maslow's "Hierarchy of Needs."
7. Explain the effects of current immigration policies on families and children.

 Visit the English CourseMate for this text at www.cengagebrain.com to find additional practice exercises.

2 Research/Sources/ Documentation

SEARCH

To obtain study resources for this section, visit the English CourseMate for this text at **www.cengagebrain.com**

6 The Research Process: A Conversation with Sources

What is research, and why do it? You think you might have the flu, and you try to find out what the symptoms are and the best way to treat them. That's research. You want to buy a new smartphone, but you don't know anything about the features, brands, and prices. You search online, talk to salespeople, go to stores, ask friends what they recommend, and read consumer magazines. That's research, too. And when your English professor asks you to write a paper on, say, the role of government in protecting the environment, research helps you as you interview experts, find reliable print and online sources, consult government documents, and get help from librarians. Doing research is finding out as much as possible about an issue, formulating a research question, and then attempting to find answers to that question. Entering into the ongoing debates around an issue is a vital part of daily life; contributing to the discussion is an essential part of academic and scholarly work.

6a Knowing what is involved in researched writing

1. Know your research context   Start by identifying the elements of your research context. Keeping your purpose, audience, voice, and medium in mind will help you make smart choices in your research, just as they will for any writing project.

See the full model on page 7.

2. Know the requirements and set a realistic schedule   Find out what the demands of the assignment are, such as length, due date, information to include, number and types of sources, documentation style, and manuscript format. Set a week-by-week or day-by-day schedule for the steps in the process as in 6b.

3. Assemble the tools you will need   Consider what will help you in your research. Do you need to create folders on your computer, identify tracking software, or set up space online so that you can access files from multiple spaces, for instance?

4. Do preliminary research to establish your topic   Make sure you understand and answer the assigned question or address the assigned topic. If you select your own topic, check with your instructor to make sure it is appropriate. Do preliminary research online or in reference works to browse for topics and become familiar with the issues. Narrow the topic so that it is manageable for the number of pages you intend to write. Also be sure to choose a topic that will engage and sustain not only readers' interests but also your own, making connections with your own experience whenever possible. If your topic is assigned, make sure you understand the terms used in the assignment.

5. Develop your research question Design a research question that establishes what you know and what you want to discover. The answer you find as you do research is likely to become your thesis (more on this in 4c and 6e).

6. Write a statement of purpose or a proposal A clearly articulated statement of purpose or a fuller research proposal will help you outline what you plan to do. Section 6f explains how to write both.

7. Determine types of sources and how to find them Decide which types of primary and secondary sources will give you the best results (use section 6c and chapter 7 to help you with this stage); then draw up a plan of action. Allow large blocks of time for locating sources. You'll likely find that this work cannot be done in just an hour or two.

8. Look for and evaluate sources, make copies, and keep full and accurate records Select only sources that fit the criteria for your research context, considering which will be most credible in that context. Record full bibliographical information for every source you consult (9e). Download, print, or make photocopies of your source material whenever possible so that you can highlight and make notes later. There are several computer applications and online tools that can help you save, tag, and annotate resources (such as *Mendeley* and *Zotero*); see 9f for more on reference tools.

9. Take precise notes (more on this in 10a–10e). Paraphrase and summarize as often as possible while taking notes. Be sure to use your own words and write down why the information is useful or how you might integrate it into your paper. Make sure you copy quotations exactly as they are written, using quotation marks or a colored font. In your notes, record all page numbers of print sources. Bookmark Web addresses through a social bookmarking application such as *Diigo* or in a specially named file for your paper; be sure to also record the date of access along with the address.

10. Establish your main idea or hypothesis   Digest your material, and determine your focus. Your paper should not simply string together what others have said with no commentary from you. Especially in the humanities, use your research to help form opinions and arrive at conclusions about your topic. Readers want to find *you* and your ideas in your paper. If you are writing in an academic genre that requires a thesis, develop a preliminary one as soon as you can, and make lists of supporting evidence and specific details from what you know and what you read. In the sciences and social sciences, it is more usual to form a hypothesis, present the evidence, and then draw conclusions (5g and 5h).

At some point, when you decide you have something to say about what you think and what your sources say, make a plan or a map, and start a rough first draft.

11. Write drafts: Revise, revise, revise   Write more than one draft. As with almost all writing for college and beyond, revision is an essential step in the writing process. You should not expect to produce a perfect first draft. Consider making an outline from each draft to check on your coverage of the main points and the logic of your argument.

12. Organize your drafts   Be sure to save copies of each draft as a new file so you can keep a record of the changes you have made. It's a good idea to develop a consistent naming convention so you can quickly see which file includes your most recent draft. You can also distinguish among your earliest rough drafts, your later revisions, and your final copyedited versions by using keywords like "rough," "revised," and "edited," along with numbers, as shown in this sample course folder:

Be sure to follow any file-naming conventions that your instructor provides if you will be turning in your work electronically.

13. Acknowledge and document all your sources Avoid plagiarism by providing information in your text every time you not only quote but also refer to the ideas you find in a source (10d, 10e).

14. Prepare a list of works cited Follow a clear and consistent set of conventions (spacing, indentation, names, order, and punctuation of entries) when you prepare a list of works cited or references (chapters 12–

See Chapters 13, 16, 18, 20 for examples of lists of works cited.

13 and 15–20). Then compare your citations with your list. Make sure that every item on your list appears in your paper and that every work referred to in your paper appears on your list. Using a system of checkmarks in both places as you read a draft is an easy way to do this.

6b Setting a schedule

Get started as early as you can. As soon as a project is assigned, set a tentative schedule for searching for sources, evaluation, and drafting, working backward from the date the paper is due and splitting your time so that you know when you absolutely must move on to the next step. On page 105 is a sample time block schedule that you can download, print, or adapt. You will find that in reality, several tasks overlap and the divisions are not neat. If you finish a block before the deadline, move on and give yourself more time for the later blocks.

6c Considering primary and secondary sources

Some college writing assignments ask student writers to engage with and write about *primary sources*—a poem, a short story, a historical document, scientific data, or a photograph. Many first-year research assignments require students to consider and include *secondary sources*—a literary analysis of a work of literature or a historical event, an interpretation of data, an art critic's commentary on a photograph—to expand, enrich, and challenge the writer's ideas.

Primary sources Primary sources are the firsthand, raw, or original materials that researchers study and analyze, such as historical documents, visuals, journals and letters, autobiographies, memoirs, government statistics, and speeches. You can examine works of art, literature, and architecture or watch or listen to performances and programs.

RESEARCH SCHEDULE

Starting date:

Date final draft is due:

Block 1: Getting started

Understand the requirements.

Select a topic or narrow a given topic.

Determine the preliminary types of sources to use.

Do preliminary research to discover the important issues.

Organize research findings in computer files.

Write a research question.

Complete by _____

Block 2: Reading, researching, and evaluating sources

Find and copy print and online sources.

Annotate and evaluate the sources.

Write summaries and paraphrases and make notes.

Set up a working bibliography.

Complete by _____

Block 3: Planning and drafting

Formulate a working thesis.

Write a purpose statement, proposal, and/or an outline.

Write a first draft.

Complete by _____

Block 4: Evaluating the draft and getting feedback

Put the draft away for a day or two—but continue collecting useful sources.

Outline the draft and evaluate its logic and completeness.

Plan more research as necessary to fill any gaps.

Get feedback from instructor and classmates.

Complete by _____

Block 5: Revising, preparing list of works cited, editing, presenting

Revise the draft.

Prepare a list of works cited.

Design the format of the paper.

Edit.

Proofread the final draft.

Complete by _____

(final deadline for handing in)

You can study or initiate case studies or scientific experiments and take extensive field notes. You can also conduct interviews and use data collected from questionnaires. The use of such primary sources can bring an original note to your research and new information to your readers.

Interviews Interview people who have expert knowledge of your topic. Plan a set of interview questions, but do not stick so closely to your script that you fail to follow up on good leads in your respondent's replies. Ask permission to record the interview; otherwise, you will have to take quick and accurate notes, particularly if you want to quote. Check the functioning of your recording device beforehand. Make note of the date, time, and place of the interview. Remember that developing good questions and performing the background research on your interviewee is equally important whether you are conducting interviews via e-mail or instant messaging or in person. Be sure to write a thank you note to follow up after your interview.

Surveys and questionnaires Designing useful questionnaires is tricky because much depends on the number and sample of respondents you use, the types of questions you ask, and the methods you employ to analyze the data. Embark on survey research only if you have been introduced to the necessary techniques in a college course or have consulted experts in this area. You may also need permission to conduct research on human subjects. If you do choose to conduct a survey, you can also use low-cost, user-friendly online survey applications, such as *Google Forms* or *SurveyMonkey*.

Secondary sources Secondary sources are analytical works that comment on and interpret other works, such as primary sources. Common in the humanities, examples include reviews, discussions, biographies, critical studies, analyses of literary or artistic works or events, commentaries on current and historical events, class lectures, and electronic discussions.

6d Consulting reference works to get started

Reference works provide basic information about a subject, often compiled from a variety of secondary sources. You can access many standard reference works online or through your library's home page. Use reference works only to get started with basic information, however, and for assistance as you explore a topic and find out what issues that topic involves. Then quickly move beyond them.

Encyclopedias   Encyclopedias provide an overview of the issues involved in a complex topic. Some may also provide extensive bibliographies of other useful sources, so they can help you develop your research and formulate a research proposal if you are asked to provide one.

General print and online encyclopedias such as *Columbia Encyclopedia, Encyclopaedia Britannica*, and subject-specific encyclopedias such as the *Internet Encyclopedia of Philosophy* or *Berkshire Encyclopedia of World History* can help you get started.

● TECH NOTE

Using *Wikipedia*

Be aware that while *Wikipedia* can be useful in getting you started with information on a topic, it is a work in progress and constantly being revised. So check any information you find there, and do not include it as a source. Even the founder of *Wikipedia*, Jimmy Wales, has said, "You're in college; don't cite the encyclopedia." If you consult *Wikipedia*, you might just scroll to the end of the article to see the list of references and follow those for potential leads. In addition, your instructor may recommend not using *Wikipedia* at all.

Bibliographies (also known as *guides to the literature*)   You can find lists of books and articles on a subject in online bibliographical databases such as the following: *Books in Print, International Medieval Bibliography, MLA International Bibliography,* and *New Books on Women, Gender and Feminism.*

Biographies   Read accounts of people's lives in biographical works such as *Who's Who, American National Biography Online, Biography Index: A Cumulative Index to Biographic Material in Books and Magazines, Contemporary Authors, Dictionary of Literary Biography, African American Biographical Database, Chicano Scholars and Writers,* and *American Men and Women of Science.*

Directories   Directories provide lists of names and addresses of people, companies, and institutions. These are useful for setting up interviews and contacting people when you need information. Examples are *Jane's Space Directory* and *Communication Media in Higher Education: A Directory of Academic Programs and Faculty in Radio-Television-Film and Related Media.*

Dictionaries   For etymologies, definitions, synonyms, and spelling, consult *The American Heritage Dictionary of the English Language*, 5th edition;

Oxford English Dictionary (multiple volumes—useful for detailed etymologies and usage discussions); *Facts on File* specialized dictionaries; and other specialized dictionaries such as *Dictionary of Literary Terms* and *Dictionary of the Social Sciences.*

Dictionaries of quotations   For a rich source of traditional quotations, go to *Bartlett's Familiar Quotations*; for more contemporary quotations, searchable by topic, go to *The Columbia World of Quotations* (both are available online). Also consult specialized dictionaries of quotations, such as volumes devoted to chess, law, religion, fishing, women, and Wall Street.

Collections of articles of topical interest and news summaries   *CQ* (*Congressional Quarterly*) weekly reports, *Facts on File* publications, and *CQ Almanac* are available in print and online by subscription. *SIRS* (*Social Issues Resources Series*) also appears in print and online.

Statistics and government documents   Among many useful online sources are *Statistical Abstract of the United States, Current Index to Statistics, Handbook of Labor Statistics, Occupational Outlook Handbook,* US Census publications, *GPO Access, UN Demographic Yearbook, Population Index,* and *Digest of Education Statistics.*

Almanacs, atlases, and gazetteers   For population statistics and boundary changes, see *The World Almanac, Countries of the World,* or *Information Please.* For locations, descriptions, pronunciation of place names, climate, demography, languages, natural resources, and industry, consult a gazetteer such as *Columbia-Lippincott Gazetteer of the World* and the *CIA World Factbook* series.

General critical works   Read what scholars have to say about works of art and literature in *Contemporary Literary Criticism* and in *Oxford Companion* volumes (such as *Oxford Companion to Art* and *Oxford Companion to African American Literature*).

For more information about finding sources beyond reference works, see Chapter 7, pages 113–127.

6e Moving from research question to preliminary thesis

Designing a research question   For a paper that draws on research, design a research question that gets at the heart of what you want to discover. Your question should contain concrete keywords that you can search rather than general terms or abstractions. The answer you find as you do research is likely to become your thesis or main idea. If you find huge amounts of material on your question and realize that you would have to write a book (or two) to cover all the issues, narrow your question.

Questions Needing Narrowing	Revised Questions
How important are families? *Too broad: important to whom and for what? No useful keywords to search.*	In what ways does a stable family environment contribute to an individual's future success?
What problems does the Internet cause? *Too broad: what types of problems? What aspects of the Internet?*	What types of Internet controls would protect individual privacy?
What are the treatments for cancer? *Too wide-ranging: volumes could be and have been written on this.*	For which types of cancer are the success rates of radiation therapy the most promising?

Formulating a preliminary thesis   If your research question is "Should Internet controls be established to protect individual privacy?" as you read and do research, you will probably move toward either a "yes" or "no" answer to the question. At this point, you might formulate a preliminary thesis in the form of a statement of opinion, which will help drive the organization of your paper. Continue, however, to look for information that will help you move beyond just "yes" or "no" to develop an informed, specific response to your question.

KEY POINTS
Writing a Preliminary Thesis

1. **Make sure it is a statement.** A phrase or a question is not a thesis: "Internet controls" is a topic, not a thesis statement. "Are Internet controls needed?" is a question, not a thesis statement.

2. **Make sure it is not merely a statement of fact.** "About 50 percent of US residents are active users of the Internet" is a statement that cannot be developed and argued. A statement of fact does not let readers feel the need to read on to see what you have to say.   *(Continued)*

(Continued)

3. **Make sure it does more than announce the topic.** "This paper will discuss Internet controls" is inadequate because your thesis statement should give information about or offer an informed opinion on the topic: "Service providers, Internet users, and parents share the responsibility of establishing Internet controls to protect an individual's privacy."

4. **Change and refine your thesis as you do more research.** Revising your thesis is essential as you discover more about what your topic entails. Remember that this is a preliminary thesis, so it will likely change as you conduct your research.

6f Writing a purpose statement or a proposal

After you have done some preliminary research, you can write a simple statement of purpose. This statement may become more developed or even change completely as you learn more about your topic, but it will serve to guide your first steps in the research process. Your purpose statement should reflect as much as you can about your research context (purpose, audience, voice, and medium) and the direction you're taking. Here is an example:

Purpose   Medium   Audience

The purpose of this documented paper is to persuade film directors and critics that films based on real-life events—such as *Moneyball*—should give precedence to the development of a good story rather than to unembellished factual accuracy; after all, adults expect entertainment rather than education when they go to the movies.

Your instructor may also ask for an outline (2d) or for a fuller proposal with a working bibliography attached (9e). Once you have your brief purpose statement, you can use it as a basis for a proposal in narrative or list form, covering background information, establishing your connection to the topic, addressing more information about your purpose and audience, discussing your voice and unique perspective on the issue, and including your research question.

6g Tips for writing, revising, and editing researched writing

WHAT NOT TO DO

- Do not expect to complete a polished draft in one sitting.

- Do not write the title and the first sentence and then panic because you feel you have nothing left to say.

- Do not necessarily begin at the beginning, and especially do not think you must first write a dynamite introduction. That is why you need to set aside time to revise!

- Do not constantly imagine your instructor's response to what you write.

- Do not worry about coherence—a draft by its nature is something that you work on repeatedly and revise.

WHAT TO DO

- Wait until you have a block of time available before you begin writing a draft of your paper.

- Turn off your cell phone, log out of Facebook, turn off the wi-fi connectivity on your laptop, close the door, and tell yourself you will not emerge from the room until you have written several pages.

- Promise yourself a reward when you meet your target—a short walk or a snack break, for instance.

- Assemble in one place your copy of the assignment, your purpose statement and thesis statement, all your copies of sources, your research notebook and any other notes, your working bibliography, and your proposal or outline. Yes, that's a lot! So start early.

- Write the parts you know most about first.

- Write as much as you can as fast as you can. If you only vaguely remember a reference in your sources, just write what you can remember and leave yourself a note to come back—but keep writing, and don't worry about gaps: *As so and so (who was it? Jackson?) has observed, malls are taking the place of city centers (check page reference).*

- Write the beginning—the introduction—only after you have some ideas on paper that you feel you can introduce.

- Write at least something on each one of the points in your outline. Start off by asking yourself: What do I know about this point, and how does it support my thesis? Write your response in your own words without worrying about who said what in which source. You can check your notes and fill in the gaps later.

- Write until you feel you have put down on the page or screen your main points and you have made reference to most of your source material.

If you can, set your draft aside and do not look at it for a while—at least a day. In the meantime, follow up on research leads, find new sources, discuss your draft with your instructor, classmates, or a tutor at your campus writing center, and continue writing ideas in your research notebook. To revise your draft, make an outline of what you have written and ask these questions:

- Have I covered the most important points?

- When I read the paper aloud, where do I hesitate to try to sort out the meaning? (Watch for those worried frowns!)

- Do I come across as someone with interesting, unique ideas on this topic? What opinions do I offer?

- Have I cited sources accurately and used summary, paraphrase, and quotation responsibly? (See chapters 9 and 10 for more on this important point.)

- Where do I need to provide more evidence from sources to support my claims?

7 How to Search for Sources

Conducting research involves looking for and collecting information on a topic to develop and refine your own views. When you conduct research for an academic project, you gather information that you need to evaluate as valid, reliable, and relevant to your research context. Then you cite this source information in your paper in ways that are specific to the discipline.

No matter how many sources you find and use, your paper should be a synthesis of the main issues you come across in your research. But a well-researched essay is not simply a mindless compilation of sources. Rather, your essay should establish your place in the ongoing conversation about the topic. Let it present you in interaction with your topic and engaged with the ways others have addressed that topic. In the sciences, the structuring of information is more important than the personal opinion of the writer. In the humanities, the writer's perspective is often more visible, so avoid the danger of listing an abundance of sources without coming to some conclusion or presenting your own point of view.

7a Starting the search for sources on a topic

Your library offers several useful starting points for a research project. This section lists categories of resources with examples of when you might find them useful. But the best resource of all remains a librarian, who can help you navigate these different resources and figure out where to start. Don't hesitate to talk to a librarian about the different resources available at your library.

Your library's catalog and interlibrary loan   The online library catalog for your college or university is the best way to find books held in the library's permanent collection. Many libraries participate in interlibrary loan programs as well, so you can access resources at other libraries by ordering them and having them sent to your school or local library. For more information about how to find books through the library catalog, see 7b.

Online library subscription databases   Databases of abstracts and full-text general and scholarly articles previously in print are a good place to start serious online searching on topics. For more information about article databases, see 7c. Access these databases by keyword searching (7f).

Web directories   Libraries, colleges, and other organizations provide valuable subject directories for researchers. These allow you to start with a subject area and drill down until you get to specific sites on specific topics.

- *Research Quickstart* at the University of Minnesota, with lists of sources in many academic subjects
- *Michigan Electronic Library* (MeL), a University of Michigan site
- *Internet Public Library*, run by librarians, offering a guide to subject collections and an "Ask an IPL Librarian" feature, which allows you to e-mail a question about a research project to librarians for evaluation and possible response within three days
- *INFOMINE*, a University of California, Riverside, site, with scholarly resources in medical sciences, business, and visual arts, along with general references
- *Voice of the Shuttle*, a University of California, Santa Barbara, site, listing research sources in the humanities
- *Library of Congress*, important for the listing of its own collections
- *Librarians' Index to the Internet*, which includes useful links to sites in cross-disciplinary subject areas, some presenting a specific viewpoint
- *Intute*, an easy-to-use database published by seven universities, with sources in science and technology, arts and humanities, social sciences, and health and life sciences
- *The WWW Virtual Library*, providing a common access point to Web catalogs/directories maintained by different institutions across the world
- *MLA International Bibliography*, providing "a classified listing and subject index for books and articles published on modern languages, literatures, folklore, and linguistics"

Free catalogs from other libraries   The Web gives you free access to the online resources of many libraries (actual and virtual) and universities, which are good browsing sites. Some useful sites are *Library of Congress*, *LibWeb*, *New York Public Library*, and *Smithsonian Institution Libraries*.

KEY POINTS
What Every Librarian Wishes You Knew

- **Libraries do more than store books.** You might think of a library as a place that holds books, but libraries do that and more. These days they provide access to information available through multiple media. For this reason, many experienced researchers make the library their first stop for any new project.

- **Not everything is accessible online.** While you can probably access your library's databases online and perhaps even see what other books are on a shelf next to one you're interested in, some things are only available in person. Go to the physical library if you can and spend some time learning about what is available.

- **Keywords should be chosen carefully.** Many students come to the library without having thought through the best way to phrase their search terms. Think of the specific words you should search for and any alternatives. Ask a librarian for help. Read through 7f for ideas about choosing keywords for searching.

- **Good researchers visit early and often.** Don't go to the library at the last minute and expect to be able to conduct solid research. You'll need time to look through the resources available, assess whether they're credible, and determine what parts you want to use. And some resources might only be available through Interlibrary Loan, which can take several days.

- **Librarians are people, too.** Librarians are specialists in finding information of all types, and they want to help you. Go with a specific question, and ask for help. You'll be glad you did.

7b Using library catalogs to find books

Library catalogs offer the option of searching by title, author, subject, or keyword (7f). Exact wording and exact spelling are essential for each kind of search.

Subject searches   To find sources focused on one topic, try subject searching. For that, you need to know the specific subject headings the catalogers used to identify and classify material, so consult a reference source such as *Library of Congress Subject Headings*, or ask a librarian for help. For example, you won't find *cultural identity* or *social identity*

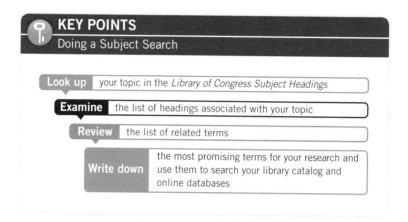

KEY POINTS
Doing a Subject Search

| Look up | your topic in the *Library of Congress Subject Headings* |

| Examine | the list of headings associated with your topic |

| Review | the list of related terms |

| Write down | the most promising terms for your research and use them to search your library catalog and online databases |

in *Library of Congress Subject Headings,* but you can look up *culture* and find a list of thirty-two associated headings, such as "language and culture" and "personality and culture."

In addition, these subject headings show related terms, which can suggest ways to narrow or broaden a topic and can help you in other searches, particularly in electronic keyword searches. The term *bilingualism,* for example, takes you to topics such as "air traffic control," "code switching," and "language attrition." An entry in a library catalog will appear with the subject descriptors, so if you find one good source, use its subject classifications to search further. A search in a library online catalog using the keywords *bilingual, education,* and *politics* comes up with fifty records. One of these sources (shown on p. 117) provides some subject terms to help with further searching: *education and state, educational change,* and *educational evaluation.*

Information in the catalog   The screens of electronic catalogs vary from one system to another, but most contain the name of the system you are using; the details of your search request and of the search, such as the number of records found; and detailed bibliographical information, which is useful for evaluating whether the book will be helpful in your research.

The screen shown on page 117 shows publication information and the library call number, as well as all the essential information you will need to document the source at the end of your paper: the author, the title, the place of publication, the publisher, and the year of publication. It also lets you know the number of pages in the book, including the number of pages (ix: nine) of introductory material, and shows that the book contains a bibliography and an index, both of which are useful research tools. In addition, the subject terms shown here indicate the subjects the book addresses; these can help you structure further searches.

LIBRARY OF CONGRESS CATALOG RECORD

View LC holdings for this title in the: LC Online Catalog *View this record in:* MARCXML | MODS | Dublin Core

Children as pawns : the politics of educational reform

LC Control No.:	2001051485
Type of Material:	Book (Print, Microform, Electronic, etc.)
Personal Name:	Hacsi, Timothy A. » More like this
Main Title:	Children as pawns : the politics of educational reform / Timothy A. Hacsi.
Published/Created:	Cambridge, Mass. : Harvard University Press, 2002.
Description:	ix, 261 p. ; 25 cm.
ISBN:	0674007441 (alk. paper)
Notes:	Includes bibliographical references (p. 217-252) and index.
Subjects:	Education and state--United States. » More like this Educational change--United States. » More like this Educational evaluation--United States. » More like this
LC Classification:	LC89 .H215 2002. —— Library call number
Dewey Class No.:	379.73 21
Geographic Area Code:	n-us---
Quality Code:	pcc

Record this information for documentation

Useful subject search terms

Library of Congress

The call number shown in the catalog entry tells you where a book is located in the library stacks (the area where books are shelved). If a book looks promising, write its call number down immediately, along with the book's title and author(s) and publication information. In a library with open stacks, you will be able to browse through books on a similar topic on the same shelf or on one nearby. Many library catalogs now offer the option of seeing other books on the same shelf as an extension of your search. Whether browsing online or in the stacks, being open to discovering new sources can reward you with options you might not have otherwise found.

Once you find a book that seems related to your topic, you do not have to read the whole book to use it for your paper. Learn what you can from the catalog entry; then skim the table of contents, chapter headings, and bibliography. Your best timesaver here is the index. Turn to it immediately, and look up some keywords for your topic. Read the section of the book in which references to your topic appear, take notes, and annotate a photocopy of the relevant pages (see 10a for a sample annotated text). A book's bibliography and references are useful, too. The research the author has done can help you in your search. It is a good idea to make a copy of the title page and the page on which the copyright notice appears. However, if you eventually find nothing connected to your research question, do not cite the book as a resource, even though you looked at it.

Books in Print and alternatives   To find a book or check on bibliographical details, use *Books in Print* (available in print and online). If your library does not subscribe to the online version, you can use the Amazon site or any other large commercial online bookseller to look up the details of a book—free. Although Amazon does not list the place of publication, it may be visible if you "search inside the book" and look at the copyright page. Complete works that are out of copyright are freely available for downloading at, for example, *Project Bartleby*, *Project Gutenberg*, *Oxford Text Archive*, and *University of Virginia Electronic Text Center. The Internet Archive* <http://www.archive.org> also includes literary and nonliterary texts as well as audio and moving-image archives.

7c Using online databases to find articles

Online databases and citation indexes owned or leased by libraries can be accessed in the library itself. Many libraries also make the databases they subscribe to available on the Internet through their home pages. For example, many libraries provide online access to the following:

- databases of abstracts in specific subject areas, such as *ERIC* (for education), *PAIS* (for public affairs), *PsycINFO* (for psychology), and *SocIndex* (for sociology)

- general databases of full texts of articles published in the last twenty or thirty years, such as *InfoTrac Expanded Academic ASAP, LexisNexis Academic,* EBSCO *Academic Search Premier,* and *ProQuest SIRS* (note that sponsors such as *EBSCO, InfoTrac, LexisNexis,* and *ProQuest* may each offer from ten to one hundred different databases covering different fields)

- databases of abstracts (with some full texts) of general, nonspecialized magazine articles, such as the *Wilson Readers' Guide to Periodical Literature*

- databases devoted to quantitative statistics, such as the *Millennium Development Goal Indicators Database*, or to images such as works of art at the J. Paul Getty Trust Web site

- the *JSTOR* database, providing access to less recent sources

- open-access databases, freely available online but often easier to find via the library catalog. These databases may include full-text scholarly or scientific articles (*PubMed Central*), catalogs of government documents, and collections of bibliographies.

Access to databases in university library Web sites, from both library and home computers, is often limited to enrolled students, who need to verify their status when they log on. Check with your college library to learn which databases it subscribes to.

New issues of periodicals will be available on your library shelves. However, you'll find most of the recent articles you need by accessing online databases. Methods for searching databases are similar to those for finding books. (Refer to 7f for help with using keywords and subject categories to search for articles through a database.) For finding earlier works for a historical study—especially for works written before 1970—you'll need to use print indexes. Check which services your library subscribes to and the dates the indexes cover.

If the periodical index does not provide the full text, you will need to find out first whether your library owns the periodical and then in which form it is available. The catalog for your library will tell you on the screen which issues are available in the library and in which location and format: in files, in bound volumes, or in film form with pages shown in a strip (microfilm) or on a sheet (microfiche), which you will need to read with a special machine. For articles in journals not available in your library, ask about interlibrary loan.

7d Finding Web sources

The democratic nature of the Internet means that many Web pages have no editorial control, so although you will probably find a great deal of material, much of it could be inaccurate. On the plus side, you will find vast resources, current material, and frequent updates—all without leaving your computer. As you plan your research, consider which of the following Internet resources might be the most appropriate for your topic. A reference librarian can help you decide.

Online magazines and online scholarly journals   Online magazines and journals are proliferating. Online scholarly journals will acknowledge their process of having all articles read and approved by experts (peer reviewers), whereas online magazines will typically have editors but no scholarly peer reviewers. You'll find a useful directory at *Librarians' Internet Index*. Some scholarly journals have no print versions. Some online journals and magazines are available free; others allow you to view only the current issue at no cost. Many, however, require either a subscription through your library computer network or a personal subscription. Most university libraries include a directory of journals in their sites.

Online literary texts   Literary texts that are out of copyright and in the public domain are increasingly available online. Try *Project Bartleby, Project Gutenberg, University of Virginia's Electronic Text Center,* or *The Internet Archive.* Be sure that the version of the text you are looking at is a reliable edition. Pay attention to the source that is making it available.

Online news sites   The Web sites of major newspapers, magazines, and television networks provide up-to-date news information; some offer archived information but often only to subscribers. *CNN* and *MSNBC* are among the sources to offer open archives. *LexisNexis* also provides access to articles from many newspapers.

Nonprofit research sites   Some nonprofit sites offer valuable and objective information. For example, see *Public Agenda Online, American Film Institute, Follow the Money,* and *San Francisco Bay Bird Observatory.* Others such as *Wikipedia* can be less accurate and reliable because of how they are written and updated.

Web home pages and hypertext links   Universities and research institutes provide information through their own Web home pages, with hypertext links that take you with one click to many other sources. Individual Web pages can provide useful information, too, but they need careful evaluation because anyone can publish on the Web (see 8c for more on how to evaluate a potential source). Be sure to pay attention to context as well; sites don't always warn you when links go out to other sites that may be less authoritative.

E-mail discussion groups   With e-mail, you have access to many discussion groups. Messages go out to a list of people interested in specific topics. Without charge, you can join a list devoted to a topic of interest. However, many lists are not refereed or monitored, so you have to evaluate carefully any information you find.

For academic research, personal blogs, Usenet newsgroups, and chat rooms provide information with widely varying reliability. Evaluating the credibility of a contributor's comments can be difficult. See Chapter 8 for tips on evaluating credibility of sources.

Using URLs   If you already know the Web address (the uniform resource locator, or URL) of a useful site, type it exactly, paying attention to underscores, dots, symbols, and capital or lowercase letters. Leave no spaces in a URL. Just one small slip can prevent access. Whenever you can, copy and paste a URL from a Web source so that you do not make mistakes when typing. If you ever get a message saying "site not found," check your use of capital and lowercase letters (and avoid inserting spaces as you type an address), and try again. Or try adding "l" to an .htm suffix or deleting "l" from .html. You may find, however, that the site really is no longer available. If a good resource appears to no longer exist, try putting the URL into the search engine at the Internet Archive, which keeps a permanent archive of a series of snapshots of the Web that begin in 1996.

7e Finding visual sources

In a research paper, consider where tables and charts could present visual data concisely and clearly. Images may also help you strengthen an argument. Use visuals to illustrate and enhance a point or to present information clearly and economically. Do not use visuals merely to fill space or to look trendy, and check with your instructor if you are unsure whether visuals are allowed in your paper.

If you look at section 4i, as well as the sample papers in 4j and in chapters 13 and 16, you'll see how photographs and Web visuals work well to highlight or illustrate specific information or to capture the essence of an argument and thus make a point convincingly. Visuals can also be used effectively to convey quantitative information in a readily comprehensible form in tables, graphs, and charts (see chapter 22 for more on visuals of this type).

Finding appropriate visuals   Several of the major search engines, including *Google, Bing, AltaVista*, and *Yahoo!,* offer specific image searches, and by using the advanced search forms there, you will be able to narrow your search to certain types of images, including those that are licensed for noncommercial use; adding that to your search parameters means you won't have to worry about copyright or whether to ask permission to use the image. Another useful source is *Flickr,* which is now owned by *Yahoo!. Flickr* is a repository for photos only, and people can put their photos in this database independent of any Web site. This is, therefore, a complementary site providing access to a large number of amateur photos.

Searching for images can often be difficult and frustrating because many "hits" may not interest you. Image searches use keywords or tags attached to the image, and often, these are not very accurate or they do not describe the image the same way you would describe it. So rather than doing a general image search, it may be more productive to look for images at the Web sites where you find relevant textual information in the first place. Many Web sites, including government sites like the US Bureau of the Census or nonprofit organizations like Public Agenda, make great efforts to present the information on their sites in a visually attractive form. In addition, the National Telecommunications and Information Administration is a good source for tables and charts analyzing Internet use; and the College Board and the UCLA Higher Education Research Institute provide annual studies of first-year students using many tables and graphs.

As a general rule, whichever style of documentation you use, you need to identify and label a visual source such as a figure or a table where you include it in your paper. Be sure to give credit to the original source of the image. Section 4j and chapters 13, 16, and 18 show examples of documenting visuals in MLA, APA, and CSE styles.

7f Using search engines and keywords

Search engines such as *Google* and *Bing* find their results in different ways, so if one does not work for you, try another. Also useful to researchers are Web directories (7a) and meta-search engines such as *Dogpile* and *MetaCrawler*, which search the results of other search engines.

KEY POINTS
Tips for Using Search Engines

1. **Don't mistake popularity for quality.** Though the exact methods that commercial search engines use to find and rank sources are trade secrets, the number of links and visits to a page play a large role in determining which sites get listed first. However, the popularity of a Web site is not necessarily an indication of quality. Search engines do not assess the quality of the content. So make your search string as specific as possible to exercise greater control of your results.

2. **Be aware of "sponsored links."** These sites often appear on the very top of a result list (often against a pale background, which may be hard to notice on some monitors) and are in addition to the easily spotted "sponsored links" in the sidebar on the right side of the screen. The site's owner pays for it to appear at the top of the page, so its inclusion there is no indication of quality, popularity, or even relevance.

3. **Try using search engines that are intended for academic work.** You probably use a search engine such as *Google* for everyday Web searches using keywords or to search for images and videos. For your academic work, branch out and use *Google Scholar* and *Book Search*, the directories listed earlier in 7a, and your library's online licensed databases, where no paid advertisements appear on the screen. To find material in journal and newspaper articles, use databases such as *Academic Search Premier, InfoTrac, LexisNexis,* and specialized subject-area databases; there you can find abstracts (when available) or full articles.

4. **Persist and be resourceful.** If a search yields only a few hits, try new keywords in new combinations. Also try variant spellings for names of people and places (such as *Chaikovsky, Tchaikovsky, Tschaikovsky*), and/or try a different search engine.

After you have decided which search engines to use for your particular task, you then have to decide how best to do the search.

TIPS FOR HOW TO DO EFFICIENT KEYWORD SEARCHES FOR ACADEMIC PURPOSES

- **Know the system of the database or search engine.** Use Search Tips or Help to learn how to conduct a search. (In *Google*, you need to scroll to the bottom of a page to find the Search Tips link.) Some systems search for any or all of the words you type in, some need you to indicate whether the words make up a phrase, and others allow you to exclude search terms or search for alternatives. Before you begin a search, read the instructions on the database to learn how to perform a simple search and an advanced search. Generally, begin a search by using keywords or subject terms if you know them. A keyword search of an online database of full-text articles will produce articles with subject terms attached, as in Source Shot 4 in section 12e, page 201. Use what the database provides to limit a search as to type of source, date, full-text articles or not, and scholarly, peer-reviewed articles, as shown in the screenshot on page 124.

- **Learn how to do Boolean searches.** Many database searches operate on the Boolean principle; that is, they use the "operators" *AND, OR,* and *NOT* in combination with keywords to define what you want the search to include and exclude. Imagine that you want to find out how music can affect intelligence. A search for "music

Advanced Search Screen: EBSCO *Academic Search Premier* Database

AND intelligence" would find sources in the database that include both the word *music* and the word *intelligence.*

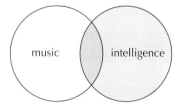

A search for "music AND (intelligence OR learning)" would expand the search. You would find sources in the database that included both the word *music* and the word *intelligence* or the word *learning.*

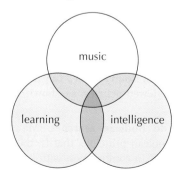

Some search engines let you use terms such as *NEAR* and *ADJ* (adjacent to) to find phrases close to each other in the searched text.

- **Know how to expand or narrow a search.** Many search engines, including *Google*, let you use signs such as + or – to include or prohibit a term, thereby expanding or narrowing your search. You do not need to insert the word *and*.

- **Use a wildcard character (* or ?) to truncate a term and expand the search.** The truncated search term *podiatr** will produce references to *podiatry*, *podiatrist*, and *podiatric*. In *Google*, however, the wildcard character * is used to stand for a whole word only, as in "Foot doctor is a *," but *Google* automatically uses "stemming" and searches for "podiatrist" as well as "podiatry" if you have entered the latter term only.

- **Narrow a search by grouping words.** Enclose search terms in quotation marks (or in some cases, parentheses) to group the words into a phrase; this is a useful technique for finding titles, names, and quotations. A collection of keywords from a half-remembered quotation from Elie Wiesel ("to write is to sow and to reap") entered as a *Google* search without quotation marks does not produce a link to Elie Wiesel's text on the first page of hits. Putting quotation marks around this phrase, however, produces a link to the text of his book *All Rivers Run to the Sea* as the first hit, and it includes the full quotation ("To cry is to sow, said the Maharal of Prague; to laugh is to reap. And to write is to sow and to reap at the same time.").

- **Be flexible.** If you don't get good results, try using synonyms. *Google* will include synonyms in the search, for example, if you type a tilde (~) immediately before the search term, as in ~ *addiction*. Or try a different search engine or database.

 ## Getting the most out of *Google*

Your college instructor may direct you away from the popular search engine *Google* and toward engines more geared to finding academic sources. However, remember that *Google* can be far more versatile, direct, and productive than the results in its basic search engine indicate.

KEY POINTS
What *Google* Can Do for You

Google provides the following useful functions for researchers. Use them.

Google Tools for Searching

- **Google Alerts** sends e-mail notifications to you about new information and content available about search terms or news stories that you are following.

(Continued)

(Continued)

- *Google Scholar,* an excellent resource for researchers, searches scholarly sources (such as research studies, dissertations, peer-reviewed papers) across many disciplines. You may also be able to customize the program to provide links to the full text of articles in your college library. Click "Scholar preferences" and enter the name of the library. You can then import local links into bibliographical programs your college may own, such as *EndNote* or *RefWorks.*

- *Google Book Search* helps you find books and provides details of the contents, even allowing you to search the full text of many books for specific content.

- *Google Blog Search* helps you find blogs that might provide interesting, current information about topics of interest.

- *Google Earth* allows you to search for maps, detailed satellite images, and 3D images.

- *Google Advanced Search* provides many options for tailoring your search to your precise needs (see the screenshot on p. 127).

Other *Google* Tools

- *Google Reader* provides a way to subscribe to specific blogs, news sites, and other Web sites that are regularly updated by subscribing to RSS (Really Simple Syndication) feeds.

- *Google Docs* allows you to create or upload existing online materials, such as documents, presentations, and spreadsheets. Others can then access the material and make comments and changes, recording their contribution. This is a useful tool for collaborative projects.

- *Google Sites* provides an easy interface for developing a Web site that is hosted for free by *Google.* You can choose from a variety of templates that help with design, or you can start with a blank template. The design interface looks much like a word processor, making it a simple alternative for Web-based development projects.

Using advanced searches Whenever you can, use a search engine's advanced search feature. This will allow you to specify results that use all the keywords in any order, just the exact phrase, or only one of the words, or that exclude unwanted words. Databases also often provide an advanced search feature that allows you to limit your search to retrieve only full-text or "peer-reviewed" articles (scholarly articles, scrutinized and approved for publication by reviewers familiar with the field). The following screenshot shows this feature.

Google Advanced Search

In addition, a *Google* Advanced Search allows you to be specific about the order and number of keywords, number of results, language of the source, and the file type (*Word, Excel, PowerPoint, Acrobat,* and so on).

How to get information to come to you—research in your pajamas   Not only can you find a vast amount of source material online, but also you can arrange to be notified when materials on your specific topic become available. For example, *Google Alerts* will e-mail search results directly to you, and *Google Reader* allows you to keep up with Web sites' RSS feeds by notifying you of the latest news items, events, or discussion postings on a given topic at the time interval you specify. In addition, several journal databases, such as those sponsored by *EBSCO, SAGE,* and *CSA,* will run a search on a topic you specify as often as you request, even daily, and alert you via e-mail about articles that meet the criteria you establish. These RSS feeds mean that you get full-text research articles brought to you 24/7 without your having to remember to redo a search.

8 How to Evaluate Sources

A critically important part of the research process is determining which sources are relevant and credible. Use the guidelines in this chapter to evaluate the potential sources that you find.

8a Reading sources critically

PURPOSE	AUDIENCE
VOICE	MEDIUM

See the full model on page 7.

To read sources critically, you follow the same process outlined in the critical thinking framework in 1c. In other words, you should think about the source's purpose, audience, voice, and medium as you read—its *context*. Understanding the context of the sources you are reading while keeping in mind your

---

🔑 KEY POINTS
Reading Sources Critically

Respond to these questions from the critical thinking framework as you read your sources.

PURPOSE	AUDIENCE
What is the author's purpose in writing this piece? Is it meant to be persuasive, informative, or something else? What influence might that purpose have on the potential usefulness of the piece as a source in your own work?	What audience is the author addressing? How do you know? Does the intended audience have any impact on what information is included in or excluded from the piece? If so, how?

VOICE	MEDIUM
What are the credentials and reputation of the author? What is the place of publication? What or whom does the author represent? Is there a particular bias that the author demonstrates? If so, where do you see it, and what is the impact on credibility?	In what medium was the piece published? Why do you think it was published in that medium? Was it peer reviewed or edited by someone else? Is the publication venue subject to rapid change (like an article in *Wikipedia*), or is it fairly static, like a printed book or an online journal article?

Other things you might do as you read your sources critically:

- Ask questions about the ideas you read. An easy way to do this is to write your annotations in the margin. If you find yourself thinking "but…" as you read, go with that sense of doubt, and make a note of what troubles you.

- Be on the lookout for assumptions that may be faulty. If you are reading an article on home-schooling and the writer favors home-schooling because it avoids subjecting students to violence in schools, the unstated assumption is that all schools are violent places.

- Make sure the writer's evidence is adequate and accurate. For example, if the writer is making a generalization about all Chinese students based on a study of only three, you have cause to challenge the generalization as resting on inadequate evidence.

- Note how the writer uses language. Which terms does the writer use with positive—or negative—connotations, signaling the values the writer holds? Does the writer flamboyantly denigrate the views of others with such phrases as "a ridiculous notion" or "laughably inept policies"?

- Be alert for sweeping generalizations, bias, and prejudice: "Women want to stay home and have children." "Men love to spend Sundays watching sports."

own research context will help you find sources that will be a good match—sources that your readers will find credible, reliable, and relevant for your research goals.

Do your reading when you are able to write—not on the treadmill or while watching TV. Note any questions, objections, or challenges on the page, as in the annotated text shown in 10a, on self-stick notes, on index cards, in a response file on your computer, or in a journal. Your critical responses to your reading will provide you with your own ideas for writing.

8b Recognizing a scholarly article

A scholarly article is not something you are likely to find in a magazine in a dentist's office. Scholarly articles are published in journals that are designed for specialists in a field. A scholarly article is reviewed by other scholars in the field for approval prior to publication, which is called peer review. Scholarly articles also share several other characteristics.

🔑 KEY POINTS
How to Recognize a Scholarly Article

1. It is reviewed by other scholars (peer reviewers) for their approval before publication.

2. It refers to the work of other scholars and includes notes, references, and/or a list of works cited, footnotes, or endnotes.

3. It names the author and may describe the author's affiliation and credentials.

4. It deals with a serious issue in depth. For example, a magazine might simply report on various findings and how they might apply to its targeted audience, but a scholarly journal would go further to discuss issues such as methodology, possible differing opinions, and potential future research directions.

5. It uses academic or technical language for informed readers.

6. If in print, it generally appears in journals that do not include colorful advertisements or eye-catching pictures. Source Shot 1 on page 186 shows a page from a scholarly journal.

(***Note:*** Not all scholarly articles will include all six of these criteria.)

Periodicals such as *Time*, *Newsweek*, and *The Economist* are serious, but they are not scholarly periodicals. Note that a scholarly article may appear in academic journals such as *College English* or the *New England Journal of Medicine*, or it might be found in a publication for the general population, such as *Psychology Today* or *Science*.

Online articles in HTML or other digital formats, aside from PDFs, do not necessarily provide the immediate signals of color, illustrations, and varied advertisements that would identify non-scholarly work in print publications. If you find an online article and wish to check its credibility, try the following:

- Follow links from the author's name (if available) to find a résumé and more information.

- In *Google Scholar*, use the author's name as a search term to see publications and citations by others.

- Do a search for the title of the periodical in which the article appears to find out that periodical's purpose and its requirements for submitting and publishing articles. In some library databases (*EBSCO's*, for example), you can limit your search to articles that are peer-reviewed; that is, they are read by other scholars working on similar topics and are found to contribute new and important knowledge before they are accepted for publication.

● TECH **NOTE**

Databases of Journal Information

- *Genamics JournalSeek* provides links to the Web sites of journals to help you identify whether journals are scholarly.

- The Cornell University Web site *Distinguishing Scholarly Journals from Other Periodicals* provides definitions and examples of four categories of periodical literature: scholarly, substantive news and general interest, popular, and sensational.

- Many academic journals available online are listed in the *Directory of Open Access Journals*. All journals listed in this directory are freely available on the internet.

- Another good resource for finding scholarly journals is the Web site for the Council of Editors of Learned Journals.

8c Evaluating potential sources

Before you make detailed notes on a source that you might use for your research, be sure it will provide suitable information to help answer your research question. As you evaluate your sources, pay careful attention to how something was vetted before it was published, especially if it is published online. Pay attention to whether the piece was peer reviewed (a scholarly article) or edited prior to publication (a magazine article).

You'll find more help with evaluating Web sources on pages 134–135, and you'll find information about how to compile summaries and evaluations of sources into an annotated bibliography in 9e.

Books Whether a book is in print or electronic form, check on who the publisher is and do a quick Web search if you don't recognize the name. Is the book published by a university press or a recognized commercial publishing house? Is it a self-published book (perhaps published through services such as *CreateSpace, Lulu,* or *XLibris*)? Check the date of publication, notes about the author, table of contents, and index. Skim the preface, introduction, chapter headings, and summaries to give yourself an idea of the information in the book and the book's theoretical basis and perspective. Do not waste time making detailed notes on a book that deals only tangentially with your topic or on an out-of-date book (unless your purpose is to discuss and critique its perspective or examine a topic historically). Ask a librarian or your instructor for help in evaluating the appropriateness of sources you discover. If your topic concerns a serious academic issue, readers will expect you to consult scholarly books and/or articles and not limit your references to popular magazines, newspapers, and Web sites.

Periodical articles Whether your access to a periodical article is in print, on the Web, or through a library's online databases, you'll need to consider similar criteria. Take into account the type of periodical, any organization with which it is affiliated, and the intended audience. Differentiate among the following types of articles (listed in descending order of reliability, with the most reliable first):

- scholarly articles (see 8b)
- articles, often long, in periodicals for non-specialists but serious, well-educated readers, such as *New York Review of Books, Atlantic Monthly, The Economist, Scientific American,* and *Nation*
- shorter articles, with sources not identified, in popular magazines for a general audience, such as *Ebony, Time, Newsweek, Parents, Psychology Today,* and *Vogue,* or in newspapers
- articles with dubious sources, written for sensational tabloid magazines, such as *National Enquirer, Globe,* and *Star*

Newspaper articles and news articles The *New York Times, Washington Post,* and *Los Angeles Times,* for example, provide mostly reliable accounts of current events; daily editorial comments; and reviews of books, film, and art. Be aware that most newspapers (as well as televised news reports such as Fox News and MSNBC) have political leanings, so perspectives on the same event may differ.

KEY POINTS
Questions to Evaluate a Source

1. **What does the work cover?** It should be long enough and detailed enough to provide adequate information.

2. **How objective is the information?** The author, publisher, or periodical should not be affiliated with an organization that has an ax to grind—unless, of course, your topic entails reading critically and making comparisons with other points of view.

3. **How current are the views?** Check the date of publication. The work should be up to date if you need a current perspective.

4. **How reputable is the publisher?** The work should be published by someone reputable in a source that is academically reliable, not one devoted to gossip, advertising, propaganda, or sensationalism. Look online for information about the publisher of the print book/journal or host of the Web site. Is it a university press? An established commercial publisher? A self-publishing Web site? Is the host of the Web site affiliated with a particular company or organization? If you are looking at a journal, is there an editorial board? If you are looking at a Web site, what kinds of ads do you see? Does it look like someone is trying to make a profit?

5. **How reputable is the author?** The author should be an authority on the subject. Find out what else the author has written (in *Google*, in *Books in Print*, or at Amazon.com) and what his or her qualifications are as an authority.

6. **Is the piece well written?** A source filled with spelling and grammatical errors should not inspire confidence. If the language has not been checked, the ideas probably haven't been given much scrutiny or thought, either. However, postings to discussion lists, though often written spontaneously, can contain useful ideas to stimulate thinking on your topic.

Other sources found online   What makes the Internet so fascinating is that it is wide open, free, and democratic. Anyone can "publish" anything, and anyone can read it. However, if you are looking for well-presented facts and informed opinion among the more than 800 million domain names registered as of January 2012 (ISC Internet Domain survey), the Internet can pose a challenge.

- **Postings found in e-mail discussion lists, blogs, and wikis** Discussion list postings, blogs (Web logs), and wiki entries (additions to or editing of a Web text appearing in a wiki) will often appear in a list of a search engine's findings. Many professionally moderated lists and other targeted discussion lists can be useful sources of information, though quality can vary considerably. Treat with caution postings in e-mail bulletin boards, newsgroups, blogs, or synchronous (real-time) communications such as chat rooms. If you look at such postings as possible sources, be sure to read and take into consideration the responses to the post you're interested in.

- **Personal or Organizational Web sites** Evaluate Web sites with particular care. Individuals on a rant, as well as serious government or research agencies, can establish a site. Because anyone can "publish" anything, and thousands or millions can read it, finding reliable information and well-presented, informed opinions on Web pages can pose a challenge. Learn to separate good information from junk.

Note: For more on the features to look for, evaluate, and record about Web sites, see the screenshot and examples of documentation in 10i: "One source, four systems of documentation."

KEY POINTS

Locating Key Information on Web Sites

1. **Scrutinize the domain name of the URL.** Reliable information can usually be found on .gov and .edu addresses that are institutionally sponsored (but also see item 2). With .com ("dot com"), .net, .info, or .org sources, always assess whether the source provides factual information or advocates a specific point of view on an issue.

2. **Assess the originator of an .edu source.** Is the educational institution or a branch of it sponsoring the site? A tilde (~) followed
by a name in the URL generally indicates a posting by an individual, with no approval from the institution. So follow up by
finding out what else the individual has published.

3. **Locate missing information.** If you can't readily find information on the actual Web site, a good way to begin an evaluation is
to look the site up on <http://www.betterwhois.com>. This site
will provide information on the author, date, sponsor, and
address, and so supply clues about the reliability of the site.

4. **Check the About page or the Home page.** If you find your way
to a Web page, always go to Home or About (if available) to find
out about the larger site. Look for the title of the site, its stated
purpose, and sponsor. Check, too, for bias. For instance, does the
site aim to persuade, convert, or sell? If you reach a page via a
search engine and no site name is visible or shown in About,
delete the URL progressively back to each single slash, and click
to see which part of the site you access.

5. **Follow the links.** See whether the links in a site take you to
authoritative sources. If the links no longer work (you'll get a 404
message: "Site Not Found"), the home page with the links has not
been updated in a while—not a good sign.

6. **Check for dates, updates, ways to respond, and ease of navigation.** A well-managed site will have recent updates, clear organization, up-to-date links, and easy-to-find contact information.

9 How to Avoid Plagiarizing

The convenience and comfort of researching online are not without a
downside. The ease of finding, copying, and downloading information
from the Internet has its attendant dangers: that researchers lose sight of
what is theirs and what isn't, that they forget where they read something,
that information seems so abundant that surely it must be there for the
taking. Unfortunately, though, that is not the case, especially in the academic world, where presenting somebody else's words or ideas without

acknowledging where those words and ideas come from is a punishable offense.

The word for the offense, *plagiarism*, is derived from a Latin verb meaning "to kidnap," and if you use someone else's words and ideas without acknowledging them, you are in effect cheating by kidnapping or stealing those words and ideas. Readers do not want to be fooled into thinking that the ideas and words you wrote actually originated someplace else. For all audiences, but especially for academic readers, honesty counts for a great deal, so much so that many colleges encourage professors and students to run papers through a plagiarism-checking program such as *Turnitin.com* to ensure that no passages in the text match any in the database of the service.

This chapter describes the various types of plagiarism, and it stresses that acknowledging the work you have done by accurately tracking your research as you do it and citing your sources (who said it, where, and when) is always the way to go.

9a The seven sins of plagiarism

The Council of Writing Program Administrators, a professional organization of writing teachers and program directors, says that plagiarism occurs "when a writer deliberately uses someone else's language, ideas, or other (not common-knowledge) material without acknowledging its source." It might be helpful to break down how such intentional use can occur into several different types of plagiarism.

KEY POINTS
Plagiarism's Seven Sins

1. **Intentional grand larceny**   Presenting as your own work a whole essay bought from a paper mill, "borrowed" or commissioned from a friend, or intentionally copied and pasted from an online source.

2. **Premeditated shoplifting**   Taking passages from a book, article, or Web site and intentionally inserting them in your paper without indicating who wrote them or where you found them. This type of plagiarism differs from intentional grand larceny only because passages, not the entire paper, are copied.

3. **Tinkering with the evidence**   Making only a few word changes to source material and inserting the slightly altered version into your paper as if you wrote it, with no acknowledgment of the

source, and trusting that those changes are enough to avoid charges of plagiarism.

4. **Idea kidnapping**   Using ideas written by others (even if you do use your own words) and neglecting to cite the source of the ideas.

5. **Unauthorized borrowing of private property**   Citing your source with a parenthetical reference or footnote/endnote but following its sentence structure and organization too closely or not indicating with quotation marks any of your source's exact words.

6. **Trespassing over boundaries**   Failing to indicate in your paper where ideas from a source end and your ideas take over (see 10d for more on this).

7. **Writing under the influence**   Being too tired, lazy, or disorganized, or facing an imminent deadline, and turning to any of the six previous sins in desperation or ignorance.

Consequences   Obviously, these "sins" vary in their severity and in the intention to deceive. The types of plagiarism described in items 4 through 6 of the Key Points box sometimes occur unintentionally, but they may be perceived as plagiarism nevertheless. You have to work hard at avoiding them, especially since the consequences of plagiarism can be severe, ranging from an F on a paper or in a course to disciplinary measures or expulsion from college. In the world at large, plagiarism can lead to lawsuits and ruined careers. Those are reasons enough to do your own work and learn to document your sources fully and correctly.

LANGUAGE AND CULTURE

Ownership Rights across Cultures

American academic culture takes seriously the ownership of words and text. It respects both the individual as author (and authority) and the originality of the individual's ideas. In some cultures, memorization and the use of classic texts are common in all walks of life. And worldwide, the ownership of language, texts, music, and videos is being called into question by the democratic, interactive nature of

(Continued)

(Continued)

the Internet. In short, therefore, plagiarism is not something universal and easy to define. In American academic culture, basic ground rules exist for the "fair use" of another writer's work without payment, but easy access to music and media sources poses interesting questions about intellectual property and the opportunities to create and remix culture.

● TECH **NOTE**

A Web Site on Plagiarism

For more on the topic of plagiarism, use the link to the excellent Georgetown University Web site *What Is Plagiarism?*

9b How to avoid even the suspicion of plagiarism

Research and clear documentation open a channel of communication between you and your audience. Readers learn what your views are and what has influenced those views. They will assume that anything not documented is your original idea and your wording.

Remember that citing any words and ideas that you use from your sources works to your advantage. Citing accurately reveals a writer who has done enough research to enter ongoing conversations in the academic world. In addition, citations show readers how hard you have worked, how much research you have done, and how the points you make are supported by experts. So be proud to cite your sources.

KEY POINTS
How to Avoid Plagiarizing

- Start your research early enough to avoid panic mode.
- Make a record of each source so that you have all the information you need for appropriate documentation. Consider using an online application such as *Zotero* to track your sources as you work.
- Set up a working annotated bibliography (9e).

- Take notes from the sources, with a systematic method of indicating quotation, paraphrase, and your own comments. For example, use quotation marks around quoted words, phrases, sentences, and passages; introduce a paraphrase with a tag, such as "Korones makes the point that…"; in your notes about a source, write your own comments in a different color. Then, later, you will see immediately which ideas are yours and which come from your source.

- Always acknowledge and document the source of any passage, phrase, or idea that you have used or summarized from someone else's work.

- Never use exactly the same sequence of ideas and organization of argument as your source.

- When you use a single key word from your source or three or more words in sequence from your source, use the appropriate format for quoting and documenting.

- Be aware that substituting synonyms for a few words in the source or moving a few words around is not enough to counter a charge of plagiarism.

- Keep in mind that paraphrasing without citing your source is plagiarism. (See 10b for more information on how to paraphrase.)

- Don't use passages in your paper that have been written or rewritten by a friend or a tutor.

- Never even consider buying, downloading, or "borrowing" a paper or a section of a paper to turn in as your own work.

9c Know why, how, and what to cite

Why you need to cite sources

- Citing sources shows your audience that you have done your homework on an issue; you will get respect for the depth and breadth of your research and for having worked hard to make your case.

- Citing responsible and recent sources lets your audience know that your arguments are both weighty and current.

- Citing sources draws your readers into the conversation about the issue and educates them. It also allows them to see you as engaged in the ongoing intellectual conversation around the issue you are writing about. With full and accurate citations, they can follow up on the same sources you used and so can learn more.

- Citation can be used to strengthen your argument, protect against counterclaims, or align your thinking with a particular scholar or institutional perspective. In other words, careful use of citations can make your writing and research stronger and more persuasive.

- Citing all sources fully and accurately is essential if you are to avoid even the suspicion of plagiarizing.

How to cite sources Citing a source means letting readers know whose words or ideas you are quoting, summarizing, or paraphrasing; where you found the information; and in the case of Web sites, when it was published or posted online. Styles of documentation vary in whether they ask initially for author and page number (MLA) or author and year of publication (APA), with a detailed list at the end of the paper of all the sources cited. Other systems (*Chicago* and CSE) use numbering systems or footnotes in the paper, with a listing of source details at the end. See comparisons of a citation in each system in 10i, and follow the detailed models in parts 3 and 4 for each of these systems.

How to cite visuals Provide a number and a source note for all tables and figures you include in your paper. In MLA style, put the visual close to the text it illustrates, with a credit line immediately beneath it. For APA papers, consult with your instructor. Some recommend including visuals within the text of a college paper; others adhere to strict APA style, with tables and figures placed at the end of the paper.

Chapters 4, 13, 16, and 18 show student papers with visuals.

What to cite Intentionally presenting another person's work as your own may be the most deceptive kind of plagiarism, but the effect is the same if you neglect to acknowledge your sources because of sloppy research and writing practices. In both cases, readers will not be able to discern which ideas are yours and which are not. Always provide full documentation of sources, with a citation in your text and an entry in your list of sources. The following Key Points box shows you what you must always cite and also points out when citing is not necessary. If you are in doubt about whether you need to cite a source, it is always safer to cite it.

KEY POINTS
Sources to Cite or Not to Cite

What to Cite

- exact words from a source (a key word or three or more words in succession), even facts, enclosed in quotation marks

- somebody else's ideas and opinions, even if you restate them in your own words in a summary or paraphrase

- each sentence in a long paraphrase if it is not clear that all the sentences paraphrase the same source

- facts, theories, and statistics

What Not to Cite

- common knowledge, especially when it is available in many sources—such as the dates of the Civil War, birth and death dates, chronological events in the lives of authors and public figures, or allusions to nursery rhymes or folktales handed down through the ages

Note how James Stalker, in his article "Official English or English Only," does not quote directly but still cites Anderson as the source of the specialized facts mentioned in the following passage:

> By 1745 there were approximately 45,000 German speakers in the colonies, and by 1790 there were some 200,000, nine percent of the population (Anderson 80).

9d Keeping track of sources

The first step toward avoiding plagiarism is keeping track of what your sources are and which ideas come from your sources and which come from you. You will find that one of the more frustrating moments for you as a researcher occurs when you find a note about an interesting point you read—but cannot remember where you found the passage or who wrote it or whether your notes represent an author's exact words. Avoid this frustration by keeping track as you go along.

- **Keep a working bibliography.** Some options: Make a bibliography card (one for each source; use one side only); save screens or print-outs from a library catalog, database listing, or Web site; or use as a research organizing tool any bibliographical software provided by your library, such as *EndNote* or *RefWorks,* or available freely online, such as *Zotero* or *Mendeley.* Record all the relevant information for each source you read and plan to use, including reference works, and remember to record inclusive page numbers for all print sources as well as the date on which you access Web sites. You may want to include annotations (notes of varying length that provide more detail) in your working bibliography either for your own benefit or to fulfill assignment requirements that include an annotated bibliography. You'll find a sample entry from an annotated bibliography in 9e.

- **Make copies of print material.** While you are in the library, scan or photocopy complete journal or magazine articles and a periodical's table of contents (which will provide date and volume number). Scan or copy book sections or chapters, too, along with the title page and copyright page of the book. You will need this information for your list of works cited.

- **Make a copy or take a screenshot of every Web source you may use.** Material you find online can change quickly, so always print a source, take a screenshot, e-mail it to yourself, add it to your bibliographical software file (9f), or save it on a flash drive, making sure you use highlighting or a special font to distinguish your own comments and notes from the material you have copied and saved.

- **Use your browser's Bookmark or Favorites feature.** Save all the links to useful sites so that you can easily find them again. If you work on a networked computer in a lab where you cannot save your work on the hard drive, export your bookmarks to your own computer or CD, or use a free online bookmark manager such as *Diigo.*

- **Record complete online document information, the URL, DOI, and the date of your access.** Bookmarking will not always last with the URLs of subscription databases. If you do not take a screenshot of the whole site, record the name of the author, title, and date posted or updated (this information is sometimes available via the Properties or Page Info commands in your browser). Recording the DOI (Digital Object Identifier) is helpful as well. The DOI provides a consistent way of identifying something you find online regardless of how you access it (for more information, see section 15c). Copy and paste to save the URL exactly on your hard drive or flash drive, and note the date on which you access the online material. In addition, although a retrieval URL is not needed for MLA documentation, it sometimes is for APA and for *Chicago.* See 10i for a screenshot and the information you need to look for on a Web site.

- **Highlight, copy, and paste.** As you read material on the Web, highlight a passage you find, copy it, and then paste it into your own file. Make sure that you indicate clearly in your new document that you have included a direct quotation. Use quotation marks and/or a bigger or colored font or highlighting along with an author/page citation, as in the following example:

> Novelist John Lanchester has made a telling point about our image of self by having his narrator declare that we **"wouldn't care so much what people thought of us if we knew how seldom they did"** (62).

Save as much information as you can about the original document in your working bibliography.

9e Recording information and setting up a working bibliography

From the first steps of your research, keep accurate records of each source in a working bibliography, with or without annotations about each source. Record enough information so that you will be able to make up a list of references in whichever style of documentation you choose, though not all the points of information you record will be necessary for every style of documentation.

Keep your list of sources in a form that you can work with to organize them alphabetically, add and reject sources, and add summaries and notes. Note cards, computer files, or your own files kept in licensed bibliographical software such as *RefWorks* or *EndNote* (9f) have the advantage over sheets of paper or a bound research journal. They don't tie you to page order.

Here is a sample bibliographical record in a computer file for a magazine article accessed in an online subscription database.

Korones, Sarah. "Don't Sneeze on Me." *Psychology Today* 45.1 (2012): 10.

Academic Search Complete. Web. 17 Jan. 2012.

Sample annotated bibliography entry   Here is a sample from Jared Whittemore's annotated bibliography that he prepared for a paper on the community college system in California. He writes the bibliographical details for future reference and ease of relocating the source, adding also useful comments about the content of the source and its relevance to his purpose in including it in his paper.

Significant Historical Events in the Development of the Public Community College. American Association of Community Colleges. 13 Feb. 2001. Web. 23 Mar. 2012.

This site provides a timeline charting the significant events in the history of community colleges, from 1862 to 2001. The timeline includes historical events, such as the founding of the first community college in 1901, and tracks important legislation and publications relating to the development and improvement of the community college system. It provides a historical perspective on the implementation and advancements made in the system in more than a century.

● TECH **NOTE**

Annotated Bibliographies

For more information on how to prepare an annotated bibliography, along with examples, go to the Purdue Online Writing Lab.

 ## Using bibliographical software and databases to help you keep records

Bibliographical software   When you are asked to write research papers, you may find that your college library owns special software (such as *EndNote* or *RefWorks*) to help you search databases, store the results of your database searches, organize your research, insert citations while you write, and prepare a bibliography in one of many styles available. If your library does not provide access to software like *EndNote* or *RefWorks*, several free applications are available online such as *Zotero, Mendeley,* and *Connotea.*

KEY POINTS
What Bibliographical Software Can (and Can't) Do

- Software can provide a way for you to record and easily save citations for sources you find in online databases.
- It will automatically create a bibliographical list or endnotes either in Cite While You Write (CWYW) mode or after completion of your text.

- It can prepare these lists in a variety of documentation styles, including those commonly required in college courses and covered in this handbook: MLA, APA, *Chicago*, and CSE. In fact, *EndNote* claims to offer 3,000 styles—more than enough for anyone.

- It does a lot but not everything. Take the time to learn the program. Using these programs requires a considerable initial investment of time and patience, but the investment will pay off eventually by making citations in research papers much easier to manage. Read the documentation and consult the Help menu whenever you need to.

- The software needs to be supplemented by your informed knowledge of the documentation system you are using. Do not let the program take over *all* the chores of recording the results of your research, inserting your citations, and preparing your list of works cited. You still need to be able to check citations for general accuracy and completeness, fix glitches, insert your anchors and hyperlinks in online papers, and handle the occasional abstruse reference yourself.

Databases Several database screens, such as those sponsored by *EBSCO*, shown here, include useful features for writers of research papers.

EBSCOhost is a registered trademark of EBSCO Publishing

From the Citation screen for an article, clicking on the third icon from the right ("Cite This Article") will take you to a screen that shows you how to cite the article in several documentation styles, including AMA, APA, *Chicago*, and MLA. The second icon from the right allows you to "Export to Bibliographic Manager." This feature enables you to save citations in a file for export to *EndNote*, *RefWorks*, and other bibliographical software. Try out these features with the article shown in Source Shot 4 on pages 200–201.

10 How to Use, Integrate, and Document Sources

10a Interacting with your sources: Annotating and making notes

Annotating your sources as you work helps you interact with the author's ideas, ask questions, write comments, and jot down your own ideas. You can annotate your online sources by printing them, saving them, or by using a social bookmarking tool such as *Diigo* to track your work. *Diigo* will allow you to post notes and highlight sections of text on any Web page.

Here is a passage from an article a student read while researching a paper about plagiarism. As the author, Amy Robillard, tells the story of a colleague whose nephew sent him a plagiarized paper to read, she begins to explore how teachers respond emotionally to student plagiarism. The passage shows the annotations that a student made as she gave the article a critical reading.

Was his nephew lazy?
Confused by the assignment?
Is there a difference between how a teacher would respond and a family member?

The bulk of our conversation centered on Aaron's anger at his nephew's actions. Some of his anger, of course, stemmed from the very fact that his nephew would plagiarize. But more anger seemed to be focused on the insult implied in his nephew's decision to send Aaron the paper to read before turning it in. Did his nephew really think Aaron wouldn't be able to tell the difference between the plagiarized work and the rest of the writing he'd been reading for him since he began college? Did he really think Aaron was that stupid? (12)

Because he breaking th rules
No way to know that's what his nephew intended
Is this reall how teache feel?

Source: Robillard, Amy E. "We Won't Get Fooled Again: On the Absence of Angry Responses to Plagiarism in Composition Studies." *College English* 70.1 (2007): 10–31. Print.

Annotating is useful for comments, observations, and questions. You also might need to make notes when you do not have a copy that you can write on or when you want to summarize, paraphrase, and make detailed connections to other ideas and other sources. Write notes on the computer, on legal pads, in notebooks, or on index cards—whatever works best for you. On the computer, you can use *Word*'s Comment function to annotate a text or insert your own comments within a text and highlight them in a color. Index cards—each card with a heading and only one note—offer flexibility: You can shuffle and reorder them to fit the organization of your paper. In your notes, always include the author's name, a short version of the title of the work, and any relevant page number(s). Include full source information in your working bibliography (9e). Then, when you write your paper, you will have at your fingertips all the information necessary for a citation.

10b Summarizing and paraphrasing

As you incorporate sources into your own writing, you can choose to summarize, paraphrase, or directly quote your sources. Summaries are useful for giving readers basic information about the work you are discussing. To summarize a source or a passage in a source, select only the main points as the author presents them, without your own commentary or interpretation. Be brief, and use your own words at all times. A good thing to remember is not to have the original source in front of you as you write. Read, understand, and put the passage away before writing your summary. Then, if you find that you absolutely need to include some particularly apt words from the original source, put them in quotation marks.

Use summaries in your research paper to let readers know the gist of the most important sources you find. When you include a summary in a paper, introduce the author or the work to indicate where your summary begins. At the end of the summary, give the page numbers you are summarizing. Do not include page numbers if you are summarizing the complete work or summarizing an online source; instead, indicate where your summary ends and your own ideas return (see 10d). When you write your paper, provide full documentation of the source in your list of works cited at the end.

Here is a passage from a *Psychology Today* article by Sarah Korones. A student's bibliographical citation for the article is shown in 9e on page 143.

Original (paragraphs from a longer source)

> The common cold results in more than a sore throat and a runny nose; new research shows that illness can actually change our personal prejudices. When we are sick, we become more aware of and repelled by people who seem unhealthy, whether or not those people are actually contagious.
>
> Researchers at the University of Kentucky and Florida State University found that study participants who had just been ill paid more attention to pictures of disfigured faces than did healthy subjects. [...]

Scientists speculate that once the immune system has been kicked into gear, it triggers cognitive processes that set off mental warning bells when we see someone who looks ill.

Sarah Korones, "Don't Sneeze on Me." *Psychology Today* 45.1 (2012): 10. *Academic Search Complete*. Web. 17 Jan. 2012.

No page number is needed in the following in-text citation as the article is only one page long and the page number will appear in the bibliographical citation. Similarly, page numbers are not needed for Web site citations. For longer articles, always include the page number(s) in parentheses before the final period.

Summary (recorded in a computer file)

Korones

Summary

"Don't Sneeze on Me"

Sarah Korones reports that we are more likely to avoid people who seem like they may be sick when we ourselves have an illness, possibly because of signals sent by our immune system.

A *paraphrase*, in contrast, is similar in length to the original material. It presents the details of the author's argument and logic, but *it avoids plagiarism by not using the author's exact words or sentence structure.* You might paraphrase instead of quoting a source if you want to translate the information into language that is more appropriate for your intended audience. If you keep the source out of sight as you write a paraphrase, you will not be tempted to use any of the sentence patterns or phrases of the original. Even if you are careful to cite your source, your writing may still be regarded as plagiarized if your paraphrase resembles the original too closely in wording or sentence structure. You can use common words and expressions without quotation marks, but if you use longer or more unusual expressions from the source, always enclose them in quotation marks.

KEY POINTS
How to Paraphrase

- Keep the source out of sight as you write a paraphrase so that you will not be tempted to copy the sentence patterns or phrases of the original.

- Do not substitute synonyms for some or most of the words in an author's passage.

- Use your own sentence structure as well as your own words. Your writing will still be regarded as plagiarized if it resembles the original in sentence structure as well as in wording.
- Do not comment or interpret. Just tell readers the ideas that the author of your source presents.
- Check your text against the original source to avoid inadvertent plagiarism.
- Cite the author (and page number if a print source) as the source of the ideas, introduce and integrate the paraphrase, and provide full documentation. If the source does not name an author, cite the title.

You can use common words and expressions such as "common cold" or "unhealthy," but if you use more unusual expressions from the source ("more aware of and repelled by those who seem unhealthy"), you need to enclose them in quotation marks. In the first sample paraphrase shown here, nothing is quoted, but the words and structure resemble the original too closely.

Paraphrase too similar to the original (similarities are highlighted)

Korones

Paraphrase, paragraph 1

Sarah Korones describes how the common cold results in more than the physical symptoms it causes. When we are sick, we can be more likely to avoid people who seem unhealthy, whether or not they truly are. Scientists speculate that our immune systems trigger warning bells when we believe someone to be sick.

Revised paraphrase

Korones describes the negative reaction we might have to others who seem unhealthy when we have an illness ourselves. Researchers have found that an individual's response to others can be altered during this time. What happens, scientists hypothesize, is that our immune systems work with our brains to warn us about possible threats.

10c Quoting accurately

Only quote sources when the exact wording of the quotation is powerful or important to the point you are trying to make. Readers should immediately realize why you are quoting a particular passage and what the quotation contributes to the ideas you want to convey. They should also learn who said the words you are quoting and, if the source is a print source, on which page of the original work the quotation appears. Then they can look up the author's name in the list of works cited at the end of your paper and find out exactly where you found the quotation.

The Modern Language Association (MLA) format for citing a quotation from an article by one author is illustrated in this chapter and in part 3. For the use of quotation marks, see chapter 47. To learn how to cite a quotation the source itself cites, see page 173 (11b, item J).

Decide what and when to quote   Quote sparingly and only when the original words express the exact point you want to make and express it succinctly and well. Ask yourself: Which point of mine does the quotation illustrate? Why am I considering quoting this particular passage rather than paraphrasing it? What do I need to tell my readers about the author of the quotation?

Quote the original exactly   Any words you use from a source must be included in quotation marks and quoted exactly as they appear in the original, with the same punctuation marks and capital letters. (For quotations of longer than 4 lines, see guidelines on pp. 152–153.) Do not change pronouns or tenses to fit your own purpose, unless you enclose changes in square brackets (as in the examples on p. 152).

Not exact quotation **Korones makes the point that "illnesses affect our personal prejudices."**

Exact **Korones makes the point that "illness can actually change our personal prejudices."**

If a quotation includes a question mark or an exclamation point, include it, and if a page number is necessary, put the final period after it: *While sick, we can "become more aware of and repelled by people who seem unhealthy" (Korones).* Note that a page number is not necessary for citing this one-page article.

How to indicate words omitted from a quotation

In the middle   If you omit as irrelevant to your purpose any words or passages from the middle of a quotation, signal this by using the ellipsis mark, three dots separated by spaces:

Korones reports, "Scientists speculate that once the immune system has been kicked into gear, it triggers... mental warning bells when we see someone who looks ill."

At the end   If you omit the end of the source's sentence at the end of your own sentence, use three ellipsis dots and put the sentence period after any necessary parenthetical citation.

▸ When people are ill, they "become more aware of and repelled by people who seem unhealthy..." (Korones).

If no citation in parentheses ends the sentence, put the sentence period, followed by three dots—four dots in all—as in the following example:

▸ Korones makes the point that when people are ill, they "become more aware of and repelled by people who seem unhealthy...."

At the beginning   If you omit any words from the beginning of a quoted sentence, do not use an ellipsis.

▸ Korones points out that "we become more aware of and repelled by people who seem unhealthy, whether or not those people are actually contagious."

Omitting a sentence or a line of poetry   If you omit a complete sentence (or more), use three dots after the previous period. For an omitted line of poetry, use a line of dots (see 49g).

Note: In MLA style, if your source passage itself uses ellipses, place your ellipsis dots within square brackets to indicate that your ellipsis mark is not part of the original text: [...].

How to split a quotation   For variety, you may want to use your own words to split a quotation:

▸ "When we are sick," the new research suggests, "we become more aware of and repelled by people who seem unhealthy, whether or not those people are actually contagious" (Korones).

Don't rig the evidence   It should go without saying that quoting means quoting an author's ideas without adding any of your own contextual material—or omitting any of the author's—that substantially changes the author's intent. For example, it would distort the author's views and present the evidence incorrectly to write this, even though the words that are quoted are in the original article:

> ▶ **Sarah Korones claims that we should "become more aware of… people who seem unhealthy."**

How to add or change words to fit into your sentence   If you add any comments or explanations in your own words or if you change a word of the original to fit it grammatically into your sentence or to spell it correctly, enclose the added or changed material in square brackets. Generally, however, it is preferable to rephrase your sentence because bracketed words and phrases make sentences difficult to read. The first example shows a word in the quotation changed to make it fit the quoter's sentence structure, and the second is a personal interjected comment; the revised example does away with the awkward square brackets.

Awkward   **Korones' article shows that "[sick people] become more aware of and repelled by people who seem unhealthy," even if "those people are [not] actually contagious."**

Revised   **Korones reports that we "become more aware of and repelled by people who seem unhealthy," when we are ill ourselves, even when we are in no danger of catching whatever illness others might have.**

How to quote a long passage   If you quote more than three lines of poetry or four typed lines of prose, do not use quotation marks.

- Begin the quotation on a new line.
- For MLA style, indent the quotation one inch from the left margin.
- For APA or *Chicago* style, indent the quotation a half inch from the left margin.
- Double-space throughout.
- Do not indent from the right margin.
- If you quote from more than one paragraph, indent the first line of a new paragraph an additional quarter inch.
- Establish the context for a long quotation and integrate it into your text by stating the point you want to make and naming the author of the quotation in your introductory statement.

Korones describes research conducted on reactions to people who seem ill:

> When we are sick, we become more aware of and repelled by people who seem unhealthy, whether or not those people are actually contagious. Researchers at the University of Kentucky and Florida State University found that study participants who had just been ill paid more attention to pictures of disfigured faces than did healthy subjects.

Note: With a long indented quotation with a parenthetical page citation, put the period before the parenthetical citation, not after it.

Avoid a string of quotations   Use quotations, especially long ones, sparingly and only when they help you make a good argument. Readers do not want a collection of passages from other writers; they could read the original works for that. Rather, they want your analysis of your sources and the conclusions you draw from your research. Quotations should not appear in a string, one after the other. If they do, your readers will wonder what purpose the quotations serve and will search for your voice in the paper.

Fit a quotation into your sentence   When you quote, use the exact words of the original, and make sure that those exact words do not disrupt the flow of your sentence and send it in another direction, with, for instance, a change of tense.

A bad fit **Just after my last illness, I noticed that, like the study participants, I avoided "people who seem unhealthy, whether or not those people are actually contagious" (Korones).**

A better fit **Just after my last illness, I noticed that, like the study participants cited in the Korones article, I was "more aware of and repelled by" sick-looking people, even though I had no way of knowing for sure if I could catch something from the individuals.**

10d Indicating the boundaries of a source citation in your text

Naming an author or title in your text tells readers that you are citing ideas from a source, and citing a page number at the end of a summary or paraphrase lets them know where your citation ends. However, for one-page print or database articles and for Internet sources, a page citation is not necessary, so it is harder to indicate where your comments about a source end. You always need to indicate clearly where your summary or paraphrase ends and where your own comments take over. Convey the shift to readers by commenting on the source in a way that clearly announces a transition back to your own views. Use expressions such as *it follows that, X's explanation shows that, as a result, evidently, obviously,* or *clearly* to signal the shift.

Unclear citation boundary

> According to promotional material on a Sony Web site more than ten years ago, the company decided to release a cassette and a CD based on a small research study indicating that listening to Mozart improved IQ. The products showed the ingenuity of commercial enterprise while taking the researchers' conclusions in new directions.

Revised citation, with source boundary indicated

> According to promotional material on a Sony Web site more than ten years ago, the company decided to release a cassette and a CD based on research indicating that listening to Mozart improved IQ. Clearly, Sony's strategy demonstrated the ingenuity of commercial enterprise, but it cannot reflect what the researchers intended when they published their conclusions.

Another way to indicate the end of your citation is to include the author's or authors' name(s) at the end of the citation instead of (or even in addition to) introducing the citation with the name.

Unclear citation boundary

> For people who hate shopping, Web shopping may be the perfect solution. Jerome and Taylor's exploration of "holiday hell" reminds us that we get more choice from online vendors than we do when we browse at our local mall because the online sellers, unlike mall owners, do not have to rent space to display their goods. In addition, one can buy almost anything online, from CDs, cell phones, and books to cars and real estate.

Revised citation, with source boundary indicated

> For people who hate shopping, Web shopping may be the perfect solution. An article exploring the "holiday hell" of shopping reminds us that we get more choice from online vendors than we do when we browse at our local mall because the online sellers, unlike mall owners, do not have to rent

space to display their goods (Jerome and Taylor). In addition, one can buy almost anything online, from CDs, cell phones, and books to cars and real estate.

10e Synthesizing sources

Large amounts of information are no substitute for a thesis or clear main idea with relevant support. Your paper should *synthesize* your sources, not just tell about them one after the other. When you synthesize, you connect the ideas in individual sources to create a larger picture, to inform yourself about the topic, and to establish your own ideas on the topic. Leave yourself plenty of time to:

- Read through your notes on your sources and think about what you have read
- Connect with the material and form responses to it
- Take into account new ideas and opposing arguments
- Find connections among the facts and the ideas your sources offer

For this last point, try drawing a map of your sources, or creating a time-line using online software, such as *Timeglider*, to show connections between your sources.

Avoid sitting down to write a paper at the last minute, surrounded by library books or stacks of photocopies. In this scenario, you might be tempted to lift material, and you will produce a lifeless paper. Remember that the paper is ultimately your work, not a collection of other people's words, and that your identity and opinions as the writer should be evident.

10f Organizing your essay by ideas, not sources

As you consider how to incorporate your sources into your paper's organization, let your ideas, not your sources, drive your paper.

Avoid Organization Like This

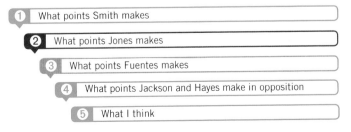

That organization is driven by sources, with the bulk of the paper dealing with the views of Smith, Jones, and the rest. Instead, let your main point and then the supporting evidence for sub-points determine the organization:

Improved Organization

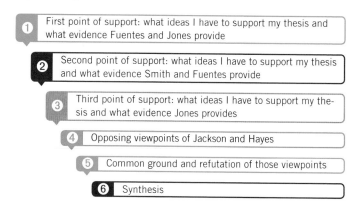

To avoid producing an essay that reads like a serial listing of summaries or references ("Crabbe says this," "Tyger says that," "Tyger also says this"), spend time reviewing your notes and synthesizing what you find into a coherent and convincing statement of what you know and believe.

- Make lists of good ideas your sources raise about your topic.
- Look for the connections among those ideas: comparisons and contrasts.
- Find links in content, examples, and statistics.
- Note connections between the information in your sources and what you know from your own experience.

If you follow these guidelines, you will take control of your material instead of letting it take control of you.

10g Introducing and integrating source material

Introduce information from your sources (summaries, paraphrases, and quotations) in a way that integrates them into the flow of your writing. They should not just pop up with no lead-in.

Source not introduced and integrated

> A recent illness can shift how we perceive other people. We can "become more aware of and repelled by people who seem unhealthy..." (Korones).

Source introduced and integrated

> In an article about how recent illness can shift how we perceive other people, Sarah Korones describes that we can "become more aware of and repelled by people who seem unhealthy...."

If you quote a complete sentence, or if you paraphrase or summarize a section of another work, introduce the source material by providing an introductory phrase with the author's full name (for the first reference to an author) and a brief mention of his or her expertise or credentials, as in the preceding example. For subsequent citations, the last name is sufficient.

Ways to introduce source material

X has pointed out that	According to X,
X has made it clear that	As X insists,
X explains that	In 2012, X, the vice president
X suggests that	of the corporation, declared

Vary the introductory phrase   The introductory verbs *say* and *write* are clear and direct. Occasionally, use one of the following verbs to express subtle shades of meaning: *acknowledge, agree, argue, ask, assert, believe, claim, comment, contend, declare, deny, emphasize, explain, insist, note, point out, propose, speculate,* or *suggest.*

10h Documenting to fit the discipline

Documentation is an integral part of a research paper. Conventions vary from discipline to discipline and from style manual to style manual—as illustrated by the inclusion of MLA, APA, CSE, and *Chicago* styles in parts 3 and 4—but the various styles of documentation are not arbitrary. The styles reflect what the disciplines value and what readers need to know.

In the humanities, for instance, many research findings offer scholarly interpretation and analysis of texts, so they may be relevant for years, decades, or centuries. Publication dates in the Modern Language Association (MLA) style, therefore, occur only in the works-cited list and are not included in the in-text citation. Such a practice also serves to minimize interruptions to the text.

The endnote/footnote system of the *Chicago Manual of Style* (along with the citation-sequence and citation-name systems of the Council of Science Editors–CSE) goes further, requiring only a small superscript number in the text to send readers to the list of sources.

Both the American Psychological Association (APA) and the CSE name-year style include the date of the work cited within the text citation itself, emphasizing that timeliness of research is an issue in the sciences and social sciences. In addition, abbreviations used in all three CSE styles (chapter 17) reflect the fact that scientists are expected to be aware of the major sources in their field.

All systems, however, aim to give enough information in the text for readers to be able to find full details of the source in a bibliographical list at the end of the work or in footnotes or endnotes.

10i One source, four systems of documentation

Note that on many sites, you may have difficulty finding a date of posting, a document title as well as a Web site name, or an exact identification of the author of the material, whether an individual or an organization. Just record whatever you can find on a thorough search of the site, always scrolling down to the bottom of a page and consulting the Home or About pages, as well as the page properties or page info tools found in your browser. Also try using the root domain of the URL—the material just before the dot preceding the first single slash—to identify the owner who is responsible for its content, also referred to as the *publisher* or *sponsor* of the site. If the Home and About links provide no useful information, consider whether you should use a source if you are unsure about the identity of the author, the author's credentials, or the owner and purpose of the site. You can also do a search to see who links to a site and what those referrers have to say about it as an additional aid to evaluation. (When using a search engine, if you put "link:" followed by a URL in the Search field and hit Return, the results will show you which sites link to that URL.)

If you find and record as many of the indicated items of information as you can, you will then be able to cite a Web source in the four most common documentation styles.

MLA STYLE

Boff, Leonardo. "Living Better or Living a 'Good Life'?" *Organic Consumers Association*. Organic Consumers Assoc., 27 Mar. 2009. Web. 23 Jan. 2012.

APA STYLE

Boff, L. (2009, March 27). Living better or living a "good life"? Retrieved from http://www.organicconsumers.org/articles/article_17378.cfm

CSE STYLE

2. Boff L. Living better or living a "good life"? [Internet]. 2009. Finland (MN): Organic Consumers Assoc.; [cited 2012 Jan 23]. Available from: http://www.organicconsumers.org/articles/article_17378.cfm

***CHICAGO* STYLE NOTE**

9. Leonardo Boff, "Living Better or Living a 'Good Life'?" Organic Consumers Assoc., March 27, 2009, http://www.organicconsumers.org/articles/article_17378.cfm.

Exercises on Research/Sources/Documentation

EXERCISE 1 Select and revise thesis statements 6e

Which of the following would make a good thesis statement for a research paper? Show how the others could be improved to make them more effective thesis statements.

1. How to discipline children.
2. The advantages and disadvantages of spanking.
3. In this paper I will discuss how parents should bring up their children.
4. Doctors' advice on the issue of spanking.
5. Children who fear spanking will behave themselves.
6. Disciplining children should involve rewards, removal of privileges, and above all, discussion of right and wrong.

EXERCISE 2 Find and narrow a topic in a search directory 7a, 7e

Access an online library database such as *InfoTrac/Expanded Academic* or *EBSCO Host/Academic Search Premier*. In the Search box, start with a subject search of any broad category: for example, "family," "health," or "music." Look at the categories until you find one you are interested in. For example, a subject search of "family" yields "family and mass media" as one of the categories. Whatever broad category you decide to search, keep narrowing the subject to a topic you could explore in a short paper.

Click on the category and access at least two sources. Then formulate a possible question that would focus your thinking and any research.

EXERCISE 3 Do a keyword search 7f

Go to *Google* at <http://www.google.com>, and do a keyword search to find reliable information on *one* aspect of *one* of the following topics.

Discuss your results with classmates.

- nonallergenic dogs
- hamstring injuries
- the digital divide
- mononucleosis
- termites
- titanium

EXERCISE 4 Find and evaluate Web sources on a topic 8c

Use a search engine to do a Web search for information on the topic "body building" or "dieting." Find one Web page that offers useful, serious information and another that you would reject as a source of balanced and objective information. Make a copy of each page, bring the copies to class, and explain your evaluation to your classmates.

EXERCISE 5 Detect plagiarism 9a–9c

The following passage is from page 142 of *His Excellency: George Washington* by Joseph Ellis:

> Whereas Cromwell and later Napoleon made themselves synonymous with the revolution in order to justify the assumption of dictatorial power, Washington made himself synonymous with the American Revolution in order to declare that it was incompatible with dictatorial power.

Consider which of the following passages use the source responsibly and avoid kidnapping its words or ideas. For each passage, explain what is or is not done correctly and what may be considered plagiarism. (If you want to review para- phrase and quotation before you do this exercise, turn to 14d–14g.) Then com- pare your results with those of your classmates, and discuss which of the seven sins you find represented here.

1. Joseph Ellis makes the point that whereas Cromwell and later Napoleon made themselves synonymous with the revolution in order to justify the assumption of dictatorial power, Washington made himself synonymous with the American Revolution in order to declare that it was incompatible with dictatorial power.

2. Joseph Ellis speculates that whereas Cromwell and later Napoleon made themselves synonymous with the revolution in order to justify the assump- tion of dictatorial power, Washington made himself synonymous with the American Revolution in order to declare that it was incompatible with dictatorial power (142).

3. As Joseph Ellis points out in *His Excellency: George Washington,* Washington was not like Cromwell or Napoleon, who led revolutions in order to become dictators themselves. Washington led the American Revolution in order that no American should ever become a dictator (142).

4. Joseph Ellis proposes that whereas Cromwell and Napoleon used their rev- olutions to justify their assumption of dictatorial power, Washington used the American Revolution to announce that it was incompatible with dicta- torial power (142).

5. It is interesting to speculate that Cromwell and Napoleon each led revolutions to become dictators. Washington, on the other hand, led the American Revolution to deny dictatorship to himself and to all other Americans.

6. As Joseph Ellis notes, Washington differed from previous great revolution- ary leaders who became dictators by seeing to it that the American Revolution, which he led, "was incompatible with dictatorial power" (142).

7. Cromwell and Napoleon identified with their revolutions so that they could become dictators, whereas Washington identified with the American Revolution so that no one could become an American dictator.

8. As Joseph Ellis observes, "Whereas Cromwell and later Napoleon made themselves synonymous with the revolution in order to justify the

assumption of dictatorial power, Washington made himself synonymous with the American Revolution in order to declare that it was incompatible with dictatorial power" (142).

9. Joseph Ellis comments that while both Cromwell and Napoleon made themselves identical with the revolution so that they could give good reason for taking on despotic authority, Washington identified with the revolution at home to show that it was irreconcilable with tyranny (142).

EXERCISE 6 Write an annotated bibliography entry **9e**

Choose a chapter from a textbook assigned for one of your courses, and write an annotated bibliography entry, with bibliographical details in MLA style (see part 3 for more on MLA style) and a brief summary of the chapter.

EXERCISE 7 Paraphrase **10b**

While Michelle Guerra was working on a paper on the English-only controversy (whether languages other than English should be banned in schools and government offices and publications) and looking for the history of the issue, she came across the following source.

ORIGINAL SOURCE

If any language group, Spanish or other, chooses to maintain its language, there is precious little that we can do about it, legally or otherwise, and still maintain that we are a free country. We cannot legislate the language of the home, the street, the bar, the club, unless we are willing to set up a cadre of language police who will ticket and arrest us if we speak something other than English.

—James C. Stalker, "Official English or English Only," *English Journal 77* (Mar. 1988): 21

1. In the following paraphrase, underline the words and structures that resemble the original too closely.
2. Revise the paragraph so that the original source is paraphrased appropriately.

PARAPHRASE OF STALKER, p. 21

As Stalker points out, if any group of languages, Greek or other, decides to keep its language, there is not much any of us can do, with laws or not, and still claim to be a free country. We cannot pass legislation about the language we speak at home, on the street, or in restaurants, unless we also want to have a group of special police who will take us off to jail if they hear us not speaking English (21).

EXERCISE 8 Quote **10c**

The sentences below incorporate quotations from the following paragraph by Ben Harder. Correct any errors or inaccuracies in the quotation, and make sure the quotation fits smoothly into the sentence. Some sentences may not need any editing.

> Using good bacteria to obstruct bad ones—a strategy known as bacterial interference—is one application of so-called probiotics, a field with growing medical promise. The name suggests a twist on antibiotics, which kill disease-causing microbes. Some probiotic bacteria do their work by competing for resources and space with pathogens inside the body and, in effect, elbowing the bad bugs out of the way.

—Ben Harder, "Germs That Do a Body Good," *Science News* 161 (2002): 72–74.

Example   Harder calls the word *probiotics* "a twist on antibiotics . . ." (72).

1. Harder says, "The use of good bacteria to obstruct bad ones is one application of probiotics . . ." (72).
2. Harder discusses one strategy of probiotic bacteria, which fight "for resources and space with pathogens inside the body and, in effect, elbowing the bad bugs out of the way" (72).
3. According to Harder, "probiotics is a field with growing medical promise" (72).
4. Harder explains that "antibiotics, which kill disease-causing microbes" (72).
5. Harder notes that probiotic bacteria can "[compete] for resources and space with pathogens inside the body . . ." (72).

EXERCISE 9 Summarize, paraphrase, and indicate a clear citation boundary 10d

1. The excerpt below is from a textbook chapter on how political power is represented in art. Summarize the excerpt. Then compare your summary with those of your classmates.

> Images of contemporary political leaders are fundamentally different from those of the past, just as the concept of "rule" has evolved. Today, almost no rulers openly consider themselves to be of divine descent, and many are not royalty. And with photography, pictures of rulers come to us not as artworks, but as a flood of newspaper or television images. There is a great difference between images that are produced under the ruler's direction and those over which the ruler has little or no control.

—Margaret Lazzari and Dona Schlesier, *Exploring Art: A Global, Thematic Approach,* Fourth Edition p. 276

2. Paraphrase the following excerpt from the same textbook chapter. Then compare your paraphrase with your classmates' versions.

> In 1934, Adolf Hitler commissioned the film *Triumph of the Will,* directed by Leni Riefenstahl, to glorify his rule, his military strength, and the Nazi order of Aryan supremacy. A work of brilliant propaganda, Riefenstahl's film established Hitler as the first media hero of the modern age.
>
> Given unlimited funding by Hitler, Riefenstahl had a staff of more than 130 people, sixteen cameras, four sound trucks, and cranes and dollies for dramatic shots. Skillfully edited into the film were speeches, parades, cheering

crowds, and the lush music of the popular German composer Richard Wagner. Although the film was a documentary covering a six-day rally celebrating Hitler at Nuremberg, the imagery was entirely staged.

—Margaret Lazzari and Dona Schlesier, *Exploring Art: A Global, Thematic Approach,* Fourth Edition p. 276

3. Revise the following two passages to create clear citation boundaries between the writer's summary or paraphrase and her own commentary.

a. Lazzari and Schlesier point out that Adolf Hitler was the first twentieth-century leader to use filmmaking to reinforce his powerful persona. China's Mao Zedong and Korea's Kim Jong-Il later relied on similar propaganda.

b. Lazzari and Schlesier observe, for example, that Leni Reifenstahl's "documentary" *Triumph of the Will* does not record real-life events but was carefully planned and staged. Americans watching Democratic and Republican delegates cheer and applaud at their national conventions must remember the producer's sometimes cynical role in creating a TV-ready show of enthusiasm.

EXERCISE 10 Use document styles to suit the discipline `10h, 10i`

1. On the Web, find an article related to your area of concentration. Record the information described in section 10i (author name, article title, Web site title, sponsor or publisher, posting date, page numbers, date of access, and URL).

2. Determine which documentation style you will use for research projects in your area of concentration. Confirm this with your instructor or a course syllabus if necessary.

3. Using the four sample listings in 10i as an example, draft a listing for the Web site. (Keep in mind that you'll learn in greater detail how to do this in the chapters that follow.)

3 MLA Documentation

© Hugo Felix/Shutterstock

CITE
MLA

3 MLA Documentation

Modern Language Association **MLA**

Modern Language Association **MLA**

For research papers and shorter documented essays, always provide detailed information about any books, articles, Web sites, or other sources that you cite. Many composition and literature courses ask you to follow the guidelines of the Modern Language Association (MLA) as recommended in the *MLA Handbook for Writers of Research Papers*, 7th edition (New York: MLA, 2009), and on the MLA Web site. See chapter 11 for an explanation of MLA style. The following three chapters illustrate this style.

11 Citing Sources in Your Paper, MLA Style

Writers and researchers in various disciplines use documentation styles to present material and acknowledge sources in ways that highlight what is most relevant to colleagues in different fields (see 10h). MLA style is used in humanities fields such as English literature, composition, foreign languages, philosophy, religion, art, theater, and music. A writer in one of these disciplines often undertakes a close study and analysis of a work, considering previous scholarly interpretations to determine how his or her view may offer a new perspective on the work. The writer may also discuss how a work is part of a particular genre. In MLA style the focus is on presenting an analysis to readers with as few interruptions as possible. To do so, MLA style uses in-text parenthetical references (see 11a and the Key Points box on p. 167) containing only enough information to help the reader find the work's full publication data at the end of the paper (see chapter 12). The conciseness of MLA style is also reflected in its use of shortened forms and abbreviations, such as giving only a shortened name of a publisher and using *P* for the word *Press* (see Source Shot 2, p. 190).

When you refer to, comment on, paraphrase, or quote another author's material, you must indicate that you have done so by inserting what is called a *citation*. In MLA style, you give the name of the author(s) and the page number(s) where you found the material, if available. You can put the author's name in your own text to introduce the material, with the page number in parentheses at the end of the sentence; or, especially for a source you have cited previously, you can put both the author and the page number in parentheses at the place in the

MLA Modern Language Association

sentence in which you cite the material. Citations most often appear at the end of the sentence, unless a writer is showing that a certain part of a sentence came from a specific source. All of the more detailed publication information about your sources then goes into a list of works cited at the end of the paper so that readers can retrieve and read the same source.

Sections 11a and 11b show you examples and variations on the basic principle of MLA citation—for instance, what to do when no author is named or how to cite an online source that has no page numbers.

Basic features of MLA style

> **KEY POINTS**
> How to Cite and List Sources in MLA Style

1. *In your paper*
   - Include the **last name(s)** of the author (or authors). Give a title (shortened) if no author is known.
   - Include the **page number(s)** where the information is located (except when the source is only one page long or an online source without page numbers), but do not include the word *page* or *pages* or the abbreviation *p.* or *pp.* For inclusive page numbers over 100 that have the same first number(s), give only the last two digits for the second number in most cases (257–58 but 658–701). In MLA style put a hyphen rather than a dash between the numbers.

Both author and page number can be given in parentheses (not separated by a comma) at the end of the sentence that makes the reference. You can also name the author in your text and put the page number in parentheses at the end of the sentence.

2. *At the end of your paper*
   - Include a **list**, alphabetized by authors' last names or by title (in italics or quotation marks) if the author is not known, of all the sources you refer to in the paper. Also include information about the publisher, date of publication, and medium of publication, reception, or source's medium of delivery (Print,

(Continued)

Modern Language Association **MLA**

(Continued)

Web, Film, Television, Performance, Lecture, CD, and so on). Begin the list on a new page and title it *Works Cited*. Sections 12c–12k provide many examples of listing different types of sources.

Illustrations of the Basic Features (MLA)

Citation in Your Paper	Entry in List of Works Cited
Author of print book named in your text with page(s) given in parentheses The renowned scholar of language David Crystal has promoted the idea of "dialect democracy" (168).	Crystal, David. *The Stories of English*. Woodstock: Overlook, 2004. Print.
Author and pages(s) of print book given in parentheses A renowned scholar of language has promoted the idea of "dialect democracy" (Crystal 168).	Crystal, David. *The Stories of English*. Woodstock: Overlook, 2004. Print.
Author of print article named in your text with page(s) in parentheses Film critic Sheri Linden sees Lisbeth, like Katniss, as "a kind of hunter in a world gone mad" (D4).	Linden, Sheri. "These Girls Come to the Rescue: A *Hunger Games* Heroine and Her Fellow Compatriots Are Challenging the Bad Guys—and Damsel Clichés." *Los Angeles Times* 8 Apr. 2012, weekend ed.: D1+. Print.

Citation in Your Paper	Entry in List of Works Cited
Author and page(s) of print article provided in parentheses Lisbeth, like Katniss, is "a kind of hunter in a world gone mad" (Linden D4).	Linden, Sheri. "These Girls Come to the Rescue: A *Hunger Games* Heroine and Her Fellow Compatriots Are Challenging the Bad Guys—and Damsel Clichés." *Los Angeles Times* 8 Apr. 2012, weekend ed.: D1+. Print.
Author of print article in an online database (no exact page numbers in HTML version) Comparing two fiction heroines now portrayed in films, Sheri Linden sees Lisbeth, like Katniss, "as a kind of hunter in a world gone mad."	Linden, Sheri. "These Girls Come to the Rescue: A *Hunger Games* Heroine and Her Fellow Compatriots Are Challenging the Bad Guys—and Damsel Clichés." *Los Angeles Times* 8 Apr. 2012, home ed.: n. pag. *LexisNexis*. Web. 19 Apr. 2012.
Author of Web magazine article named in your text Dahlia Lithwick of *Slate* magazine notes, "The standard argument against allowing cameras into the Supreme Court is that mere mortals can't be exposed to all that weighty gravitas and live to tell about it."	Lithwick, Dahlia. "Lights! Cameras! It's the Supreme Court!" Jurisprudence: The Law, Lawyers, and the Court. *Slate*. Washington Post, 30 Mar. 2012. Web. 6 Apr. 2012.

11b How to cite sources in your paper, MLA author/page style

MLA recommends that you create a draft list of your works cited (see chapter 12) before you begin writing your paper so that you can insert the correct information in your parenthetical references. For example, you will want to plan ahead to correctly cite works by authors with the same last name or two works by the same author. The information in a parenthetical reference must exactly match the information about that source in your works-cited list. The following section gives examples of the various formats used for in-text citations.

THE BASICS OF CITATIONS: INCORPORATING QUOTED MATERIAL INTO YOUR PAPER

A. Author named in your text You can cite an author in a sentence in your paper, or you can put the author and page number in parentheses at the end of your sentence. Naming the author as you introduce the source material allows you to supply information about the author's credentials as an expert and so increases the credibility of your source for readers. Another advantage of naming your source in your text is that readers then know that everything between the mention of the author and the cited page number is a reference to your source material and not your own ideas. Put a page number only within parentheses, not in the text of your paper.

For the first mention of an author in a text sentence, use the full name and any relevant credentials. After that, use only the last name. Generally, use the present tense to cite an author. See Source Shot 2 on pp. 190–191 for the entry for the following text in a works-cited list.

author and credentials

National Book Award winner Paul Fussell points out that even people in

low-paying jobs show "all but universal pride in a uniform of any kind" (5).

page number

B. Punctuation of the quotation and citation When a quotation ends the sentence, as in the previous example, put the closing quotation marks after the last word and before the parentheses, and place the sentence period after the parentheses. (Note that this rule differs from the one for undocumented writing, which calls for a period before the closing quotation marks.)

When a quoted sentence ends with a question mark or an exclamation point, also include a period after the parenthetical citation:

> Paul Fussell reminds us of our equating uniforms with seriousness of purpose when he begins a chapter by asking, "Would you get on an airplane with two pilots who are wearing cut-off jeans?" (85).

For more information on incorporating quotations into your paper, see 10c and 10d. To cite sequential references to the same work in one text paragraph, see item D.

C. Author named in parentheses   If you have referred to an author previously or if you are citing statistics, you do not need to mention the author in your text to introduce the reference. Simply include the author's last name before the page number within the parentheses, with no comma between them.

> The army retreated from Boston in disarray, making the victors realize that they had defeated the "greatest military power on earth"
>   author   page number
> (McCullough 76).

D. Sequential references to the same source   If you use several quotations from the same page of your source within one of your paragraphs, one parenthetical reference after the last quotation is enough, but make sure that no quotations from other works intervene. If you are paraphrasing from and referring to one work several times in a paragraph, mention the author in your text. Then give the page number at the end of a paraphrase and again if you paraphrase from a different page. Make it clear to a reader where the paraphrase ends and your own comments take over (10d).

E. A long quotation   For a quotation longer than four lines, indent the quoted material one inch, double-space it, and do not enclose it in quotation marks. You may want to introduce the quotation with a text sentence naming the author, followed by a colon. Put the period ending the last sentence of the quotation (and one space) before the parenthetical citation, not after it. For an example and more information on a long quotation, see 10c, p. 152.

CITING A WORK WITH AN INDIVIDUAL AUTHOR OR AUTHORS (MLA)

Note: Items A–E give examples of the basic conventions for citing a work by one author. Items F–K that follow provide more details about a wider variety of authored sources.

F. Work written by two or more authors For a work with two or three authors, include all the names either in your text sentence or in parentheses, with no comma between the last name and any available page number.

> Lakoff and Johnson have pointed out . . . (42)
>
> (Baumol, Litan, and Schramm 18-20)

For a work with four or more authors, either put the first author's name followed by *et al.* (for the Latin *et alii*, meaning "and others")—with no comma before *et al.*—in your text sentence or name all of the authors as found on the book's title page. In the parenthetical citation, give either the first author's last name and *et al.* or all of the authors' last names. The listing must match the form you use for the authors in your works-cited entry.

> (Roberts et al. 10)
>
> (Roberts, Smith, Jones, and Morgan 10)

See 12d, item 11, for how to list a print work with several authors in a works-cited list.

G. Work by author(s) with more than one work cited Include the author and title of the work in your text sentence.

> Alice Walker, in her book *In Search of Our Mothers' Gardens*, describes
> revisiting her past to discover more about Flannery O'Connor (43-59).

If you do not mention the author in your text, include in your parenthetical reference the author's last name followed by a comma, an abbreviated form of the title (not followed by a comma), and the page number.

comma
> O'Connor's house still stands and is looked after by a caretaker (Walker,
> abbreviated title page number
> *In Search* 57).

H. Work by two authors with the same last name Include each author's first initial or the complete first name if the authors' initials are the same.

> A writer can be seen as both "author" and "secretary," and the two roles
> can be seen as competitive (F. Smith 19).

I. Author of work in an edited anthology Cite the author of the included or reprinted work (not the editor of the anthology) and the page number(s) you refer to in the anthology (see Source Shot 3, p. 192).

Mention the editor of the anthology only in the entry in the works-cited list, as shown in 12d, item 14, p. 189.

> Saunders predicts that Bill Clinton will eventually be seen "as the
> embodiment of a certain strain of ornery, compassionate, complicated
> American energy" (300).

J. Author of work quoted in another source If an author is quoted in a different source, and you quote or paraphrase that author's words, write *qtd. in* (for "quoted in") in your parenthetical citation, followed by the last name of the author of the source in which you found the reference (the indirect source) and the page number where you found the quotation. List the author of the indirect source in your list of works cited. In the following example, the indirect source Hofstadter, not Harry Williams, would be included in the list of works cited.

> Harry Williams argues that Lincoln waged the war "for the preservation of
> the status quo which had produced the war" (qtd. in Hofstadter 31).

See 12d, item 14, for this entry in the works-cited list.
However, note that MLA encourages you to quote a direct source whenever possible.

K. More than one work in one citation Use semicolons to separate two or more sources named in the same citation.

> The links between a name and ancestry have occupied many writers and
> researchers (Waters 65; Antin 188).

To avoid using a long parenthetical citation that disrupts the flow of your text, you can put multiple sources in a bibliographic note (see 11c, p. 179).
However, if you quote sources that refer to different points made in one sentence, cite each source after the point it supports.

CITING A WORK WITH NO INDIVIDUAL AUTHOR(S) NAMED (MLA)

L. Work by a corporation, government agency, or organization as author When you use material authored not by an individual but by a corporation, government agency, or organization, cite that entity as the author, making sure its name corresponds with the alphabetized entry in your works-cited list (see 12d, item 18). Use the complete name in your text sentence or a shortened form in the parenthetical citation. Begin a government source citation with the name or abbreviation of the country or state. Then follow with the name of the agency and any additional divisions. (If the author(s) or compiler(s) are named, you may still begin with the name of the government source as author and put *By* and the author(s) or compiler(s) after the document title in the works-cited list.) The following examples have been listed with the government agency as author in the works-cited entry and cite a page number in the introduction (a specific section) of a PDF version of a government report on a Web site (see Source Shot 6 in 12f, p. 208).

> full name
> The United States Department of the Interior US Geological Survey recognizes "a need for clear methods to identify tsunami deposits in the geologic record" since deposit studies are an important element in assessing tsunami risk for localities (Introd. 1).
>
> During the past twenty years, the examination of tsunami deposits has proven to be an essential means of assessing tsunami risk for areas
>
> shortened name
> (US Dept. of the Interior, USGS Introd. 1).

See the Key Points box in 8c on p. 134 for help finding the author of a Web site document.

M. No author or editor named If no author or editor is named for a source, refer to the title of the book (italicized), the article title (within quotation marks), or the title of the Web site (italicized).

> *The Chicago Manual of Style* advises that "breaking or bending rules to fit a particular case" when writing is sometimes necessary (xii).

Within a parenthetical citation, shorten the title to the first word (if possible) by which it is alphabetized in the works-cited list (12d, item 19).

> When writing, one may find that "breaking or bending rules to fit a particular case" is sometimes necessary (*Chicago* xii).

For help reading a Web site to determine its author, see the Key Points boxes in 8c on pages 133 and 134. If no author is indicated, use the name of the site.

N. Unauthored entry in a dictionary or encyclopedia For an unsigned entry, give the title of the entry. A page number is not necessary for an alphabetized work. Begin the entry in the works-cited list with the title of the alphabetized entry (see 12d, item 17).

> Drypoint differs from etching in that it does not use acid ("Etching").

If you are citing a specific definition in a dictionary entry, add a comma after the term and write *def.* and the letter or number: ("Mimesis," def. 3).

CITING A WORK WITH PAGE NUMBERS NOT AVAILABLE OR RELEVANT (MLA)

O. Reference to an entire work and not to one specific page   If you are referring not to a quotation or idea on one specific page but rather to an idea that is central to the work as a whole, name the author in your text. Include publication details of the work in your works-cited list.

> Mallon insists that we can learn from diaries about people's everyday lives
> and the worlds they create.

P. Work only one page long   If a print article is only one page long, you may give the author's name alone in your text but include the page number in your works-cited list. However, a page reference in parentheses clearly indicates where quoted or paraphrased material ends, so it may be helpful for your reader if you also include the page number in your text.

Q. Web or electronic source with no page numbers   Electronic database material and Web sources, which appear on a screen, have no stable page numbers that apply across systems or when printed unless you access them in PDF (portable document format) files.

> *author named in text*
> Science writer Stephen Hart describes how researchers Edward Taub and
> *no page citation: online source has no numbered pages or paragraphs*
> Thomas Ebert conclude that for musicians, practicing "remaps the brain,"
> thus maybe suggesting that it is better to start practicing at an early age.

With no page number to mark where a parenthetical citation would go (at "brain," above, or at the end of the sentence?), you need to define the point at which the material from your source ends and your own commentary takes over, so it may be advisable to give the author's name in a parenthetical citation to mark the end of the reference.

> Researchers Edward Taub and Thomas Ebert conclude that for musicians,
> practicing "remaps the brain" (Hart), thus maybe suggesting that . . .

Section 10d shows how to define the boundaries of a citation.

If your source as it appears on the screen includes no visible numbered pages or numbered paragraphs, include *n. pag.* in your works-cited list, as shown in 12f, item 39.

For an online source with no author or page numbers, in your parenthetical citation give the title of the Web page or posting either in full (if short) or abbreviated to begin with the first word by which it is alphabetized in the works-cited list (see 12f, items 37 and 38).

> A list of frequently asked questions about documentation and up-to-date instructions on how to cite online sources in MLA style can be found on the association's Web site (*MLA*).

If there are no page numbers to refer to, you may cite online scholarly material by the abbreviated internal headings of the source, such as *introduction* (*introd.*), *chapter* (*chap. or ch.*), or *section* (*sec.*) (see example in item L, p. 174). Give paragraph numbers only if they are supplied in the source and you see the numbers on the screen, using the abbreviation *par.* or *pars.* Then include the total number of numbered paragraphs in your works-cited list (see 12f, item 39).

> Hatchuel discusses how film editing "can change points of view and turn objectivity into subjectivity" (par. 6).

If the parenthetical citation contains the author's name, put a comma after it and before *par.* or *sec.* and the number—something you do *not* do before a page number.

> Film editing provides us with different perceptions of reality (Hatchuel, par. 6).

CITING MULTIMEDIA AND MISCELLANEOUS SOURCES (MLA)

R. Multimedia source For radio or TV programs, interviews, live performances, films, computer software, recordings, works of art, and other multimedia sources, include only the author (or contributor such as the producer, actor, and so on) or title. Make sure that your text reference corresponds to the first element of the information you provide in the entry in your works-cited list. See 12i, item 62, for examples of documenting the following performance in a works-cited list.

> The audience of *In Paris* may themselves feel isolated while watching Baryshnikov, who portays an aging exiled Russian guard, since translations of the play's sparse Russian dialogue are projected on and behind the actors, along with videos and postcard images of 1930s Paris.

MLA Modern Language Association

S. Multivolume work   If you refer to more than one volume of a work in your paper, in the parenthetical citation give the author's name and the volume number, followed by a colon, a space, and the page number: (Einstein 1: 25). Do not use the word or abbreviation for *volume* or *page*. Give the total number of volumes in the works-cited list entry. If you refer to only one volume in your paper, just give the page number in your in-text citation and give the volume number in the works-cited entry (see 12d, item 24, for examples in the list).

T. Lecture, speech, personal communication (letter, e-mail, memo), or interview   In your text, give the name of the person delivering the communication. In your works-cited list, state the type of communication at the end of the citation, in this case "E-mail" (see also 12k, items 72 and 73).

> According to Roberta Bernstein, professor of art history at the University of Albany, the most challenging thing about contemporary art is understanding that it is meant to be challenging. This may mean that the artist wants to make us uncomfortable with our familiar ideas or present us with reconceived notions of beauty.

U. Frequently studied literary works: Fiction, poetry, and drama
For well-known works published in several different editions, include information in your parenthetical citations that will allow readers to locate the material in whatever edition they are using. For a short story or novel with no divisions or chapters, simply give the author's last name and page number. For other works, particularly classic works appearing in many editions, the following guidelines will allow your readers to find your reference in any edition. In your works-cited list include details about the edition you used.

For a novel   First give the page number(s) in the edition that you used, followed by a semicolon. Then give the chapter or section (abbreviated) number: (104; ch. 3).

For a poem   Give line numbers, not page numbers (lines 62-73), spelling out the word *lines* in the first citation. Omit the word *lines* and just give the line numbers in subsequent references.
   Include up to three lines of poetry sequentially in your text, separating them with a slash (/) with a space on each side (see 49f). For four or more lines of poetry, begin on a new line, indent the whole passage one

inch from the left, double-space throughout, and omit quotation marks from the beginning and end of the passage (see 10c).

For classic poems, such as the *Iliad*, with divisions into books or parts   Give the book or part number, followed by a period; then, with no space, give the line numbers, not page numbers, separated by a hyphen: (8.21-25).

For a play   With dialogue, set the quotation off from your text, indented one inch with no quotation marks, and in all capital letters write the name of the character speaking, followed by a period. Indent subsequent lines of the same speech another one-quarter inch. Give act, scene, and line numbers in Arabic numerals (see the following example).

For a new play available in only one published edition, cite author and page numbers as you do for other MLA citations.

For a classic work   For classic plays published in several different editions (such as plays by William Shakespeare or Oscar Wilde), omit page numbers and cite in parentheses the act, scene, and line numbers of the quotation in Arabic numerals separated by periods.

> Shakespeare's lovers in *A Midsummer Night's Dream* appeal to
> contemporary audiences accustomed to the sense of loss in love songs:
>
> > LYSANDER. How now, my love! Why is your cheek so pale?
> >
> > How chance the roses there do fade so fast?
> >
> > HERMIA. Belike for want of rain, which I could well
> >
> > Beteem them from the tempest of mine eyes. (1.1.133-36)

In your works-cited list, list the bibliographical details of the edition you used.

For classic literary works by Shakespeare, Chaucer, and others, MLA style uses abbreviated titles cited in parentheses, such as the following: *Tmp.* for *The Tempest; 2H4* for *Henry IV, Part 2; MND* for *A Midsummer Night's Dream; GP* for the *General Prologue; PrT* for *The Prioress's Tale; Aen.* for *Aeneid; Beo.* for *Beowulf; Prel.* for Wordsworth's *Prelude.*

V. The Bible and other sacred texts   In a parenthetical citation, give the title of the sacred text (italicized), along with the book of the Bible (abbreviated) and chapter and verse numbers. Note, though, that in a reference to a sacred text that is not directing readers to a specific citation in the list of works cited, the title of the sacred text is not italicized, as in the example that follows (see also 50b).

not a reference: no italics

Of the many passages in the Bible that refer to lying, none is more apt

today than the one that says that a wicked person "is snared by the

transgression of his lips" (*Holy Bible*, Prov. 12.13).

italics for a reference name of book abbreviated

See 12d, item 30, for this entry and others in a list of works cited.

W. Historical or legal document Cite any article and section number of a familiar historical document, such as the Constitution, in parentheses in your text, with no entry in the works-cited list. Abbreviate the title and section(s) and separate them with commas: (US Const., art. 2, sec. 4). Italicize the name of a court case (*Roe v. Wade*) but not the names of laws and acts. List cases and acts in your works-cited list (see 12k, item 74).

X. A footnote or footnotes To cite a footnote in a source, give the page number followed by *n* or *nn* (as in "65n"). For a footnote in an annotated edition of a sacred text, give the edition (with the word *The* omitted from your citation), book, chapter, and verse(s), followed by *n* or *nn*: (*New Oxford Annotated Bible*, Gen. 35.1-4n). See 12d, item 30, for this entry in a works-cited list.

11c MLA explanatory footnotes and endnotes

The MLA parenthetical style of documentation uses a footnote (at the bottom of the page) or an endnote (on a separate numbered page at the end of the paper before the works-cited list) only for notes giving supplementary bibliographic information or content information that clarifies or expands a point. You can use a note to cite multiple bibliographic sources instead of putting them in an in-text citation that would interrupt the flow of your text (see item K., p. 173) or to evaluate or give additional information about sources. You can also use a note to provide a comment that is interesting but not essential to your argument. Indicate a note with a raised number (superscript) in your text after the word or sentence to which your note refers.

- Begin the first line of each note one-half inch from the left margin. Put the note number (followed by a space) on the same line as the rest of the note content.
- Do not indent subsequent lines of the same note.
- Double-space endnotes.
- Single-space within each footnote, but double-space between notes.

NOTE NUMBER IN TEXT

Ethics have become an important part of many writing classes.[1]

CONTENT FOOTNOTE OR ENDNOTE

one-half inch ————————number on line followed by a space and text

1. For additional discussion of ethics in the classroom, see Stotsky

799-806; Knoblauch 15-21; Bizzell 663-67; Friend 560-66.

12 The MLA List of Works Cited

The references you make in your text to sources are brief—usually only the author's last name and a page number—so they allow readers to continue reading without interruption. For complete information about the source, readers use your brief in-text citation to direct them to the full bibliographical reference in the list of works cited at the end of your paper. For formatting instructions for articles, books, databases, Web sources, and multimedia sources, see the sample listings in 12c–12k.

12a How to set up and organize the MLA list

KEY POINTS
How to Cite and List Sources in MLA Style

Guidelines for the MLA List of Works Cited

1. **What to list**   List only works you actually cite in the text of your paper, not works you read but did not mention, unless your instructor requires you to include all the works you consulted as well as those mentioned in your text.

2. **Format of the list**   Begin the list on a new numbered page after the last page of the paper or any endnotes. Center the heading (*Works Cited*) without quotation marks, italicizing, or a period. Double-space within and between entries. Do not number the entries.

3. **What to put first in an entry (author or title)**   List works alphabetically by the author's last name or the name of an organization as author. List works with no stated author by the first main word of the title.

4. **Indentation**   To help readers find a source and to differentiate one entry from another, indent all lines of each entry—except the first—one-half inch. A word processor can provide these *hanging indents* (go to your Help menu). See the Tech Note on p. 182 on posting your paper online.

5. **Periods**   Separate the main parts of an entry with a period, followed by one space.

6. **Capitals in titles**   Capitalize the first letter of all words in titles of books and articles except *a, an, the*, coordinating conjunctions, *to* in an infinitive, and prepositions (such as *in, to, for, with, without, against*) unless they begin the title or subtitle.

7. **Titles in italics**   Italicize the titles of books, periodicals, databases, and Web sites as well as the titles of films, CDs, performances, and so on.

8. **Titles in quotation marks**   Put in quotation marks shorter titles contained within larger works (articles, stories and poems, Web pages) and unpublished works (letters, speeches).

9. **Abbreviations**   Use shortened forms of some publishers' names (as in Source Shot 2, p. 190); well-known religious and literary works; some common words in references, such as *fig., assn., ser., dept.,* and *introd.*; and common terms such as *e.g.* and *i.e.* Use postal abbreviations for states, and do not use periods in abbreviations such as *US*. When Web or other sources are missing information that MLA style usually requires, use *n.p.* for *no publisher* (or no Web site sponsor); *n.p.* for *no place* of publication given for a book; *n.d.* for *no date* of publication; and *n. pag.* for *no pagination* of a print or database work. More examples are in 12d.

10. **Page numbers**
    - Give inclusive page numbers for print articles and sections of books.
    - Do not use *p.* (or *pp.*) or the word *page* (or *pages*) before page numbers in any reference.

(Continued)

(Continued)

- For inclusive page numbers greater than 100 that share the same first number (or more), in most cases use only the last two digits for the second number (for instance, 683-89, but 798-805). Separate the numbers with a hyphen rather than a dash in MLA style.
- For a work in print or in a database with no pagination information given, write *n. pag.* (See item 35.)
- Do not include page numbers for online works unless they are in PDF format or are provided on the screen as part of an original print source. If a Web source has sections, then providing the name of a section (*Introd.*) may help your readers locate the exact place in the source.

11. **Genre label**   Include a label identifying the type of source if it will help your reader locate information. Labels include *Advertisement, Afterword, Cartoon, Chart, Comic strip, Foreword, Home page, Interview, Introduction, Map, Online posting,* and *Preface.*

12. **Publication medium**   Include in each entry (usually as the last item) the medium of publication, reception, or delivery of the source, such as *Print, Web, Film, Television, CD, DVD, Lecture, MS, E-mail, MP3 file, Performance,* and so forth. For a work of visual art, give the medium of composition (*Oil on canvas, Encaustic, Bronze, Styrofoam, and so on*). Specific examples are in 12c–12k.

13. **Scholarly journals**   Include the volume and issue number for all scholarly journals.

   NOTE on URLs   As of 2009, the *MLA Handbook* recommends using a URL only "when the reader probably cannot locate the source without it or when your instructor requires it" (182). If you need to include a URL, remove any automatically inserted hyperlinks. Then you will be able to enclose the URL in angle brackets, followed by a period. Break a URL for a new line only after the double slashes or a single slash. Never insert a hyphen into a URL (see 12h items 52 and 53 for examples).

● **TECH NOTE**

Posting Your Paper Online

For an online list of works cited, do not use indentation, which HTML does not support well. Instead, keep all lines flush left and follow each entry with a line space.

12b How to list authors in the MLA list of works cited

Name of author(s)

- Put the last name first for a single author or the first author: *Fussell, Paul.*

- For two or more authors, reverse the names of only the first author: *Nichols, John, and Robert W. McChesney.*

- For four or more authors, either use *et al.* (Latin for "and others") after the reversed name of the first author or give all of the authors' names as listed in the source.

- When a corporation, agency, or organization is the author, begin your entry with that name.

- Include a title such as *Jr.* or a numeral such as *II* after the first name, separating the two with a comma: *King, Martin Luther, Jr.*

Alphabetical order   Alphabetize entries in the list by authors' last names. Note the following:

- Alphabetize by the exact letters in the spelling: *MacKay* precedes *McHam.*

- Let a shorter name precede a longer name beginning with the same letters: *Linden, Ronald* precedes *Lindenmayer, Arnold.*

- With last names using a prefix such as *le, du, di, del*, and *des*, alphabetize by the prefix: *Le Beau, Bryan F.*

- When *de* occurs with French names of one syllable, alphabetize under *D: De Man, Paul.* Otherwise, alphabetize by last name: *Maupassant, Guy de.*

- Alphabetize by the first element of a hyphenated name: *Sackville-West, Vita.*

- Alphabetize by the last name when the author uses two names without a hyphen: *Thomas, Elizabeth Marshall.*

Author not known   For a work with no author named, alphabetize by the first word in the title of the work other than *A, An,* or *The.*

Several works by the same author(s)   For all entries after the first, replace the name(s) of the author(s) with three hyphens followed by a period, and alphabetize according to the first significant word in the title. If an author serves as an editor or translator, put a comma after the three hyphens, followed by the appropriate abbreviation (*ed.* or *trans.*). If, however, the author has coauthors, repeat all authors' names in full and put the coauthored entry after all the single-name entries for the author.

Goleman, Daniel. *Destructive Emotions: A Scientific Dialogue with the Dalai Lama.* New York: Bantam-Dell, 2003. Print.

---. *Working with Emotional Intelligence.* New York: Bantam, 2000. Print.

Goleman, Daniel, Richard E. Boyatzis, and Annie McKee. *Primal Leadership: Learning to Lead with Emotional Intelligence.* Cambridge: Harvard Business School, 2004. Print.

Authors with the same last name Alphabetize by first names: *Smith, Adam* precedes *Smith, Frank.*

12c Sample MLA listings: Articles in periodical print publications (scholarly journals, magazines, newspapers)

Periodical publications—scholarly journals, magazines, and newspapers—are issued regularly on scheduled dates. The conventions for listing information about a print article in a works-cited entry depend on whether the article appears in a newspaper, popular magazine, or scholarly journal.

For information on how to distinguish scholarly journals from other periodicals, see 8b. Scholarly journal articles are some of the most common sources used in academic research.

1. Article in a scholarly journal After the author and title of the article, give the name of the journal (in italics), volume and issue numbers (separated by a period), year of publication (in parentheses), a colon, inclusive page numbers, and medium of publication (*Print*), followed by a period (see Source Shot 1, p. 186).

2. Article in a magazine

- Do not include *The* in the name of a magazine: *Atlantic*, not *The Atlantic.*

- For a magazine published every week or biweekly, give the complete date (day, month, and year, in that order, with no commas between them), followed by a colon. Abbreviate all months except May, June, and July.

- For a monthly or bimonthly magazine, give only the month and year (followed by a colon), as in the first example that follows. In either case, do not include volume and issue numbers.
- If the article is on only one page, give that page number. If the article covers two or more consecutive pages, list inclusive page numbers. If pages are not consecutive, indicate this with a plus sign (+) immediately after the first page number, for example, 16+.
- End with the medium of publication, *Print*.

Wilson, E. O. "What's Your Tribe?" *Newsweek* 9 Apr. 2012: 43-48. Print.

Schnayerson, Michael. "A Question of Provenance." The Art World. *Vanity Fair* May 2012: 111-21. Print.

3. Article in a newspaper   Give the author, article title (in quotation marks), and newspaper's name (in italics, omitting the word *The*). If the city isn't part of the name, put it in square brackets (not italicized) after the name. Then give the day, month, and year, with no punctuation and abbreviating all months except May, June, and July. Follow with any edition given at the top of the first page (*late ed., natl. ed., intl. ed.*) and a colon. For a newspaper that uses letters to designate sections, give the letter that appears on the page before the page number: "A23." For a numbered or titled section, write, for example, *sec. 2: 23* or *Arts and Leisure sec: 3*. End with the medium of publication, *Print*.

Barron, James. "The Titanic Fascinated New York, the Port It Never Reached." *New York Times* 9 Apr. 2012, natl. ed.: A16-17. Print.

4. Article that skips pages   When a periodical article does not appear on consecutive pages, give only the first page number followed by a plus sign. The following newspaper article by Rein is on pages C1 and C4 (in section C) of the *Washington Post*.

Rein, Lisa. "Not That Simple: The Plain Writing Act Requires Bureaucrats to Lay Off the Jargon—but It's Still a Work in Progress." *Washington Post* 9 Apr. 2012: C1+. Print.

5. Unsigned article   If the author's name is not given, begin with the title of the article, ignoring *A, An,* or *The* when alphabetizing.

"Put Out to Pasture: Controversy Surrounds the Government's Management of Wild Horses." *Economist* 24 Sept. 2011: 40. Print.

Modern Language Association MLA

SOURCE SHOT 1

Listing a Scholarly Print Journal Article in MLA Style MLA

Include the following when listing a scholarly print journal article:

① **Name of author(s)** Last name, first name, followed by a period

② **"Title of Article: Subtitle."** Followed by a period, within quotation marks

③ **_Name of journal or periodical_** In italics, omitting any _A_, _An_, or _The_, with no period following. Then give **volume** and **issue numbers** in regular (roman) print, separated by a period (with no spaces). Do not use the abbreviation _vol._ (_volume_) or _no._ (for issue number).

④ **Date of publication** The year—in parentheses, followed by a colon

⑤ **Page number or range of pages** (such as 24-27; 365-72), separated by a hyphen and concluding with a period (see Key Points box, p. 180).

⑥ **Medium of publication** Here, _Print_ followed by a period.

     ①   **②**

Bhatia, Tej K. "Super-Heroes to Super-Languages: American

       Popular Culture through South Asian Language Comics."
           ③   **④**   **⑤**   **⑥**
       World Englishes 25.2 (2006): 279-98. Print.
                      colon

---

6. Review Begin with the name of the reviewer and the title of the review article in quotation marks if these are available. Then add _Rev. of,_ the title of the work being reviewed in italics, a comma, the word _by_ or the abbreviation _ed._ (for _edited by_), and the author or editor of that work. Follow with the publication information for the review and the word _Print_.

Delbanco, Nicholas. "Dickens, as Exuberant in Private as in Public." Rev.

    of _The Selected Letters of Charles Dickens,_ ed. Jenny Hartley. _Los Angeles_

    Times 8 Apr. 2012, weekend ed.: E6. Print.

7. Editorial (signed or unsigned) Begin with the author (if available) or the title. Include the label _Editorial_ after the title. Follow with the

Table of Contents of a Scholarly Journal

Vol. 25, No. 2   **WORLD ENGLISHES**   2006

3 Journal, volume, and issue   **4 Year**

CONTENTS

1 Author

SYMPOSIUM ON
WORLD ENGLISHES IN POP CULTURE
Guest editors: Jamie Shinhee Lee and Yamuna Kachru

2 Title

5 Page span

6 Medium of publication: Print

---

rest of the publication information. In alphabetizing, ignore an initial *A,
An,* or *The* in the editorial title.

"A Bad Bet on Online Gambling." Editorial. *San Francisco Chronicle* 13 Apr.

     2012: A11. Print.

8. Letter to the editor   Write *Letter* or *Reply to letter of* . . . after the
name of the author (or after the title, if there is one). Follow with the
publication information.

Levin, Michael. "Books with Not Much to Say." Letter. *Economist* 24 Sept. 2011:

     22. Print.

9. Abstract in an abstracts journal For abstracts (brief summaries) of articles, provide exact publication information for the original work, and add information about your source for the abstract: the title of the abstract journal (italicized), volume and issue numbers, year, and page number and/or item number (preceded by the word *item*). End with the word *Print*. For a dissertation abstract, see 12d, item 31.

Powers, R. S., and R. A. Wojtkiewicz. "Occupational Aspirations, Gender, and

　　Educational Attainment." *Sociological Spectrum* 24.5 (2004): 601-22.

　　Studies on Women and Gender Abstracts 23.8 (Dec. 2005): 435, item

　　05W/710. Print.

12d Sample MLA listings: Nonperiodical print publications (print books, parts of books, pamphlets, etc.)

10. Book with one author See Source Shot 2 (p. 190) for an explanation and example.

11. Book with two or more authors List the authors' names in the order in which they appear on the title page. Separate the names with commas. Reverse the order of only the first author's name.

　　comma　　　　　　　name(s) of last author(s) not reversed
Baumol, William J., Robert E. Litan, and Carl J. Schramm. *Good Capitalism, Bad*

　　Capitalism, and the Economics of Growth and Prosperity. New Haven:

　　Yale UP, 2007. Print.

For a work with four or more authors, either list all the names (in the order listed on the title page) or use only the first author's name followed by *et al.* (Latin *et alii*, meaning "and others"). The form must match the form you use for in-text parenthetical citations. See 11b, item F, for an example.

Bellah, Robert N., et al. *Habits of the Heart: Individualism and Commitment in*

　　American Life. Berkeley: U of California P, 1985. Print.

12. Book with editor(s) or compiler(s) For an anthology or compilation, list the editor(s) or compiler(s), a comma, and the abbreviation *ed.* (or *eds.*) or *comp.* (or *comps.*).

Gates, Henry Louis, Jr., ed. *Classic Slave Narratives*. New York: NAL, 1987. Print.

For a work with four or more editors or compilers, use the name of only the first, followed by a comma and *et al.*, or name them all.

13. Book with author and editor   When an editor has prepared an author's work for publication, list the book under the author's name if you cite the author's work. Then, in your listing, include the name(s) of the editor(s) after the title, introduced by *Ed.* for one or more editors. *Ed.* stands for *edited by* in the following entry.

author of letters   name of editor
Bishop, Elizabeth. *One Art: Letters*. Ed. Robert Giroux. New York: Farrar, 1994.

    Print.

If you cite a section written by the editor, such as an introduction or a note, list the source under the name of the editor, and give the page numbers for the section.

name of editor   editor (abbrev.)   author of letters
Giroux, Robert, ed. Introduction. *One Art: Letters*. By Elizabeth Bishop.

    New York: Farrar, 1994. vii-xxii. Print.

14. One work in an anthology (original or reprinted)   See Source Shot 3 on pages 192–193 for an example and an explanation.

    If the work in the anthology is a reprint of a previously published scholarly article or chapter, supply the complete information (including the page numbers) for both the original publication and the reprint in the anthology. Add the words *Rpt. in* before the anthology details.

Hofstadter, Richard. "Abraham Lincoln and the Self-Made Myth." *American*

    Political Tradition: And the Men Who Made It. New York: Knopf, 1948.

    119-74. Rpt. in *The Best American History Essays on Lincoln*. Ed. Sean

    Wilentz. New York: Palgrave-Macmillan, 2009. 3-40. Print.

15. More than one work in an anthology, cross-referenced   If you cite more than one work from the same anthology, list the anthology separately in a complete entry, alphabetized by the name of the editor(s) in the works-cited list. Also list each work in a brief entry with a cross-reference to the anthology. This entry only needs the author's complete name, the title of the work, the last name(s) of the editor(s) of the anthology, and the inclusive page numbers of the work (not preceded by a comma). Alphabetize the entries in the usual way, as in the following examples. Include the medium of publication (*Print*) only with the anthology entry.

(Continued)

Modern Language Association | MLA

SOURCE SHOT 2

Listing a Book in MLA Style MLA

Find the necessary information for documenting a book on its title page. If the date is not on the title page, look on the copyright page. Include the following:

1 Name of author(s) Last name first (followed by a comma) for the first author. Normal order of any other author names. End with a period.

2 *Title of Book: Subtitle.* In italics, with capitals for main words (see p. 181), followed by a period

3 City of publication The first city mentioned on the title page, followed by a colon. Give the state or country (abbreviated) only if the city is not well known.

4 Name of publisher The short form of the name, usually one word (*Cengage*, not *Cengage Learning*; *Basic*, not *Basic Books*; *Abrams*, not *Harry N. Abrams*), followed by a comma. (***Note:*** Omit words such as *Press* or *Books* and omit any abbreviations such as *Co.* and *Inc.*: *Simon*, not *Simon & Schuster, Inc.* For university presses, however, use the abbreviations *U* and *P*, with no periods: *Columbia UP, U of Chicago P,* and so on.)

5 Year of publication Available after © on the copyright page of the book, ending with a period. Give the most recent year if several are listed.

6 The medium of publication For a print book, *Print*.

Items 11–30 give examples of and provide information on variations.

       comma period   period   colon

    1 / /   **2**   **3** /

Fussell, Paul. *Uniforms: Why We Are What We Wear.* Boston:

                  comma period

Indented   **4** /**5** / **6**

½ inch   ◄———► Houghton, 2002. Print.

---

editor of anthology   title of anthology

Eggers, Dave, ed. *The Best American Non-Required Reading 2008*. Boston:

    Houghton, 2008. Print.

author of   title of work   editor of page numbers
  work   in anthology anthology of work

King, Stephen. "Ayana." Eggers 200-15.

MLA Modern Language Association

Title Page of Print Book

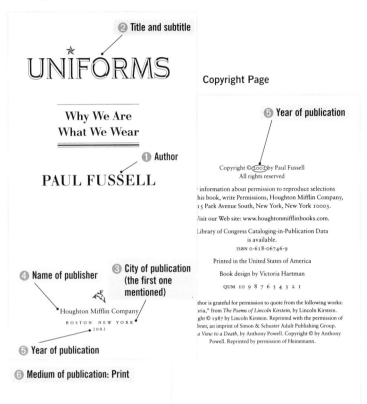

2 Title and subtitle

UNIFORMS

Why We Are
What We Wear

1 Author

PAUL FUSSELL

4 Name of publisher

3 City of publication (the first one mentioned)

Houghton Mifflin Company
BOSTON   NEW YORK
2002

5 Year of publication

6 Medium of publication: Print

Copyright Page

5 Year of publication

author of work   title of work in anthology   editor of page numbers anthology of work

Saunders, George. "Bill Clinton, Public Citizen." Eggers 267-300.

16. Foreword, preface, introduction, or afterword   List the name of the author of the book element cited, followed by the name of the

(Continued on page 194)

Modern Language Association **MLA**

SOURCE SHOT 3

Listing a Work in an Anthology in MLA Style **MLA**

Look on the title page and copyright page for publication information for the anthology. Look on the appropriate page of the table of contents (and on the pages themselves) for the details and inclusive page numbers of the specific work that you are documenting.

1 Author of work Last name, comma, first name, period

2 "Title of Short Work" Title of short work (poem, short story, essay) in quotation marks with main words capitalized, followed by a period. (Put the title of a play, which could be published separately, in italics when it is contained in an anthology.)

3 _Title and subtitle of anthology_ In italics, separated by a colon, with a period after the subtitle.

4 Editors of anthology List _Ed._ (for _Edited by_) and the editors' names in normal order, followed by a period.

5 Edition of anthology Number and _ed._ (for _edition_)

6 City of publication The first city mentioned on the title page, followed by a colon. If not found, look on the copyright page.

7 Imprint and publisher Separate these with a hyphen, putting the name of the imprint (division within a larger publishing house) first (see 12d, item 27). Follow with a comma.

8 Year of publication Available after © on the copyright page of the book, ending with a period. Give the most recent year if several are listed.

9 Inclusive page numbers of work Give all of the pages of the work, separated by a hyphen, not just the ones that you quote. (See Key Points box, p. 180.) End with a period.

10 Medium of publication For a print book, write _Print_ and end with a period.

1 comma period   **2** period   **3** colon
Hardy, Thomas. "The Man He Killed." _Compact Literature: Reading,_
                         period   **4**   period
Reacting, Writing. Ed. Laurie G. Kirszner and Stephen R. Mandell.
                                        Separated   Separated
                          colon   by hyphen   period   by hyphen   period
5   **6**   **7**   **8** **9**   **10**
8th ed. Boston: Wadsworth-Cengage, 2013. 689-90. Print.
                                                      comma   period

MLA Modern Language Association

Title Page

③ Title and subtitle of anthology

Compact Literature

READING ■ REACTING ■ WRITING

⑤ Edition of anthology — Eighth Edition

④ Editors of anthology
— Laurie G. Kirszner
— Stephen R. Mandell

WADSWORTH
CENGAGE Learning

Copyright Page

⑦ Imprint and publisher

⁞⁞ WADSWORTH
CENGAGE Learning

Literature: Reading, Reacting, Writing, Compact Eighth Edition
Laurie G. Kirszner
Stephen R. Mandell

Senior Publisher: Lyn Uhl
Publisher: Michael Rosenberg
Development Editor: Karen Mauk
Assistant Editor: Erin Bosco
Editorial Assistant: Rebecca Donahue
Media Editor: Janine Tangney
Marketing Manager: Melissa Holt
Marketing Coordinator: Brittany Blais
Content Project Manager: Corinna Dibble
Art Director: Marissa Falco
Manufacturing Planner: Betsy Donaghey
Rights Acquisition Specialist: Jen Meyer Dare
⁞ Service: Nesbitt ⁞s, Inc.
⁞ner: Nesbitt Graphics,
⁞igner: Walter Kopec
⁞lt Image: Greta Vaught
⁞or: Nesbitt Graphics,

© 2013, 2010, 2007 Wadsworth, Cengage Learning
ALL RIGHTS RESERVED. No part of this work covered ⁞ans-⁞leans ⁞t not ⁞digitiz-⁞works, or information storage and retrieval systems, except as permitted under Section 107 or 108 of the 1976 United States Copyright Act, without the prior written permission of the publisher.

⑥ Year of publication (most recent)

For product information and technology assistance, contact us at **Cengage Learning Customer & Sales Support, 1-800-354-9706**

For permission to use material from this text or product, submit all requests online at **www.cengage.com/permissions**. Further permissions questions can be emailed to **permissionrequest@cengage.com**.

Library of Congress Control Number: 2011943246
Student Edition:
ISBN-10: 1-111-83901-8
ISBN-13: 978-1-111-83901-7

Wadsworth
20 Channel Center Street
Boston, MA 02210
USA

⑥ City of publication

Cengage Learning is a leading provider of customized ⁞Australia, Mexico, Brazil and Japan. Locate your local office at **international.cengage.com/region**

Cengage Learning products are represented in Canada by Nelson Education, Ltd.

For your course and learning solutions, visit **www.cengage.com**.

Purchase any of our products at your local college store or at our preferred online store **www.cengagebrain.com**. Instructors: Please visit **login.cengage.com** and log in to access instructor-specific resources.

⁞e United States of America
⁞ 6 7 15 14 13 12 11

⑨ Inclusive page numbers of work

① Author of work

② Title of work

Janice Mirikitani

Photo of Janice Mirikitani by David Paul Morris/Getty Images

Table of Contents Page

element (*Foreword, Introduction,* and so on), with no quotation marks. Give the title of the work; then use *By* to introduce the name of the author(s) of the book (first name first). After the publication information, give inclusive page numbers for the book element cited, and conclude with the medium of publication.

Trillin, Calvin. Foreword. *Eat Me: The Food and Philosophy of Kenny Shopsin*.

    By Kenny Shopsin and Carolynn Carreño. New York: Knopf, 2008. xiii-xxi.

    Print.

17. Entry in a reference book Cite an entry in an encyclopedia as you would a work in an anthology or collection (shown in Source Shot 3). For a well-known reference book, such as a dictionary or encyclopedia, give the title and author of the entry (if available), title of the reference work, edition number, year of publication, and medium of publication, with no editor or publication details. When entries within the reference book are arranged alphabetically, omit volume and page numbers.

"Etching." *The Columbia Encyclopedia*. 6th ed. 2000. Print.

Kahn, David. "Cryptology." *Encyclopedia Americana*. Int. ed. 2001. Print.

If you are citing the *New Encyclopedia Brittanica*, in the title add a colon and indicate whether you used the *Micropaedia* or *Macropaedia* set of volumes.

"Fauvism." *New Encyclopedia Brittanica: Micropaedia*. 15th ed. 2010. Print.

For reference works that are not widely known, also give details of editors, volumes, place of publication, and publisher.

18. Corporation, organization, or government agency as author
Alphabetize by the name of the corporate author or branch of government. If the publisher is the same as the author, include the name again as publisher.

Hoover's Inc. *Hoover's Handbook of World Business*. Austin: Hoover's Business,

    2008. Print.

If no individual author is named for a government publication, begin the entry with the name of the national, state, or local government, followed by the name of the agency. Note that you can use an abbreviated form for a term referring to a US government agency (such as *dept., natl.,* and *Cong. House*).

United States. Natl. Commission on Terrorist Attacks upon the US. *The 9/11*
    Commission Report. New York: Norton, 2004. Print.

See item 43 and Source Shot 6 (p. 208) for an online government publication.

19. Work with no author named   Put the title first. Do not consider the words *A, An*, and *The* when alphabetizing the entries. The following entry would be alphabetized under C.

The Chicago Manual of Style. 16th ed. Chicago: U of Chicago P, 2010. Print.

20. Pamphlet, brochure, or press release   Document a pamphlet or brochure as you would a book.

Consumer Action. *Internet Safety: A Computer User's Guide to Privacy and*
    Security. San Francisco: Consumer Action, 2009. Print.

Document a press release similarly, but add the day and month as well as the year.

21. Translation   After the title, add *Trans.* (*Translated by*) and the name of the translator, first name first.

Pastoureau, Michel. *The Bear: History of a Fallen King*. Trans. George Holoch.
    Cambridge: Belknap-Harvard UP, 2011. Print.

22. Graphic narrative or illustrated work   For collaboratively created graphic narratives, use labels to indicate contributors' roles (e.g. writer, and short forms for other roles, such as illus., adapt., trans., and so on). Begin your entry with the name of the person(s) whose work you want to emphasize. List other contributors and their roles after the title, using the order and descriptions of roles given in the source.

McCulloch, Derek, writer. *Gone to Amerikay*. Art by Colleen Doran. Colors by
    José Villarruba. Letters by Jared K. Fletcher. New York: Vertigo-DC
    Comics, 2012. Print.

If the work is part of a multivolume work, see item 24. If it is part of a series, see item 25. If the work does not have page numbers, see the example in item 29.

If the graphic narrative was created by one person, cite it as you would any other nonperiodical print work. In the following example, Corman is both the writer and the illustrator.

Corman, Leela. *Unterzakhn*. New York: Schocken-Random, 2012. Print.

If illustrations are part of a literary work and you are citing the writers, give *Illus.* and the illustrator's name after the title.

Pekar, Harvey, and Joyce Brabner. *Our Cancer Year*. Illus. Frank Stack. New
York: Four Walls, 1994. Print.

If you are citing the work of the illustrator, begin the entry with that person's name.

23. Book in second or subsequent edition After the title, give the edition number, using the abbreviation *ed.* for *edition*.

Raimes, Ann. *Pocket Keys for Writers*. 4th ed. Boston: Wadsworth-Cengage,
2013. Print.

24. Multivolume work If you refer to only one volume of a multivolume work in your paper, give the author and page number in your intext citation, and give only the volume number for that book in the works-cited entry.

Richardson, John. *A Life of Picasso*. Vol. 2. New York: Random, 1996. Print.

If you refer to more than one volume of a multivolume work in your paper (as in 11b, item S), give the number of volumes (abbreviated *vols.*) after the title in your list of works cited.

Einstein, Albert. *Collected Papers of Albert Einstein*. 10 vols. Princeton:
Princeton UP, 1987-2006. Print.

25. Book in a series If the title page or an earlier page identifies a book as part of a series, after the medium of publication (*Print*), end the entry with the name of the series (abbreviated as *ser.*) and any series number given.

Connor, Ulla. *Contrastive Rhetoric: Cross-Cultural Aspects of Second Language
Writing*. New York: Cambridge UP, 1996. Print. Cambridge Applied
Linguistics Ser.

26. Republished book   For a paperback edition of a hardcover book, give the original date of publication after the title. Then cite publication information about the current book, ending with the medium of publication.

King, Stephen. *On Writing*. 2000. New York: Pocket, 2002. Print.

For a book republished under a different title, give the date and publication facts of both titles. Put the information about the new book and the medium (*Print*) first. Then add *Rpt. of* (*Reprint of*) and the original book's publication information.

Raimes, James. *An Englishman's Garden in America*. London: Frances Lincoln,

2007. Print. Rpt. of *Gardening at Ginger*. Boston: Houghton, 2006.

27. Book published under a publisher's imprint   State the names of both the imprint (the publisher within a larger publishing enterprise) and the larger publishing house, separated by a hyphen.

Atwood, Margaret. *Negotiation with the Dead: A Writer on Writing*. New York:

Anchor-Doubleday, 2003. Print.

For other examples, see 12d, items 14, 21, 22, and 23.

28. Book title including a title   Do not italicize a book title (or a journal name) included in the title of the work you list. (However, if the title of a short work, such as a poem or short story, is included, enclose it in quotation marks.)

book title within title not in italics

Hays, Kevin J., ed. *The Critical Response to Herman Melville's* Moby Dick.

Westport: Greenwood, 1994. Print.

29. Book without stated publication information or pagination   If a book does not provide some publication information, add any details about it that you may have found elsewhere in square brackets to indicate that they were not in the source: [2008]. If you cannot supply missing information, use the abbreviations *N.p.* (*no place* of publication) before the colon that otherwise follows the city, *n.p.* (*no publisher*) after the colon, *n.d.* (*no date*), or *n. pag.* (*no pagination*) before the medium of publication (see Key Points box, p. 181).

Kirkman, Robert, writer. *The Walking Dead, Vol. 1: Days Gone By*. Inking by

Tony Moore. Additional gray tones by Cliff Rathburn. Berkeley: Image

Comics, 2010. N. pag. Print.

More examples are in 12d, item 30.

30. The Bible and other sacred texts　Take the information from the title page and give the usual bibliographical details for a book. Also include the edition and the name of a translator or editor where appropriate. When no date of publication is given, use *n.d.* for *no date.* Ignore any *The* in the title for alphabetizing purposes in the works-cited list: Put *The Holy Bible* under *H.* Put the name of a version (abbreviated as *Vers.*) at the end of the entry after *Print*, as in the second example that follows.

Enuma Elish. Ed. Leonard W. King. Escondido: Book Tree, 1998. Print.

The Holy Bible. Peabody: Hendrickson, 2003. Print. King James Vers.

The Koran. Trans. George Sales. London: Warne, n.d. Print.

The New Oxford Annotated Bible. 3rd ed. Ed. Michael D. Coogan. Oxford: Oxford UP, 2001. Print.

31. Dissertations　Cite a published dissertation as you would a book, with place of publication, publisher, and date, but also include dissertation information after the title (for example, *Diss. U of Missouri, 2012.*).

If the dissertation is published by University Microfilms International (UMI), italicize the title and include *Ann Arbor: UMI,* the year, and the medium of publication.

Jerskey, Maria. *Writing Handbooks, English Language Learners, and the Selective Tradition.* Diss. New York U, 2006. Ann Arbor: UMI, 2006. Print.

For an unpublished dissertation, follow the title (in quotation marks) with *Diss.* and then with the university and year, ending with the medium of publication.

Hidalgo, Stephen Paul. "Vietnam War Poetry: A Genre of Witness." Diss. U of Notre Dame, 1995. Print.

If you cite an abstract published in *Dissertation Abstracts International*, abbreviated as *DAI,* give the volume number, issue number, year, and item or page number, and end with the medium of publication.

Hidalgo, Stephen Paul. "Vietnam War Poetry: A Genre of Witness." Diss. U of Notre Dame, 1995. *DAI* 56.8 (1995): item 0931A. Print.

12e Sample MLA listings: Periodical publications in online databases

Libraries subscribe to large information services to gain access to extensive databases of online articles (such as *Academic Search Premier, InfoTrac, LexisNexis, WorldCat,* and others) as well as to specialized databases (such as *ERIC, Contemporary Literary Criticism, JSTOR,* and *Project Muse*). You can use these databases to locate abstracts and full texts of thousands of articles that were originally published in print. And because many of the articles will have been previously accepted for publication, you will be able to find reliable materials for your papers.

> **KEY POINTS**
> MLA Guidelines for Listing Print Periodical Works in Online Databases
>
> Include the following:
> - **Print publication details** Give information for the print periodical publication of the work as shown in the examples in 12c, but omit the medium *Print*.
>
> - **Page numbers** Access a PDF version if possible so that you can include the inclusive page numbers. If no information about pagination is available, use *n. pag.* Use a plus sign after the first page number if the database indicates that pagination is not continuous.
>
> - **Database information** Italicize the name of the database. Do not include the name of the service providing the database (such as *EBSCO*), and do not include the name and place of the library system.
>
> - **Medium of publication and date of access** End with the word *Web* (the medium of publication) and the date (day, month, year) when you accessed the source. (Do not include the URL of the home page of the database.)
>
> To cite an article published in an online periodical that you have accessed through a database, see 12e, item 35.

SOURCE SHOT 4

Listing a Print Magazine Article Found in an Online Database [MLA]

❶ Name of author(s) Last name, first name, followed by a period

❷ "Title of Article: Any Subtitle." In quotation marks

❸ Print publication details
- *Name of magazine* In italics, excluding any volume or issue number
- **date of publication** (month and year, or day, month, year), followed by colon
- inclusive **page numbers** of the print document if given or shown on the screen. When no complete information about the page span appears, write *n. pag.* (see Key Points box on p. 199). When only the number of the first page is given, you may give that page number followed by a plus sign. Use page numbers from a printout only if you cite a PDF document.

❹ *Title of the database* In italics (for example, *Academic Search Premier*), followed by a period

❺ The medium of publication Here, *Web* (not in italics)

❻ Your date of access Day, month (all abbreviated except May, June, July), and year, as shown on a printout of the work, with a period at the end

See items 32–35 for examples of how to cite a variety of articles found in online databases.

❶   ❷   ❸
Lindsey, Brink. "Culture of Success." *New Republic* 12 Mar. 2008: 30-31.

     ❹   ❺   ❻
Academic Search Premier. Web. 13 May 2012.

---

32. Print scholarly article in an online database First give the article's print publication information (see 12c, item 1), but do not list *Print* as the medium of publication. Give the inclusive page numbers if they are visible on the screen (if the article is in PDF format); otherwise indicate *n. pag.* (*no pagination*). Follow with the name of the database (italicized), the medium of publication (*Web*), and your date of access. See Key Points box on p. 199.

Academic Search Premier Citation Page for a Print Magazine Article

The citation page indicates that the full text of the article is available in HTML or PDF. Always choose PDF as your source when available so that you can provide an exact page number for a citation.

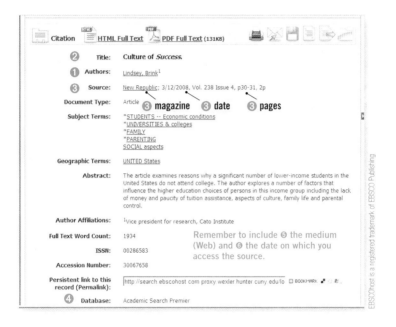

Lowe, Michelle S. "Britain's Regional Shopping Centres: New Urban Forms?"
      journal, volume and issue
      numbers (year): page span   title of database   medium
      Urban Studies 37.2 (2000): 261-74. *Academic Search Premier*. Web.
      date of access
      4 Feb. 2012.

33. Print magazine article in an online database First give the article's print publication information (as in 12c, item 2), but do not list

Print as the medium of publication. Give the inclusive page numbers if they are visible. See Source Shot 4 on page 200, for more information to include and an example.

34. Print newspaper article in an online database   First give the article's print publication information (see 12c, item 3), but do not list *Print* as the medium of publication. Give the inclusive page numbers if they are visible; otherwise indicate *n. pag.* (*no pagination*). Follow with the name of the database (italicized), the medium of publication (*Web*), and your date of access. See Key Points box on p. 199.

"A Painful Betrayal." Editorial. *New York Times* 3 Feb. 2012, late ed., sec. A: n. pag.

    LexisNexis. Web. 16 Feb. 2012.

35. Article in an online periodical accessed in an online database
If you use a database to access an article first published in an online scholarly journal, magazine, or newspaper, first give all of the information for the article's publication in the online periodical (see 12f, items 39–41). Indicate the absence of page numbers with *n. pag.* Then give the name of the database (italicized), the medium of publication (*Web*), and your date of access.

Apter, Emily. "Technics of the Subject: The Avatar Drive." *Postmodern Culture*

    18.2 (2008): n. pag. *Project Muse*. Web. 22 Mar. 2012.

12f Sample MLA listings: Sources found only on the Web

If a work is available only on the Web (that is, not also existing in print or in another medium), in addition to information about the author, title, and other details that you would list for a print publication, in your works-cited entry you will also need to include the name of the Web site or database, the sponsor (publisher) of the site, and the date of posting or update. Most work found on Web sites is nonperiodical, that is, not published on a regular schedule (as an online newspaper would be), so the date of posting or update is important. Sometimes you have to search hard on a Web site to find this information, and you may discover that the information just isn't there. Missing information could be a factor in persuading you not to use a site as a source. (You'll find the two Key Points Boxes in 8c on pp. 133 and 134 helpful as you look for this information.)

Since Web site material can change over time and may be available in different versions, you will also need to list your date of access. Always save or print a copy of a Web source that you are using since it will display your date of access.

Source Shot 5 (p. 204) shows you how to provide and format the information needed to cite a Web source that has no print equivalent. (For listing works on the Web that have print sources, see 12g.) **Note:** Include a URL as supplementary information in your citation only if the source could not otherwise be located. Include the URL at the end of the entry, within angle brackets, and split across lines only after a slash, as in items 52 and 53.

Items 36–47 that follow show examples of works-cited entries for sources available only on the Web.

36. Authored document with no print version on a nonperiodical Web site For an article on a nonperiodical Web site (one not published on a regular schedule as an online magazine, newspaper, or scholarly journal would be), begin with the name of the author. Follow with the title of the source. Put titles of Web pages and articles in quotation marks and titles of reports in italics. Then give the title of the Web site (in italics). Web sites often comprise many pages, each with its own URL, so list the primary site on which the document is found. (See the Key Points box in 8c for help identifying the site title.) Continue with other details of the site: sponsor/publisher, date of publication or posting, medium of publication (*Web*), and your date of access.

Rogers, Felisa. "Lessons of a Reluctant Hunter." *Salon.com*. Salon Media Group,

14 Apr. 2012. Web. 16 Apr. 2012.

Groeger, Lena. "And You Thought It Was Just 'Pink' Slime." *ProPublica*.

ProPublica, 12 Apr. 2012. Web. 16 Apr. 2012.

37. Document with no author named and no print version on a nonperiodical Web site For a Web site document for which no author is named, begin with the title of the document. Continue with other details: name of the site, sponsor/publisher, date of publication or posting, medium of publication (*Web*), and your date of access. Source Shot 5 on page 204 shows an example of how to cite one Web page on the National Trust for Historic Preservation Web site that has no named author and no print version.

38. Entire Web site, no author named Begin with the name of the site. Then give the sponsor/publisher, date of publication or update (or *n.d.* if there is none), medium of publication (*Web*), and your date of access.

(Continued)

SOURCE SHOT 5

Listing a Web Source with No Author and No Print Version **MLA**

Include these six basic items if they are available:

1 **Title and subtitle of the Web page or article.** If you find no author credited on the site, begin with the title (and subtitle if there is one). Use quotation marks for the title of an article or Web page (part of a larger work) on a Web site. Use italics for a report or other longer independent document. End with a period.

2 *Title of Web site* (in italics) + any version or edition number, if available, ending with a period

3 **Sponsor/publisher** of the site (often found at bottom of Web page; if not available anywhere, use *n.p.*). Follow with a comma. *Note:* A Webmaster is not the sponsor of the site (see 8c). See the Key Points box on p. 134 for more on finding the sponsor of a site.

4 **Date of online posting or update** (or *n.d.* if no date is given).

5 **The medium of publication** Here, *Web* with a period after it

6 **Your date of access** Day, month (abbreviated except May, June, and July), and year, with a period at the end

If you make a copy of the Web page as soon as you find it or save it to your computer, your date of access will appear on your printout or with your saved file.

1
"11 Most Endangered Historic Places: National Soldiers Home Historic
2   **3**
    District." *National Trust for Historic Preservation*. National Trust for
              4   **5**   **6**
    Historic Preservation, 2012. Web. 13 Mar. 2012.

Penn: University of Pennsylvania. University of Pennsylvania, 2011. Web. 28
    Mar. 2012.

Modern Language Association. MLA, 20 Apr. 2012. Web. 21 Apr. 2012.

39. Article in an online scholarly journal Give the author, title of article, name of online journal (which is also the name of the Web site),

A Document with No Author Named on a Web Site

Bottom of Web Page

volume and issue numbers, and date of publication as you would for an article in a print journal (see Source Shot 1, p. 186). Give paragraph numbers in your in-text citations (see 11b, item Q) or give the total number of paragraphs in your works-cited entry only if paragraphs are numbered in the source (visible on screen), as they are for the first example that follows. Otherwise indicate *n. pag.* Add the medium of publication (*Web*) and end with your date of access. You do not list a sponsor for an online scholarly journal.

author   title of article

Hatchuel, Sarah. "Leading the Gaze: From Showing to Telling in Kenneth

                                 volume and

                name of online journal   issue numbers

     Branagh's Henry V and Hamlet." *Early Modern Literary Studies* 6.1

date of online   total number of paragraphs

    publication   (numbered on screen)   date of access

      (2000): 22 pars. Web. 1 Aug. 2012.

           author   title of article

Ferris, Sharmila Pixy. "Writing Electronically: The Effects of Computers on

                              volume and   date of electronic

             title of online journal   issue numbers   publication

     Traditional Writing." *Journal of Electronic Publishing* 8.1 (2002)

no numbered pages   medium of   date of

or paragraphs   publication   access

     n. pag. Web. 3 Feb. 2012.

For an article from an online scholarly journal that is included in a database, see 12e, item 35.

40. Article in an online magazine   Give the author, title of the article (enclosed in quotation marks), title of the section of the Web site where the article is housed (if applicable), title of the magazine (in italics), which also is the name of the Web site, its sponsor (followed by a comma), the date of posting, the medium of publication, and your date of access. If you are citing an editorial, review, or letter to the editor, list that designation after the article title (as in 12c, items 6–8). For an article in a special section, give the name of the special section, as in the following example. It is not necessary to indicate n. pag. (*no pagination*).

Lithwick, Dahlia. "Lights! Cameras! It's the Supreme Court!" Jurisprudence:

     The Law, Lawyers, and the Court. *Slate*. Washington Post, 30 Mar. 2012.

     Web. 4 Apr. 2012.

41. Article in an online newspaper   Give the author (if known), title of the article, title of the newspaper (in italics), which is also the name of the Web site, sponsor of the site, and date of online publication. If you are citing an editorial, review, or letter to the editor, list that designation after the article title (see 12c, items 6–8). Note that for a newspaper article on the Web, it is not necessary to include *n. pag.* End with the medium of publication (*Web*) and your date of access.

Heim, Joe. "On Emancipation Day in DC, Two Memorials Tell Very Different
Stories." *Washington Post*. Washington Post, 15 Apr. 2012. Web. 15 Apr. 2012.

Semple, Kirk. "Many U.S. Immigrants' Children Seek American Dream Abroad."
New York Times. New York Times, 15 Apr. 2012. Web. 15 Apr. 2012.

42. Entry in an online encyclopedia, dictionary, or other reference work   When entries are not individually authored, begin with the title of the entry. Give the most recent date of posting. Provide details of the publisher or sponsor, date of publication, medium of publication, and your date of access.

"Vicarious." *Cambridge Advanced Learner's Dictionary*. Cambridge UP, 2004.
Web. 6 Feb. 2012.

43. Government publication available only online   If no author or authors are named, begin with the national or state government, name of agency (can be abbreviated), and title of the work. Follow these with the name of the government Web site, date of electronic posting or update, medium of publication, and your date of access (see Source Shot 6 on p. 208).

   If an author or authors (or compiler or compilers) are named, you may either begin with the government and agency (as illustrated in Source Shot 6) or begin with the author(s) or compiler(s).

   To cite a government publication on the Web that is also available in print, see 12g.

44. Scholarly project online   If the site shows the name of an editor, give it after the title. Give the sponsor after the title (or name of editor), followed by a comma. If no date is given for site creation or updating, write *n.d.*

                           sponsor
Victorian Women Writers Project. Ed. Angela Courtney and Michelle Dalmau.

          date of   medium of   date of
          posting   publication   access
Trustees of Indiana U, 2010. Web. 2 Mar. 2012.

45. Book published online only   Cite a book that is only published electronically (that is, online) as you would a print book by listing the author, title, and other bibliographic details. Next give the name of the Web site, the sponsor of the site, date of posting, the medium of publication (*Web*), and your date of access.

(Continued)

SOURCE SHOT 6

Listing an Online Government Publication MLA

Include the following:

❶ **Name of national or state government and name of agency,** along with any office or institute posting the publication (abbreviated)

❷ ***Title and subtitle of the work*** in italics for a report or other independent publication and in quotation marks for a shorter piece (a form, chart, fact sheet, etc.)

❸ Follow the title with *By* . . . and the **name(s)** of any **author(s)** or **compiler(s)** (*comp.*).

❹ Any **report number** or other identifying information

❺ **Inclusive page numbers** only if you used the document in PDF format with numbered pages and cited page numbers in your paper (see examples in 11b, item L, for how to cite this Department of the Interior source within a paper).

❻ ***Title of the Web site*** (*in italics*)

❼ **Sponsor of the site,** followed by a comma

❽ **Date of online posting or update** of document (or *n.d.* if no date is given)

❾ **Medium of publication,** here *Web*

❿ **Your date of access**

    ❶   Department of government   Name of agency   ❷
United States. Dept. of the Interior. US Geological Survey. *Identification*

    of Tsunami Deposits in the Geologic Record: Developing Criteria Using
                               ❸
    Recent Tsunami Deposits. By Robert Peters and Bruce Jaffe. USGS
       ❹   ❺   ❻   ❼
    Open-File Report 2010-1239. 1-39 PDF. *USGS*. US Dept. of the Interior,
      ❽   ❾   ❿
    USGS, 19 Nov. 2010. Web. 21 Apr. 2012.

MLA Modern Language Association

An Online Government Publication

⑥ Title of Web site   ② Title of work

④ Report number and identifying information

⑧ Date of online posting

⑤ Report available in PDF format, so page numbers available

③ Names of authors

Report only available on the Web

Bottom of Web Page   Sample citation given in another documentation style, so it needs to be changed to MLA style

① Name of government + name of agency and   ⑧ Date of most recent update
⑦ Sponsor of site

Goldberg, David Theo, Stretka Hristova, and Erik Loyer. *Blue Velvet: Re-dressing New Orleans in Katrina's Wake. Vectors Journal.* Vectors Journal, 2008. Web. Mar. 2012.

To cite a book with a print source that is available online, see 12g, item 48.

46. Poem published online only   For a poem only published on a Web site, give the author, title, name of Web site, name of site sponsor, date of posting, medium of publication (*Web*), and your date of access.

Aechtner, Chris D. "Goddess of the Night." *PoetrySoup.* Poetry Soup, 2011. Web. 2 Feb. 2012.

To cite a poem with a print source that is available online, see 12g, item 49.

47. Review published online only   After the name of the reviewer and title (if there is one), add *Rev. of . . .* and the title of the work being reviewed, a comma, and the author of that work (see 12c, item 6). Then add the name of the Web site, sponsor of the site, date of posting, medium of publication (*Web*), and your date of access.

Miller, Laura. "'The Queen and the Maid': Joan of Arc's Secret Backer." Rev. of *The Maid and the Queen*, by Nancy Goldstone. *Salon.com.* Salon Media Group, 1 Apr. 2012. Web. 20 Apr. 2012.

To cite a review found online that was previously published in print, see 12g.

12g Sample listings: Sources on the Web with print publication data

If a nonperiodical source (one not published on a regular schedule, such as a book or a brochure) you find on the Web was previously or is currently also published in print, first list all of the print publication information (see examples in 12d, items 10–31), but do not list *Print* as the medium of publication. Then list the Web site or name of the database (italicized) where you found the work, the medium of publication (*Web*), and your date of access. You do not need to list the sponsor of the Web site, but you may add it as supplementary information.

To cite a print periodical article (or editorial, review, letter to the editor, and so on) found in a database, see 12e, items 32 (scholarly journal), 33 (magazine), and 34 (newspaper). For an example of a newspaper editorial found in a database, see 12e, item 34.

48. Online book with print source   Give whatever is available of the following: author, title, editor or translator, and print publication information (as shown in 12d, items 10–30), but do not give *Print* as the medium of publication. Follow this with the electronic publication information: name of the Web site or database, medium of publication (*Web*), and your date of access.

    author   title of work   print publication information
Darwin, Charles. <i>The Voyage of the Beagle</i>. New York: Collier, 1909.
                        medium of   date of
  title of database   publication   access
  Oxford Text Archive. Web. 22 Jan. 2012.

49. Online poem with print source   Give the author, title, and print publication information (see 12d, item 14), but do not list *Print* as the medium of publication. If the print work was first published in an anthology or collection and had a page number(s) there, but none are visible on-screen, put *N. pag.* after the date. Then list the Web site or database, the medium of publication (*Web*), and your date of access.

                                                              no page
                                         print publication   numbers in
  author   title of poem   print source   information   Web source
Levine, Philip. "What Work Is." <i>What Work Is</i>. New York: Knopf, 1991. N. pag.
                        medium of   date of
  name of database   publication   access
  Internet Poetry Archive. Web. 19 Sept. 2012.

12h Sample listings: Other Web sources

Other sources only available online should contain the name of the author, the title of the Web site, the sponsor of the site, the date of posting, your date of access, and any other necessary descriptive details.

50. Personal Web site or home page   First list the site creator or editor. If a personal Web site has a title, supply it, in italics. If the home page is part of a larger Web site, use the designation *Home page* before the name of the Web site. If no publisher/sponsor is named, write *N.p*. Use *n.d.* when no date of posting or updating is available. End with the medium of publication (*Web*) and your date of access.

Ferraro, Janet. *The Art of Janet Ferraro*. N.p., n.d. Web. 23 Mar. 2012.

Pollitzer, Sally. Home page. *Architectural Glass*. Pharus Design, 2006. Web.
    22 Mar. 2012.

51. Course or department home page For a course home page, give the name of the instructor(s), the course number and title (in quotation marks), the words *Course home page*, the dates of the course, the department, the title of the Web site, the division and institution sponsoring the site, date of posting, the medium of publication (*Web*), and your access date.

Casana, Jesse. "ANTH 3023: Approaches to Archaeology." Course home page.

Spring 2012. Dept. of Anthropology. *University of Arkansas*. Fulbright

College of Arts and Sciences, U of Arkansas, 2012. Web. 22 Apr. 2012.

For a department home page, start with the name of the department and the description *Department home page*.

52. Online posting on a blog, discussion list, wiki, and so on Give the author's name and the document title (in quotation marks) as visible on-screen or written in the subject line in a discussion list. If there is no title, use the label *Online posting* (not in quotation marks). Continue with the name of the list or forum or the title of the blog (in italics unless the blog is part of a Web site) or wiki, the name of the sponsor/publisher, the date of posting, the medium of publication, and your date of access. Add a URL only if the source would otherwise be difficult for others to find (as in the first example that follows). Include online postings as references in a paper only if you assess the sources as reliable—always check the authors and their qualifications.

Althouse, Ann. "Do Poor Urban Neighborhoods Lack Places to Buy Fresh

Produce, and Is That Contributing to Obesity?" *Althouse*. Althouse, 19

Apr. 2012. Web. 21 Apr. 2012. <http://althouse.blogspot.com>.

The following entry by Nick Bilton is a posting on the blog Bits: The Business of Technology (blog title not in italics), which is found on the *New York Times* Web site (an online newspaper; see 12f, item 41).

Bilton, Nick. "Disruptions: Time to Review FAA Policy on Gadgets." Bits: The

Business of Technology. *New York Times*. New York Times, 18 Mar. 2012.

Web. 19 Mar. 2012.

If a wiki entry is unsigned, begin with the title of the entry.

"Katherine Anne Porter." *Wikipedia*. Wikimedia Foundation, 30 Mar. 2012. Web.

23 Apr. 2012.

To make it easy for readers to find a posting in a discussion list, refer whenever possible to one stored in Web archives.

Kuechler, Manfred. "Google Docs: A New Tool for Collaborative Writing."

5 Dec. 2007. Hunter-L Archives. Web. 22 Jan. 2012.

<http://hunter.listserv.cuny.edu/scriptshc/

wa-hc.exe?A2=ind0712A&L=HUNTER-L&P=R2013>.

53. Forwarded online document   To cite a forwarded document in an online posting, include the author, title, and date, followed by *Fwd. by* and the name of the person forwarding the document. End with the date of forwarding, the name of the discussion group, the medium of publication, and your date of access.

Beaky, Lenore A. "Chronicle Article." 18 Mar. 2012. Fwd. by Jack Hammond.

18 Mar. 2012. Hunter-L. Web. 20 Mar. 2012. <http://hunter.listserve.cuny.edu>

12i Sample MLA listings: Visual, audio, and multimedia sources

For visual, audio, and multimedia sources, list the medium of reception (*Radio, Television,* etc.), format (*Film, DVD,* etc.), or descriptive label (*Map, Photograph,* etc.) as illustrated in the following examples.

54. Work of visual art or photograph (and image reproduction or slide)   List the name of the artist; the title of the work (in italics); the date of the work's creation—or *n.d.* if no date is available; the medium of composition used by the artist; the name of the museum, gallery, or private collection; and the city where it is located.

Duchamp, Marcel. *Bicycle Wheel.* 1951. Metal wheel mounted on painted wood

stool. Museum of Mod. Art, New York.

Johns, Jasper. *Racing Thoughts.* 1983. Encaustic and collage on canvas.

Whitney Museum of Amer. Art, New York.

For an image of a work of art in a print book, in addition to details about the work and its location, give complete publication information for the book containing the reproduction, including the number of the page on which the photograph appears and any figure, slide, or plate number.

Johns, Jasper. *Racing Thoughts.* 1983. Whitney Museum of Amer. Art, New

York. *The American Century: Art and Culture 1950–2000.* By Lisa Phillips.

New York: Norton, 1999. 311. Print.

For an image of a work of art on the Web, see 12j, item 66; for an image on CD-ROM, see 12i, item 64.

For a slide in a collection, include the slide number (as in *Slide 17*).

55. Museum wall placard   For a placard such as a museum wall label, include the label *Placard* after the title or name of the work. Also give the name of the exhibition, the name of the museum, its location, and the dates of the show, followed by the medium of publication (*Print*).

Aphrodite's Children. Placard. *Aphrodite and the Gods of Love*. Boston:
    Museum of Fine Arts, 26 Oct. 2011-20 Feb. 2012. Print.

56. Cartoon or comic strip   After the name of the artist and the title (within quotation marks), include the label *Cartoon* or *Comic strip*. Follow this with information about the source and the medium of publication. Include the page number for a print source.

Chast, Roz. "New Chess Pieces." Cartoon. *New Yorker* 27 Sept. 2010: 65. Print.

57. Advertisement   Give the name of the product, company, or organization, followed by the label *Advertisement*. If a print page is not numbered, write *n. pag.* Use *n.d.* if the source is not dated. End with the medium of publication or reception.

American Indian College Fund. Advertisement. *New York Times Style*
    Magazine 25 Sept. 2011: 91. Print.

Acura automobile. Advertisement. Comedy Central. 24 Mar. 2012. Television.

58. Map or chart   Italicize the title of the map or chart, and include the genre designation *Map* after the title. Also include the medium of publication (*Print, Web,* etc.).

Los Angeles Region. Map. N.p.: Automobile Club of Southern California, 2009.
    Print. California Regional Ser.

For a map or chart accessed on the Web, include the date of posting and your date of access.

"Attack Map." *Remembering Pearl Harbor*. Multimedia map.
    Nationalgeographic.com. National Geographic Soc., 2001. Web.
    1 Mar. 2012.

MLA Language Map. Map. *Modern Language Association*. MLA, 12 Apr. 2012.
    Web. 12 Apr. 2012.

59. Film or video recording   For a film, begin with the title (italicized) unless you are citing the work of a specific contributor (director, writer, etc.), whom you would list first. Otherwise, after the title, list the director, performers, and any other contributors or pertinent information. Follow with the name of the distributor (and a comma), the year of distribution, and the medium of publication (*Film*).

A Dangerous Method. Dir. David Cronenberg. Perf. Michael Fassbinder, Viggo

Mortensen, and Keira Knightley. Sony, 2011. Film.

Cronenberg, David, dir. *A Dangerous Method.* Perf. Michael Fassbinder, Viggo

Mortensen, and Keira Knightley. Sony, 2011. Film.

Cite a DVD, laser disc, videocassette, filmstrip, or slide program as you would a film. Include the date of the original film, if relevant, but do not list *Film* as the medium of publication. Follow with the name of the distributor of the DVD, laser disc, or other format; the year of the new release; and the medium of publication (*DVD, Laser disc, Videocassette, Filmstrip, Slide program*).

Casablanca. Dir. Michael Curtiz. Perf. Humphrey Bogart and Ingrid Bergman.

1943. MGM, 1998. DVD.

The Iron Lady. Dir. Phyllida Lloyd. Perf. Meryl Streep. 2011. Weinstein, 2012.

Laser disc.

To cite a digitized version of a film that you viewed on the Web, see 12j, item 67.

For an online video, add the label *Video* after the title. Provide the name of the distributor (followed by a comma) and date of publication. Follow with the name of the Web site (here, *YouTube*), the medium of publication (*Web*), and your date of access.

Phillips, Barnaby, narr. *South Africa's Threatened Rhinos.* Video.

AlJazeeraEnglish, 28 Sept. 2010. *YouTube.* Web. 1 May 2012.

60. Television or radio program   Give the title of the program episode or segment (in quotation marks), the name of the program or series (in italics), the network, the call letters and city of the local station (if any), and the date of broadcast. Put a comma between the call letters and city and between the city and broadcast date; separate other details with periods. End with the medium of reception (*Television* or *Radio*). After the title of the episode or program, include any pertinent information about individual contributors, such as a performer, narrator, or director.

"The Vaccine War." Dir. Jon Palfreman. *Frontline.* PBS. KVIE, Sacramento, CA,

20 Mar. 2012. Television.

Howe, Marie. Interview by Terry Gross. *Fresh Air.* Natl. Public Radio. WGBH,

Boston, 20 Oct. 2011. Radio.

"Take the Money and Run for Office." *This American Life.* Narr. Ira Glass.

Public Radio Intl. KQED, San Francisco, 30 Mar. 2012. Radio.

To refer to the work of a particular person, begin the entry with the person's name and contribution (dir., narr., perf., etc.).

Fellowes, Julian, writer. "Downton Abbey: Season Two." Perf. Hugh Bonneville, Maggie Smith, and Elizabeth McGovern. 7 episodes. *Masterpiece Theatre.* PBS. KCRB, Cotati, CA, 8 Jan.-19 Feb. 2012. Television.

To cite a live radio program listened to on the Web or on a radio, or a TV program accessed from an online archive, see 12j, item 68. If you listened to a podcast or MP3 recording of a radio program, see 12i, item 63.

To cite a transcript of a radio or television program, see 12k, item 71, and Source Shot 7 on p. 222.

61. Sound recording   Begin the entry with the person whose role you want to emphasize: composer or writer, performer, conductor, etc. Then list the title of the work (with album titles in italics and song titles in quotation marks), name(s) of artist(s), manufacturer (followed by a comma), year of issue, and medium of publication (*CD, LP, Audiocassette*, or *Audiotape*).

If you cite a specific song on an album, give the song title (in quotation marks) and then the album title (in italics) to indicate a work contained within a larger work (as you would cite a short work contained in an anthology). If the performer also wrote the song, you begin with the performer and do not need to list *By* . . . and the name after the song title.

Welch, Kevin. "Andaman Sea." *A Patch of Blue Sky.* Music Road Records, 2010. CD.

Brooks, Gwendolyn. "We Real Cool." *The Norton Anthology of African American Literature Audio Companion.* Disc 2. Norton, 2004. CD.

Walker, Alice. Interview by Kay Bonetti. Columbia: American Audio Prose Library, 1981. Audiocassette.

62. Live performance   Give the title of the performance (play, concert, dance, etc.), the author, any pertinent information about the director and performers, the theater and city (separated by a comma), and the date of the performance. End with the word *Performance.* If you are citing an individual's role in the performance, begin your citation with the person's name, as in the second example that follows.

In Paris. By Ivan Bunin. Dir. and Adapt. Dmitry Krymov. Perf. Mikhail Baryshnikov. Broad Stage, Santa Monica, 15 Apr. 2012. Performance.

Mikhail Baryshnikov, perf. *In Paris.* By Ivan Bunin. Dir. Dmitry Krymov. Broad Stage, Santa Monica, 15 Apr. 2012. Performance.

63. Podcast (online audio recording)   If you listen to or view a podcast online, cite it as you would a document or page on a Web site (12f, items 36 and 37).

Cite a podcast that you download and access on an audio player as you would cite a work in its original medium (sound recording [CD, etc.], lecture, concert performance, online newspaper, and so on), but give *MP3 file* as the medium. You do not need to give your date of access.

Lehrer, Jonah. "How Creativity Works." Interview by June Thomas. *Slate.*

Washington Post, 30 Mar. 2012. MP3 file.

Also see item 65 (on digital files).

64. CD-ROM or DVD-ROM Cite material from a CD-ROM or DVD-ROM published as a single edition (that is, with no regular updating or revising) in the same way you cite a book, an article in a book, or a work of art (see 12i, item 54), but include any version or release number and end with the medium of publication (*CD-ROM* or *DVD-ROM*).

Flanner, Janet. "Führer I." *New Yorker* 29 Feb. 1934: 20-24. *The Complete New*

Yorker. New York: Random, 2005. DVD-ROM.

Keats, John. "To Autumn." *Columbia Granger's World of Poetry.* Rel. 3. New

York: Columbia UP, 1999. CD-ROM.

If there is more than one disc and you used only one, after the medium of publication, give the number of that disc (*Disc 3*); otherwise, give the total number of discs (*4 discs*).

If you cite a work in a scholarly journal, abstracts journal (see 12c, item 9), magazine, newspaper, or reference book that is published periodically in print as well as on CD-ROM or DVD-ROM as a database or as part of a database, first give the publication information for the print source (check the disc's publication booklet for this). Follow with the medium of publication for your source (*CD-ROM* or *DVD-ROM*). Then list the title of the database (italicized), the name of the vendor (such as *Silver Platter*), and the publication date of the database.

65. Digital files A digital file is an image, performance, or document (such as a photograph, video recording of a concert, or typed word-processing file) that can exist in digital form on your computer or another device or that can be published on a disc and played without the support of a Web site. For digital files that you download, receive, or create, document the source according to the publication information of the original work, but do not list the original medium (*CD*, etc.). Instead, give the medium of publication as the type of file: *PDF file, MP3 file, JPEG file, Word file,* and so on. If you do not know the type of file, write *Digital file.* Do not give your date of access.

Byrne, David. "A Walk in the Dark." *Uh-Oh.* Luaka Bop/Warner Bros., 1992. MP3 file.

Cite a published disc that can be played on an MP3 audio device as you would cite a book, but give MP3-CD as the medium of publication.

More, Thomas. *Utopia*. 1516. Read by James Adams. Blackstone Audio, 2008. MP3-CD.

Cite an e-book as you would cite a print book, but give the medium of publication as the kind of electronic file (such as *Nook file, Kindle file, EPUB file,* or *PDF file*).

Brooks, David. *The Social Animal: The Hidden Sources of Love, Character, and Achievement*. New York: Random, 2011. EPUB file.

12j Sample listings: Works on the Web from another medium (besides print)

Cite online versions of interviews, maps, charts, films and film clips, videos, television programs, radio programs, sound recordings, works of art, cartoons, advertisements, and other sources that were previously or are also presently available in another format (other than print) by first listing the publication information for the original source, but do not list the original medium of publication or transmission (*Film, Radio,* etc.) for that source. Then add the title of the Web site or database, the medium of publication (*Web*), and your access date. (For online sources that were previously or are concurrently available in print, see 12g.)

66. Image of a work of art on the Web   Indicate the digitized image of a work of art accessed on the Web by first giving details about the work (see 12i, item 54), but do not include the medium of composition. Then add the name of the Web site, the medium of publication (*Web*), and your date of access.

Christo and Jeanne-Claude. *The Umbrellas*. 1984-1991. Japan-USA. *National Gallery of Art*. Web. 3 Mar. 2012.

Wolfgang Volz/Laif/Redux © 1991 Christo

67. Film on the Web For a digitized version of a film that you viewed online, first give all of the film publication information, but do not put *Film* as the medium of reception. Instead, add the title of the Web site or database where you viewed the film, the medium of reception (*Web*), and the date you accessed and viewed the film online.

Alice in Wonderland. Dir. Cecil Hepworth. Hepworth Mfg., 1903. *Internet*

Archive. Web. 13 Mar. 2012.

For sources on digital files (MP3 files), see 12i, items 63 and 65.

68. Radio or television program on the Web For a live (streaming) radio program accessed online, give all of the broadcast information, including the date of broadcast (see 12i, item 60), but do not give *Radio* as the medium of reception. Next give the name of the Web site, the medium of reception (*Web*), and your date of access.

Bonnie Simmons Show. KPFA, Berkeley. 19 Apr. 2012. *Archives for the Bonnie*

Simmons Show. Web. 19 Apr. 2012.

Follow the same format for a radio or television program accessed from an online archive.

(Continued)

 KEY POINTS

Nine Ways to Document a Jay-Z and Kanye West Song

Daniel Boczarski/Getty Images

CD

Jay-Z, and Kanye West, perf. "Otis." *Watch the Throne.* Roc-A-Fella, 2011. CD.

(Continued)

(Continued)

MP3 file

Jay-Z, and Kanye West, perf. "Otis." *Watch the Throne.* Roc-A-Fella, 2011. MP3 file.

LP record

Jay-Z, and Kanye West, perf. "Otis." *Watch the Throne.* Roc-A-Fella, 2011. LP.

Lyrics in print (print booklet with CD)

Carter, Shawn [Jay-Z], Kanye West, et al. "Otis." Booklet. *Watch the Throne.* Roc-A-Fella, 2011. CD.

Lyrics on the Web

Carter, Shawn [Jay-Z], Kanye West, et al. "Otis." *Watch the Throne.* Roc-A-Fella, 2011. *Direct Lyrics.* DirectLyrics, 2012. Web. 8 May 2012.

Music video on the Web

Jay-Z, and Kanye West, perf. "Otis." *Watch the Throne.* Dir. Spike Jonze. Roc-A-Fella, 11 Aug. 2011. Music video. *YouTube.* Web. 8 May 2012.

Live performance

Jay-Z, and Kanye West, perf. "Otis." *Watch the Throne.* Watch the Throne Tour. Toyota Center, Houston. 5 Dec. 2011. Performance.

Live performance broadcast on television

Jay-Z, and Kanye West, perf. "Otis." *Watch the Throne. 2011 MTV Video Music Awards.* Nokia Theatre, Los Angeles. MTV. 28 Aug. 2011. Television.

Video on the Web of live performance

Jay-Z, and Kanye West, perf. "Otis (Live)." *Watch the Throne.* 2011 MTV Video Music Awards. Nokia Theatre, Los Angeles. *MTV.* Viacom, 28 Aug. 2011. Web. 9 May 2012.

"Mystery of Edwin Drood." By Charles Dickens. Dir. Diarmuid Lawrence. Adapt. Gwyneth Hughes. Perf. Matthew Rhys and Julia MacKenzie. *Masterpiece Theatre.* PBS. 16 Apr. 2012. *Masterpiece: The Mystery of Edwin Drood.* Web. 20 Apr. 2012.

69. Documenting across media The previous Key Points box shows nine different publication, performance, and broadcast sources for one song by rap artists Jay-Z and Kanye West, documented in MLA style. The sources include lyrics in print, online, on CD, on DVD, on LP

MLA Modern Language Association

record, and in an MP3 file and sung in a live performance and on videos. URLs are included for sources that may otherwise be difficult to find.

12k Sample listings: Other common sources

70. Interview (personal, published, broadcast, or online) Begin with the name of the person interviewed. For an interview that you conducted, include the type of interview (telephone, e-mail, personal [in person], etc.).

Earle, Steve. Telephone interview. 4 Apr. 2012.

For a published interview, give the name of the person interviewed and then the title (if any) in quotation marks. If there is no title, put the label *Interview* or *Interview by . . .* and the name of the interviewer. Then give the print publication information (see 12c, items 1–3, and 12d, item 10).

Parker, Dorothy. Interview by Marion Capron. *Writers at Work:* The Paris

Review *Interviews.* London: Secker and Warburg, 1958. 66-75. Print.

For a broadcast (television or radio) interview, provide information about the source and date of the interview (see 12i, item 60).

Howe, Marie. Interview by Terry Gross. *Fresh Air.* Natl. Public Radio. WGBH,

Boston, 20 Oct. 2011. Radio.

Spurlock, Morgan. Interview by Bruce Sylvester. *Troubadour.* WMBR,

Cambridge, 5 May 2011. Radio.

For a radio interview broadcast simultaneously on the Web or a radio or television interview archived on the Web, see 12j, item 68. For a podcast of an interview, see 12i, item 63.

For a transcript of a radio or television interview, see item 71 and Source Shot 7 on p. 222.

For a sound recording of an interview, see item 12i, item 61.

71. Transcript of a radio or television program To cite a transcript of a radio or television program, first give all of the program information (see 12i, item 60). Then give the medium of publication (*Print*). End the entry with the word *Transcript.*

Howe, Marie. Interview by Terry Gross. *Fresh Air.* Natl. Public Radio. WHYY,

n.p., 20 Oct. 2011. Print. Transcript.

Note that this entry lists WHYY, the original station on which the program was broadcast (as noted on the transcript), rather than the station on which you may have listened to it (see item 70).

(Continued)

> **SOURCE SHOT 7**

Listing a Transcript of a Television Interview in an Online Archive **MLA**

If you have listened to a radio interview or watched one on television, you may want to refer to a transcript of the program to quote or paraphrase material from the interview in your paper. Many transcripts of interviews and other programs are archived online and can be downloaded and printed. Look for the following information on the Web site to include in your citation.

❶ **Name of the person interviewed,** last name first

❷ The words *Interview by* and the **name of the interviewer** (in normal order)

❸ *Name of the television program* (in italics)

❹ **Name of the network of the original broadcast**

❺ **Date of the original broadcast of the program**

❻ *Web site where the transcript of program is archived* (in italics)

❼ **Publisher or sponsor of the Web site**

❽ **Date transcript was posted in the online archive**

❾ **Medium of publication** (Web)

❿ **Your date of access** (day month year)

⓫ End with the label **Transcript** and a period.

    ❶   ❷   ❸   ❹
Hillary Clinton. Interview by Barkha Dutt. *We the People* . NDTV,
       ❺   ❻   ❼
7 May 2012. *US Depart. of State.* Bureau of Public Affairs,
 ❽   ❾   ❿   ⓫
2012. Web. 9 Nov. 2012. Transcript.

To cite a transcript of a radio or television program accessed from an online archive, see item 68 and Source Shot 7.

72. Lecture, reading, speech, or address Give the author and title, if known. Also give the name of any organizing sponsor, the venue, the city, and the date. For the medium of delivery, include an appropriate label at the end.

Top of Web Page

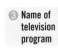
③ Name of television program

⑤ Original broadcast date

Bottom of Web Page

Singer, Peter. "Happiness and Ultimate Good." Graduate Council Lectures. Alumni House, U of California, Berkeley. 17 Apr. 2012. Lecture.

73. Letter (published or personal), e-mail, memo, or other personal communication Cite a personal letter by giving the name of the letter writer, the description *Letter to the author* (not in quotation marks), and the medium of publication—*MS* (*manuscript*) for a handwritten letter, *TS* (*typescript*) for a typed one.

Rogan, Helen. Letter to the author. 3 Feb. 2012. TS.

Cite a published letter in a collection as you would cite a work in an anthology. After the name of the author, include any title or number that the editor gives the letter and then the date of the letter. Follow with the inclusive page numbers, the book's publication information, and the medium of publication (*Print*).

Bishop, Elizabeth. "To Robert Lowell." 26 Nov. 1951. *One Art: Letters*. Ed.

Robert Giroux. New York: Farrar, 1994. 224-26. Print.

Cite an e-mail by listing the writer, the title of the message (from the subject line) in quotation marks, a phrase that names the recipient (*Message to the author*), the date, and the medium of delivery (*E-mail*).

Bernstein, Roberta. "Challenges." Message to the author. 12 Feb. 2012. E-mail.

Treat a memo similarly, putting any title in quotation marks and indicating the recipients (for example, *Memo to senior class officers*). End with the medium of delivery (*Memo*).

Follow the same format for any other type of personal communication, ending with the medium of delivery (for example, *Telephone call*).

74. Legal or historical document   For a court case, give the name of the case (with no italics or quotation marks) in the short form, listing the first plaintiff and defendant, the number of the case, the name of the court deciding the case, the date of the decision, and the medium of publication. End with your access date for a Web source. Use familiar abbreviations. (Note, however, that if you mention the case in the text of your paper, you should italicize the name: "Chief Justice Burger, in *Roe v. Wade,* noted that . . .".)

Roe v. Wade. No. 70-18. Supreme Ct. of the US. 22 Jan. 1973. Print.

To cite an act, give its Public Law (abbreviated as *Pub. L.*) number, its Statutes at Large volume and inclusive page numbers, the date it was enacted, and the medium of publication that you consulted.

USA Patriot Act. Pub. L. 107-56. 115 Stat. 272-402. 26 Oct. 2001. Web. 10 Apr. 2012.

Well-known historical documents (such as the U.S. Constitution) should not be included in your works-cited list (see 11b, item W).

75. Article on microform (microfilm and microfiche)   Some early newspaper and magazine articles still are available only on microfiche or microfilm, so you will need to use this medium for historical research; however, be aware that such collections may be incomplete and difficult to read and duplicate clearly.

To cite these sources that are neither in hard copy nor in electronic form, provide as much of the original print publication information as is available and follow with the medium of publication (*Microform*). Then add details about the microform—title of the source (in italics), volume number, year (in parentheses), and identifying numbers. *Newsbank* offers large collections of microfiche indexed by subject area. In the example that follows, *FTV* stands for *Film and Television*.

Bass, Alison. "Do Slasher Films Breed Real-Life Violence?" *Boston Globe* 19

 Dec. 1988: 33. Microform. *Newsbank:* FTV (1989): fiche 5, grids B2-4.

12l Bibliographical software

Your college may provide free access to bibliographical software that can help you compile and format citations and bibliographies in any documentation style. Follow your instructor's directions to see if you should ask a librarian about the availability of a program such as *EndNote* or *RefWorks* or explore these functions of free online software such as *Mendeley* and *Zotero*. With these programs, you enter details in specific fields, and the program then formats your book or journal citations into a bibliography according to MLA, APA, or another documentation style. Some will also transfer the bibliographical references for titles found during a literature search directly into the user's Web-based account (see 9d, 9f). However, whether you use such a program or do the formatting yourself, you still have to find—and type—the information necessary for citations not directly transferred. Such programs sometimes produce incorrect or incomplete citations, so you will still need to learn the specified formats and check any computer-generated entries to be sure that they are correctly styled and contain all of the required information.

13 Sample Paper 4: A Student's Research Paper, MLA Style

Here is Patti Suchan's research paper written for her first-year composition course at High Point University in North Carolina. For this essay, students were asked to develop an argument that presented a radical perspective, or "re-seeing," on the topic of globalization. The citations and the list of works cited are in the style recommended in the 2009 *MLA Handbook for Writers of Research Papers,* 7th edition.

Note: Annotations have been added here to point out features of her paper that you may find useful when you write your own research paper in MLA style. Blue annotations point out issues of content and organization. Red annotations point out MLA format issues.

½"

Suchan 1   Last name
and page
number

1"

Patti Suchan

1"
Dr. Kozma

ENG-1103-10

September 12, 2012

**Paper
double-
spaced
throughout**

Originality Died and Made Profit King

There was a time when the theater was known for

dramatics and creativity, but also for being an unstable and

unprofitable way to make a living. Only a few truly gifted people

could survive in such an industry, where freedom of expression

did not always achieve public resonance and equate to a regular

payday, or even an occasional paycheck. The renowned American

playwright Arthur Miller remarked, "The theater is so endlessly

fascinating because it's so accidental" ("Arthur Miller"), and

many believe that this is undoubtedly true. But those days of

**Establishing
argument as
chronological**

spontaneity and insecurity have been on the wane, unbeknownst

to the world's hoi polloi. Although they are often not included

in discussions about how globalization is changing the world,

the arts are actually an area that is leading the charge. Back in

the Elizabethan age William Shakespeare created a worldwide

theater phenomenon that has resulted in both positive and

negative repercussions in modern times. Thomas Friedman, a

journalist for the *New York Times*, notes in his book *The Lexus

and the Olive Tree* that the present era of globalization began in

1989, with the end of the Cold War (xvii). Jonathan Burston, a

**No author
named, short
form of Web
page title, no
page number**

**Author, his
credentials,
and source
named in
sentence**

**Page number
at end of
paraphrase**

1"

Suchan 2

scholar, also connects history and theater to argue that globally

driven changes to theater, and "cultural industries in general,"

began in the early 1980s ("Recombinant" 161). With the advent

of globalization, the destruction of the art form that is theater has

been almost completely actualized for the benefit of increased

profitability and the ruination of originality.

Thesis

Author with more than one work cited— shortened title in parentheses

Globalization is a difficult subject to define. There are

many different elements that together create the concept

of globalization. The coming together of cultures, ideas,

religions, and industries are some of the more essential pieces

of globalization. The most important aspect of globalization is

the maximizing of profits in a market that has a broader reach

than ever before, regardless of what that particular market may

be. Michael Moore wrote an article about American business

owners who would frequently "tell [him] that 'a company must

do whatever is necessary to create the biggest profit possible'"

(410). This ideology is not limited to major businesses in the

United States, though. It is a mindset that has spread around

the world and into atypical market sectors, such as theater, as

globalization has become prevalent.

Defining term so that audience can follow argument

Quotation in source quoted by student writer; word changed in brackets within quotation and page numbers in parentheses after quotation and before period

Sentence connects the writer's two main ideas: globalization and the theater.

In the history of theater, going as far back as the origins and

as recently as about a half century ago, productions of shows were

vastly different from others done previously. The script of the show

would be the same, but since the actors would be different, the

Modern Language Association MLA

Suchan 3

whole show would have a different essence. The sets, costumes, and props could all be different as well, but what would really make the critical difference was the new life that each actor's interpretation breathed into a character. Since this was how the theater worked for such a long period of time, theater became irrevocably known as a creative art form. One of the most important and formative time periods for theater was the Elizabethan age of William Shakespeare. His legacy has been a blessing and a curse to theater worldwide. (See fig. 1.)

Shakespeare greatly contributed to the prominence of theater in not just English speaking countries but around the globe, which has been very beneficial to the theater community. The popularity becomes a problem when many new shows are just repetitions of common themes. Shakespeare's works have been adapted into many modern works, such as *West Side Story* and *Kiss Me, Kate,* but even his "original" works are not thought to be original ideas. *The Taming of the Shrew*, known as a tale of "achieving rapid dominance" (Fhloinn 188), is based on a common story of the time. Jan Harald Brunvand believes that "Shakespeare's source for the taming plot was most likely an oral text of the folklore" (qtd. in Fhloinn 190), but it has also been suggested that the "story originated in the east" (Fhloinn 191). The possible origin comes from the famous fifth century BC Chinese strategist and philosopher, Sun Tzu, by way of Chinese historian Sima Qian. Sun

Indirect source: cites work in which another author is quoted

Suchan 4

The Bridgeman Art Library/Getty Images

Fig. 1. The First Globe Theatre, where many of Shakespeare's plays were performed, from Visscher's View of London (1616); rpt. in Joseph Quincy Adams, *Shakespearean Playhouses: A History of English Theatres from the Beginnings to the Restoration* (Gloucester, MA: Peter Smith, 1960; print; 254). *Project Gutenberg eBook*. Web. 6 Apr. 2012.

Suchan 5

Tzu, author of *The Art of War*, is said to have performed acts of violence to "achieve rapid dominance," which, in turn, inspired such a tale (Fhloinn 192). Shakespeare's works themselves can therefore be said to represent globalization long before globalization was even acknowledged, which helped with their popularity, but which has also created world-renowned clichés. With the continued success of all things Shakespearean, though, the clichés have been oft-repeated, which is unsurprising. When profit is king, a popular storyline is the surest route to success.

There are new shows created every year that are re-creations of already well-liked stories. International blockbusters are frequently being brought to the stage, especially since the Disney Company achieved such wide success with the productions of *Beauty and the Beast* and *The Lion King*. Broadway producers are "choosing bankable titles more and more regularly in order to reduce risk" because, even if the show does poorly, it will attract enough attention to run for an adequate period of time and, more importantly, boost global sales of related products (Burston, "Recombinant" 166). *Shrek the Musical* is a fairly recent adaptation that joined the lineup on the Great White Way (fig. 2). Many negative critiques of the show, by both experts and audience members, revolved around the fact that the storyline of the show was exactly the same as that of the movie. While this is true, it is also true for the Disney musicals, in which no fault is generally found.

Clear transition from "popular storylines" to "re-creations of well-liked stories." Writer is forming an evidence chain.

Quotation from source and paraphrase both used in sentence

Author's name and short form of work's title (separated by comma) when two works by same author cited

Blue = content issues, **Red = format issues**

Suchan 6

Fig. 2. Publicity photograph from *Shrek the Musical*. By David Lindsay-Abaire. Dir. Jason Moore and Rob Ashford. 2012 Touring Performance.

The difference, I believe, comes from the musical nature of the movie on which a show is based, which Disney has and Dreamworks does not. Regardless, *Shrek the Musical* characters are portrayed in a manner similar to their counterparts in the movie. This is especially surprising since Daniel Breaker, the actor playing Donkey, and possibly the character that was most similar

Suchan 7

between the two mediums, said in an interview that he had

Ellipsis points indicate part of quoted sentence omitted

"never seen the movies . . . and didn't want to [because he] didn't

Substituted words in brackets within quotation

want to be lost in trying to re-create Eddie Murphy's role." Is his

portrayal so similar to that of Eddie Murphy because the part is

Web source, no page number for quotation

written in such a way as to lend itself to such an interpretation,

or is it that the director of the show was guiding the actor into

making the character the same as is found in the movie? Either

way, the actor was not organically creating the character.

Someone else, either the writer or the director, was pushing

him to act in such a way, and it wasn't of his own volition. This

repetition of characters from silver screen to stage has become

a popular trend, possibly in part because foreign audiences who

have seen the movie can enjoy the show despite the language

barrier, since they already know the storyline.

Another type of show, those that do not have storylines

that are popular from films, is becoming widely famous for

another reason: they are being designed for worldwide success.

Jonathan Burston, a professor in the Department of Information

Establishing author's credentials is important to demonstrate his ethos and the writer's ethos.

and Media Studies at the University of Western Ontario who

specializes in music, media, globalization, and "social uses

of spectacle in contemporary life," wrote an article entitled

"Recombinant Broadway" that discusses the changes that have

occurred in the field of theater, particularly the changing origins

of shows and the methods in which these shows are

Blue = content issues, **Red = format issues**

Suchan 8

reproduced on a global scale ("Faculty Member"). Starting in the early 1980s, when the theater industry was struggling, Andrew Lloyd Webber and Cameron Mackintosh discovered a way to take the theater industry from a risky endeavor and make it into a largely profitable business. Their new musical *Cats* had become a smashing success on Broadway in London's West End and on tours of both North America and Europe, but they realized that the demand to see the show was greater than what they were meeting. They decided to create permanent productions in "emerging major markets like Hamburg, Tokyo, and Toronto" (Burston, "Recombinant" 161) for as long as they were attracting a sufficient audience. The decisive factor about these productions that changed theater forever is that "Lloyd Webber and Mackintosh also concluded that each show should look, feel, and sound *exactly* like the originating production...if the producers were to maximize the new levels of profitability" (Burston, "Recombinant" 161). Thus, the megamusical, designed for mega-profits by stifling originality, was born.

Today, productions of shows that are running in different parts of the world are exactly the same, "based upon a *template* of an original production whose cast and creative team have already completed all the exciting collaborative work of turning written page into breathing performance" (Burston, "Recombinant" 166). The actors and musicians now have greater

Quotation
integrated
into writer's
sentence

Ellipsis
points signal
part of
quoted
material
omitted

Modern Language Association **MLA**

First source cited locates the direct quotation. Sources following provide additional evidence for persistence of these ideas.

job security, but they complain about having to work "McTheater jobs," where they are more "acting machines" and less artists (Burston, "Recombinant" 162; also Burston, "Spectacle"; Russell). Have the global audiences' expectations become such that actors can compare their profession to that of a fast-food worker? Sadly, this has become a trending phenomenon in the theater worldwide.

Academic writing can use the first-person "I," depending on audience expectation.

    I know from experience that people going to a show for a repeat viewing expect the performance to be identical to the first time that they went. When I saw the show *Wicked* for the first time, I was enraptured by the characters and the story, and I was blown away by the sincerity of the actress playing the main character, Elphaba. When I saw *Wicked* for the fifth time, I did not enjoy the performance as much. The new leading actress was portraying the character of Elphaba with slightly different emotional motives than I was used to, and these emotions did not fit in with the version of the story, and the character within it, that I had seen four times previously. A person seeing the show for the first time would not have noticed the nuances, but for me the performance wasn't magical. This is not to say that free expression in the theater is a bad thing and that it is good that globalization is making it rare. The point of this anecdote is to illustrate that in order for this actress to make the show feel like her own, she had to change the traits of her character. Originality

Writer builds her credibility as a theater goer.

Writer's personal experience as primary-source evidence, supported by secondary sources

Blue = content issues, **Red = format issues**

Suchan 10

in the theater is getting so rare that it takes theater lovers by surprise.

There is some originality left in the theater, and when it is witnessed it is truly wonderful. Every year there are shows created that are brilliantly pure and unique, but they often go unnoticed. These shows are either not designed for widespread public resonance, or they are simply overshadowed by the unoriginal names lighting up marquees around the world. One such show is *Next to Normal*, which is a mental whirlwind of a show, the likes of which has never been experienced on Broadway before, but it did not achieve lasting success because it did not fit into the category of "megamusical." Even a Pulitzer Prize could not save this theatrical masterpiece.

There are also shows that are written in such a way as to inspire creativity, even though they are not new. *Godspell* is an example of a show that exemplifies the joy that is live theater. I was the stage manager when my high school performed this show. The script contains the lines and songs, but ultimately it is up to the cast to decide what the acting in the show will be like. Every parable is performed in a new way by the cast members, who even use their own names on stage. *Godspell* recently reopened on Broadway, and I had the privilege to attend one of the preview showings. The show had all the same stories and songs as what we had performed at school, but it was a

Having established a pattern of re-creation in the theater, the writer moves to offer examples of shows that seek to defy this trend.

Blue = content issues, **Red = format issues**

Modern Language Association **MLA**

Suchan 11

completely different experience. It was incredible to experience the magic that a small group of people can create on a stage. It was wonderful to see the personalities of the characters and slightly different interpretations of the plot, but this show is a rare exception when it ought to be, and used to be, the rule. Broadway used to be about new drama, but now "for every daring producer risking an *In the Heights* there are two *Legally Blondes* being mounted by corporate suits. All these adaptations are crowding out the authentically *Broadway* Broadway" (Burston, "Recombinant" 166). The Broadway of old is slowly dying to make way for the profitable and unoriginal reproductions that globalization demands.

The magic of theater still exists, but the magic is often not the invention of the actors performing. The story they are acting out is clichéd and the characters are hackneyed. Shakespeare helped the theater become a globally recognized art form and kept it prevalent for many years, but he also damaged theater by starting the trend of reusing ideas to create new shows. The business of Broadway, and its counterparts worldwide, is booming for both the producers and the actors, with profits that were unimaginable several decades ago. Nevertheless, many actors resist the death of creativity and try to keep the originality of the theater alive in our new, globalized world.

Writer emphasizes that this kind of show is an exception, further reinforcing her claim.

Narrow summary sentence restates the writer's claim that originality is dead.

Blue = content issues, **Red = format issues**

Suchan 12

Works Cited

"Arthur Miller Quotes." *BrainyQuote*. BookRags Media Network, 2011. Web. 2 Dec. 2011.

> No author named; entry begins with Web page title

Breaker, Daniel. "Daniel Breaker on Fatherhood, Donkey-hood (in *Shrek*), and His Strange New Movie." Interview by Melissa Rose Bernardo. *Broadway.com*. Key Brand Entertainment, 27 July 2009. Web. 13 Nov. 2011.

> Interview posted on Web site; no print version

Burston, Jonathan. "Recombinant Broadway." *Continuum: Journal of Media and Cultural Studies* 23.2 (2009): 159-69. *Academic Search Premier*. Web. 14 Nov. 2011.

> Two works by same author cited; entries listed by author and then alphabetically by title.

> Three hyphens used instead of author's name for second work by same author.

----. "Spectacle, Synergy, and Megamusicals: The Global-Industrialisation of Live-Theatrical Production." *Media Organisations in Society*. Ed. James Curran. London: Arnold, 2000. 69-81. Print.

> Print scholarly journal article accessed in online database

> Original British English spelling of title maintained

> Editor of book named after title.

"Faculty Member Profile: Jonathan Burston." *Faculty of Information and Media Studies at the University of Western Ontario*. U of Western Ontario, 2010. Web. 30 Nov. 2011.

> Sponsor of Web site, date site last updated, medium of publication (Web), date student writer accessed site

Fhloinn, Bairbre Ní. "From Medieval Literature to Missiles: Aspects of ATU 901 in the Twenty-First Century." *Fabula* 51.3/4 (2010): 187-200. *Academic Search Premier*. Web. 14 Nov. 2011.

Friedman, Thomas L. *The Lexus and the Olive Tree*. New York: Anchor-Doubleday, 1999. Print.

> Place of publication: Publisher and imprint, year of publication, medium of publication (Print)

Blue = content issues, **Red = format issues**

Modern Language Association MLA

Moore, Michael. "Why Doesn't GM Sell Crack?" *The Composition of Everyday Life: A Guide to Writing.* Ed. John Mauk and John Metz. 3rd ed. Boston: Cengage, 2010. 410-11. Print.

Russell, Susan. "The Performance of Discipline on Broadway." *Studies in Musical Theatre* 1.1 (2007): 97-108. Print.

Page range for essay in anthology

Journal title, no comma, volume and issue numbers separated by period

4

APA, CSE, and *Chicago* Documentation

CITE
APA

4 APA, CSE, and *Chicago* Documentation

20 Sample Paper 7: Student's Research Paper, *Chicago*
Style 325

APA AT-A-GLANCE: INDEX OF APA STYLE FEATURES

15d Sample APA listings: Print and online books, parts of books, and reference
     books 268

15e Sample APA listings: Reports and presentations—print, online, and live 274

15f Sample APA listings: Other online sources 276

American Psychological Association

APA

16   Sample Paper 5: A Student's Research Paper, APA Style 282

Part 4 covers documentation styles other than the MLA system. Chapters 14 and 15 focus on the style recommended for the social sciences and some sciences by the *Publication Manual of the American Psychological Association*, 6th edition (Washington, DC: Amer. Psychological Assn., 2010), and on the APA Web site. A student's paper written in APA style is in chapter 16. Chapter 17 describes the citation-sequence and the citation-name styles, two of three documentation styles recommended for all natural and applied sciences by the Council of Science Editors (CSE) in *Scientific Style and Format: The CSE Manual for Authors, Editors, and Publishers*, 7th edition (Reston, VA: Council of Science Eds., 2006). Chapter 18 shows an excerpt from a student's CSE research paper in the citation-sequence style. Chapter 19 illustrates the endnote and footnote style and discusses the bibliography format recommended in *The Chicago Manual of Style*, 16th edition (Chicago: U of Chicago P, 2010), for writing in the humanities, a style sometimes used as an alternative to MLA style. Chapter 20 presents a student's paper with endnotes and bibliography in *Chicago* style. The order of categories in which the citation examples for each style are discussed follows the order of categories in its respective style manual.

14 Citing Sources in Your Paper, APA Style

APA style for documenting and formatting publications, which is described in the *Publication Manual of the American Psychological Association,* 6th edition (2010), is used in the social sciences—psychology, sociology, anthropology, education, management, business, economics, criminal justice, ethnic studies, women's and gender studies, and political science—as well as in geography, communications, linguistics, nursing, allied health, and other medical disciplines. In these fields new research results in new theories and interpretations of materials that update and replace earlier ones. Therefore, it is essential for readers to know the publication date of a source when it is introduced so that they can place the information in the continuum of research or views on an issue necessary to understand the writer's analysis or argument.

In order to let the reader know when the source's research or theories were presented, APA uses an author-date system. Each time the source is mentioned, the date is given either immediately after the author's name in the text or with the author's name in parentheses (along with any page number) after quoted or paraphrased material. The reader can then refer to an alphabetical list of sources, the References, at the end of the paper for full source information. The prominent placement and repetition of the date in each source citation underscores the need for readers to be aware of the timeliness and relevance of the source's information as they follow the author's presentation.

APA style uses the past or past perfect verb tenses for introducing quoted material: "Smith (2012) reported," "Previous studies have demonstrated." It only uses the present tense when discussing results ("This study illustrates") or generally accepted facts ("Scientists acknowledge"). The passive voice is often used since the results of a study or experiment are important whereas the names of the lab assistants who conducted it, for example, are not ("An elevated blood pressure reading was noted for the majority of subjects").

14a Basic features of APA style

KEY POINTS
How to Cite and List Sources in APA Style

1. **In the text of your paper,** include at least two pieces of information each time you cite a source:
   - the last name(s) of the author (or authors) or first words of the title if no author's name is available

- the year of publication or posting online

Also give the page number(s) (using the abbreviation *p.* or *pp.*) for a quotation, summary, or paraphrase.

2. **At the end of your paper**, on a new numbered page, include a list with the title *References* (centered and not in italics or quotation marks). The list should be double-spaced and arranged alphabetically by authors' last names, followed by the initials of first and the other names (also last name first and with initials), the date in parentheses, and other bibliographical information. See sections 15c–15h for fifty-six sample entries.

Illustrations of APA Style's Basic Features

Citation in Text	Entry in List of References
Print journal article, author's name in text introduces comment [Page number included for quotation]	
In their study Giordano and Giordano (2011) found that despite their profession's concerns about privacy and security, "an overwhelming majority of health students prefer to get their information online" (p. 80).	Giordano, C., & Giordano, C. (2011). Health professions students' use of social media. *Journal of Allied Health, 40*(2), 78–81.
Print journal article, citation in parentheses [Page number included for quotation]	
Although such tools may be useful for recruiting and informing students, "universities may be hesitant to adopt social media due to fear of privacy, security, and inability to measure success and usage with great precision" (Giordano & Giordano, 2011, p. 80).	Giordano, C., & Giordano, C. (2011). Health professions students' use of social media. *Journal of Allied Health, 40*(2), 78–81.

Citation in Text	Entry in List of References

Print book, author and year in your text
[Page number included for quotation]

According to Charles Emmerson (2010), "as the natural environment of the north begins to change out of all recognition, the idea of the Arctic as an impenetrable physical barrier will be overturned" (p. 158).

Emmerson, C. (2010). *The future history of the Arctic.* New York, NY: Public Affairs Press.

Article on a Web site, author paraphrased
[no page or paragraph numbers for online source]

Amanda Enayati (2012) speculates that people may not want to admit that in uncertain times they are biased against creative ideas and instead prefer known procedures and solutions.

Enayati, A. (2012). Is there a bias against creativity? Retrieved from http://www.cnn.com/2012/03/28/health/enayati-uncertainty/index.html?hpt=he_bn2

Journal article with digital object identifier (DOI) in an online database, parenthetical citation

Research has shown that cross-cultural identification does not begin before 8 years of age (Sousa, Neto, & Mullet, 2005).

[See the Key Points box in 15c, p. 258, for more on DOIs, and see 15a for when to include an issue number.]

Sousa, R. M., Neto, F., & Mullet, E. (2005). Can music change ethnic attitudes among children? *Psychology of Music, 33*(3), 304–316. doi:10.1177/0305735605053735

14b How to cite sources (author/date) in your paper

CITING AN AUTHOR OR AUTHORS (APA)

A. Author quoted and named in your text   If you mention the author's name in your own text, include the year in parentheses directly after the author's name. Put any page number in parentheses after a quotation or paraphrase; end with a period.

> author   year
> Martinot (2010) maintains that whenever society seems to be minimizing
>
> racism, "it comes back wearing different language, speaking an up-to-date
>
> lingo, while creating more of the 'same old' effects" (p. 2).

See 15d, item 17, and Source Shot 11 for this work in a reference list.

B. Author cited in parentheses   If you do not name the author in your own text (perhaps because you have referred to the author previously), include both the name and the year, separated by a comma, in parentheses.

> We can only comprehend the full impact of infectious diseases by viewing
>
> them in the contexts of culture and history (Reagan, 2010).
> author   comma   year

C. Author quoted or paraphrased   If you use a direct quotation or a paraphrase, follow it with parentheses containing the author's name and the date (if not already given in the text, as in item A) and the abbreviation *p.* or *pp.*, a space, and the page number(s). Use commas to separate items within the parentheses, and end the sentence with a period.

> It is important to note that "naming a disease is an essential component
>
> of diagnosis and treatment" (Reagan, 2010, p. 25).
> comma   comma   page number

D. A long (block) quotation   If you quote more than forty words of prose, do not enclose the quotation in quotation marks. Start the quotation on a new line, and indent the whole quotation half an inch from the left margin. If there are other paragraphs within the block quotation, indent the first line of each paragraph an additional half inch. Double-space the quotation. Any necessary parenthetical citation should come after the final period of the quotation. See 10c for more information on quoting long passages.

E. A work with more than one author

Two authors For a work by two authors, name both in the order in which their names appear on the work and give the year of publication every time that the authors are cited in your text. Use the word *and* between the names for a reference made in your text. Within parentheses, use an ampersand (&) between the names in place of *and*.

> the word *and* in your text
>
> Kanazawa and Still (2000) in their analysis of a large set of data show that the statistical likelihood of being divorced increases if one is male and a secondary school teacher or college professor.
>
> Analysis of a large set of data shows that the statistical likelihood of being divorced increases if one is male and a secondary school teacher or college professor (Kanazawa & Still, 2000).
>
> ampersand in parentheses

See 15c, item 1, for a work by two authors in a reference list.

Three to five authors Identify all authors the first time you mention the work in either your running text or in a parenthetical citation.

> Baumol, Litan, and Schramm (2007) posit the existence of several types of capitalist economies around the world.

In subsequent in-text or parenthetical citations, use the last name of the first author and *et al.* (*et alii*—Latin for "and others") in place of the other names.

> In the United States, the dominant type of capitalism, called "entrepreneurial capitalism," shows significant differences from the capitalism in Japan and Europe, which tends to avoid "radical entrepreneurship" (Baumol et al., 2007, p. viii).

See 15d, item 18, for this work in a list of references.

Six or more authors Cite the name of only the first author followed by *et al.* for all citations in your text and for all parenthetical citations. However, in your reference list include the names of up to seven authors. For eight or more authors, list the first six and use ellipsis dots to indicate additional authors; end with the name of the last author. See 15c, item 3 for a reference list entry for more than seven authors.

F. More than one work within same parentheses
List the sources by author in alphabetical order as they appear in the list of references

APA American Psychological Association

(including those that shorten to *et al.*), separated by semicolons. List two or more works by the same author chronologically (earliest source first); only give the author's name once. See item G for citing multiple works by the same author published in the same year.

> Criticisms of large-scale educational testing are anything but new. They have been appearing repeatedly for many years (Crouse & Trusheim, 1988; Nairn, 1978, 1980; Perelman, 2007; Raimes, 1990a, 1990b; Sacks, 2003).

G. Author with more than one work published in the same year　In a parenthetical reference, after the author's name identify each work with a lowercase letter after the year: (Schell, 2007a, 2007b). The letters are assigned in the reference list, where the works are arranged alphabetically by their titles after the author's name and the year (repeated in each entry). Separate the dates with commas. See 15b for how to order such entries in the list of references.

H. Author of work in an edited anthology　In your text, refer to the author of the work, not to the editor of the anthology (however, include information about the anthology in your list of references). The essay in the following example is in an anthology of writing about identifying and treating psychiatric problems in general medical environments.

> Geoffrey Lloyd (2007) notes that *post-traumatic stress disorder* (PTSD) is usually defined as "a delayed and/or protracted response to a stressful event or situation of a threatening or catastrophic nature" (p. 73).

In the reference list entry, also include details about the anthology, including its editors (see 15d, item 23, to see how to cite this source).

I. Author's work cited in another source (secondary source)　APA advises you to quote primary sources whenever possible. If you do use a secondary source, in your text sentence name the author whom you are quoting. After the quoted or paraphrased material, put in parentheses the words *as cited in*, the name of author of the work in which you found the material (the secondary source), the year, and the page number. List that secondary source in your list of references. In the following example, *Martinot* will appear in the list of references with details of the source; *Goldberg* will not.

> David Goldberg calls this phenomenon the "inherently homogenizing logic of institutions" (as cited in Martinot, 2010, p. 59).

J. Entire work or an idea in a work   Use only an author and the year to refer to a complete work. For a paraphrase or a comment on a specific idea, a page number is not required but is recommended.

> Leslie Reagan (2010) recounts the 1960s German measles epidemic to illustrate the extent of society's fear of disability—a fear that is still evident today.

K. Two authors with the same last name   Include the authors' initials, even if the publication dates of their works differ, in all citations.

> F. Smith (2011) first described a writer as playing the two competitive roles of author and secretary.

For the order of entries of such works in the list of references, see 15b.

L. Specific part of a source   After listing the author and year within parentheses, cite any specific relevant part of the source such as page number, chapter, section, table, or figure. Abbreviate *page* or *pages* (*p.* or *pp.*) but not *Chapter* (capitalizing the first letter). For citing electronic sources that do not have page numbers, see item P on p. 251.

> (Cutler, 2011, Introduction)

> (Robinson, 2012, Chapter 5)

M. Multivolume work   In your citation, give the publication date of the volume you are citing: (Einstein, 1987). If you refer to more than one volume, give inclusive dates for all the volumes you cite: (Einstein, 1998–2004). See 15d, item 28, for how to list this work in your reference list.

CITING A WORK WITH NO INDIVIDUAL AUTHOR NAMED (APA)

N. No author named   If a print or Web source has no named individual or organization as author, use the first few words of the title in your text (capitalizing major words). Within the body of the paper (including parenthetical citations), put quotation marks around the title of an article, chapter, or Web page; italicize the title of a book, report, or brochure.

> Many Hurricane Katrina survivors were located to trailers whose materials caused health problems from breathing disorders to cancer (*World Almanac*, 2009, p. 55).

Narcolepsy is defined as "a disabling sleep disorder that mixes the nervous system's messages about when to sleep and when to be awake" ("Narcolepsy," 2011).

See 15d, item 29, and 15f, item 42, for how to list these sources.

O. Work by a corporation, association, government agency, study group, or organization   If the first citation is an in-text reference, use the organization's full name and immediately following put in parentheses the abbreviation, a comma, and the year; in subsequent in-text references, just use the abbreviation and the year.

first text mention: full name with abbreviation and year in parentheses

In its annual survey of college costs, the College Board (CB, 2011) gives examples of rapid increases. In 4-year colleges, in particular, tuition and fees increased 35% in just five years.

In the first parenthetical citation give the organization's full name, the abbreviation in brackets, a comma, and the year. In subsequent parenthetical citations, just give the abbreviation and year.

In 4-year colleges, tuition and fees increased 35% in just five years (College Board [CB], 2011).

first parenthetical citation: full name, abbreviation in brackets, comma, year

Section 15d, item 30, shows how to list this work.

CITING ONLINE VISUAL, MULTIMEDIA, AND MISCELLANEOUS SOURCES (APA)

P. Internet source

Web page or article   Give the author's name, if it is available, or a short form of the title, followed by the year of electronic publication or update. In your text, put titles of Web pages in quotation marks as you would an article title. Use *n.d.* if no date is given. Give any page numbers (from the PDF, if available in portable document format, which is used for photographed print works available online) or paragraph numbers that you see on the screen (using the abbreviation *para.*). For a section of text you quote, paraphrase, or comment on in a source with no page or paragraph numbers visible on the screen, give any available section heading or a shortened title, and indicate the paragraph within the section (in this case you would determine the paragraph's number): (Conclusion section, para. 2).

Entire Web site   When citing an entire Web site rather than a specific document or page on the site, only name the Web site in your text (not in italics) and give the Web address (URL) in parentheses after the cited material. Do not list the Web site in your reference list.

> The Arthritis Foundation website contains much valuable information about treatments for the disease (http://www.arthritis.org).

E-mail messages   Be wary of citing e-mail messages (personal, bulletin board, discussion list, or Usenet group) because they are not peer-reviewed or easily retrievable. If you need to refer to an e-mail message, cite from an archived list whenever possible (see the example in 15f, item 44); otherwise, cite the message in your text as a personal communication (see item R), but do not include it in your list of references.

Q. Visual, multimedia, or nonprint source   For a film, television or radio broadcast, podcast, MP3 file, video recording, live performance, map, photo, artwork, or other static object or nonprint source, include in your citation the name of the originator or main contributor (such as the creator, writer, narrator, director, performer, artist, or producer), along with the year of production.

> An Al Jazeera video highlights the plight of the African rhino (Phillips, 2010).

R. Personal communication (telephone conversation, unarchived letter, unpublished interview, e-mail, or unarchived electronic discussion group)   Cite only sources that have scholarly content. Mention these sources only in your paper with the label *personal communication* and the date in parentheses; do not include them in your list of references. Give the last name and initial(s) of the author of the communication and the complete date of posting, publication, or occurrence.

> According to V. Sand, former executive director of the Atwater Kent Museum of Philadelphia, "Museums engage our spirit, help us understand the natural world, and frame our identities" (personal communication, February 7, 2012).

For including archived sources in the list of references, see 15f, item 44.

S. A classical or religious work   If the date of publication of a classical work is not known, cite the year of translation (preceded by *trans.*) or the year of the version you used (followed by *version*): (Plato, trans. 1965).

You do not need a reference list entry for major classical works such as ancient Roman and Greek works or religious works such as the Bible or the Qu'ran. Parts of these works are numbered similarly in all editions, so just give information about book, chapter, verse, and line numbers in your text, and identify the version you used in your first citation: Gen. 35: 1–4 (Revised Standard Version).

14c Notes, tables, and figures (APA)

Content notes   In APA style, you can use content notes to amplify or supplement information in your text. For example, you might want to indicate where additional material can be found online. Number notes consecutively throughout the paper with superscript Arabic numerals. Footnotes should be double-spaced and placed at the bottom of the page where the material is discussed. Alternately, you can attach a separate page containing your numbered notes after the list of references and title it *Footnotes* (centered). Use notes sparingly and only if they are essential to your analysis; include all important information in your text, not in footnotes.

Tables and figures   APA style for manuscripts submitted for publication asks that all tables and figures be placed on separate pages at the end of the paper, after the references and any notes. However, college instructors may prefer that you insert tables and figures within your paper, as shown on pages 282–292 in the sample research paper in chapter 16. Follow your instructor's directions about placement of tables and figures.

Number all tables and figures consecutively with labels containing Arabic numbers (Table 1, *Figure 2*) in the order in which they appear in your paper. If you include them within the paper, place them close to their discussion in the text.

For tables, include a label (Table 1), followed by a brief title in italics (*Increases in Student Enrollment 2000–2010*) and any explanatory information, such as source information (detailed in "Citing copyrighted material," below).

For graphs, charts, maps, diagrams, drawings, photographs, or other visual elements known as *figures,* place a caption below the visual. Begin with the numbered label (*Figure 1*), in italics and followed by a period. Then, on the same line, give a brief description (not in italics) of the figure that functions as its title; end with a period. If you did not create the figure yourself, follow with any source information (beginning with the word *From,* as in the sample student paper figure captions in Chapter 16 on pp. 289–290).

Citing copyrighted material When you reproduce a copyrighted table or figure in your paper, you must give complete source details in a specific format in your table notes or figure caption (see examples on pp. 289–290). Notice that this format differs from the one for a citation in a reference list. You can find the copyright information under the original table or figure in your source. If you want to publish your paper or post it online using copyrighted material, you will have to obtain written permission to use it and will have to add these words after the copyright information: *Reprinted* [or *Adapted*] *with permission.*

14d Sections and their headings (APA)

APA-style papers begin with a separate title page; the Abstract and References are also on separate pages, and their titles are centered but not boldfaced. Major headings within the main text, such as Review of the Literature, Experiment, Results, or Conclusion, should be centered and boldfaced. The next level of subheading should be boldfaced and flush left. A third level should be bold, indented to begin a new paragraph, and followed by a period. See chapter 16 for a student's research paper in APA style.

15 APA List of References

15a How to set up an APA list of references

The sixth edition of the APA *Publication Manual* (2010) and the association's Web site <http://www.apastyle.org> provide guidelines for submitting professional papers for publication, and many instructors ask students to follow those guidelines to prepare them for advanced work. The following section explains and illustrates APA guidelines for reference list entries. The APA Web site also provides additional citation examples, periodic updates, and tips. Check with your instructor, however, for any specific course requirements for preparation of the paper and the reference list.

KEY POINTS
Guidelines for the APA List of References

- **What to list** List only the works you cited (quoted, summarized, paraphrased, or commented on) in the text of your paper, not every source you examined.

- **Format** Start the list on a new numbered page after the last page of the text of your paper. Center the heading *References,* without quotation marks; not boldfaced, underlined, or italicized; and not followed by a period. Double-space throughout the list, with no additional space between entries.

- **Indentation** Use hanging indents. Begin the first line of each entry at the left margin; indent subsequent lines one-half inch.

- **How to list authors and works** List the works alphabetically by the last names of primary authors or by the name of a corporation or organization that acts as the author. Do not number the entries. Begin each entry with the first author's name, last name first, followed by an initial or initials. Give any additional authors' names after the first in the same inverted form, separated by commas (see 15b and 15c, item 3, for more than seven authors). Connect the last two names with an ampersand (&) instead of the word *and.* List works with no author by title, alphabetized by the first main word.

- **Date** Put the year in parentheses after the authors' names; follow with a period. For magazines, newspapers, and newsletters, also add the month and day (if available) after a comma; do not abbreviate the names of the months: (2012, January 8).

- **Periods** Use a period and one space to separate the main parts of each entry.

- **Titles and capitals** In titles of books, reports, articles, Web documents, and Web pages, capitalize *only* the first word of the title and of any subtitle and any proper nouns or adjectives. For journals, magazines, newspapers, and newsletters, give the periodical title in full, using uppercase and lowercase letters.

- **Titles and italics** Italicize the titles of books, reports, and documents, but do not italicize or use quotation marks around the titles of articles, chapters, or Web pages (however, if the title quotes certain words, as in 15c, item 5, put quotation marks around them). Italicize the titles of newspapers (including the word *The*), newsletters,

(Continued)

(Continued)

journals, and magazines. Identify a specific format in square brackets immediately after the title, followed by a period. Do not italicize the format, and capitalize only the first word: [Brochure], [Letter to the editor], [Editorial], [Audio file].

- **Volume and issue numbers** For journals and magazines, also italicize the comma following the title and the volume number (not preceded by *Vol.*)—but not the issue number contained next in parentheses (with no space between volume and issue numbers): *Wired, 17*(2). For more information on volume and issue numbers, see 15c, item 1.

- **Page numbers** Give inclusive page numbers for print and PDF articles (portable document format, which is used for photographed print works available online) and for sections of books, repeating all digits and separating the numbers with an en dash: 251–259. Use the abbreviation *p.* or *pp.* only for newspaper articles and sections of books (such as chapters or anthologized short works).

- **Online sources** Give as much information as you would for a print source, with the addition of a DOI or URL to enable your readers to find the same source. Use a DOI (digital object identifier)—a permanent identification number that enables easy retrieval—rather than a URL if one is available. See the Key Points box on page 258 for more information on DOIs and URLs. Split a DOI or URL across lines only before a punctuation mark such as a period or a slash (except for the double slash that follows *http:*). Do not underline the URL as a hyperlink unless you are posting the paper online, and do not put a period after a DOI or URL, which will be the last item in the entry. Provide page numbers only for documents accessed as PDF files. Instead, use names of sections for articles written for online use (in HTML): Introduction. See 15f for more on listing online sources.

15b How to list authors in the APA reference list

Name of author(s) Put the last name first, followed by a comma and then the initials.

Gould, S. J.

Reverse the names of all authors listed, except the editors of an anthology or a reference work, and separate them with commas. Use an ampersand (&),

not the word *and*, before the last author's name (15c, item 2). For eight or more authors, give the reversed names of the first six, then use three ellipsis dots and add the name of the last author (as in the example in 15c, item 3).

Alphabetical order   Alphabetize letter by letter. Treat *Mac* and *Mc* literally, by letter.

MacKay, M.	D'Agostino, S.
McCarthy, T.	De Cesare, P.
McKay, K.	DeCurtis, A.

A shorter name precedes a longer name beginning with the same letters, whatever the first initial: *Black, T.* precedes *Blackman, R.*

For a work with no known author, list by the first word in the title other than *A, An,* or *The.* Alphabetize numerals according to their spelling: 5 (*Five*) precedes 2 (*Two*).

Organization or group as author   If the author is an organization, corporation, agency, group, or institution, give its official name, alphabetized by the first important word (see 15d, item 30). Use complete names, not abbreviations.

No author named   If no author or group is named, alphabetize by the first main word of the title (15d, item 29).

Several works by the same author   List the author's name in each entry. Arrange entries chronologically by year of publication from past to present. Entries published in the same year should be arranged alphabetically by title and distinguished with lowercase letters after the date (*a, b,* and so on). Note that entries for one author precede entries listing the same author with coauthors.

> Goleman, D. (1996a, July 16). Forget money; nothing can buy happiness, some researchers say. *The New York Times,* p. C1.

> Goleman, D. (1996b). *Vital lies, simple truths.* New York, NY: Simon & Schuster.

> Goleman, D. (2007). *Social intelligence: The new science of social relationships.* New York, NY: Bantam.

> Goleman, D., Boyatzis, R. E., & McKee, A. (2004). *Primal leadership: Learning to lead with emotional intelligence.* Cambridge, MA: Harvard Business School Press.

Authors with the same last name   List alphabetically by first initial: Smith, A. precedes Smith, F.

American Psychological Association **APA**

15c Sample APA listings: Articles in print and online periodicals with or without a DOI

Periodicals—scholarly journals, magazines, newspapers, and newsletters—are published on a regularly scheduled basis. After the author and year, give the periodical article title. Do not put quotation marks around the title, and only capitalize the first letter of the first word of the title and of any subtitle and proper nouns or adjectives. After the article title, include the italicized periodical name in uppercase and lowercase letters. Items 1–16 describe the rest of the information needed to cite articles in the various types of periodicals.

1. Article in a print scholarly journal   For a scholarly journal article, begin with the authors' names, reversed and connected with an ampersand (for more than two authors, see 15b; for more than seven authors, see 15c, item 3). Then give the date (in parentheses), article title, and journal title; add a comma, the volume number, and another comma (all italicized); and then give the inclusive page numbers, repeating all digits and separating the numbers with an en dash (–). Include the issue number only if each issue is paged separately (each issue begins with page 1). Put the issue number (not in italics) in parentheses immediately after the volume number, with no space between them, as in the following example. Then add a comma and the inclusive page numbers, repeating all digits. Do not use *p.* or *pp.* with page numbers.

Giordano, C., & Giordano, C. (2011). Health professions students' use of

social media. *Journal of Allied Health, 40*(2), 78–81.

2. Article with a DOI in an online scholarly journal   See Source Shot 8 on p. 260 for how to locate and cite an article with a DOI found in an online scholarly journal.

> **KEY POINTS**
> **DOIs and URLs: Locating and Citing Electronic Sources**
>
> A DOI (digital object identifier) or URL (uniform resource locator) is listed at the end of a citation for an online source to enable readers to access the same source. Since a URL, a Web address on the Internet, can easily be changed or deleted, resulting in an unreliable link, APA recommends using a DOI, a permanent identification number for a source as published in any medium, rather than a URL if one is available. The DOI for the source will never change, even if its URL does. APA advises listing an available DOI for print as well as electronic sources.

How a DOI Works

The publisher assigns a persistent DOI number to a published article or other work when it is made available electronically. The DOI both identifies the content and provides a link for readers to locate the article on the Internet through registration services such as CrossRef (<http://www.crossref.org>) or the DOI resolver at <http://www.doi.org>. If you give a DOI in your citation, readers can then easily turn the DOI string into a link by going to CrossRef or appending the string to <http://dx.doi.org> to access the work. For example, appending the DOI in the citation in Source Shot 9 (p. 262) so that it becomes <http://dx.doi.org/10.1542/peds.2011-1434> would take readers directly to a page on the Web site of the journal *Pediatrics* containing the article's abstract; they could then either purchase the full text in PDF format there or access the article free by logging into a library database.

The DOI is usually found on the first page of an online journal article near the copyright notice (see Source Shot 8) or on the citation page for the article in a library subscription database (see Source Shot 9). A DOI in a database listing or in an electronic document reference may also function as a live direct link to the article. However, the DOI might be lurking behind a button labeled *CrossRef, Article, PubMed,* or the name of a supplier of full-text articles (see item 4). Remember to search the site fully for the DOI.

Listing a DOI or URL

1. Copy and paste a DOI or URL from its source to be sure it is accurate. Many can be long and complex.

2. When a DOI is given, no additional retrieval information is necessary.

3. In your reference list entry, add the DOI after the period following the inclusive page numbers. Write *doi* (lowercase) and add a colon (not followed by a space) and the DOI numbers.

4. If the article has no DOI, list the URL of the home page of the journal. After the inclusive page numbers, write *Retrieved from* and add the URL. Write *Available from* when a URL does not provide the actual source but instead tells how to retrieve it.

5. Split a DOI or URL across lines only before a slash, a period, or other punctuation mark (exception: split after double slashes in *http://*). Do not add a hyphen at the end of the first split line.

6. Do not italicize or underline a DOI or URL, which will be the last item in your reference list entry, and do not follow it with a period. (Only underline URLs as hyperlinks if you are posting your paper online.)

SOURCE SHOT 8

Listing an Online Scholarly Journal Article (PDF Format) APA

The following scholarly journal article was published in *Preventing Chronic Disease*, an electronic journal published by the Centers for Disease Control and Prevention. It is available in a downloadable PDF version, so page numbers of the PDF version are given. (Always use a PDF version if one is available.) When listing a journal article found online either in a database (see Source Shot 9 on p. 262) or on the journal's Web site, include the following information in your reference list entry. Do not list your retrieval date or the name of the database if you found the article there.

❶ **Author(s)** Last name, initials (see Key Points box, p. 255.)

❷ **(Date of publication)** In parentheses, give the year of online publication. Put a period after closing parenthesis.

❸ **Title: Subtitle of article** Do not use quotation marks or italics; capitalize only the first word of title and of any subtitle and proper nouns and adjectives. End with a period.

❹ *Journal Title, volume* **(issue number)** Capitalize all major words in the title. Italicize the title, comma, and volume number, but not the issue number (contained in parentheses). For journals with each issue paged separately (beginning with page 1), put the issue number immediately following the volume number, with no space between them. Follow with a comma before the page numbers. (The cited journal volume in this example has no issue number.)

❺ **Inclusive range of page numbers** Repeat all digits (as in 167–188) and separate numbers with an en dash. Do not use the abbreviation *p.* or *pp.* End with a period.

❻ **Digital object identifier (DOI)** End with the article's DOI for retrieval information (see Key Points box on p. 258). Only break a DOI before a punctuation mark (such as a slash or a hyphen in this example's DOI), but do not add a hyphen to break a DOI at the end of a line. Do not add a period after the DOI.

    ❶   ❷   ❸

Kemp, C. B. (2012). Public health in the age of health care reform.

              ❹   ❺   ❻

Preventing Chronic Disease, 9, 1–4. doi:10.5888/pcd9.120151

APA American Psychological Association

Online Scholarly Journal Article (PDF Format)

Preventing Chronic Disease | Public Health in the Age of Health Care Reform - CDC   Page 1 of 4

⑤ **Inclusive page numbers**

CDC Centers for Disease Control and Prevention
CDC 24/7: Saving Lives. Protecting People.™

PREVENTING CHRONIC DISEASE
PUBLIC HEALTH RESEARCH, PRACTICE, AND POLICY

④ **Journal volume**

ESSAY   ③ **Title of article**   Volume 9 — October 11, 2012

Journal title

Public Health in the Age of Health Care Reform

Catherine B. Kemp, RN, BScN, DOHS   ② **Date of publication**

Suggested citation for this article: Kemp CB. Public Health in the Age of Health Care Reform. Prev Chronic Dis 2012;9:120151. DOI: http://dx.doi.org/10.5888/pcd9.120151 .

① **Authors**

Preventive medicine has vast unused possibilities for improving the health of the population, partly in ways that require compulsory controls, like quarantine and compulsory immunization, partly through systematic arrangements for personal check-ups and early diagnosis and treatment. Without going into the controversial question of socialized medicine, it is clear that health is a national asset, and the undisputed judgment of the people is that it is worth conserving, more or less regardless of whether it can be done on purely commercial principles. JM Clark, 1950 (1)

⑥ **Digital object identifier (DOI)**

One might assume that the foregoing quotation is from recent debates on the Patient Protection and Affordable Care Act (PPACA) (2); however, it actually appeared in an article written more than 60 years ago. The author, an economist, was articulating his perspective on the effect of President Franklin Roosevelt's New Deal and the influences of Keynesian economics. His remarks illustrate that issues related to health care reform — now the PPACA — are long-standing. Discussions of health care reform have been a major part of American public discourse in nearly every decade since President Theodore Roosevelt's 1912 platform for re-election included a proposal for universal health insurance (3). Historically and currently, the health care debate has emphasized the treatment of people once they become ill. This emphasis ignores the basic fact that maintaining the health of the population is essential to our economy, our national security, and our success as a nation. The benefits of a healthy population extend far beyond health care costs. Although treating illness is an indispensable part of health care, reforming and strengthening our public health system are equally important to improving the health of individuals and of our population as a whole and to managing finite resources effectively.

To define "public health," many turn to Dr. C.E.A. Winslow, a pioneer instrumental in the development of this discipline, who described it as: the science and the art of preventing disease, prolonging life, and promoting physical health and efficiency through organized community efforts for the sanitation of the environment, the control of community infections, the education of the individual in principles of personal hygiene, the organization of medical and nursing service for the early diagnosis and preventive treatment of disease, and the development of the social machinery which will ensure to every individual in the community a standard of living adequate for the maintenance of health (4).

Indeed, the Partnership for Prevention defines the 3 main goals of public health as protection of the population's health and safety, promotion of improved health for everyone, and prevention of the consequences and suffering resulting from disease (5).

Although there is some overlap, the discipline of public health differs from health care practice, which involves assessing health, diagnosing symptoms, treating diseases, and managing chronic impairments. Public health's primary function is to protect and promote the population's health through prevention, environmental protection, and public regulations and policies. Kenneth Arrow made this very point in a 1963 essay (6) when he described how medical care is but 1 aspect of health care and that other aspects such as sanitation, shelter, nutrition, and clothing are perhaps even more important to health, especially when a person lacks them (6). Discussions about disease prevention and health promotion today are too frequently overshadowed by politics and debates about medical interventions and technologies. Meanwhile, the American health care system is expensive; its costs are rising and consistently outpacing inflation, from 5.2% of gross domestic product in 1960 to 17.6% in 2009, a trajectory that is expected to persist (7).

Our population is aging. Projected demographic shifts over the next 20 years underscore the need to incorporate effective preventive health services into public health. The US Department of Health and Human Services indicates that in 2009, 39.6 million Americans were aged 65 years or older and accounted for 12.9% of the total population. By

American Psychological Association **APA**

SOURCE SHOT 9

Locating a Scholarly Journal Article in an Online Database **APA**

You can use your school library's databases to locate articles for your research (see 7c). The citation page for an article in a database will tell you if the article has been published in a scholarly journal and has been peer-reviewed (see Key Points box in 8b on p. 130) and if it is available in PDF format so that you can cite page numbers. It will also give you the necessary information for your reference list entry.

Include the following in your reference list entry:

❶ Author(s) Last name, initials

❷ (Publication date) Year in parentheses followed by a period

❸ Title of work: Any subtitle No quotation marks or italics; only capitalize the first word of the title and of any subtitle and proper nouns and adjectives; end with a period.

❹ *Periodical Title, volume* (issue number) Capitalize all major words in the title. Italicize the title, comma, and volume number, but not the issue number (contained in parentheses). If each issue of the periodical is paged separately (beginning with page 1, not the case here), put the issue number immediately after the volume number, with no space between them. Follow with a comma.

❺ Inclusive range of page numbers Repeat all digits, and separate numbers with an en dash. Do not use the abbreviation *p.* or *pp.* End with a period.

❻ Digital object identifier (DOI) End with the article's DOI (see Key Points box on p. 258). Only break a DOI before a punctuation mark, and do not add a hyphen to break a DOI at the end of a line. Do not add a period after the DOI.

Do not list the name of the database or your date of retrieval of the article.

        ❶   ❷

Burstein, M., Ameli-Grillon, L., & Merikangas, K. (2011). Shyness

          ❸   ❹   ❺

    versus social phobia in U.S. youth. *Pediatrics, 128,* 917–925.

          ❻

    doi:10.1542/peds.2011-1434

---

3. Journal article with DOI, more than seven authors If a scholarly journal article has more than seven authors, list the first six (last name, comma, initials), separated by commas. Insert three ellipsis dots and add the last author's name.

Online Database Citation Page (from ProQuest PsycINFO database)

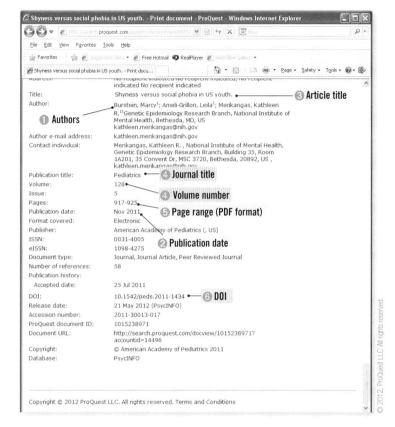

Stoloff, M., McCarthy, M., Keller, L., Varfolomeeva, V., Lynch, J., Makara, K....
    Smiley, W. (2010). The undergraduate psychology major: An examination of
    structure and sequence. *Teaching of Psychology, 37*(1), 4–15. doi:10.1080
    /00986280903426274

4. Journal article with DOI in an online database Universities and libraries subscribe to large searchable databases of print publications, such as Gale InfoTrac, EBSCO Academic Search Premier, ERIC, LexisNexis, ProQuest PsycINFO, and WilsonWeb Education Full Text, providing access to full-text articles and abstracts. Cite a journal article in an online database the same way that you would cite one found in an online journal (see item 2), listing page numbers if the article is in PDF format. After the publication information, give the DOI for electronic retrieval. Do not give the name of the database. Source Shot 9, page 262, shows the relevant part of the ProQuest PsycINFO database citation page that provides information about the journal article needed to create the reference list entry on the opposite page.

5. Article with no DOI in an online-only journal The following article is published in an online journal with no print version. However, the journal provides downloadable PDF versions of articles, so the inclusive page range is cited. If the article does not have a DOI, after the inclusive page numbers, write *Retrieved from* and give the URL of the home page of the journal. Do not list your date of access.

Boudiny, K., & Mortelmans, D. (2011). A critical perspective: Towards a broader
    understanding of "active ageing." *E-Journal of Applied Psychology, 7*(1),
    8–14. Retrieved from http://ojs.lib.swin.edu.au/index.php/ejap

6. Abstract of a journal article in a database or online Although it is best to cite full articles, you can use an abstract as a source and cite it in your references. For an abstract in an online database, cite the journal publication details, including the page numbers (but not the DOI). Then add *Abstract retrieved from* and the name of the database. You may add an identifying number (if available).

Ann Cameron, C. (2009). Associations between shyness, reluctance to engage,
    and academic performance. *Infant and Child Development, 18*, 299–305.
    Abstract retrieved from ProQuest PsycINFO database.

For an abstract on a Web site, give the URL of the site's home page (not followed by a period).

Schmitt, D., Realo, A., Voracek, M., & Allik, J. (2008). Why can't a man be more
    like a woman? Sex differences in Big Five personality traits across 55
    cultures. *Journal of Personality and Social Psychology, 94*(1), 168–182.
    Abstract retrieved from http://psycnet.apa.org

7. Print magazine article Include the year and any exact date of publication in parentheses. Do not abbreviate months. Italicize the name of the magazine, the comma following it, and the volume number. Then give the issue number in parentheses and the page number(s), not italicized. See Source Shot 10 (p. 266) for an example.

8. Online magazine article with no print source If only an HTML version is available, with no page numbers, give available publication information and the URL.

Marshall, M. (2012, June 14). Oldest cave art is a single red dot. *New Scientist.*
Retrieved from http://newscientist.com

9. Newsletter article Cite a newsletter article as you would cite an article in a magazine, giving the volume and issue numbers if available. If no author is named, as in the following citation, begin with the article title. See item 11 for an article that skips pages.

Major fat-burning discovery: Harvard researchers discover a hormone released
by exercise. (2012, June). *Harvard Health Letter, 32*(8), 1, 7.

10. Print newspaper article In parentheses, include the month and day of publication after the year. Give the section letter or number before the page, if applicable. Do not omit *The* from the newspaper title. Note that with newspaper articles only, use *p.* and *pp.* with page numbers. See item 13 for an article with no author named.

Tanner, L. (2012, April 10). Study links autism to obesity during pregnancy. *The*
Washington Post, p. A3.

11. Article that skips pages When an article does not appear on continuous pages, give all page numbers, separated by commas. Use *p.* and *pp.* for newspapers only.

Strom, S. (2012, April 6). A case long ripening: For two food giants, defining
fresh fruit is not cut and dried. *The New York Times*, pp. B1, B3.

12. Online newspaper article Newspaper articles are often available from several sources, in several databases, and in a variety of formats, such as in the newspaper's database or a library subscription database. Give the URL of the newspaper's home page in your entry. Do not insert a period at the end of the URL. A date of retrieval is not necessary.

SOURCE SHOT 10

Listing a Print Magazine Article **APA**

When listing a print magazine article, include the following:

❶ Author(s) Last name, initials (see 15b on how to list authors)

❷ (Date of publication) In parentheses: year, comma, month (not abbreviated) and day (if given), followed by a period.

❸ Title of article: Any subtitle Not in quotation marks or italics; capitalize only the first word of the title and subtitle and proper nouns or adjectives; end with a period.

❹ *Periodical Title, volume* (issue number) All italicized, except for the issue number. For periodicals with each issue paged separately, put the issue number in parentheses immediately following the volume number, with no space between. Use a comma (italicized) to separate a periodical title from the volume number, and use another before the page numbers.

❺ Inclusive range of page numbers All digits included and separated by an en dash (as in 167–168). Do not use *p.* or *pp.* End with a period.

    ❶   ❷   ❸   ❹
Del Frate, J. (2005, Winter). Old journey, new heights. *ASK Magazine, 6*(21),
    ❺
    6–9.

---

                 year, month and day in parentheses
Belluck, P. (2012, May 15). New drug trial seeks to stop Alzheimer's

    before it starts. *The New York Times.* Retrieved from

    www.nytimes.com —— no period at end after URL

13. Unsigned article or editorial   For an article with no author named, begin with the title and follow with the date in parentheses.

Go with the flow: Removing old dams benefits American's rivers economically

    and ecologically. (2011, October 1–7). *The Economist, 401*(8753), 35.

For an unsigned editorial, add the label *Editorial* in square brackets after the title.

Title page and Table of Contents of a Magazine (APA)

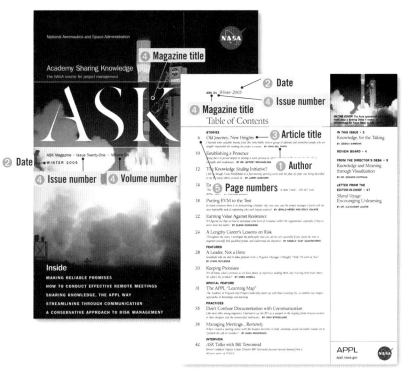

Who owns the past? [Editorial]. (2012, April). *Scientific American, 306*(4), 9.

If the editorial is signed, begin with the author's name.

14. Review   After the title of the review (if any), add in square brackets (with no intervening punctuation) *Review of* and a description of the work reviewed, including the author or creator, and identify the medium: book, film, or video, for example.

Ayala, F. J. (2012, Spring). All for one and one for all? An eminent scientist reconsiders natural selection [Review of the book *The social conquest of Earth,* by E. O. Wilson]. *The American Scholar, 81*(2), 112–113.

15. Published interview Begin with the writer of the published interview and the date. After the title (with no intervening punctuation), in brackets write *Interview with* and the name of the person interviewed.

Jeffery, C. (2009, January/February). The Maddow knows [Interview with

Rachel Maddow]. *Mother Jones, 34*(1), 72–73.

16. Letter to the editor Put the label *Letter to the editor* in brackets after the date or the title of the letter, if it has one.

Bogorad, H. C. (2012, April 10). The price of not voting [Letter to the editor].

The Washington Post, p. A12.

For an editorial, review, interview, letter to the editor, or other feature in an online periodical, end with *Retrieval from* and the URL.

15d Sample APA listings: Print and online books, parts of books, and reference books

- Look for the necessary information on the title page and the copyright page of a book.
- Use the most recent copyright date or *n.d.* if no date is given.
- Include the city (or the first city if two or more are given) and the state of publication (two-letter U.S. Postal Service abbreviation).
- Write complete names of foreign countries (see item 22).
- Give the publisher's name in a shortened but intelligible form, including *Books* or *Press* but omitting *Publishers, Co.,* or *Inc.*
- If a DOI has been assigned to the book, list it. (See the Key Points box on p. 258.)
- If a book or chapter is only available online, either give the DOI or give a retrieval statement and the URL in place of the name and location of the publisher (see item 19).

17. Book with one author Give the last name first, followed by the initial(s). See Source Shot 11 on page 270 for an example.

18. Book with multiple authors For two to seven authors, list all names in the order in which they appear on the book's title page. Reverse the order of each name: last name first, followed by initials. Separate all names with commas, and insert an ampersand (&) before the last name.

American Psychological Association

all names reversed ampersand

Baumol, W. J., Litan, R. E., & Schramm, C. J. (2007). *Good capitalism, bad*

indented *capitalism, and the economics of growth and prosperity.* New Haven,
a half inch
⟵⟶ CT: Yale University Press.

For eight or more authors, list the first six names (reversed), add three ellipsis dots, and list the name of the last author, also reversed (see 15c, item 3).

19. Electronic version of print book (e-book) To cite an electronic version of a print book that can be read on an e-reader such as the Nook, Kindle, iPad, or Sony Reader, give the author, date, and book title. Then, with no intervening punctuation, add in brackets the e-reader version; follow with a period. Then list the book's DOI if available. Do not list the place of publication or publisher for an electronic book. If you download the e-book from a Web site, and it does not have a DOI, write *Retrieved from* and the URL. Do not give your date of retrieval.

Epstein, P. R. (2012). *Changing planet: How the climate change crisis threatens our health and what we can do about it* [Adobe Digital Editions version]. Retrieved from http://www.ucpress.edu/ebook/

20. Electronic version of print book in online library If the book was read or accessed through an online library such as NetLibrary, Google Books, or ebrary instead of on an e-reader, just give the retrieval information after the title. Do not give your date of access.

Galanti, G.-A. (2008). *Caring for patients from different cultures* (4th ed.). Retrieved from http://books.google.com/books

21. Electronic-only book If a book has only been published online (with no print edition), list the retrieval information after the title. The following book can be downloaded in PDF format.

Shrout, R. N. (2012). *True hypnotism: Understanding its science and mastering its art.* Retrieved from http://www.onlineoriginals.com/showitem .asp?itemID=253

22. Edited book After the reversed name(s) of the editor(s), add *Ed.* or *Eds.* in parentheses and follow with a period. Continue with the year, title, and publication details of the book. Give the city and state (abbreviated) or country (spelled out, as in the example that follows).

American Psychological Association **APA**

SOURCE SHOT 11

Listing a Print Book **APA**

On the title page and copyright page of the book, you will find the information you need for an entry in the list of references.

❶ **Author(s)** Last name, initials (see 15b on how to list multiple authors).

❷ **(Year of publication)** In parentheses, followed by a period; the most recent copyright (©) date or *n.d.* if no date is supplied.

❸ *Title of book: Any subtitle* In italics, with capital letters only for the first word of the title and subtitle and any proper nouns or adjectives.

❹ **Place of publication** City and state (two-letter U.S. Postal Service abbreviation) or country, omitting the state when its name appears in the name of the publisher, as in *University of Illinois Press*. Cite only the first city if more than one is listed. Write complete names of foreign countries. Follow with a colon.

❺ **Publisher** In a short but intelligible form, including *Books* or *Press* but omitting *Publishers, Co.,* or *Inc.* and ending with a period

See 15d, items 18–33, for more examples.

    ❶   ❷   ❸

Martinot, S. (2010). *The machinery of whiteness: Studies in the structure*

                  ❹   ❺

of racialization. Philadelphia, PA: Temple University Press.

Lloyd, G., & Guthrie, E. (Eds.). (2007). *Handbook of liaison psychiatry.* Oxford,
    England: Cambridge University Press.

If the book has both an author and an editor, begin with the author's name (reversed), the date, and the book title. After the title, with no intervening punctuation, in parentheses add the editor's name in normal order, a comma, and the abbreviation *Ed.* (or *Eds.* for more than one editor). Put a period after the closing parenthesis and continue with the publication details.

23. Work or chapter in an edited book (collection) List the author of the work or chapter, the date of publication of the edited book, and the title of the work. Follow this with *In* and the names of the editors (not inverted), the title of the book, and (in parentheses) the inclusive page

Title Page

1 Author

Steve Martinot

Copyright Page

4 City and state (abbreviated) of publication

3 Title: Subtitle

The Machinery
of Whiteness

Studies in the Structure of Racialization

TEMPLE UNIVERSITY PRESS
Philadelphia, Pennsylvania 19122
www.temple.edu/tempress

Copyright © 2010 by Temple University
All rights reserved
Published 2010 ●————— **2 Year of publication**

Library of Congress Cataloging-in-Publication Data

Martinot, Steve.
  The machinery of whiteness : studies in the structure of racialization /
Steve Martinot.
    p.   cm.
  Includes bibliographical references and index.
  ISBN 978-1-4399-0051-2 (cloth : alk. paper)
  ISBN 978-1-4399-0052-9 (pbk. : alk. paper)
  1. Whites—Race identity. 2. Racism—United States—History.
4. United States—Race relations—History. I. Title.
  HT1575.M436 2010
  305.8—dc22   2009048505

♾ The paper used in this publication meets the requirements of the American
National Standard for Information Sciences—Permanence of Paper for Printed
Library Materials, ANSI Z39.48-1992

Printed in the United States of America

2 4 6 8 9 7 5 4 3

5 Publisher

TEMPLE UNIVERSITY PRESS
Philadelphia

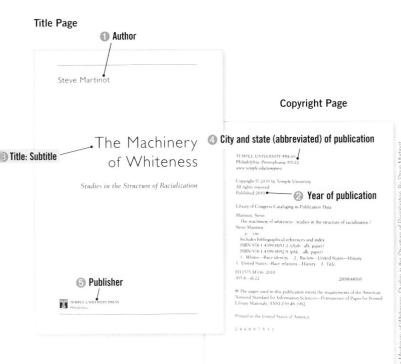

numbers (preceded by *pp.*) of the work or chapter. End with the place of publication and the publisher for a print book (as in the following example) or the DOI or URL for an electronic book. If you cite more than one work from an edited book in your reference list, include the full bibliographical details in each entry.

Lloyd, G. (2007). Understanding psychological reactions to physical illness. In

G. Lloyd & E. Guthrie (Eds.), *Handbook of liaison psychiatry* (pp. 64–82).

Oxford, England: Cambridge University Press.

24. Foreword, preface, introduction, or afterword   List in reverse order (last name first, initials) the name(s) of the author(s) of the book element. Follow the date with the name of the element, the word *In*, the names of the author(s) of the book in normal order (initials, last name), the book title, and in parentheses, the page number or numbers of the element, preceded by *p.* or *pp.*

Simon, J. (1997). Introduction. In K. Washburn & J. F. Thornton (Eds.), *Dumbing down: Essays on the strip-mining of American culture* (pp. 43–54). New York, NY: Norton.

25. Translated book   After the title of the work (with no intervening punctuation), in parentheses give the initials and last name of the translator (in normal order), followed by a comma and the abbreviation *Trans.* Put a period after the closing parenthesis.

name of translator not reversed

Jung, C. G. (1960). *On the nature of the psyche* (R. F. C. Hull, Trans.). Princeton, NJ: Princeton University Press.

26. Edition after the first   For an edition of a book after the first, give the edition number in parentheses after the title, with no intervening punctuation.

Raimes, A. (2013). *Pocket keys for writers* (4th ed.). Boston, MA: Wadsworth.

For a revised edition, put *Rev. ed.* in parentheses instead of the edition number.

27. Republished or reprinted work—print and online   For a republished book, give the most recent date of publication after the author's name and at the end in parentheses add *Original work published* and the date. Do not add a final period. In the citation in your paper, give both dates: (Smith, 1793/1976).

Smith, A. (1976). *An inquiry into the nature and causes of the wealth of nations.* Chicago, IL: University of Chicago Press. (Original work published 1793)

For an electronic version of a republished book, give the date of online publication. In place of the location and publisher, give the retrieval information and URL. Add the information about the original publication last.

Freud, S. (2007). *A young girl's diary.* Retrieved from http://books.google.com /books (Original work published 1923)

For a reprint of a work published in a different source, first give the complete publication information for the reprinted work. Begin the details in the parentheses with *Reprinted from* and give the title of the original work, inclusive page numbers (if part of a book), *by* and the author or editor, date, place, and publisher.

28. Multivolume work Give the number of volumes after the title, in parentheses. The date should indicate the range of years of publication, when appropriate.

Einstein, A. (1987–2006). *Collected papers of Albert Einstein* (Vols. 1–10).

Princeton, NJ: Princeton University Press.

If you cite only one volume, give only that volume number and its date.

29. No author identified Put the title first. Ignore *A, An,* and *The* when alphabetizing. Alphabetize the following under *W.*

The world almanac and book of facts 2012. (2012). Pleasantville, NY: World

Almanac Books.

30. Print or online book, pamphlet, or brochure by a corporation, government agency, or other organization Give the name of the corporate author first. If the publisher is the same as the author, write *Author* for the name of the publisher. For a brochure or pamphlet, include the format *Brochure* or *Pamphlet* in square brackets after the title.

College Board. (2011). *Trends in college pricing 2011.* Washington, DC: Author.

East Bay Municipal Utility District. (2012). *2011 annual water quality report*

[Brochure]. Oakland, CA: Author.

If no author is named for a government publication, begin with the name of the federal, state, or local government department (if given), followed by the agency. If the work is available online (as is the following example in PDF format), give the retrieval information in place of the location and publisher.

U.S. Substance Abuse and Mental Health Services Administration. (2011).

Disaster training and technical assistance [Brochure]. Retrieved from

http://store.samhsa.gov/product

31. Signed entry in a print reference work Cite the entry as you would cite a work in an edited collection, giving complete publication information (see item 23).

Bedford, V. H., & Diderich, M. (2009). Sibling relationships in adulthood. In

H. T. Reis & S. Sprecher (Eds.), *Encyclopedia of Human Relationships:*

Vol. 1 (pp. 41–44). Thousand Oaks, CA: Sage.

32. Signed entry in an online reference work Cite an entry for an online reference work as you would cite one for a print source, but give the retrieval information in place of the location and publisher.

Hilpinen, R. (2011). Artifact. In E. N. Zalta (Ed.), *The Stanford encyclopedia of philosophy* (Spring 2012 ed.). Retrieved from http://plato.stanford.edu /entries/artifact/

33. Unsigned entry in a print or online reference work.   Begin an unsigned print entry with the title of the work. Put the edition and page numbers in parentheses after the title, and give complete publication information.

Antarctica. (2000). In *The Columbia encyclopedia* (6th ed., pp. 116–118). New York, NY: Columbia University Press.

For an unsigned online entry, give the edition number in parentheses after the title if the online version of the book is based on a print edition.

Gerrymander. (n.d.). In *Merriam-Webster's online dictionary* (11th ed.). Retrieved from http://www.m-w.com/dictionary/gerrymander

15e Sample APA listings: Reports and presentations— print, online, and live

34. Print report   Italicize the title of a technical or research report; list the location and publisher as you would for a print book.

Blash, L., Chapman, S., & Dower, C. (2011). *WellMed's medical assistant training program prepares students for health care career ladder.* San Francisco: Center for the Health Professions, University of California.

35. Online report on a government Web site.   If no author is named for a government publication, begin with the name of the federal, state, or local government department, followed by the agency. Provide any identifying number in parentheses after the title. In the retrieval statement, name the publisher (*Retrieved from U.S. Census Bureau website*) before the URL unless it has already been listed as author, as in the following example.

U.S. Department of Commerce, Census Bureau. (2012). *Educational attainment in the United States: 2009* (Report No. P20-566). Retrieved from http:// www.census.gov/prod/2012pubs/p20-566.pdf

36. Task force report on a university Web site   If no individual authors are named, give the university and the name of the task force or similar group as author. In the following example, the name of the task force is capitalized in the report title.

Harvard University, Task Force on University Libraries. (2009). *Report of the*
　　　　Task Force on University Libraries. Retrieved from http://provost.harvard
　　　　.edu/reports/Library_Task_Force_Report.pdf

37. Issue brief　Cite issue briefs, working papers, and other documents as you would a longer report, giving the document number in parentheses after the title. Give the month as well as the year of publication. Add retrieval information and the URL for documents accessed online.

U.S. Department of Commerce, Census Bureau. (2011, November). *Lifetime*
　　　　mobility in the United States: 2010 (American Community Survey Brief
　　　　No.10-07). Retrieved from http://www.census.gov/prod/2011pubs
　　　　/acsbr10-07.pdf

38. Unpublished conference paper　Cite unpublished papers or symposia presentations by listing the presenter, date (year and month), title (italicized), name of the meeting, and location (city and state or province/country).

Leavitt, S. (2006, May). *Something to think about when I can't sleep: The*
　　　　development of rubella vaccine. Paper presented at the American Association
　　　　for the History of Medicine Annual Meeting, Halifax, Nova Scotia, Canada.

39. Conference paper or proceedings in print or online　Cite a conference paper published in a print volume of conference proceedings as you would a work in an edited collection (see 15d, item 23). If the proceedings are published regularly, cite as a journal article. If a DOI is available, include it. If you accessed the work on a Web site, add the retrieval information and URL.

Kennedy, F. A., McWhorter, L. B., Troyer, J., & Stroup, C. (2006). *An empirical*
　　　　investigation of changes in charity care spending by nonprofit hospitals
　　　　in response to mandatory threshold law. Presentation to the 2006 annual
　　　　meeting of the American Accounting Association, Washington, DC.
　　　　Retrieved from http://aaahq.org/GNP/newsheadline/MYM2006
　　　　/_afk%20Charity%20Care%20Spending%20GNP%20Submission
　　　　%202006%20B.pdf

40. Poster session

Szenher, M. (2005, September). *Visual homing in natural environments.* Poster
　　　　session presented at the annual meeting of Towards Autonomous
　　　　Robotic Systems, London, England.

Give the retrieval information and URL for a poster session accessed online.

15f Sample APA listings: Other online sources

Include in your citation whatever information is available of the following to enable your readers to locate your online source:

1. **Name(s) of author(s)** If not available, begin with the title.
2. **Year and date** of online posting or update in parentheses (or *n.d.* if no date is available).
3. **Title and any subtitle** Italicize titles of documents that stand alone (such as reports) but not items that are part of a larger entity (such as Web pages, articles, or sections). If there is no title, begin with the description of the source contained in brackets (see 4 below).
4. **Format** List the format or other identifying description of the source in square brackets after the title: [Web log post], [Newsgroup message].
5. **Any print publication information** if the document has a print source.
6. **Retrieval statement**: Write *Retrieved from* and the URL. Include your retrieval date (day, month, year) for material from sites that are likely to be frequently updated or changed or are otherwise unstable.

41. Authored article on a Web site Cite a Web page or article as you would a print article, without italics or quotation marks. Do not name the Web site in the entry. Give the date of retrieval only for content that may be changed or updated.

Enayati, A. (2012). Is there a bias against creativity? Retrieved from http://www
.cnn.com/2012/03/28/health/enayati-uncertainty/index.html?hpt=he_bn2

42. Web page, no author identified Alphabetize by the first major word of the title. Put identifying information in brackets after the title. Follow the date with the retrieval information.

The heavy burden of arthritis in the U.S. [Prevalence fact sheet]. (2011).
Retrieved from http://www.arthritis.org/media/newsroom
/Arthritis_Prevalence_Fact_Sheet_5-31-11.pdf

Narcolepsy. (2011). Retrieved from http://www.health.com/library/mdp
/0,,stn166193,00.html

43. Entire Web site, no author Name the site (not italicized) and then give the complete URL in parentheses only in the text of your paper, not in your list of references (see 14b, item P).

44. Blogs, discussion boards, wikis, newsgroups, and archived mailing lists Include in your list of sources only academic material posted on archived lists or blogs. If no archives exist, cite an entry on a discussion or message board as a personal communication (see 14b, item R). List the author's last name and initials, if available. If only a screen name is given, use that. Cite the complete date of posting. Give the subject line (the "thread") of the posting (not in italics), followed by a description in brackets. Always give the retrieval date for wiki pages, which may change constantly.

Myers, P Z. (2012, June 12). A well-informed citizenry is the only true repository of the public will [Web log post]. Retrieved from http:// scienceblogs.com/pharyngula/2012/06/12/a-well-informed-citizenry -is-the-only-true-repository-of-the-public-will/

Love, R. (2012, June 17). Re: Does anyone realistically think that an International Space Agency can be formed and maintained? [online newsgroup comment]. Retrieved from http://groups.google.com/group /sci.space.policy/browse_thread/thread/e1886d6ddfe9efb9#

Landscape architecture. (2012, May 2). Retrieved June 17, 2012, from Wikipedia, http://en.wikipedia.org/wiki/Landscape_architecture

15g Sample APA listings: Visual and multimedia sources (live, print, and online)

Multimedia sources include audiovisual media such as motion pictures, television and radio broadcasts, and podcasts; and music recordings such as CDs and LPs. Visual sources include static objects such as artwork and visual representations such as maps, charts, photos, illustrations, and graphs. To cite a multimedia or visual source, begin with the primary contributor, artist, or creator in the author position and identify the person's role in parentheses. In brackets after the title (with no intervening punctuation) give the format or description of the source. If the source was retrieved online, end with *Retrieved from* and the URL.

45. Map in a print book   Cite a map included in a print book as you would cite an article contained in one. Give the location and publisher (which is the same as the creator of the map in the following example).

National Geographic Society (Cartographer). (2009). World time zones [Map]. In *Visual atlas of the world* (pp. 310–311). Washington, DC: Author.

46. Online map   See Source Shot 12 for an example.

American Psychological Association **APA**

SOURCE SHOT 12

Listing an Online Visual (Figure) **APA**

APA cites visual elements such as maps, graphs, charts, photographs, illustrations, and cartoons in a format similar to the one used for multimedia sources. Within a paper or published text, these elements are labeled as *figures* and identified by number (see 14c, p. 253). Include the following elements, most separated by periods, in your citation.

① **Creator of the work** Begin with the creator in the author position.

② **(Type of creator)** Follow with a description of the person or organization's role—cartographer, illustrator, and so on—in parentheses, and add a period. In this example, the creator is a cartographer.

③ **(Year of publication or creation)** contained in parentheses and followed by a period.

④ **Title of figure or other visual work** No italics for titles of maps, graphs, illustrations, and similar visual elements; italics for works of art (painting, sculpture, artistic photograph) and for visual representations of them (such as a photograph of a painting published in a book or online).

⑤ **[Format or description of visual work]** contained in brackets and followed by a period.

⑥ **Retrieval information and URL** If the visual work was accessed online, write *Retrieved from* and give the URL, not ending with a period.

The screen shots on the opposite page show you where to find the information necessary to cite a map downloaded from the state of California's online map gallery.

             ①   **②**

CA.gov Cal-Atlas Geospatial Clearinghouse (Cartographer).
     ③   **④**   **⑤**

   (2010). Demographic population growth [Demographic map].

      No punctuation between title and description in brackets
                  ⑥

   Retrieved from http://atlas.ca.gov/view/gallery.html

                         No period after URL

An Online Map

Top of Web Page

6 Retrival information (URL)

Creator of figure

4 Title of figure

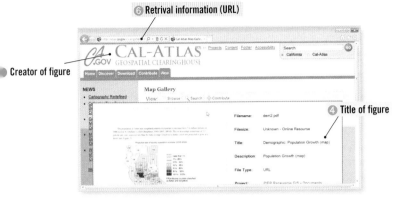

Middle of Web Page

5 Description of figure (map) in brackets

3 Year of online publication

47. Film or video Begin with the primary contributors (producer and director, if known). Identify the medium or format (motion picture, videocassette, DVD, etc.) in brackets after the italicized title. Give the country where a film was released, or give the city and state or country for other formats. End with the location and name of the studio or publisher.

Pitt, B. (Producer), & Miller, B. (Director). (2011). *Moneyball* [Motion picture].
United States: Columbia Pictures.

Jacquet, L. (Director). (2005). *The march of the penguins* [DVD]. Burbank, CA:
Warner Home Video.

48. Television or radio program Begin with the writer and director in the author position and the producer as editor, if known. Cite an episode of a television series or radio program as you would an article in a book. Put the description in brackets after the title. End with the location and network of the broadcast.

Knutson, R., & Day, L. (Writers). (2012, May 22). Cell tower deaths [Television
series episode]. In D. Fanning (Executive producer), *Frontline*. Boston,
MA: WGBH.

49. Music recording Cite a song on an album as you would an article in a book. Begin with the writer and put the copyright year in parentheses. Give the song title and put information in brackets if the song was recorded by someone else. Cite the album title (italicized) and put the medium of recording (LP, CD, etc.) in brackets. End with the location and record label (publisher). In the following example, the songwriter is also the performing artist, so recording information is not needed.

Ely, J. (2007). July blues. On *Happy songs from Rattlesnake Gulch* [CD]. Austin,
TX: Rack 'em Records.

50. Podcast or MP3 download For a podcast, give the producer or editor, complete date, italicized title, identification of format and any other supplementary information in brackets, and *Retrieved from* and the URL.

Rehm, D. (Producer). (2012, June 4). *The Diane Rehm Show* [Interview with
Jordan Smoller about his book *The other side of normal: How biology*

is providing the clues to unlock the secrets of normal and abnormal behavior] [Audio podcast]. Retrieved from http://www.npr.org/rss /podcast/podcast_detail.php?siteId=5495237

Davis, A. (2007, October 2). Angela Davis speaks. *Panel discussion with Burnham, Mitchell, and Noble* [MP3 download]. Washington, DC: Folkways Records. Retrieved from http://www.amazon.com

51. Video blog posting   Use a screen name if it is the only one available.

nnnicck. (2007, February 7). *The march of the librarians* [Video file]. Retrieved from http://www.youtube.com/watch?v=Td922l0NoDQ

52. CD-ROM or DVD-ROM   Identify the format in square brackets after the title.

U.S. Substance Abuse and Mental Health Services Administration. (2012). *Shared decision making in mental health decision aid: Considering the role of antipsychotic medications in your recovery plan* [CD-ROM]. Washington, DC: Author.

15h Sample APA listings: Miscellaneous sources

53. Dissertation or abstract—print, online, multimedia   Italicize the dissertation or master's thesis title and identify the work as such in parentheses. If you retrieved it from a commercial database, add *Available from* here and the database name, with the order or accession number in parentheses at the end of the entry (not followed by a period).

Jerskey, M. (2006). *Writing handbooks, English language learners, and the selective tradition* (Doctoral dissertation). Available from ProQuest Dissertation and Theses database. (UMI No. 3235697)

If you retrieved the work from an institutional database or Web site, add the words *Retrieved from* and the URL. For a Web source, add a comma and the granting institution's name after the identifying phrase in the parentheses.

For an abstract published in *DAI*, give the author, date, and dissertation title (not in italics), followed by *Dissertation Abstracts International* and the name of the section (*Section B. Sciences and Engineering*). After a comma, add the volume, issue, and page number: 35(20), 3315.

For a dissertation on microfilm (with the format in brackets), also include in parentheses at the end of the entry the University Microfilms number. For a dissertation on CD-ROM, include *CD-ROM* in brackets after the title and provide any access number.

54. Presentation slides

Norvig, P. (2000). *The Gettysburg PowerPoint presentation* [PowerPoint slides].
Retrieved from http://norvig.com/Gettysburg/index.htm

55. Personal communication (letter, telephone conversation, unpublished interview, e-mail, message on discussion board)
Cite only in the body of your text as *personal communication*. Do not include these communications in your list of references (see 14b, item R).

56. Computer software
Do not use italics for the name of the software.

Snaglt (Version 9.0) [Computer software]. (2008). Okemos, MI: TechSmith.

16 Sample Paper 5: A Student's Research Paper, APA Style

The following paper was written by Maria Saparauskaite in a required first-year course at Hunter College. The assignment was to explore a current issue in the news. Using the APA style of documentation, she provides a title page, an abstract, and section headings (see 14d). Her citations and the list of references at the end follow APA guidelines and serve to answer any questions readers may have about the authors, dates, and publication details of her source material. Her instructor asked for tables and figures to be included within the paper rather than attached separately at the end in normal APA style. See 14c for more on figures and their captions.

Note: Blue annotations point out issues of content and organization; red annotations point out APA format issues.

Title Page (APA)

Running head (brief title) flush left and in capitals on every page

Running head: SECRET OF SAVANT   1

Page number flush right on every page

Midway on page, centered, capital and lowercase letters

The Secret of the Savant

Maria Saparauskaite

Hunter College of the City University of New York

Blue = content issues, **Red = format issues**

Abstract Page (APA)

American Psychological Association APA

Heading
centered,
not in
boldface

Double-
space
throughout
paper

Abstract

This paper investigates the phenomenon of savants, people with
unusual mental talents, and describes some of their extraordinary
feats. Theories of the development of the rare savant syndrome
are explored, especially the connection between a savant's
abilities and whether the effects of brain damage on the
hemispheres of the brain cause savant talents to emerge
spontaneously. A study by Snyder, Bahramali, Hawker, and
Mitchell (2006) is explored in detail. The researchers wanted to
examine how stimulation of the brain affected mental functions,
with participants experiencing either brain stimulation or a sham
session and then being asked to make judgments about what
they saw. The study suggests that the savant condition could
be stimulated, thus raising questions about not only whether
rewiring of the brain is advisable but also to what ends any
newfound intelligence may be applied.

Length:
137 words
(aim for
150–250)

Passive
voice
common in
APA style

All four
authors
named in
first text
citation to
work; year in
parentheses

Summary of
findings

Essay (APA)

SECRET OF SAVANT   3

The Secret of the Savant

Many of us struggle with learning and memorization. We
may long to be able to do math problems quickly in our heads, play
a favorite song on the piano after hearing it only once, or recapture
details from an event we have observed. We may wish we could
learn a second language as easily as we did our first. For a few
individuals among us, these talents are as natural as breathing.
These individuals are *savants,* and they are capable of unusual
mental feats. Some recent studies have shown that there may be
a savant within all of us, which means that our brains may be
capable of the same abilities as those of savants. Through artificial
means these talents can in some cases be accessed temporarily.

Background Review of the Literature

Savants and Their Accomplishments

Savants exhibit extraordinary talents. Researchers Treffert
and Wallace (2004) have reported that at the age of 14, Leslie
Lemke was able to play Tchaikovsky's Piano Concerto No. 1
without a single mistake after hearing it only once. He had never
had a piano lesson in his life but today he tours all over the world
playing in concerts even though he is blind and developmentally
disabled. Lemke even composes his own music. Another savant,
Kim Peek, the inspiration for the Oscar-winning film *Rain Man*,
has memorized more than 7,600 books. It would take him less
than three seconds to tell you which day of the week your
birthday fell on and which day of the week you will be

Margin annotations:

Title centered, not bold or underlined

Indent first line after headings

Double-space text of paper

1" Margin

Main headings in body of paper bold and centered

Subheads in body of paper bold and flush left

Area of research and hypothesis

No extra space around headings

Word *and* connects authors' names in text sentence

Blue = content issues, **Red = format issues**

American Psychological Association   APA

collecting your first pension. Like Lemke, Peek is also

developmentally disabled. The artwork of another savant, Richard

Wawro, is known all over the world. His childhood oil paintings

left people speechless (Treffert & Wallace, 2004). He is an

autistic savant, as is David Tammet, who can calculate 37 to

the power of four in his head (Heffernan, 2005).

Ampersand (&) connects authors' names in parenthetical citation

The Savant Syndrome

The savant syndrome is an extremely rare condition, most

often found in people with IQs ranging from 40 to 70, though

sometimes it can occur in people with IQs up to 114 or higher

(Treffert & Wallace, 2004). Most savants are physically disabled

or suffer from autism, which is a "pervasive development disorder

[that] is characterized by a severe disturbance of communication,

social, and cognitive skills, and is often associated with mental

retardation" (Sternberg, 2004, p. 352). Despite that situation, savants

Word enclosed in brackets added in quotation

Page number for a quotation from a book; period after closing parenthesis

exhibit amazing mental superiority in specific areas, such as

arithmetic, drawing, music, or memory. However, their way of

thinking is very literal, and they have problems understanding

abstract concepts. Their abilities emerge spontaneously and

cannot be improved over time. Also savants cannot explain how

they do what they do (Snyder et al., 2006).

Parenthetical citation uses *et al.* because all authors are named in first citation to work on page 2 of essay

Theories of Development of the Syndrome

Scientists have only a vague idea of how the savant

syndrome develops. Recent studies have illustrated that developmental

problems in the left brain hemisphere are most commonly seen in

savants. Bernard Rimland of the Autism Research Institute

Mentions authority of source

Blue = content issues, **Red = format issues**

SECRET OF SAVANT   5

has observed that most abilities in autistic savants are associated

with the right hemisphere, whereas the abilities they are deficient

in are associated with the left hemisphere (Treffert & Wallace,

2004). The left hemisphere is thought to be responsible for forming

hypotheses and concepts. This observation helps to explain why

savants tend to be so literal. Another set of evidence for this theory

is the occasional emergence of savantlike talents in people suffering

from dementia. Bruce Miller of the University of California observed

five elderly patients who spontaneously developed exceptional artistic

skills in music and painting. All of these patients had what is

called *frontotemporal dementia* (FTD). Miller discovered that most

brain damage caused by FTD was localized in the left hemisphere

(Treffert & Wallace, 2004). In another case of brain damage,

psychologist T. L. Brink reported that a nine-year-old boy developed

"unusual savant mechanical skills" (Treffert & Wallace, 2004, p.18)

after a bullet damaged his left hemisphere. According to Treffert and

Wallace, these reports of spontaneous emergence of the savant

syndrome in people with brain damage could point to a possibility

that savant talents may be innate to everyone. So, as reporter

Lawrence Osborne (2003) provocatively asked, "Could brain

damage, in short, actually make you brilliant?"

Snyder's Experiment

Allan Snyder of the University of Sydney, "one of the world's

most remarkable scientists of human cognition" (Osborne, 2003), became

interested in the prospect of hidden genius when observing patients

who underwent a procedure called *transcranial magnetic stimulation*

(TMS). TMS was "originally developed as a tool for brain surgery:

Present perfect tense used to introduce source

Past tense used when discussing a completed research study

Question for research

New section of paper: heading centered

Credentials of researcher

No page numbers available for quotation from online newspaper article

Blue = content issues, **Red = format issues**

American Psychological Association APA

by stimulating or slowing down specific regions of the brain, it allowed doctors to monitor the effects of surgery in real time" (Osborne, 2003). Interestingly enough, this procedure had very noticeable side effects on the patients' mental functioning. A patient would either temporarily lose his ability to speak or make odd mistakes while speaking. But one side effect intrigued Snyder the most: Some patients undergoing TMS would gain savantlike intelligence for a limited amount of time. With his colleague Mitchell, he came up with the theory that savants have a privileged access to lower levels of cognition, whereas normal persons do not (Snyder & Mitchell, 1999).

Claim of researchers

Participants and Method

To test this theory, Snyder, along with Bahramali, Hawker, and Mitchell (2006), led an experiment that was based on the finding that some savants are able to guess the exact number of items, such as matches, just by glancing at them. He tells of autistic twins who were able to estimate correctly the number of matches (111) fallen on the floor. By using TMS on the brains of 12 volunteers, Snyder wanted to find out if a normal person could accomplish the same thing. The goal was to create virtual lesions in the left anterior temporal lobes of the volunteers, thus suppressing mental activity in that region of the brain (see Figure 1).

First reference to figure in parentheses; figure placed nearby

The participants underwent two sessions. During one of them, they received TMS stimulation, while during the other, or "sham," session, they did not. The participants were not able to tell the difference. During each session, the participants were shown a

Description of the experiment

Blue = content issues, **Red = format issues**

Figure 1. Diagram of the brain. From *Psychology* (p. 91), by
R. J. Sternberg, 2004, Boston, MA: Wadsworth. Copyright 2004
by Cengage Learning.

Source
information
in caption
separated by
commas; note
APA use of
capital letters
in a caption

random number of dots on a computer screen (as shown in Figure
2) and then told to estimate the number of dots they saw. They
were asked to do this before the TMS stimulation, then 15
minutes afterward, and finally an hour later. The same procedure
was used in both real and sham sessions.

Results of the Experiment

The results, summarized in Figure 3, are surprising. Eight
of the 12 participants improved their ability to estimate the
number of dots within an accuracy range of five after the TMS
stimulation. The probability for this to happen merely by chance
alone is less than 1 in 1,000. Clearly there is a significant increase
in the number of correct estimations after the TMS stimulation.
The sham session shows relatively little variation.

Purpose
of figure
explained

Blue = content issues, **Red = format issues**

SECRET OF SAVANT   8

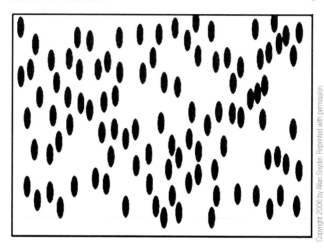

Figure 2. The task—to estimate the number of dots. From A. Snyder et al., 2006, p. 838.

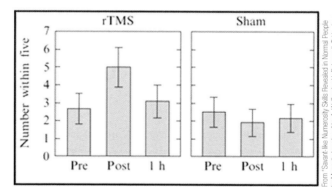

Figure 3. Participants' ability to make guesses within an accuracy range of 5, both with repetitive transcranial magnetic stimulation and without (the sham session). From A. Snyder et al., 2006, p. 841.

Blue = content issues, **Red = format issues**

SECRET OF SAVANT   9

Snyder and the other researchers concluded that the

confirmation of hypothesis

experiment "demonstrated an enhanced ability of healthy normal

individuals to guess the absolute number of discrete elements by

Authors named at beginning of sentence; year and page number in parentheses after quotation

attempting to artificially stimulate the savant condition" (2006,

p. 842). They described savants as being able to see the parts of

the holistic picture, thus having access to raw information, unlike

other individuals.

Conclusion

The line separating a neurotypical person from a savant

may thus be less "hard wired" than previously assumed. If a

Questions for further research

person could become brilliant by having his or her brain rewired,

how would this newfound intelligence be used? For personal

Thesis

gain or for selfless good? Whatever directions and possibilities

such research may reveal, understanding the savant syndrome

brings us closer to understanding the human brain. Perhaps, in

the future, research on savants will not only teach us more about

what intelligence is and where it lies but will also help people

who are born mentally retarded or brain damaged. The research

that is just beginning opens up many possibilities.

Blue = content issues, **Red = format issues**

American Psychological Association   APA

SECRET OF SAVANT   10

Heading centered, not in boldface   References   New page, double-spaced

Heffernan, V. (2005, February 23). A savant aided by the sparks

that he sees inside his head. *The New York Times.*

Retrieved from http://www.nytimes.com

Osborne, L. (2003, June 22). Savant for a day. *The*

New York Times Magazine. Retrieved from http://

www.nytimes.com

Snyder, A. W., Bahramali, H., Hawker, T., & Mitchell, D. J. (2006).

Savant-like numerosity skills revealed in normal people by

magnetic impulses. *Perception, 35,* 837–845. doi:10.1068

/p5539

Snyder, A. W., & Mitchell, D. J. (1999). Is integer arithmetic

fundamental to mental processing? The mind's secret

arithmetic. *Proceedings of the Royal Society B: Biological*

Sciences, 266, 287–292. doi:10.1098/rspb.1999.0676

Sternberg, R. J. (2004). *Psychology* (4th ed.). Boston, MA:

Wadsworth.

Treffert, D. A., & Wallace, G. L. (2004, January). Islands of genius.

Mind [Special issue]. *Scientific American, 14*(1), 14–23.

Retrieved from http://scientificamerican.com

Entries organized alphabetically by author

Complete date given in parentheses for newspaper article

All four authors' names (reversed) listed in entry; ampersand (&) before last author's name

Scholarly journal title, comma, and volume number italicized

Volume and issue numbers and page range of print magazine article

Retrieval information: URL for home page of online newspaper

No period after URL

All digits repeated in page range

DOI of the article given last in entry, not followed by period

Edition of book in parentheses after title

Name of special issue followed by label in brackets

Blue = content issues, **Red = format issues**

CSE Style of Documentation

CSE AT-A-GLANCE: INDEX OF CSE STYLE FEATURES

This chapter describes the documentation style recommended for all natural and applied science disciplines by the Council of Science Editors (CSE) in *Scientific Style and Format: The CSE Manual for Authors, Editors, and Publishers*, 7th edition (Reston, VA: Council of Science Eds., 2006). This edition describes three systems of documentation for citing the elements necessary to "ensure retrievability of the cited documents" (p. xii):

- a *name-year system* similar to APA style (see chapters 14 and 15), in which the in-text citation includes author(s) and year of publication and the reference list is arranged alphabetically by author

- a *citation-sequence system* that numbers and lists sources in the order in which they are cited in the paper

- a *citation-name system* that also gives numbers to citations but organizes and numbers the list of references alphabetically by author or title, differing from the citation-sequence system only in the method of assigning numbers to the entries (both use the same number when citing a source throughout the paper)

This last option is the one used in *The CSE Manual* itself. Because the name-year system is so similar to APA and because citations for the citation-sequence and citation-name systems differ only in the ordering of the reference list, this chapter concentrates on examples of entries for those last two citation systems.

Basic features of CSE style

Always check with your instructors about documentation style guidelines. Some may not specify a particular style but will ask you to select one and use it consistently.

KEY POINTS

How to Number and List Sources in the CSE Citation-Sequence or Citation-Name Style

1. **In the text of your paper**, number each reference with a superscript number in a smaller size than the font for the text, or place the reference number on the line within parentheses. Place punctuation *after* the superscript number.

2. **At the end of your paper**, list the references on a new page titled *References* or *Cited References*.

For the *citation-sequence system*, arrange and number the references in your list in the order in which you cite them in your paper. The first citation that appears in your paper will be *1*, and the first reference in your list (also number *1*) will give information about that first citation. Therefore, an author's name beginning with *Z* could be number *1*

CSE Council of Science Editors

and listed first if it is the first source cited in your paper. Each time you cite this source in your paper, you will use the same number (in this case, *1*).

For the *citation-name system*, first arrange your list of references alphabetically by author (or by title if no author is known); then number that list. Whenever you cite the source numbered *1* in your paper, you will insert a superscript *1* (and so on). Therefore, a source with an author's name beginning with *Z* is likely to appear near the end of your list and be numbered accordingly.

Example of Documenting a Print Periodical Article

In-Text Number Citation	Numbered Entry in List of References
The mutation may prevent degradation of unknown substrates leading to their accumulation in Lewy bodies in neuronal cells[6].	6. De Silva HR, Khan NL, Wood NW. The genetics of Parkinson's disease. Curr Opin Genet Dev. 2000; 10(3):292–298.

17b How to cite CSE sources in your paper (citation-sequence and citation-name styles)

Use superscript numbers to refer readers to the list of references at the end of your paper. Note that the superscript number goes before a punctuation mark.

superscript number

A recent fruit fly study has produced interesting results[2].

One summary of studies of the life span of the fruit fly[3] has shown . . .

Refer to more than one entry in the reference list as follows:

Two studies of the life span of the fruit fly[1,5] have shown that . . .

Several studies of the life span of the fruit fly[1-4] have shown that . . .

Studies of the fruit fly are plentiful[1-6], but the most revealing is . . .

17c   How to list CSE references (citation-sequence and citation-name systems)

KEY POINTS
Setting Up the CSE List of Cited References

1. After the last page of your paper, attach the list of references, titled *References* or *Cited References*.

2. Arrange and number the works either (1) consecutively in the order in which you mention them in your paper (citation-sequence system) or (2) alphabetically (citation-name system). Invert all authors' names, and use the initials of first and middle names. Use no punctuation between last names and initials, leave no space between initials, and do not use *and* or & before the last author's name.

3. Begin each entry with the note number followed by a period and a space. Do not indent the first line of each entry; indent subsequent lines to align beneath the first letter of the previous line.

4. Do not italicize, underline, or use quotation marks for the titles of articles, books, or journals and other periodicals.

5. Capitalize only the first word of a book or article title and any proper nouns.

6. Abbreviate titles of journals, organizations, and words such as *volume* (*vol.*) or *series* (*ser.*).

7. Use a period between major divisions of each entry.

8. Put a semicolon and a space between the name of the publisher (not abbreviated) and the publication year of a book. Use a semicolon with no space between the date and the volume number of a journal.

9. For books, you may give the total number of pages, followed by a space and *p.* For journal articles, give inclusive page spans, using all digits: 135–136.

10. For online sources provide (as applicable) author; title; *Internet* in brackets; any print publication information; date, place, and publisher or sponsor; date of online publication or update; the word *cited* and your date of access in brackets; the length (pages, paragraphs, and so on) in brackets; and a DOI or URL (see the Key Points box in 15c on p. 258). Only break a DOI or URL after a slash, and do not end one with a period (unless it ends with a slash).

17d Sample CSE listings: Print and online books and parts of books (citation-sequence or citation-name system)

1. Whole book with one author

no punctuation

title not italicized; only first word capitalized

1. Finch CE. Longevity, senescence, and the genome. Chicago:

initials with no period between

publisher   semicolon   number of pages in book (optional)

University of Chicago Press; 1990. 922 p.

Give the city of publication, and include the state in parentheses if the city is not well known (see item 3).

2. Book with two or more authors

For up to ten authors, list all names (separated by commas). For eleven authors or more, list the first ten and follow with a comma and *et al.*

all authors' names reversed   edition after the first

2. Siebert L, Simkin T, Kimberly P. Volcanoes of the world. 3rd ed. Berkeley:

University of California Press; 2011. 568 p.

3. Book with editor(s)

Spell out the word *editors.*

3. Aluja M, Norrbom AL, editors. Fruit flies (tephritidae): phylogeny and

evolution of behavior. Boca Raton (FL): CRC Press; 2000. 984 p.

4. Part of a book

For a work in an edited book, first give the author and name of the work. Then write *In* (followed by a colon) and give the publication information for the edited book. End with the page numbers for the work.

4. Tallacchini M. Risks and rights in xenotransplantation. In: Jasanoff S, editor.

Reframing rights: bioconstitutionalism in the genetic age. Cambridge: MIT

Press; 2011. p. 169–192.

For a chapter or section of a book written by the author(s), first give the book's regular publication details (but not the total number of pages); then give the name of the chapter or section and its inclusive page numbers.

5. Online book (e-book)

Give the publication information as you would for a print book, adding *Internet* in brackets after the title. Then add the electronic publication date as a copyright date and give online source information (see 17f).

5. Macdougall D. Nature's clocks: how scientists measure the age of almost everything [Internet]. Berkeley: University of California Press; c2008 [cited 2012 Jun 29]. Available from: http://www.ucpress.edu/ebook.php?isbn=9780520933446

17e Sample CSE listings: Articles in print and online periodicals

6. Article in a print scholarly journal

6. Bonar EE, Young KM, Hoffman E, Gumber S, Cummings JP, Pavlick M, Rosenberg H. Quantitative and qualitative assessment of university students' definitions

volume complete page span

of binge drinking. Psych Add Behav. 2012;26:187–193.

no spaces in information about journal

For a journal paginated by issue, include the issue number in parentheses after the volume number.

7. Newspaper or magazine article   Give the name of the newspaper (not including *The*), the edition, the complete date, the section, and the first page and column numbers of the article. Abbreviate months to three letters with no period.

7. Gorman J. In the human genome, hearing echoes of opera's intricacies. New York Times (National Ed.). 2012 Apr 10;Sect D:3 (col. 1).

For a magazine article, give the complete date but not volume and issue numbers. Give the complete page span.

8. Article with no author identified   Begin with the title of the article.

9. Online journal article with a print source and DOI   Cite as for a print journal article and include the type of medium (*Internet*) in brackets after the journal title. After the publication date give your date of access (*cited . . .*) in brackets, followed by a semicolon. Then give the volume and issue numbers and inclusive page numbers. End with the DOI (not followed by a period). (See the Key Points box on p. 296.)

9. Pawitan JA. Prospect of cell therapy for Parkinson's disease. Ant Cell Biol [Internet]. 2011 [cited 2012 Jun 24];44(4):256–264. doi:10.5115/acb.2011.44.4.256

10. Online journal article with no print source   If no print source is available, after the volume or issue number provide in square brackets an estimate of the article's length in paragraphs, screens, lines, or bytes: [15 paragraphs], [172 lines].

10. Rosco C. A neurological virus. Vectors Journ [Internet]. 2007 [cited 2012 Jun 9];2(2); [about 2 screens]. Available from: http://vectors.usc.edu/issues/ 4/malperception/virus.html

11. Article in an online database   After your date of access in brackets and the print publication information, write *In:* and the name of the database, the identification *database on the Internet* in brackets, and any date of posting or modification or the copyright (©) date. Follow this with the article's approximate length in brackets, the URL, and any document number.

11. Verhoeven JTA, Setter TL. Agricultural use of wetlands: opportunities and limitations. Ann Bot. 2010 [cited 2012 Jun 19];105(1):155–163. In: PubMed Central [database on the Internet]; c2010; [about 10 screens]. Available from: http://www.ncbi.nlm.nih.gov/pmc/articles/PMC2794053/. Document no. PMC 2794053.

17f Sample CSE listings: Other online and audiovisual sources

For other online sources indicate *Internet* in brackets after the title. Give the city, publisher or site sponsor, and full date of publication or copyright year. In brackets put any update or modification date and your date of access. Indicate in brackets the number of screens, paragraphs, lines, or bytes. End with *Available from:* and the URL.

12. Web page   Give full dates (abbreviating months).

12. Hill LO. Seizures: when "electrical brainstorm" hits [Internet]. Atlanta: Cable News Network; 2012 Jun 21 [cited 2012 Jun 28]. Available from: http://www.cnn.com/2012/06/18/health/seizures-epilepsy-myths/ index.html?hpt=he_bn2

13. Posting to a discussion list   After the author's name and the subject line of the message, give any available information about the discussion list, including *In:* and the name of the list; description *discussion list on the Internet*; place and sponsor; year, date, and time of posting; your date of access; and approximate length of the posting. End with the URL.

13. Grubb B. Tsunami sensor network going up in June off Vancouver Island. In: sci.geo.earthquakes [discussion list on the Internet]. Mountain View, CA: Google Groups; 2012 May 27 [cited 2012 Jun 27]; [about 1 screen]. Available from: https://groups.google.com/forum/?fromgroups&hl=en#!topic/ sci.geo.earthquakes/g4O2XrIQrPo

14. DVDs, CD-ROMs, and other audiovisual sources Begin with the title and include the medium in brackets. Follow this with details of producer, author, or editor; place; publisher; and date. Include a brief description, such as length (of a film), color (of a work of art), number of discs, and type of accompanying material. End with *Available from:* and the name, city, and state of the distributor or the URL for online sources.

18 Sample Paper 6: Excerpt from a Student's Research Paper, CSE Style

The following excerpt from a paper titled "Longaeva: The Scientific Significance of the Ancient Bristlecone Pine" was written by Andrew Dillon for a first-year course on "Volcanoes of the Eastern Sierra Nevada" at Indiana University. He uses the CSE citation-sequence documentation style as required by his instructor and divides his paper into sections with headings: Abstract, Introduction, Phenotype and Physiology, Natural Range and Growing Adversities, Contributions to Science, Conclusion, and References. He also illustrates his twenty-one-page paper with photographs and images that show some features and settings of the huge ancient trees. Dillon's title page, numbered page 1, provides the essay title, the running head (*Bristlecone Pine*), his name, the name of the course, the instructor, and the date. Shown here are pages excerpted from the paper: the abstract, the beginning of the Phenotype and Physiology section, and the references, all of which demonstrate key features of the CSE citation-sequence system.

Note: Blue annotations point out issues of content and organization. Red annotations point out CSE format issues.

Abstract

CSE Council of Science Editors

Running
head and
page number
on every page
(title page is
page 1)

Bristlecone Pine   2

Abstract

Section
heading
centered

More than any other species of tree, the bristlecone pine

(*Pinus longaeva*), of the White Mountains in California, helps

scientists to understand the environmental conditions of the

past. With some living specimens attaining ages nearing 5,000

years, and dead matter persisting for another several thousand,

these ancient trees have provided climatologists, geologists, and

dendrochronologists with a continuous tree-ring chronology that

dates back to the last Ice Age. This paper examines the complex

Summary
of paper

physiology and habitat of the species and considers what

scientists have learned from the bristlecone about the earth's

history. Research from the past half century illuminates the

magnificence of bristlecone pines as living evidence of

past millennia.

Blue = content issues, **Red = format issues**

Council of Science Editors CSE

Excerpt from third section of paper, pages 6 and 7

Bristlecone Pine   6

Phenotype and Physiology

Section heading centered

Like all pines, bristlecones belong to the phylum

1" margins

Coniferophyta: the conifers. Classified within this phylum are

almost 50 genera and roughly 550 species. Evidence suggests

that the *Coniferophyta* developed some 300 million years ago in

the Carboniferous Period, developing the pine family after 165

million years. Now approximately 135 million years old, this family

Includes data on age and size

includes bristlecones and coastal redwoods, respectively holding

records for the oldest and tallest trees in the world[1].

Superscript number referring to source #1 in references (citation-sequence style)

Although maintaining easily identifiable conifer traits,

the bristlecone pine has a distinctive, even odd, appearance.

Many of these trees have been gnarled, bent, and twisted over

time, resulting in ghostly entangled forms of both living and

dead material. Some researchers believe that in fact, "over the

millennia bristlecones genetically programmed to twist may

have been better adapted to survive"[2], potentially explaining the

unusual contortions, as shown in Figure 1.

Figure placed near first mention in text

Figure 1. Bristlecone Pine (*Pinus aristata*), among the oldest

known trees (Lola B. Graham, The National Audubon Society

Collection/Photo Researchers).

Blue = content issues, **Red = format issues**

Bristlecone Pine   7

Deadwood colors range from white to dark gray or black, living

from light to dark brown. Because these trees grow for so long

and at such slow rates, wood tends to be tightly compact,

resinous, and highly resistant to disease, infestation, or rot[3].

For their old age they are also remarkably small, hardly ever

exceeding thirteen meters tall by four meters around[4].

unctuation
ark after
perscript
tation
umber

Blue = content issues, **Red = format issues**

Council of Science Editors CSE

List of references (selected here to match the excerpt)

Bristlecone Pine   20

References

1. Allaby M. Plants and plant life. Vol. 8, Conifers. Danbury (CT): Grolier; 2001. 49 p.

2. Little JB. Time line. Amer Forests [Internet]. 2004 [cited 2012 May 6];109(4):22–27. Available from: https://www.americanforests.org/productsandpubs/ magazine/archives/2004winter/feature1_1.php

3. Ferguson CW. Bristlecone pine: science and esthetics. Science New Ser. 1968;159(3817):839–846.

4. Gidwitz T. Telling time. Archaeology [Internet]. 2001 [cited 2012 May 4];54(2):36–41. Available from: http://www.archaeology.org/0103/abstracts/time.html

Online source: date of access in brackets

Split URL or DOI only after a slash

Issue number in parentheses

No period after URL

Blue = content issues, **Red = format issues**

19 *Chicago Manual of Style*: Endnotes, Footnotes, and Bibliography

CHICAGO AT-A-GLANCE: INDEX OF *CHICAGO* STYLE FEATURES

The Chicago Manual of Style, 16th ed. (Chicago: U of Chicago P, 2010) describes two documentation systems, an author-year parenthetical system of references similar to the APA system and a system in which sources are documented in footnotes or endnotes and usually listed in a bibliography. This second system, sometimes called *Chicago* humanities style, discussed in this chapter and chapter 20, is used widely in the humanities, especially in history, art history, literature, and the arts. Because works in these fields are most concerned with presenting content without interruption, sources are cited within the text with only superscript numbers that refer the reader to footnotes or endnotes for source information. All publication details are given either in a complete first footnote or endnote for the source or in a bibliography at the end of the work.

19a Basic features of the *Chicago* note style

KEY POINTS
How to Number and Document Sources in the
Chicago Endnote/Footnote Style

1. **In your text,** place a superscript numeral at the end of the quotation or the clause or sentence in which you mention source material; place the number after all punctuation marks except a dash.

2. **On a separate numbered page at the end of the paper,** list all endnotes, and number the notes sequentially, as they appear in your paper. If you use footnotes, a word processing program will automatically place them at the bottom of a page (see 21g on using computer programs such as Word for formatting an academic paper).

Example of an Endnote or Footnote for a Book

In-text Citation with Numeral	Numbered Endnote or Footnote

Numeral only
Mondrian planned his
compositions with colored tape.[3]

Source mentioned in your paper
According to Arnason and
Prather, Mondrian planned his
compositions with colored tape.[3]

3. H. Harvard Arnason and
Marla F. Prather, *History of Modern Art* (New York: Abrams, 1998), 393.

19b How to cite sources and prepare notes (*Chicago*)

To cite a source in your paper   Use the following format and number your notes sequentially. If you use endnotes and not footnotes, mention the source in your text whenever possible so that readers do not have to flip to the end to find the source.

> George Eliot thought that *Eliot* was a "good, mouthfilling, easy to pronounce word."[1]

First note for a source when no bibliography is attached   Long-form source notes can supply full publication details of a source, so a separate list of references is not necessary. However, if your instructor requires one, see 19d and the sample student paper in chapter 20. See the Key Points box on p. 306 for more on the format of a note.

author's name in normal order   comma   book title italicized; all major words capitalized   place, publisher, and date in parentheses

1. Margaret Crompton, *George Eliot: The Woman* (London: Cox and

page number

Wyman, 1960), 123.

comma

Short form first note for a source if a bibliography is provided   If you are required to attach a separate bibliography listing the complete publication information for all the sources you cited or consulted, the note citation can be concise. It gives just enough information to enable your reader to find the source in the bibliography.

1. Crompton, *George Eliot*, 123.

For the format of a bibliography entry see 19d; for a sample bibliography, see chapter 20.

Note referring to the immediately preceding source In a reference to the immediately preceding source, you may use *Ibid.* (Latin *ibidem*, meaning "in the same place") instead of repeating the author's name and the title of the work; follow with a comma and the page number(s). All the details except the page number(s) must be the same as those in the previous citation. If the page number is the same, too, just write *Ibid.*

> 2. Ibid., 127.

However, avoid using a series of *Ibid.* notes. These are likely to irritate your reader. Instead, place additional page references within your text: *As Crompton points out (127), . . .*

Any subsequent reference to a previously cited source For a reference to a source cited in a previous note but not in the immediately preceding note, give only the author and page number:

> 6. Crompton, 124.

If you cite more than one work by the same author, however, include a short title to identify the source.

19c How to format *Chicago* endnotes and footnotes

KEY POINTS
Guidelines for *Chicago* Endnotes and Footnotes

1. **Numbering** In the list of endnotes, place each number on the line (not as a superscript), followed by a period and one space. Follow the same format for a footnote. For footnotes, word processing software will often automatically make the number a superscript—just be consistent with whatever format you use.

2. **Spacing and indentation** Indent the first line of each note as you would the first line of a paragraph. Single-space within a note and double-space between notes unless your instructor prefers double-spacing throughout.

3. **Authors' names** Use the author's full name, not inverted, followed by a comma and the title of the work.

4. **More than one author** In section 19e, items 2–3 show how to cite multiple authors of books. Follow these examples for articles, online sources, multimedia, and miscellaneous works.

5. **Titles of works** Put quotation marks around titles of articles and Web pages, and italicize titles of books, periodicals, and blogs. Capitalize all first letters of words in the titles of books, periodicals, and articles except *a*, *an*, *the*; coordinating conjunctions such as *and*, *but*, and *so*; *to* in an infinitive; and prepositions. These words are capitalized only when they are the beginning words of titles.

6. **Publishing information** After a book title, in parentheses give the city (and state for a city not well known), name of publisher, and year. Follow this with a comma and the page number(s), with no *p.* or *pp.* After an article title, give the name of the periodical and pertinent publication information (volume, issue, date, and page numbers where appropriate). You may abbreviate or spell out months in the date of publication—just be consistent.

7. **Punctuation** Separate major parts of the citation with commas, not periods.

8. **Online sources** Provide a DOI or a URL and date of posting or revision. If there is none, list your access date (not otherwise needed) before the URL.

9. **Quotations and specific references** Provide the page number(s) for cited material following the publication details and after a comma, as in Source Shot 13. No page numbers are needed when referring to a work as a whole.

19d The *Chicago* bibliography

A bibliography is an alphabetical list arranged by author (or by title if no author is named) of all the works cited (or consulted) in your paper. It is placed at the end of the paper after any endnotes. A bibliography contains the same elements as those listed in a long-form note (see 19c), but they are separated by periods rather than commas. In entries the first author's name is inverted, and a book's publication details are not put in parentheses (see Source Shot 13 on page 312). Inclusive page numbers are given for periodical articles and for short works and chapters in books, but no page range or total is given for complete books. Entries are single-spaced, with a double-space between them. The first line of an entry begins flush left, and subsequent lines are indented (called a *hanging indent*).

If you include a bibliography, you only need to use short-form notes (see 19b), but check to see what your instructor prefers. See an example of a bibliography in the sample student paper in chapter 20.

Note how the bibliography form differs from the note form:

Note Form	Bibliography Form
commas separate 3 major parts of note; note number, first line indented	periods separate 3 major parts of entry; no note number, indented after first line
7. Martha Hollander, "Public and Private Life in the Art of Pieter de Hooch," *Nederlands Kunsthistorisch Jaarboek* 51 (2000): 274.	Hollander, Martha. "Public and Private Life in the Art of Pieter de Hooch." *Nederlands Kunsthistorisch Jaarboek* 51 (2000): 272–93.
page number of cited material	page range of article

19e Sample *Chicago* notes: Print and online books, parts of books, and reports

1. Print book with one author See Source Shot 13. Always include a page number or numbers to cite a specific page or specific pages of a book.

2. Book with two or three authors

> 2. George Lakoff and Mark Johnson, *Metaphors We Live By*, 2nd ed. (Chicago: University of Chicago Press, 2003), 55–61.

List three authors in the order in which they appear on the title page, separated by commas. In a bibliography entry, invert only the first author's name.

3. Book with four or more authors In a note for a book with multiple authors, use the name of only the first author followed by *et al.* (abbreviation for Latin *et alli,* "and others").

> 3. Randolph Quirk et al., *A Comprehensive Grammar of the English Language* (London: Longman, 1985), 132.

In a bibliography, for a work with ten authors or fewer, include all the names; for a work with more than ten authors, list only the first seven and *et al.*

4. Book with no author identified For a note, begin with the title.

> 4. *Chicago Manual of Style*, 16th ed. (Chicago: University of Chicago Press, 2010).

5. Book with editor, translator, or compiler

> 5. John Updike, ed., *The Best American Short Stories of the Century* (Boston: Houghton Mifflin, 1999).

For a translated or compiled work, after the title write *trans.* or *comp.* and the name of the translator or compiler. For more than one editor, translator, or compiler, add the appropriate abbreviation and treat as multiple authors (see items 2 and 3).

If the book has both an author and an editor or translator, begin with the author; then add *ed.* or *trans.* after the title of the book and give that person's name.

6. Work in an edited volume or anthology (essay, story, chapter, poem, letter)
Begin with the author and title of the work, and follow with the title of the anthology. Include *ed.* for *edited by*. For a letter, also include the addressee and the date (Elizabeth Bishop to Marianne Moore, January 5, 1945). End with any relevant page number(s).

> 6. Adrienne Rich, "Split at the Root," in *The Art of the Personal Essay*, ed. Phillip Lopate (New York: Anchor/Doubleday, 1994), 649.

7. Preface, introduction, foreword, or afterword
Give the name of the writer of the material when this is different from the author of the book.

> 7. David Remnick, introduction to *Politics*, by Hendrik Hertzberg (New York: Penguin, 2004), xviii.

8. Subsequent and reprint editions
For an edition after the first, add the number and *ed.* (for *edition*) after the title. Use *rev. ed.* for a revised edition.

> 8. Jim Leach, *Film in Canada*, 2nd ed. (New York: Oxford University Press, 2010), 40.

If a work has been reprinted, in a note in parentheses give the year of the original publication and a semicolon and then add the abbreviation *repr.*, a comma, and the publication details for the work.

9. Multivolume work
Give the number of any specific volume you cite, followed by a colon (with no space) and the page number. If the author's name is part of the title, the note may begin with the title.

> 9. *Collected Papers of Albert Einstein*, ed. John Stachel, David C. Cassidy, and Robert Schulmann (Princeton, NJ: Princeton University Press, 1987), 1:107.

(Continued)

SOURCE SHOT 13

Listing a Print Book in *Chicago* Style

Find the necessary information for documenting a book on its title page or copyright page.

Format for a footnote or endnote:

① Name of author First and last name in normal order, followed by a comma

② *Title of Book: Subtitle* In italics, with capitals for main words (see the Key Points box on p. 308); not followed by punctuation

In parentheses after the title (or subtitle if there is one), list items 3–5.

③ City of publication The first city mentioned on the title page, followed by a colon. Give the state (two-letter postal abbreviation) or country (abbreviated) only if the city is not well known or could be confused with another one.

④ Name of publisher Either give the name in full or in a somewhat short-ened form, omitting abbreviations such as *Co.* and *Inc.* (*Little, Brown,* not *Little, Brown & Co.*), followed by a comma. (**Note:** Usually list the word *Books* (*Basic Books*) and list *Press* if omitting it could cause misunderstanding (*New Press*). Always list *Press* for a university press: *University of Missouri Press.*)

⑤ Year of publication Available after © on the copyright page. Give the most recent year if several are listed. End with closing parentheses.

⑥ To cite a page or pages in the source, put a comma after the closing parentheses and add the number(s) and a period.

Items 2–15 give examples of cited books.

Indented
½ inch
       ①   ②
⟵⟶1. Fariba Zarinebaf, *Crime and Punishment in Istanbul: 1700–1800*
           Elements separated by commas   colon

    ③   ④   ⑤ ⑥
(Berkeley: University of California Press, 2010), 79.
Publication details 'colon   comma
  in parentheses

Format for a bibliography entry

In a bibliography entry give the same full publication information that you would in the first note for a source, but invert the first author's name, separate the elements with periods instead of commas, and do not put the publishing details in parentheses. Do not list the total page numbers of the book. Begin the first line flush left (at the margin) and indent all subsequent lines.

Author's name inverted — Elements separated by periods

Zarinebaf, Fariba. *Crime and Punishment in Istanbul: 1700–1800.*

First line begins at left margin

    Berkeley: University of California Press, 2010.

Title Page of Print Book

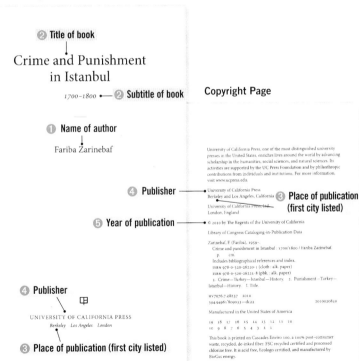

② **Title of book**

Crime and Punishment in Istanbul

1700–1800 —② **Subtitle of book**

① **Name of author**

Fariba Zarinebaf

④ **Publisher**

⑤ **Year of publication**

④ **Publisher**

⊞

UNIVERSITY OF CALIFORNIA PRESS

Berkeley Los Angeles London

③ **Place of publication (first city listed)**

Copyright Page

University of California Press, one of the most distinguished university presses in the United States, enriches lives around the world by advancing scholarship in the humanities, social sciences, and natural sciences. Its activities are supported by the UC Press Foundation and by philanthropic contributions from individuals and institutions. For more information, visit www.ucpress.edu.

University of California Press
Berkeley and Los Angeles, California ③ **Place of publication**
University of California Press, Ltd.   **(first city listed)**
London, England

© 2010 by The Regents of the University of California

Library of Congress Cataloging-in-Publication Data

Zarinebaf, F. (Fariba), 1959–.
  Crime and punishment in Istanbul : 1700/1800 / Fariba Zarinebaf.
    p.   cm.
  Includes bibliographical references and index.
  ISBN 978-0-520-26220-1 (cloth : alk. paper)
  ISBN 978-0-520-26221-8 (pbk. : alk. paper)
  1. Crime—Turkey—Istanbul—History. 2. Punishment—Turkey—Istanbul—History. I. Title.

HV7076.7.Z8Z37 2010
394.94961'809033—dc22   2010020820

Manufactured in the United States of America

19 18 17 16 15 14 13 12 11 10
10 9 8 7 6 5 4 3 2 1

This book is printed on Cascades Enviro 100, a 100% post-consumer waste, recycled, de-inked fiber. FSC recycled certified and processed chlorine free. It is acid free, Ecologo certified, and manufactured by BioGas energy.

If you refer to the work as a whole, the part of the citation after the title should look like this: *13 vols. (Princeton, NJ: Princeton University Press, 1987–2012).*

10. Author's work quoted in another work (secondary source)

10. E. M. Forster, *Two Cheers for Democracy* (New York: Harcourt, Brace, and World, 1942), 242, quoted in Phyllis Rose, *Woman of Letters, A Life of Virginia Woolf* (New York: Oxford University Press, 1978), 219.

List both works in your bibliography, giving *quoted in* and the name of the secondary source in the entry for the author's work. Note, however, that *The Chicago Manual of Style* recommends that whenever possible a reference be cited from the original work.

11. E-book (electronic book)
Cite an e-book downloaded from a bookseller or library as you would a print book, but add the format: Kindle edition, Microsoft Reader e-book, and so on. Because page numbers are usually not stable, cite a chapter, section heading, or other division of the work.

11. Luis Alvarez, *The Power of the Zoot: Youth Culture and Resistance During World War II* (Berkeley: University of California Press, 2009), Adobe PDF e-book, chap. 2.

12. Book accessed online
Cite as you would a print book, but end with the DOI (if available) or URL (see Key Points box on p. 316). For citing specific material, give a chapter number or section heading (as in item 11).

12. Mary Wollestonecraft Shelley, *Frankenstein, or, the Modern Prometheus* (London: Dent, 1912), http://ota.ahds.ac.uk.

13. Religious works and classics
Provide the citation in parenthetical text references or in a note. For the Bible, include the book (in abbreviated form, along with chapter and verse, but no page number) and in parentheses give the version used (spelled out in full on first mention).

13. Gen. 27:29 (New Revised Standard Version).

For Greek and Roman works and for classic plays in English, put a comma between the author and title but add no punctuation after the title. Locate the work by the number of book, section, and line or by act, scene, and line (separated by periods with no space following). Cite a classic poem by book, canto, stanza, and line, whichever is appropriate. Specify the edition used only in the first note referring to the work.

Do not include the Bible or classical works in a bibliography.

14. Entry in a print reference work   Begin with the work's title and edition, but include no page number, publication information, or date. Precede the title of an alphabetized entry with the initials *s.v.* (*sub verbo*— Latin for "under the word").

> 14. *Chambers Biographical Dictionary,* 7th ed., s.v. "Fuller, Margaret."

Do not include dictionary or encyclopedia entries in a bibliography.

15. Entry in an online reference work   Cite an online reference work entry as you would cite one in a print reference work (see item 14), and give the date of posting or update and the URL. If there is no date, give your date of access before the URL.

> 15. *Columbia Encyclopedia,* 6th ed., s.v. "symbolists," accessed July 10, 2012, http://education.yahoo.com/reference/encyclopedia/entry/symbolists.

16. Print organization or government report   Cite reports, pamphlets, and similar documents as you would cite books. If no individual author is named, list the organization or government department and agency as author. Give any report number after the title.

> 16. U.S. Department of Education, National Center for Education Statistics, *The National Indian Education Study: 2011,* Report No. 2012466 (Washington, DC: Government Printing Office, 2012), 15.

17. Online organization or government report   Cite as you would a print report (see item 16), but give the date of online publication and the URL.

> 17. U.S. Department of Education, National Center for Education Statistics, *Trends in High School Dropout and Completion Dates in the United States 1972–2009,* Report No. 2012006, 2011, http://nces.ed.gov/pubsearch/pubsinfo .asp?pubid=2012006.

19f Sample *Chicago* notes: Articles in print and online periodicals

When citing periodicals (scholarly journals, magazines, and newspapers), give the full name of the author or authors, title and subtitle of the article (in quotation marks), italicized title of the periodical, volume and issue numbers (for journals), date (complete dates for newspapers), specific page numbers (for notes) or inclusive page numbers (for bibliography entries), and the DOI or URL for online periodicals (see Key Points box on p. 316). Most online journals have page numbers. When there are none, you may cite material by visible paragraph number or section heading. Cite multiple authors for articles as you would cite them for books (see 19e, items 2 and 3).

18. Article in a print scholarly journal, continuously paged If journal volumes are paged continuously through issues (for example, if issue 1 ends on page 188 and issue 2 of the same volume begins with page 189), you need to give only the volume number, not the issue number (although in *Chicago* style it is never wrong to list it as well), and year (in parentheses). If you refer to a specific page, put a colon and a space after the year, and then add the page number(s). To cite an abstract, include the word *abstract* after the title of the article. For more on scholarly journals, see 8b.

18. Meir Zamir, "MI6: The History of the Secret Intelligence Service: 1909–1949," *Middle Eastern Studies* 48 (2012): 682.

19. Article in a print scholarly journal, each issue paged separately When each issue of a journal begins on page 1, after the volume number, add a comma, *no.* (for *number*), and the issue number. Follow with the year in parentheses, a colon and space, and the specific page number(s) of the cited material. See Source Shot 14 for an example.

KEY POINTS
Using DOIs and URLs in *Chicago* Style

Chicago recommends using a DOI (digital object identifier) or URL (uniform resource locator) for any electronic source, including periodicals, accessed online. Use a DOI, a unique, permanent identifying number that applies to a work in any medium in which it is published, rather than a URL if one is available. Put a DOI at the end of an entry, with *doi* (lowercase) and a colon (with no intervening space) before the number. See the Key Points box in 15c on p. 258 for more on using a DOI to locate sources.

When citing a URL, put the date of posting or update before the URL. You do not need to give your date of access (placed immediately before the URL) unless there is no date of posting or update, the site material changes frequently, or your instructor or field requires it.

Only break a DOI or URL that continues to a second line **after** a colon or double slash; **before** a single slash, a comma, period, hyphen, or most other punctuation marks; or **before** or **after** an ampersand or equals sign. Never add a hyphen at the end of a line. Put a period after the DOI or URL, which will end the citation.

20. Article with a DOI in an online scholarly journal Most articles published in online journals have DOIs, which go at the end of the citation. See the Key Points box on p. 316.

> 20. Sunanda K. Sanyal and Kizito Maria Kasule, "Modernism and Cultural Politics in East Africa: Cecil Todd's Drawings of the Uganda Martyrs [With Commentary]," *African Arts* 39, no. 1 (2006): 57, doi:10.2307/20447751.

21. Scholarly journal article in an online database Many articles published in print are also archived and available through free or subscription databases. To cite one, use a DOI rather than a URL if one is available. Otherwise, cite a stable or persistent, shorter URL that is listed with the article (as in the following example) instead of the URL you see in your browser's address bar when viewing the article. If listing the DOI or stable URL, do not name the database. If no stable URL is given, just list the name of the database and (in parentheses) any identification number.

> 21. Dianne Sachko Macleod, "Rossetti's Two Ligeias: Their Relationship to Visual Art, Music, and Poetry," special issue on the works of Dante Gabriel Rossetti, *Victorian Poetry* 20, no. 3/4 (1982): 93, http://www.jstor.org/stable/40002989.

Put information about a special issue (often a double issue, as in this example) before the journal title.

22. Online scholarly journal article with URL If an article published in an online journal does not have a DOI (sometimes the case if a journal does not also have a print version), give the URL. The following example cites an article in an online-only journal with numbered paragraphs rather than page numbers.

> 22. Anna Feuer, "Fair Foul and Right Wrong: The Language of Alchemy in *Timon of Athens*," *Early Modern Literary Studies* 16, no. 1 (2012): paragraphs 5–6, http://extra.shu.ac.uk/emls/16-1/feuetimo.htm.

23. Article in a print magazine Do not give volume or issue numbers, even if they are available. Include the month (abbreviated or spelled out) for monthly magazines and the complete date (with commas) for weekly magazines (month, day, year). Cite only a specific page number in a note (after a comma), not the range of pages. In a bibliography, provide the range of pages of the whole article.

> 23. Sam Tanenhaus, "The Electroshock Novelist," *Newsweek,* July 2 and 9, 2012, 52.

Chicago Manual of Style **CHICAGO**

SOURCE SHOT 14

Listing a Scholarly Print Journal Article in *Chicago* Style

In a note include the following when listing an article in a scholarly print journal with each issue paged separately:

❶ Name of author First and last names in normal order, followed by a comma

❷ "Title of Article: Any Subtitle." In quotation marks, with major words capitalized, followed by a comma

❸ *Title of journal* In italics, omitting *The* and with no comma following

❹ The **volume number** (with no abbreviation *vol.*) in regular (roman) print, followed by a comma

❺ The abbreviation *no.* and the **issue number**, not followed by a comma

❻ (Year of publication) in parentheses, followed by a colon

❼ Specific page number or **numbers** of cited material, followed by a period

Endnote or footnote format for a print article

First line
indented
½ inch
        ❶   ❷   ❸   ❹ ❺
⟵⟶19. Matthew Moten, "Out of Order," *Foreign Affairs* 89, no. 5
❻ ❼
(2010): 5.
   Elements separated by commas

Colon and space

Bibliography entry format

In a bibliography entry, separate the elements with periods. Begin the first line flush left and indent all other lines. List the author's last name, a comma, and first name (for alphabetizing). End with the range of pages for the article.

Author's name
inverted

Moten, Matthew. "Out of Order." *Foreign Affairs* 89, no. 5 (2010): 2–8.

First line   Elements separated with periods   Complete page
begins at   range of article
left margin

Journal Table of Contents

FOREIGN AFFAIRS
③ Journal title

⑥ Year of publication

SEPTEMBER / OCTOBER 2010

④ Volume number ———• VOLUME 89, NUMBER 5 •——— **⑤ Issue number**

Comments

② Title of article

⑦ Page span

Out of Order *Matthew Moten* 2

> The ouster of General Stanley McChrystal for his disparaging comments about civilian leaders does not suggest that U.S. political-military relations are in crisis. But it should remind the military's highest officers of the the need for, and the requirements of, appropriate professional behavior.

① Author

Smaller and Safer *Bruce Blair, Victor Esin, Matthew McKinzie, Valery Yarynich, and Pavel Zolotarev* 9

> The proposed nuclear arms reductions in the New START treaty are sensible, but the United States and Russia can and should go much further. In the next round of negotiations, the two countries should pursue deep cuts in their stockpiles and agree on maintaining a lower level of launch readiness.

Essays

Beyond Moderates and Militants
Robert Malley and Peter Harling 18

> When it comes to the Middle East, U.S. policymakers tend to apply yesterday's solutions to today's problems. In doing so, they miss realistic chances to help reshape the region. President Barack Obama must recognize that there is not a clean divide between a moderate, pro-American camp and an extremist, militant axis and take into account the Middle East's rapidly shifting dynamics—including the complex and competing interests of newly engaged players, such as Iran, Syria, and Turkey.

SOURCE SHOT 15

Listing an Article in an Online Newspaper in *Chicago* Style

In a note include the following:

1 **Name of author** First and last names in normal order, followed by a comma

2 **"Title of Article: Any Subtitle."** In quotation marks, with major words capitalized, followed by a comma

3 Any **section name** (not in quotation marks), followed by a comma

4 *Name of newspaper* In italics, omitting *The*, followed by a comma

5 **Complete date of publication** Month, day, year, separated by commas

6 **URL** End with a period

First line indented ½ inch

Items separated by commas

1 **2**
26. Maggie Severns, "Illinois Offers Lessons in Teaching English
3 **4**
as a Second Language," Opinions, *Washington Post,*
5 **6**
May 31, 2012, http://www.washingtonpost.com/opinions

/illinois-lessons-in-teaching-preschool.html.

Period at end of URL

---

24. Article in an online magazine   Cite as for a print publication, but add the URL. Add the name of a department or section (not in quotation marks) before the magazine title.

24. Brian Palmer, "Living Legends: Do Mythical Creatures Like Bigfoot Ever Turn Out to Be Real?," Explainer, *Slate,* May 23, 2012, http://www.slate .com/articles/health_and_science/explainer/2012/05/bigfoot_dna_analysis _how_often_do_scientists_discover_mythical_creatures_.htm.

CHICAGO *Chicago Manual of Style*

An Article in an Online Newspaper

Top of Article Web Page   ⑥ **URL**

③ **Special section**

⑥ **URL**

Opinions

Illinois offers lessons in teaching English as a second language

② **Article title**

Text Size   Print   E-mail   ⑤ **Date of publication (month and day)**

By Maggie Severns, Published: May 31

① **Author**   *Maggie Severns is a policy analyst for the New America Foundation's Early Education Initiative and the author of "Starting Early With English Language Learners: First Lessons From Illinois."*

The news that minority babies make up a majority of all births in the United States should be a wake-up call. This shift to a majority-minority population has been taking place for years, while the way minorities are educated in our public schools has stayed the same. It's time to think about next-generation America — a young, unprecedentedly diverse group with different needs, and strengths, from generations past.

Immigrant youths and the children of immigrants are one of the lowest-performing groups in U.S. public schools. But they will account for virtually all growth in the workforce over the next 40 years, the Brookings Institution has estimated, based on census data. In California, the state with the country's largest Hispanic population, more than half of all 3- and 4-year-

Bottom of Web Page   ⑤ **Date of publication (year)**

④ **Name of newspaper**

The Washington Post   Politics Opinions Local Sports National World Business Tech Lifestyle Entertainment Photo Video Blogs Classifieds

More ways to get us   Contact Us   About Us   Partners
Home delivery   Newsletter & Alerts   Help & Contact Info   The Washington Post Company
Mobile & Apps   Washington Post Live   Careers   In the community
RSS   Reprints & Permissions   Digital Advertising   PostPoints
Facebook   Post Store   Newspaper Advertising   Newspaper in Education
Twitter   e-Replica
Social Reader   Archive

Web site   washingtonpost.com   © 1996-2012 The Washington Post   Terms of Service   Privacy Policy   Submissions and Discussion Policy   RSS Terms of Service   Ad Choices

---

25. Article in a print newspaper   Cite newspaper articles in notes or in parentheses in running text but not in a bibliography. Do not include an initial *The* in the newspaper title. If the city is not part of the title, add it (italicized). Add the state (abbreviated) or province in parentheses (italicized) if the city is not well known. You may give an edition or section number, but do not give page numbers.

25. Jenny Anderson, "New Rules Seek to Stop Cheating on SAT and ACT," *New York Times*, March 28, 2012, national edition, sec. A.

26. Article in an online newspaper   Cite as for a print publication, adding the URL. See Source Shot 15 for an example.

27. Editorial   For an unsigned editorial, begin with the title. Cite a signed editorial as you would an article.

> 27. "A Rockier Pathway to Work," Editorial, *New York Times,* April 10, 2012, national edition, sec. A.

28. Letter to the editor   Do not list a title even if one is given.

> 28. Robert Appin, letter to the editor, *Economist*, June 30, 2012, 19.

29. Review (of a book, play, film, performance, etc.)   Give the name of the reviewer (if signed); title (if any); words *review of* and title of the reviewed work; name of the author, director, or other creator; location and date (for a performance); and publication details of the periodical.

> 29. Joe Morgenstern, "'Tattoo': Raw, Rousing and Rather Redundant," review of *The Girl with the Dragon Tattoo,* directed by David Fincher, *Wall Street Journal,* December 23, 2011, sec. D.

19g Sample *Chicago* notes: Other online sources

See the Key Points box on p. 316 on formatting URLs and publication dates. Do not give an access date unless there is no date of posting or update, site material is frequently updated, or your instructor or discipline requires one.

30. Web page or article   To cite a Web page or article that is not a formally published document, give the author of the content, if known; the title of the page or article (in quotation marks); the Web site name, if necessary (not in quotation marks, italics only if the name of a publication); the owner or sponsor of the site; the date of posting or update; and the URL. If there is no publication date or if the material is often updated, give your date of access before the URL.

> 30. Douglas O. Linder, "The Pentagon Papers (Daniel Ellsberg) Trial: An Account," Famous Trials, Douglas O. Linder, 2011, http://www.law2.umkc.edu /faculty/projects/ftrials/ftrials.htm.

Web site content is not usually listed in a bibliography.

31. Personal home page If a Web page does not have a title, use a descriptive phrase such as *home page.*

> 31. Alfred Gingold, home page, July 2, 2012, http://www.alfredgingold.com.

32. Posting on a blog Cite an entry on a blog as you would cite an article in a periodical. Give the author, entry title in quotation marks, blog title in italics, date of posting, and URL. Put the word *blog* in parentheses after the title unless the word is part of the blog's name. If the blog is part of a larger publication (such as an online newspaper or magazine), also list that publication.

> 32. Katy Waldman, "The Problem with Scientific Studies of Music,"
> *Browbeat: Slate's Culture Blog, Slate,* June 26, 2012, http://www.slate.com
> /content/slate/blogs/browbeat.7.html.

To cite a comment on a blog, give the commenter, date of comment, and words *comment on* with information about the related entry. Blog entries are usually only cited in notes, but you may list a blog you cite often in a bibliography.

33. Posting on a discussion board, archived electronic mailing list, or wiki Whenever possible, include the name of the list, date of posting, and URL for archived material.

> 33. David Schwalm to WPA-L mailing list, August 30, 2010, https://lists.asu
> .edu/cgi-bin/wa?AO=WPA-L.

34. E-mail or other personal communication Mention within your text or in a note, noting type of message (telephone, etc.).

> 34. Toby Gingold, e-mail message to the author, February 17, 2012.

19h Sample *Chicago* notes: Visual, multimedia, and miscellaneous sources

35. Sound recording (LP, compact disc, audiocassette, audiobook, etc.) Give the performer, writer, or other creator of the content; title; name of recording company or publisher; any identifying number; date of copyright, publication, or recording; medium (LP, etc.), and any optional supplementary information (number of discs, etc.). If accessed online, include a URL or DOI.

35. W. E. B. DuBois, *The Souls of Black Folk,* read by Richard Allen, Tantor Media, 2008, MP3-CD audiobook.

36. Video recording (DVD, CD-ROM, videocassette, film, filmstrip, etc.) List pertinent identifying details (see item 35) and identify the medium (DVD, slides, etc.). Give facts of publication as for print media where needed.

36. *World of Warcraft,* Irvine, CA: Blizzard Entertainment, 2004, CD-ROM.

37. Podcast and other online multimedia Cite a podcast, video blog, or other electronic format as you would cite a blog posting (see item 32). List performers, writers, or other creators of the content; pertinent identifying and publication or broadcast details (including information about original performance or source); the medium (MPEG video, MP3 file, etc.); and the URL.

37. John S. Allen, author of *The Omnivorous Mind: Our Evolving Relationship with Food,* interview with Chris Gondek, Harvard University Press website, podcast audio, July 15, 2012, http://www.hup.harvard.edu/news/audio/HUP_Allen.mp3.

38. Interview Treat a published interview like a periodical article or book chapter, including the phrase *interview with.*

38. Rachel Maddow, "The Maddow Knows," interview with Clara Jeffery, *Mother Jones,* January/February, 2009, 72–73.

If conducted online, include the URL. If on an audiovisual source, indicate the medium (see item 37).

For an unpublished interview, include in your text the names of the interviewer and person interviewed, date, and type of interview (such as *telephone interview*).

39. Lecture, speech, or debate In addition to the speaker(s) and title, in parentheses give the type of presentation, sponsor, location, and date.

39. Maria Jerskey, "At Their Point of Strength: Teaching Multilingual Writers of English" (paper presented at the 2009 Conference on College Composition and Communication, San Francisco, March 14, 2009).

20 Sample Paper 7: Student's Research Paper, *Chicago* Style

Here is a paper in *Chicago* style written by Ashley Hanson for Dr. Erik Trump's political science course Race and the U.S. Political System at Saginaw Valley State University in Michigan. The assignment was to write an introduction to Richard Wright's autobiographical book *American Hunger,* analyzing it as a political work rather than as an emotional record, as Wright calls it. Wright's complete text, which recounts his early life in Mississippi and his experiences after moving to Chicago in 1927, was to be published in 1944 with the original title, *American Hunger.* However, after the Book-of-the-Month Club requested that the politically focused second half be dropped, only the first part was published in 1945 as *Black Boy.* The second part was published posthumously in 1977 as *American Hunger.* In it, Wright tells of the social isolation, economic distress, and political concerns of black Southerners who had moved north. Hanson's class was asked to examine how the surrounding political context of the 1920s and 1930s affected the plight of African Americans and, more specifically, how the book reveals the political unrest of the time.

The paper is formatted and documented in *Chicago* style. Note that a *Chicago*-style paper begins with a title page, which is unnumbered, containing the paper title (centered and in all capital letters) and the author's name, course title, and date. The first full page of the text of the paper is numbered 1. Some instructors also request that the title be put above the first paragraph on page 1, as is done here. Because the paper contains a bibliography, short-form endnotes are used. The endnotes and bibliography pages are numbered consecutively after the text pages. For more information on formatting college papers in *Chicago* style, see Kate L. Turabian, *A Manual for Writers of Research Papers, Theses, and Dissertations,* 7th ed. (Chicago: U of Chicago P, 2007).

Note: Blue annotations point out issues of content and organization. Red annotations point out formatting features in *Chicago* style.

Chicago Manual of Style   **CHICAGO**

No page
number on
title page

AMERICAN HUNGER: A POLITICAL INTRODUCTION

Title (all
capitals)
centered,
1/3 way
down page

Ashley Hanson

Political Science 270: Race and the U.S. Political System

Fall 2011

Author's
name,
course
title, date
(centered,
capital and
lowercase
letters)

American Hunger: A Political Introduction

"Politics was not my game; the human heart was my game,
but it was only in the realm of politics that I could see the
depths of the human heart."

—Richard Wright, *American Hunger*[1]

In his book *American Hunger,* author Richard Wright
describes himself as a conveyer of human emotions, especially
those shared by African Americans, rather than a political writer.
This book, set in the late 1920s and 1930s, describes Wright's
experiences and hardships as a young African American man in
Chicago. On the surface, it is obvious that Wright delivers his story
in an emotional context. However, when one examines the book
from a deeper perspective, it becomes clear that this text not only is
an emotional depiction of African American life in the 1930s but also
is set in a much larger political context that greatly influences the
structure and transformation of the African American community.
Through his descriptions of his experiences, Wright exposes much of
the political unrest that African Americans endured during this time,
which resulted in political transformations, Communist allegiance,
and new artistic visions shaped by the New Deal programs.

American Hunger begins with Wright's journey from the
South to the northern city of Chicago. Between 1920 and 1930,
the time that Wright migrated north, approximately 872,000
African Americans left the South to move northward. Much

Title centered, capital and lowercase letters, double space below

1" margins on all four sides

Paper double-spaced throughout

Introduction establishes context

Superscript note numbers refer readers to citations in endnotes.

Thesis

Blue = content issues, **Red = format issues**

2

of this move could be attributed to the extreme political disenfranchisement, segregation, and violence that black people suffered in the southern states. Many black people believed that the North held more opportunity and possibility than they would ever be able to obtain in the South. Wright's recounting of his journey gives his reasoning for leaving the South and describes his adjustment to the northern city of Chicago.[2]

Like most black people, Wright believed that the North held greater opportunities; however, once he settled in Chicago, he quickly discovered that the North, too, was extremely racist. Although the North was not quite as openly prejudiced as the South, black people were still segregated into ghettos and suffered political limitations such as excessive unemployment.[3] In addition, the political significance of the migration had a potentially much more devastating effect on the black community. Just as Wright describes, once the African Americans began to settle into their northern homes, they became increasingly conscious of their race. In his book, Wright states that "color hate defined the place of black life as below that of white life; and the black man . . . strove to bury within his heart his awareness of this difference because it made him lonely and afraid."[4] As Wright explains, although black people migrated north to escape the hate and disenfranchisement, the harsh political effects of the move still overwhelmed them and left them feeling helpless and isolated.

As black Southerners began to experience isolation even in the northern cities, they also began to feel neglected by

Margin annotations:

Background information telling why black people moved north

Superscript note number placed after punctuation mark

Quotes Wright to illustrate point

Ellipsis points indicate part of quotation omitted

Blue = content issues, Red = format issues

3

the Republican Party. For years, African American allegiance had remained with the Republican Party because of Lincoln's support for ending slavery during the Civil War.[5] However, in the years following, the Republican Party disregarded the support of its black constituents, an action that forced them to rethink their loyalty to the party. Richard Wright himself wrote on a ballot for Republican candidate "Big Bill" Thompson the words *I protest this fraud!*[6] African Americans all over the country felt as though their loyalty to the party was being taken for granted, and they grew bitter toward the failed promises of the Republican Party.

In 1928, black allegiance to the Republican Party began to shift.[7] Slowly, the Democratic Party gained more support from the black community. In 1932, presidential candidate Franklin Delano Roosevelt promised to impose national relief programs and make "Negro" appointments to provide benefits to African Americans and promote their equality. In addition to stressing the relief programs in his campaign, he also appointed black cabinet members, and his wife, Eleanor Roosevelt, sat with the leading members of national African American groups.[8] To black people, FDR became known as a symbol of economic and political freedom.

Presents examples found through research to illustrate point

In a 1936 African American journal, a campaign advertisement was published for the reelection of Roosevelt under the slogan "Not Promise but Performance."[9] The advertisement outlined his relief programs and black appointments and encouraged black people to "Read what he has done . . . [and] vote for his re-election!"[10] One political cartoon, also published in 1936, showed FDR physically

Word in brackets added to quotation

4

Fig. 1: FDR Promises Economic Freedom.
Source: Originally published in *New York Amsterdam News,*
October 1936. Reprinted in Weiss, *Farewell to the Party of
Lincoln* (Princeton, NJ: Princeton University Press, 1983), 215.

leading a suppressed African American to economic freedom

(see Fig. 1). This shift of African American allegiance from the

Republican to the Democratic Party depicted a major change that

influenced blacks in the 1930s, and the hardships and neglect

that are so vividly illustrated in Wright's book accurately coincide

with the reason for the African Americans' political party shift.

The disregard and inequality they suffered forced them to shift

their political loyalty from the Republicans to the Democrats in

search of a much needed feeling of unity and usefulness.

One significant reason for African Americans' political

change from the Republicans to the Democrats was the New Deal

programs initiated by President Franklin Delano Roosevelt; the

Blue = content issues, **Red = format issues**

CHICAGO *Chicago Manual of Style*

5

experiences described in *American Hunger* are deeply intertwined with many of these programs. The New Deal programs that were established by FDR were essentially an attempt by the federal government to manage the economy and provide assistance to unemployed and poor citizens, including African Americans. Organizations such as the Works Progress Administration (WPA) and the Public Works Administration (PWA) were established and employed a large number of black people in the country.[11] For example, a Democratic campaign advertisement that was published in an African American journal confirmed that the "unemployment relief inaugurated by the Roosevelt Administration saved millions of Negro men, women, and children from extreme want by direct relief, WPA and PWA."[12] These New Deal programs created by Roosevelt provided many new economic and political opportunities for African American citizens in the United States.

Wright's experiences with the New Deal programs not only coincided with the greater political context of the era but also provide a window to view how these programs intersected with African Americans' artistic visions. For example, one of the jobs Wright was given by the government was working in the Federal Negro Theater, an art division under the WPA. While working in this theater, Wright describes his larger goal, one of great political importance, which was to create a genuine Negro theater to depict the realities of African American life. He believed that the "heart of the Negro actor was pining for adult expression in the American theater,"[13] and he wanted to be able to help black people express their feelings.

Transition: Expands discussion to show significance of New Deal arts programs for black people's artistic aspirations

Quotation incorporated into sentence

Blue = content issues, **Red = format issues**

6

Wright's goal was shared by the overall objective found in these Federal Arts relief programs. These political arts programs did many things to document the experience of the African American. For example, the theater produced all-black performances of *Macbeth,* the writing division produced an oral history project that included southern ex-slaves' stories, and guidebooks were created by black people that included a history of African Americans.[14] Overall, Wright's explanation of his experiences with the relief programs and his artistic visions that resulted from his experiences intersect with the New Deal programs and the larger political framework of the time period.

Despite these New Deal programs and the exposure to art that Wright and other African Americans received, many black people began to turn to the Communist Party as a means to pursue their artistic endeavors. The Communist Party was a great supporter of African American art. Wright himself said, "I owe my literary development to the Communist Party and its influence, which has shaped my thoughts and creative growth."[15] In a sense, African Americans turned to the Communist Party because it gave them a feeling of hope within America when everyone else had abandoned them. For example, the lynching of black people became a very prominent issue in the early 1900s, yet the response of the Democratic Party to brutal lynchings was one of disregard. Although Roosevelt claimed to oppose lynching, his fear of losing the support of southern Democrats kept him from pushing any anti-lynching bills through the Senate.[16] Conversely, in 1928,

Provides transition from discussion of New Deal art programs to Communist support of African American art and broader political support of African Americans

Blue = content issues, **Red = format issues**

7

the Communist Party publicly denounced lynching in its party

platform and urged black people to organize against the practice.

In a 1934 election leaflet titled *Why Every Negro Should Vote Communist,* the author points out that "[the Communist Party] is the only party that fights against lynching, jim-crowism, [and] discrimination, and for complete equality and freedom of the Negro people."[17] In addition, in 1925 the Communist Party integrated their black and white memberships, long before the two major parties did so, in order to advance the Communist Party's political well-being. As a result, some African Americans began to show greater allegiance to the Communist Party in the 1930s. In Wright's discussion of his ties to the Communist Party, he states, "It was not the economics of Communism, nor the great power of trade unions, nor the excitement of underground politics that claimed me; my attention was caught by the similarity of the experiences of workers in other lands, by the possibility of uniting scattered but kindred peoples into a whole."[18] Just as Wright's search for unity and integration, as recounted in this book, led him to the Communist Party, African Americans as a whole in the 1930s were drawn to the Communist Party because of the support it provided for black artists and because of its sense of unity and kinship, a feeling many African Americans had never known before.

Overall, the early 1900s were a time of unrest and political turmoil for many African Americans. Even those who had moved north to escape the hatred and isolation of the South were still unhappy and felt abandoned. Wright's book *American Hunger*

Words in brackets added in quotation

Transition: Expands discussion and presents examples to show why black people, including Wright, turned to the Communist Party

Superscript note number placed after period and closing quotation mark

8

does an excellent job of shaping this feeling and opening the reader's eyes to the larger issues of the era. Although Wright claims he is neither a political person nor a political writer, the issues he exposes in his book seem to express the overall plight of African Americans in a largely political manner. Wright's words and experiences resonate in a way that allows his readers not only to sympathize with the emotions and sentiments he felt but also to understand his hardships, and those of other African Americans, in a much broader political culture. Just as African Americans in the 1930s continued searching for a feeling of unity and equality even during times of struggle, Wright's main goal when writing this book was to "send other words to tell, to march to fight, to create a sense of the hunger for life that gnaws in us all, to keep alive in our hearts a sense of the inexpressibly human."[19] And he succeeded.

Conclusion restates thesis and expands on it to discuss significance of Wright's book for readers.

CHICAGO

Chicago Manual of Style

Double-space twice between head and first note.

9

Notes page numbered consecutively

NOTES

Short-form notes used because complete details of sources in bibliography

Single-space notes; double-space between notes.

1. Wright, *American Hunger*, 46.

2. Trump, class lecture.

3. Ibid.

Ibid. indicates source is same as one in previous note.

4. Wright, *Black Boy*, 266.

5. Trump, class lecture.

6. Wright, *Black Boy*, 298.

Indent first line of note ½ inch (paragraph indent).

7. Trump, class lecture.

8. Ibid.

9. Democratic campaign advertisement, in Weiss, *Farewell to the Party*, 188.

Source contained within a larger source

10. Ibid.

Short-form note: Author's last name, shortened title, page number

11. Trump, class lecture.

12. Democratic campaign advertisement, in Weiss, *Farewell to the Party*, 188.

13. Wright, *Black Boy*, 365.

Secondary source: Author quoted in another source. Both sources listed in bibliography.

14. Trump, class lecture.

15. Wright, *Daily Worker*, February 25, 1938, quoted in Naison, *Communists in Harlem*, 210–11.

16. Trump, class lecture.

17. Communist Party, *Why Every Negro*.

No page number for Web source

18. Wright, *Black Boy*, 318.

19. Ibid., 384.

Blue = content issues, **Red = format issues**

Chicago Manual of Style   CHICAGO

Entries listed
alphabetically.
Periods
separate major
components.

Double-space
twice between
head and first
entry.

Hanging
indent: First
line flush left;
subsequent
lines indented
½ inch.

Access date
given when
no date of
posting or
update;
period after
URL ends
entry.

Author's name
inverted for
alphabetizing

No periods in
abbreviations
in notes or
bibliography

Head centered,
all capital
letters

BIBLIOGRAPHY

Page number
(consecutive)
in right-hand
corner

Communist Party. *Why Every Negro Should Vote Communist.*
    Leaflet, 1934. A. E. Forbes Communist Collection.
    Archives Service Center. Digital Research Library,
    University of Pittsburgh. Accessed October 17, 2012.
    http://images.library.pitt.edu/a/aeforbes/.

Democratic campaign advertisement, in *Opportunity,* October
    1936. Reprinted in Nancy J. Weiss, *Farewell to the
    Party of Lincoln: Black Politics in the Age of FDR,* 188.
    Princeton, NJ: Princeton University Press, 1983.

"FDR Promises Economic Freedom." Political Cartoon. *New
    York Amsterdam News,* October 1936. Reprinted in Weiss,
    Farewell to the Party of Lincoln,* 188.

Naison, Mark. *Communists in Harlem During the Depression.*
    New York: Grove, 1984.

Trump, Erik. Class lecture. Political Science 270: Race and
    the U.S. Political System, Fall 2009. Saginaw Valley State
    University, University Center, MI. October 7, 2009.

Weiss, Nancy. *Farewell to the Party of Lincoln: Black Politics in the
    Age of FDR.* Princeton, NJ: Princeton University Press, 1983.

Wright, Richard. *American Hunger: The Compelling Continuation
    of Richard Wright's Autobiographical Work, Black Boy.*
    New York: Harper, 1977.

———. *Black Boy.* 60th anniversary ed. New York: Harper
    Perennial Modern Classics, 2007.

———. [Unknown article title]. *Daily Worker.* February 25, 1938.

Organization
as author

Entry lists
information
about leaflet
and details
about
collection,
archive, online
source, and
sponsor.

Source
reprinted in
another source

Single-space
entries;
double-space
between
entries.

Reprint
edition—
pertinent
details given
about
previous
editions.

Only sources
used in the
paper are
listed

5 Design, Media, and Presentation

DESIGN

To obtain study resources for this section, visit the English CourseMate for this text at **www.cengagebrain.com**

5 Design, Media, and Presentation

There's no getting around it: medium (such as print, online, video, etc.) is an important part of your writing context, which is why it's part of the Critical Thinking Framework introduced in Part 1. Your choice of medium, and how well you use its capabilities, will leave an impression on your audience. Your audience will have expectations about what a particular type of communication should look like, and, to make an impression that inspires their interest and confidence in what you have to say, you will want to fulfill those expectations. Straying from those expectations is also an option, but you only want to do that if you have a specific reason for doing so that will communicate with your audience. Whether it's an English essay or a scientific report, a Web-based résumé or a post on a community-based blog, the design and presentation of your writing communicates to your readers that you understand the conventions required by your writing context. Equally important, it can help you communicate your message as effectively as possible.

While the design of texts and presentation of information have always been important, the expansion of digital media has enhanced our ability to make strong, media-rich impressions and skillfully convey information to our readers and listeners. It's not unusual to see text (in words) joined by pictures, photographs, tables, graphs, sound, and video to convey information and emotion, often more immediately and dramatically than is possible with words alone. During presentations, audiences are accustomed to visuals that are digital slides, often with other media embedded into the slides to enhance and illustrate what they are hearing and seeing in the presentation.

Whether you are tweeting to readers around the globe or sending a message to an older family member who just discovered *Facebook*, whether you are formatting your English professor's six-page essay assignment or putting the final touches on

See the full model on page 7.

your e-portfolio before sending the link to a prospective employer, you will want to ask yourself (or your professor) this: What medium is most appropriate for my writing context, what will my audience's expectations be for that medium, and how can I communicate my message with the most impact?

21 Document Design

21a Formatting academic writing in print

As you draft, revise, and edit your writing, you can think about how you'll prepare it for presentation to readers. Guides are available for presenting academic essays in specific disciplines and media. Frequently used style guides are those published by the Modern Language Association (MLA), American Psychological Association (APA), Council of Science Editors (CSE), and *The Chicago Manual of Style*. The features of these guides are covered in parts 3 and 4 of this handbook. However, commonalities exist among the differences. Basic guidelines are in the Key Points box for preparing your essay on paper, whichever style guide you follow. See 21g for a table and detailed instructions for *Word* functions that can help with formatting academic writing, including tips for navigating the function in whichever version you may have installed on your computer.

> ### KEY POINTS
> ### Guidelines for College Essay Format
>
> - **Paper** White bond, unlined, 8½" × 11". Clip or staple the pages.
> - **Print** Dark black printing ink—an inkjet or laser printer if possible.
> - **Margins** One inch all around. In some styles, one and one-half inches may be acceptable. Lines should have justified left but ragged right margins.
> - **Space between lines** Uniformly double-spaced, including any list of works cited. Footnotes (in *Chicago* style) may be single-spaced.
> - **Spaces after a period, question mark, or exclamation point** One space, as suggested by most style manuals. Your instructor may prefer two in the text of your essay.
> - **Type font and size** Standard type font (such as Times New Roman or Arial), not a fancy font that looks like handwriting. Select a regular size of 10 to 12 points.
> - **Page numbers** In the top right margin. (In MLA style, put your last name before the page number. In APA style, put a short version of the title, called a running head, on the left and the page

number on the right.) Use Arabic numerals with no period. (See p. 347; 21g shows the header formatting tools available in *Word*.)

- **Paragraphing** Indent one-half inch (five spaces) from the left.
- **Title and identification** On the first page or on a separate title page. See the examples below and on pages 226 and 283.
- **Parentheses around a source citation** MLA and APA style, for any source you refer to or quote, including the textbook for your course; then add at the end an alphabetical list of works cited.

Note: Your instructor may prefer a separate title page or ask you to include the identification material on the first page of the essay.

Title and identification on the first page   The following sample of part of a first page shows one format for identifying a paper and giving it a title. The MLA recommends this format for papers in the humanities.

Croasdale 1

Yulanda Croasdale

Professor Raimes

English 120, Section 13

5 April 2012

Jamaican-American: A New Culture

To outsiders, the emergence of a strong Jamaican-

American community is probably not a noticeable occurrence,

though insiders are all too well aware of their growing population

and spread of notoriety.

At the top of subsequent pages, write the page number in the upper right corner, preceded by your last name (21g shows you how to make this header). No period or parentheses accompany the page number.

Title and identification on a separate title page　In the humanities, include a title page only if your instructor requires one or if you include an outline. (For the social sciences or other academic areas, see part 4.) On the title page include the following, all double-spaced:

> **Title:** Centered, about one-third of the way down the page. Do not enclose the title in quotation marks, do not italicize or underline it, and do not put a period at the end.
>
> **Name:** Centered, after the word *by*, on a separate line.
>
> **Course information:** College course and section, instructor, and date, each centered on a new line, either directly below your name or at the bottom of the title page.

With a title page, you do not need the title and identification on your first page.

21b Formatting academic writing online

You may be required to submit an essay for a course online rather than in hard copy. Your instructor may ask you to e-mail an attachment, or in a hybrid or distance-learning course, you may be required to submit your essays in a dropbox or post them on a class online discussion board for the instructor and other students to read and comment on. Alternatively, you may have your own e-portfolio (25b) where you display your work. In any of these cases, keep in mind the following general guidelines, and ask your instructor for instructions specific to the course, format, and type of posting.

Guidelines for posting academic writing online　Recent versions of word processing programs can automatically convert a document and save it as an HTML file for the Web. In *Word*, for example, you simply produce your document in the usual way but then, when you save it, go to "Save As" and change "Save as type" from "Word" to "Web page." The HTML commands are done for you automatically. The automatic coding can create some formatting issues because the code is not clean, but it can be a useful alternative if you do not know how to code in HTML yourself. If you would prefer to write the document in an HTML editor instead of *Word, KompoZer* is a free, open-source application you can download that is easy to use.

KEY POINTS
Posting Academic Writing Online

- **Structure** Set up a structure with sections and subsections, all with headings, that allows each section to be accessed directly through a link—for example, from your table of contents (see the next point) and from any other part of your paper as well. So instead of saying diffusely, "See above" or "See below," you can provide a specific link allowing readers to jump directly to this part (see the *internal hyperlinks* list entry).

- **Links to sections from a table of contents** Provide a table of contents, with an internal link to each section. Readers can then click and go directly to any section they are interested in.

- **Internal hyperlinks** Use internal hyperlinks (Insert/Bookmark) to connect readers directly to relevant sections of your text, content notes, and visuals. Also provide a link from a source cited in the body of your paper to the entry in your list of works cited.

- **External hyperlinks** Use external hyperlinks (Insert/Hyperlink) to connect to Web documents from references in the body of your paper and from your list of works cited. Useful for the works-cited list, *Word* has a function that will automatically convert any string starting with <http://> into a hyperlink.

- **No paragraph indentation** Do not indent new paragraphs when writing online. Instead, leave a line space between paragraphs.

- **Attribution of sources** Make sure that the link you give to an online article in a database is a persistent link, not a link that works for only a few hours or days. Typically, you shouldn't just link to where you got an article in a library database, but find the link to get to the article directly without going through the database. You might need to copy the link, open a new browser, and try it. It is often difficult to determine at first glance whether a link is persistent. Some databases are explicit; others are not. Double-check your links after a few days to see whether they are still working. Some sites such as *Thomas* at the Library of Congress <http://thomas.loc.gov> and *EBSCO* databases provide persistent links.

- **List of works cited or list of references** Give a complete list, even if you provide some external links to the sources from the body of your paper. If a reader prints your paper, the exact references will then still be available.

21c Typefaces

What's in a typeface? A lot. It's not just what you write but also how it looks when it's read. Fitting the typeface to the content of a public document can be seen as an aesthetic challenge, as it was for the choice of the simple and legible Gotham typeface for the Freedom Tower cornerstone at the site of the former World Trade Center. The silver-leaf letters, with strokes of uniform width with no decorative touches, have been described by David Dunlap in the *New York Times* as conjuring "the exuberant, modernist, midcentury optimism of New York even as they augur the glass and stainless-steel tower to come." That's what's in a typeface. The cornerstone, according to Dunlap, looks "neutral enough so that viewers could impose their own meanings" on a site of profound historical and emotional impact.

James Estrin/The New York Times

Of course, designing the presentation of a college essay is not the same as designing a historic monument. However, you can still make a choice that emphasizes simplicity and legibility.

For college essays in hard copy, consider using the following:

For the body of the text: Times New Roman or some other *serif* font. (A *serif* font has little strokes—serifs—at the top and bottom of individual characters.)

For captions and headings: Arial or some other *sans serif* font. (The word *sans* is French for "without"; a sans serif font does not have the little strokes at the top and bottom of the characters.)

Avoid ornamental fonts such as *Monotype Corsiva* and **𝓑𝓻𝓾𝓼𝓱 𝓢𝓬𝓻𝓲𝓹𝓽**. They are distracting and hard to read.

Note that if you are designing a Web page or other online communication, your readers' computer settings determine which fonts can be displayed. The simpler the font you choose (Times, **Arial**, Georgia, and **Verdana** all work well on both PC and Mac browsers), the more likely readers are to see your chosen font.

For the body of your text in a college essay or a piece of business communication, stick to 10- to 12-point type. Use larger type only for headings and subheadings in business, technical, or Web documents (see 21b and chapter 24). Never increase or decrease font size (or margins) to achieve a required page length. You will convey desperation, and you will certainly not fool your instructor.

Note: MLA and APA guidelines do not recommend typeface changes or bold type for titles and headings.

21d Color

Color printers and online publication have made the production of documents an exciting enterprise for both writers and readers. You can include graphs and illustrations in color, and you can highlight headings or parts of your text by using a different color typeface. However, simplicity and readability should prevail. Use color only when its use will enhance your message. Certainly, in the design of business reports, newsletters, brochures, and Web pages, color can play an important and eye-catching role. Color can be expensive to print, however, so minimize use of color for documents that must be reproduced for a large number of people. For college essays, the leading style manuals ignore and implicitly discourage the use of color. Also keep in mind that many people may not have a color printer, and printing color charts on a black-and-white printer may produce shades that are difficult to distinguish.

21e Headings

Headings divide text into helpful chunks and give readers a sense of your document's structure. Main divisions are marked by first-level headings, subdivisions by second-level and third-level headings. In the heading structure of chapter 21, for example, the main heading is "Document Design," and the subheadings include "Formatting academic writing in print," "Formatting academic writing online," "Typefaces," "Color," "Headings," "Lists," and "Academic design features in *MS Word*."

For headings, bear in mind the following recommendations:

- If you use subheadings, use at least two—not just one. If you think you only need one subheading, the point can probably be incorporated under the main heading.

- Whenever possible, use your word processing program's Style feature to determine the level of heading you need: heading 1, 2, 3, and so on. This will make it easy to produce a Table of Contents with internal links when your document is finished and will help you maintain consistency throughout the document.
- Style manuals, such as the one for APA style, recommend specific formats for typeface and position on the page for levels of headings. Follow these recommended formats. See chapter 16 for an APA paper with headings.
- Keep headings clear, brief, and parallel in grammatical form (for instance, all commands: "Set Up Sales Strategies"; all beginning with *-ing* words: "Setting Up Sales Strategies"; or all noun-plus-modifier phrases: "Sales Strategies").

21f Lists

Lists are particularly useful in business reports, proposals, and memos. They direct readers' attention to the outlined points or steps. Decide whether to use numbers, dashes, or bullets to set off the items in a list. Introduce the list with a sentence ending in a colon. Items in the list should be parallel in grammatical form: all commands, all *-ing* phrases, or all noun phrases, for example. Listed items should not end with a period unless they are complete sentences.

21g Academic design features in *MS Word*

As a college student in the twenty-first century, you probably find it second nature to use the functions of a word processing program to add, delete, move material, and check your spelling. But a word processor also can help you fulfill the conventions of academic writing and the formatting functions that your audience may expect.

This section outlines the features of *Word* that are most useful in academic writing. You'll find a table on page 350 with brief instructions for accessing the features in different versions of *Word*. (*WordPerfect* provides similar functions, as does a free alternative to *Word*, *OpenOffice*. For full details on the following list of tasks, consult your word processing program's written documentation, built-in "Help" files, or online training and customer support.)

1. Formatting a document using templates and styles No matter which version you are using—*Word 2007* or *2010* for PC; or *Word 2011* for Mac—*Word* provides useful ready-made design formats called *templates* for an MLA essay, APA paper, and a term paper. It also has templates for many other documents you may need to produce in college and beyond, including résumés, brochures, and newsletters. In addition, you can create and save your own templates. Most word processing programs also use *styles*—a mechanism for setting document format choices that apply to the entire document rather than to individual parts. In *Word 2010* for PC, the styles feature is easier to use than previous versions. Using the styles feature lets you establish the default look and feel of your document and maintain a consistency of design so you don't have to worry about formatting choices while you are writing or editing.

2. Adding a header or footer on every page   The Header and Footer options allow you to (1) include a page number along with any text, such as your name or a short running head; (2) include the date and time; and (3) toggle between the choice of headers or footers. Headers and footers will adjust automatically to any changes in the pagination of your document. You type the information once only, and it appears in the place you specify on every page, however much material you add or delete.

Header Screen, *Word 2011* for Mac

© 2012 Microsoft

3. Inserting visuals, charts, and graphs   The Insert menu provides access to useful functions. Here, you can insert into your text a page number, a footnote, or a hyperlink to a URL, though you can also set up *Word* to hyperlink all the URLs automatically (Tools/AutoCorrect/AutoFormat As You Type). You can insert Comments into your own or someone else's document, a useful feature for writing collaboratively and giving feedback.

It is also possible to insert into your text a picture, caption, diagram, or chart. For presentation of data, the chart feature is particularly helpful and easy to use: You simply type your data into a data grid and then choose from a wide variety of charts, such as bar, line, pie, doughnut, scatter, and pyramid. One click—and your chart appears. (On pages 354 and 356 in 22b, Figures 2 and 5 show a graph and a chart made in *Word*.)

4. Inserting a table Tables can help you organize your data into easy-to-read columns and rows.

Word 2011 **for Mac**

Word 2010 **for PC**

5. Formatting your document As you move toward your final draft, you will want to format your document using some of the following features:

- **Font** Options are available for changing typeface, styles, and size as well as using superscripts, useful for *Chicago Manual of Style* citations; see also 21c
- **Paragraph** Options are given for line spacing and indenting (see the screen capture below for how to set the special command for the hanging indents used in an MLA list of works cited)
- **Bullets and Numbering** Options are given for lists, Borders and Shading, Columns, Tabs, Dropped Capitals (just highlight the text to be formatted)
- **Change Case** Options are provided for changing text from capital letters to lowercase, or vice versa

Format Manager, *Word 2011* for Mac

6. Editing with *Word*: Checking, correcting, and changing All versions of *Word* give you access to a word count, to spelling and grammar checkers and a thesaurus, and to AutoCorrect and AutoFormat functions (such as turning off the automatic hyperlinks when you do not need them underlined for an MLA list of works cited). Note that you can set a grammar checker to look for specific features, such as "Punctuation with quotes" and "Passive sentences." You may also find the Track Changes feature to be a useful tool for adding editing suggestions to your own or somebody else's text.

7. Using *Word* to format citations   *Word 2007* or *2010* and *Word 2011* for Mac will format a citation you include in your paper into MLA, APA, or *Chicago* style and add the source to a list that will be used for your bibliography. *Word* will form a bibliography in the style you determine, using only sources you have cited in your paper via the Bibliography command on the References tab. There are also some tools available that extend the functionality of earlier versions of *Word*, and other word processors, such as *OpenOffice*, also include the citation/bibliography feature in their latest versions.

Accessing Formatting Options in Different Versions of *MS Word*

	Word 2007 (PC)	*Word 2010* (PC)	*Word 2011* (Mac)
Margins	Formatting Toolbar	Page Setup/Page Layout	View Menu
Headers/Footers	Insert Tab	Insert Tab	View Menu
Page Numbers	Insert Menu	Insert Menu	Insert Menu
Footnotes/Endnotes	Insert Menu	Insert Menu	Insert Menu
Comments	Review Tab	Review Tab	Insert Menu and Review Tab
Track Changes	Review Tab	Review Tab	Review Tab
Visuals	Insert Menu	Insert Menu	Insert Menu
Tables	Table (on toolbar)	Table (on toolbar)	Table Menu
Font Style	Home Tab	Home Tab	Home Tab and Format Menu
Paragraph Formatting	Home Tab	Home Tab	Format Menu
Bullets/Numbering	Home Tab	Home Tab	Home Tab and Format Menu
Word Count	Review Tab	Review Tab	Tools Menu
Citations	References Tab	References Tab	View Menu/Citations
Spelling and Grammar Check	Review Tab	Review Tab	Tools Menu

● TECH NOTE

Versions of *Word* for PC and Mac

It is not unusual to find both Mac and PC computers in college computer laboratories, so you may need to become familiar with both *Word* for PCs and *Word* for Mac. If you are a PC user and have recently upgraded to *Word 2010* from *Word 2007*, go to <http://technet.microsoft.com/en-us/library/cc179199.aspx> to learn more about the changes in *Word 2010*. If you're a Mac user, take advantage of the interactive tutorials for *Word for Mac 2011* features at <http://www.microsoft.com/mac/word/getting-started-with-word>.

22 Visuals

The technology of scanners, photocopiers, smart phones, digital cameras, and downloaded images provides the means of making documents more functional and more attractive by allowing the inclusion of visual material. Frequently, when you are dealing with arguments using complicated data, the best way to get information across to readers is to display it visually.

For a college paper, you can download visuals from the Web (with a source acknowledgment) to strengthen an argument or to present data clearly and efficiently. Alternatively, computers make it easy for you to take data from your own research and present the data in a table, graph, or chart (22a, 22b).

KEY POINTS
On Using Visuals

1. **Plan** Decide which type of visual presentation best fits your data, and determine where to place your visuals; these are usually best within your text. However, APA style for printed papers requires visuals to be placed in an appendix.

2. **Introduce** Whenever you place a visual in your text, introduce it and discuss it fully before readers come across it. Do not just make a perfunctory comment like "The results are significant, as seen in Figure 1." Rather, say something like "Figure 1 shows an increase in the number of accidents since 2005." Keep in mind

(Continued)

(Continued)

that the visual should supplement your words but not replace them. In your discussion, indicate where the visual appears ("In the table below" or "In the pie chart on page 8"), and carefully interpret or analyze the visual for readers, using it as an aid that supports your points, not as something that can stand alone.

3. **Compress** When you include a visual in an online document, make sure the image file is not so large that it will take a long time for readers to download.

4. **Identify** Give each visual a title, number each visual if you use more than one of the same type, and credit the source.

5. **Avoid filler** Do not include visuals simply to fill space or make your document look colorful. Every visual addition should enhance your content and provide an interesting and relevant illustration.

22a Tables

Tables are useful for presenting data in columns and rows. They help readers keep track of and comprehend data that might otherwise be confusing if included just in the text itself. They can be created easily with word processing programs using figures from large sets of data, as in the following table.

Table 1 **Party Affiliation among Hispanic Registered Voters in Florida, 2006 to 2012**

	Republicans	Democrats	Other Party	No Party Affiliation	Total
2012*	452,619	564,513	25,657	431,131	1,473,920
2010	445,353	550,799	25,082	404,570	1,425,804
2008	445,526	513,252	23,500	372,992	1,355,270
2006	414,185	369,902	16,915	312,881	1,113,883

Note: *Data for 2012 as of January 3, 2012, the presidential preference primary book closing date. The Florida presidential preference primary election date is Tuesday January 31, 2012. For all other years, data reflect general election book closing dates.
Source: Florida Division of Elections http://election.dos.state.fl.us/voter-registration/statistics/elections.shtml

22b Graphs and charts

Graphs and charts are useful for presenting data and comparisons of data. Many software products allow you to produce graphs easily, and even standard word processing software gives you several ways to present your numbers in visual form. In *Microsoft Office*, you can create graphs and charts in *Word* or *Excel*. Whether you work in *Word* for Mac or for PC, you are able to select a type of chart, such as a pie chart or a bar chart, and enter your own details, such as title, labels for the vertical and horizontal axes of a bar chart, numbers, and data labels.

Chart Menu, *Word 2011* for Mac

Simple line graph   Use a line graph to show changes over time. Figure 1 has a clear caption and is self-explanatory.

Figure 1 Relationship of Income to Education

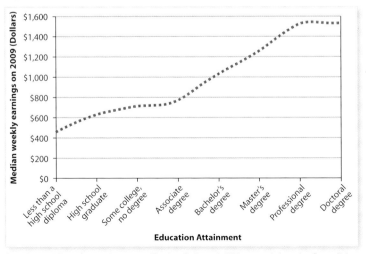

Source: Data are 2009 annual averages for persons age 25 and over. Earnings are for full-time wage and salary workers. Bureau of Labor Statistics, Current Population Survey. BLS has some data on the employment status of the civilian noninstitutional population 25 years and over by educational attainment, sex, race, and Hispanic origin online. The Bureau of the Census also has some data on the educational attainment online at <http://www.bls.gov/emp/p_chart_001.txt>.

Comparative line graph Line graphs are especially useful for comparing data over time. Figure 2, for example, compares unemployment rates in the European Union, European Area, the United States, and Japan from 2000–2012.

Figure 2 Unemployment Rates in the European Union, European Area, the United States, and Japan

Source: http://epp.eurostat.ec.europa.eu/statistics_explained/index.php/Unemployment_statistics

 KEY POINTS
Using Graphs and Charts

- Use a graph or chart only to help make a point.
- Set up a graph or chart so that it is self-contained and self-explanatory.
- Make sure that the items on the time axis of a line graph are proportionately spaced.
- Always provide a clear caption.
- Use precise wording for labels.
- Always give details about the source of the data or the chart itself if you download from the Web.
- Choose a value range for the axes of a graph that does not exaggerate or downplay change (see 22e).

Pie chart Use a pie chart to show how fractions and percentages relate to one another and make up a whole. Figure 3 shows petroleum imports in the United States in 2011.

Figure 3 Sources of US Net Petroleum Imports, 2011

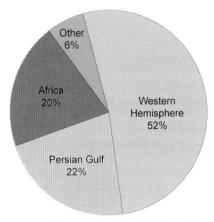

Source: U.S. Energy Information Administration, *Petroleum Supply Monthly* (February 2012), preliminary data.

Bar chart A bar chart is useful to show comparisons and correlations and to highlight differences among groups. The bar chart in Figure 4, created in *MS Word*, displays the number of students who frequently or occasionally discussed politics during the presidential election years since 1988. The chart shows that in 2008 the number of students who frequently discussed politics was at its highest level (35.6%) in twenty years.

Figure 4 Discussion of Politics among Freshmen during Election Years
(vertical bar chart)

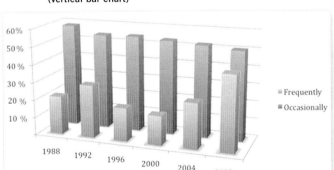

Source: Data are from Sylvia Hurtado and John H. Pryor, *The American Freshman: National Norms for Fall 2008*, Los Angeles, Higher Education Research Institute, University of California, 2009 at <http://www.gseis.ucla.edu/heri/heri/html>, slide 14; sample size varies over the years; for 2008, data are based on the responses of 240,580 first-time, full-time freshmen at 340 four-year colleges and universities.

A bar chart can also be presented horizontally, which makes it easier to attach labels to the bars. Figure 5 was produced in *MS Office* using the data from Table 1 on page 352.

Figure 5 **Party Affiliation among Hispanic Registered Voters in Florida (horizontal bar chart)**

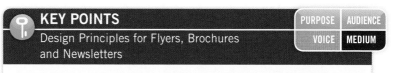

Source: Data are from the Florida Division of Elections, http://election.dos.state.fl.us/voter-registration/statistics/elections.shtml

22c Flyers, brochures, and newsletters

Although it is generally better to use document design software (such as *Adobe InDesign*) for creating publishable document formats, it is certainly possible to create simple flyers, brochures, and newsletters using word processing software. Templates for flyers, brochures, and newsletters are available on your word processor, and they provide layouts that must be customized with text and images. Careful attention to the elements of design increases the chance that your flyer, brochure, or newsletter will be read and have the effect you hoped.

KEY POINTS | PURPOSE | AUDIENCE
Design Principles for Flyers, Brochures and Newsletters | VOICE | MEDIUM

Some basic principles can help you design a successful print communication in academic, community, or business settings:

- **Plan:** Consider the writing situation of your document. Who is the audience? What is the purpose? What is the most important message you are communicating?
- **Experiment:** Leave time to play with the design—colors, type-faces, images, white space, and so on—and get feedback from sample audience members.

- **Value readability and clarity:** Give priority to important information.
- **Be consistent:** Keep all design elements consistent (headers, margins, typefaces, captions, and so on).
- **Consider standard design principles**
  - Type size and font: Choose a readable type size. Serif typefaces (the ones with the little strokes at the top and bottom of each letter) are more readable and are thus the best choice for the main body of the document. For headlines and headings, use a limited number of other larger type sizes.
  - Use of white space: Allow for a generous amount of white space in your margins and borders. Adequate line spacing is important, too, to make the text easy to read.
  - End-of-line alignment: Justified lines (lines that are all the same length to create a squared-off box of text) appear more formal, have a greater type density, and can create a lot of hyphenated words; lines that are ragged right create a less formal and more open look.
  - Column width and line length: Shorter columns and shorter lines of type are easier to read (but too many columns on one page may overwhelm your readers).
  - Boxes and sidebars: Boxing a part of your document can give it extra emphasis or attention.

22d Images and copyright issues

Your computer software provides many standard images (clip art) and photographs that you can use free in your documents without any copyright concerns. Web sites offer images to download, either free or at a small cost. Keep in mind, however, that unless the creator of the image has explicitly stated that it is free for noncommercial use (either by a statement on the Web site or by using a Creative Commons license), you should assume that the image is copyrighted and not free for the taking.

Note that if your document is to be posted on the Web, readers who have slow Internet connections may find it time-consuming or even impossible to download images with a large file size. Use a lower quality setting for .jpg files or the .gif or .png format instead (resave if necessary).

Sophisticated and original graphics are usually copyrighted, so if you intend to use an image in a document that you post on the Web or make widely available in print, you must do more than download the image and cite the source. The "fair use" principle of copyright law allows use of a small portion of a source in a noncommercial work, but you may need to write to the originator for permission to use an image or text.

For a college paper intended for your classmates and instructor alone and not posted publicly on the Web, you may want to include an illustration you find on the Web, such as a graph, a map, a photograph of an author or artist, a work of art, or an illustration from an online encyclopedia. You can do so without getting permission, but you must cite the source in your paper.

22e Honesty in visuals

With the ability to use software programs such as *Photoshop* to crop, combine, juxtapose, erase, and enhance images come attendant dangers and innumerable opportunities for comedy. Late night talk-show hosts show edited photos and video clips from the day's news to hilarious effect. Image manipulation can also be used for political effect (such as Josef Stalin's order to delete Leon Trotsky from photographs that show Lenin). In academic work, the changing of images is never acceptable. Falsifying data can reach the level of fraud, as in the case of a scientist who manipulated images of stem cells to achieve personal ambition. Scientific journals are beginning to check photos that are submitted with research to ensure that they have not been manipulated to remove images, change the contrast, or combine images from several slides into one.

The lesson here is a simple one: Be ethical in your use of visuals.

Charts and graphs can also be manipulated—not by changing the original data but simply by selectively plotting the axes of a graph. Take care when choosing the value range for the axes to avoid exaggerating or downplaying changes over time. For example, for comparative data on population projections ranging between a 50% and 60% increase, a vertical axis of 0% to 100% will show the lines as almost flat, indicating little change over time. However, a vertical axis of 40% to 70% will emphasize and maybe exaggerate the small projected increase—one that could be attributable solely to a sampling fluctuation.

23 Online Communication Forums

23a E-mail in academic and business settings

Communicating online to professors or supervisors in academic or business contexts is different from writing personal e-mail. Observe the following conventions.

Salutations   Although e-mail can seem like an informal medium, when communicating with your professor or with individuals that you do not know well, you should begin your e-mail with an appropriate salutation. Unless your instructor tells you otherwise, you should use "Dear Professor [Name]:" to start your e-mail. If you are addressing an individual in an organization, find out and use that person's title. Don't address someone who is not your peer and whom you don't know well by a first name unless instructed to do so.

Subject line   Be clear and concise when composing a subject line so that readers will know at a glance what your message is about. Well-written subject lines will also make it easier to find a message if you want to refer to it later.

Length and readability   Be brief, and state your main points clearly at the start. One screen holds about 250 words, and online readers do not want to scroll repeatedly to find out what you are saying. Keep paragraphs short and manageable so that readers can take in the information at a glance. Use numbered or bulleted lists to present a sequence of points as brief items that can be readily seen and absorbed. Avoid multiple colors, fonts, and graphics unless you are certain readers can receive and read these features.

Capitals   Avoid using all capital letters in an e-mail message. To readers, it looks as if you are SHOUTING. But do use capitals when appropriate, especially for "I."

Accuracy   Use a spelling checker and edit your e-mail before sending if you are writing to people you do not know well and you want them to take your ideas seriously.

Signing off   Always put your actual name (not just <cutiepie3@gmail.com>) at the end of your online message. You can also construct a "signature file," which will appear automatically at the end of every message you send. Find out how to do this from the Help or Tools menu of your e-mail program.

E-mail accounts If possible, send your e-mail from an account that the receiver will take seriously. Beware of e-mailing important information from accounts with addresses that seemed "cute" in one context (like the <cutiepie3@gmail.com> address above) or might sound overly personal. In an academic setting, use your account from the school if you have one. If not, you can easily set up separate e-mail accounts for social and professional/academic contexts.

Attachments Attachments can harbor computer viruses, so always be cautious about opening any attachments to an e-mail message. Open attachments only from known senders, and keep your own antivirus software up to date so that you will not spread a virus. If you need to send a large attachment, condense it or send it as a zipped file so you don't overload the inbox of the receiver.

Spam Make sure you add your instructor or business associates to your safe list so that their messages are not classified as spam.

The following two e-mail examples show some of these principles in action. See if you can identify the ways in which the first is an improvement over the second.

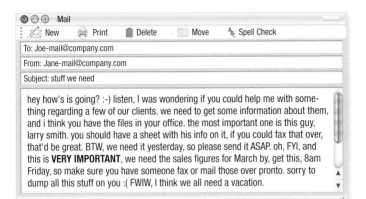

23b E-mail discussion lists, discussion boards, and online communities

E-mail discussion lists, discussion boards on the Web and within course sites such as *Blackboard* or *Moodle*, and online communities provide a forum for a virtual community of people sharing interest in a topic. Thousands of these forums exist—some public, some private—providing opportunities for you to find information and to enter discussions with others and make your own contributions. Since many of the groups and forums may not be moderated or refereed in any way, you must always be careful about evaluating the reliability of a source of information. However, any discussion group can be valuable not only for the information it provides but also for the ideas that emerge as participants discuss an issue and tease out its complexities. As a general rule, e-mail lists to which it is necessary to first subscribe or register tend to be more substantive and professional than lists or boards with no access control.

E-mail discussion lists The administrators of even a public list may screen potential subscribers carefully, although generally there is no fee for subscribing. (To participate in an e-mail list, you need only an e-mail address and a mail program.) Private lists and professionally moderated lists, especially those with a technical focus, can be reliable sources of factual information and informed opinion. In an online discussion group, all the messages posted are sent automatically to the e-mail accounts of everyone who has registered as a subscriber. Subscribing simply means registering, not paying a fee. Lists are managed by specific software programs, such as *LISTSERV®*, *Listproc,* and *Majordomo*, which have similar but not identical procedures.

Caution: Discussion lists often sell e-mail addresses, so you may get huge amounts of spam. Be careful about allowing your e-mail address to be circulated. If there is a box you can check to prohibit giving out your address, be sure to check it.

KEY POINTS
Guidelines for Participating in Online Discussion Lists

1. **If a Web interface is available for an e-mail discussion list, use it.** Subscription management and posting, each with its own address, will be all in one place and therefore easier to manage.

2. **If you do subscribe via e-mail, remember that a list has two addresses:** the *posting* address (to send messages to all subscribers) and the *subscription* address (to send commands about managing your subscription). To differentiate between them, think of the difference between sending a letter to the editor of a printed newspaper for publication and sending a note to the circulation manager about a vacation suspension of your subscription. Use the subscription address (not the posting address) to subscribe to a list, suspend your subscription, unsubscribe from a list, or make other changes to your subscription details. The wording you use must be exact. Follow the list's directions for the commands, and save a copy.

3. **Lurk before you post!** Spend time reading and browsing in the Web archives to learn the conventions and the types of topics before you start sending messages to everyone on the list.

4. **Manage the volume of mail.** A mailing list may generate thirty, one hundred, or more messages a day, so after a few days away from the list, you may feel overwhelmed. Use the options the list provides to select—for example—Nomail, Digest, or Index. Nomail temporarily suspends the sending of messages to your mailbox; Digest allows you to get only one bundle of mail every day; Index simply lists the messages once a day, and you retrieve the ones you want to read. However, not all options are available for all lists. You can also use filters to put messages into a special folder so that you can read them when you are ready.

5. **Pay close attention to who the actual recipient is.** Is it the whole list or the person who posted the original message? Make sure you know who will actually receive your message. If you want to

reply to only the individual sender of a message, do not send your message to the entire list. Instead, manually type in the individual's address you wish to respond to. This way you won't complain to Manuel about Bob's views and then by mistake send your reply to the whole list, including Bob! Some lists automatically send a message to everyone if you hit "Reply." Find out the policy of your list.

6. **Do not quote the complete original message.** Select only a short passage, the one you immediately refer or reply to. Similarly, if you subscribe to a list in digest form, don't send all of the day's messages back with your reply—edit those out first.

7. **Avoid sending a message like "I agree" to the many subscribers to the list.** Make your postings substantive and considerate so that subscribers find them worth reading.

8. **Do not forward.** Only forward a posting from one list to another if you ask the sender for permission or the posting is a general informational announcement.

Discussion boards and online communities Like discussion lists, discussion boards are Web pages to which you can post messages directly, but messages are not sent to your e-mail inbox. Sometimes, you post spontaneously; in other instances, you have to register first. Discussion boards are included in many online magazine and media Web sites, such as the Kindle Forums on the Amazon Web site. Course management software, such as *Blackboard* and *Moodle*, also provide a forum for students' discussions that is generally restricted to students registered in the class. In these venues, follow the e-mail advice in 23a.

23c Other forums: Blogs, wikis, and virtual classrooms

Blogs Blogs are publicly posted observations on a topic initiated by the author or authorized group; they cover a range from personal diaries, family photos, and stories about pets to statements of political/religious/cultural views and observations of social issues. Typically open to everyone, they have been called the soapbox of the electronic age; they can be initiated with little technical expertise, thus making contributing to the Web truly democratic.

More and more, blogs such as the *Huffington Post* (<http://www.huffingtonpost.com>) and those hosted by the *New York Times* (<http://www.nytimes.com/ref/topnews/blog-index.html>) provide insight into the state of our society and other societies at a particular point, and they broaden from the personal not only in content but also by including images, videos, and links to other sites. Blogs provide an opportunity to learn how others are thinking and to express your own views for a special audience or for anyone who happens to read your entries. Blogs can be set up so that groups as well as individuals can have posting and discussion rights, so they are useful and affordable discussion venues for student course sites and clubs (for a student's blog for a course, see 2b). Because blogs are often spontaneous, personal, unedited, and written frequently (often daily), they may not be reliable sources of information for researchers. But they serve as a corrective to a self-censoring press, and from them, you can learn about how people view current issues and react to actions taken by individuals, political parties, and governments. Several providers, such as *Blogspot, Wordpress,* and *Edublogs*, offer free server space for blogs.

Wikis Wikis are dynamic Web texts with open editing access to anyone, allowing information to be instantaneously added and corrected or otherwise changed with minimal technical expertise. Pages are created as a team or community effort. Some college instructors use wikis in their courses as a venue for student-instructor discussion, to support collaborative writing, or to serve as the platform for course portfolios. Some course management systems such as *Blackboard* and *Moodle* offer wikis in the course Web site, and these are generally restricted to editing and viewing only by other students enrolled in the course.

You are probably familiar with the collaborative encyclopedia *Wikipedia,* one of the best-known wikis. In collaborative writing situations such as a report assigned to a group of students or a team of employees, wikis can be a fast way to work together on generating and editing text. Most wikis can be set up so that contributors have to log in; this is useful for tracking who made specific changes. One of the key features of wikis is that you can easily see what changes have been made and even compare versions throughout the entire history of a document using the "page history" function. In a word processing program, you have to be careful to keep copies of the iterations of your revised work; a wiki will take care of that aspect of composition for you. However, because wikis are server based, it is a good idea to always draft text in your word processor and save it before posting it to the wiki (that way, in the event of a server crash or a network disconnect, you won't lose your work). See 6d for guidelines on using wikis as a research source.

Virtual classrooms Course management systems such as *Blackboard, Moodle,* and *Eluminate* provide synchronous cyberspaces in which a whole class or a group of students can log in at the same time and communicate in real time in chat rooms. Virtual classrooms exist at different levels of sophistication:

- no more than a chat room, but typically archiving all entries
- adding a "whiteboard," a display/draw space that can be used by both instructor and student (upon permission)
- adding an audio channel to allow verbal exchange
- adding two-way video (including live feed from instructor to students, and vice versa)
- adding slideshow capability for presentations

Virtual classrooms are used for serious instruction in distance learning, with some providing videoconferencing tools for group projects and opportunities for online discussions.

23d Social media: *Twitter, Facebook,* and virtual worlds

Some instructors use social media such as *Twitter, Facebook,* and virtual worlds like *Second Life* as instructional spaces. Although you probably use social media for a more informal purpose, you might find that you need to think about multiple audiences when you're posting in spaces like *Facebook.* This poses a challenge for many students, so keep a few guidelines in mind.

- If your instructor sets up a virtual space in a social media site for your class, follow the same guidelines for writing that we mention in 23a when you are communicating with your teacher and other students in your class in these spaces.

- When you post images, status updates, and other information in *Facebook,* everyone can see them (unless you have made them private). Because images of you can be posted and tagged by others, they can be especially compromising. Consider whether you want your teacher or other students in your class (or a future employer, for that matter) seeing images and information about you posted online. Stay vigilant and keep track of what you are sharing about yourself publicly.

- *Twitter,* unlike *Facebook,* is a completely public, searchable space. Tweets are posted for the world to see, and they can be found by search engines such as *Google.* Only post tweets that you are comfortable having a wide audience read. If you are posting tweets for a class, use the hashtag set up by your teacher (such as #eng101).

- Virtual worlds like *Second Life* can be useful spaces for class discussions, but some of the features in these worlds can be distracting when you're trying to pay attention. Focus on the content of the discussion and don't get distracted by backchannel chats or other features of the space.

- Take advantage of privacy controls. *Facebook* has sophisticated privacy settings, but you need to keep up to date because they change frequently. You can control who views and posts on your wall, who views and comments on your images, who can see your profile, and who can search your timeline, among other things. *Twitter* accounts can be made private so that tweets are not searchable or viewable by anyone not authorized by the account holder.

24 Oral and Multimedia Presentations

You may be asked to give oral presentations in writing courses, in other college courses, and in the work world. Usually, you will do some writing as you prepare your talk, and you might deliver your oral report either from notes or from a manuscript text written especially for oral presentation.

24a Preparing an oral presentation

PURPOSE AUDIENCE VOICE MEDIUM

See the full model on page 7.

Use the Critical Thinking Framework in chapter 1 to consider the background and expectations of your audience and other elements of your writing situation. Jot down what you know about your listeners and what stance and tone will best convince them of the validity of your views. For example, what effect do you want to have on the members of your audience? Do you want to inform, persuade, move, or entertain them? What do you know about your listeners' age, gender, background, education, occupation, political affiliation, beliefs, and knowledge of your subject? What do listeners need to know? In a college class, your audience will be your classmates and instructor. You can often help build a sense of community with your audience by asking questions and using the inclusive pronoun *we*.

Making an effective oral presentation is largely a matter of having control over your material, deciding what you want to say, and knowing your subject matter well. Preparation and planning are essential.

KEY POINTS
Tips for Preparing an Oral Presentation

1. **Select a topic you are committed to, and decide on a clear focus.** If you are assigned a topic, concentrate on what aspect of the topic is most interesting and relevant to you. Think about ways you can help your audience connect with your topic.

2. **Prepare a strong introduction.** Quickly capturing your audience's attention will increase your confidence and help to ensure that your entire talk gets heard.

3. **Make a few strong points.** Back up your ideas with specific details. Have a few points that you can expand on and develop with interesting examples, quotations, and stories.

4. **Provide listening cues.** Include signposts and signal phrases to help your audience follow your ideas (*first, next, finally; the most important point is…*).

5. **Structure your talk clearly.** Present the organizational framework of your talk along with illustrative materials in handouts, *PowerPoint* slides (24e), posters, charts, or other visuals (22a and 22b).

6. **Use short sentences, accessible words, memorable phrases, and natural language.** In writing, you can use long sentences with one clause embedded in another, but these are difficult for listeners to follow.

7. **Use repetition.** An audience listening, rather than reading, will appreciate being reminded of the structure of the talk and of points you referred to previously.

8. **Follow the guidelines.** To be effective, you will want to meet the requirements set for the presentation in terms of time available for preparation, length of presentation, and possible questions from the audience.

9. **Prepare a strong ending.** To ensure that you have an impact on the audience, deliver a strong conclusion. Do not simply stop or trail off. Consider connecting your introduction to your conclusion to frame your presentation for the audience.

24b Speaking from notes or manuscript

Speaking from notes You will be able to be more spontaneous and to look your audience in the eye if you speak from notes, instead of a full manuscript. Think of your presentation as a conversation. For this method, notes or a key-word outline must be clear and organized so that you feel secure about which points you will discuss and in what order. Also, practice is essential so that you don't lose your place in your notes. Here are a speaker's notes for a presentation on paternity leave.

PATERNITY LEAVE

1. Children's needs

   Benefits

   Bonding

2. Issue of equity

   Equal treatment for men and women

   Cost

Your notes or outline should make reference to specific illustrations and quotations to help you keep your place as you present (as in Key Points box, page 367, item 4). You can also use either slides prepared with your word processor or *PowerPoint* slides to guide the direction and structure of your presentation (24e). For a short presentation on a topic that you know very well, use notes with or without the visual aid of slides. Do not read aloud the text on your slides though, especially in front of a small audience. Try to limit the amount of text you put on slides and use them primarily for visual support to your presentation.

Speaking from a manuscript Writing out a complete speech may be necessary for a long formal presentation. Still, even if you do this, you should practice and prepare so that you do not have to labor over every word. Remember, too, to build in places to pause and make spontaneous comments. This gives you the opportunity to make frequent eye contact with the audience. The advantages of speaking from a prepared manuscript are that you can time the presentation exactly and that you will never wonder what to say next. The disadvantage is that you have to read the text, and reading aloud is not easy, especially if you want to maintain eye contact. If you prefer to speak from a complete manuscript text, prepare the text for oral presentation as follows:

- Triple-space your text and use a large font.
- When you reach the bottom of a page, begin a new sentence on the next page. Do not start a sentence on one page and finish it on the next.

- Highlight key words in each paragraph so that you will be able to spot them easily.
- Underline words and phrases that you want to stress.
- Use slash marks (/ or //) to remind yourself to pause. Read in "sense groups" (parts of a sentence that are read as a unit—a phrase or clause, for example—often indicated by a pause when spoken and by punctuation when written). Mark your text at the end of a sense group.
- Number your pages so that you can keep them in the proper sequence.
- Do not staple the pages, but rather place them face down as you finish each page.

24c Practicing and presenting

Whether you speak from notes or from a manuscript, practice is essential.

- **Practice not just once, but many times.** Try recording yourself, watching or listening to the recording, and asking a friend for comments.
- **Speak at a normal speed and at a good volume.** Speaking too quickly and too softly is a common mistake.
- **Imagine a full audience.** Use gestures, and practice looking up to make eye contact with people in the audience. Practice in front of a mirror and critique yourself, or practice in front of a friend and ask for feedback.
- **Beware of filler words and phrases.** Avoid terms such as *OK, well, you know*, and *like*. These verbal tics, when repeated during a presentation, annoy and distract the audience.
- **Do not punctuate pauses with "er" or "uhm."** These verbalized pauses may undermine your confidence, and they will almost certainly annoy and distract your audience.
- **Beware of nervous habits when you speak.** Avoid pacing too quickly, playing with your hair, or other nervous habits. They can be distracting to your audience.

It is natural to feel some anxiety before the actual presentation, but most people find that their jitters disappear as soon as they begin talking, especially when they are well prepared.

Look frequently at your listeners. Work the room so that you gaze directly at people in all sections of the audience. In *Secrets of Successful*

Speakers, Lilly Walters points out that when you look at one person, all the people in a V behind that person will think you are looking at them. Bear in mind that no matter how well prepared a report is, listeners will not respond positively if the presenter reads it too rapidly or in a monotone or without looking up and engaging the audience. If your topic is lighthearted, remember to smile.

24d Preparing a multimedia presentation

The possibilities for supplementing a presentation with multiple media can seem almost limitless. You can use slide presentation software such as *PowerPoint, Prezi,* or *Google Docs* to embed graphics, photos, charts, video, audio, or any combination of these to support and enhance your presentation. Many audiences expect some type of multimedia presentation as part of the listening experience, and it is important to pay attention to what your audience's expectations are.

© Charlie Schuck/Photodisc/Getty Images

When you prepare an oral presentation, think about your writing and *speaking* situation: what type of media would be appropriate and effective for your purpose, your audience, the length of your presentation, and the media you have available. The goal of your presentation is to effectively communicate to your audience. You want them to leave thinking about *what* you said and not only *how* you said it. Use multimedia aids to help your audience grasp an important point and eliminate them when they are not legitimately needed.

KEY POINTS
Common Types of Multimedia Aids

- **Digital slides of video** are run directly from a computer and shown on a screen via a digital projector. On the one hand, digital slides are flexible and provide the possibility of easily embedding other media such as photographs, video, and audio. On the other hand, you are limited by your equipment and the facility where you will be presenting.

- **Video clips, audio clips, and DVDs** require a moderate amount of production but can be particularly effective for orientations and training purposes. Presentation software makes integrating audio and video quite easy, as it eliminates a speaker's need to transport and manage additional equipment. Because of their relatively low reproduction cost, DVDs are increasingly provided to audience members so they can review the presentation long after it is over. They are, today, the ultimate "handout."

- **Flipcharts** are best used in informal presentations with a smaller audience. They are easy to prepare, easy to update, and require no equipment.

- **Posters** are common for presentations in the sciences and social sciences, especially during "poster sessions" where several speakers display their posters at the same time, and the audience circulates to hear informal presentations of the speakers' research. Posters typically contain visuals or graphics to represent the research with limited amounts of texts so that the audience can see the main points without reading too much up close.

- **Handouts** can provide the audience with printed copies of notes, tables, or illustrations from your presentation. They also can provide the audience with a permanent record of the presentation's major points and bibliographic information for any sources you cite. Not only do they help your audience follow your presentation, but also they can provide a review and new information for the audience after the presentation is over. Many presenters will provide a URL to their audience so participants can access materials online.

Using multimedia equipment smoothly does not come naturally, so be sure to practice your presentation. And because bulbs can burn out, cords can be forgotten, and computers can crash, always be prepared to give your presentation without visuals if necessary. Use the following guidelines to prepare yourself for any presentation situation:

- **Use multimedia to enhance what you have to say—not to replace it.** Your words should still be the star of your presentation, and the media should enhance and support what you have to say.

- **Keep it simple.** Flashy doesn't always mean effective. Sometimes the simplest media can make the most effective impact.

- **Know the technical requirements/limitations.** Don't plan a presentation that requires Internet access if there's no connection. If you use a Mac, find out whether you need to bring an adapter if you are projecting images. Avoid using platform-specific software (like *Keynote* for the Mac) if you don't know whether it will be available for your presentation. If you are using common software such as *PowerPoint*, make sure a compatible version is available.

- **Have a backup plan.** You never know what might go wrong, so have a backup in case your technology does not work. Handouts are the safest backup in case all technology fails. An alternate presentation technology (like *Google Docs*, which works on any platform with Internet access) is helpful if you have compatibility issues or the right software isn't available.

In preparing a live or online multimedia presentation, consider the effectiveness of positioning images near your words and of conveying emotion and meaning through pictures. Imagine, for instance, how you might present an argument against genetic engineering of food crops to classmates or colleagues. In addition to your well-formed argument, you could show graphs of public opinion data on the issue, pictures of chemicals that are used on crops and how they are applied, and a video clip of interviews with shoppers as they read labels and buy produce. If you use media imaginatively, you can do what writing teachers have long advised for printed essays: Show; don't tell.

● TECH **NOTE**

Multimedia Presentation Design

An excellent online resource that covers a wide range of issues for designers of multimedia presentations is Garr Reynolds's *Presentation Zen* site <http://www.presentationzen.com/>. For examples of compelling multimedia presentations, check out *TED*: "Riveting talks by remarkable people, free to the world" <http://www.ted.com/>.

24e Using *PowerPoint, Prezi,* and *Google Docs*

Using presentation software like *PowerPoint, Prezi,* and *Google Docs* gives you access to organizing and design tools. It also allows you to seamlessly integrate audio and visual components to produce a dynamic multimedia presentation.

Presentation software as an organization tool   Presentation software allows you to prepare slides that illustrate the logic of your presentation and helps you separate the main points from the supporting details. That way, the slides keep you focused as you give your presentation. Your audience follows your ideas not only because you have established a clear principle of organization but also because the slide on the presentation screen reminds people of where you are in your talk, what point you are addressing, and how that point fits into your total scheme.

PowerPoint Slide

> ### Slide Structure – Good
>
> - Use 1-2 slides per minute of your presentation
> - Write in point form, not complete sentences
> - Include 4-5 points per slide
> - Avoid wordiness: use key words and phrases only

Slides as visual evidence and support   Many speakers incorporate slides in their presentations as evidence, support, and even as counterpoints to their presentations. Slides containing well-timed quotes, visual images, graphs, and charts can have the same rhetorical effect as well-placed visuals in an argument essay (4j). If you decide to include sound, music, and video clips to illustrate and drive home the points you want to make, be careful not to overdo these effects. Embedded media can easily become distracting bells and whistles, and your audience may suspect you have used them to make up for lack of content. They should enhance your work, not dominate it.

Creating Slides*   When you create slides, keep in mind the following:

KEY POINTS
Tips for Creating Digital Slides

Using Slides as an Outline	• Make your first or second slide an outline of your presentation.
	• Follow the order of your outline for the rest of the presentation.
	• Place only main points on the outline slide.
Slide Structure	• When possible, choose visuals instead of text.
	• Write in point form, never in complete sentences.
	• Include no more than 4–5 points per slide.
	• Consider the 6×6 rule:
	○ No more than 6 words across
	○ No more than 6 lines down
	• Avoid wordiness: use key words and phrases only.
Slide Timing	Use one or two slides per minute of your presentation and show one point at a time to:
	• help your audience concentrate on what you are saying
	• prevent your audience from reading ahead
	• help you keep your presentation focused
Animation	• Do not use distracting animation.
	• Do not go overboard with the animation.
	• Be consistent with the animation that you use.

*Adapted from *Making PowerPoint Slides: Avoiding the Pitfalls of Bad Slides* at: <http://www.iasted.org/conferences/formatting/Presentations-Tips.ppt>.

Fonts	• Use at least an 18-point font.
	• Use different size fonts for main points and secondary points.
	• Use a standard font like Times New Roman or Arial.
Color	• Use a color of font that contrasts sharply with the background. For example, use a blue font on a white background.
	• Use color to reinforce the logic of your structure. For example, use a dark blue text under a light blue title.
	• Use color to emphasize a point (but only do so occasionally).
Background	• Use backgrounds that are attractive but simple.
	• Use backgrounds that are light.
	• Use the same background consistently throughout your presentation.
Graphs	• Use graphs rather than just charts and words because
	○ data in graphs are easier to comprehend and retain than are raw data
	○ trends are easier to visualize in graph form
	• Always title your graphs.
Spelling and Grammar	• Proof your slides for
	○ spelling mistakes
	○ the use of repeated words
	○ grammatical errors
	• If English is not your first language, have someone else check your presentation.

Portfolios

25a Preparing a hard-copy portfolio

Portfolios are used by artists, writers, and job hunters to demonstrate their range of skills and accomplishments. In your college writing courses, your instructors may ask you to select work to include in a portfolio that allows you and your instructor an opportunity to review and assess your progress over time. If your instructor does not issue specific guidelines for presenting your portfolio, use those in the following Key Points box.

KEY POINTS
Presenting a Course Writing Portfolio

- Number and date drafts; clip or staple all drafts and final copy together.
- Include a cover sheet describing the contents of the package for each separate package in your portfolio (for example, "In-class essay" or "Documented paper with three prior drafts").
- Include a brief cover letter to introduce the material and yourself.
- Pay special attention to accuracy and mechanics. Your semester grade may depend on the few pieces of writing that you select for evaluation, so make sure that the ones you include are carefully edited and well presented.

Regardless of whether a portfolio is required, consider collecting in your own portfolio academic writing that indicates both the range of topics covered in your courses and the types of writing you have done. To show prospective professors, graduate schools, or employers that you are able to produce several kinds of writing, use the list in the following Key Points box (adapted from Carleton College's writing portfolio requirements for its graduates) as a guideline in preparing your portfolio. Don't leave it up to your readers to deduce what you have accomplished. Be sure to include at the beginning a cover letter, an essay, and/or a table of contents that explicitly states what you have included and why.

> ## KEY POINTS
> ### Preparing a Portfolio of Your Academic Writing
>
> An effective academic writing portfolio will demonstrate to your readers
>
> - your breadth of interests by showing writing that you have produced in multiple courses from a range of departments or disciplines: the humanities, business, education, social sciences, mathematics, and the natural sciences
> - your ability to construct, develop, and effectively support an argument
> - your ability to observe and report by showing writing such as interviews from a sociology class, field notes from an education class, a laboratory report from the natural sciences, a description of a work of art you observed, or a concert you attended
> - your ability to analyze complex information by showing writing that includes, for example, numeric data, multiple texts, or multiple observations
> - your ability to interpret diverse material, whether it's a film you saw, a poem you read, or a set of data you analyzed
> - your ability to conduct effective research by including writing that shows a range of well-identified, integrated, and documented sources

25b Preparing an e-portfolio

Increasingly, individual instructors as well as college-wide programs require or strongly encourage students to construct an e-portfolio. Space is allotted on a server where students can store writing samples, a résumé, information about their experience, and relevant images. Students can also reflect on their work as they present it to readers. The specific charges or tasks vary with the course. While an English instructor will probably focus on writing samples, a social science instructor may ask students to locate primary sources about a specific research topic (like the environment or laws and court cases related to civil unions). In education, e-portfolios have become quite common to document a student's progress through a course of study—for example, to file lesson plans, lesson evaluations, and so on.

● TECH **NOTE**

For examples of college programs that assign e-portfolios, see the following:

- Penn State includes instructions on building e-portfolios and examples of students' e-portfolios (including video and audio clips) that they used when applying for jobs. See <http://portfolio.psu.edu/>.

- LaGuardia Community College includes a useful e-portfolio flowchart, instructions for developing a portfolio, resources, student samples, and advice about the language to use, the information to provide, and ways to avoid plagiarizing images and sounds found on the Web. See <http://www.eportfolio.lagcc.cuny.edu>.

- Florida State University has a useful Career Portfolio guide to help students develop online portfolios to show instructors and prospective employers what they have learned and what skills they possess. See <http://career.fsu.edu>.

Whatever software your school may use to support e-portfolios, typically you will have control over the material that goes onto your pages on the (Web) server. In your private storage area, you'll be able to make material available to your instructors and/or other students for review so that these "reviewers" can add their comments to the material. Also, you may have the option of publishing the document online so that future employers or friends and family can also see the work. You can make specific documents—aimed at particular audiences— available for viewing at any time. One advantage of e-portfolios is that you have the flexibility to remix the materials for different purposes. In addition, you can include a variety of materials that you produce, such as HTML documents, graphics, images, audio files, and film clips, rather than simply printed college essays that make up more conventional portfolios. If you use an e-portfolio system at your school to upload and design your portfolio, find out what access you'll have to it after you graduate.

25c A student's e-portfolio

Daniel Familia prepared this unedited first draft of his e-portfolio in a course at LaGuardia Community College, City University of New York. The seven-part structure of the portfolio was provided by templates offered by his college; the actual appearance of the template, with its unifying color scheme throughout the site, is his own design. The screenshots show an excerpt from two pages—Welcome and About Me/Photography—both combining text and images and providing internal links to his photography, an area of interest for him, and other sections of his Web site. Note that the links to the home page and all the other pages appear across the top of each screen, allowing easy access to all parts of the site at all times.

26 Résumés and Letters of Application

In business, knowing how to prepare documents for the screen and the page is a valuable skill whether you are applying for a job or communicating with colleagues and clients.

26a How to write a résumé

Résumés can be presented on paper, posted on the Web, or delivered electronically through e-mail or a dropbox. Designs differ, and no one format works for everybody. However, in all formats, you need to convey to a prospective employer what you have accomplished and when, providing details of your education, work experience, honors or awards, interests, and special skills. Above all, you need to show that your qualifications and experience make you suitable for the job you are applying for.

KEY POINTS
Writing a Résumé

1. Decide how to deliver your résumé, or follow a prospective employer's instructions: on paper, posted online, sent as an e-mail attachment, uploaded to a dropbox—or all of these. Start with a word processed version and save it as .rtf or .doc. Convert it to HTML or to PDF to post online. If you send it as an e-mail attachment or upload to a dropbox, save it as a PDF first to preserve the formatting.

2. For a hard-copy version, print on standard-size paper of good quality, white or off-white.

3. Use headings to indicate the main sections.

4. Highlight section headings and important information with boldface, italics, bullets, indentation, or different fonts. Use a clear, simple design. Do not use overly elaborate fonts, colors, or design features. Keep a print résumé at 1-2 pages. Do not include extraneous information to add length, but do not cram by using single-spacing between sections, a small font, or tiny margins.

5. Include information and experience relevant to the job you are applying for. Use reverse chronological order (begin with your most recent work experience and education).

6. Proofread your résumé several times, and ask someone else to examine it carefully as well. Make sure it contains no errors. Avoid howlers such as "rabid typist" and "responsible for ruining a five-store chain."

7. Accompany your résumé with a cover letter (26c), also carefully checked to avoid an error such as "Thank you for considering me. I look forward to hearing from you shorty."

Note: *Microsoft Word* provides résumé templates that set up headings for you—a useful guide. If you are converting your résumé to HTML, however, the formatting might not translate exactly.

26b Sample print or Web page résumé

Notice how Marcus Benini organized his résumé into clear divisions, using bold headings and a space between sections. This résumé presents the most recent education and job experience first and works backward.*

Uses a simple, creative design; includes clear contact information and a professional email address.

Starts with educational background, most relevant for a graduating student.

Highlights experience to differentiate his candidacy.

Uses bold type to emphasize job title, which is more important than the names of this applicant's employers.

Chooses present tense verbs to describe current responsibilities.

Chooses past tense verbs to describe previous experience.

Includes relevant skills and hobbies (optional).

Marcus C. Benini
1445 College Avenue
Palos Hills, IL 60465
708.555.4539
mbenini@555.com

Education

Moraine Valley Community College, Palos Hills, IL
- Associate in Science Degree (A.S.), 3.8 G.P.A., Expected Graduation 2012
- Dean's List All Semesters
- Coursework: International Business, Fundamentals of Accounting, Business Mathematics, Financial Accounting, Computer Applications in Accounting

The American International University in Rome
Study Abroad, High School Program, Summer 2010
- Lived with a host family for three weeks
- Studied Italian and Introduction to Business Management

Employment

Moraine Valley Community College
Teaching Assistant, Computer Applications in Accounting, (2011-present)
- Assist professor with grading 150 papers each semester
- Hold daily office hours for students
- Provide tutoring on challenging course material

Lakewatch Apartments
Property Accountant (2009-2012)
- Processed all accounts payable including taxes, mortgages, and monthly bills
- Maintained cash receipt journals for various properties
- Processed and deposited rental income
- Maintained general ledger and reconciled all bank statements
- Produced special reports for the partners and investors

Other
- Notary Public, State of Illinois
- Proficient in Peachtree and Microsoft Word, Excel, and Outlook
- Proficient Italian
- Hobbies include guitar, tennis, model airplanes

---

*Sample documents in 26b, 26c, and 27b are adapted from Amy Newman and Scot Ober's *Business Communication: In Person, In Print, Online*, 8th edition (Boston: South-Western, 2012). Used with permission.

26c Cover letter and sample

Accompany your print or e-mail résumé with a cover letter that explains what position you are applying for and why you are a good candidate. Find out as much as you can about the potential employer and type of work; then, in your letter, emphasize the connections between your experience and the job requirements. (Below is an example of a solicited application letter; it accompanies the résumé on p. 382.) Let the employer

---

October 13, 2012

Ms. Jane Wu, Partner
Ross, Russell & Weston
452 S. Michigan Avenue
Chicago, IL 60605

Dear Ms. Wu:

Subject: EDP Specialist Position (Reference No. 103-G)

My varied work experience in accounting, coupled with my associate's degree earned in May 2012, has prepared me for the position of EDP specialist that you advertised in the October 9 *Chicago Sun-Times.*

In addition to taking required courses in accounting and international business at Moriane Valley Community College, I took an elective course in EDP auditing and control. The training I received in this course in applications, software, systems, and service-center records would enable me to immediately become a productive member of your EDP consulting staff.

My college training has been supplemented by experience as a teaching assistant in computer applications in accounting, a position that gave me leadership experience among my fellow business and accounting students. I also noticed that you have a branch office in Milan, and I hope that my native fluency in Italian and my training in internaional business would be of use as you continue to grow your overseas accounts.

After you have reviewed my enclosed résumé, I would appreciate having the opportunity to discuss with you why I believe I have the right qualifications and personality to serve you and your clients. I can be reached by e-mail or phone after 3 p.m. daily.

Sincerely,

Marcus C. Benini

Marcus C. Benini
1445 College Avenue
Palos Hills, IL 60465
Phone: 708.55.4539
E-mail: mbenini@555.com

Addresses the letter to a specific person

Identifies the job position (EDP, or Electronic Data Processing, Specialist) and source of advertising

Emphasizes a qualification that might distinguish him from other applicants

Relates his work experience to the specific needs of the employer

Provides a telephone number and an email address (may be done either in the body of the letter or at the end of the address block) see that you understand what type of person he or she is looking for. State when, where, and how you can be contacted. As you do with the résumé itself, proofread the letter carefully.

Once you have had an interview, write a short note to thank the interviewer and emphasize your interest in the position.

27 Business Letters and Memos

27a Features of a business letter

A good business letter usually has the following qualities:

1. It is brief.
2. It clearly conveys to the reader information and expectations for action or response.
3. It lets the reader know how he or she will benefit from or be affected by the proposal or suggestion.
4. It is polite.
5. It is written in relatively formal language.
6. It contains no errors.

27b Sample business letter

LANGUAGE AND CULTURE

Business Letters across Cultures

The basic features of business letters vary from culture to culture. Business letters in English avoid both flowery language and references to religion, elements that are viewed favorably in some other cultures. Do not assume that there are universal conventions. When writing cross-cultural business letters, follow these suggestions:

1. Use a formal style; address correspondents by title and family name.
2. If possible, learn about the writing conventions of your correspondent's culture.
3. Use clear language and a summary to get your point across.
4. Avoid humor; it may fall flat and could offend.

The sample letter uses a block format, with all parts aligned at the left. This format is commonly used with business stationery.

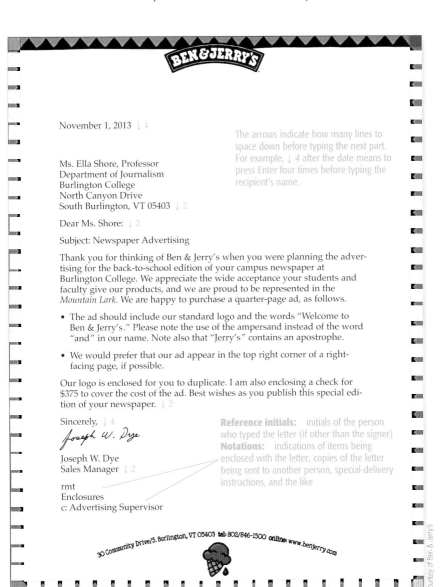

BEN&JERRY'S

November 1, 2013 ↓ 4

> The arrows indicate how many lines to space down before typing the next part. For example, ↓ 4 after the date means to press Enter four times before typing the recipient's name.

Ms. Ella Shore, Professor
Department of Journalism
Burlington College
North Canyon Drive
South Burlington, VT 05403 ↓ 2

Dear Ms. Shore: ↓ 2

Subject: Newspaper Advertising

Thank you for thinking of Ben & Jerry's when you were planning the advertising for the back-to-school edition of your campus newspaper at Burlington College. We appreciate the wide acceptance your students and faculty give our products, and we are proud to be represented in the *Mountain Lark*. We are happy to purchase a quarter-page ad, as follows.

- The ad should include our standard logo and the words "Welcome to Ben & Jerry's." Please note the use of the ampersand instead of the word "and" in our name. Note also that "Jerry's" contains an apostrophe.

- We would prefer that our ad appear in the top right corner of a right-facing page, if possible.

Our logo is enclosed for you to duplicate. I am also enclosing a check for $375 to cover the cost of the ad. Best wishes as you publish this special edition of your newspaper. ↓ 2

Sincerely, ↓ 4

Joseph W. Dye

Joseph W. Dye
Sales Manager ↓ 2

rmt
Enclosures
c: Advertising Supervisor

> **Reference initials:** initials of the person who typed the letter (if other than the signer)
> **Notations:** indications of items being enclosed with the letter, copies of the letter being sent to another person, special-delivery instructions, and the like

30 Community Drive/S. Burlington, VT 05403 **tel:** 802/846-1500 **online:** www.benjerry.com

27c Technical requirements of a business letter

Paper and page numbering   Use 8½" × 11" white unlined paper. If your letter is longer than one page, number the pages beginning with page 2 in the top right margin.

Spacing   Type single-spaced, on one side of the page only, and double-space between paragraphs. Quadruple-space below the date. Double-space below the inside address and the salutation. Double-space between the last line of the letter and the closing. Quadruple-space between the closing and the typed name of the writer, and then double-space to *Enclosure* (or *Enc.*) or *c*: (indicating that you are enclosing materials or are sending a copy to another person).

Left and right margins   The sample letter on letterhead in 27b uses a block format: the date, inside address, salutation, paragraphs, closing, and signature begin at the left margin. The right margin should not be justified; it should be ragged (with lines of unequal length) to avoid awkward gaps in the spacing between words. A modified block format places the date, closing, and signature on the right.

Return address   If you are not using business letterhead, give your address as the return address, followed by the date. Do not include your name with the address. (If you are using business letterhead on which an address is printed, you do not have to write a return address.)

Inside address   The inside address gives the name, title, and complete address of the person you are writing to. With a word processing program and certain printers, you can use this part of the letter for addressing the envelope.

Salutation   In the salutation, mention the recipient's name if you know it, with the appropriate title (*Dr., Professor, Mr., Ms.*) or just the recipient's title (*Dear Sales Manager*). If you are writing to a company or institution, use a more general term of address (*Dear Sir* or *Madam*) or the name of the company or institution (*Dear British Airways*). Use a colon after the salutation in a business letter.

Closing phrase and signature   Capitalize only the first word of a closing phrase, such as *Yours truly* or *Sincerely yours*. Type your name four lines below the closing phrase (omitting *Mr.* or *Ms.*). If you have a title

(*Supervisor, Manager*), type it underneath your name. Between the closing phrase and your typed name, sign your name in ink.

Other information   Indicate whether you have enclosed materials with the letter (*Enclosure* or *Enc.*) and to whom you have sent copies (*cc: Ms. Amy Ray*). The abbreviation *cc:* previously referred to "carbon copy" but now refers to "courtesy copy" or "computer copy." You may, however, use a single *c:* followed by a name or names to indicate who besides your addressee is receiving the letter.

The envelope   Choose an envelope that fits your letter folded from bottom to top in thirds. Use your computer's addressing capability to place the name, title, and full address of the recipient in the middle of the envelope and your own name and address in the top left corner. Remember to include ZIP codes. Word processing programs include a function that allows you to create labels for envelopes.

27d Basic features of a memo

A memo (from the Latin *memorandum,* meaning "to be remembered") is a message from one person to someone else within an organization. It can be sent on paper or by e-mail. A memo usually reports briefly on an action, raises a question, or asks permission to follow a course of action. It addresses a specific question or issue in a quick, focused way, conveying information in clear paragraphs or numbered points.

Begin what will be a hard-copy memo with headings such as *To, From, Date*, and *Subject*; such headings are frequently capitalized and in boldface type. If you will be sending a memo via e-mail, be sure to fill in the "Subject" field. For both formats, tell readers what your point is in the first sentence. Then briefly explain and give reasons or details. Single-space the memo. If the body of your memo is long, divide it into short paragraphs, or include headings and numbered or bulleted lists (see 21e and 21f) to draw attention to and organize and essential points. Most computer programs provide a standard template for memo format. The design and headings are provided; you just fill in what you want to say. Keep in mind that the features of a memo pertaining to considerations such as tone and correctness are essentially the same as for a business letter (27a).

Exercises on Design, Media, and Presentation

EXERCISE 1 Format a piece of academic writing in print. 21a

Select a piece of writing that you've completed for one of your courses. Format and print the piece according to the guidelines in this chapter. Check with your instructor, or the style guide for your discipline, about variables such as documentation style and whether to use a title page. Have a peer check your work for style and accuracy.

EXERCISE 2 Format a piece of academic writing to be published online. 21b

Select a piece of writing that you've completed for one of your courses and adapt the piece to be published on a Web site. Follow the instructions in the Key Points box for creating section headings, internal hyperlinks, and external hyperlinks. Format paragraphs in a block style, attribute sources with persistent links, and provide a list of references or works cited. Have a peer check the paper and test the links. Consider submitting the piece to a Web-based publication related to your topic, or publish it on your own or in a class blog.

EXERCISE 3 Suggest visuals to support a paper. 22

Read the list of college papers below. Then suggest visuals that would add to or support each paper.

- An argument that CPR training should be compulsory for every United States citizen.
- A critical review comparing the success and artistic achievement of Johnny Cash's albums to other artists' recordings of his songs.
- An analysis of the change in traffic that would result from building a shopping mall where there is now a school.
- Instructions for creating a compost pile.
- An explanation of the failure of NASA's first Orbiting Carbon Observatory satellite.

EXERCISE 4 Create a pie chart and a bar chart. 22b

Suppose that at a college 43 percent of the students live on campus, 29 percent commute by car, 18 percent commute by bicycle, and 10 percent live near enough to walk to the campus. Using your word processing program, create a pie chart to display these data. Then create a bar chart using the same data.

EXERCISES

EXERCISE 5 Consider sources for visuals. **22d–22e**

Look back at your answers for Exercise 3, Suggest Visuals to Support a Paper. Indicate which of these visuals you would create and where you would find the others. Then indicate which items would require permission, a source credit, or a copyright line.

EXERCISE 6 Revise an e-mail message. **23a**

Rewrite the second message in section 23a so that it follows the guidelines for e-mail in a business setting. Create any details that you need to complete the message.

EXERCISE 7 Create a plan for an oral presentation. **24a**

Select one aspect of your school or community that you think needs to be changed. Then write up a plan for convincing the people who can make this change:

1. Identify where the audience currently stands on your issue.
2. Decide on the main points you should make to bring decision makers around.
3. Select the right medium for the presentation (in-person talk, video, slides, podcast).
4. Assess what visuals you would need.
5. Choose a tone that would alert listeners to the need for change without alienating them, and draft a sample paragraph of the presentation.

EXERCISE 8 Select items for an academic portfolio. **25a**

Choose five items that you would put in a college portfolio (either print or online). Select items that demonstrate your interests and abilities, as described in the Key Points box "Preparing an Academic Writing Portfolio." Write a cover letter describing each assignment and why you've selected it.

EXERCISE 9 Select items for a résumé. **26a**

Decide on a job or training program that you would like to apply for, either this year or in the near future. Select five or six experiences that you believe qualify you for this opportunity, and expand them into items for a résumé. Exchange your list of items with a classmate, and critically evaluate how well your classmate presents her- or himself. Which items are most relevant and compelling? What improvements would you suggest?

 Visit the English CourseMate for this text at www.cengagebrain.com to find additional practice exercises.

6 Style: The Five C's

SHAPE

To obtain study resources for this section, visit the English CourseMate for this text at **www.cengagebrain.com**

6 Style: The Five C's

Readers sometimes suffer from what has been called the MEGO—
"My Eyes Glaze Over"—reaction to a piece of writing even when
ideas are well organized and there are no grammatical errors. This happens when readers are turned off by a style that obscures meaning—a
style characterized by wordiness, flatness, inappropriate word choice,
clichés, or sentences constructed without interesting variations. Do
your readers a favor: When you read your own draft prior to revision,
use the convenient mnemonic of the five C's to remind you what to
consider for revision: **C**ut, **C**heck for Action, **C**onnect, **C**ommit, and
Choose the Best Words. Keep clarity and directness in mind as the
basics of academic writing. Of course, graceful and elegant writing
may ultimately be your aim, but grace and elegance always need an
underlay of clarity.

Try this quick test: Read your draft aloud. If you have to pause
anywhere to make sense of what you have written (watch out for a
stumble, a pause, discomfort, or the occasions when "huh?" flashes
through your mind), use the five C's to revise for style and to get rid of
the glitch.

LANGUAGE AND CULTURE

Style Across Cultures

It is impossible to identify one style as the best. What is considered
good (or appropriate) style varies according to the writer's purpose
and the expectations of the anticipated readers. Country, culture,
region, ethnic heritage, language, gender, class can all play a role in
influencing what readers define as *style*. What may please readers in
one language and culture in one setting in one part of the world
may seem too flat or too adorned in another. Good style is relative
and culture-bound. The Japanese novelist Junichuro Tanizaki, for
example, gives writers this advice: "Do not try to be too clear; leave
some gaps in the meaning." Western cultures, on the other hand,
tend to value clarity.

With acknowledgment to Joseph Williams's *Style: Lessons in
Clarity and Grace*, 9th edition, chapters 28 to 32 examine five anti-
MEGO strategies, called here the "five C's of style": cut, check for action, connect, commit, and choose the best words. Chapters 33 and 34
provide a sample of a passage revised for style and some handy tips for
writers.

28 The First C: Cut

When you write, do not underdevelop your ideas because you fear taxing readers' patience. Work on developing ideas and presenting material that has substance, persuasive detail, explanation, and original expression, and make sure you don't pad your work to fill an assigned number of pages. However, once you have a draft that has ideas and content you are happy with, scrutinize it for obvious redundancies, fumbling phrases, weak expressions, and obscurities that can easily creep into a first draft.

28a Cut repetition and wordiness

Say something only once and in the best place.

> The Lilly Library ~~contains many rare books.~~
>
> ~~The books in the library are~~ carefully preserved, s
>
> many rare books and manuscripts.
> ~~The library also houses a manuscript collection.~~

> ~~In my own personal opinion,~~ I believe that bail should never be granted to anyone who has ~~ever~~ committed a violent crime ~~in which a gun was used by the criminal.~~

> In 1998, California residents voted to abolish bilingual education, ~~The main reason for their voting to abolish~~
>
> because
> ~~bilingual education was that~~ many children were being
>
> placed indiscriminately into programs and kept there too long.

If your draft says something like "As the first paragraph states" or "As previously stated," beware. Such phrases indicate that you have repeated yourself.

28b Cut formulaic phrases

Replace wordy phrases with shorter and more direct expressions.

Formulaic	Concise
at the present time	now
at this point in time	
in this day and age	
in today's society	

because of the fact that due to the fact that	because
are of the opinion that	believe
have the ability to	can
in spite of the fact that	although, despite
last but not least	finally
prior to	before
concerning the matter of	about

Be watchful for the phrase "the fact that." Edit when you can.

▷ Few people realize ~~the fact~~ that the computer controlling the
Eagle lunar module in 1969 had less memory than a cheap
wristwatch does today.

28c Cut references to your intentions

Eliminate references to the organization of your text and your own planning, such as *In this essay, I intend to prove...* or *In the next few paragraphs, I hope to show...* or *In conclusion, I have demonstrated....* In a
short essay, there's no need to announce a plan.

However, in the social or physical sciences, information is often
provided in a set order, so such signals are more appropriate and occur more frequently: *This paper describes three approaches to treating
depression.*

28d Cut redundant words and phrases

Trim words that simply repeat an idea expressed by another word in the
same phrase: *basic* essentials, *true* facts, circle *around*, cooperate
together, *final* completion, return *again*, refer *back*, *advance* planning,
consensus *of opinion*, *completely* unanimous, *free* gift. Also edit redundant pairs: *various and sundry, hopes and desires, each and every.*

▷ Before deciding to cancel classes, the program director sought a
consensus ~~of opinion~~ among the teachers.

▷ His surgeon ~~is a doctor with~~ a great deal of clinical experience.
   has

▷ ~~A total of 97~~ students completed the survey.
   Ninety-seven

29 The Second C: Check for Action

Vigorous sentences show clearly who or what is doing the action. Use vivid, expressive verbs when you can. Do not overuse the verb *be* (*be, am, is, are, was, were, being, been*) or verbs in the passive voice.

29a Show "Who's doing what" as subject and verb

In the following sentence, the subject (*approval*) and verb (*was*) tell readers very little:

Wordy **The mayor's approval of the new law was due to voters' suspicion of the concealment of campaign funds by his deputy.**

The subject and verb of this dull thud of a sentence tell us that "the... approval...was"—not a very powerful statement! Ask "Who's doing what?" and you come up with a tougher, leaner sentence.

Who's Doing What?

Subject	Verb
the mayor	approved
the voters	suspected
his deputy	had concealed

Revised **The mayor approved the new law because voters suspected that his deputy had concealed campaign funds.**

The revision is shorter and more direct; it gets rid of three nouns formed from verbs (*approval, suspicion,* and *concealment*) as well as five phrases using prepositions (words used before nouns and pronouns): *of, to, of, of, by.*

29b Scrutinize sentences beginning with *there* or *it*

For a lean, direct style, rewrite sentences in which *there* or *it* occupies the subject position (as in *there is, there were, it is, it was*). Revise by using verbs that describe an action and subjects that perform the action.

Wordy   There was a discussion of the health care system by the politicians. [Who's doing what here?]

Revised The politicians discussed the health care system.

Wordy   There is a statue of a lion standing in the center of the square.

Revised A statue of a lion stands in the center of the square.

Wordy   It is a fact that Arnold is proudly displaying a new tattoo.

Revised Arnold is proudly displaying a new tattoo.

● TECH NOTE

Searching for *There* and *It*

Use the Find function of your computer to locate all instances in your draft of *it is*, *there is*, and *there are* in the initial position in a clause. If you find a filler subject with little purpose, revise.

29c Avoid unnecessary passive voice constructions

The *passive voice* tells what is done to someone or something: "The turkey *was cooked* too long." Extensive use of the passive voice can make your style seem pedantic and wordy, especially if you use a "by…" phrase to tell about who is doing the action.

Passive   The problem will be discussed thoroughly by the committee.

Active   The committee will discuss the problem thoroughly.

Note: The passive voice occurs frequently in scientific writing because readers are primarily interested in data, procedures, and results, not in who developed or produced them. In a scientific report, you are likely to read, for example, *The rats were fed,* not *The researchers fed the rats.* For other acceptable uses of the passive voice, see section 30a and chapter 40.

30 The Third C: Connect

When you read your draft, pay attention to a smooth flow, with clear connections between sentences and paragraphs. Avoid a series of grasshopper-like jumps.

30a Connect with consistent subjects and topic chains

Readers need a way to connect the ideas beginning a sentence with what has gone before. So when you move from one sentence to the next, avoid jarring shifts of subjects by maintaining a topic chain of consistent subjects, as in the revised example that follows.

Shift of subject
> *Memoirs* are becoming increasingly popular. *Readers* all over North America are finding them appealing.

Revised
> *Memoirs* are becoming increasingly popular. *They* appeal to readers all over North America.

In the revised version, the subject of the second sentence, *they*, refers to the subject of the previous sentence, *memoirs*; the new information about "readers all over North America" comes at the end, where it receives more emphasis.

Examine your writing for awkward topic switches. Note that preserving a connected topic chain may mean using the passive voice, as in the last sentence of the revision that follows (see also 40c).

Frequent topic switches
> *I* have lived all my life in Brooklyn, New York. *Park Slope* is a neighborhood that has many different ethnic cultures. *Harmony* exists among the people, even though it does not in many other Brooklyn neighborhoods. *Many articles in the press* have praised the Slope for its ethnic variety.

Revised with topic chain
> *Many different ethnic cultures* flourish in Park Slope, Brooklyn, where I have lived all my life. *These different cultures* live together harmoniously, even though they do not in many other Brooklyn neighborhoods. In fact, *the ethnic variety* of the Slope has often been praised in the press.

30b Use logical connections with coordination, subordination, and transitions

When you write sentences containing two or more clauses, consider where you want to place the emphasis.

Coordination You give two or more clauses equal emphasis when you connect them with one of the following coordinating conjunctions: *and,* *but, or, nor, so, for,* or *yet.* (For more on coordination, see 30c, 35d, and 45b.)

▸ ┌─────independent clause─────┐ ┌─────independent clause─────┐
The waves were enormous, but the surfers approached them

with glee.
└──┘

Subordination   When you use subordinating conjunctions such as *when, if,* or *because* to connect clauses, you give one idea more importance by putting it in the independent clause (35d, p. 429; and 36c).

▸ We cannot now end our differences. At least we can help make the world safe for diversity. [Two sentences with equal importance]

▸ ┌────────dependent clause────────┐ ┌──independent clause──┐
If we cannot now end our differences, at least we can help

make the world safe for diversity.
└─────────────────────────────┘

—John F. Kennedy

[Two clauses connected by *if*; emphasis on the independent clause at the end of the sentence]

Transitional expressions   Use words such as *however, therefore,* and *nevertheless* (known as *conjunctive adverbs*) and phrases such as *in addition, as a result,* and *on the other hand* to signal the logical connection between independent clauses (for a list of transitional expressions, see 2f). A transitional expression can move around in its own clause—yet another stylistic option for you to consider.

▸ The children collected bags full of candy on Halloween; *however,* their parents would allow them to eat only one piece per day.

▸ The children collected bags full of candy on Halloween; their parents, *however,* would allow them to eat only one piece per day.

KEY POINTS
Options for Connecting Clauses

COORDINATING CONJUNCTION	SEMICOLON AND TRANSITIONAL EXPRESSION	SUBORDINATING CONJUNCTION
and (addition)	also, further, furthermore, moreover, in addition	

(Continued)

(Continued)

COORDINATING CONJUNCTION	SEMICOLON AND TRANSITIONAL EXPRESSION	SUBORDINATING CONJUNCTION
but, yet (contrast)	however, nevertheless, on the other hand	although, even though, whereas, while
or, nor (alternative)	instead, otherwise, alternatively	unless
so, for (result)	therefore, as a result, hence, consequently, thus, accordingly, then	because, as, since, so/such that, now that, once

Know your options To avoid a series of short, choppy sentences, consider the logical connection between ideas. Frequently, you will have several alternatives: a transition, a coordinator (*and, but, or, nor, so, for,* or *yet*), or a subordinator (a word such as *because, if, although, while, who,* or *which* used to introduce a dependent clause), as in the following examples. Note the punctuation in each.

▶ **Grant has traveled all over South America and Asia. He has seen little of his own country.**

Transition   **Grant has traveled all over South America and Asia;** *however*, **he has seen little of his own country.**

      Grant has traveled all over South America and Asia; he has seen little of his own country, *however*.

Coordination   **Grant has traveled all over South America and Asia,** *but* **he has seen little of his own country.**

Subordination   *Although* **Grant has traveled all over South America and Asia, he has seen little of his own country.**

Avoid excessive coordination or subordination Too much of any one stylistic feature will become tedious to readers.

Excessive coordination with *and*   **I grew up in a large family, and we lived on a small farm, and every day I had to get up early and do farm work, and I would spend a lot of time cleaning out the stables, and then I would be exhausted in the evening, and I never had the energy to read.**

Revised	Because I grew up in a large family on a small farm, every day I had to get up early to do farm work, mostly cleaning out the stables. I would be so exhausted in the evening that I never had the energy to read.
Excessive subordination	Because the report was weak and poorly written, our boss, who wanted to impress the company president by showing her how efficient his division was, to gain prestige in the company, decided, despite the fact that work projects were piling up, that he would rewrite the report over the weekend.
Revised	Because the report was weak and poorly written, our boss decided to rewrite it over the weekend, even though work projects were piling up. He wanted to impress the company president by showing her how efficient his division was; that was his way of gaining prestige.

30c Perhaps begin a sentence with *and* or *but*

People who consider *and* and *but* conjunctions whose purpose is join two or more independent clauses within a sentence may frown when they see these words starting a sentence. Nevertheless, examples of this usage can be found in literature from the tenth century onward. As with any other stylistic device, it is not wise to begin a sentence with *and* or *but* too often. And, given the difference of opinion on this usage, check with your instructor, too.

LANGUAGE AND CULTURE

Sentences Beginning with *And* or *But*

Occasionally, writers choose to start a sentence with *and* or *but*, either for stylistic effect of emphasis or contrast or to make a close connection to the previous sentence:

▶ **You can have wealth concentrated in the hands of a few, or democracy. But you cannot have both.** ——Justice Louis Brandeis

The usage is found often in journalism. Note, though, that the culture of academia is more conservative, and some readers may raise an eyebrow when they see *and* or *but* starting a sentence in an academic paper, especially if it happens often.

30d Connect paragraphs

Just as readers appreciate a smooth flow of information from sentence to sentence, they also look for transitions—word bridges—to move them from paragraph to paragraph. A new paragraph signals a shift in topic, but careful readers will look for transitional words and phrases that tell them *how* a new paragraph relates to the paragraph that precedes it. Provide your readers with steppingstones; don't ask them to leap over chasms.

> **KEY POINTS**
> A Checklist for Connecting Paragraphs
>
> ☐ **Read your draft aloud.** When you finish a paragraph, make a note of the point you made in the paragraph. Then, check your notes for the flow of ideas and logic.
>
> ☐ **Refer to the main idea of the previous paragraph as you begin a new paragraph.** After a paragraph on retirement, the next paragraph could begin like this, moving from the idea of retirement to saving: *Retirement is not the only reason for saving. Saving also provides a nest egg for the unexpected and the pleasurable.*
>
> ☐ **Use adjectives like *this* and *these* to provide a link.** After a paragraph discussing urban planning proposals, the next paragraph might begin like this: *These proposals will help. However,...*
>
> ☐ **Use transition words.** Words and phrases such as *also, too, in addition, however, therefore,* and *as a result* signal the logical connection between ideas (2f).

31 The Fourth C: Commit

E. B. White tells us that William Strunk, Jr., author of *The Elements of Style*, "scorned the vague, the tame, the colorless, the irresolute. He felt it was worse to be irresolute than to be wrong." This chapter focuses on ways to be detailed, bold, colorful, and resolute.

31a Commit to a personal presence

Academic writing is certainly not the same as personal accounts of feelings, events, and opinions. But it is not writing from which you as the writer should fade from sight. The best academic writing reveals personal engagement with the topic and details of what you (the writer) have observed and read—an unmistakable *you*. Always ask yourself: Where am *I* in this draft? What picture of me and my world do readers get from my writing? Do they see clearly what I base my opinions on? If you use sources, readers should be able to perceive you in conversation with your sources; they should see not just a listing of what sources say but also your responses to and comments on those sources.

Showing a personal presence does not necessarily mean always using *I* or repeatedly saying "in my opinion." It means writing so that readers see *you* in what you write and recognize that you have integrated any research findings into your views on a topic. See 1d for more on voice.

31b Commit to an appropriate and consistent tone

PURPOSE AUDIENCE
VOICE MEDIUM

See the full model on page 7.

Readers will expect the tone of your document to fit its purpose. The tone of your piece of writing reflects your attitude toward your subject matter and is closely connected to your audience's expectations and your purpose in writing. If you were, for example, writing about a topic such as compensation for posttraumatic stress disorder suffered by soldiers who have served in Iraq or Afghanistan, anything other than a serious, respectful tone would be inappropriate.

For most academic writing, commit resolutely to an objective, serious tone. Avoid sarcasm, colloquial language, name calling, or pedantic words and structures, even for the sake of variety. Make sure you dedicate a special reading of a draft to examining your tone; if you are reading along and a word or sentence strikes you as unexpected and out of place, flag it for later correction. In formal college essays, watch out especially for sudden switches to a chatty and conversational tone (see 32d), as in "Willy Loman surprises his family and the theater audience when his frustration makes him suddenly become *mad as all hell*." Since tone is really an indicator of how you anticipate your readers' expectations, ask a tutor or friend to read your document and note any lapses in consistency of tone.

31c Commit to a confident stance

Your background reading, critical thinking, and drafting will help you discover and decide upon a perspective and thesis that seem correct to you (2a–2c). Once you have made those decisions, commit to that point of view. When you are trying to persuade readers to accept your point of view, avoid the ambivalence and indecisiveness evident in words and phrases like *maybe, perhaps, it could be, it might seem*, and *it would appear*.

Hedging will not heighten readers' confidence in what you say:

> ~~You may not agree with me, but~~ I believe it ~~might be~~ ^is^ time for the
>
> city council to replace Chief Yates with a leader who is unafraid
> to crack down on corruption in the ranks.

Aim for language that reflects accountability and commitment: *as a result, consequently, of course, believe, need, demand, should, must.* It's important, however, to use the language of commitment only after thoroughly researching your topic and satisfying yourself that the evidence is convincing.

In addition, convey to readers an attitude of confidence in your own abilities and judgment. Make an ethical appeal to readers by stressing your evenhanded expertise (4g). Avoid apologies. One student ended a first draft this way:

Too
apologetic
> **I hope I have conveyed something about our cultural differences. I would like my reader to note that this is just my view, even if a unique one. Room for errors and prejudices should be provided. The lack of a total overview, which would take more time and expertise, should also be taken into account.**

If you really have not done an adequate job of making and supporting a point, try to gather more information to improve the draft instead of adding apologetic notes. The writer revised the ending after reading section 2h on conclusions.

Revised
version
> **The stories I have told and the examples I have given come from my own experience; however, my multicultural background has emphasized that cultural differences do not have to separate people but can bring them closer together. A diverse, multicultural society holds many potential benefits for all its members.**

31d Commit to sentence variety

Variety in sentence length   Readers appreciate variety, so aim for a mix of long and short sentences. If your editing program can print out your text in a series of single numbered sentences, you will easily be able to examine the length and structure of each. Academic writing need not consist solely of long, heavyweight sentences—in fact, it should not. Short sentences interspersed among longer ones can have a dramatic effect.

This passage from a student's course blog demonstrates the use of short sentences to great effect:

> I once had a baseball team-mate who said to me, "Mathematics is like whipped cream." I never fully understood what he meant, but I knew I liked whipped cream on anything, and as far as I was concerned mathematics could get lost. It was one of the very few disagreements I ever had with him. He was a nice guy, but he had a problem. He loved math.

Variety in sentence functions: Statements, questions, commands, and exclamations *Declarative* sentences make statements (Poems are to be read slowly with concentration), *interrogative* sentences ask questions (What does the author intend?), *imperative* sentences give commands (Forget about trying to understand Barthelme), and *exclamatory* sentences express surprise or some other strong emotion (The ending was a total shock!). Most of the sentences in your college writing will be declarative. However, the occasional question or command provides a sense of contact between writer and reader. Beware, though, of sprinkling an academic text with exclamations.

Variety of sentence types Vary the structure of your sentences throughout any piece of writing. Aim for a mix of simple, compound, complex, and compound-complex sentences.

A *simple sentence* contains one independent clause.

▶ **Kara raised her hand.**

A *compound sentence* contains two or more independent clauses connected with one or more coordinating conjunctions (*and, but, or, nor, so, for, yet*), with a semicolon alone, or with a semicolon and a transitional expression (2f).

┌──independent clause──┐ ┌───────independent clause────────┐
▶ **Kara raised her hand, and the whole class was surprised.**

┌──independent clause──┐ ┌───independent clause───┐
▶ **Kara raised her hand, but nobody else responded.**

┌──independent clause──┐ ┌───────independent clause───────┐
▶ **Kara raised her hand; the whole class was surprised.**

┌───independent clause───┐ ┌───────────independent clause───────────┐
▶ **Kara raised her hand; as a result, the whole class was surprised.**

If you read these sentences aloud, you may notice the longer pause in the last two; consider how that pause may affect a reader. Consider, too, how your expectations as a reader change as you move to a comma or a semicolon.

A *complex sentence* contains an independent clause and one or more dependent clauses.

    ┌────────dependent clause────────┐ ┌────────independent clause────────┐
▸ **When Kara raised her hand, the whole class was surprised.**

    ┌────────independent clause────────┐ ┌────────dependent clause────────┐
▸ **The whole class was surprised when Kara raised her hand.**

When you decide which of the two previous types to write, consider the sentences that precede and follow. Avoiding repetition or following through with a subject or topic chain (see 30a) may help determine which element should come first and which last.

A *compound-complex sentence* contains at least two independent clauses and at least one dependent clause.

    ┌────────dependent clause────────┐ ┌────────independent clause────────┐
▸ **When Kara raised her hand, the whole class was surprised,**

    ┌────────independent clause────────┐ ┌────────dependent clause────────┐
and the professor waited eagerly as she began to speak.

Sentences structured with several clauses are common in academic writing. Just make sure that you keep track of where you are in the sentence and check the relationship between dependent and independent clauses.

In addition, be aware of *cumulative* and *periodic sentences.* Cumulative (or loose) sentences begin with the independent clause and add on to it. Periodic sentences begin with words and phrases that lead to the independent clause, giving emphasis to the end of the sentence. The cumulative sentence is the norm in English prose. Use a periodic sentence to make a specific stylistic impact.

Cumulative   *The experienced hunter stood stock still for at least five minutes,* sweat pouring from his brow, all senses alert, and waiting to hear a twig snap.

Periodic   Sweat pouring from his brow, all senses alert, and waiting to hear a twig snap, *the experienced hunter stood stock still for at least five minutes.*

Variety of word order in a sentence   Sometimes, inverted word order of verb followed by subject (v + s) helps achieve coherence, consistent subjects, emphasis, or a smooth transition:

            V   ┌────S────┐
▸ **Next to the river runs a superhighway.**

        V S V
▸ **Never have I laughed so hard.**

▸ V ┌─S─┐ V
Not only does the novel entertain, but it also raises our
awareness of poverty.

▸ V S
So eager was I to win that I set off before the starter's gun.

▸ V ┌─S─┐ V
Rarely has a poem achieved such a grasp on the times.

Using an occasional rhetorical question will also help drive a point home:

▸ V S V
How did she think she could get away with such a lie?

Variety of sentence beginnings   Consider using some of these variations to begin a sentence, but remember that beginning with the subject will always be clear and direct for readers. Any of the following
beginnings repeated too often will seem like a stylistic tic and may annoy readers.

Begin with a dependent or condensed clause

┌─────────────dependent clause─────────────┐
▸ While my friends were waiting for the movie to begin, they ate
three tubs of popcorn.

┌───── clause condensed to phrase ─────┐
▸ While waiting for the movie to begin, my friends ate three tubs
of popcorn.

Begin with a participle or an adjective   A sentence can begin with a participle or an adjective but only if the word is in a phrase that refers to the
subject of the independent clause. If the phrase does not refer to
the subject, the result is a *dangling modifier* error (38c).

-ing participle
▸ Waiting for the movie to begin, my friends ate popcorn.

past participle
▸ Wanted by Interpol, the spy fled Europe and hid out in South
America.

adjective
▸ Aware of the problems, they nevertheless decided to continue.

Begin with a prepositional phrase

┌─prepositional phrase─┐
▸ With immense joy, we watched our team win the pennant.

You can also occasionally use inverted word order after a prepositional phrase (but see 41d on agreement of subject and verb).

┌──────prepositional phrase──────┐ verb ┌────── subject ──────┐
▶ **At the bottom of the trunk lay a satin wedding dress.**

32 The Fifth C: Choose the Best Words

Word choice, or *diction*, contributes a great deal to the effect your writing has on your readers. Do not give readers puzzles to solve.

32a Word choice checklist

KEY POINTS
Checklist for Word Choice

☐ Underline words whose meaning or spelling you want to check and words that you might want to replace. Then spend some time with a dictionary and a thesaurus (32b).

☐ Look for words that might not convey exactly what you mean (*thrifty* vs. *stingy*, for example), and look for vague words (32c).

☐ Check figurative language for appropriateness, think about where a simile (a comparison) might help convey your meaning, and find original substitutes for any clichés (32e, 32g).

☐ Check for level of formality and for the appropriateness of any colloquial, regional, ethnic, or specialized work terms (32d).

☐ Check for gender bias in your use of *he* and *she* and other gender-related words (32f).

☐ Look for language that might exclude or offend (such as *normal* to mean people similar to you). Build community with your readers by eliminating disrespectful or stereotyping terms referring to race, place, age, politics, religion, abilities, or sexual orientation (32f).

32b Use a dictionary and a thesaurus

Dictionary   The dictionary built into your word processing program informs you about spelling, pronunciation, and definitions. Sometimes, though, you need more than that. Don't forget about the comprehensive dictionaries such as the *Oxford English Dictionary* (OED), available online in many libraries or in print form. In the OED, you can explore the historical development of the meaning and usage of a word (its etymology), find synonyms and antonyms (words of similar and opposite meaning), and learn about grammatical functions and current usage. If you have no easy online access to the OED, invest in a good desk dictionary such as *The Merriam-Webster Dictionary*.

Use a dictionary to learn or confirm the *denotation*—the basic meaning—of a word. Some words that appear similar are not interchangeable. For example, *respectable* has a meaning very different from *respectful*; *emigrant* and *immigrant* have different meanings; and so do *defuse* and *diffuse*, *uninterested* and *disinterested*, and *principal* and *principle*.

Thesaurus A thesaurus is useful when you want to find alternatives to words that you know. Exercise caution, however, to make sure that the word you choose fits your context. Suppose you use the word *privacy* a few times and want an alternative in the sentence "She values the privacy of her own home." You could consult a thesaurus and might find words such as *aloofness, seclusion,* and *isolation* listed. The word *aloofness* would not work as a replacement for *privacy* in the example sentence, and the

others do not capture the idea of *privacy*. You might, in the end, want to use two words to convey your meaning: *She values the* safety *and* seclusion *of her own home,* or you might stick with *privacy*.

Thesaurus programs built into word processing programs typically offer lists of synonyms but little guidance on *connotation*—the meaning associated with a word beyond its literal definition. Using a thesaurus alone is not enough. Always check a word in a dictionary that provides examples of usage.

32c Use exact words and connotations

When you write, use words that convey exactly the meaning you intend. Two words that have similar dictionary definitions (*denotation*) can also have additional positive or negative implications and emotional overtones (*connotation*). Readers will not get the impression you intend if you describe a person as *lazy* when the more positive *relaxed* is what you have in mind.

Select words with appropriate connotations. Hurricanes *devastate* neighborhoods; construction workers *demolish* buildings. Writing "Construction workers devastated the building" would be inappropriate. Note how the connotations of words can affect meaning:

Version 1 **The crowd consisted of young couples holding their children's hands, students in well-worn clothes, and activist politicians, all voicing support of their cause.**

Version 2 **The mob consisted of hard-faced workers dragging children by the hand, students in leather jackets and ragged jeans, and militant politicians, all howling about their cause.**

Some words do little more than fill space because they are so vague. The following oh-so-general words signal the need for revision: *area, aspect, certain, circumstance, factor, kind, manner, nature, seem, situation, thing.*

Vague **Our perceptions of women's roles differ as we enter new *areas*. The girl in Kincaid's story did many *things* that are commonly seen as women's work.**

Revised **Our perceptions of women's roles differ as we learn more from what we *see, hear, read, and experience*. The girl in Kincaid's story did many *household chores* that are commonly seen as women's work. She washed the clothes, cooked, swept the floor, and set the table.**

Some words are abstract and general; other words are concrete and specific. Notice the increasing concreteness and specificity in this list: *tool, cutting instrument, knife, penknife. Tool* is a general term; *penknife* is more specific. If you do not move away from the general and abstract, you will give readers too much imaginative leeway. "Her grandmother was shocked by the clothing she bought" leaves a great deal to readers' imaginations. What kind of clothing do you mean: a low-necked dress, high-heeled platform shoes, and black fishnet stockings or a conservative navy blue wool suit? Choose words that convey exact images and precise information.

32d Monitor the language of speech, region, and workplace

The language of speech In a formal college essay, avoid colloquial language and slang unless you are quoting someone's words. Use the level of diction appropriate for the academic world, not for the world of hip-hop, *Facebook*, or texting. Don't enclose a slang expression in quotation marks to signal to readers that you know it is inappropriate. Instead, revise to reach an appropriate level of formality.

▸ The solution to the problem ~~was a no-brainer~~. *required little thought*

▸ The jury returned the verdict that the ~~guy~~ was guilty. *defendant*

▸ Nutrition plays a large part in whether people ~~hang on to~~ their own teeth as they age. *retain*

▸ The music at the party was ~~dope~~. *excellent*

▸ The class was ~~a drag~~, so I stopped attending after the second week. *tedious*

In formal writing, avoid colloquial words and expressions, such as *folks, guy, OK, okay, pretty good, hassle, kind of interesting/nice, a ways away, no-brainer.*

Note that the synonyms of the italicized words listed next convey different eras, attitudes, and degrees of formality:

child: kid, offspring, progeny

friend: dog, peeps, buddy, mate, brother/sister, comrade

jail: slammer, cooler, prison, correctional institution

angry: pissed off, ticked off, furious, mad, fuming, wrathful

computer expert: geek, hacker, techie, programmer

threatening: spooky, scary, eerie, menacing

fine: rad, phat, dope, fly, cool, first-rate, excellent

Some of these words—*kid, slammer, ticked off, geek, spooky, rad*—are so informal that they would rarely if ever be appropriate in formal academic writing or business letters, though they would raise no eyebrows in most journalism, advertising, or e-mail. Overuse of formal words—*progeny, comrade, wrathful*—on the other hand, could produce a tone that suggests a stuffy, pedantic attitude (see 32g).

For more on levels of diction and Standard English, see 35c.

Regional and ethnic language Use regional and ethnic dialects in your writing only when you are quoting someone directly ("*Your car* *needs fixed," the mechanic grunted.*) or you know that readers will understand why you are using a nonstandard phrase.

▶ I bought ~~me~~ a backpack.
  myself

▶ They ~~done~~ finished painting the house.
  have

▶ ~~They're~~ here three years already.
  They have been

▶ She used to ~~could~~ run two miles, but now she's out of shape.
  be able to

LANGUAGE AND CULTURE

Dialect and Dialogue in Formal Writing

Note how Paule Marshall uses Standard English for the narrative thread of her story while reproducing the father's Barbadian dialect and idioms in the dialogue, thus combining the formal and the informal, the academic and the personal into a rich whole:

> She should have leaped up and pirouetted and joined his happiness. But a strange uneasiness kept her seated with her knees drawn tight against her chest. She asked cautiously, "You mean we're rich?"
> "We ain rich but we got land."
> "Is it a lot?"
> "Two acres almost. I know the piece of ground good. You could throw down I-don-know-what on it and it would grow. And we gon have a house there—just like the white people own. A house to end all house!"
> "Are you gonna tell Mother?"
> His smile faltered and failed; his eyes closed in a kind of weariness.
>
> —Paule Marshall, *Brown Girl, Brownstones*

The jargon of the workplace   People engaged in most areas of specialized work and study use technical words that outsiders perceive as jargon. A sportswriter writing about baseball will refer to *balks, ERAs, brushbacks,* and *cutters.* A linguist writing about language for an audience of linguists will use terms like *phonemics, sociolinguistics, semantics, kinesics,* and *suprasegmentals.* If you know that your audience is familiar with the technical vocabulary of a field, specialized language is acceptable. But, if you are writing for a more general audience, try to avoid jargon. If you must use technical terms, provide definitions that will make sense to your audience.

32e Use figurative language for effect, but don't overuse it

Figures of speech can enhance your writing and add to imaginative descriptions. Particularly useful are similes and metaphors. A simile is a comparison in which both sides are stated explicitly and linked by the words *like* or *as*. A metaphor is an implied comparison in which the two sides are indirectly compared. When figurative language is overused, however, it can become tedious and contrived.

Simile: An explicit comparison with both sides stated

▶ America is *not like a blanket*—one piece of unbroken cloth, the same color, the same texture, the same size. America is more *like a quilt*—many pieces, many colors, many sizes, all woven and held together by a common thread.
—Rev. Jesse Jackson

▶ He was reading, leaning so far back in the chair that it was balanced on its two hind legs *like a dancing dog*.
—Barbara Kingsolver

Metaphor: An implied comparison, without *like* or *as*

▶ All the world's a stage,
And all the men and women merely players
—William Shakespeare, *As You Like It*

▶ Some television programs are so much chewing gum for the eyes.
—John Mason Brown

Mixed metaphors   Take care not to mix (illogically combine) metaphors.

▶ As she walked onto the tennis court, she was ready to sink or swim. [Swimming on a tennis court?]

▶ You need to wake up and smell the music. [The mix of metaphors—*wake up and smell the coffee* and *face the music*—creates a confusing clash for the reader.]

▶ **He was a whirlwind of activity, trumpeting defiance whenever anyone crossed swords with any of his ideas.** [The three metaphors—*whirlwind, trumpet, crossed swords*—obscure rather than illuminate.]

For more examples of figurative language in literature, see 5e.

32f Avoid sexist, biased, and exclusionary language

You cannot avoid writing from perspectives and backgrounds that you know about, but you can avoid divisive terms that reinforce stereotypes or belittle other people. Be sensitive to differences. Consider the feelings of members of the opposite sex, racial or ethnic minorities (now sometimes called "world majorities"), and special-interest groups. Do not emphasize differences by separating society into *we* (people like you) and *they* or *these people* (people different from you). Use *we* only to be truly inclusive of yourself and all your readers. Be aware, too, of terms that are likely to offend. You don't need to be excessive in your zeal to be PC (politically correct), using *underachieve* for *fail*, or *vertically challenged* for *short*, but do your best to avoid alienating readers.

Gender   The writer of the following sentence edited to avoid gender bias and sexist language in the perception of women's roles and achievements.

▶ **Running for the position of ~~councilman~~ were Stan Foster, an** ^council member

accountant, and ~~Mrs.~~ Julia Estes, a community organizer ~~and mother.~~

Choice of words can reveal gender bias, too.

Avoid	Use
chairman	chairperson
female astronaut	astronaut
forefathers	ancestors
foreman	supervisor
mailman	mail carrier
male nurse	nurse
man, mankind (meaning any human being)	person, people, our species, human beings, humanity, humankind
poetess	poet
policeman, policewoman	police officer
salesman	sales representative, salesclerk
veterans and their wives	veterans and their spouses

Pronouns *he* or *she* Pronoun use is especially vulnerable to gender bias. See 42e for more on gender pronouns, the use of the phrase *he or she*, and the use of *they* to avoid tricky decisions.

Race Mention a person's race only when it is relevant. If you write, "Attending the meeting were three doctors and an Asian computer programmer," you reveal more about your own stereotypes than you do about the meeting. When the newly appointed Supreme Court Justice Sonia Sotomayor referred to one of her judicial decisions as made by a "wise Latina," this angered her opponents who saw race as irrelevant in matters of legal precedent.

Aside from avoiding gratuitous comments about race, try to use the names that people prefer for their racial or ethnic affiliations. The *Columbia Guide to Standard American English* advises: "It is good manners (and therefore good usage) to call people only by the names they wish to be called." Consider, for example, that *black* and *African American* are preferred terms; *American Indian*, or better still, the particular group (*Sioux* etc.) is now often preferred to *Native American*, though this usage has swung back and forth. *Asian* is preferred to *Oriental,* while *Latino/Latina* vies with *Hispanic* to refer to Americans originating in Latin America.

Place Avoid stereotyping people according to where they come from. Some British people may be stiff and formal, but not all are (one of the authors of this book is from London, so take her word for it). Not all Germans eat sausage and drink beer; not all North Americans carry cameras and chew gum.

Be careful, too, with the way you refer to countries and continents. The Americas include both North and South America, so you need to make the distinction. England, Scotland, Wales, and Northern Ireland make up Great Britain, or the United Kingdom. In addition, shifts in world politics and national borders have resulted in the renaming of many countries. Always consult a current atlas, almanac, or reliable reference Web site.

Age Avoid derogatory or condescending terms associated with age. Refer to a person's age or condition neutrally if at all: not *well-preserved little old lady* but *woman in her eighties* or just *woman*.

Politics Words referring to politics are full of connotations. Consider, for instance, the positive and negative connotations of *liberal* and *conservative* in various election campaigns. Take care when you use words like *radical, left-wing, right-wing*, and *moderate*. How do you want readers to interpret them? Are you identifying with one group and implicitly criticizing other groups?

Religion An older edition of an encyclopedia referred to "devout Catholics" and "fanatical Muslims." A newer edition refers to both Catholics and Muslims as "devout," thus eliminating the bias of a sweeping generalization. Examine your use of the following: words that sound derogatory or exclusionary, such as *cult* or *fundamentalist*; expressions, such as *these people*, which emphasize difference; and even the word *we* when it implies that all your readers share your beliefs.

Health and abilities Avoid expressions such as *confined to a wheelchair* and *AIDS victim* so as not to focus on difference and disability. Instead, write *someone who uses a wheelchair* and *a person with AIDS*, but only if the context makes it necessary to include that information. Do not unnecessarily draw attention to a disability or an illness.

Sexual orientation Mention a person's sexual orientation only if the information is relevant in context. To write that someone accused of stock market fraud was "defended by a homosexual lawyer" would be to provide gratuitous information. The sexual orientation of the attorney might be more relevant in a case involving discrimination against homosexuals. Since you may not know the sexual orientation of your readers, do not assume it is the same as your own.

The word *normal* Be especially careful about using the word *normal* when referring to your own health, ability, or sexual orientation. Some readers might justifiably find that usage offensive.

32g Avoid tired expressions (clichés) and pretentious language

Avoiding clichés *Clichés* are tired, overly familiar expressions that anyone can complete: *as cool as a* _____. Common clichés are *hit the nail on the head, crystal clear, better late than never,* and *easier said than done.* They never contribute anything fresh or original. Avoid or eliminate them as you revise your early drafts.

▶ ~~Last but not least,~~ Finally, the article recommends the TeleZapper.

▶ My main ambition in life is not to make a fortune, since

I know that~~, as they say, "money is the root of all evil."~~ having money does not guarantee a good life.

> After five months of daily exercise and twice-weekly sessions

with a trainer, Mallick is ~~fit as a fiddle~~ and healthy.
 physically fit

Distinguishing the formal from the stuffy *Formal* does not mean stuffy and pretentious. Writing in a formal situation does not require you to use obscure words and long sentences. In fact, convoluted writing is not a sign of brilliance or of a powerful mind. It is usually just a sign of bad writing. Pretentious language makes reading difficult, as the following example shows:

> When a female of the species ascertains that a male with whom she is acquainted exhibits considerable desire to extend their acquaintance, that female customarily will first engage in protracted discussion with her close confidantes.

Simplify your writing if you find sentences like that in your draft. Aim for clear, direct expression of ideas. Here are some words to watch out for:

Stuffy	Direct	Stuffy	Direct
ascertain	find out	optimal	best
commence	begin	prior to	before
deceased	dead	purchase	buy
endeavor	try	reside	live
finalize	finish	terminate	end
implement	carry out	utilize	use

Avoiding euphemisms *Euphemisms* are expressions that try to conceal a forthright meaning and make the concept seem more delicate, such as *change of life* for *menopause* or *downsized* for *fired*. Because euphemisms often sound evasive or are unclear, avoid them in favor of direct language. Similarly, avoid *doublespeak* (evasive expressions that seek to conceal the truth, such as *incendiary device* for *firebomb*, *combat situation* for *battle*, and *collateral damage* for *civilian casualties*). Examples of such language are easy to find in advertising, business, politics, and especially, in war reporting. Do not equate formality with these indirect expressions.

> Six ~~freedom fighters~~ were intercepted as they attempted to set ~~an~~
 terrorists   *a*
 incendiary device under the general's car.
 bomb

33 Revising for Style: A Student's Drafts

While focusing on the style features discussed in this chapter, several classmates analyzed one of their peer's writing on the topic of books and the Web. The writer's paragraphs and analysis, along with his classmates' responses, are shown below.

Student's passage for peer review

Classmates' analysis, using part 6 on style

Books are becoming obsolete. More and more guys are turning to the Web for both information and entertainment. Web sites are accessed when people need to check a fact or even when they just want to read and relax.

Switch in subject
Slang? Or sexist language?

Unnecessary passive; switch in subject

In this paragraph, I will turn to explaining the many advantages to the Web. At this point in time, books are losing in popularity due to the fact that they are expensive and not easy to take from place to place. The main reason for the fact that people prefer the Web is that it is there when it's needed. It offers great variety. It also can be informative. A friend of mine reads the news on his iPad. He sends messages to his friends on his iPad. It is very versatile. It's a pretty snazzy tool for everyday life.

Reference to intentions
Formulaic phrase
Switch in subject
Formulaic phrase
Wordy

No sentence variety in this paragraph
Good examples here

Tone too conversational

Last but not least, despite the many advantages to the Web, people still purchase books to endeavor to improve themselves. There is so much handy and portable information in books. Books have passed the test of getting published, so they can be more reliable. With books you can move from being an ignorant numbskull to dissing all your friends about their ignorance.

Formulaic cliché

Use "try" instead
There is—action verb better

Good point here

Language of speech

The student worked with his group to revise the paragraphs for style. This is a better version, which the student took as the basis for his next two revisions.

As increasingly more people turn to the Web for information and entertainment, books seem to be fading in popularity. The Web rather than a book is now what we all use to check a fact, communicate with others, or just relax.

Nowadays, the Web wins out over books in several ways. First, books are expensive and not easy to take from place to place. Second, the Web is always there when people need it to answer a question. In addition, it is versatile enough to provide not only information but also entertainment. Many students use their handy little portable iPad to read the news, send messages to friends, make notes for essays, and play video games.

However, in spite of the advantages the Web offers, people are still buying books to improve their skills and knowledge. They know that the information they find on the Web posted by individuals or organizations may be biased, wrong-headed, or even inaccurate. They know, though, that with a book, some publisher has been impressed enough by the author and the content to put money behind the publication. So they tuck a handy book into a pocket to read on a bus or train on the way to work. That way, they have instant access to information as well as to entertainment, knowing that a published book will usually offer more reliability than a published Web site.

34 Style Tips

As you write and revise, keep in mind the five C's of style, and aim for sentence variety. For a final quick review of your style, read your draft aloud and use these tips.

KEY POINTS
Tips for Style

1. **Be adaptable.** Consider the style your readers will expect. Don't work on developing a figurative style for short stories and then continue to use the same style in business communications or e-mail. Choose a style as you choose your clothes: the right outfit for the occasion.

2. **When in doubt, favor a plain style.** Be clear and straightforward. Don't search for the big words or the obscure turn of phrase. The following sentences, part of an e-mail message to the author of this book from an online service provider, are decidedly overdressed and stuffed with bureaucratic nothings: "It has been a pleasure assisting you. It is my hope that the information provided would be of great help with regards to your concern."

3. **Less is often better.** Details and descriptions are interesting, but don't overload your writing with adjectives and adverbs: *The perky little redheaded twin sat languidly in the comfortable overstuffed green-striped armchair and bit enthusiastically into a red and yellow fleshy, overripe peach.* Such prose is as overripe as the peach. Also avoid intensifying adverbs such as *very, really, extremely, terribly,* and *enormously.* Find a stronger word to use in place of the two words, such as *terrified* in place of *extremely scared.*

4. **Focus on rhythm, not rules.** Heed the advice of *The New York Times Manual of Style and Usage:* "One measure of skill is exceptions, not rules." And keep in mind this remark by novelist Ford Madox Ford: "Carefully examined, a good—an interesting—style will be found to consist in a constant succession of tiny, unobservable surprises." Ask yourself how you can provide pleasant surprises for your readers.

Exercises on Style: The Five C's

EXERCISE 1 Cut wordiness and formulaic phrases. 28a–28b

Edit the following sentences to eliminate wordiness and formulaic phrases.

Example   ~~In spite of the fact that~~ *Although* Michael Jordan retired from basketball

twice, fans held out hope that their hero would return ~~back~~ to the
court ~~again~~.

1. Michael Jordan first retired from basketball in 1993 and tried to begin a
   career in the game of baseball, but he returned to the Chicago Bulls in the
   spring of 1995 because of the fact that he had not been successful enough
   in baseball to reach the major leagues.
2. When Jordan retired again in 1999, he told reporters that he was
   "99.9 percent" sure that he would never return to basketball, but basketball fans who loved the game were of the opinion that he had meant to
   leave himself a loophole.
3. Jordan bought for himself a part of the Washington Wizards, a team with a
   poor record of wins and losses in the 2000–2001 season.
4. At the point in time when Jordan began working out on a basketball court
   again, many people thought he was planning a comeback, but Jordan insisted that he was simply and solely trying to lose weight.
5. Then, in the fall of 2001, Jordan, who at the time was then thirty-eight
   years old, revealed that he would sell his stake in the Wizards and reprise
   his role as a player in the game of basketball.
6. He played with the Wizards for two seasons, and called his 2009 induction
   into the Hall of Fame "bittersweet" because it meant he had undoubtedly
   retired for sure.

EXERCISE 2 Cut redundant words and phrases. 28d

Edit to eliminate redundant words and phrases.

Example   The Strangler cases terrified ~~and unnerved~~ Bostonians until 1965,
when Albert DeSalvo confessed to the eleven murders.

1. The nephew of one of the Boston Strangler's murder victims began to
   investigate his aunt's case in 1999 to prove to his own mother that the
   Strangler had been caught, but he eventually became mentally certain that
   Albert DeSalvo, the confessed killer of the victims, was not guilty.
2. In the 1960s, the public was told that DeSalvo had admitted details in his
   confession that only the murderer or killer would have known.
3. DeSalvo was never convicted of the Strangler murders, but he went to prison,
   where he was jailed for another crime and was fatally stabbed there in 1973.

4. DeSalvo seemed to have exclusive and inside knowledge of the murders, but others have since noted that he had heard many details from lawyers and police officials, and DeSalvo was known for his complete and total recall of each and every thing he had been told.
5. Once the victim's nephew got involved, lawyers and forensic specialists began cooperating together to investigate new leads and DNA evidence that could either exonerate DeSalvo or finally prove him guilty at last.

EXERCISE 3 Revise sentences beginning with *there* or *it*. `29b`

Rewrite each sentence to eliminate *there* or *it* wherever possible.

Families
Example   ~~There are families~~ known as "travelers" ~~who~~ live in mobile homes in
              ^

Ireland and are constantly on the move.

1. It is traditional for some families in Ireland to travel from place to place instead of settling permanently in one location.
2. There are deep-seated prejudices among many Irish people against the traveler families.
3. Although most travelers share the Catholic faith and the Celtic background of the majority of Irish people, it is not unusual for travelers to face discrimination and accusations of thievery.
4. There have been instances in which parents have removed children from local schools after traveler children arrived.
5. There was a law instituted in Ireland requiring communities to begin providing water and other basic services to traveler populations by 2004, but few districts made plans to comply.

EXERCISE 4 Avoid unnecessary passive voice constructions. `29c`

Rewrite any passive voice constructions in the active voice.

Poachers   wild animals
Example   ~~Wild animals~~ have ~~been~~ hunted ~~by poachers~~ in national parks all
              ^   ^

over the world.

1. In some wildlife preserves abroad, a radical new strategy has been adopted by conservationists.
2. Even in preserves that are supposed to be safe, many threatened wild species are either captured by poachers for the thriving black market in exotic pets or killed for their valuable body parts.
3. Poachers have been asked by wildlife organizations to use their knowledge of animals and animal habitats to contribute to wildlife preservation.
4. Many poachers have agreed to stop hunting endangered animals in exchange for a living wage and health benefits for themselves and their families; instead, information about the animals in the preserves is now collected by former poachers.

5. Local economies in poor areas near the preserves have long been supported by poaching, but with this new approach, local young people can see that working to support wildlife conservation is a better and safer way to earn a living than illegal poaching.

EXERCISE 5 Use different options for connecting ideas.

In each of the following sentences, rewrite the two independent clauses as a single sentence, giving the information appropriate emphasis by using coordination, subordination, or a transitional expression. Then identify the method that you used.

> Example   Environmental groups have often portrayed American Indians as
>
>   , but some
>   conservationists. ~~Some~~ tribes feel that such portrayals are simplistic
>
>   and culturally insensitive. [coordination]

1. Environmentalists believe that drilling for oil in the Arctic National Wildlife Refuge will damage a wilderness area. They have also cast drilling for oil as a human rights issue.
2. The Gwich'in Indians rely on a caribou herd in the wildlife refuge. Drilling for oil on the caribou's calving ground could disrupt the herd and the tribe's way of life.
3. The Gwich'in are not categorically opposed to oil drilling on tribal lands. They have permitted an oil company to drill on their lands in Canada.
4. Many tribes around the United States have turned to allowing drilling for oil and gas, gambling, and even nuclear waste storage on their reservations in an effort to achieve economic independence. The Gwich'in are not alone in trying to use their land to make money.
5. The view of American Indians as stewards of the land may be based more on myth than on fact. Some feel that this view denies natives a place in the modern world.

EXERCISE 6 Commit to sentence variety. `31d`

Select a piece of your own writing. Using your word processing program, print out your text in a series of single numbered sentences. Examine the length, word order, and sentence beginnings, and consider how they might be revised for greater effect.

EXERCISE 7 Monitor word choices. `32a–32d`

Revise the following sentences to eliminate inappropriately colloquial language, regional or community dialect, non-Standard English, or workplace jargon. Some sentences may not need revision.

Example   Organic farmers have ~~a rough time~~ protecting their corn crops from
                       difficulty

genetic contamination by corn ~~produced through bioengineering~~
            that has been genetically modified

because ~~corn is open-pollinating.~~
*wind and insects carry pollen from one plant to
other plants that can be miles away.*

1. A common agricultural genetic modification introduces *Bacillus thurengensis* into corn plants.
2. These bacteria bump off caterpillars; the bacteria, also called *Bt,* are sometimes spread on organic corn plants to rid them of corn borers and other destructive insects.
3. Organic farmers have been testing their corn crops for the presence of genetic modifications, and many of these guys are discovering that their crops have been contaminated by genetically modified corn grown up the road.
4. Some farmers are getting stuck with unsold corn, and others are selling it on the open market for less than half the price they would have gotten for a purely organic crop.
5. The problem of cross-pollination of genetically modified corn with organic corn—known as "genetic drift"—troubles many nonfarmers as well.
6. A lot of other countries buy organic produce from the United States, and few of them countries allow genetically modified foods to cross their borders.
7. If genetically modified corn can contaminate organic corn naturally, pretty soon there won't be hardly any corn without genetic modifications, and exports of American corn will be greatly reduced.
8. Genetic drift also bugs people who believe that maintaining crops' genetic diversity is important to avoid massive crop failures caused by disease and pests.
9. Most of the dozens of unique corn types found in the world come from Central America.
10. Genetic drift has gotten to lots of the unique corn types in parts of Mexico that scientists have studied, and some folks fear that eventually there will be no untainted corn.

EXERCISE 8 Use figurative language appropriately. `32e`

Revise any of the following items that contain mixed metaphors or other inappropriate figurative language. Some sentences may not need revision.

Example   Grade inflation may have begun as a ~~salve to~~ students' self-esteem,
                       way to promote

but some professors believe that it has now become ~~a tidal wave.~~
                 a self-perpetuating force.

1. Dr. Harvey C. Mansfield, a professor at Harvard University, argued that college students are too often allowed to coast easily along in the sea of courses and arrive in a harbor protected by unrealistically high grade point averages.

2. According to Mansfield's article in the *Chronicle of Higher Education,* half of the grades given at Harvard are either A's or A-minuses, so some professors, and even students, complain that there is no way to distinguish the cream from the chaff or to tell where students stand in relation to one another.

3. Faculty members who lack tenure are often handicapped in their grading because they know that good student evaluations can help them in the ceaseless competition for scarce teaching appointments.

4. Instructors who do not offer the carrot of A's and B's to students whose work is below par are likely to be bludgeoned with poor evaluations.

5. Mansfield wards off the minefield of grade inflation by keeping two grades for each student, an official inflated one that appears on the transcript and a privately communicated one that tells the student how well his or her work compared with that of other students in the class and with Dr. Mansfield's standards.

EXERCISE 9 Avoid biased language. `32f`

In each of the following sentences, revise any biased or exclusionary language.

> Example   Some comic strips, such as *Doonesbury,* written by Garry Trudeau, and *The Boondocks,* created by ~~the African American~~ Aaron McGruder, can be considered political satires.

1. Many normal people have found *Doonesbury* offensive throughout its long history, for Trudeau has depicted premarital sex and drug use and criticized respectable politicians from Richard Nixon to Rick Perry.

2. The radical leftist Aaron McGruder's comic strip offended some readers with its claim that the United States had helped to arm and train Osama bin Laden.

3. In the fall of 2001, the main character in McGruder's comic strip argued that the ultra-conservative Reagan administration had aided Osama bin Laden and other fanatical Muslims fighting against the Soviet Union.

4. In March of 2012, Trudeau published a series of strips criticizing new laws that required loose women to have ultrasounds before undergoing an abortion.

5. Several papers chose not to run the strip that week, displaying their squeamish Midwestern sensibilities.

EXERCISE 10 Avoid tired expressions (clichés) and pretentious language. `32g`

Edit the following sentences to eliminate clichés and pretentious language.

> Example   I have found a new ~~employment opportunity~~ ^{job} that is
> ~~truly a dream come true.~~ _{exactly what I wanted.}

1. It is with a heavy heart that I terminate my employment situation at Liberty Fixtures.

2. I have accepted a new position at Holt Manufacturing that not only fits me like a glove but is more remunerative.
3. My new position in the credit department involves making "friendly reminders" to customers who are allowing our bills to collect dust.
4. I will everlastingly recollect my years with my Liberty "band of brothers," and I hope that our paths cross often.
5. If you are ever within proximity of my new office, please don't be a stranger.

 Visit the English CourseMate for this text at www.cengagebrain.com to find additional practice exercises.

7 Common Sentence Problems

SOLVE

PART 7 Common Sentence Problems

To obtain study resources for this section, visit the English CourseMate for this text at **www.cengagebrain.com**

7

Common Sentence Problems

35 Trouble Spots and Terms

35a Students' FAQs—and where to find answers

Questions	Short Answer	More Information
Can I begin a sentence with *and* or *but*?	Occasionally, yes	30c, p. 399
Can I interchange *but* and *however*?	No. Meanings are similar; usage and punctuation differ.	37c, 45e: pp. 435, 505
Is it *would have drank* or *would have drunk*?	*Drunk:* past participle verb form after *have*	39a, p. 444
How do I know whether to use *I* or *me* with *and*? (The boss promoted *Tom and I* or *Tom and me*?)	Use the "drop the noun in the *and* phrase" test: The boss promoted *me*.	42a, p. 474
When do I use *who, whom, which*, or *that*?	For people: *who, whom* For things: *which, that* This is a complex issue; turn to the sections in column 3.	44a, 44b, 44d: pp. 492, 493, and 495
What is the difference between *who* and *whom*?	Use *whom* in formal writing as an object form	42i, 44a: pp. 483, 492
When do I use *good* or *well, bad* or *badly*?	*Good* and *bad* modify nouns. *Well* and *badly* modify verbs. But there are tricky exceptions.	43a, 43b, 43c: pp. 485, 486
What are the errors called fragments, run-ons, and comma splices?	A fragment is an incomplete sentence; a run-on or a comma splice is wrongly written as one sentence but needs to be separated or rewritten.	chapters 36 and 37: pp. 430, 433

Questions	Short Answer	More Information
What is the difference between		
a. *it's* and *its*?	*It's* stands for *it is* or *it has*. *Its* is a possessive adjective.	46f, p. 511
b. *who's* and *whose*?	*Who's* stands for *who is* or *who has*. *Whose* is a possessive relative pronoun.	Glossary of Usage, p. 587
c. *lay* and *lie*?	*Lay* is used only with a direct object, and *lie* with no direct object.	39b, p. 448

Grammar-check programs: Uses, dangers, and suggestions

Set aside time for a separate reading of your draft to check for the common problem areas covered in this part of the book and to make corrections. Do not rely on computer tools for editing. Spelling checkers and grammar-check programs are not complete or sophisticated enough to cover all the options. Spelling checkers will catch typographical errors, such as *teh* in place of *the*, but they will not catch missing *s* or *-ed* endings, nor will they find a misspelled word that forms another word: *affect/effect, expect/except, then/than,* or *peek/peak/pique,* for example. You can check out many of these problem areas in the Glossary of Usage at the end of this book.

A grammar-check program analyzes sentences and makes suggestions about what might need to be fixed, tightened, or polished. But technology has not advanced enough for it to be able to take context, meaning, and cultural diversity into account.

KEY POINTS
Grammar-Check Programs: Uses, Dangers, and Suggestions

Uses

A grammar-check program provides helpful observations about simple mechanical matters, such as pointing out

- commas and periods that you may need to place inside quotation marks
- quotation marks or parentheses that you may need to close

(Continued)

(Continued)

- passive verbs that you may wish to revise as active
- clichés
- verb problems such as in the sentence, "Can the mayor wins?"

You may find it worthwhile to activate a grammar-check program solely to catch these basic errors. But before you do, be aware of the following dangers.

Dangers

The capabilities of grammar-check programs are limited. They cannot recognize some errors because they do not "understand" the context or your intention. For example, if you wrote "The actors were boring" but meant to write "The actors were bored," a grammar-check program would not reveal your mistake. Some correct sentences can even be made wrong upon the advice of such a program, as shown in the Note for Multilingual Writers in 3c, p. 43.

Suggestions

If you use a grammar-check program, review all its points of advice before you make any changes based on its recommendations. Never make a suggested change in your draft before verifying that the change is really necessary. Or more radically, consider deactivating the checking feature while you write. Its constant reminders may interrupt your train of thought, introduce errors, and keep you from developing confidence in your own judgment and grammatical expertise.

35c Standard English/Edited American English

Science fiction writer and editor Teresa Neilson Hayden, in *Making Book*, characterizes English as "a generous, expansive, and flexible language" but adds, "a less charitable description would characterize it as drunk and disorderly." The task of editing, she claims, is to try to impose "a degree of regularity on something that is inherently irregular." A set of conventions referred to as Standard English can help you move away from irregularities in your writing; the term Edited American English more directly relates to academic writing in the United States.

The American Heritage Dictionary (AHD), 4th edition, defines *Standard English* as "the variety of English that is generally acknowledged as the model for the speech and writing of educated speakers."*

---

*Definition of "Standard English," Copyright © 2009 by Houghton Mifflin Harcourt Publishing Company. Adapted and reproduced by permission from *The American Heritage Dictionary of the English Language*, Fourth Edition.

A Usage Note in the *AHD,* however, continues, "A form that is considered standard in one region may be nonstandard in another" and points out that *standard* and *nonstandard* are relative terms, depending largely on context.

In short, the concept of Standard English is complex. It is entwined with the region, race, class, education, and gender of both the speaker (or writer) and the listener (or reader). Standard English is far from monolithic. It is constantly supplemented and challenged by other ways of speaking and writing, such as those coming from technology, hip-hop, the worlds of gender and sexual politics, popular culture, and conventions in use in different parts of the English-speaking world.

Nevertheless, Standard English, with all its quirks, irregularities, rules, and exceptions, is politically and sociologically branded as the language of those in power. Its practices are what most readers still expect in the academic and business worlds. However insightful and original your ideas may be, readers will soon become impatient if those ideas are not expressed in sentences that follow conventions determined by the history of the language and the prescriptive power of its educated users.

Attention to accuracy is important in the business world as well as in college. A study of 120 corporations found that one third of the employees of major companies had poor writing skills, leading an executive to say, "It's not that companies want to hire Tolstoy. But they need people who can write clearly."

To meet readers' expectations in academic and business settings, use the version of Edited American English represented in this book and stressed in parts 7–10.

35d Terms for the parts of a sentence

To think about and discuss how sentences work, it is useful to have a shared vocabulary. Here are some of the basic terms covering the parts of speech and the parts of a sentence. The Glossary of Grammatical Terms on page 601 provides further definitions and examples.

Parts of speech   Words are traditionally classified into eight categories called *parts of speech.* Note that the part of speech refers not to the word itself but to its function in a sentence. Some words can function as different parts of speech.

> verb
▶ They respect the orchestra manager.

> noun
▶ Respect is a large part of a business relationship.

Nouns   Words that name a person, place, thing, or concept—*teacher, valley, furniture, Hinduism*—are called *nouns*. When you use a noun, determine the following: Is it a proper noun, requiring a capital letter? Does it have a plural form? If so, are you using the singular or plural form?

Pronouns   A pronoun represents a noun or a noun phrase. In writing, a pronoun refers to its antecedent—that is, a noun or noun phrase appearing just before it in the text.

(compound.

▶ My sister loves *her* new car, but *she* dented *it* last week.

   Pronouns fall into seven types: personal (42a), possessive (42b), demonstrative (41j), intensive or reflexive (42h), relative (44a), interrogative (42i), and indefinite (41h). When you use a pronoun, determine the following: What word or words in the sentence does the pronoun refer to? Does the pronoun refer to a noun or pronoun that is singular or plural?

Verbs   Words that tell what a person, place, thing, or concept does or is—*smile, throw, think, seem, become, be*—are called *verbs*. Verbs change form, so when you use a verb, determine the following: What time period does the verb refer to? What auxiliary or modal verbs are needed for an appropriate tense? Is the subject of the verb singular or plural? Is the verb in the active voice or passive voice? What are the five forms of the verb (*sing, sings, singing, sang, sung*), and are you using the correct form?

   Main verbs often need auxiliary verbs (*be, do, have*) or modal auxiliaries (*will, would, can, could, shall, should, may, might, must*) to complete the meaning.

Adjectives   Words that describe nouns—*purple, beautiful, big*—are called *adjectives*. An adjective can precede a noun or follow a linking verb:

▶ Renee Fleming has a *magnificent* singing voice.

▶ Her singing voice is *magnificent.*

   Descriptive adjectives have comparative and superlative forms: *short, shorter, shortest*. Also functioning as adjectives (before a noun) are *a, an,* and *the,* as well as possessives and demonstratives: *a* cabbage, *an* allegory, *their* poems, *this* book. For more on adjectives, see chapter 43.

Adverbs   Words that provide information about verbs, adjectives, adverbs, or clauses are called *adverbs*. Many but not all adverbs end in *-ly: quickly, efficiently.* Adverbs also provide information about how or when: *very,* *well, sometimes, often, soon, never.* Adverbs modify verbs, adjectives, other adverbs, or clauses.

▸ Federer served brilliantly. He played spectacularly well.

modifies verb ... *modifies adverb*

▸ He is a very energetic player. Undoubtedly, he is a genius.

modifies adjective ... *modifies whole clause*

Conjunctive adverbs—such as *however, therefore, furthermore*—make connections between independent clauses.

Conjunctions Words that connect words, phrases, and clauses are called *conjunctions.*

▸ Martin loves ham *and* eggs.

▸ Kathryn requested an aisle seat *and* a vegetarian meal.

▸ To brighten up her room, she bought a red bowl, a blue jug, *and* yellow cushions.

▸ The magazine was published, *and* his article won acclaim.

The seven coordinating conjunctions—*and, but, or, nor, so, for, yet*—connect ideas of equal importance. Subordinating conjunctions—*because, if, when, although,* for instance—make one clause dependent on another. Consider meaning and style when deciding whether to use a conjunction or a transition.

Prepositions Words used before nouns and pronouns to form phrases that usually do the work of an adjective or adverb are called *prepositions.*

▸ A bird with a red crest flew onto the feeder.

preposition ... preposition

Some common prepositions are *against, around, at, behind, between, except, for, from, in, into, like, on, over, regarding, to,* and *without.* Prepositional phrases are often idiomatic: *on occasion, in love.* To understand their use and meaning, consult a good dictionary. See also chapter 61.

Interjections Words that express emotion and can stand alone—*Ha! Wow! Ugh! Ouch! Say!*—are called *interjections.* Interjections are not used frequently in academic writing. The more formal ones (such as *alas, oh*) are sometimes used in poetry:

But she is in her grave, and, Oh,
The difference to me!   —William Wordsworth, "She Dwelt among the Untrodden Ways"

A sentence and its parts You have probably heard various definitions of a *sentence*, the common one being that "a sentence is a complete thought." Sometimes it is. Sometimes it is not, depending on what one expects by "complete." In fact, that definition is not particularly helpful. How complete is this thought?

▶ **He did not.**

You probably do not regard it as complete in the traditional sense because it relies on text around it, on other sentences, to tell who he is and what it was he did not do, as in the following example.

▶ **Sarah was always competitive with her brother. She studied hard. He did not.**

However, each of these sentences can be said to be *grammatically* complete, containing a subject and verb in an independent clause.

Subject and predicate A sentence needs at the very least a *subject* (the person or thing doing or receiving the action) and a *predicate* (a comment or assertion about the subject). Only a command (such as "Run!") will not state the subject (*you*). A predicate must contain a complete verb, expressing action or state.

Direct and indirect object Some verbs are followed by a *direct object*, a word that receives the action of a verb.

▶ **Many people wear glasses.** [A verb that is followed by a direct object is known as a *transitive verb. Intransitive verbs* such as *sit, happen, occur,* and *rise* are never followed by a direct object.]

Verbs such as *give, send,* and *offer* can be followed by both a direct and an *indirect object* (see 60c).

      ┌─indirect object─┐ ┌─────direct object─────┐
▶ **He gave his leading lady one exquisite rose.**

Complement   Verbs such as *be, seem, look,* and *appear* are *linking verbs,* not action verbs. They are followed by a *subject complement* that renames or describes the subject.

subject complement

▶ The instructor seems troubled.

An *object complement* renames or describes the direct object.

direct object object complement

▶ We appointed a student the chairperson of the committee.

Phrase   A *phrase* is a group of words that lacks a subject, a verb, or both. A phrase is only a part of a sentence. It cannot be punctuated as a sentence.

> an elegant evening gown
>
> singing in the rain
>
> on the corner
>
> worried by the news
>
> with her thoughts in turmoil
>
> to travel around the world

Clause   Clauses can be independent or dependent. A sentence must contain a *main clause,* also called an *independent clause,* which is one that can stand alone. A clause introduced by a word such as *because, when, if,* or *although* is a *dependent clause.* Every clause, whether independent or dependent, needs its own subject and predicate.

dependent (subordinate) clause   independent clause

▶ Because her eyesight is deteriorating, she wears glasses.

Dependent clauses can function as adverbs, adjectives, or nouns.

▶ *When the sun shines,* the strawberries ripen. [Adverb clause expressing time]

▶ The berries *that we picked yesterday* were delicious. [Adjective clause modifying *berries*]

▶ The farmers know *what they should do.* [Noun clause functioning as a direct object]

See 36c for more on dependent clause fragments.

36 Fixing a Sentence Fragment

A *fragment* is a group of words incorrectly punctuated as if it were a complete sentence.

36a What a sentence needs

Check that your sentences contain the following:

1. a **capital letter** at the beginning

2. an **independent (main) clause**—one that can stand alone—containing both a **subject** and a **complete verb** and not introduced by a word such as *when, because, although, which,* or *until* (such words, known as *subordinators* or *subordinating conjunctions*, introduce dependent clauses and are common culprits in fragments)

3. appropriate **end punctuation:** period, question mark, exclamation point, or semicolon

Note that a semicolon indicates the end of one independent clause with a close meaning attachment to another independent clause: *The senator explained the budget items; her assistants helped by displaying explanatory charts.*

Most problems occur when what is presented as a sentence has no complete independent clause.

┌a phrase fragment: no subject or verb┐
▸ He wanted to make a point. To prove his competence.

┌not an independent clause┐
▸ The *Titanic* sank in 1912. Because it hit an iceberg.

(*Because* is a subordinating conjunction connecting to an idea in the previous sentence.)

36b How to fix a phrase fragment with no subject and/or verb

1. Connect the fragment to what comes before or after, removing a period and the following capital letter:

                                                      to
   ▸ Architects recommend solar panels/~~To~~ save on heating bills.
                                        ^

▸ In a valiant attempt to save some money/ ~~The~~ family moved into
  their RV and rented their house. *, the*

▸ The police found a knife and an Uzi/ ~~An~~ Israeli-made
  submachine gun. *an*

▸ The sculptor described his ~~proposal. An~~ innovative plan for an
  abstract fountain in the middle of the town square.

▸ A prize was awarded to Ed/ ~~The~~ best worker in the company. *the*

2. Revise so that each group of words between a capital letter and a
   period contains a subject and a verb.

▸ Many people try to lose weight. ~~Is~~ wise for them to avoid sugary
  snacks. *It is*

36c How to fix a dependent clause fragment

A *dependent clause* begins with a word that makes the clause subordinate
and dependent upon another clause. Unable to stand alone, a subordinate clause must be attached to an independent clause. Here are the
words that introduce subordinate adverb clauses:

SUBORDINATING CONJUNCTIONS

time: when, whenever, until, till, before, after, while, once, as soon
  as, as long as

place: where, wherever

cause: because, as, since

condition: if, even if, unless, provided that

contrast: although, though, even though, whereas, while

comparison: than, as, as if, as though

purpose: so that, in order that

result: so...that, such...that

Whenever you begin a sentence with one of these words, make sure you
see a comma at the end of the clause and then the subject and verb of the
independent clause:

▸ When Jane Austen describes people, she emphasizes all their
  little foibles.

Words introducing other types of dependent clauses (adjective or noun clauses) include *who, whom, whose, which, that, what, when,* and *whoever.*

Methods of correcting a dependent clause fragment   Two methods are available:

1. Connect the fragment to an independent clause before or after it.

   ▸ Lars wants to be a stand-up comic/~~Because~~ ^{because} he likes to make people laugh.

   ▸ Comedians like to perform in small clubs/~~In~~ ⁱⁿ which they can connect with their audience.

   ▸ She made many promises to her family/~~That~~ ^{that} she would write to them every day.

   ▸ The name *Google* comes from the word *googol*/~~Which~~ ^{which} is the

   mathematical term for a one followed by a hundred zeros.

   For the use of commas before clauses beginning with *who, whom,* or *which,* see 44b and 45d.

2. Delete the subordinating conjunction. The dependent clause then becomes an independent clause, which can stand alone.

   ▸ Lars plans to become a stand-up comic. ~~Because he~~ ^{He} likes to make people laugh.

Note: It is a myth that a sentence should never begin with *because.* A word like *because* at the beginning of a sentence does not always signal a fragment. The following sentence is perfectly grammatical, beginning with a dependent clause and ending with an independent clause.

   ▸ **Because Lars likes to make people laugh, he plans to become a stand-up comic.**

36d How to fix a fragment with a missing subject after *and, but,* or *or*

Two separate sentences need two separate subjects. In academic English, one subject is enough for a compound predicate (two verbs after the subject in the same sentence), but it cannot do the work of a subject across two sentences.

Fragment

   ▸ **After an hour, the dancers changed partners. And easily adapted**
   ———fragment: no subject of *adapted*———
   from rock and roll to the tango.

Possible revisions

▶ After an hour, the dancers changed partners and easily adapted from rock and roll to the tango.

▶ After an hour, the dancers changed partners. They easily adapted from rock and roll to the tango.

▶ After an hour, the dancers changed partners, adapting easily from rock and roll to the tango.

▶ After an hour, the dancers changed partners. And they adapted easily from rock and roll to the tango. [See the Language and Culture box in 30c for more on sentences beginning with *and* or *but*.]

36e Intentional fragments

Fragments are used frequently in advertisements to keep the text short. In academic writing, you will sometimes see a fragment used intentionally for emphasis, after a question, as an explanation, or at a point of transition.

▶ **Man is the only animal that blushes. Or needs to.**

—Mark Twain, *Following the Equator*

▶ He [Dylan Thomas] **lived twenty-four years after he began to be a poet. Twenty-four years of poetry, dwindling rapidly in the last decade.**

—Donald Hall, *Remembering Poets*

By all means, use fragments to achieve a specific effect. However, edit fragments that serve no identifiable rhetorical purpose.

 # **37** Run-ons and Comma Splices

37a How to identify run-on (or *fused*) sentences and comma splices

A writer who takes two independent clauses and rams them up against each other, end to end, creates the error of a *run-on sentence*, also known as a *fused sentence*. Academic readers expect two independent clauses to be separated by more than a comma alone.

Run-on error

┌─────────────────── independent clause ───────────────────┐
▶ Blue jeans were originally made as tough work clothes

┌─────────────── independent clause ───────────────┐
they became a fashion statement in the 1970s.

Inserting a comma between the two clauses is no help. That would then be a *comma splice* error.

Comma splice error

▶ Blue jeans were originally made as tough work clothes, they became a fashion statement in the 1970s.

Note: Comma splices are often used in advertising and journalism for stylistic effect to emphasize a contrast: *Obama and Hillary Clinton campaigned on different issues. He looked for ways to create change in the future, she looked back to her husband's presidency.* Take this stylistic risk only if you are sure of the effect you want to achieve.

37b Five ways to correct run-on sentences and comma splices

You can correct run-ons and comma splices in the following five ways. Select the one that works best for the sentence you are editing.

KEY POINTS
Options for Editing a Run-on or Comma Splice

1. When the two clauses are quite long, simply separate them.

▶ Blue jeans were originally made as tough work clothes. *They* became a fashion statement in the 1970s.

▶ Blue jeans were originally made as tough work clothes; *they* became a fashion statement in the 1970s.

2. Include a comma, but make sure it is followed by *and, but, or, nor, so, for,* or *yet.*

▶ Blue jeans were originally made as tough work clothes, *but* they became a fashion statement in the 1970s.

3. If you are switching direction or want to stress the second clause, separate the clauses with a period or a semicolon, followed by a transitional expression such as *however* or *therefore,* followed by a comma (see also 37c and 43f).

> **Blue jeans were originally made as tough work clothes; *however*, they became a fashion statement in the 1970s.**

4. Rewrite the sentences as one sentence by using, for example, *because, although,* or *when* to make one clause introduce or set up the clause containing the important point.

> ***Although* blue jeans were originally made as tough work clothes, they became a fashion statement in the 1970s.**

5. Condense or restructure the sentence.

> **Blue jeans, *originally* made as tough work clothes, became a fashion statement in the 1970s.**

37c How to avoid a run-on or a comma splice when using a transition

Run-ons and comma splices often occur with transitional expressions such as *in addition, however, therefore, for example,* and *moreover* (you'll find a list in 2f). When one of these expressions precedes the subject of its own clause, end the previous sentence with a period or a semicolon. Put a comma after the transitional expression, not before it.

Corrected
run-on error

Martha cleaned her closets ~~in~~ addition, she reorganized the kitchen. In

The house was remodeled ~~moreover~~ the new owners added a guest wing. Moreover

Corrected
comma splice
error

The doctor prescribed new pills, however she did not alert the patient to the side effects.

Note: You can use the coordinating conjunctions *and, but,* and *so* after a comma to connect two independent clauses, but *in addition, however,* and *therefore* do not follow the same punctuation pattern.

Compound

▸ The stock market was falling, so he decided not to invest his savings.

Complex

▸ The stock market was falling; therefore, he decided not to invest his savings.

Commas should both precede and follow a transitional expression that does not appear at the beginning of its own clause:

▸ The weekend guest apologized for breaking a vase. She did not, however, offer to pay for a replacement.

38 Sentence Snarls

Snarls, tangles, and knots are as difficult to deal with on a bad writing day as on a bad hair day, though they may not be as painful. Sentences with structural inconsistencies give readers trouble. They make readers work to untangle the meaning.

38a Tangles: Mixed constructions, confusing comparisons, and convoluted syntax

Mixed constructions   A mixed construction is a sentence with parts that do not match grammatically. The sentence begins one way and then veers off in an unexpected direction. Check to ensure that the subject and verb in your sentence are clear and work together, and note that a phrase beginning with *by* can never be the subject of a sentence. Do not use a pronoun to restate the subject as shown in the third example that follows.

The

▸ ~~In the~~ excerpt by Heilbrun and the story by Gould are similar.

Working

▸ ~~By working~~ at night can create tension with family members.

▸ My neighbors ~~they~~ speak Farsi among themselves.

When you start a sentence with a dependent adverbial clause (beginning with a word like *when, if, because,* and *since*), make sure you follow that clause with an independent clause. A dependent clause cannot serve as the subject of a verb.

Swimming

▶ ~~Because she swims~~ every day does not guarantee she is healthy.

Trading

▶ ~~When~~ a baseball player ~~is traded~~ every few years causes

family problems.

Confusing comparisons   When you make comparisons, readers need to know clearly what you are comparing. See also 42a for faulty comparisons with personal pronouns.

Confusing comparison	**When you finish the exercise, compare your answers with a partner.** [Don't compare your answers with your partner; compare them with your partner's answers.]
Revised	**When you finish the exercise, compare your answers with your partner's.**

Convoluted syntax   Revise sentences that ramble on to such an extent that they become tangled. Make sure they have clear subjects, verbs, and connections between clauses.

Tangled	**The way I feel about getting what you want is that when there is a particular position or item that you want to try to get to do your best and not give up because if you give up you have probably missed your chance of succeeding.**
Possible revision	**To get what you want, keep trying.**

38b Misplaced modifiers: Phrases, *not*, *only*, split infinitives

A modifier is a word or words describing a noun, verb, or clause. A misplaced modifier is a word, phrase, or clause that is wrongly placed so that it appears to modify the incorrect word or words.

Place a phrase or clause close to the word it modifies

Misplaced	**She proudly showed the iPhone to her colleagues that her boss had given her.**
Revised	**She proudly showed her colleagues the iPhone that her boss had given her.**

Take care with modifiers such as *only* and *not* Place a word such as *only, even, just, nearly, not, merely,* or *simply* immediately before the word it modifies. The meaning of a sentence can change significantly as the position of a modifier changes, so careful placement is important.

▸ Next year, everyone in the company will ~~not~~ get a raise. [The
   not

   unrevised sentence says that nobody at all will get a raise. If you move *not*, the sentence now says that although not all workers will get a raise, some will.]

▸ *Only* Rafael planned to visit Disney World. [no one else]

▸ Rafael *only* planned to visit Disney World. [but didn't visit]

▸ Rafael planned to visit *only* Disney World. [and nowhere else]

What you need to know about splitting an infinitive When you place a word or phrase between *to* and the verb (the infinitive), the result can be awkward. Avoid splitting an infinitive when the split is unnecessary or clumsy, as in the following:

▸ Upon hearing the news, she began ~~to uncontrollably cry.~~
   to cry uncontrollably.

▸ We want ~~to honestly and in confidence inform~~ you of our plans.
   to inform   *honestly and in confidence.*

Traditionally, a split infinitive was frowned upon, but it is now acceptable, as in the *Star Trek* motto "To boldly go where no man has gone before…." Sometimes, however, splitting may be necessary to avoid ambiguity.

▸ We had *to stop* them from talking *quickly.* [Were they talking too quickly? Did we have to stop them quickly? The meaning is ambiguous.]

▸ We had *to quickly stop* them from talking. [The split infinitive clearly says that we were the ones who had to do something quickly.]

38c Dangling modifiers

When a modifier beginning with a word ending in *-ing* or *-ed* is not grammatically connected to the noun or phrase it is intended to describe, it is said to *dangle*.

Dangling   *Driving* across the desert, the saguaro *cactus* appeared eerily human. [Who or what was driving? The cactus?]

Usually, you can fix a dangling modifier by either (1) making the modifier refer to the person or thing performing the action or (2) rewriting the modifier as a dependent clause.

Possible   *Driving* across the desert, *the naturalists* thought the
revisions   saguaro cactus appeared eerily human.

When the naturalists were driving across the desert, the saguaro cactus appeared eerily human.

38d Shifts: From statements to commands, from indirect to direct quotation, and in point of view

Sudden shifts in your sentences can be disconcerting to readers. See also 39h on avoiding unnecessary shifts in verb tense.

Do not shift abruptly from statements to commands

▶ Participants should discuss the questions in small groups.
   They should inform
   ~~Inform~~ the facilitator if there are questions.
          ^

Do not shift from indirect to direct quotation   See 39i and 60d for more on tenses in indirect quotations.

▶ The client told us that he wanted to sign the lease and
   asked us to
   ~~would we~~ prepare the papers.
       ^

▶ She wanted to find out whether any interest had accumulated on
                    whether she was
   her account and ~~was she~~ receiving any money.
              ^

Do not shift point of view in pronouns   Be consistent in using first, second, or third person pronouns. For example, if you begin by referring to *one,* do not switch to *you* or *we.* Also avoid shifting unnecessarily between third person singular and plural forms.

Shift   *One* needs a high salary to live in a city because *you* have to spend so much on rent and transportation.

Possible   *One* needs a high salary to live in a city because *one* has
revisions   to spend so much on rent and transportation.

Possible
revisions *We all* **need high salaries to live in a city because we have to spend so much on rent and transportation.**

A high salary is necessary in a city because rent and transportation cost so much.

38e Mismatch of subject and predicate

To avoid confusing readers, never use a subject and predicate that do not make sense together (see 35d, p. 428, for the definition of a predicate). This error is known as *faulty predication*.

Building
▶ ~~The decision to build~~ **an elaborate extension onto the train station made all the trains arrive late.** [It was not the decision that delayed the trains; building the extension did.]

▶ **According to the guidelines,** ~~people in~~ **dilapidated public housing will be demolished this year.** [Surely the housing, not people, will be demolished!]

38f Definitions and reasons ("is when" and "is because")

When you write a definition of a term, use parallel structures on either side of the verb *be*. In formal writing, avoid defining a term by using *is when* or *is where* (or *was when, was where*).

▶ **A tiebreaker in tennis** *is* ~~when there is~~ **a final game to decide a set.**

In giving reasons in both speech and writing, the expression *the reason is because* is becoming common. However, many readers of formal prose traditionally prefer *the reason is that* or simply *because* by itself. Decide what your readers may expect, and consider your options.

that
▶ *The reason* **the young executive lost the account** *is* ~~because~~ **clients had little confidence in his judgment.**

The
▶ ~~*The reason*~~ **the young executive lost the account** *is because* ~~that~~ **clients had little confidence in his judgment.**

38g *Because* and *when* clauses as subject

A dependent adverb clause (35d) beginning with *because* or *when* cannot function as the subject of a sentence.

> *Swimming*
> ▶ ~~Just because she swims~~ every day does not mean she is healthy.
>   ^

[The subject is now a noun phrase, *Swimming every day*, instead of a clause, *Because she swims every day*.]

> *they*
> ▶ When people eat too much fat, increases their cholesterol.
>   ^

[The dependent clause *When people eat too much fat* is now attached to an independent clause with its own subject, *they*.]

38h Omitted words

Include necessary words in compound structures If you omit a verb form from a compound verb, the main verb form must fit into each part of the compound; otherwise, you must use the complete verb form (see 38j on parallelism).

> *been*
> ▶ The person we could hear coughing has always and will always
>   ^
>   be a cigar smoker. [*Be* fits only with *will*, not with *has*.]

Include necessary words in comparisons

> *as*
> ▶ The volleyball captain is as competitive or even more
>   ^
>   competitive than her teammates. [The comparative structures
>   are *as competitive as* and *more competitive than*. Do not merge
>   them.]

If you omit the verb in the second part of a comparison, ambiguity may occur.

> *did.*
> ▶ He liked baseball more than his son. [Omitting *did* implies he
>   ^
>   liked baseball more than he liked his son.]

For more on faulty comparisons, see 43i. For sentence snarls caused by omitting an apostrophe, see 46c.

38i Unnecessary restated subject

Do not insert a pronoun between the subject and the verb to restate the subject (see also 60f).

subject   verb

▶ **The businessmen who supported the candidate they felt betrayed when he lost the election.** [The stated subject is "The businessmen."]

subject   verb

▶ **What may seem funny to some it can be deadly serious to others.** [The subject is the clause "What may seem funny to some."]

38j Structures not parallel

Parallel structures are words, phrases, or clauses that use similar grammatical form. Balance your sentences by using similar grammatical constructions in each part.

Not parallel	**The results of reform were that class size decreased, more multicultural courses, and being allowed to choose a pass/fail option.**
Parallel clauses after *that*	**The results of reform were that class size decreased, more multicultural courses were offered, and students were allowed to choose a pass/fail option.**
Parallel noun phrases	**The results of reform were a decrease in class size, an increase in the number of multicultural courses, and the introduction of a pass/fail option for students.**

The use of parallel structures helps produce cohesion and coherence in a text. Aim for parallelism in sentences and in longer passages, too. The structures can be clauses or phrases, as shown in the following passages from "Maintenance" by Naomi Shihab Nye.

Parallel structures: clauses

We saw one house *where walls and windows had been sheathed in various patterns of gloomy brocade.* We visited another *where the kitchen had been removed* because the owners only ate in restaurants.

Parallel structures: verb phrases

Sometimes I'd come home to find her *lounging* in the bamboo chair on the back porch, *eating* melon, or *lying* on the couch with a bowl of half-melted ice cream balanced on her chest.

Use parallel structures with paired (correlative) conjunctions When your sentence contains *correlative conjunctions*—pairs such as *either…or, neither…nor, not only…but also, both…and, whether…or,* and *as…as*—the structure after the second part of the pair should be exactly parallel in form to the structure after the first part.

▸ He made up his mind *either* to paint the van *or* ~~sell~~ it to
  to

  another buyer. [*To paint* follows *either*; therefore, *to sell* should follow *or*.]

▸ She loves *both* singing in a choir *and* ~~to dance~~ with a folk-dance
  dancing

  troupe. [An *-ing* form follows *both*; therefore, an *-ing* form should also follow *and*.]

▸ **The drive to Cuernavaca was *not only* too expensive *but also* ~~was~~ too tiring to do alone.** [*Too expensive* follows *not only*; therefore, *too tiring* should follow *but also*.]

Use parallel structures in comparisons with *as* or *than* and in lists

▸ **Talking to a child in a stroller is more important than ~~to text~~**
  texting

  and ~~check~~ e-mail.
  checking

▸ **~~To find~~ a life partner is infinitely more complex than**
  Finding

  choosing a new pair of shoes.

▸ **Writing well demands the following: (1) planning your time,**

  (2) paying attention to details, (3) ~~the need for revision,~~ and
  revising,
  (4) proofreading.

39 Verbs

A verb expresses what the subject of the sentence is or does. Verbs may change form according to person, number, and tense; can be regular or irregular; and may require auxiliary verbs (forms of *be, do,* or *have*) or modal verbs (*will, would, can, could, shall, should, may, might,* and *must*) to complete their meaning.

A verb will fit into all four of the following:

1. They want to _____.   3. It is going to _____.

2. They will _____.   4. It might _____.

Identify a verb by checking that the *base form* (that is, the form listed as a dictionary entry) fits these sentences. Note, however, that modal verbs (see 39c) follow a different pattern. Although you may use a variety of verb forms when you speak, readers generally expect verbs in formal writing to follow predictable patterns.

39a Regular and irregular verb forms in Edited American English

Regular Verbs Regular verbs follow a predictable pattern. From the base form—that is, the dictionary form—you can construct all the forms.

Regular Verbs

Base	-s	-*ing* Present Participle	Past Tense	Past Participle
paint	paints	painting	painted	painted
smile	smiles	smiling	smiled	smiled

Irregular verbs Irregular verbs also have the -*s* and the present participle (-*ing*) forms, but they do not use -*ed* to form the past tense and the past participle. (For *be, do,* and *have,* see 39c; for *rise, lie,* and *sit/set,* see 39b.) However, there are many more verbs, so use a dictionary to check irregular past tense and past participle forms if you are unsure. Always refer to 39c for help in deciding which form to use in tenses after auxiliary verbs (such as *has swam* or *has swum?*—the latter is correct).

Note, too, that verbs such as *bet, burst, cost, cut, hit, hurt, let, put, quit, set, slit, split, spread,* and *upset* are irregular only in that they make no change for their past tense or past participle form.

Common Irregular Verbs

Base Form	Past Tense	Past Participle
arise	arose	arisen
be	was/were	been
bear	bore	born, borne
beat	beat	beaten
become	became	become
begin	began	begun
bend	bent	bent
bind	bound	bound

Base Form	Past Tense	Past Participle
bite	bit	bitten
bleed	bled	bled
blow	blew	blown
break	broke	broken
bring	brought	brought
build	built	built
buy	bought	bought
catch	caught	caught
choose	chose	chosen
cling	clung	clung
come	came	come
creep	crept	crept
deal	dealt	dealt
dig	dug	dug
do	did	done
draw	drew	drawn
drink	drank	drunk
drive	drove	driven
eat	ate	eaten
fall	fell	fallen
feed	fed	fed
feel	felt	felt
fight	fought	fought
find	found	found
flee	fled	fled
fly	flew	flown
forbid	forbad(e)	forbidden
forget	forgot	forgotten
forgive	forgave	forgiven
freeze	froze	frozen

(Continued)

(Continued)

Base Form	Past Tense	Past Participle
get	got	gotten, got
give	gave	given
go	went	gone
grind	ground	ground
grow	grew	grown
hang*	hung	hung
have	had	had
hear	heard	heard
hide	hid	hidden
hold	held	held
keep	kept	kept
know	knew	known
lay	laid	laid (39b)
lead	led	led
leave	left	left
lend	lent	lent
lie	lay	lain (39b)
light	lit, lighted	lit, lighted
lose	lost	lost
make	made	made
mean	meant	meant
meet	met	met
ride	rode	ridden
ring	rang	rung
rise	rose	risen (39b)
run	ran	run
say	said	said
see	saw	seen
seek	sought	sought

*Hang meaning "put to death" is regular: hang, hanged, hanged.

Base Form	Past Tense	Past Participle
sell	sold	sold
send	sent	sent
shake	shook	shaken
shine	shone, shined	shone, shined
shoot	shot	shot
shrink	shrank	shrunk
sing	sang	sung
sink	sank	sunk
sit	sat	sat (39b)
sleep	slept	slept
slide	slid	slid
speak	spoke	spoken
spend	spent	spent
spin	spun	spun
spit	spit, spat	spit
spring	sprang	sprung
stand	stood	stood
steal	stole	stolen
stick	stuck	stuck
sting	stung	stung
stink	stank, stunk	stunk
strike	struck	struck, stricken
swear	swore	sworn
sweep	swept	swept
swim	swam	swum
swing	swung	swung
take	took	taken
teach	taught	taught

(Continued)

(Continued)

Base Form	Past Tense	Past Participle
tear	tore	torn
tell	told	told
think	thought	thought
throw	threw	thrown
tread	trod	trodden, trod
understand	understood	understood
wake	woke	waked, woken
wear	wore	worn
weave	wove	woven
weep	wept	wept
win	won	won
wind	wound	wound
wring	wrung	wrung
write	wrote	written

39b Verbs commonly confused

Give special attention to verbs that are similar in form but different in meaning. Some of them, called *transitive verbs,* can take a direct object. Others, called *intransitive verbs*, never take a direct object (see 60c).

1. *rise:* to get up, to ascend (intransitive; irregular)
   raise: to lift, to cause to rise (transitive; regular)

Base	-s	-ing	Past Tense	Past Participle
rise	rises	rising	rose	risen
raise	raises	raising	raised	raised

▶ **A strong wind *rose* out of the west.**

▶ **The historian *raised* the issue of accuracy.** [The direct object answers the question "raised what?"]

2. *sit:* to occupy a seat (intransitive; irregular)
   set: to put or place (transitive; irregular)

Base	-s	-ing	Past Tense	Past Participle
sit	sits	sitting	sat	sat
set	sets	setting	set	set

▶ The audience *sat* on hard wooden seats.

▶ The waiter *set* the steaming plates in front of the diners.

3. *lie:* to recline (intransitive; irregular)
   lay: to put or place (transitive; regular)

Base	-s	-ing	Past Tense	Past Participle
lie	lies	lying	lay	lain
lay	lays	laying	laid	laid

      lay

▶ She ~~laid~~ down for an hour after her oral presentation.

      lying

▶ I was just ~~laying~~ down for a nap when the phone rang.

    Lay

▶ ~~Lie~~ the map on the floor.

In addition, note the verb *lie* ("to say something untrue"), which is intransitive and regular.

Base	-s	-ing	Past Tense	Past Participle
lie	lies	lying	lied	lied

▶ He *lied* when he said he had won three trophies.

39c Auxiliary verbs

An auxiliary verb is used with a main verb and sometimes with other auxiliaries. The auxiliary verbs are *do, have,* and *be,* and the nine modal verbs are *will, would, can, could, shall, should, may, might,* and *must* (59b). Note the irregular forms of *do, have,* and *be.*

Base	Present Tense Forms	-ing	Past	Past Participle
do	do, does	doing	did	done
have	have, has	having	had	had
be	am, is, are	being	was, were	been

See 41a for agreement with present tense forms of *do, have,* and *be.*

Language and Dialect Variation with *Be*

In some languages (Chinese and Russian, for example), forms of *be* used as an auxiliary ("She *is* singing") or as a linking verb ("He *is* happy") can be omitted. In some spoken dialects of English (African American Vernacular, for example), subtle linguistic distinctions not possible in Standard English can be achieved: The omission of a form of *be* and the use of the base form in place of an inflected form (a form that shows number, person, mood, or tense) signal entirely different meanings.

VERNACULAR		STANDARD
He busy.	(temporarily)	He is busy now.
She be busy.	(habitually)	She is busy all the time.

Edited American English always requires the inclusion of a form of *be*.

    are
▶ Latecomers ˄always at a disadvantage.

Auxiliary verbs can be used in combination. Whatever the combination, the form of the main verb is determined by the auxiliary that precedes it.

Verb Forms Following Auxiliaries

Last Auxiliary and Its Forms	+ base	+ *ing*	+ past participle
do	*did* write		
modals (*can, could, will, would, shall, should, must, might, may*)	*might* go *would* fall		
have			has/have/had written should *have* seen would *have* gone

Last Auxiliary and Its Forms	+ base	+ ing	+ past participle
be (active)		*is* writing *were* singing might *be* driving has *been* running should have *been* thinking	
be (passive)			*are* grown *was* taken was *being* stolen would *be* eaten has *been* written might have *been* worn

Pay careful attention to the tricky editing points here:

1. Make sure you use a past participle form after *have*. In speech, we run sounds together, and the pronunciation may be mistakenly carried over into writing.

   > He could ~~of~~ ^{have} run faster.

   > We should ~~of~~ ^{have} replaced the roof before it started leaking.

   The contracted forms *could've, should've, would've,* and so on are probably responsible for the nonstandard substitution of the word *of* in place of *have*. Watch out for this as you edit.

2. With modal verbs and the verbs *do* and *have*, the verb form following is fixed. It is only with *be* that a conscious choice of active or passive voice comes into play.

   > Laura *is taking* her driving test. [active]

   > Laura *was taken* to the hospital last night. [passive]

● **NOTE** **FOR MULTILINGUAL WRITERS**

What Comes before *Be*, *Been*, and *Being*

Be requires a modal auxiliary before it to form a complete verb (*could be jogging; will be closed*). *Been* requires *have*, *has*, or *had* (*have been driving; has been eaten*). *Being* must be preceded by *am*, *is*, *are*, *was*, or *were* to form a complete verb and must be followed by an adjective or a past participle: *You are being silly. He was being followed.*

39d Verb tenses: Overview

Tenses indicate time as perceived by the speaker or writer. The following examples show active voice verbs referring to past, present, and future time. For passive voice verbs, see chapter 40.

Past Time

Simple past	They *arrived* yesterday./They *did* not *arrive* today.
Past progressive	They *were leaving* when the phone rang.
Past perfect	Everyone *had left* when I called.
Past perfect progressive	We *had been sleeping* for an hour before you arrived.

Present Time

Simple present	He *eats* Wheaties every morning./ He *does* not *eat* eggs.
Present progressive	They *are working* today.
Present perfect	She *has* never *read* Melville.
Present perfect progressive	He *has been living* here for five years.

Future Time (using *will*)

Simple future	She *will arrive* soon.
Future progressive	They *will be playing* baseball at noon tomorrow.
Future perfect	He *will have finished* the project by Friday.
Future perfect progressive	By the year 2015, they *will have been running* the company for twenty-five years.

Other modal auxiliaries can substitute for *will* and thus change the meaning: *must arrive, might be playing, may have finished, should have been running* (see also 59b).

● NOTE **FOR MULTILINGUAL WRITERS**

Verbs Not Using -*ing* Forms for Progressive Tenses

Use simple tenses, not progressive forms, with verbs expressing mental activity referring to the senses, preference, or thought, as well as with verbs of possession, appearance, and inclusion (for example, *smell, prefer, understand, own, seem, contain*).

don't understand

► Sorry, I ~~am not understanding~~ the point of the story.

possess

► They ~~are possessing~~ different behavior patterns.

39e Present tenses

Simple present   Use the simple present tense for the following purposes:

1. To make a generalization

    ► Gardening *nourishes* the spirit.

2. To indicate a permanent or habitual activity

    ► The poet *uses* rhyme and meter in an innovative way.

    ► Young snakes *shed* their skins as often as once every two weeks.

3. To express future time in dependent clauses (clauses beginning with words such as *if, when, before, after, until, as soon as*) when *will* is used in the independent clause

    ► When the newt colony *dies* in the cold weather, building construction will begin.

4. To discuss literature and the arts (called the *literary present*) even if the work was written in the past or the author is no longer alive

    ► In *Zami*, Audre Lorde *describes* how a librarian *introduces* her to the joys of reading.

    However, when you write a narrative of your own, use past tenses to tell about past actions.

    walked   kissed

    ► Then the candidate ~~walks~~ up to the crowd and ~~kisses~~ all the babies.

● NOTE **FOR MULTILINGUAL WRITERS**

No *Will* in Time Clause

In a dependent clause beginning with a conjunction such as *if, when, before, after, until,* or *as soon as,* do not use *will* to express future time. Use *will* only in the independent clause. Use the simple present in the dependent clause.

▸ As soon as they ~~will~~ get married, they will return to their hometown.

Present progressive   Use the present progressive to indicate an action in progress at the moment of speaking or writing.

▸ Publishers *are getting* nervous about Internet copyright issues.

However, do not use progressive forms with intransitive verbs such as *believe, know, like, prefer, want, own, seem, appear,* and *contain.*

               believe
▸ Many people ~~are believing~~ that there may be life on other planets.

Present perfect and present perfect progressive   Use the present perfect in the following instances:

1. To indicate that an action occurring at some unstated time in the past is related to present time

   ▸ They *have worked* in New Mexico, so they know its laws.

2. To indicate that an action beginning in the past continues to the present

   ▸ She *has worked* for the same company since I *have known* her.

   If you state the exact time when something occurred, use the simple past tense, not the present perfect.

        planted
   ▸ Sandra ~~has planted~~ tulips, marigolds, and daffodils last fall.

3. To report research results in APA style

   ▸ Feynmann *has shown* that science can be fun.

   Use the present perfect progressive when you indicate the length of time an action has been in progress up to the present time.

   ▸ Researchers *have been searching* for a cure for arthritis for many years. [This implies that they are still searching.]

39f Past tenses

Use past tenses consistently. Do not switch from past to present or future for no reason (see 39h).

Simple past   Use the simple past tense when you specify a past time or event.

▶ The tornado *destroyed* hundreds of structures and *left* three people dead.

When the sequence of past events is indicated with words like *before* or *after,* use the simple past for both events.

▶ She *knew* how to write her name before she *went* to school.

Use past tenses in an indirect quotation (a reported quotation, not in quotation marks) introduced by a past tense verb.

▶ His chiropractor *told* him that the adjustments *were* over.

Past progressive   Use the past progressive for an activity in progress over time or at a specified point in the past.

▶ Abraham Lincoln *was attending* the theater when he was assassinated.

Past perfect and past perfect progressive   Use the past perfect or the past perfect progressive only when one past event was completed before another past event or stated past time.

▶ *Ben had cooked* the whole meal by the time Sam arrived.
[Two events occurred: Ben cooked the meal; then Sam arrived.]

▶ He *had been cooking* for three hours when his sister finally offered to help. [An event in progress—cooking—was interrupted in the past.]

Make sure that the past tense form you choose expresses your exact meaning.

▶ When the student protesters marched into the building at noon, the administrators *were leaving*. [The administrators were in the process of leaving. They began to leave at, say, 11:57 a.m.]

▶ When the student protesters marched into the building at noon, the administrators *had left*. [There was no sign of the administrators. They had already left at 11 a.m.]

> **When the student protesters marched into the building at noon, the administrators *left*.** [The administrators saw the protesters and then left at 12:01 p.m.]

39g *-ed* endings: Past tense and past participle forms

Both the past tense form and the past participle of regular verbs end in *-ed*. Edited American English (see 35c) requires the *-ed* ending in the following instances:

1. To form the past tense of a regular verb

   > The new trainee ask^ed^ to take on more responsibility.

2. To form the expression *used to*, indicating past habit

   > Cell phones use^d^ to be larger and heavier than they are now.

3. To form the past participle of a regular verb after the auxiliary *has, have,* or *had* in the active voice or after forms of *be* (*am, is, are, was, were, be, being, been*) in the passive voice (see chapter 40)

   > The sheriff has live^d^ in this town for over 30 years. [active]

   > Their work will not be finish^ed^ soon. [passive]

4. To form a past participle used as an adjective

   > The nurses rushed to help the injure^d^ toddler.

   > The trainer was surprise^d^ to learn that the skier had been hurt.

● NOTE **FOR MULTILINGUAL WRITERS**

The *-ed* Ending

The *-ed* ending is particularly troublesome for learners of English because in speech the ending is difficult to hear and may seem to be dropped—particularly when it blends into the next sound.

> They wash^ed^ two baskets of laundry last night.

This is an area that will always need careful editing.

The following *-ed* forms are used with *be: concerned, confused, depressed, divorced, embarrassed, married, prejudiced, satisfied, scared, supposed* (to), *surprised*, *used (to)*, *worried*. Some can also be used with *get*, *seem*, *appear*, and *look*. Do not omit the *-d* ending.

- ▸ People are often confuse when driving around a rotary in England. *(d)*

- ▸ The candidate was embarrass not to know the answer to the reporter's question. *(ed)*

Do not confuse the past tense and past participle forms of an irregular verb (39a). A past tense form occurs alone as a complete verb, and a past participle form must be used with a *have* or *be* auxiliary.

- ▸ He ~~drunk~~ the liquid before his medical tests. *(drank)*

- ▸ She ~~done~~ her best to learn how to count in Japanese. *(did)*

- ▸ The explorers could have ~~went~~ alone. *(gone)*

- ▸ The employees were badly ~~shook~~ up after the unexpected news. *(shaken)*

39h Tense shifts

If you use tenses consistently throughout a piece of writing, you help readers understand what is happening and when. Check that your verbs consistently express present or past time, both within a sentence and from one sentence to the next. Avoid unnecessary tense shifts.

Tense shifts	Selecting a jury *was* very difficult. The lawyers *ask* many questions to discover bias and prejudice; sometimes, the prospective jurors *had* the idea they *are acting* in a play.
Revised	Selecting a jury *was* very difficult. The lawyers *asked* many questions to discover bias and prejudice; sometimes, the prospective jurors *had* the idea they *were acting* in a play.

When you write about events or ideas presented by another writer, use the literary present consistently (see 39e).

- ▸ The author ~~illustrated~~ the images of women in two shows using advertisements and dramas on TV. One way shows women who advanced their careers by themselves, and the other shows those who used beauty to gain recognition. *(illustrates)*

Tense shifts are appropriate in the following instances:

1. When you signal a time change with a time word or phrase

   signal for switch from past to present
   ▶ We *bought* our house at the wrong time, and *now*

   signal for switch back to the past
   it *is* worth less than we *paid* for it *two years ago.*

2. When you follow a generalization (present tense) with a specific example of a past incident

   ─ generalization ─
   ▶ Some bilingual schools *offer* intensive instruction in English.

   ─ specific example ─
   My sister, for example, *went* to a bilingual school where she *studied* English for two hours every day.

39i Tenses in indirect quotations

An indirect quotation reports what someone said. It does not use quotation marks, and it follows the tense of the introductory verb. For example, when the verb introducing an indirect quotation is in a present tense, the indirect quotation should preserve the tense of the original direct quotation (see also 60d).

Direct   "The economic outlook has improved."

                  present   ─ indirect quotation ─
Indirect   Only one reporter *says* that the economic outlook has

improved.

When the introductory verb is in a past tense, use forms that express past time in the indirect quotation.

Direct   "The banks are lending and the economic outlook has improved."

                 past   ─ indirect quotation ─
Indirect   The reporter *announced* that the banks were lending

and the economic outlook *had improved.*

In a passage of more than one sentence, preserve the sequence of tenses showing past time throughout the whole passage.

▶ The reporter announced that the banks were lending and the economic outlook *had improved.* His newspaper *had reassigned* him to another case, so he *was ending* his daily reports on the crisis.

Note: Use a present tense after a past tense introductory verb only if the statement is a general statement that holds true in present time.

▶ The reporter *announced* that he *is* happy with his new assignment.

Verbs in conditional sentences, wishes, requests, demands, and recommendations

Conditions When *if* or *unless* introduces a dependent clause, the sentence expresses a condition. There are four types of conditional sentences: two refer to actual or possible situations, and two refer to speculative or hypothetical situations.

🔑 KEY POINTS
Verb Tenses in Conditional Sentences

MEANING EXPRESSED	*IF* CLAUSE	INDEPENDENT CLAUSE
1. Fact	Simple present	Simple present

▶ **If mortgage rates *go* down, house sales *increase*.**

MEANING EXPRESSED	*IF* CLAUSE	INDEPENDENT CLAUSE
2. Prediction/possibility	Simple present	*will, can, should, might* + base form

▶ If I *hear* someone misuse the word "literally" one more time, I *will scream.*

▶ If we *don't speak* ill of the dead, who *will*? —Harold Bloom

3. Speculation about present or future	Simple past or subjunctive *were*	*would, could, should, might* + base form

▶ If he *had* an iPhone, he *would download* music. [But he does not have one.]

▶ If she *were* my lawyer, I *might win* the case. [But she is not.]

4. Speculation about past	Past perfect (*had* + past participle)	*would have* *could have* *should have* *might have* } + past participle

▶ If Jane *had attended* the book signing, she *could have met* her favorite author. [But she did not attend.]

Use of subjunctive *were* in place of *was* With speculative conditions about the present and future using the verb *be, were* is used in place of *was* in the dependent *if* clause. This use of *were* to indicate hypothetical situations involves what is called the *subjunctive mood.*

▶ If my aunt *were* sixty-five, she *could get* a discount airfare.
[My aunt is sixty.]

Blending Some blending of time and tenses can occur, as in the case of a condition that speculates about the past in relation to the effect on the present.

▶ If we *hadn't taken out* a second mortgage, we *would own* the house free and clear by now.

Use of *would* When writing in an academic setting, use *would* only in the independent clause, not in the conditional clause. However, *would* occurs frequently in the conditional clause in speech and in informal writing.

showed
▶ If the fish-fry committee ~~would show~~ more initiative, people
might attend their events more regularly.

had
▶ If the driver ~~would have~~ heard what the pedestrian said, he
would have been angry.

had
▶ If you ~~would have~~ paid attention in class, you wouldn't have
done the wrong assignment.

Would, could, and might with conditional clause understood *Would, could,* and *might* are used in independent clauses when no conditional clause is present. These are situations that are contrary to fact, and the conditional clause is understood.

▶ I *would* never *advise* her to leave college without a degree. She *might come back* later and blame me for her lack of direction.

Wishes Like some conditions, wishes deal with speculation. For a present wish—about something that has not happened and is therefore hypothetical and imaginary—use the past tense or subjunctive *were* in the dependent clause. For a wish about the past, use the past perfect: *had* + past participle.

A wish about the present

▶ I wish I *had* your attitude.

▶ I wish that Shakespeare *were* still alive.

A wish about the past

▶ Addicted to cigarettes, the patient wishes she *had* never *taken* that first puff.

Requests, demands, and recommendations   The subjunctive also appears after certain verbs, such as *request, command, insist, demand, move* (meaning "propose"), *propose,* and *urge.* In these cases, the verb in the dependent clause is the base form regardless of the person and number of the subject.

▶ The dean suggested that students *be* allowed to vote.

▶ He insisted that she *submit* the report.

▶ The boss is demanding that everyone *work* overtime.

Some idiomatic expressions preserve the use of the subjunctive, for example, *far* be *it from me, if need* be, *as it* were.

Passive Voice

In the active voice, the grammatical subject is the doer of the action, and the sentence tells "who's doing what." The passive voice tells what "is done to" the subject of the sentence. The person or thing doing the action may or may not be mentioned but is always implied: "My car was repaired" (by somebody at the garage).

Active

subject	active voice verb	direct object
▶ Alice Walker	wrote	*The Color Purple.*

Passive

subject	passive voice verb	doer or agent
▶ *The Color Purple*	was written	by Alice Walker.

40a How to form the passive voice

The complete verb of a passive voice sentence consists of a form of the verb *be* followed by a past participle.

receiver   verb: *be* +
┌─ as subject ─┐ ┌─ past participle ─┐ doer omitted or named after *by*

▸ The windows *are cleaned* [by someone] every month.

▸ The windows *were being cleaned* yesterday afternoon.

▸ The windows *will have been cleaned* by the end of the workday.

Auxiliaries such as *would, can, could, should, may, might,* and *must* can also replace *will* when the meaning demands it.

▸ The windows *might be cleaned* next month.

40b When to use the passive voice

Use the passive voice sparingly. A general rule is to use the passive voice only when the doer or agent in your sentence (the person or thing acting) is unknown or is unimportant or when you want to connect the topics of two clauses (see 30a and 40c).

▸ The pandas are rare. Two of them *will be returned* to the wild.

▸ He had a lot of people working for him, maybe sixty, and most of them liked him most of the time. Three of them *will be* seriously *considered* for his job.   —Ellen Goodman, "The Company Man"

Notice how in the first example, the pandas are the topic of the sentences. It doesn't really matter who is returning them to the wild, but rather that they are being returned.

In scientific writing, the passive voice is often preferred to indicate objective procedures. Scientists and engineers are interested in analyzing data and in performing studies that other researchers can replicate. The individual doing the experiment is therefore relatively unimportant and usually is not the subject of the sentence.

▸ Sixty volunteers *were given* a placebo while another sixty received the experimental treatment. Participants *were not told* which group they had been assigned to.

● NOTE FOR MULTILINGUAL WRITERS

Passive Voice with Transitive Verbs

Use the passive voice only with verbs that are transitive in English (that is, they can be followed by a direct object). Intransitive verbs such as *happen*, *occur*, and *try* (*to*) are not used in the passive voice.

▶ The accident ~~was~~ occurred on a deserted street.

▶ Morality is an issue that ~~was~~ *have* tried to explain by

⏜many philosophers⟋

40c The passive voice as connector

In the following passage, notice how the passive voice preserves the topic chain of *I* subjects (see also 30a):

▶ I remember to start with that day in Sacramento...when I first entered a classroom, able to understand some fifty stray English words. The third of four children, I *had been preceded* to a Roman Catholic school by an older brother and sister.

—Richard Rodriguez, *Hunger of Memory*

40d Overuse of the passive voice

In the humanities, your writing will generally be clearer and stronger if you name the subject and use verbs in the active voice to explain who is doing what. If you overuse the passive voice, the effect will be heavy and impersonal (see 29a).

Unnecessary passive **He *was alerted* to the danger of drugs by his doctor and *was persuaded* by her to enroll in a treatment program.**

Revised **His doctor alerted him to the danger of drugs and persuaded him to enroll in a treatment program.**

41 Subject-Verb Agreement

The principle of agreement means that when you use the present tense of any verb or the past tense of the verb *be* in academic writing, you must make the subject and verb agree in person (first, second, or third) and number (singular or plural): *A baby cries. Babies cry.*

41a Basic principles for an *-s* ending

The ending *-s* is added to both nouns and verbs but for very different reasons.

1. An *-s* ending on a noun is a plural signal: *her brothers* (more than one).

2. An *-s* ending on a verb is a singular signal; *-s* is added to a third person singular verb in the present tense: *Her plumber wears gold jewelry.*

🔑 KEY POINTS
Two Key Points about Agreement

1. Follow the "one *-s* rule" in the present tense. Generally, you can put an *-s* on a noun to make it plural, or you can put an *-s* on a verb to make it singular. (But see the irregular forms *is* and *has* on p. 465.) Do not add an *-s* to both subject and verb.

   No   **The articles explains the controversy.** [Violates the "one *-s* rule"]

   Possible   **The article explains the controversy.**
   revisions   **The articles explain the controversy.**

2. Do not omit a necessary *-s*.

   > deals
   ▸ **Whitehead's novel deal with issues of race and morality.**
                        ^

   > reports
   ▸ **The report in the files describe the housing project in detail.**
                        ^

Most simple present verbs show agreement with an *-s* ending. The verb *be,* however, has three instead of two present tense forms. In addition, *be* is the only verb to show agreement in the past tense, where it has two forms: *were* and the third person singular *was.* The table shows agreement forms for a regular verb and for the three auxiliary verbs *have, be,* and *do.*

Subject-Verb Agreement

Base Form	like (regular)	have	be	do
Simple Present: Singular				
First person: I	like	have	am	do
Second person: you	like	have	are	do
Third person: he, she, it	likes	has	is	does
Simple Present: Plural				
First person: we	like	have	are	do
Second person: you	like	have	are	do
Third person: they	like	have	are	do

LANGUAGE AND CULTURE

Issues of Subject-Verb Agreement

Many languages make no change in the verb form to indicate number and person, and several spoken versions of English, such as African American Vernacular (AAV), Caribbean Creole, and London Cockney, do not observe the standard rules of agreement.

▶ **AAV: She *have* a lot of work experience.**

▶ **Cockney: He *don't* never wear that brown whistle.** [The standard form is *doesn't;* other nonstandard forms in this sentence are *don't never* (a double negative) and *whistle*—short for *whistle and flute,* rhyming slang for *suit.*]

Use authentic forms like these when quoting direct speech; for your formal academic writing, though, follow the subject-verb agreement conventions used in academic English.

41b What to do when words come between the subject and verb

When words separate the subject and verb, find the verb and ask "who?" or "what?" about it to determine the subject. Ignore any intervening words.

▶ **The general discussing the attacks looks tired.** [Who looks tired? The subject, *general*, is singular.]

▶ **A box containing valuable old books was accidentally tossed into the dumpster.** [What was tossed? The subject, *box*, is singular.]

▶ **The government's proposals about preserving the environment cause controversy.** [What things cause controversy? The subject, *proposals*, is plural.]

Do not be confused by intervening words ending in -*s*, such as *always* and *sometimes.* The -*s* ending still must appear on a present tense verb if the subject is singular.

▶ **A school play always get the parents involved.**

Phrases introduced by *as well as, along with, together with,* and *in addition to* that come between the subject and the verb do not change the number of the verb.

▶ **The dog, as well as the two cats, spend most of the day outdoors.**

▶ **The article, together with the books, make a significant contribution to the topic.**

41c Agreement with linking verbs (*be, seem, appear*)

Linking verbs such as *be, become, look,* and *appear* are followed by what is called a *complement,* and a subject complement should not be confused with a subject (see 35d). Make the verb agree with the subject.

plural   plural   singular
┌— subject —┐ verb ┌————complement————┐
▶ **The drinks *were* the most expensive item on the restaurant bill.**

          singular   singular plural
┌———————— subject ————————┐ verb ┌complement┐
▶ **The most expensive item on the restaurant bill *was* the drinks.**

▶ **My favorite part of dorm life *has become* the parties.**

▶ **Parties *have become* my favorite part of dorm life.**

41d What to do when the subject follows the verb

When the subject follows the verb in the sentence, you must still make the subject and verb agree.

1. Questions In a question, make the auxiliary verb agree with the subject, which follows the verb.

▸ *Does* the editor agree to the changes?

▸ *Do* the editor and the production manager agree to the changes?

2. Initial *here* or *there* When a sentence begins with *here* or *there,* make the verb agree with the subject.

▸ There *is* a reason to rejoice.

▸ There *are* many reasons to rejoice.

However, avoid excessive use of an initial *there* (see 29b): *We have a reason to rejoice.*

● NOTE **FOR MULTILINGUAL WRITERS**

Singular Verb after *It*

It does not follow the same pattern as *here* and *there.* The verb attached to an *it* subject is always singular.

▸ It *is* hundreds of miles away.

3. Inverted word order When a sentence begins with a phrase placed before the verb, not with the subject, the verb still agrees with the subject (see also 31d, p. 404).

```
                          plural
                           verb
 ┌──prepositional phrase──┐ │ ┌──plural subject──┐
```
▸ In front of the library sit two stone lions. [Who or what performs the action of the verb? Two stone lions do.]

41e Eight tricky subjects with singular verbs

1. *Each* and *every* *Each* and *every* may seem to indicate more than one, but grammatically, they are singular words. Use them with a singular verb, even if they are parts of a compound subject (41g) using *and* or *or*.

▶ *Each* of the poems *employs* a different rhyme scheme.

▶ *Every* seat in the theater *has* a good view of the stage.

▶ *Every* essay and quiz *counts* in the grade.

2. -*ing* or infinitive form as subject   With a subject beginning with the -*ing* verb form used as a noun (a *gerund*) or with an infinitive, always use a singular verb form.

singular
subject

▶ *Speaking* in public *causes* many people as much fear as death.

▶ *To fly* across the country with small children *requires* patience and stamina.

3. Singular nouns ending in -*s*   Some names of disciplines that end in -*s* (*economics, physics, politics, mathematics, statistics*) are not plural. Use them and the noun *news* with a singular verb.

▶ The news *has* been bad lately.

▶ Politics *is* dirty business.

4. Phrases of time, money, and weight   When the subject is regarded as one unit, use a singular verb.

▶ Fifteen pounds *is* a lot of weight to lose in one month.

▶ Seven years *was* a long time to spend at college.

But

▶ Seven years *have* passed.

5. Uncountable nouns   An uncountable noun (such as *furniture, jewelry, equipment, advice, happiness, honesty, information,* and *knowledge*) encompasses all the items in its class. An uncountable noun does not have a plural form and is always followed by a singular verb (58b).

▶ That advice *makes* me nervous.

▶ The information found in the press *is* not always accurate.

6. *One of* *One of* is followed by a plural noun (the object of the preposition *of*) and a singular verb form. The verb agrees with the subject *one*.

▶ **One of her friends *loves* to tango.**

▶ **One of the reasons for his difficulties *is* that he spends too much money.**

For agreement with *one of* and *the only one of* followed by a relative clause, see 44c, page 495.

7. *The number of/a number of* The phrase *the number of* is followed by a plural noun (the object of the preposition *of*) and a singular verb form.

▶ **In the US, the number of television sets *exceeds* the number of people.**

However, with the phrase *a number of*, meaning "several," use a plural verb.

▶ **A number of reasons *are* listed in the letter.**

8. The title of a long work or a word referred to as the word itself Use a singular verb with the title of a long, whole work or a word referred to as the word itself. Use a singular verb even if the title or word is plural in form (see also 50a and 50d).

▶ *Cats was* based on a poem by T. S. Eliot.

▶ In her story, the *word* "dudes" *appears* five times.

41f Collective noun as subject

A collective noun names a collection of people or things: *class, government, family, jury, committee, group, couple,* or *team.* If you refer to the group as a whole, use a singular verb.

▶ The class *begins* every school day with a song.

Use a plural verb if you wish to emphasize differences among the individuals or if members of the group are thought of as individuals.

▶ His family *are* mostly artists and musicians.

▶ The committee *are* taking on many different jobs around the county.

If that seems awkward to you, revise the sentence.

▶ His close relatives *are* mostly artists and musicians.

▶ The members of the committee *are* taking on many different jobs around the county.

However, with the collective nouns *police, poor, elderly,* and *young,* always use plural verbs.

▶ The elderly *deserve* our respect.

41g Subjects containing *and, or,* or *nor*

Subjects with *and* When a subject consists of two or more parts joined by *and,* treat the subject as plural and use a plural verb.

—————plural subject————— plural verb
▶ His instructor and his advisor *want* him to change his major.

However, if the parts of the compound subject refer to a single person or thing, use a singular verb.

————singular subject (one person)———— singular verb
▶ The film's director and producer *has* a fearsome temper.

—singular subject— singular verb
▶ Fish and chips *is* a popular dish in England, but it is no longer served wrapped in newspaper.

Also use a singular verb with a subject beginning with *each* or *every.*

▶ Every claim and conclusion *deserves* consideration.

With *or* or *nor* When the parts of a compound subject are joined by *or* or *nor,* the verb agrees with the part nearer to it.

▶ Her sister or her parents *look* after her children every Friday.

▶ Neither her colleagues nor her boss *remembers* her name.

41h Indefinite pronouns (*anyone, everybody, nobody,* etc.)

Words that refer to nonspecific people or things (indefinite pronouns) can be tricky. Most of them take a singular verb. Usage may differ in speech and writing, so when you write, it is important to pay attention to the conventions of agreement between subject and verb.

Indefinite pronouns used with a singular verb

someone, somebody, something

anyone, anybody, anything

one, no one, nobody, nothing

everyone, everybody, everything

each, either, neither

▸ Nobody *knows* the answer.

▸ Everyone *agrees* on the author's intention.

▸ Everything about the story *makes* me suspicious.

▸ Both films are popular; neither *contains* gratuitous violence.

▸ Each of the chess games *promises* to be exciting.

See 42d, page 480, on the personal pronouns to use (*he? she? they?*) to refer to indefinite pronouns.

A note on *none* and *neither*

None   Some writers prefer to use a singular verb after *none* (of) because *none* means "not one": *None of the contestants has smiled.* However, as *The American Heritage Dictionary* (4th ed.) points out, a singular or a plural verb is technically acceptable: *None of the authorities has* (or *have*) *greater tolerance on this point than H. W. Fowler.* Check to see if your instructor prefers the literal singular usage.

Neither   The pronoun *neither* is, like *none*, technically singular: *The partners have made a decision; neither wants to change the product.* In informal writing, however, you may come across *neither* with a plural verb, especially when followed by an *of* phrase: *Neither of the novels reveal a polished style.*

41i Quantity words

Some quantity words are singular, and some are plural. Others can be used to indicate either singular or plural depending on the noun they refer to.

Words Expressing Quantity

With Singular Nouns and Verbs	With Plural Nouns and Verbs
much	many
(a) little	(a) few
a great deal (of)	several
a large amount of	a large number of
less	fewer
another	both

See 62c for more on the difference between *few* and *a few*.

▸ **Much** *remains* **to be done before our departure.**

▸ **Much of the machinery** *needs* **to be repaired.**

▸ **Many** *have* **gained from the recent economic swings.**

▸ **Fewer celebrities than anticipated** *have* **agreed to attend the gala.**

You will see and hear *less* used in place of *fewer*, especially with numbers ("5 items or less"), but in formal writing, use *fewer* to refer to a plural word.

▸ **More** *movies* **have been made this year than last, but** *fewer have* **made a large profit.**

Quantity words used with both singular and plural nouns and verbs The following quantity words take their cue from the number (singular or plural) of the noun they refer to: *all, any, half (of), more, most, no, other, part (of), some.*

▸ **You gave me** *some information. More is* **necessary.**

▸ **You gave me** *some facts. More are* **needed.**

▸ *All the water is* **contaminated.**

▸ *All the students look* **healthy.**

41j Agreement with *this, that, these, those, mine, ours,* etc.

Demonstratives agree in number with a noun: *this solution, these solutions; that problem, those problems.*

plural

▸ **The mayor is planning changes. These will be controversial.**

Singular	Plural
this	these
that	those

Possessives such as *mine, his, hers, ours, yours,* and *theirs* can refer to both singular and plural antecedents (see 42d).

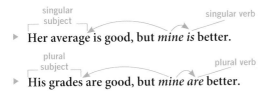

▶ Her average is good, but *mine is* better.

▶ His grades are good, but *mine are* better.

41k Agreement with subject clauses beginning with *what* or other question words

When a clause introduced by *what* or other question words, such as *how, who,* and *why,* functions as the subject of an independent clause, use a third person singular verb in the independent clause.

▶ What you eat in the morning *affects* your mood all day long.

▶ How the players train *makes* all the difference.

When the verb is followed by the linking verb *be* and a plural complement, some writers use a plural verb. However, some readers may object.

▶ What I need *are* black pants and an orange shirt.

You can avoid the issue by revising the sentence to eliminate the *what* clause.

▶ I need black pants and an orange shirt.

42 Pronouns

A pronoun is a word that substitutes for a noun, a noun phrase, or another pronoun.

▶ Rebecca's headaches are so bad that *they* are affecting *her* ability to function.

42a Forms of personal pronouns (*I* or *me*, *he* or *him*?)

Personal pronouns change form to indicate person (first, second, or third), number (singular or plural), and function in a clause.

KEY POINTS
Forms of Personal Pronouns

PERSON	SUBJECT	OBJECT	POSSESSIVE (+ NOUN)	POSSESSIVE (STANDS ALONE)	INTENSIVE AND REFLEXIVE
1st person singular	I	me	my	mine	myself
1st person plural	we	us	our	ours	ourselves
2nd person singular and plural	you	you	your	yours	yourself/ yourselves
3rd person singular	he	him	his	his	himself
	she	her	her	hers	herself
	it	it	its	its [rare]	itself
3rd person plural	they	them	their	theirs	themselves

In a compound subject or compound object with *and*: *I* or *me*; *he* or *him*? In speech, the forms *I* and *me*, *he* and *him*, *she* and *her* are often interchanged even by educated people (the fourth example sentence below was said by President Obama in an impromptu interview), but you should take care to edit them in formal writing. To decide which pronoun form to use with a compound subject or compound object, mentally recast the sentence with only one pronoun in the subject or object position.

▶ **Richard and ~~me~~ play in our school's marching band.** [Drop the
   I
   words *Richard and*. Then you will have *I play*, not *me play*. Here
   you need the subject form, *I*.]

▶ **~~Him~~ and his whole family decided to move to Oregon.** [He
   He
   decided to move.]

> She   I
> ~~Her~~ and ~~me~~ tried to solve the problem. [She tried. I tried.]
>   ^   ^

>   me
> The ambassador invited Michelle and ~~I~~ to join the celebration.
>   ^

[If the words *Michelle and* are dropped, the sentence would be *The ambassador invited me*, not *The ambassador invited I*. The object form is needed here. He invited *me*, not "He invited I."]

After a preposition   After a preposition, you need an object form.

>   me
> Between you and ~~I~~, the company is in serious trouble.
>   ^

>   me
> Rachid stared at my colleague and ~~I~~. [He stared at my colleague.
>   ^
> He stared at me.]

After a linking verb   In formal academic writing, use the subject form of a personal pronoun after a linking verb, such as *be*, *seem*, *look*, or *appear*.

> Was that Oprah Winfrey? It was *she*. [Informal: "It was her."]

> It was *they* who hosted the benefit. [Many writers would revise this sentence to sound less formal: "They were the ones who hosted the benefit" or simply "They hosted the benefit."]

After a verb and before an infinitive   Use the object form of a personal pronoun after a verb and before an infinitive. When a sentence has only one object, this principle is easy to apply.

> The dean wanted *him* to lead the procession.

Difficulties occur with compound objects.

>   him and me
> The dean wanted ~~he and I~~ to lead the procession.
>   ^

In appositive phrases and with *we* or *us* before a noun   When using a personal pronoun in an appositive phrase (a phrase that gives additional information about a preceding noun), determine whether the noun that the pronoun refers to functions as subject or as object in its own clause.

>   appositive
>   ┌─ direct object   ┌─phrase─┐
> The supervisor praised only two employees, Ramon and me.
> [She praised me.]

appositive
subject phrase

▶ **Only two employees, Ramon and I, received a bonus.** [I received a bonus.]

Similarly, when you consider whether to use *we* or *us* before a noun, use *us* when the pronoun is the direct object of a verb or preposition; use *we* when it is the subject.

object of preposition

▶ **LL Cool J waved to us fans.**

subject

▶ **We fans have decided to form a club.**

In comparisons   In comparisons with *than* and *as*, decide when to use the subject or object form of the personal pronoun by mentally completing the meaning of the comparison.

▶ **You have more information about the project than I.** […than I do.]

▶ **Matt and Juanita work in the same office; Matt criticizes his boss more than she.** […more than Juanita does.]

▶ **Matt and Juanita work in the same office; Matt criticizes his boss more than her.** […more than he criticizes Juanita.]

42b **Possessive forms of pronouns (*my* or *mine*, *her* or *hers*?)**

Distinguish between adjective and pronoun forms (*her* and *hers*)

▶ **The large room with three windows is *her* office.** [*Her* is an adjective.]

▶ **The office is *hers*.** [*Hers*, the possessive pronoun, can stand alone.]

When a possessive pronoun functions as a subject, the word it refers to (its antecedent) determines singular or plural agreement for the verb (see 41j).

▶ **My purse is leather; hers *is* plastic.** [*purse* is singular; it needs a singular verb.]

▶ **My gloves are black; hers *are* yellow.** [plural antecedent and plural verb]

Note: The word *mine* does not follow the pattern of *hers, theirs, yours,* and *ours*. The form *mines* is nonstandard.

▶ **The little room on the left is *mine*.**

No apostrophe with possessive personal pronouns   Even though possessive in meaning, the pronouns *yours, ours, theirs, his*, and *hers* should never be spelled with an apostrophe. Use an apostrophe only with the possessive form of a noun.

- ▶ That swim cap is *Nancy's.*

- ▶ That is *her* swim cap.

- ▶ That swim cap is *hers.*

- ▶ These books are the *twins'.* (46c)

- ▶ These are *their* books.

- ▶ These books are *theirs.*

No apostrophe with *its* as a possessive pronoun   The word *it's* is not a pronoun; it is the contraction of *it is* or *it has*. An apostrophe is never used with *its*, the possessive form of the pronoun *it* (see also 46f).

- ▶ The paint has lost *its* gloss.

- ▶ *It's* not as glossy as it used to be. [It is not as glossy…]

Possessive pronoun before an *-ing* form   Generally, use a possessive personal pronoun before an *-ing* verb form used as a noun.

- ▶ I appreciate *your* thinking of me.
- ▶ *Their* winning the marathon surprised us all.

Sometimes, the *-ing* form is a participle functioning as an adjective. In that case, the pronoun preceding the *-ing* form should be in the object form.

- ▶ I saw *him* rummaging through the trash.

Comparisons using possessive forms   Note how using *them* in place of *theirs* in the following sentence would change the meaning by comparing suitcases to roommates, not suitcases to suitcases.

- ▶ It's really hard to be roommates with people if your suitcases are much better than *theirs.*   —J. D. Salinger, *The Catcher in the Rye*

Forgetting to use the appropriate possessive form in the next example, too, could create a misunderstanding. Is the writer comparing a house to a person or his house to her house?

- ▶ I like his house more than I like her.

42c **Pronoun reference to a clear antecedent**

A pronoun substitutes for a noun, a noun phrase, or a pronoun already mentioned. The word or phrase that a pronoun refers to is known as the pronoun's *antecedent*. Antecedents should always be clear and explicit.

▶ Psychiatrist Edward Hallowell, a leading expert on

   ADD, suspects that some of the greatest minds in history

   had the condition, and that *it* enhanced *their* creativity.

State a specific antecedent   Be sure to give a pronoun such as *they, this,* or *it* an explicit antecedent.

No specific antecedent	When Mr. Rivera applied for a loan, they outlined the procedures for him. [The pronoun *they* lacks an explicit antecedent.]
Revised	When Mr. Rivera applied to bank officials for a loan, *they* outlined the procedures for him.

When you use a pronoun, make sure it does not refer to a possessive noun or to a noun within a prepositional phrase.

                                                          George Orwell
▶ In ~~George Orwell's~~ "Shooting an Elephant," he reports an incident

   that shows the evil effects of imperialism. [The pronoun *he* cannot refer to the possessive noun *Orwell's.*]

                 Lance Morrow's essay
▶ ~~In the essay by Lance Morrow, it~~ points out the problems of

   choosing a name. [*It* refers to *essay,* which functions as the object of the preposition *in* and therefore cannot function as an antecedent.]

Avoid ambiguous pronoun reference   Your readers should never be left wondering which *this, they,* or *it* is being discussed.

Ambiguous	My husband told my father that he should choose the baby's name. [Does *he* refer to *husband* or *father*?]
Revised	My husband told my father to choose the baby's name.
Revised	My husband wanted to choose the baby's name and told my father so.

42d Making a pronoun agree with its antecedent

A plural antecedent needs a plural pronoun; a singular antecedent needs a singular pronoun.

▶ Listeners heard *they* could win free tickets. The ninth caller learned *she* was the winner.

Make a demonstrative pronoun agree with its antecedent The demonstrative pronouns *this* and *that* refer to singular nouns; *these* and *those* refer to plural nouns: *this/that house, these/those houses* (41j).

singular antecedent

▶ He published his autobiography two years ago. This was his first book.

plural antecedent

▶ One reviewer praised his honesty and directness. These were qualities he had worked hard to develop.

Make a pronoun agree with a generalized (generic) antecedent Generic nouns name a class or type of person or object, such as *a student* meaning "all students" or *a company* meaning "any company" or "all companies." Sometimes, writers use *they* to refer to a singular generic noun, but the singular/plural mismatch annoys some readers.

	singular antecedent	plural pronoun

Mismatch When a student is educated, they can go far in the world.

singular antecedent   singular pronoun

Revised but somewhat stilted When a student is educated, he or she can go far in the world.

plural antecedent   plural pronoun

Best When students are educated, they can go far in the world.

Increasingly, in advertising, journalism, and informal writing you will see (and you will certainly hear this usage in speech, too) a plural pronoun referring to a singular antecedent, as in the following station wagon advertisement:

▶ One day *your child* turns sixteen, and you let *them* borrow the keys to the wagon.

However, in formal academic writing, many readers may still expect a pronoun to agree with its antecedent. Even though usage may be changing, you can avoid problems by making the antecedent plural.

>   *people*   *stand*
> ▸ I respect ~~a person~~ who ~~stands~~ by their word.

Make a pronoun agree with an indefinite pronoun Indefinite pronouns, such as *everyone, somebody, each,* and *nothing* (see the list in 41h), are singular in form. A singular antecedent traditionally needs a singular pronoun to refer to it, but which one: *he, she,* or *he or she?* The *Oxford English Dictionary* points out that for centuries, *they* has often been used "in reference to a singular noun made universal by *every, any, no,* etc., or applicable to one of either sex (= 'he or she')."

Despite the increasingly widespread use of *they,* some readers may still object to it, so revising the sentence is a good idea.

Singular pronoun	*Everyone* picked up *his* assignments and raced off to write *his* parts of the report. [Sentence needs revision because of the sexist bias.]
Revised but clumsy	*Everyone* picked up *his or her* assignments and raced off to write *his or her* parts of the report.
Revised but some may object	*Everyone* picked up *their assignments* and raced off to write *their* parts of the report. [The plural pronoun *their* refers to a singular antecedent, *everyone.*]
Probably best	**The lawyers all picked up** *their* **assignments and raced off to write** *their* **parts of the report.**

Make a pronoun agree with the nearer antecedent when you use *or* or *nor* When an antecedent includes *or* or *nor,* a pronoun agrees with the element that is nearer to it. If one part of the compound is singular and the other part is plural, put the plural antecedent closer to the pronoun and have the pronoun agree with it.

> ▸ Either my tutor or my professor has left *his* wallet on the table.

> ▸ Neither Bill nor the campers could find *their* soap.

Make a pronoun agree with a collective noun Use a singular pronoun to refer to a collective noun (*class, family, jury, committee, couple, team*) if you are referring to the group as a whole.

> ▸ The jury reached *its* decision in less than an hour.

> ▸ The committee has not yet completed *its* report.

Use a plural pronoun if members of the group named by the collective noun are considered to be acting individually.

▸ **The committee began to cast *their* ballots in a formal vote.**

42e Gender bias

For many years, the pronoun *he* was used routinely in generic references to unspecified individuals in certain roles or professions, such as student, teacher, doctor, lawyer, and banker, and *she* was used routinely in generic references to individuals in roles such as nurse, secretary, or typist. This usage is now considered sexist language.

Not appropriate   **When an accountant learns a foreign language, *he* gains access to an expanded job market.**

To revise such sentences that make general statements about people, roles, and professions, use one of the following methods:

1. Use a plural antecedent plus *they* (see also 32f and 42d).

▸ **When accountants learn a foreign language, *they* gain access to an expanded job market.**

2. Avoid the issue by rewriting the sentence to eliminate the pronoun.

▸ **An accountant who learns a foreign language gains access to an expanded job market.**

3. Use a singular antecedent and the phrase *he or she*.

▸ **When an accountant learns a foreign language, *he or she* gains access to an expanded job market.**

The problem with option 3 is that awkward and repetitive structures can result when such a sentence is expanded.

▸ **When an accountant learns a foreign language, *he or she* gains access to an expanded job market once *he or she* has decided on *his or her* specialty.**

That's clumsy. Use the *he or she* option only when a sentence is relatively short and does not repeat the pronouns. On the whole, though, revision is usually the best:

▸ **Accountants who learn a foreign language gain access to expanded job markets once they choose a specialty.**

See also pronoun agreement with indefinite pronouns (p. 480).

42f   Consistent point of view

Always write from a consistent perspective. Pronouns can help maintain consistency. Consider the person and number of the pronouns you use:

- Are you emphasizing the perspective of the first person (*I* or *we*)?
- Are you primarily addressing the reader as the second person (*you*)?
- Are you, as is most common in formal academic writing, writing about the third person (*he, she, it, one,* or *they*)?

Avoid confusing readers by switching from one perspective to another.

Inconsistent   *The company* decided to promote only three midlevel managers. *You* had to have worked there for ten years to qualify.

Revised   *The company* decided to promote only three midlevel managers. *The employees* had to have worked there for ten years to qualify.

42g   The use of the pronoun *you*

In formal writing, do not use the pronoun *you* when you mean "people generally." Use *you* only to address readers directly and to give instructions.

Not appropriate   Credit card companies should educate students about how to handle credit. *You* should not have to find out the problems the hard way. [A reader addressed directly in this way might think, "Who, me? I don't need to be educated about credit, and I have no problems."]

Appropriate   Turn to the next page, where *you* will find an excerpt from Edith Wharton's novel that will help *you* appreciate the accuracy of the details in this film.

Edit uses of *you* if you are making a generalization about a group or if using *you* entails a switch from the third person.

> While growing up, ~~you~~ teenagers face arguments with ~~your~~ their parents.

> It doesn't matter if young professionals are avid music admirers or comedy fans since ~~you~~ they can find anything ~~you~~ they want in the city.

42h Intensive and reflexive pronouns

Intensive pronouns emphasize a previously mentioned noun or pronoun. Reflexive pronouns identify a previously mentioned noun or pronoun as the person or thing receiving the action (see the Key Points box in 42a).

Intensive   **The president *himself* appeared at the gates.**

Reflexive   **He introduced *himself*.**

Do not use an intensive pronoun in place of a personal pronoun in a compound subject:

▸ **Joe and ~~myself~~ will design the brochure.**

Forms such as *hisself, theirself,* and *theirselves* occur in spoken dialects but are not Standard English.

42i *Who/whom, whoever/whomever*

In all formal writing situations, distinguish between the subject and object forms of the pronouns used to form questions (interrogative pronouns) or to introduce a dependent noun clause.

Subject	Object
who	whom (or informally, *who*)
whoever	whomever

In questions   In a question, ask yourself whether the pronoun is the subject of its clause or the object of the verb. Test the pronoun's function by rephrasing the question as a statement, substituting a personal pronoun for *who* or *whom*.

▸ **Who wrote that fascinating book?** [*He* wrote that fascinating book. Subject: use *who*.]

▸ **Whoever could have written it?** [*She* could have written it. Subject: use *whoever*.]

▸ **Who[m] were they describing?** [*They* were describing *him*. Object: *whom* (formal), though *who* is common in such contexts both in speech and in writing.]

When introducing a dependent clause with a pronoun, determine whether to use the subject or object form by examining the pronoun's function in the clause. Ignore expressions such as *I think* or *I know* when they follow the pronoun; they have no effect on the form of the pronoun.

subject of clause

▶ They want to know who runs the business.

subject of clause (who runs the business)

▶ They want to know who I think runs the business.

object of *to* (the manager reports to him or her)

▶ They want to know whom the manager reports to.

subject of clause

▶ I will hire whoever is qualified.

object of *recommends*

▶ I will hire whomever my boss recommends.

For uses of *who* and *whom* in relative clauses, see 44a.

43 Adjectives and Adverbs

Adjectives describe, or modify, nouns or pronouns. They do not add -*s* or change form to reflect number or gender. For the order of adjectives, see 60g.

▶ A recent article in the journal *Nature* discussed the *toxic* effects of sugar on our health.

▶ The director tried a *different* approach to a documentary.

▶ The depiction of rural life is *accurate*.

▶ The reporter keeps her desk *tidy*.

● NOTE **FOR MULTILINGUAL WRITERS**

No Plural Form for Adjectives

Do not add -*s* to an adjective that modifies a plural noun.

▶ Only bilinguals candidates will be interviewed for the job.

Adverbs modify verbs, adjectives, and other adverbs, as well as whole clauses.

▶ The financial analyst settled down *comfortably* in her new job.

▶ The patient is demanding a *theoretically* impossible treatment.

▶ *Inevitably*, the projector failed five minutes before the start of

our presentation.

43a Forms of adjectives and adverbs

No single rule indicates the correct form of all adjectives and adverbs.

Adverb: adjective + -ly   Many adverbs are formed by adding *-ly* to an adjective: *soft/softly; intelligent/intelligently*. Sometimes, when *-ly* is added, a spelling change occurs: *easy/easily; terrible/terribly*.

Adjectives ending in -ic   To form an adverb from an adjective ending in *-ic*, add *-ally* (*basic/basically; artistic/artistically*), except for *public*, whose adverb form is *publicly*.

Adjectives ending in -ly   Some adjectives, such as *friendly, lovely, timely*, and *masterly*, already end in *-ly* and have no distinctive adverb form.

adjective

▶ She is a friendly person.

— adverbial phrase —

▶ She spoke to me in a friendly way.

Irregular adverb forms   Certain adjectives do not add *-ly* to form an adverb:

Adjective	Adverb
good	well
fast	fast
hard	hard

adjective

▶ He is a hard worker.

adverb
▶ **He works hard.** [*Hardly* is not the adverb form of *hard*. Rather, it means "barely," "scarcely," or "almost not at all": *I could* hardly *breathe in that stuffy room.*]

Note: *Well* can also function as an adjective, meaning "healthy" or "satisfactory": *A* well *baby smiles often. She feels* well.

43b When to use adjectives and adverbs

In speech, adjectives (particularly, *good, bad*, and *real*) are often used to modify verbs, adjectives, or adverbs. This is nonstandard usage. Use an adverb to modify a verb or an adverb.

well
▶ **The webmaster fixed the link good.**

really well
▶ **The chorus sings real good.**

nicely
▶ **She sings nice.**

badly
▶ **They dance bad.**

43c Adjectives after linking verbs

After linking verbs (*be, seem, appear, become*), use an adjective to modify the subject.

▶ **Sharon Olds's poems are** *lyrical.*

▶ **The book seems** *repetitive.*

Some verbs (*appear, look, feel, smell, taste*) are sometimes used as linking verbs and other times as action verbs. If the modifier tells about the subject, use an adjective. If the modifier tells about the action of the verb, use an adverb.

Adjective **The analyst looks** *confident* **in her new job.**

Adverb **The lawyer looked** *confidently* **at all the assembled partners.**

Adjective   The waiter feels *bad*.

        The steak smells *bad*.

Adverb   The chef smelled the lobster *appreciatively*.

Note: Use a hyphen to connect two words used as an adjective when they appear before a noun. Do not use a hyphen when the words follow a linking verb with no noun complement.

▶ Wynton Marsalis is a *well-known* trumpet player.

▶ Wynton Marsalis is *well known*.

43d Compound adjectives

A compound adjective consists of two or more words used as a unit to describe a noun. Many compound adjectives contain the past participle *-ed* verb form: *flat-footed, barrel-chested, broad-shouldered, old-fashioned, well-dressed, left-handed*. Note the form when a compound adjective is used before a noun: hyphen, past participle (*-ed*) form where necessary, and no noun plural (*-s*) ending.

▶ They have a *five-year-old* daughter. [Their daughter is five years old.]

▶ She gave me a *five-dollar* bill. [She gave me five dollars.]

▶ The actress was accompanied by a *well-dressed* older man. [The man was dressed well.]

For more on hyphenation with compound adjectives, see 54b.

43e Position of adverbs

An adverb can be placed in various positions in a sentence.

▶ *Enthusiastically*, she ate the sushi.

▶ She *enthusiastically* ate the sushi.

▶ She ate the sushi *enthusiastically*.

● NOTE **FOR MULTILINGUAL WRITERS**

Adverb Placement

Do not place an adverb between a verb and a short direct object (60b).

▶ She ate | *enthusiastically* | the sushi.

Put adverbs that show frequency (*always, usually, frequently, often, sometimes, seldom, rarely, never*) in one of four positions:

1. At the beginning of a sentence

   ▶ *Sometimes*, **he rides his bike to work instead of driving.**

When *never, seldom,* or *rarely* occurs at the beginning of the sentence, word order is inverted (see also 41d).

   ▶ *Never* **will I let that happen.**

2. Between the subject and the main verb

   ▶ **They** *always* **arrive half an hour late.**

3. After a form of *be* or any auxiliary verb (such as *do, have, can, will, must*)

   ▶ **The writing center is** *always* **closed on Saturdays.**

   ▶ **The tutors are** *seldom* **late for training.**

   ▶ **There has** *never* **been an available computer during exam week.**

4. In the final position

   ▶ **Amira checks her e-mail** *frequently*.

Note: Don't place the adverb *never* in the final position.

43f Conjunctive adverbs (*however*, *therefore*, etc.)

There are two important points to remember about conjunctive adverbs such as *however, therefore,* and *moreover*.

1. When a conjunctive adverb occurs in the middle of a clause, set it off with commas.

   ▶ **The mayor's course of action has, therefore, been severely criticized.**

2. When it occurs between independent clauses, use a semicolon to end the first clause and put a comma after the adverb.

   ▶ **The hearings were contentious; however, the Supreme Court justice was approved.**

   See also 2f, 30b, 37c, and 45e.

43g No double negatives

Adverbs like *hardly, scarcely*, and *barely* are considered negatives, and the contraction *-n't* stands for the adverb *not*. Some languages and dialects allow the use of more than one negative to emphasize an idea, but the standard form is for only one negative in a clause. Avoid double negatives.

Double
negative

We *don't* have *no* excuses.

Revised

We *don't* have *any* excuses. [or] We have *no* excuses.

Double
negative

She did*n't* say *nothing*.

Revised

She did*n't* say *anything*. [or] She said *nothing*.

Double
negative

City residents ca*n't hardly* afford the sales tax.

Revised

City residents can *hardly* afford the sales tax.

43h Comparative and superlative forms of adjectives and adverbs

Adjectives and adverbs have three forms: positive, comparative, and superlative. Use the comparative form when comparing two people, places, things, or ideas; use the superlative form when comparing more than two.

Regular forms Add the ending *-er* (or just *-r* for an adjective already ending in *-e*, such as *feeble*) to form the comparative and *-(e)st* to form the superlative of both short adjectives (those that have one syllable or those that have two syllables and end in *-y* or *-le*) and one-syllable adverbs. (Change *-y* to *-i* if *-y* is preceded by a consonant: *icy, icier, iciest*.) Generally, a superlative form is preceded by *the* (*the shortest distance*).

Positive	Comparative (Comparing two)	Superlative (Comparing more than two)
short	shorter	shortest
pretty	prettier	prettiest
simple	simpler	simplest
fast	faster	fastest

With longer adjectives and with adverbs ending in -*ly*, use *more* (for the comparative) and *most* (for the superlative). Note that *less* (comparative) and *least* (superlative) are used with adjectives of any length (*less bright, least bright; less effective, least effective*).

Positive	Comparative	Superlative
intelligent	more intelligent	most intelligent
carefully	more carefully	most carefully
dangerous	less dangerous	least dangerous

If you cannot decide whether to use -*er*/-*est* or *more*/*most*, consult a dictionary. If there is an -*er*/-*est* form, the dictionary will say so.

Note: Do not use the -*er* form along with *more* or the -*est* form along with *most*.

▶ The pizza from the store is ~~more~~ better than the pizza we make at home.

▶ Boris is the ~~most~~ fittest person I know.

Irregular forms   The following common adjectives and adverbs have irregular comparative and superlative forms:

Positive	Comparative	Superlative
good	better	best
bad	worse	worst
much/many	more	most
little	less	least
well	better	best
badly	worse	worst

***Than* with comparative forms**   To compare two people, places, things, or ideas, use the comparative form and the word *than*. If you use a comparative form in your sentence, you need the word *than* to let readers know what items you are comparing.

than the previous one.

▶ This course of action is more efficient⟋

Comparative forms are also used without *than* in an idiomatic way.

▸ The *longer* the wait, the *more anxious* she becomes.

▸ The *more*, the *merrier*.

Absolute adjectives   Do not use comparative and superlative forms of adjectives that imply absolutes: *complete, empty, full, equal, perfect, priceless*, or *unique*. In addition, do not add intensifying adverbs such as *very, totally, completely*, or *absolutely* to these adjectives. To say that something is "perfect" implies an absolute rather than something measured in degrees.

▸ He has ~~the most~~ perfect view of the ocean.
          a

▸ They bought a ~~totally~~ unique quilt at an auction.

43i Faulty or incomplete comparisons

Make sure that you state clearly what items you are comparing. Some faulty comparisons can give readers the wrong idea (see 38h and 42b).

Incomplete   **He likes the parrot better than his wife.**

Do you really want to suggest that he prefers the parrot to his wife? If not, clarify the comparison by completing the second clause.

Revised   **He likes the parrot better *than his wife does*.**

Edit sentences like the following:

▸ **In winter, New York's weather is colder than London.** [Compare
                                                       's
   the weather in both places, not the weather in New York and the
   city of London.]

▸ **Williams's poem gives a more objective depiction of the**

   painting than Auden. [To compare Williams's poem with
                      's
   Auden's poem, you need to include an apostrophe and -*s*;
   otherwise, you compare a poem to the poet W. H. Auden.]

Comparisons must also be complete. If you say that something is "more efficient," your reader wonders, "More efficient than what?"

▸ **Didion shows us a home that makes her feel more tied to her roots.**
                                          than her home in Los Angeles does
   [Include the other part of the comparison.]

44 Relative Clauses and Relative Pronouns (*who, whom, whose, which, that*, etc.)

A relative clause relates to an antecedent in a nearby clause.

——relative clause——

▶ The girl *who* can't dance says the band can't play. —Yiddish proverb

44a Relative pronouns

When deciding whether to use *who, whom, which,* or *that,* use the following table as a guide. Your choice of pronoun will depend on these three factors:

1. The function of the relative pronoun in its clause

2. Whether the relative pronoun refers to a human or nonhuman antecedent

3. Whether the clause is restrictive or nonrestrictive (see 44b for this distinction)

Relative Pronouns and Antecedents

Antecedent	Function of Relative Pronoun		
	Subject	Object	Possessive
Human antecedent	*who*	*whom* (can be omitted)	*whose*
Nonhuman antecedent	*that* or *which* (see 44b)	*that* (can be omitted) or *which* (see 44b)	*of which* (formal); *whose* (informal)

Examples: Human

Subject **The teachers *who* challenge us are the ones we remember.**

Object **The players [*whom*] the spectators boo often end up in the minor leagues.**

Possessive **Spectators *whose* cell phones ring will be asked to leave.**

Examples: Nonhuman

Subject **The dog *that* kept barking all night drove the neighbors crazy.**

Object **They stayed at a hotel [*that*] their friends had recommended.**

Possessive **We stayed in a picturesque town the name *of which* I can't remember.**

We stayed in a picturesque town *whose* name I can't remember.

Watch out! Do not rename the subject in the independent clause.

▸ **The teachers who challenge us ~~they~~ are the ones we remember.**

Remember that an inserted phrase does not affect the function of a pronoun.

▸ **Let's reward contestants who we realize have not been coached.**

Do not use *what* as a relative pronoun.

that
▸ **The deal ~~what~~ the CEO was trying to make turned out to be crooked.**

44b Restrictive and nonrestrictive relative clauses

The two types of relative clauses, restrictive and nonrestrictive, fulfill different functions and need different punctuation (45d).

Restrictive **The people *who live in the apartment above mine* make a lot of noise at night.**

Nonrestrictive **The Sullivans, *who live in the apartment above mine*, make a lot of noise at night.**

Restrictive relative clause   A restrictive relative clause provides information essential for identifying the antecedent and restricting its scope.

FEATURES

The clause is not set off with commas. It is needed to understand what the subject is.

An object relative pronoun can be omitted.

That (rather than *which*) is used for reference to nonhuman antecedents.

▶ **The teachers *who challenge us* are the ones we remember.** [The independent clause—"The teachers are the ones we remember"—leads us to ask, "Which teachers?" The relative clause provides information that is essential to completing the meaning of the subject; it restricts the meaning from "all teachers" to "the teachers who challenge us."]

▶ **The book [*that*] *you gave me* was fascinating.** [The relative pronoun *that* is the direct object in its clause ("You gave me the book") and can be omitted.]

Nonrestrictive relative clause   A nonrestrictive relative clause provides information that merely adds descriptive information.

FEATURES

The antecedent is a unique, designated person or thing.

The clause is set off by commas; it provides additional nonessential information, a kind of aside. It could be omitted, and the sentence would make sense without it.

Which (not *that*) is used to refer to a nonhuman antecedent.

An object relative pronoun cannot be omitted.

▶ **The book *War and Peace*, which you gave me, was fascinating.** [The independent clause—"The book *War and Peace* was fascinating"—does not promote further questions, such as "Which book?" The information in the relative clause ("which you gave me") is almost an aside and not essential for understanding the independent clause.]

A nonrestrictive relative clause with a quantity word   Relative clauses beginning with a quantity word such as *some, none, many, much, most,* or *one* followed by *of which* or *of whom* are always nonrestrictive.

▶ **They selected five candidates, *one of whom* would get the job.**

▶ **The report mentioned five names, *none of which* I recognized.**

● **NOTE** **FOR MULTILINGUAL WRITERS**

Relative versus Personal Pronouns

Do not add a personal pronoun in addition to the relative pronoun.

most of which

▶ **We harvested fifty pounds of tomatoes,** ~~**which most of them**~~ **we**
   ^
   plan to give away.

44c Agreement of verb with relative pronoun

Determine subject-verb agreement within a relative clause by asking whether the antecedent of a subject relative pronoun is singular or plural.

—————relative clause—————
▶ **The book that *is* at the top of the bestseller list gives advice about health.** [The singular noun *book* is the antecedent of *that*, the subject of the singular verb *is* in the relative clause.]

—————relative clause—————
▶ **The books that *are* at the top of the bestseller list give advice about health, success, and making money.** [The plural noun *books* is the antecedent of *that*, the subject of the plural verb *are* in the relative clause.]

Note: The phrase *one of* is followed by a plural noun phrase. However, the verb can be singular or plural depending on the meaning.

▶ **Juan is one of the employees who *work* long hours.** [Several employees work long hours. Juan is one of them. The plural noun *employees* is the antecedent of *who*, the subject of the plural verb *work* in the relative clause.]

—antecedent—   singular verb
▶ **Juan is the only one of the employees who *works* long hours.** [Only Juan works long hours.]

44d Relative clauses with prepositions

When a relative clause contains a relative pronoun within a prepositional phrase, do not omit the preposition. Keep in mind these three points:

1. Directly after the preposition, use *whom* or *which*, never *that*.

—————relative clause—————
▶ **The family *to whom* the package is addressed no longer lives here.**

2. In a restrictive clause (44b), if you place the preposition after the verb, use *that* (or you can omit *that*), but do not use *whom* or *which*.

[that]
▶ **The security measures ~~which~~ the mayor had insisted on made him unpopular.**

3. Do not add an extra personal pronoun object after the preposition at the end of the relative clause.

▶ **The theater company [that] they are devoted to ~~it~~ has produced six new plays this season.**

44e Position of relative clause

To avoid ambiguity, place a relative clause as close as possible to its antecedent (see also 38b on misplaced modifiers).

Ambiguous   **He searched for the notebook all over the house that his friend had forgotten.** [Had his friend forgotten the house?]

Revised   **He searched all over the house for the notebook that his friend had forgotten.**

44f *Where* and *when* as relative pronouns

When you refer to actual or metaphoric places and times, you can use *where* to replace *in which, at which,* or *to which,* and you can use *when* to replace *at which, in which,* or *on which.* Do not use a preposition with *where* or *when.*

▶ **The day on which I was born was cold and snowy.**

▶ **The day *when* I was born was cold and snowy.**

▶ **The village in which he was born honored him last year.**

▶ **The village *where* he was born honored him last year.**

Use *where* or *when* only if actual time or physical location is involved.

                                     according to which

▶ **The influence of the Sapir-Whorf hypothesis, ~~where~~ behavior is regarded as influenced by language, has declined.**

Exercises on Common Sentence Problems

EXERCISE 1 Identify the subject and predicate in a simple sentence. 35d

In each of the following sentences, underline the complete subject once and underline the predicate twice. Then write *S* over the simple subject and *V* over the verb. Remember that the verb may consist of more than one word and that sentences can have more than one subject or verb.

Example   Many people in the United States carry too much credit-card debt.

1. Most experts consider some types of debt, such as a mortgage, financially necessary.
2. However, credit-card debt never benefits an individual's long-term financial goals.
3. Today even college students without jobs or credit records can usually acquire credit cards easily.
4. Unfortunately, many students charge expensive purchases and pay only the minimum balance on their cards every month.
5. Graduating from college with a large credit-card debt can severely limit a person's opportunities.

EXERCISE 2 Identify and correct phrase fragments. 36a–36e

In each of the following items, identify any phrase fragment, and correct it either by attaching it to a nearby independent clause or by changing it to an independent clause. Some sentences may be correct.

Example   American popular music has had an enthusiastic following around

the world. ~~Since~~ the early days of rock and roll.
since

1. Every country has its own musical styles. Based on the traditional music of its people.
2. Having its own tradition as the birthplace of jazz, blues, and rock music. The United States has long been one of the world's leading exporters of popular music.
3. In spite of enjoying enormous popularity in their own countries. Many performers from Europe, South America, Africa, and Asia have had a hard time attracting American fans.
4. Some American musicians have championed their favorite artists from abroad. Examples include the hip-hop artist Jay-Z's collaboration with South Asian artist Punjabi MC on the hit song "Beware of the Boys" and Beck's tribute to the late French singer-songwriter Serge Gainsbourg.

5. Although some US music fans pay attention to foreign musical styles, most Americans buy the music they know from American top-40 radio and MTV. Songs also loved by fans around the world for sounding typically American.

6. However, not all Americans are native English speakers. Listening exclusively to English-language music.

7. Latin music has had some crossover success in the United States. Propelled, at least at first, by the high percentage of Spanish-speaking people in this country.

8. On American radio and television today, some of the most popular male acts are Latin pop stars. Singing sensations such as Marc Anthony, Ricky Martin, and Enrique Iglesias.

9. These singers are considered crossover artists because they have achieved mainstream success by singing in English. After making earlier recordings in Spanish.

10. Perhaps there will be a time when artists can have big hits with songs sung in a foreign language. At present, however, singing in English is almost always required for being successful in America.

EXERCISE 3 Identify run-on sentences and comma splices. 37a, 37b

For each of the following items, write *CS* on the line before the sentence if it is a comma splice, *RO* if it is a run-on sentence, and *OK* if the sentence is correctly written.

Example   _CS_ Many consumers want to buy American cars, unfortunately, choosing an American car is not as easy as it sounds.

1. ____ Often a car's parts are made in one country and assembled in another, can the car be considered American if the whole thing is not manufactured in this country?

2. ____ Sometimes car companies manufacture parts in the United States and also put cars together here however, these companies may have their headquarters in Japan.

3. ____ People who buy cars sold by Ford, an automaker whose name implies "made in the United States" to many Americans, may not know that the vehicles may have been assembled in Mexico.

4. ____ On the other hand, most Honda Accords are made in Ohio in fact, the Honda Corporation now manufactures more cars in the United States than in Japan.

5. ____ As several American auto manufacturers have become part of multi-national corporations, globalization has made "buying American" increasingly difficult, consumers can no longer simply rely on the make of a car to determine its country of origin.

EXERCISE 4 Avoid a run-on or comma splice when using a transition. 37c

Correct the run-ons and comma splices in these sentences by changing punctuation and capitalization.

Example If you have a proper place for everything in your house or apartment,

you may be able to turn that knack into a profit/that is, you may

want to consider becoming a professional organizer.

1. Many people need help making the most of their space and eliminating clutter from their homes and offices in fact the demand is so great that the National Association of Professional Organizers now has 4,200 members in thirteen countries.
2. Many of NAPO's clients are businesspeople, however, organizers also create plans for homemakers, retired adults, hobbyists, and school-age children.
3. Paper is the major source of clutter in most homes, says organizer Jennifer Hunter, incidentally, Hunter's business has the humorous name of "Find Your Floor."
4. Disorganized people often waste time searching for keys, documents, and other items they've misplaced as a result, organizers help their clients save not only space but time.
5. Getting organized can be a matter of life and death accordingly, for several years NAPO has joined with the US Department of Homeland Security to educate the public about how households can prepare for emergencies.

EXERCISE 5 Correct sentence "tangles." 38a

In each of the following items, correct mixed constructions and faulty comparisons.

Example *Adopting*
By adopting the poetic techniques popular in colonial America

enabled Phillis Wheatley to find an audience for her writings.

1. Phillis Wheatley's education, which was remarkable mainly because she received one, a rare luxury for a slave girl in the American colonies.
2. Wheatley, kidnapped from her homeland and sold into slavery when she was about seven, an experience that must have been traumatic.
3. By learning to read and write gave Phillis an opportunity to demonstrate her aptitude for poetry.
4. Like Alexander Pope, iambic pentameter couplets were Phillis Wheatley's preferred poetic form.
5. Publishing a book of poems, Phillis Wheatley, becoming famous partly because she was an African slave who could compete as a poet with well-educated white men.

6. Her work, poems in a very formal eighteenth-century style that found aris-
   tocratic admirers in America and England.
7. With the deaths of Mr. and Mrs. Wheatley, when Phillis was in her twenties, left her free but also penniless.
8. Like Zora Neale Hurston in the twentieth century, an impoverished,
   lonely death followed a loss of public interest in Wheatley's writings, but
   scholars discovered her work posthumously and realized her contribution
   to American literature.

EXERCISE 6 Correct inappropriate shifts: mood, pronoun person and number, and direct and indirect quotations. 38d

On the line after each of the following sentences, identify inappropriate shifts
in mood by writing *M*, inappropriate shifts in pronoun person by writing *PP*,
inappropriate shifts in pronoun number by writing *PN*, and inappropriate
shifts in direct and indirect quotations by writing *Q*. Then revise each inappropriate shift.

>   *people*
>
> Example   Sharks do occasionally attack swimmers, but ~~you~~ are more
>
>   likely to be killed by a falling television than by a shark bite. _PP_

1. When a tourist in Florida wants an underwater adventure, you can swim in
   the ocean with sharks._____
2. A series of shark attacks on the east coast of the United States made Florida
   Fish and Wildlife Conservation commissioners ask whether swimmers
   were being too careless or were tourist attractions that feature swimming
   with sharks the cause of the problem? _____
3. When a tour operator puts bait in the water before a shark swim, they may
   be teaching sharks to associate people with food. _____
4. If sharks were fed too frequently by human beings, the commissioners
   wondered, will the big fish be more likely to endanger swimmers? _____
5. The curator of the International Shark Attack File told commissioners that
   the feeding probably didn't contribute to the attacks and would they tell
   people more about the good behavior of sharks. _____
6. The shark attacks shocked people around the country, and you heard
   about the attacks constantly at the beach and in coastal regions. _____
7. A shark can seem ferocious, but they are often in more danger from
   humans than humans are from the sharks. _____
8. People should not be frightened by the shark's torpedo-like body,
   scaly skin, and sharp teeth. Try to learn about the shark's habits
   instead. _____
9. Some scientists believe that if a person studies sharks, they will understand
   ocean ecosystems better. _____
10. Some species of sharks have become endangered because so many people
    like the taste of it. _____

EXERCISE 7 Use correct form of regular and irregular verbs. `39a`

Replace any incorrect verb forms with the correct form. Some sentences may be correct as written.

Example   Kenrick ~~broken~~ *broke* his elbow when he ~~fall~~ *fell* off his skateboard.

1. I lent Miranda my *Hunger Games* books, and she red all three of them.
2. Sacha ment to leave the party early.
3. Sir William Wallace led the Scots in their rebellion against English rule.
4. Surgeons were pleased that the tumor had shrunken considerably.
5. Some of the campers were bitten by snakes or stang by bees.

EXERCISE 8 Use auxiliary verbs correctly. `39c`

Revise these two paragraphs to eliminate errors in auxiliary verbs or the verb forms following auxiliaries. Some sentences may be correct.

Example   Syria ~~be~~ *is* located north of Jordan.

Paragraph 1

   We living in an era when antibiotics and other antimicrobial medicines can be use to treat diseases that just a few decades ago would of been fatal. Nevertheless, the world health community is still concern about the rise of "superbugs"—microorganisms that have develop resistance to the medications that are most commonly prescribe to treat them. Antimicrobial resistance may occur when medicines are used inappropriately: for example, a tuberculosis patient might of taken substandard doses of a medication or fail to finish a prescribed course of treatment. Superbugs must become a worldwide health priority, because a resistant infection can spread uncontrollably, imposing huge costs on individuals and society. On April 7, World Health Day, the World Health Organization will calls for a greater global commitment to educating people about the correct use of antimicrobials so that these drugs will continues to be effective.

Paragraph 2

   Todd's Market in Silverlake, California, has became slightly less friendly now that cashiers have been instruct not to refer to customers by the name printed on the customers' credit cards. One shopper complained that a man who had been standen behind her in line followed her out of the store and used her first name to try to strike up a conversation. Cashiers can see the name of any shopper who pays with a debit or credit card, and the store manager had instruct cashiers to use a customer's name in order to personalize the shopping experience and make a good impression. The woman in the Silverlake incident was not harm, but she did felt worried enough to tell the company it should discontinued the practice. "When someone uses your name, you think they know you, and you let down your guard," said the woman, who preferred to remain anonymous. "I'm lucky," she added, noting that the situation could of ended differently. Todd's Market has announce that although cashiers will no longer say aloud the name on a credit card, they will continue to wish departing customers a good day.

EXERCISE 9 Use present tenses correctly. `39e`

In each of the following sentences, correct any errors in the use of present tense verb forms. Some sentences may be correct.

Example   What did babies *observed* when they look at faces?
do   *observe*

1. Within a few hours of birth, newborn babies are showing a preference for looking at human faces.
2. Cognitive psychologists determine what has interested babies by measuring how long they look at certain patterns or objects.
3. Recent studies have shown that babies' brains have been forming the ability to differentiate faces by the time the babies are a few months old.
4. Scientists have not yet come to an agreement on whether babies are born with the ability to recognize faces or whether they are simply born with a preference for certain shapes and contours.
5. Scientific debate on the subject is raging, but as further studies will be completed, our understanding of how humans learn face recognition will continue to grow.

EXERCISE 10 Identify active and passive voices. `40a–40d`

In each of the following sentences, write *P* on the line before each sentence that is in the passive voice and *A* before each sentence that is in the active voice. Then rewrite each passive voice sentence as active whenever it is possible or advisable to do so, and underline the verb that you changed.

Example   *P* More than a thousand pounds of rice. is yielded by each acre of fertile rice fields of southern China.
Each acre of the fertile rice fields of southern China yields more

1. ___ The sticky rice that brings the highest prices in China is often attacked by rice blast, a fungus that destroys the rice crop.
2. ___ A farmer in Yunnan province discovered that he could nearly eliminate rice blast by planting alternating rows of sticky rice and long-grain rice.
3. ___ The technique of alternating rows of rice was then adopted widely.
4. ___ The application of expensive and toxic fungicides that had been used to fight the rice blast was discontinued by most farmers.
5. ___ Healthier fields, bigger rice yields, and more money for the farmers were subsequently produced by this low-tech, environmentally sound agricultural method.

EXERCISE 11 Make subjects and verbs agree and identify linking verbs. 41c

In the following passage, underline the subject in each independent clause. Then correct any errors in subject-verb agreement. Write *LV* over any linking verbs.

Example   There *are*
             There is many security questions involved in cryptography.

Do the government have the right to keep certain kinds of information out of the hands of the public? There is no easy answers to this question. When the science of cryptography was being developed, the National Security Agency wanted to restrict access to powerful, unbreakable codes. After all, using codes are one way that a government keeps information from its enemies, and breaking codes allows a government to find out what its enemies are planning. NSA agents worried that unbreakable codes would allow enemies of the United States to conceal their activities from US intelligence. Cryptographers won the right to develop and distribute their new codes to the general public, and unbreakable codes have certainly been a boon to the computer science and communications industries. Does these codes also hamper efforts to discover what terrorists are doing? Probably, say cryptographers. However, technologies that scientists decide not to develop out of fear of the results is a potential danger: if someone else develops these technologies, they can be used against anyone who has not considered their potential. There is dangers in cryptography, but perhaps there is even more problems in avoiding the issue. Somewhere in the future is the answers to these and other urgent security questions.

EXERCISE 12 Make subject and verb agree when the subject follows the verb. 41d

Correct the subject-verb agreement in these sentences. Some sentences may be correct as written.

Example   *Does*
             Do every civilization have some kind of horticulture?

1. At the US National Arboretum is the miniature trees that are called *bonsai* in Japanese.
2. There is three pavilions where visitors can view specimens from Japan, China, and several other Asian countries.
3. On display in the gardens and pavilions are approximately 150 perfect miniature trees.
4. For example, there are a Japanese white pine that was presented to the people of the United States in celebration of the US bicentennial in 1976.
5. It are hundreds of years old.
6. In the Special Exhibits Wing is seasonal displays of bonsai, flower arrangements, stones, and wood block prints.

EXERCISE 13 Correct subject-verb agreement in sentences with indefinite pronouns (*anyone*, *nobody*, etc.). 41h

Correct these sentences so that the verb agrees with the subject in number. Some sentences may be correct as written.

Example   Nobody ~~have~~ to be afraid to sing in public. *(has)*

1. Do everybody have the ability to sing?
2. Not everyone are born with great natural talent.
3. However, most voice teachers believe no one has to avoid singing.
4. The key is to find the range of notes in which someone feel most comfortable.
5. Somebody who sing professionally probably have a wide range.
6. Each of us amateurs need a range of only fifteen notes to sing most songs.

EXERCISE 14 Use the correct form of personal pronouns. 42a

In the following passage, correct any errors in the form of personal pronouns.

Example   Although Marie and Pierre Curie made important scientific discoveries,

both ~~her~~ and ~~him~~ spent years being unable to afford a decent *(she)* *(he)*

laboratory to work in.

    Marie Curie, born Maria Sklodowska in Poland in 1867, devoted her life to pure science in the hope that humans would benefit from what she discovered. Her parents, poor teachers, wanted she and her siblings to get an education. Marie went to Paris to study at the Sorbonne when she was twenty-four; her work as a governess had earned her enough money to educate she and her older sister. Marie struggled to learn French and overcome her deficient early education in physics and mathematics—subjects that girls in Poland such as her and her sister had not been allowed to study. When she completed her master's degree in physics in 1894, she placed first in her class. Pierre Curie, who was doing research on magnetism, and her met when Marie was searching for a laboratory she could use. Although Pierre did not have space for Marie in his lab, him and her fell in love and married.

    The Curies did much of their innovative research in a small lab set up in an abandoned shed because both she and him believed that scientists should not waste valuable research time trying to make money. Marie did work on uranium and thorium, and it was her who invented the term *radioactivity*. In 1903, three scientists, Pierre and her, along with Henri Becquerel, shared the Nobel Prize in Physics. At around the same time, Pierre and Marie discovered the elements polonium (named after Marie's homeland) and radium. In 1911, after her husband's death, an unprecedented second Nobel Prize, this time in chemistry, was awarded to she alone. Marie Curie died in 1934 as a result of years of exposure to radiation, but her legacy continued. The Curies' daughter Irene, who had learned physics and chemistry from Marie and was nearly as skilled in scientific research as her, shared a Nobel Prize in Chemistry with her husband, Frederic Joliot-Curie, in 1935.

EXERCISE 15 Use the correct possessive pronoun form. `42b`

In the following sentences, correct any errors in the use of possessive forms of pronouns. Some sentences may be correct.

Example   Bonhoeffer tried to convince other Germans to oppose Nazi views of

racial purity, and h<del>im</del> ^his^ playing gospel records in Nazi Germany

required courage.

1. When Dietrich Bonhoeffer was a visiting pastor at Harlem's Abyssinian Baptist Church in 1931, the congregation was pleased with him learning to love gospel music.
2. As a white German Protestant among African American worshippers, Bonhoeffer at first worried that his life was too different from them.
3. When Bonhoeffer returned to Germany, something of their's went with him: members of the church gave him several gospel records.
4. Dietrich Bonhoeffer's opposition to the Nazi regime led to him putting his life on the line by participating in the plot to assassinate Hitler in 1944; it's failure resulted in his imprisonment and execution.
5. Bonhoeffer's influence still appears in today's Germany, where the popularity of gospel music is still growing as a result of his championing of it decades ago.

EXERCISE 16 Use correct pronoun-antecedent agreement. `42c, 42d`

In each of the following sentences, correct any errors in pronoun-antecedent agreement, revising sentences as necessary. Some sentences may be correct.

Example   In wartime, a country's intelligence community ~~finds that their work~~ ^the work of^

has tremendous importance and urgency.

1. If a historian studies World War II, they will learn how important intelligence was for the Allied victory.
2. At first, however, US intelligence was unable to identify the risk of a Japanese attack, and their failure brought the country into the war.
3. Neither the head of the FBI nor his counterparts at the State Department, Army, and Navy allowed other government officials access to secrets their agents had discovered, and the result was American unpreparedness for the attack on Pearl Harbor.

4. In December 1941, an American could easily have felt that his country might lose the war against the Japanese military and the still-undefeated German army.
5. Everyone involved in decoding German and Japanese messages deserves their share of the credit for the ultimate defeat of the Axis powers in 1945.

EXERCISE 17 Use correct forms of adjectives and adverbs. `43a`

In each of the following sentences, correct any errors in adjective or adverb forms. Some sentences may be correct.

> Example   Amish adolescents face issues of independence and conformity that
>
> *basically*
> are ~~basicly~~ the same as those confronting other young Americans.

1. People in Amish communities live without electricity or cars, in isolation from the modern world, where technology makes activities such as work and travel go swift.
2. Members of the church live strict by its rules, but a young person in an Amish household does not join the church until adulthood.
3. Amish teenagers are allowed to break church rules and experiment with the outside world; many non-Amish are shocked to learn how widely accepted such behavior is in the Amish community.
4. The great majority of young Amish people do eventually join the church, and those who feel that they are not suited good to a highly regulated life may decide to join a more tolerant Amish group in another area.
5. A church member who breaks the rules faces excommunication and shunning by others in the community, so Amish groups try hardly to encourage young people to get over their interest in experimentation before they join the church.

EXERCISE 18 Use adjectives and adverbs correctly after linking verbs. `43c`

In each of the following sentences, correct any errors in adjective and adverb use. Some sentences may be correct.

> *suddenly*
> Example   The aurora borealis appeared ~~sudden~~ in the sky.

1. The Norwegian scientist Kristian Birkeland felt certainly about the cause of the aurora borealis (or northern lights).
2. The lights, which hang like a brightly colored curtain in the night sky, look spookily to most observers.
3. Birkeland looked careful at the lights from a Norwegian mountaintop in midwinter during his 1899 expedition to study the phenomenon.

4. His two expeditions to observe the northern lights appeared successful, but some members of his scientific teams were badly injured or killed in the severe winter conditions.
5. He appeared madly to some colleagues, but Birkeland finally determined that sunspots caused the aurora borealis.

EXERCISE 19 Identify restrictive and nonrestrictive clauses. 44b

In the following sentences, underline each relative clause and write *R* (restrictive) or *NR* (nonrestrictive) on the line before the sentence. There may be more than one relative clause in a sentence. Then edit to make sure that each clause is punctuated correctly and that the correct form of the relative pronoun is used.

> Example   _R_ People who speak a pidgin language are finding away to bridge the communication gap.

1. ___ When a person who speaks only English and a person, who speaks only Spanish, must communicate, they will find common ground by using the simple grammar and vocabulary of pidgin.
2. ___ Pidgin which is not spoken as a native tongue by anyone is different from creolized language.
3. ___ When a language, that started out as pidgin, becomes the common speech of a community, that language has been creolized.
4. ___ For example, Haitian Creole that is a language with its own complex grammar and vocabulary came from the pidgin speech created by slaves from many cultures, who were forced to live and work together.
5. ___ Creolized languages which often develop when pidgin speakers raise children in a multicultural community demonstrate both the creativity of human beings—even in terrible hardship—and the depth of the human need to communicate with other people.

EXERCISE 20 Make verb and antecedent of subject relative pronouns agree. 44c

In each of the following sentences, correct any subject-verb agreement errors within the relative clauses. Then draw an arrow from any subject relative pronoun to its antecedent. Some sentences may be correct.

> Example   Keeping costs down is one of the reasons that ~~makes~~ *make* most health
>
> maintenance organizations require approval for certain treatments.

1. Most people who participate in group insurance plans now use some form of managed care.
2. Many insurance companies require any patients who participates in managed care plans to get a referral from their primary care physician before seeing an expensive specialist.

3. This practice, which are known as "gatekeeping," often infuriates both patients and physicians.
4. In some cases, patients may believe that a particular specialist is the only one of the doctors in the group who know how to treat a particular condition.
5. Everyone in the plan who need to see a specialist must first make an appointment with a primary care physician to get his or her referral; many patients resent having to make this extra visit.
6. In addition, many insurance companies pay lower fees to any doctor in a managed care plan who refer patients to a specialist for treatment, so doctors are often reluctant to make referrals.
7. Any patients in managed care who sees a specialist without a referral usually have to pay for the full cost of the visit.
8. According to some analysts, feeling angry about being forced to get a primary care physician's permission to see a specialist is one of the situations that causes patients to sue their doctors.
9. One of the surprises that has come from a recent study of health maintenance organizations is the finding that few patients made unnecessary visits to specialists when referrals were not required.
10. In spite of this finding, many experts still support some version of gatekeeping because they think that patients who get a specialist's care should nevertheless let the primary care physicians who knows them best participate in decisions about treatment.

EXERCISE 21 Use *where* and *when* appropriately. `44f`

In each of the following sentences, revise any inappropriate uses of *where* and *when* as relative pronouns. Some sentences may be correct.

Example Spelunking is one name for the profession or hobby ~~where~~ *in which* people

explore caves, but most cave explorers prefer the term *caving*.

1. In 1838, Stephen Bishop, a seventeen-year-old slave, arrived at Kentucky's Mammoth Cave, to where he had been sent to work as a guide.
2. Bishop was a popular guide, but he was also a fearless explorer, squeezing through tight passages in which no humans had been for centuries.
3. In a single year where Bishop explored previously unknown parts of the cave, he doubled the explored portion of Mammoth Cave, earning fame—but not freedom—and attracting hundreds of tourists to the site.
4. Bishop discovered the underground river in Mammoth Cave, in which blind fish and crustaceans live, and in 1842 he drew a careful map of the cave that was used by explorers for the next forty years.
5. In 1972, cave explorers found a passage called Hanson's Lost River that led from another Kentucky cave system into Mammoth Cave; the explorers later discovered that the passage through where they had crawled to make the connection was marked on Bishop's 130-year-old map.

8 Punctuation, Mechanics, and Spelling

EDIT

To obtain study resources for this section, visit the English CourseMate for this text at **www.cengagebrain.com**

8 Punctuation, Mechanics, and Spelling

Punctuation serves to regulate the flow of information through a sentence, showing readers how to read your ideas. The following headline from the *New York Times*, "Stock Fraud Is Easier, and Easier to Spot," says that stock fraud is not only easy to engage in but also easy to detect. Without the comma, however, the sentence would send a different message: It would say that detecting stock fraud is becoming increasingly easy.

Try reading the following without the benefit of the signals a reader usually expects.

When active viruses especially those transmitted by contact can spread easily within the world health organization hard working doctors are continually collaborating to find treatments for several infectious diseases sars avian flu and hepatitis.

Conventional punctuation and mechanics clarify the meaning:

When active, viruses—especially those transmitted by contact—can spread easily; within the World Health Organization, hard-working doctors are continually collaborating to find treatments for several infectious diseases: SARS, avian flu, and hepatitis.

Commas

A comma separates parts of a sentence. It does not separate one sentence from another. When readers see a comma, they know that the parts of the sentence are separated for a reason. When you really can't decide whether to use commas, follow this general principle: "When in doubt, leave them out." Readers find excessive use of commas more distracting than a few missing ones.

45a Checklists: Comma yes and comma no

Use the following guidelines, but note that variations can occur. Details and more examples follow in the rest of the chapter. Throughout chapter 45, note the comma where there is blue shading.

> **KEY POINTS**
> Comma Yes

1. Between two independent clauses connected by a coordinating conjunction: *and, but, or, nor, so, for,* or *yet,* but optional in British English (45b)

   ▶ **The food was beautifully displayed, but no one felt like eating.**

   A comma is optional if the clauses are short.

   ▶ **She finished speaking and she left.**

2. After most introductory words, phrases, or clauses (45c)

   ▶ **After the noisy party, the neighbors complained. When the police came, the guests left.**

3. To set off extra (nonrestrictive) information included in a sentence ("extra commas with extra information"—see 45d)

   ▶ **Her husband, a computer programmer, works late at night.**

4. To set off a transitional expression or an explanatory insert (45e)

   ▶ **The ending of the film, however, is disappointing. In fact, it is totally predictable.**

5. To separate three or more items in a series (45f)

   ▶ **The robot vacuums, makes toast, and plays chess.**

6. Between adjectives that can be reversed and connected with *and* (coordinate adjectives—45g)

   ▶ **When people move, they often discard their worn, dilapidated furniture.**

7. Before or after a quotation (45h)

   ▶ **"Whales are color-blind," the professor declared. The student replied, "I didn't know that."**

In the following box and in 45b–45i, yellow shading indicates "no comma here."

KEY POINTS
Comma No

1. Not between subject and verb

   ▶ **The debate between the two contestants became more acrimonious as the evening wore on.**

   Note: Use paired commas, however, to set off any extra information inserted between the subject and verb (see 45d).

   ▶ **The fund manager, a billionaire, has been married five times.**

2. Not before the word *and* that connects two verbs to the same subject

   ▶ **She won the trophy and accepted it graciously.**

3. Not *after* a coordinating conjunction (*and, but, or, nor, so, for, yet*) connecting two independent clauses, but *before* it (see 45b)

   ▶ **The prisoner begged for mercy, but the judge was unmoved.**

4. Not between two independent clauses without any coordinating conjunction such as *and* or *but* (use either a period or a semicolon instead)

   ▶ **The harvest was meager; it had been a dry winter.**

   Some writers, however, use a comma between two independent clauses when the clauses use parallel structures (38j) to point out a contrast.

   ▶ **She never insults, she just criticizes.**

   (Continued)

(Continued)

5. Not between an independent clause and a following dependent clause introduced by *after, before, because, if, since, unless, until,* or *when* (no comma before the subordinating conjunction)

▶ **Test results tend to be good when students study in groups.**

6. Not before a clause beginning with *that*

▶ **The dean warned the students that the speech would be long.**

Note: A comma can appear before a *that* clause when it is the second comma of a pair before and after extra information inserted as a nonrestrictive phrase.

▶ **He skates so fast, despite his size, that he will probably break the world record.**

7. Not before or after essential, restrictive information (see 45d)

▶ **Alice Walker's essay "Beauty: When the Other Dancer Is the Self" discusses coping with a physical disfigurement.** [Walker has written more than one essay. The title restricts the noun *essay* to one specific essay.]

Similarly, a restrictive relative clause introduced by *who, whom, whose, which,* or *that* is never set off by commas. The clause provides essential, identifying information (see 45b and 45d).

▶ **The teachers praised the children who finished on time.** [The teachers didn't praise all the children. The clause "who finished on time" restricts the meaning to only those who finished on time.]

8. Not between a verb and its object or complement

▶ **The best gifts are food and clothes.**

9. Not after *such as*

▶ **Popular fast-food items such as hamburgers and hot dogs tend to be high in cholesterol.**

10. Not separating cumulative adjectives (adjectives that cannot be connected by *and* and whose order cannot be reversed—see 45g for more examples)

▶ **many little white ivory buttons**

45b Use a comma before a coordinating conjunction (*and, but*, etc.) that connects independent clauses

When you connect independent clauses with a coordinating conjunction (*and, but, or, nor, so, for, yet*), place a comma before the conjunction.

▶ The managers are efficient, **but personnel turnover is high.**

▶ The winner was announced, **and the audience erupted in cheers.**

However, when the clauses are short, many writers omit the comma.

45c Use a comma after most introductory phrases and clauses

The comma signals to readers that the introductory part of the sentence has ended. It says, in effect, "Now wait for the main point in the independent clause."

▶ **Just as we began eating, there was a knock at the door.**

▶ **As recently as twenty years ago, very few students had computers or cell phones.**

The comma after the introductory material tells readers to expect the subject and verb of the independent clause. After one word or a short phrase, the comma can be omitted: *Immediately the fun began.* However, in some sentences, omitting the comma can lead to a serious or humorous misreading:

▶ **While the guests were eating a mouse ran across the floor.**

45d Use commas to set off an extra (nonrestrictive) phrase or clause

A phrase or clause may provide extra information that can be omitted without changing the meaning of the independent clause by restricting its meaning. Such information may be included almost as an aside—a "by the way." If the insertion comes midsentence, think of the commas as handles that can lift the extra information out without inconveniencing your reader.

Nonrestrictive **We'll attend, even though we'd rather not.** [We will definitely attend. The *even though* clause does not restrict the meaning of the independent clause.]

Restrictive **We'll attend if we have time.** [We will attend only if circumstances permit. The *if* clause restricts the meaning.]

Commas around appositive phrases Use commas to set off a descriptive or explanatory phrase, called an *appositive phrase*. If the phrase were omitted, readers might lose some interesting details but would still be able to understand the message.

appositive
phrase
▶ **She loves her new phone, a Droid.**

appositive phrase
▶ **His dog, a big Labrador retriever, is afraid of mice.**

▶ **Salinger's first novel,** *The Catcher in the Rye,* **captures the language and thoughts of teenagers.** [The commas are used because the title provides supplementary information about the first novel, not information that identifies which novel the writer means.]

Commas around nonrestrictive participle phrases Nonrestrictive participle phrases add extra descriptive, but not essential, information.

▶ **My boss, wearing a red tie and a green shirt, radiated the holiday spirit.** [The participle phrase does not restrict the meaning of *boss* by distinguishing one boss from another.]

Commas around extra information in nonrestrictive relative clauses When you give nonessential information in a relative clause introduced by *who, whom,* or *which* (never *that*), set off the clause with commas.

▶ **The trainee's new shoes, which cost more than $300, were too fancy to wear to work.** [The independent clause "The trainee's new shoes were too fancy to wear to work" does not lead readers to ask "Which shoes?" The relative clause does not restrict the meaning of *shoes.*]

Note: Do not use commas to set off essential, restrictive information.

restricts *people* to a subgroup
▶ **People who wear bright colors send an optimistic message.** [The relative clause, beginning with *who,* restricts "people" to a subgroup: Not all people send an optimistic message; those who wear bright colors do.]

45e **Use commas to set off transitional expressions and explanatory insertions**

Transitional expressions and conjunctive adverbs connect or weave together the ideas in your writing and act as signposts for readers. See 2f for a list of these expressions. Use commas to set off a transitional expression from the rest of the sentence.

▸ **Most Labrador retrievers, however, are courageous.**

Note: When you use a transitional expression such as *however, therefore, nevertheless, above all, of course,* or *in fact* at the beginning of an independent clause, end the previous clause with a period or a semicolon. Then place a comma after the transitional expression.

▸ **The patient suffered from both diabetes and high blood pressure. Nevertheless, she lived to be 93.**

You may sometimes choose to insert a phrase or a clause to make a comment, offer an explanation, drive a point home, or indicate a contrast. Insertions used for these purposes are set off by commas.

▸ **The consequences will be dire, I think.**

▸ **The best, if not the only, solution is to apologize and start over.**

▸ **Seasonal allergies, such as those caused by ragweed, are common.**

▸ **Unlike silver, gold does not tarnish.**

45f **Use commas to separate three or more items in a series**

Readers see the commas between items in a series (words, phrases, or clauses) and realize "this is a list." If you said the sentence aloud, you would pause between items; when writing, you use commas to separate them. However, journalists and British writers often omit a comma before the final *and*.

▸ **In the hour between appointments, the salesperson managed to eat lunch, phone his mother, buy a potted plant, and have his shoes shined.**

See also 48a for when to use semicolons in place of commas in a list.

45g Use commas to separate certain (coordinate) adjectives

Adjectives are *coordinate* when their order can be reversed and the word *and* can be inserted between them without any change in meaning. Coordinate adjectives (such as *beautiful, delicious, exciting, noisy*) make subjective and evaluative judgments rather than provide objectively verifiable information about, for instance, size, shape, color, or nationality. Separate coordinate adjectives with commas.

▸ Buyers like to deal with energetic, efficient, and polite salespeople.

Do not, however, put a comma between the final adjective of a series and the noun it modifies.

▸ Energetic, efficient, and polite salespeople are in demand.

Note that no comma is necessary to separate adjectives that are cumulative, modifying the whole noun phrase that follows (see 60g for the order of these adjectives).

▸ An old blue Persian rug sold for the auction's highest price.

45h Use a comma between a direct quotation and the preceding or following clause

The independent clause may come either before or after the quotation.

▸ When asked what she wanted to be later in life, she replied, "An Olympic swimmer."

▸ "I want to be an Olympic swimmer," she announced confidently. [The comma is inside the quotation marks.]

However, omit the comma if the quotation is a question or exclamation.

▸ "Would you like to sit down?" the interviewer asked.

In addition, do not insert a comma before a quotation that is integrated into your sentence:

▸ In our family, a ten-year-old car was considered "new."

45i Special uses of commas

To prevent misreading Use a comma to separate elements in a sentence that may otherwise be confusing.

▶ **He who can, does. He who cannot, teaches.**

—George Bernard Shaw, *Man and Superman*

[Usually, a comma is not used to separate a subject from the verb. Here, the comma is necessary to prevent confusion.]

With an absolute phrase Use a comma to set off a phrase that modifies the whole sentence (an absolute phrase).

```
┌──────────── absolute phrase ────────────┐
```
▶ **Her arms folded defiantly across her chest, the four-year-old announced that she would not take a bath.**

With a date Use a comma to separate the day from the year in a date.

▶ **On May 14, 1998, the legendary singer Frank Sinatra died.** [Do not use a comma before the year when the day precedes the month: 14 May 1998.]

With numbers Use a comma (never a period) to divide numbers into thousands.

▶ **1,200**   ▶ **515,000**   ▶ **34,000,000**

No commas are necessary in years (*2012*), numbers in addresses (*3501 East 10th Street*), or page numbers (*page 1008*).

With titles Use commas around a person's title or degree when it follows the name.

▶ **Stephen L. Carter, PhD, gave the commencement speech.**

With the parts of an address

▶ **Ronald Reagan was born in Tampico, Illinois, in 1911.**

However, do not use a comma before a ZIP code: Newton, MA 02159.

With a conversational tag, tag question, or insert

▶ **Yes, Salinger's daughter, like others before her, has produced a memoir.**

▶ Mark Zuckerberg is the chief executive of Facebook, isn't he?

▶ The show dwelt on tasteless, not educational, details.

With a direct address or salutation

▶ Whatever you build next, Mr. Trump, will cause controversy.

 Apostrophes

An apostrophe indicates ownership or possession: *Fred's books, the government's plans, a year's pay* (the books belonging to Fred, the plans of the government, the pay for a year). It can also signal omitted letters in contractions.

46a Checklists: Apostrophe yes and apostrophe no

> **KEY POINTS**
> Apostrophe Yes
>
> 1. Use -'s for the possessive form of all nouns except plural nouns that end with -s: *the hero's misfortunes, the nation's capital, the people's advocate.*
> 2. Use an apostrophe alone for the possessive form of plural nouns that end with -s: *the heroes' misfortunes, the states' governors, liberal politicians' efforts.*
> 3. Use an apostrophe to indicate the omission of letters in contracted forms such as *didn't, they're, can't,* and *let's.* However, some readers of formal academic writing may object to such contractions.

Note: If you do use a contraction, use *it's* only for "it is" or "it has": *It's a good idea; it's been a slow process* (see 46f).

KEY POINTS
Apostrophe No

1. Generally, do not use an apostrophe to form the plurals of nouns (see 46e for rare exceptions).

2. Never use an apostrophe before an -s ending on a verb. Note that *let's* is a contracted form for *let us*; the -s is not a verb ending.

3. Do not write possessive pronouns (*hers, its, ours, yours, theirs*) with an apostrophe.

4. Do not use an apostrophe to form the plural of names or numbers: *the Browns; the 1990s [not 1990's]; the '90s [not 90's].*

5. With inanimate objects and concepts, *of* is often preferred to an apostrophe: *the cost of service, the top of the mountain, the back of the desk.*

46b When to use -'s to signal possession

As a general rule, to signal possession, use -'s with singular nouns, with indefinite pronouns (41h), with names, and with plural nouns that do not form the plural with -s: *the gardener's tools, anybody's opinion, the men's department, today's world, this week's schedule, Mr. Jackson's voice, someone else's idea, their money's worth.* Also note the following uses:

With individual and joint ownership   To indicate individual ownership, make each owner possessive.

▸ **Sam's and Pat's houses are across the street from each other.**

To show joint ownership, make only the last owner possessive: *Sam and Pat's house.*

With compound nouns   Add -'s to the last word in a compound noun.

▸ **her sister-in-law's purse**

With singular proper nouns ending in -s   When a name ends in -s, add -'s as usual for the possessive.

▸ **Dylan Thomas's imagery conjures up the Welsh landscape.**

When a name has more than one syllable and ends in *-s* with a *z* pronunciation, you can use an apostrophe alone: *Moses' law, Euripides' dramas.*

In all words that need an apostrophe to signal possession

▶ **Yosemite National Park's vegetation differs from Sequoia.** 's
[meaning the vegetation of Sequoia National Park]

46c Use only an apostrophe to signal possession in plural nouns already ending in *-s*

Add only an apostrophe when a plural noun already ends in *-s*.

▶ **the students' suggestions** [more than one student]

▶ **my parents' friends** [more than one parent]

Remember to include an apostrophe in comparisons with a plural noun understood:

▶ **His views are different from other professors'.** [...from other professors' views]

46d Use an apostrophe in contractions

In a contraction (*shouldn't, don't, haven't*), the apostrophe appears where letters have been omitted. To test whether an apostrophe is in the correct place, mentally replace the missing letters. The replacement test, however, will not help with the following:

won't   will not

Note: Some readers may object to contractions in formal academic writing, especially scientific writing, because they view them as colloquial and informal. It is safer not to use contractions unless you know the conventions of the genre and your readers' preferences.

can't	cannot	'd	had, would, did (They'd already
didn't	did not		left. I'd try. Where'd you go?)
he's	he is *or* he has	're	are (you're, we're, they're)
's	is, has, does	it's	it is *or* it has
	(He's happy. She's moved. How's it taste?)	let's	let us (as in "Let's go.")

Never place an apostrophe before the *-s* ending of a verb:

▸ **The author let's his characters take over.**

An apostrophe can also take the place of the first part of a year or decade.

▸ **the radical rebellion of the '60s** [the 1960s]

▸ **the floods of '04** [the year 2004]

Note: Fixed forms spelled with an apostrophe, such as *o'clock* and the poetic *o'er*, are contractions ("of the clock," "over").

46e Two occasions to use -'s to form a plural

1. Use -'s for the plural form of letters of the alphabet Italicize only the letter, not the plural ending (50d).

▸ **Maria picked all the *M*'s out of her alphabet soup.**

▸ **Georges Perec's novel called *A Void* has no *e*'s in it at all.**

2. Use -'s for the plural form of a word referred to as the word itself Italicize the word named as a word, but do not italicize the -'s ending (50d).

▸ **Her speech was punctuated with *um*'s.**

MLA and APA prefer no apostrophe in the plural form of numbers, acronyms, and abbreviations (52f).

the 2000s   the terrible twos   DVDs   FAQs   MAs

However, you may see such plurals spelled with -'s. In all cases, be consistent in your usage.

Never use an apostrophe to signal the plural of common nouns or personal names: *big bargains, the Jacksons.*

46f Distinguish between *it's* and *its*

Its is the possessive form of the pronoun *it* and means "belonging to it." Use the apostrophe only if you intend *it is* or *it has* (see also 42b, p. 477).

▸ **It's a hilarious play.**   ▸ **The committee took its time.**

Many writers slip up with these forms. Use your spell checker to search your entire document for both *its* and *it's*. Then check each one by asking "Am I saying *it is* or *it has* here?" If the answer is yes, use *it's* or *it is*. If the answer is no, use *its*.

Quotation Marks

In American English, double quotation marks indicate where someone's exact words begin and end. (British English, however, uses single quotation marks.) For long quotations, see 47f.

47a Guidelines for using quotation marks

> ### KEY POINTS
> Quotation Marks: Basic Guidelines

1. Quote exactly the words used by the original speaker or writer.
2. Pair opening quotation marks with closing quotation marks to indicate where the quotation ends and your ideas begin.
3. Use correct punctuation to introduce and end a quotation, and place other marks of punctuation carefully in relation to the quotation marks.
4. Enclose the titles of articles, short stories, songs, and poems in quotation marks.
5. Enclose any added or changed material in square brackets (49e); indicate omitted material with ellipsis dots (49g).

47b Punctuation introducing and ending a quotation

After an introductory verb, such as *say, state,* or *write,* use a comma followed by a capital letter to introduce a direct quotation

▶ It was Tolstoy who wrote, "Happy families are all alike, [but] every unhappy family is unhappy in its own way."
—Anna Karenina

Use a colon after a complete sentence introducing a quotation, and begin the quotation with a capital letter

▶ Woody Allen always tries to make us laugh even about serious issues like wealth and poverty: "Money is better than poverty, if only for financial reasons."

—Without Feathers

When a quotation is integrated into the structure of your own sentence, use no special introductory punctuation other than the quotation marks

▶ Phyllis Grosskurth says of Lord Byron that "anxiety over money was driving him over the brink."

—Byron

Put periods and commas inside quotation marks, even if these punctuation marks do not appear in the original quotation

▶ When Henry Rosovsky characterizes Bloom's ideas as "mind-boggling," he is not offering praise.

—The University

In a documented paper, when you use parenthetical citations after a short quotation at the end of a sentence, put the period at the end of the citation, not within the quotation. See 10c and 47f for how to handle long quotations.

▶ Geoffrey Wolff observes that when his father died, there was nothing to indicate "that he had ever known another human being" (11).

—The Duke of Deception

Put question marks and exclamation points inside the quotation marks if they are part of the original source, with no additional period   When your sentence is a statement, do not use a comma or period in addition to a question mark or exclamation point.

▶ The attorney asked her secretary, "Where did you put my report?"

Put a question mark, exclamation point, semicolon, or colon outside the closing quotation marks   If your sentence contains punctuation that is your own, not part of the original quotation, do not include it within the quotation marks.

▶ What does the author mean when she describes the heroine as a "carnivorous spider"?

47c Quotation marks in dialogue

Do not add closing quotation marks until the speaker changes or you interrupt the quotation. Begin each new speaker's words with a new paragraph.

interruption
of quotation

▶ **"I'm not going to work today," he announced. "Why should I?
I worked all weekend. My boss is away on vacation. And I have a
headache."**

change of speaker

▶ **"Honey, your boss is on the phone," his wife called from the
bedroom.**

If a quotation from one speaker continues for more than one paragraph, place *closing* quotation marks only at the end of the *final* paragraph of the quotation. However, place *opening* quotation marks at the beginning of every paragraph so that readers realize that the quotation is continuing.

47d A quotation within a quotation

Enclose quotations in double quotation marks. Use single quotation marks to enclose a quotation or a title of a short work within a quotation. (The reverse is the case in British English.)

▶ **"I read 'The Turn of the Screw' in ninth grade," Jorge recalled.**

▶ **The comedian Steven Wright once said, "I have an existential
map. It has 'You are here' written all over it."**

47e Quotation marks with titles, definitions, and translations

For a translation or definition, use quotation marks:

▶ **The abbreviation *p.m.* means "after midday."**

KEY POINTS
Titles: Quotation Marks or Italics/Underlining?

1. **Quotation marks** with the title of an article, short story, poem, song, or chapter: "Ode on a Grecian Urn"; "Candle in the Wind"; "The Yellow Wallpaper"; "America: The Multinational Society"

2. Italics (or underlining in a handwritten manuscript) with the title of a book, journal, magazine, newspaper, film, play, or long poem published alone: *The Atlantic, Time, District 9, Beowulf* (50a)

3. No quotation marks and no italics or underlining with the title of your own essay

For more on capital letters with titles, see 51d.

47f When not to use quotation marks

In the sample sentences, yellow shading means "no quotation marks here."

1. Do not put quotation marks around indirect quotations

▶ Some astrophysicists claim that the world is headed for a new Ice Age.

2. Do not put quotation marks around clichés, slang, or trite expressions   Instead, revise. See also 32d and 32g.

involvement.

▶ All they want is "a piece of the action."
             ^

3. Do not put quotation marks at the beginning and end of long indented quotations   When you use MLA style to quote more than three lines of poetry or more than four typed lines of prose, indent the whole passage one inch from the left margin. For 40 or more words in APA style or for 100 words (eight lines or two or more paragraphs) in *Chicago* style, indent the passage one-half inch. Do not enclose the quoted passage in quotation marks, but retain any internal quotation marks. See 10c, 13, and 14b, item R for examples.

4. On the title page of your own paper, do not put quotation marks around your essay title   Use quotation marks in your title only when your title contains a quotation or the title of a short work.

Charles Baxter's "Gryphon" as an Educational Warning

48 Semicolons and Colons

A colon (:) looks somewhat like a semicolon (;). However, they are used in different ways, and they are not interchangeable.

48a Checklists: Semicolon yes and semicolon no

A period separates independent clauses with finality; a semicolon, such as the one you just saw in this sentence, provides a less distinct separation and indicates that an additional related thought or item will follow immediately. As essayist Lewis Thomas comments in his "Notes on Punctuation":

> The period tells you that that is that; if you didn't get all the meaning you wanted or expected, anyway you got all the writer intended to parcel out and now you have to move along. But with a semicolon there you get a pleasant little feeling of expectancy; there is more to come.

KEY POINTS
Semicolon Yes

1. Between closely connected independent clauses when no coordinating conjunction (*and, but, or, nor, so, for, yet*) is used

   ▶ **Biography tells us about the subject; biographers also tell us about themselves.**

   Do not overuse semicolons in this way. They are more effective when used sparingly. Do not use a capital letter to begin a clause after a semicolon.

2. Between independent clauses connected with a transitional expression like *however, moreover, in fact, nevertheless, above all,* or *therefore* (see the list in 2f)

   ▶ **Chocolate may have some benefit as a mood enhancer; however, it is high in calories.**

   (If the transitional expression is in the middle or at the end of its clause, the semicolon still appears between the clauses:

The results support the hypothesis; further research, however, is necessary.)

3. To separate items in a list containing internal commas

▶ **When I cleaned out the refrigerator, I found a chocolate cake, half-eaten; some canned tomato paste, which had a blue fungus growing on the top; and some possibly edible meat loaf.**

KEY POINTS
Semicolon No

1. Not in place of a colon to introduce a list or an explanation

▶ **Ellsworth Kelly has produced a variety of works of art; drawings, paintings, prints, and sculptures.**

2. Not after an introductory phrase or dependent clause, even if the phrase or clause is long. A semicolon would produce a fragment. Use a comma instead.

▶ **Because the training period was so long and arduous for all the players; the manager allowed one visit by family and friends.**

3. Not before an appositive phrase

▶ **The audience cheered the Oscar winner; Meryl Streep.**

4. Not in place of a comma before *and, but, or, nor, so, for,* or *yet* joining independent clauses

▶ **The thrift shop in the church basement needed a name; and the volunteers chose Attic Treasures.**

48b Checklists: Colon yes and colon no

A colon signals anticipation. It follows an independent clause and introduces information that readers will need. A colon tells readers, "What comes next will define, illustrate, or explain what you have just read." Use one space after a colon.

KEY POINTS
Colon Yes

1. After an independent clause to introduce items in a list

   ▶ **The students included three pieces of writing in their portfolios: a narrative, an argument, and a documented paper.**

2. After an independent clause to introduce an explanation, expansion, or elaboration

   ▶ **After winning seven Tour de France cycling titles, Lance Armstrong was deprived of his titles: he was accused of taking part in a doping program.**

   Note: Some writers may prefer to use a capital letter after a colon introducing an independent clause. Whatever you choose to do, be consistent in your usage.

3. To introduce a rule or principle (a capital is usually used here)

   ▶ **The main principle of public speaking is simple: Look at the audience.**

4. To introduce a quotation not integrated into your sentence and not introduced by a verb such as *say*

   ▶ **Emily Post has provided an alternative to attempting to outdo others: "To do *exactly as your neighbors do* is the only sensible rule."**

   Note the capital for the first word of a sentence quotation. A colon also introduces a long quotation set off from your text (see 10c).

5. In salutations, precise time notations, titles, and biblical citations of chapter and verse

   ▶ **Dear Doctor Faber:**

   ▶ **To: The Chancellor**

   ▶ **8:30 p.m.**

   ▶ *Backlash: The Undeclared War against American Women*

   ▶ **Exodus 3:11–14** [In MLA style, a period is used in place of the colon.]

KEY POINTS
Colon No

(Note that in the sample sentences, yellow shading means "no colon here.")

1. Not directly after a verb (such as a form of *be* or *include*)

▶ **The two main effects were the improvement of registration and an increase in the numbers of advisers.**

▶ **A classical sonata typically includes exposition, development, recapitulation, and coda sections.**

2. Not after a preposition (such as *of, for, except,* and *regarding*) or the phrase *such as*

▶ **Southern California is known for its beautiful beaches, mild weather, crowded freeways, and dirty air.**

▶ **The novel will please many readers except linguists and lawyers.**

▶ **They packed many different items for the picnic, such as taco chips, salsa, bean salad, pita bread, and egg rolls.**

3. Not after *for example, especially,* or *including*

▶ **His varied taste is shown by his living room furnishings, including antiques, modern art, and art deco lighting fixtures.**

 Other Punctuation Marks

 Periods

In British English, a period is descriptively called a "full stop." The stop at the end of a sentence is indeed full—more of a stop than a comma provides. Periods are also used with abbreviations, decimals, and amounts of money, as in items 3 and 4 below.

1. Use a period to end a sentence that makes a statement or gives a command

▸ The interviewer asked the manager about the company's finances.

▸ Remember to log out at the end of the day.

The Web site of the Modern Language Association (MLA), in its list of Frequently Asked Questions about the *MLA Handbook*, recommends leaving one space after a concluding punctuation mark but sees "nothing wrong with using two spaces" if your instructor approves. For periods used with sentences within parentheses, see 51a.

2. Use a period, not a question mark, to end a sentence concluding with an indirect question

▸ The reporter asked the company treasurer how much the company had spent on gifts.

3. Use a period to signal an abbreviation

Mr.   Dr.   Rev.   Tues.   etc.

Use only one space after the period: Mr. Lomax. When abbreviations contain internal periods, do not insert a space after any internal periods.

e.g.   i.e.   a.m.   p.m.   (or A.M.   P.M.)

Note: For some abbreviations with capital letters, you can use periods or not. Just be consistent.

A.M. or AM   P.M. or PM   U.S.A. or USA (but note that MLA style prefers USA.)

When ending a sentence with an abbreviation, do not add an extra period: *The plane left at 7 a.m.*

However, MLA style recommends that no periods be used with initials of names of government agencies (HUD) or other organizations (ACLU), acronyms (abbreviations pronounced as words: NASA, AIDS), Internet abbreviations (URL), abbreviations for states (CA, NJ), or common time indicators (BC, AD). See also 52c.

4. Use a period with decimals and with amounts of money over a dollar

▸ 3.7, $7.50

49b Question marks and exclamation points

Question marks (?)   A question mark at the end of a sentence signals a direct question. Do not use a period in addition to a question mark.

> ▶ **Was anyone hurt in the accident?**

If questions in a series are not complete sentences, you still need question marks. A question fragment may begin with a capital letter or not. Just make your usage consistent.

> ▶ **Are the characters in the play involved in the disaster? Indifferent to it? Unaware of it?**

> ▶ **Are the characters in the play involved in the disaster? indifferent to it? unaware of it?**

However, after an indirect question, use a period, not a question mark (49a, item 2).

> ▶ **We'd like to know what you expect us to do.**

Questions are useful devices to engage readers' attention. You ask a question and then provide an answer.

> ▶ **Many cooks nowadays are making healthier dishes. How do they do this? For the most part, they use unsaturated oil.**

A question mark is sometimes used to express uncertainty about a date or a query about an incident.

> ▶ **"A noise outside woke her up?" the detective wondered.** [Note that no comma is needed after a question mark that is part of a quotation.]

> ▶ **Plato (427?–347 BC) founded the Academy at Athens.**

Exclamation points (!)   An exclamation point at the end of a sentence indicates that the writer considers the statement amazing, surprising, or extraordinary. As novelist F. Scott Fitzgerald said, "An exclamation point is like laughing at your own joke." Let your words and ideas carry the force of any emphasis you want to communicate.

No   **The last act of her play is really impressive!**

Yes   **The last act of her play resolves the crisis in an unexpected and dramatic way.**

If you feel you absolutely have to include an exclamation point to get your point across in dialogue or with an emphatic command or statement, do not use it along with an additional comma or period.

▶ "Get off my property!" the farmer yelled at the teenage couple.

Note: An exclamation point (or a question mark) *can* be used with a period that signals an abbreviation:

▶ The match didn't end until 1 a.m.!

Avoid using a question mark or an exclamation point enclosed in parentheses to convey irony or sarcasm.

No   My father, Mr. Diplomatic (!), regularly insulted my sister by commenting on her weight.

Yes   My father, who could be tactless, regularly insulted my sister by commenting on her weight.

49c Dashes

A dash (—) alerts readers to an explanation, to something unexpected, or to an interruption. Form a dash by typing two hyphens with no extra space before, between, or after them. Some word processing software will transform the two hyphens into one continuous dash. Dashes should enclose a phrase, not a clause.

▶ She bragged that her dog--a Pomeranian--had a complete wardrobe of sweaters.

▶ The accused gasped, "But I never—" and fainted.

▶ In America there are two classes of travel—first class and with children.
                                        —Robert Benchley, in Robert E. Drennan, *The Algonquin Wits*

Commas can be used to set off an appositive phrase, but a pair of dashes is preferable when appositive phrases form a list already containing commas.

▶ The contents of his closet—torn jeans, frayed jackets, and suits shiny on the seat and elbows—made him reassess his priorities.

Overusing the dash may produce a staccato effect. Use it sparingly.

49d Parentheses

Use parentheses to mark an aside or provide additional information.

> ▸ **Everyone admires Rafael Nadal's feat (winning Grand Slam finals on all court surfaces).**

Also use parentheses to enclose citations in a documented paper and to enclose numbers or letters preceding items in a list.

> ▸ **(3) A journalist reports that in the course of many interviews, he met very few people who were cynical about the future of the country (Lamb 5).**

At the end of a sentence, place the period inside the last parenthesis only when a separate new sentence is enclosed (see examples in 51a).

> ▸ **Meryl Streep burst out laughing when it was announced that she had won the 2012 Oscar for Best Actress. (Her previous win had taken place almost 30 years earlier.)**

49e Brackets

Square brackets ([ ]) When you insert words or comments or make changes to words within a quotation, enclose the inserted or changed material in square brackets. Be careful to insert only words that help the quotation fit into your sentence grammatically or that offer a necessary explanation. Do not insert words that substantially change the meaning.

> ▸ **According to Ridley, "the key to both of these features of life [the ability to reproduce and to create order] is information."**

On occasion, you may need to use brackets to insert the Latin word *sic* (meaning "thus") into a quoted passage in which an error occurs. Using *sic* tells readers that the word or words that it follows were present in the original source and are not your own.

> ▸ **Richard Lederer tells of a man who did "exercises to strengthen his abominable [sic] muscles."**

Square brackets can also be used in MLA style around ellipsis dots that you add to signal an omission from a source that itself contains ellipsis dots (49g).

Angle brackets (< >) Use angle brackets to enclose e-mail addresses and URLs when you need to include them in an MLA works-cited list (see 12a, 12f, and 55a).

49f Slashes

Use a slash (/) to separate two or three lines of poetry quoted within your own text. For quoting more than three lines of poetry, see 10c and 49g.

> ▶ **Elizabeth Barrett's most romantic poem begins with the famous question: "How do I love thee? / Let me count the ways."**

Slashes are also used in expressions such as *and/or* and *he/she* to indicate options. Be careful not to overuse these expressions.

49g Ellipsis dots

When you omit material from a quotation, indicate the omission—the ellipsis—by three dots with a space between each dot (...). (MLA style recommends using square brackets around ellipsis dots if the passage you quote from already contains an ellipsis.) The following passage by Ruth Sidel, on page 27 of *On Her Own,* is used in some of the examples that follow.

> These women have a commitment to career, to material well-being, to success, and to independence. To many of them, an affluent lifestyle is central to their dreams; they often describe their goals in terms of cars, homes, travel to Europe. In short, they want their piece of the American Dream.

Words omitted from the middle of a quotation   Use three ellipsis dots when you omit material from the middle of a quotation.

> ▶ **Ruth Sidel reports that the women in her interviews "have a commitment to career . . . and to independence" (27).**

Words omitted at the end of your sentence   When you omit part of a quotation and the omission occurs at the end of your own sentence, insert ellipsis dots after the sentence period, followed by the closing quotation marks, making four dots in all.

> ▶ **Ruth Sidel presents interesting findings about jobs and money: "These women have a commitment to career, to material well-being. . . ."**

When a parenthetical reference follows the quoted passage, put the final sentence period after the parenthetical reference:

> ▶ **Ruth Sidel presents interesting findings about jobs and money: "These women have a commitment to career, to material well-being . . ." (27).**

Complete sentence omitted   When you omit a complete sentence or more, insert three ellipsis dots.

▶ Sidel tells us how "an affluent lifestyle is central to their dreams; . . . they want their piece of the American Dream" (27).

Line of poetry omitted   When you omit one or more lines of poetry from a long, indented quotation, indicate the omission with a line of dots.

My good Lysander!
I swear to thee, by Cupid's strongest bow,
By his best arrow with the golden head,
By the simplicity of Venus' doves,
By that which knitteth souls and prospers loves,
. . . .
By all the vows that ever men have broke,
In number more than ever women spoke,
In that same place thou hast appointed me,
To-morrow truly will I meet with thee.

— William Shakespeare, *A Midsummer Night's Dream*

When not to use ellipsis dots   Do not use ellipsis dots when you quote only a word or a phrase because it will be obvious that material has been omitted:

▶ The women Sidel interviewed see an "affluent lifestyle" in their future.

Note: Use three dots to indicate a pause in speech or an interruption.

▶ Professor Lang got as far as "Economists disagree on the wisest course . . ." before he was overtaken by a fit of coughing.

50 Italics/Underlining

Italics and underlining serve the same function: to highlight a word, phrase, or title. Use underlining only in a handwritten or typed manuscript. In all other material written with a word processor or online, use italics. In some e-mail postings and discussion lists, you may need to indicate italics by a single underscore at the beginning and end of the passage you would usually italicize.

50a When to italicize the titles of long, whole works

In the body of an essay, italicize the titles of books, journals, magazines, newspapers, plays, films, TV series, long poems, musical compositions, Web sites, online databases, and works of art

- *Pride and Prejudice*
- *The Daily Show*
- *Mad Men*
- *American Gothic*
- *Newsweek*
- *About.com*

50b When not to italicize titles

- In the body of your text, do not italicize the names of sacred works such as the Bible and the Koran (Qur'an). Note, though, that these will be italicized in an MLA citation (11b, item V) and in an MLA works-cited list (12d, item 30).
- Do not italicize the books of the Bible (Genesis, Psalms) or the titles of documents and laws, such as the Declaration of Independence, the Constitution, and the Americans with Disabilities Act. However, follow style guides for the use of italics for titles of works in bibliographical lists or notes: CSE, for example, does not use italics for titles.
- Do not italicize the titles of short works, such as poems, short stories, essays, and articles. (MLA and *Chicago* styles use quotation marks for short works in their list of works cited or notes.)
- Do not italicize the title of your own essay (see 47f).
- See MLA, APA, CSE, and *Chicago* styles for the conventions of using italics and quotation marks in a list of references (chapters 11–20).

50c Italicize names of ships, trains, airplanes, and spacecraft

- *Titanic*
- *Silver Meteor*
- *Mir*
- *Gemini*

However, do not italicize any abbreviation preceding the name: USS *Constitution*.

50d Italicize letters, numerals, and words referring to the words themselves, not to what they represent

- The sign had a large *P* in black marker and a *3* in red.
- Many publications now write *website* as one word, uncapitalized.

50e Italicize words from other languages not yet adopted in English

Expressions not commonly used in English should be italicized. Do not overuse such expressions because they tend to sound pretentious.

▶ **The Marshall Plan was instrumental in creating the** ***Wirtschaftswunder*** **in West Germany after World War II.**

Do not italicize common expressions: et al., croissant, film noir, etc.

50f Do not use italics for emphasis

Select a word that better conveys the idea you want to express.

hilarious.
▶ **The joke was** *too funny!*
         ^

51 Capitalization

51a Capitalize *I* and the first word of a sentence

Always use a capital letter for the pronoun *I* and for the first letter of the first word of a sentence. E-mail correspondence without any capitals may look sloppy and annoy some readers (see also 55b). However, do not use a capital letter for the first word after a semicolon even when it begins a complete sentence. In addition, do not use a capital letter if you insert a complete sentence into another sentence using parentheses:

▶ **Dr. Elana Fisher was recently appointed Chief of Surgery (previously she was a staff surgeon at the Cleveland Clinic).**

If you want to give the material within the parentheses a little more emphasis, make it a sentence with a capital letter and place the period before the closing parenthesis.

▶ **Dr. Elana Fisher was recently appointed Chief of Surgery. (Previously she was a staff surgeon at the Cleveland Clinic.)**

51b Capitalize proper nouns and proper adjectives

Begin the names of specific people, places, and things with a capital letter. For the use of *the* with proper nouns, see 58f.

Types of Proper Nouns and Adjectives	Examples
People	Albert Einstein, Adele, T. S. Eliot, Bill Gates (but bell hooks), Selena Gomez
Nations, continents, planets, stars, and galaxies	Hungary, Asia, Mercury, the North Star, the Milky Way
Mountains, rivers, and oceans	Mount Everest, the Thames, the Pacific Ocean
Public places and regions	Golden Gate Park, the Great Plains, the Midwest, the South (but no capital for direction, as in "Drive south on the turnpike")
Streets, buildings, and monuments	Rodeo Drive, the Empire State Building, the Roosevelt Memorial
Cities, states, and provinces	Toledo, Kansas, Nova Scotia
Days of the week and months	Wednesday, March
Holidays	Labor Day, the Fourth of July
Organizations, companies, and search engines	the Red Cross, Microsoft Corporation, eBay (internal capital), Yahoo!
Institutions (including colleges, departments, schools, government offices, and courts of law)	University of Texas, Department of English, School of Business, Department of Defense, Florida Supreme Court
Historical events, named periods, and documents	the Civil War, the Renaissance, the Roaring Twenties, the Declaration of Independence
Religions, deities, revered persons, and sacred texts	Buddhism, Islam, Muslim, Baptist, Jehovah, Mohammed, the Torah, the Koran (Qur'an)
Races, tribes, nations, nationalities, and languages	the Navajo, Greece, Greek, Spain, Spanish, Syrian, Farsi
Registered trademarks	Kleenex, Apple, iPod, Nike, Xerox
Names of ships, planes, and spacecraft	the USS *Kearsarge*, the *Spirit of St. Louis*, the *Challenger*
Titles of courses	English Composition, Introduction to Sociology

Note: Do not capitalize nouns naming general classes or types of people, places, things, or ideas: *government, jury, mall, prairie, utopia, traffic court, the twentieth century, goodness, reason.* Also, do not capitalize the names of seasons (*next spring*) or subjects of study, except for languages (*She is interested in geology and Spanish.*). For the use of capital letters in online writing, see 55b.

51c Capitalize a title before a person's name

▸ **Voters were surprised to hear of Senator Snowe's retirement.**

▸ **The residents cheered Grandma Jones.**

Do not use a capital letter when a title is not attached to a person's name.

▸ **Maine has had the same senator since 1994.**

▸ **My grandmother is ninety years old.**

When a title substitutes for the name of a known person, a capital letter is often used.

▸ **Have you spoken with the Senator [senator] yet?**

51d Capitalize major words in a title

In titles of published books, journals, magazines, essays, articles, films, poems, and songs, use a capital letter at the beginning of all words. Exceptions: articles (*the, a, an*), coordinating conjunctions (*and, but, or, nor, so, for, yet*), *to* in an infinitive (*to stay*), and prepositions unless they begin or end the title or subtitle.

▸ **"With a Little Help from My Friends"**

▸ *Reflections from the Keyboard: The World of the Concert Pianist*

For more on titles, see the Key Points box in 47e, p. 514.

51e Capitals with colons and quotations

Writers often ask how to use capital letters with colons and quotations.

Should a capital letter be used at the beginning of a clause after a colon? Usage varies. Usually, a capital letter is used if the clause states a rule or principle (p. 518, item 3). Make your usage consistent.

Should a capital letter be used at the beginning of a quotation? Capitalize the first word of a quoted sentence if it is capitalized in the original passage.

> ▶ When Quindlen writes, "The world is full of women blindsided by the unceasing demands of motherhood, still flabbergasted by how a job can be terrific and torturous," is she writing from experience?

Do not capitalize when you quote part of a sentence.

> ▶ When Quindlen writes that motherhood can be both "terrific and torturous," it makes me wonder how her own children turned out.

52 Abbreviations

For abbreviations commonly used in online writing, see 55d.

52a Abbreviate titles used with people's names

Use an abbreviation, followed by a period, for titles before or after names. The following abbreviated titles precede names: *Mr., Mrs., Ms., Prof., Dr., Gen.,* and *Sen.* The following abbreviated titles follow names: *Sr., Jr., PhD, MD, BA,* and *DDS.* Do not use a title both before and after a name: *Dr. Benjamin Spock* or *Benjamin Spock, MD.* Do not abbreviate a title if it is not attached to a specific name.

> professor
> ▶ The ~~prof.~~ is supposed to hold office hours twice a week, but he
>   ^
> never shows up.

52b Abbreviate the names of familiar institutions, countries, tests, diseases, diplomas, individuals, and objects

Use capitalized abbreviations of the names of well-known institutions (*UCLA, YWCA, FBI, UN*), countries (*USA* or *U.S.A.*), tests and diplomas (*SAT, GED*), diseases (*MS, HIV*), individuals (*FDR*), TV and radio networks and stations (*PBS, WQXR*), and objects (*DVD*). If you use a specialized abbreviation, first use the term in full followed by the abbreviation in parentheses; then use the abbreviation.

▶ The Test of English as a Foreign Language (TOEFL) is taken by more than 800,000 students a year. However, our college does not offer a TOEFL preparation class.

52c Abbreviate terms used with numbers

Use abbreviations such as *BC, AD, a.m., p.m., $, mph, wpm, mg, kg,* and other units of measure only when they occur with specific numbers.

▶ **35 BC** [meaning "before Christ," now often replaced with *BCE,* "before the Common Era"]

▶ **AD 1776** [*anno domini,* "in the year of the Lord," now often replaced with *CE,* "Common Era," used after the date: 1776 CE]

▶ **2:00 a.m./p.m.** [*ante* or *post meridiem,* Latin for "before or after midday"] Alternatives are A.M./P.M. or AM/PM. Be consistent.

Do not use these abbreviations and other units of measure when no number is attached to them.

▶ The keg weighed about forty ~~lbs.~~ *pounds.*

▶ They arrived late in the ~~p.m.~~ *afternoon.*

52d Abbreviate common Latin terms

In notes, parentheses, and source citations, use abbreviations for common Latin terms. In the body of your text, use the English meaning.

Abbreviation	Latin	English Meaning
etc.	et cetera	and so on
i.e.	id est	that is
e.g.	exempli gratia	for example
cf.	confer	compare
NB	nota bene	note well
et al.	et alii	and others

52e Do not abbreviate familiar words to save time and space

In formal writing, write in full expressions such as the following:

&	and
bros.	brothers [Use "Bros." only if it is part of the official name of a business, such as Warner Bros. Studio.]

chap.	chapter
lb.	pound
Mon.	Monday
nite	night
NJ	New Jersey [Abbreviate the name of a state only in an address, a note, or a reference.]
no.	number [Use the abbreviation only with a specific number: "No. 17 on the list was deleted."]
Oct.	October [Write names of days and months in full, except in some works-cited lists, such as in MLA format.]
soc.	sociology [Write names of academic subjects in full.]
thru	through
w/	with

52f Use -*s* (not -'*s*) for the plural form of an abbreviation

Do not use an apostrophe to make an abbreviation plural (46e).

▶ **We packed away our old Springsteen LPs.**

▶ **Both his SUVs are at the repair shop.**

53 Numbers

Conventions for using numerals (actual figures) or words vary across the disciplines.

53a Use the conventions of the discipline in which you are writing

In the humanities and in business letters

Use words for numbers expressible in one or two words and for fractions (*nineteen, fifty-six, two hundred, one-half*).

Use numerals for longer numbers (*326; 5,625; 7,642,000*).

Use a combination of words and numerals for whole millions, billions, and so on (*45 million, 1 billion*).

In scientific and technical writing

Use numerals for all numbers above nine.

Use numerals for numbers below ten only when they show precise measurement, as when they are grouped and compared with other larger numbers (*5 of the 39 participants*) or when they precede a unit of measurement (*6 cm*), indicate a mathematical function (*8%; 0.4*), or represent a specific time, date, age, score, or number in a series.

Use words for fractions: *two-thirds.*

53b Spell out numbers that begin a sentence

▸ **One hundred twenty-five members voted for the new bylaws.**

▸ **Three thousand residents were evacuated in anticipation of the flood.**

● NOTE **FOR MULTILINGUAL WRITERS**

Number before *Hundred, Thousand,* and *Million*

Even after plural numbers, use the singular form of *hundred, thousand,* and *million.* Add *-s* only when there is no preceding number.

▸ **Five *hundred* books were damaged in the flood.**

▸ ***Hundreds* of books were damaged in the flood.**

53c Use numerals for giving the time and dates and in other special instances

In nonscientific writing, use numerals for the following:

Time and dates	6 p.m. on 31 May 2009
Decimals	20.89
Statistics	median score 35
Addresses	16 East 93rd Street
Chapter, page, scene, and line numbers	chapter 5, page 97

Quantities appearing with abbreviations or symbols	6°C (for temperature Celsius), $21, 6' 7"
Scores	The Yankees beat the Orioles 3–2 to win the Division Series.

For percentages and money, numerals and the symbol (*75%, $24.67*) are usually acceptable, or you can spell out the expression if it is fewer than four words (*seventy-five percent, twenty-four dollars*).

53d Use -*s* (not -*'s*) for the plural form of numerals

▶ Housing prices skyrocketed in the 1980s.

▶ Most of the graduating class scored in the 700s on the SATs.

54 Hyphens

Use hyphens to divide a word or to form a compound. For the use of hyphens online, see 55c.

54a Hyphens with prefixes

Many words with prefixes are spelled without hyphens: *cooperate, nonrestrictive, unnatural.* Others are hyphenated: *all-inclusive, anti-intellectual, self-effacing.* Always use a hyphen when the main word is a number or a proper noun: *all-American, post-2010.* If you are unsure about whether to insert a hyphen after a prefix, check a big dictionary to see if it lists the word as hyphenated.

54b Hyphens in compound words

Some compound nouns are written as one word (*toothbrush*), others as two words (*coffee shop*), and still others with one or more hyphens (*role-playing, father-in-law*). Always check an up-to-date dictionary. Similarly, check a dictionary for compound verbs (*cross-examine, overemphasize*).

Hyphenate compound adjectives preceding a noun: *a well-organized party, a law-abiding citizen, a ten-page essay.* When the modifier follows the noun, no hyphen is necessary: *The party was well organized. Most citizens try to be law abiding. The essay was ten pages long.*

Do not insert a hyphen between an *-ly* adverb and the word it modifies or after an adjective in its comparative (*-er*) or superlative (*-est*) form: *a tightly fitting suit, an expertly written essay, a sweeter sounding melody.*

Treat a series of hyphenated prefixes like this:

▶ **A verdict of either first- or second-degree murder was expected.**

54c Hyphens in spelled-out numbers

Use hyphens when spelling out two-word numbers from twenty-one to ninety-nine. (See 53b for more on spelling out numbers.)

▶ **Twenty-two applicants arrived early in the morning.**

Also use a hyphen in spelled-out fractions: *two-thirds of a cup.*

54d End-of-line hyphens

Most word processors either automatically hyphenate words or automatically wrap words around to the next line. Choose the latter option to avoid the strange and unacceptable word division that sometimes appears with automatic hyphenation. Do not insert a hyphen into a URL to split it across lines (see 55a).

55 Online Guidelines

55a Punctuation in URLs

Punctuation marks communicate essential information in Web site addresses—uniform resource locators (URLs)—and in e-mail addresses. Be sure to include all marks when you write an address, and if you need to spread a URL over more than one line in your text, split it after a slash (MLA, CSE, and *Chicago* styles) or before a punctuation mark such as a period (APA and *Chicago* styles). Do not split the protocol (<http://>). In a print source in MLA style, use angle brackets to enclose e-mail and Web addresses.

▶ **The Modern Language Association, whose Web site is at <http://www.mla.org>, provides examples of documenting Web sources.**

Do not include any additional punctuation within the angle brackets.

When you write an online paper, URLs are hyperlinked and therefore appear as underlined on the screen. Do not use angle brackets for a paper published online.

55b Capital letters online

Don't let the speed and informal nature of e-mail delude you into thinking that no rules or conventions matter anymore. Especially in academic and business settings, e-mail messages written with no capitals for the first letter of the first word of a sentence, for proper nouns, or for *I* will send readers the somewhat insulting signal that you have not bothered to check what you send them.

Overdoing capitals is as bad as (maybe worse than) including none at all. Writing a whole message in capital letters can be perceived by readers as the online equivalent of shouting. In order not to offend readers in e-mail communications and online discussion groups, avoid the prolonged use of capital letters.

55c Hyphens online

Some e-mail addresses and URLs include hyphens, so never add a hyphen to indicate that you have split an address between lines. When an online address includes a hyphen, do not break the line at a hyphen because readers will not know whether the hyphen is part of the address. Break the line after @ or after a slash.

Technological vocabulary changes quickly. You will find both *e-mail* and *email*. The MLA prefers the hyphenated spelling, *e-mail* (as do the authors of this book), but the tendency is for common words like this to move toward closing up. Whichever form you use, use it consistently.

55d Abbreviations online

Many abbreviations in the electronic world have become standard fare: CD-ROM, RAM, PIN, and more. In addition, the informal world of online communication leads to informal abbreviations, at least in personal e-mail and text messages. Abbreviations such as *BTW* ("by the way"), *IMHO* ("in my humble opinion"), and *TTYTT* ("to tell you the truth") are used in texting and informal e-mail, but you should avoid them in formal contexts.

55e Italics online

If you are using a social networking Web site or other technology that provides no italics, you can indicate a title and other types of words usually italicized by inserting an underscore before and after the words to be italicized:

▶ I loved the cinematography in Scorsese's film _Hugo_.

56 Spelling

Get into the habit of using a dictionary and a word processor with a spelling-check program. Even if you check your spelling with computer software, you still need to proofread. A program will not alert you to a correctly spelled word used in the wrong place (such as *cite* used in place of *sight* or *site*). However, you may be called upon to write spontaneously without access to a spelling program or a dictionary, so learn the basic rules in this chapter.

56a Plurals of nouns

Regular plural forms   The regular plural of nouns is formed by adding *-s* or *-es* to the singular word.

essay, essays   match, matches

To form the plural of a compound noun, attach the *-s* to the main noun in the phrase.

mothers-in-law   passersby

Proofread carefully for words that form the plural with *-s* but make other changes, too, such as the following:

-f or *-fe* → *-ves*
thief, thieves
wife, wives
Exceptions: beliefs, roofs, chiefs

-o → *-oes*   *-o* → *-os*
potato, potatoes   hero (sandwich), heros
tomato, tomatoes   photo, photos
hero (human), heroes   piano, pianos

Consonant + *-y* → *-ies*	Vowel + *-y* → *-ys*
family, families	toy, toys
party, parties	monkey, monkeys

Irregular plural forms (no *-s* ending)

man, men	foot, feet
woman, women	tooth, teeth
child, children	mouse, mice

Plural forms borrowed from other languages   Words borrowed from other languages, particularly Greek and Latin, frequently borrow the plural form of the language, too.

basis, bases	nucleus, nuclei
thesis, theses	vertebra, vertebrae
hypothesis, hypotheses	alumnus (m.), alumni
criterion, criteria	alumna (f.), alumnae

Plural forms with no change   Some words have the same form in singular and plural: *moose, deer, sheep, species.*

56b Doubling consonants

Doubled consonants form a link between spelling and pronunciation because the doubling of a consonant signals a short vowel sound.

Double the consonant when the verb stem contains one vowel plus one consonant in one syllable

slip, slipping, slipped   hop, hopping, hopped

The doubled consonant preserves the short vowel sound. Compare the pronunciation of *hop, hopping, hopped* with *hope, hoping, hoped.* Compare the vowel sounds in *write, writing,* and *written.*

Double the consonant when the verb stem contains two or more syllables with one vowel plus one consonant in the final stressed syllable

refer, referring, referred   control, controlling, controlled

Compare *traveling* and *traveled* with the stress on the first syllable. (British English usage, however, is *travelling* and *travelled.*)

Double the consonant when the suffix *-er* or *-est* is added to one-syllable adjectives ending in one vowel plus one consonant

big, bigger, biggest   hot, hotter, hottest

Double the *l* when adding *-ly* to an adjective that ends in one *-l*

careful, carefully   successful, successfully

56c Spelling with *-y* or *-i*

Verb Ends in Consonant + *-y*	*-ies*	*-ying*	*-ied*
cry	cries	crying	cried
study	studies	studying	studied

Verb Ends in Vowel + *-y*	*-ys*	*-ying*	*-yed*
play	plays	playing	played

Exceptions: pay/paid, say/said, lay/laid

Verb Ends in Vowel + *-e*	*-ies*	*-ying*	*-ied*
die	dies	dying	died

Two-Syllable Adjective Ends in *-y*	*-i* with a Suffix	
happy	happier, happily, happiness	

Two-Syllable Adjective Ends in *-ly*	*-lier*	*-liest*
friendly	friendlier	friendliest

56d Internal *ie* or *ei*

This traditional rhyme helps with the decision about whether to use *ie* or *ei*: "*I* before *e* / Except after *c* / Or when sounded like *ay* / As in *neighbor* and *weigh*." The following examples illustrate those guidelines:

i before *e*	*e* before *i* after *c*	*e* before *i* when sounded like *ay*
believe	receive	vein
relief	ceiling	reign
niece	deceive	sleigh

But note the exceptions:

i before *e* even after *c*	*e* before *i*, not after *c*	
conscience	height	seize
science	either/neither	foreign
species	leisure	weird

56e Adding a suffix

Keep a silent -*e* before an -*ly* suffix

immediate, immediately   sure, surely

Exceptions: true, truly; whole, wholly; due, duly

Keep a silent -*e* before a suffix beginning with a consonant

state, statement   force, forceful   rude, rudeness

Exceptions: acknowledge, acknowledgment; judge, judgment; argue, argument

Drop a silent -*e* before a suffix beginning with a vowel

hope, hoping   observe, observant

write, writing   remove, removable

Exceptions: enforce, enforceable; change, changeable. Retaining the -*e* preserves the soft sound of the preceding consonant.

With adjectives ending in -*le*, drop the -*le* when adding -*ly*

sensible, sensibly

With adjectives ending in -*ic*, add -*ally* to form the adverb

basic, basically   characteristic, characteristically

Exception: public, publicly

Pay attention to the suffixes *-able, -ible, -ant, -ent, -ify,* **and** *-efy*
More words end in *-able* than in *-ible*. Here are some of the most common *-ible* words:

eligible	incredible	irresistible	legible
permissible	responsible	terrible	visible

Unfortunately, there are no rules of thumb to help you decide whether to use the suffix *-ant* or *-ent*. Learn common words with these suffixes, and have your dictionary handy for others.

-ant	*-ent*
defiant	confident
observant	convenient
relevant	existent
reluctant	imminent
resistant	independent

The suffix *-ify* is more common than *-efy*. Learn the four *-efy* words:

liquefy	putrefy	rarefy	stupefy

56f Multinational characters: Accents, umlauts, tildes, and cedillas

Words and names in languages other than English may be spelled with special marks over or under a letter, such as an accent (é or è), an umlaut or dieresis (ö), a tilde (ñ), or a cedilla (ç). Your word processing program probably provides these characters (in Microsoft Word, go to Insert/Symbol). If it does not, insert them by hand.

● TECH NOTE

A Useful Web Site for Writing in Other Languages

International Accents and Diacriticals: Theory, Charts, and Tips, prepared by Irene Starr of the Foreign Language Resource Center at the University of Massachusetts, is a useful site that provides charts of how to produce multinational characters; instructions on accessing and using the International English keyboard; and links to sites useful for those writing non-Roman alphabets.

Exercises on Punctuation, Mechanics, and Spelling

EXERCISE 1 Use commas after introductory material or with nonrestrictive elements 45c

Add any necessary commas. Some sentences may be correct.

> Example   Working for a major chemical manufacturer, Charles Baldwin, an
>
> engineer, helped to develop the symbol that identifies biohazards.

1. Realizing that laboratories and medical facilities around the world all needed to dispose of biohazards researchers wanted a symbol that would indicate to everyone which material was infectious.
2. Designers who create symbols want them to be memorable.
3. However the biohazard symbol needed to be unlike any other symbol.
4. In 1966 the symbol which is three-sided so that it looks the same if seen upside-down or sideways was chosen.
5. With its vivid orange color, a shade determined to be the most visible of all colors under most conditions the symbol was soon accepted by the Centers for Disease Control, the Occupational Safety and Health Administration, and the National Institutes of Health.

EXERCISE 2 Use commas in special situations 45i

Add commas to the correct places in these sentences.

> Example   The Mayan calendar ends a major sequence on December 21, 2012,
>
> and then begins a new sequence.

1. Yes some people believed that this date also known as the winter solstice signalled the end of human civilization.
2. Many books and Internet sites said that a planet called Nibiru discovered by the Sumerians would collide with Earth at that time.
3. The village of Bugarach France was overrun by visitors who believed aliens in the mountains there would lead them to safety.
4. Scientists such as Mary A. Voytek PhD of NASA sought to reassure the public that the frightening predictions were unfounded.
5. It's exciting to speculate about cataclysmic events isn't it?

EXERCISE 3 Know when to use an apostrophe 46a

Correct the use of the apostrophe in these sentences.

> Example   Some of Rihanna's fan's applauded her songs about domestic violence.

1. The farmer's market offers the freshest honeydew melon's, watermelon's, and cantaloupe's.

2. Let's jump in the water before it get's too cold.
3. The orange parka is Sara's and the blue one is your's.
4. When we're in New Orleans we can stay with my friends the Abbott's.
5. The mountain's sides are beginning to erode.

EXERCISE 4 Use apostrophes to signal possession 46b, 46c

Correct any errors in the use of apostrophes.

Example   In parts of Africa that have been devastated by AIDS, doctors who

practice Western-style medicine are looking at traditional ~~healer's~~ healers'
roles in treating the sick.

1. Doctors and healers' ideas about useful treatments for people infected with
the AIDS virus sometimes conflict with each other.
2. For example, traditional healers often prescribe emetics to cause vomiting,
and if a patients' treatment also includes retroviral drugs, the patient may
expel the drugs before they take effect.
3. Because many doctors in Africa understand their patients faith in traditional healing, some doctors are trying to work with healers rather than
fighting them.
4. Some healers have agreed to attend conferences' at hospitals, where they
learn to wear latex gloves when treating patients and to use alcohol to clean
razor blades' edges and porcupine quills that have contacted any patients'
body fluids.
5. Many patients trust healer's more than they trust doctor's, so hospitals in
some areas have deputized traditional healers to monitor their patients intake of AIDS drugs and their mental well-being.

EXERCISE 5 Use apostrophes correctly with contractions in special instances and with *it's* 46d, 46f

Correct any errors in the use of apostrophes.

Example   Trainspotting has ~~it's~~ its fans in Great Britain, and airplane spotters
~~are'nt~~ aren't unusual either.

1. Although theyre often regarded as geek's by people who do'nt share their
passion, trainspotters are devoted to their hobby of watching trains and
noting engine numbers.
2. Planespotting, a variation of trainspotting, resulted in legal difficulties for a
group of vacationing Briton's who were arrested and accused of spying on
airfields in Greece.
3. The arrests led to a diplomatic rift between Great Britain and Greece, with
the Britons claiming that theyd merely been enjoying the Greek Air Force
celebrations and the Greeks claiming that the spotters were illegally

monitoring pilots conversations and observing high-security military installations.

4. Its not surprising that the Greek police were unfamiliar with planespotting, since the hobby attracts few people outside of it's British birthplace.
5. "Its an embarrassment," said one Greek official; the detained Britons may have been accustomed to seeing their passions ridiculed at home, but they probably were'nt expecting to meet such a reception abroad.

EXERCISE 6 Use quotation marks in dialogue 47c

Correct the use of quotation marks in these sentences.

> Example "Are you going to the play this weekend? Marj asked.

1. Bao isn't coming to the theater," Aidan said. "He can't stand comedies.
2. "Why didn't he say that, Marj asked, before I paid for the tickets?"
3. "When you said this was a Shakespeare play, Bao assumed you meant a tragedy." Aidan explained. "You should have been more specific."
4. But no big tragedy, he joked. "Right?
5. "Small tragedy, grumbled Marj. "I'm still out fifteen dollars.

EXERCISE 7 Punctuate a quotation within a quotation 47d

Correct the use of quotation marks in these sentences. Some sentences may be correct as written.

> Example The article stated, "Indiana University's eight-minute flag routine
>
> has been called "the best timeout in college basketball."

1. "I get chills when I hear the song "Lay Your Head Down,"" Pam said.
2. Randy asked, 'Do you like that song better than "Molly Malone"?'
3. Writes Jack De Bellis in *The John Updike Encyclopedia,* "Updike has explained that he writes every day but Sunday for three hours in the morning. As he notes, Like snowflakes falling an accumulation will result."
4. Jayne's dating book advised, "When a man says 'I'll call you, reply, No, I'll call you.'"
5. I was fascinated by this *Huffington Post* headline: 'Mirlande Wilson, McDonald's Worker, 'Loses' Mega Millions Ticket.'

EXERCISE 8 Use quotations with titles, definitions, and translations 47e

Use quotation marks and italics to correct these sentences.

> Example My grandfather used the word *stripling* to mean "young man."

1. Did you know that alfresco means in the fresh air?
2. A. M. Homes's short story The Safety of Objects became a film with the same name.

3. After Joao heard the song Mamma Mia on the radio, he found himself singing it all day.
4. The article Unsinkable in this week's issue of The New Yorker reviews Jeannette Winterson's memoir Why Be Happy When You Could Be Normal?
5. The word that means government by a few is oligarchy.

EXERCISE 9 Know when to use and when not to use a semicolon 48a

Add semicolons and change commas to semicolons as needed.

Example   Jan Harold Brunvald is the man who coined the term *urban legend*⨟

        he once said that the truth never stands in the way of a good story.

Many urban legends are the kinds of stories that people use to frighten one another around a campfire. Some of the best-known ones are about escaped lunatics and murderers such as the man with a hook for a hand who terrorizes a young couple who, while parked on a deserted road, hear a radio broadcast about him, the man who telephones a babysitter with dire warnings, finally revealing that he is calling from another extension in the same house, and the killer who hides in the back seat of a woman's car or under the bed in her dorm room. These stories are chilling but faintly unbelievable, we all realize, eventually, that they are not true.

EXERCISE 10 Know when to use and when not to use a colon 48b

Make any changes so that colons and semicolons are used correctly.

Example   Turtles are a unique life form for one reason⨟ no other creature has a rigid shell made of vertebrae and ribs.

1. The professor required each student to have a copy of *Herpetology An Introductory Biology of Amphibians and Reptiles.*
2. Turtles are divided into two main types according to the way they retract their necks into their bodies, the *cryptodire*, or "hidden neck," turtles can pull their heads completely into their shells, but the *pleurodire*, or "side neck," turtles can only partially retract their heads.
3. Turtles are different from other reptiles because: their chest cavities cannot expand when they inhale.
4. Turtles can survive without air much longer than other reptiles; sometimes as long as thirty-three hours.
5. Many species of turtles can take in oxygen through sacs which emerge from the turtle's digestive and urogenital cavity; turtles share this unusual method of breathing with life forms such as: dragonfly nymphs and sea cucumbers.

EXERCISE 11 Use end punctuation correctly `49a, 49b`

Mark with "X" the sentence (A or B) that uses more appropriate end punctuation. Explain your choice to your classmates.

Example

___ A. The Web site asks users whether they are so afraid of flying that they avoid airplanes in all circumstances?

_X_ B. The Web site asks users whether they are so afraid of flying that they avoid airplanes in all circumstances.

1. ___ A. With modern technology come modern fears, and thousands of people in industrial societies are terrified of air travel.

   ___ B. With modern technology come modern fears, and thousands of people in industrial societies are terrified of air travel!

2. ___ A. If people who must fly for business or family reasons are too frightened to board an airplane, where can they turn for help.

   ___ B. If people who must fly for business or family reasons are too frightened to board an airplane, where can they turn for help?

3. ___ A. Although most fearful fliers know that flying is statistically safer than driving a car, many of them cannot overcome the part of the mind that says, "What if the plane crashes?"

   ___ B. Although most fearful fliers know that flying is statistically safer than driving a car, many of them cannot overcome the part of the mind that says, "What if the plane crashes?".

4. ___ A. Self-help classes and Web sites help fearful fliers to become more familiar with airplanes; the idea is that familiar things are less frightening.

   ___ B. Self-help classes and Web sites help fearful fliers to become more familiar with airplanes; the idea is that familiar things are less frightening!

5. ___ A. After a plane crash has been in the news, enrollment in self-help classes for fearful fliers tends to decline; psychologists believe that such events convince people that their irrational fears are based in reality, so they say to themselves, "See? I was right to avoid airplanes."

   ___ B. After a plane crash has been in the news, enrollment in self-help classes for fearful fliers tends to decline; psychologists believe that such events convince people that their irrational fears are based in reality, so they say to themselves, "See? I was right to avoid airplanes!"

EXERCISE 12 Use italics and underlining correctly `50a–50f`

Underline any words that need italicization or underlining, and remove any unnecessary underlining or quotation marks.

In the nineteenth century, phrenology—the study of bumps on the skull and their relation to the personality—was a popular pseudoscientific practice, and one of the best-known phrenologists was Lorenzo Fowler. Along with his brother Orson, Lorenzo Fowler headed the Phrenological Institute in New York City, where the two trained other phrenologists, and Lorenzo gave readings to celebrities such as Julia Ward Howe, author of The Battle Hymn of the Republic. The Fowler brothers saw themselves as leaders of a progressive movement; they ran the publishing company that put out the first edition of Walt Whitman's "Leaves of Grass." They also published the Phrenological Journal, hoping that phrenological analysis could lead people to correct defects of character that had been revealed by their cranial protrusions.

In 1872, Samuel Clemens, who had written Huckleberry Finn and many other works under the nom de plume Mark Twain, visited Fowler under an assumed name and obtained a reading and a phrenological chart. Clemens, who was an early champion both of scientific innovations like fingerprinting (which is featured in his novel "Pudd'nhead Wilson") and of inventions that proved to be dismal failures, wanted to put phrenology to the test. The results amused him: in "The Autobiography of Mark Twain," Clemens notes that Fowler found a spot on his skull that "represented the total absence of the sense of humor." Months later, Clemens returned for a second reading, identifying himself both as Clemens and as Mark Twain, and was given a reading and a chart that "contained several sharply defined details of my character, but […] bore no recognizable resemblance to the earlier chart."

Clemens remained convinced that phrenology was quackery, and others soon agreed. By 1900, phrenology had fallen out of favor. Even in the twenty-first century, however, the use of terms such as highbrow and lowbrow, which came from phrenology, demonstrates the influence that this idea once had.

EXERCISE 13   Use capital letters correctly   `51a–51e`

Capitalize any letters that are incorrectly lowercase, and change any incorrect capital letters to lowercase letters.

>   Civil War   doctor   virus
> **Example**   During the ~~civil war~~, a ~~Doctor~~ from Kentucky tried to spread a ~~Virus~~
>
>   North
> to cities in the ~~north~~.

1. Biological warfare may strike modern Americans as Barbaric, but during the French and Indian war, smallpox-infected blankets given to Native Americans helped to decimate their numbers.
2. in the 1860s, Dr. Luke blackburn tried the same tactic, giving or selling clothing from patients with Yellow fever to Soldiers in the Union Army.
3. According to some historians, the Doctor hoped to spread Yellow Fever in washington and new York; president Jefferson Davis of the confederate States of America probably knew about and approved of the plan.
4. Fortunately for citizens of the north, yellow fever cannot be passed from one person to another by skin contact. although Dr. Blackburn's plot was

discovered on the day of Lincoln's Assassination, he was never prosecuted in a Court of Law.
5. Blackburn eventually became the Governor of Kentucky, where he worked for penal and educational reform. A statue of the good samaritan marks his grave in frankfort cemetery.

EXERCISE 14 Use abbreviations correctly 52a–52f

Correct any errors in the use of abbreviations.

> Example According to ~~Mister~~ Sid Green, who teaches ~~H.S. hist.~~ in ~~CA,~~ some
>   Mr.   high school history California
>
>   U.S. colleges and universities no longer require students to take
>
>   the SAT.

1. An early adopter—someone who buys new devices and gadgets as soon as they are available—probably owned CD's when most people still bought records, rented DVD's while others still watched videos on their VCR's, and picked out iPod's as holiday gifts.
2. The acupuncturist's receptionist referred to him as Doctor Loren Selwyn, but I later discovered that he was Loren Selwyn, doctor of philosophy, not Loren Selwyn, medical doctor.
3. Ms Krebs could type so many w.p.m. that the computer printer was spewing out pp. long after she had stopped working for the eve.
4. Sen Hammond helpfully told us that the New Year's Eve party would be held on Dec. 31, but he neglected to say what time we should arrive.
5. Akhenaton, orig. known as Amenhotep, ruled ancient Egypt until his death in about 1358 before the Common Era.

EXERCISE 15 Use hyphens correctly 54a–54d

Correct the use of hyphens in these sentences.

> Example My friend Suzette is great at do it yourself projects.

1. Suzette's mother- and father-inlaw got a postHalloween visit from their grand-children.
2. Suzette dressed her kids in home-made were-wolf costumes.
3. They were un-recognizable in heavy, furcovered masks.
4. Their lethal-looking paws were creatively-designed too.
5. Their grandfather pretended to be terror-stricken.

EXERCISE 16 Correct misspelled words 56a–56e

In each of the following sentences, correct any misspelled words. Some sentences may not contain any errors.

> Example In the wake of ~~violant~~ incidents at high schools, many
>   violent
>
>   schools have adopted a "zero ~~tolerence~~" policy toward weapons.
>   tolerance

1. After a slew of school shootings in Arkansas, Kentucky, and elsewhere, some schools decided to crack down on students carrieing weapons.
2. In many schools, students face suspension if they are caught with guns, knifes, or any potential weapon.
3. One seven-year-old boy was suspended when other childrens saw a two-inch toy gun on a keychain fall out of his pocket.
4. His mother made the arguement that suspending students for carrying toys was a violation of common sense.
5. Schools have also been declareing zero-tolerance policys toward possession of drugs and other controled substances.
6. It's hard to beleive, but one child was suspended for shareing candy with friends when teachers did not recognize the brand.
7. A declareation of zero tolerance means that a school automaticly punishs any student who even appears to have broken the rules.
8. These policys allow employees no leeway to decide for themselfs whether the student's behavior warrants punishment.
9. Some of the grislyest incidents of school violence have occured in schools that had already adopted zero-tolerance policies, such as Columbine High School in Littleton, Colorado.
10. Can a zero-tolerance policy realy help schools, familys, and nieghborhoods avoid tragedy?

 Visit the English CourseMate for this text at www.cengagebrain.com to find additional practice exercises.

9 Writing across Languages and Cultures

GO GLOBAL

To obtain study resources for this section, visit the English CourseMate for this text at **www.cengagebrain.com**

© ra2studio/Shutterstock

9 Writing across Languages and Cultures

Language Diversity and Edited American English: Challenges for Multilingual Writers

College students in North America are a linguistically diverse group: monolingual English-speaking students who have little experience with other cultures and who may speak a local dialect of English; students who grew up in North America among family and friends with their own languages and cultures; students who learned English in formal or informal situations either in their own countries or after they immigrated from other countries; students who speak several languages fluently; and various mixes and remixes of these categories. For college students, Edited American English consists of the language used in formal written documents, for example, in course essays, assignments, and term papers. The rigorous editing required for those tasks is not as necessary in more informal writing, such as journal entries, freewriting, blogs, and first drafts—nor on Twitter or Facebook. The chapters in this part of the handbook are specifically designed to help you write and edit your college work.

57a Englishes and other languages

At the same time that travel and the Internet make us more aware of diversity and other countries' languages and cultures, we are also experiencing a spread in the use of English. Worldwide estimates now show three nonnative speakers of English for every native speaker. It is estimated that more than 400 million people speak English as their native language, and more than a billion use English as a common language for special communicative, educational, and business purposes within their own communities. And by 2017, the estimated number of people speaking English will be about three billion—that is, half the world.

But languages are not fixed and static, and the users of English in their various locations adapt the language for their own purposes.

The concept of one English or a "standard" language is becoming more fluid; it is more focused on the situation and the readers of a particular piece of writing rather than on one set of rules. Consequently, the English regarded as standard in North America is not necessarily standard in Australia, the United Kingdom, Hong Kong, Singapore, Indonesia, India, or Pakistan. Scholars see Englishes—varieties of English—in place of one monolithic language, and these Englishes claim their own names, such as Spanglish, Singlish, Hindlish, and Taglish. English is constantly

The Circle of World English (used with permission)

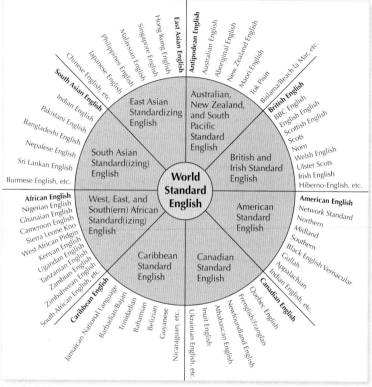

Source: Tom McArthur, "The English Languages?" *English Today* (July 1987), p. 11.

being reinvented around the world, sometimes to the dismay of academics and government officials and sometimes with the approval of individuals who see the adaptation as an act of freedom, even rebellion. The Filipino poet Gemino Abad has gone so far as to make this claim: "The English language is now ours. We have colonized it."

In the United States, too, the Conference on College Composition and Communication as early as 1974 passed a resolution on *Students' Right to Their Own Language* <http://www.ncte.org/library/NCTEFiles/Groups/CCCC/NewSRTOL.pdf>. The report on this resolution stresses the differences between speech and writing, affirming the viability of spoken dialects. However, the report makes the point that students "who want to write EAE [Edited American English] will have to learn the forms identified with that dialect as additional options to the forms they already control." The concept of *addition* and not *replacement* is important.

Therefore, despite the complexity and fluidity of varieties of English, with all their quirks, irregularities, rules, and exceptions, in the academic and business worlds the conventions of what is often called Edited American English remain relatively constant in grammar, syntax, and vocabulary (though not in spelling), with only subtle variations from country to country, region to region. Whether you are monolingual—familiar only with American English—or grew up multilingual or learned English in classes designated for English as a Second Language (ESL) students, in everyday life you, too, constantly switch the Englishes you use depending on whether you are texting a friend, tweeting, compiling a report for a supervisor, or writing a research paper in college. In all instances, it is *you* in the writing, but they are different *you*s, different voices of you. The formal voice of Edited English is the one to use in most academic contexts. More on the importance of voice can be found in sections 1b and 1c.

57b Difference, not deficit, in academic writing

Students in colleges in North America who grew up speaking another language are often called English as a Second Language learners, and the ESL abbreviation is commonly used in college curricula, professional literature, and the press. However, this term is not broad enough. Many so-called second-language students speak three or four languages depending on their life and educational circumstances and the languages spoken at home. Along with being bilingual or multilingual, such students frequently are multicultural, equipped with all the knowledge and experience that those terms imply.

Whether your first language is a variety of English or a totally different language, it is a good idea to view your knowledge of language and culture as an advantage rather than a problem. Unlike many monolingual writers (individuals who know only one version of one language), you are familiar with different cultures in depth and can switch at will among varied linguistic and rhetorical codes. Rather than having only one language, one culture, and one culturally bound type of writing, you have a broader perspective—more to think about, more to write about, more resources to draw on as you write, and far more comparisons to make among languages, writers, writing, and culture. You bring your culture with you into your writing, and as you do so, you help shape and reshape the culture of North America.

Remember, too, that in many situations, the readers you write for will be culturally and linguistically diverse, not all emerging from one educational background. In formal settings, always aim to make your ideas clear to *all* readers by using standard forms of edited English, avoiding slang and jargon, and choosing a style appropriate to your subject matter.

57c Learning about difference as you write

Even for students who have been learning a new language or the conventions of academic writing for some time, departures from the standard language forms are inevitable. Welcome and embrace what others describe as errors. Study them and learn from them. Having errors pointed out can help you become aware of differences among languages. In fact, errors show learning in progress. If you make no errors while you are learning to speak or write a new language or a standard version of English, perhaps you are being too careful and using only what you know is correct. Be willing to take risks and try new words, new expressions, new combinations. Expand your repertoire.

● TECH NOTE

Web Sites on Language and Writing

The Web sites listed here provide useful information.

* ESL Resources, Handouts, and Exercises from Purdue University's Online Writing Lab at <http://owl.english.purdue.edu/handouts/esl/index.html>.
* Guide to Grammar and Writing at <http://grammar.ccc.commnet.edu/grammar>. On this Capital Community College site, you will find information and quizzes on words, paragraphs, and essays. The Grammar Logs in "Ask Grammar" contain questions and answers and cover interesting points.

When somebody points out an error in your writing, write a note about it. Consider why you made the error—was it, for example, a transfer from your home language, a guess, a careless mistake? Or was it the employment of a logical but erroneous hypothesis about the rules of edited English (such as "many verbs form the past tense with -*ed*; therefore, the past tense form of *swear* is probably *sweared*")? Analyzing the causes of errors will help you understand how to edit them and avoid them in the future. (By the way, the past tense form of *swear* is *swore*.)

57d Editing guide to multilingual transfer patterns

Nonstandard forms can occur while you are writing in a new language, especially when you are grappling with new subject matter and difficult subjects. You concentrate on ideas and clarity, but because no writer can do everything at once, you fail to concentrate on editing.

The editing guide that follows identifies several problem areas for multilingual writers. It shows grammatical features (column 1) of specific languages (column 2) and features that lead to an error when transferred to English (column 3). An Edited American English version appears in column 4. Of course, the guide covers neither all linguistic problem areas nor all languages. Rather, it lists a selection, with the goal of being useful and practical. Use the guide to raise your awareness about your own and other languages.

Editing Guide

Language Features	Languages	Sample Transfer Errors in English	Edited Version
Articles (58c–58f)			
No articles	Chinese, Japanese, Russian, Swahili, Thai, Urdu	*Sun is hot. I bought book. Computer has changed our lives.*	*The sun is hot. I bought a book. The computer has changed our lives.*
No indefinite article with profession	Arabic, French, Japanese, Korean, Vietnamese	*He is student. She lawyer.*	*He is a student. She is a lawyer.*
Definite article with days, months, places, idioms	Arabic	*She is in the bed. He lives in the Peru.*	*She is in bed. He lives in Peru.*
Definite article used for generalization	Farsi, French, German, Greek, Portuguese, Spanish	*The photography is an art. The books are more expensive than the disks.*	*Photography is an art. Books are more expensive than disks.*
Definite article used with proper noun	French, German, Portuguese, Spanish	*The Professor Brackert teaches in Frankfurt.*	*Professor Brackert teaches in Frankfurt.*

(Continued)

(Continued)

Language Features	Languages	Sample Transfer Errors in English	Edited Version
No definite article	Hindi, Turkish	*Store on corner is closed.*	*The store on the corner is closed.*
No indefinite article	Korean (uses *one* for *a*; depends on context)	*He ran into one tree.*	*He ran into a tree.*
Verbs and Verb Forms (chapter 59)			
A form of the verb *be* can be omitted	Arabic, Chinese, Greek, Russian	*India hotter than Britain.* *They working now.* *He cheerful.*	*India is hotter than Britain.* *They are working now.* *He is cheerful.*
No progressive forms	French, German, Greek, Russian	*They still discuss the problem.* *When I walked in, she slept.*	*They are still discussing the problem.* *When I walked in, she was sleeping.*
No tense inflections	Chinese, Thai, Vietnamese	*He arrive yesterday.* *When I was little, I always walk to school.*	*He arrived yesterday.* *When I was little, I always walked to school.*
No inflection for third person singular	Chinese, Japanese, Korean, Russian, Thai	*The singer have a big band.* *She work hard.*	*The singer has a big band.* *She works hard.*
Past perfect formed with *be*	Arabic	*They were arrived when I called.*	*They had arrived when I called.*
Different tense boundaries from English	Arabic, Chinese, Farsi, French	*I study here for a year.* *He has left yesterday.*	*I have been studying here for a year.* *He left yesterday.*

Language Features	Languages	Sample Transfer Errors in English	Edited Version
Different limits for passive voice	Japanese, Korean, Russian, Thai, Vietnamese	*They were stolen their luggage.*	*Their luggage was stolen.*
		My name base on Chinese characters.	*My name is based on Chinese characters.*
		The mess clean up quick.	*The mess was cleaned up quickly.*
		A miracle was happened.	*A miracle (has) happened.*
No -*ing* (gerund)/ infinitive distinction	Arabic, Chinese, Farsi, French, Greek, Portuguese, Spanish, Vietnamese	*She avoids to go.*	*She avoids going.*
		I enjoy to play tennis.	*I enjoy playing tennis.*
Infinitive not used to express purpose	Korean	*People exercise for losing weight.*	*People exercise to lose weight.*
Overuse of progressive forms	Hindi, Urdu	*I am wanting to leave now.*	*I want to leave now.*
Sentence Structure and Word Order (chapter 60)			
Verb precedes subject	Arabic, Hebrew, Russian, Spanish (optional), Tagalog	*Good grades received every student in the class.*	*Every student in the class received good grades.*
Verb-subject order in dependent clause	French	*I knew what would propose the committee.*	*I knew what the committee would propose.*

(Continued)

(Continued)

Language Features	Languages	Sample Transfer Errors in English	Edited Version
Verb after subject and object	Bengali, German (in dependent clause), Hindi, Japanese, Korean, Turkish	*... (when) the teacher the money collected.*	*... (when) the teacher collected the money.*
Coordination favored over subordination	Arabic	Frequent use of *and* and *so*	
Relative clause or restrictive phrase precedes noun it modifies	Chinese, Japanese, Korean, Russian	*The enrolled in college student...*	*The student (who was) enrolled in college...*
		A nine-meter-high impressive monument...	*An impressive monument that is nine meters high...*
		He gave me a too difficult for me book.	*He gave me a book that was too difficult for me.*
Adverb can occur between verb and object or before verb	French, Spanish, Urdu (before verb)	*I like very much clam chowder.*	*I like clam chowder very much.*
		They efficiently organized the work.	*They organized the work efficiently.*
That clause rather than an infinitive	Arabic, French, Hindi, Russian, Spanish	*I want that you stay.*	*I want you to stay.*
		I want that they try harder.	*I want them to try harder.*
Inversion of subject and verb (rare)	Chinese	*She is leaving, and so I am.*	*She is leaving, and so am I.*

Language Features	Languages	Sample Transfer Errors in English	Edited Version
Conjunctions occur in pairs	Chinese, Farsi, Vietnamese	*Although she is rich, but she wears simple clothes.* *Even if I had money, I would also not buy that car.*	*Although she is rich, she wears simple clothes.* *Even if I had money, I would not buy that car.*
Subject (especially *it* pronoun) can be omitted	Chinese, Italian, Japanese, Portuguese, Spanish, Thai	*Is raining.*	*It is raining.*
Commas set off a dependent clause	German, Russian	*He knows, that we are right.*	*He knows that we are right.*
No exact equivalent of *there is/there are*	Japanese, Korean, Portuguese, Russian, Thai (adverb of place and *have*)	*This article says four reasons to eat beans.* *In the garden has many trees.*	*This article says [that] there are four reasons to eat beans.* *There are many trees in the garden.*
Nouns, Pronouns, Adjectives, Adverbs (chapters 42, 43, 58)			
Personal pronouns restate subject	Arabic, Gujarati, Spanish (optional)	*My father he lives in California.*	*My father lives in California.*
No human/nonhuman distinction for relative pronoun (*who/which*)	Arabic, Farsi, French, Russian, Spanish, Thai	*Here is the student which you met her last week.* *The people which arrived…*	*Here is the student [whom] you met last week.* *The people who arrived…*
Pronoun object included in relative clause	Arabic, Chinese, Farsi, Hebrew	*The house [that] I used to live in it is big.*	*The house that I used to live in is big.*

(Continued)

(Continued)

Language Features	Languages	Sample Transfer Errors in English	Edited Version
No distinction between subject and object forms of some pronouns	Chinese, Gujarati, Korean, Thai	*I gave the forms to she.*	*I gave the forms to her.* Or *I gave her the forms.*
Nouns and adjectives have same form	Chinese, Japanese	*She is beauty woman.* *They felt very safety on the train.*	*She is a beautiful woman.* *They felt very safe on the train.*
No distinction between *he* and *she, his* and *her*	Bengali, Farsi, Gujarati, Spanish (*his* and *her* only), Thai	*My sister dropped his purse.*	*My sister dropped her purse.*
No plural form after a number	Creole, Farsi	*He has two dog.*	*He has two dogs.*
No plural (or optional) forms of nouns	Chinese, Japanese, Korean, Thai	*Several good book…*	*Several good books…*
No relative pronouns	Korean	*The book is on the table is mine.*	*The book that is on the table is mine.*
Different perception of countable/ uncountable	Japanese, Russian, Spanish	*I bought three furnitures.* *She has red hairs.*	*I bought three pieces of furniture.* Or *I bought three chairs.* *She has red hair.*
Adjectives show number	Russian, Spanish	*I have helpfuls friends.*	*I have helpful friends.*
Negative before verb	Spanish	*Jack no like meat.*	*Jack does not like meat.*
Double negatives used routinely	Spanish	*They don't know nothing.*	*They don't know anything.* Or *They know nothing.*

57e Editing guide to vernacular Englishes

Many of the varieties of English shown in the Circle of English in section 57a differ from what is known as a standard form of the language in their use of words and grammatical conventions. Speakers of these Englishes have to do a kind of translating, called *code switching*, when they speak or write, just as we all switch codes between levels of formality when we interact with different audiences. Consider, for example, situations in which you might say, "'Sup?" ("What's up?") rather than "Good morning." As David Crystal, author of *The Stories of English*, points out, "We need to be very sure of our ground (or very drunk) before we say, 'Yo, Officer.'"

The following table shows some of the common language features that confront speakers of African American Vernacular (AAV), Creole, and other varieties of English in North America when they move back and forth between their home culture and the academic world.

Vernaculars and Standard English

Linguistic Feature of Vernacular	Example (Nonstandard)	Edited for Standard English
Omitted form of *be*	*Maxine studying.*	*Maxine is studying.*
Use of *be* for habitual action	*Ray be working at home.*	*Ray usually works at home.*
Use of *been* without *have*	*I been sleeping all day.*	*I have (I've) been sleeping all day.*
Omitted *-ed*	*The books arrive this morning.*	*The books arrived this morning.*
No *-s* ending for third person singular present tense verb	*That model have a big smile.*	*That model has a big smile.*
No plural form after a plural number	*Jake own two dog.*	*Jake owns two dogs.*
Verb inversion before indefinite pronoun subject	*Can't nobody do that.*	*Nobody can do that.*
They instead of possessive *their*	*The players grabbed they gear.*	*The players grabbed their gear.*
Hisself instead of *himself*	*That musician promote hisself too much.*	*That musician promotes himself too much.*

(Continued)

(Continued)

Linguistic Feature of Vernacular	Example (Nonstandard)	Edited for Standard English
Personal pronoun restates subject	*His instructor, she strict.*	*His instructor is strict.*
No apostrophe + -s for possessive	*She my brother wife.*	*She is my brother's wife.*
It used in place of *there*	*It's a gate at the entrance.*	*There is (There's) a gate at the entrance.*
Double negative	*You don't know nothing.*	*You don't know anything.* Or *You know nothing.*

57f Tips for multilingual writers

Get help   Use the resources available at your college. Librarians and Writing Center tutors are there to assist you. Don't be afraid to ask. And make sure that you go to your instructor during assigned office hours to get advice and clarification on any of the assignments and on your progress in the course.

Participate in class   It isn't always easy to join a discussion with a group of students who speak English fluently, but if you prepare well for class, you will find that your fellow students will be eager to hear the comments and observations of somebody who knows more than one language and has lived in more than one country. In class or in a group, listen attentively to others and offer informative responses. Your instructor and classmates will be delighted to hear comments from a cross-cultural perspective.

Follow the conventions   Be aware of the conventions associated with writing papers in North America. Readers expect you to take a stand on a controversial issue, and they value direct expression of your opinions, authoritatively backed up by appropriately cited evidence. Academic readers will expect you to express your point of view clearly in a thesis statement somewhere close to the beginning of your paper and back up your claim with concrete points of evidence. Some students find that making an outline helps with organizing a paper. See section 2d for sample outlines.

Don't lapse into informality and slang   It is often difficult for learners of a language to decide exactly how and when to use the new language forms they hear and read. By all means, try out new words and expressions, but do so in safe situations before you use them in an academic setting where they might be inappropriate or even cause offense. When you are in doubt about whether you should use a new expression, check its connotations first with a friend, tutor, or your instructor.

Keep a learning log   In a notebook or a computer file, keep a log of language errors that your instructor or peer editors comment on. If you enter in your log a sentence with an error and then correct the error there on the page, you will create a record of your own editing and learning. In addition, keep special logs of prepositions (rely *on*, afraid *of*) and of idioms, those expressions that defy rules and follow no patterns, such as *burn up* and *burn down*.

Consult learners' dictionaries   Make use of an English dictionary specifically designed for multilingual writers, such as *Cambridge Advanced Learner's Dictionary* or *Oxford ESL Dictionary for Students of American English*. Such dictionaries provide useful information to language learners, including example sentences.

Learn from Web sites   Use sites specially designed for language learners, such as the ones listed on page 548. In addition, go to *Activities for ESL Students* at <http://a4esl.org>, which includes quizzes and crossword puzzles in English as well as bilingual quizzes in more than forty languages.

Acknowledge sources   In some cultures, the citing of classic, often memorized texts without acknowledgment of the exact source is accepted and common. However, academic conventions in North America require all writers to cite their sources of information other than the common knowledge of dates and events in the lives of public figures. Failing to do so can lead to a serious charge of academic plagiarism. Whatever you do, always cite your sources to avoid plagiarism. For more on the important issues of textual ownership and plagiarism, go to 9a–9c.

58 Nouns and Articles

58a Categories of nouns

Nouns in English fall into two categories: proper nouns and common nouns. A *proper noun* names a unique person, place, or thing and begins with a capital letter: *Walt Whitman, Lake Superior, Grand Canyon, Vietnam Veterans Memorial, Tuesday* (51b, 58f).

A *common noun* names a general class of persons, places, or things and begins with a lowercase letter: *bicycle, furniture, plan, daughter, home, happiness.* Common nouns can be further categorized as countable and uncountable.

- A *countable noun* has a plural form. Countable nouns frequently add *-s* to indicate the plural: *picture, pictures; plan, plans.* Singular countable nouns are used after *a, an, the, this, that, each, every.* Plural countable nouns are used after *the, these, those, many, a few, both, all, some, several.*

- An *uncountable noun* cannot be directly counted. It has no plural form: *furniture, advice, information.* Uncountable nouns are used after *the, this, that, much, some,* and other singular expressions of quantity.

Common Nouns

Countable	Uncountable
tool, hammer (tools, hammers)	equipment
chair, desk (chairs, desks)	furniture
necklace, earring (necklaces, earrings)	jewelry
view, scene (views, scenes)	scenery
tip, suggestion (tips, suggestions)	advice

The concept of countability varies across languages. Japanese, for example, makes no distinction between countable and uncountable nouns. In French, Spanish, and Chinese, the word for *furniture* is a countable noun; in English, it is not. In Russian, the word for *hair* is countable and used in the plural.

58b Uncountable nouns

Some nouns are usually uncountable in English and are commonly listed as such in a language learners' dictionary such as *The American Heritage English as a Second Language Dictionary.* Learn the most common uncountable nouns, and note the ones that end in *-s* but are nevertheless singular:

A *mass made up of parts:* clothing, equipment, furniture, garbage, homework, information, jewelry, luggage, machinery, money, scenery, traffic, transportation

Abstract concepts: advice, courage, education, fun, happiness, health, honesty, information, knowledge

Natural substances: air, blood, cotton, heat, ice, sunshine, water, wood, wool

Diseases: diabetes, influenza, measles

Games: checkers, chess, soccer, tennis

Subjects of study: biology, economics, history, physics

Note the following features of uncountable nouns.

1. An uncountable noun has no plural form:

   ▸ She gave me ~~several~~ informations. [*some* above *several*]

   ▸ The couple bought a lot of new furnitures.

2. An uncountable noun subject is always followed by a singular verb:

   ▸ Their advice ~~are~~ useful. [*is* above *are*]

3. You can give an uncountable noun a countable sense—that is, indicate a quantity of it—by adding a word or phrase that indicates quantity. The noun itself will always remain singular: three pieces of *furniture*, two items of *information*, many pieces of *advice*.

4. Some nouns can be countable in one context and uncountable in another. Always examine the context.

General class (uncountable)

   ▸ He loves *chocolate.* [all chocolate, in whatever form]

   ▸ *Time* flies.

   ▸ He has red *hair.*

A countable item or items

   ▸ She gave him a *chocolate.* [one piece of candy from a box of many chocolates]

   ▸ They are having *a good time.*

   ▸ There is a *long gray hair* on her pillow.

> **KEY POINTS**
> What to Use before an Uncountable Noun

USE

The zero article (generalization)	Furniture is expensive.
The (specific reference)	*The* furniture in the new office is hideous.
This, that	*This* furniture is tacky.
A possessive pronoun: *my, his, their*, etc.	*Their* furniture is modern.
A quantity word: *some, any, much, less, more, most, a little, a great deal (of), all, other* (41i)	She has bought *some* new furniture.

DO NOT USE

A/an (except in phrases *a little* or *a great deal of*)	The room needs ~~a~~ new furniture.
Each, every, another	All furniture ~~Every furniture~~ should be practical.
These, those	That furniture is ~~Those furnitures are~~ elegant.
Numerals: *one, two, three*, etc.	two pieces of furniture. They bought ~~two furnitures.~~
A plural quantity word: *several, many, a few*	a little furniture She took only ~~a few furniture~~ with her to her new apartment.

58c Basic rules for *a*, *an*, and *the*

1. Use *the* whenever a reference to a common noun is specific and unique for both writer and reader (see 58d).

   the
   ▶ He loves museum that Rem Koolhaas designed.

2. Do not use *a* or *an* with a plural countable noun.

   ▶ They cited ~~a~~ reliable surveys.

3. Do not use *a* or *an* with an uncountable noun.

 ▸ He gave a̷ helpful advice.

4. Use *a* before a consonant sound: *a bird, a house, a sonnet.* Use *an* before a vowel sound: *an egg, an ostrich, an hour, an ugly vase.* Take special care with the sounds associated with the letters *h* and *u*, which can have either a consonant or a vowel sound: *a housing project, an honest man; a unicorn, an uprising.*

5. To make a generalization about a countable noun, do one of the following:

 • Use the plural form: *Lions are majestic.*

 • Use the singular with *a* or *an: A lion is a majestic animal.*

 • Use the singular with *the* to denote a classification: *The lion is a majestic animal.*

6. Make sure that a countable singular noun is preceded by an article or by a demonstrative pronoun (*this, that*), a number, a singular word expressing quantity, or a possessive.

 A (Every, That, One, Her) nurse
 ▸ ~~Nurse~~ has a difficult job.
      ^

7. In general, though, note that there are exceptions, use no article with a singular proper noun (*Mount Everest*), and use *the* with a plural proper noun (*the Himalayas*) (see 58f).

58d *The* for a specific reference

When you write a common noun that both you and your readers know refers to one or more specific persons, places, things, or concepts, use the article *the.*

 ▸ I study *the* earth, *the* sun, and *the* moon. [the ones in our solar system]

 ▸ She closed *the* door. [of the room she was in]

 ▸ Her husband took *the* dog out for a walk. [the dog belonging to the couple]

 ▸ *The* song that won *the* prize was written by a first-year student. [a specific song—the one that won a specific prize]

▶ Jorge wrote *a* song last night for his music class assignment.
He was delighted when he was asked to perform *the* song in class.

▶ He bought *the most expensive* bicycle in the store. [A superlative
makes a reference to one specific item.]

58e Which article? Four basic questions to ask

Multilingual writers often have difficulty choosing among the articles *a, an,* and *the* and the *zero article* (no article at all). Languages
vary greatly in their representation of the concepts conveyed by
English articles (see the Editing Guide to Multilingual Transfer
Patterns in 57d). The Key Points box below should provide a useful
guide.

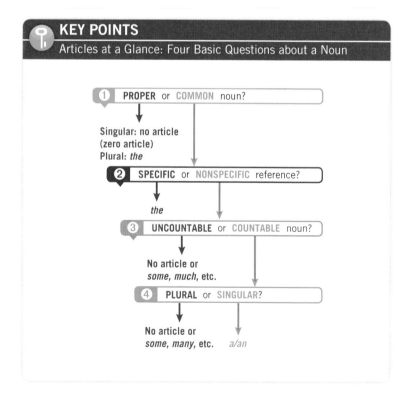

KEY POINTS
Articles at a Glance: Four Basic Questions about a Noun

① **PROPER** or COMMON noun?

Singular: no article
(zero article)
Plural: *the*

② **SPECIFIC** or NONSPECIFIC reference?

the

③ **UNCOUNTABLE** or COUNTABLE noun?

No article or
some, much, etc.

④ **PLURAL** or SINGULAR?

No article or
some, many, etc.   *a/an*

You can use the questions to decide which article, if any, to use with the noun *poem* as you consider the following sentence:

▶ Milton wrote ___?___ moving poem about the blindness that afflicted him before he wrote some of his greatest works.

1. Is the noun (*poem*) a proper noun or a common noun?

Common **Go to question 2.**

2. Does the common noun refer to a specific person, place, thing, or idea known to both writer and reader as unique, or is the reference nonspecific?

Nonspecific [*Poem* is not identified to the reader in the same way that *blindness* is. We know the reference is to the blindness that afflicted Milton before he wrote some of his greatest works. However, there is more than one "moving poem" in literature. The reference would be specific for readers only if the poem had been previously discussed.] **Go to question 3.**

3. Is the noun uncountable or countable?

Countable [We can say *one poem, two poems.*] **Go to question 4.**

4. Is the noun plural or singular?

Singular [The first letter in the noun phrase *moving poem is m*, a consonant sound.] **Use *a* as the article.**

▶ Milton wrote *a* moving poem about the blindness that afflicted him before he wrote some of his greatest works.

58f Proper nouns and articles

Singular proper nouns: Use no article   As a general rule, capitalize singular proper nouns and use no article: *Stephen King, Central America, Africa, Islam, Golden Gate Park, Hollywood Boulevard, Cornell University, Lake Temagami, Mount St. Helens, Thursday, July.* However, note the many exceptions.

EXCEPTIONS: SINGULAR PROPER NOUNS WITH *THE*

Proper nouns with a common noun and *of* as part of the name: *the University of Texas, the Fourth of July, the Museum of Modern Art, the Statue of Liberty*

Highways: *the New Jersey Turnpike, the Long Island Expressway*

Buildings: *the Eiffel Tower, the Prudential Building*

Bridges: *the Golden Gate Bridge*

Hotels and museums: *the Hilton Hotel, the Guggenheim Museum*

Countries named with a phrase: *the United Kingdom, the Dominican Republic, the People's Republic of China*

Parts of the globe: *the North Pole, the West, the East, the Riviera*

Seas, oceans, gulfs, rivers, and deserts: *the Dead Sea, the Atlantic Ocean, the Persian Gulf, the Yangtze River, the Mojave Desert*

Historical periods and events: *the Enlightenment, the October Revolution, the Cold War*

Groups: *the Taliban, the Chicago Seven*

Plural proper nouns: Use *the* Examples are *the United States, the Great Lakes, the Himalayas, the Philippines, the Chinese* (people) (51b).

59 Verbs and Verb Forms

A clause needs a complete verb consisting of one of the five verb forms (39a) and any necessary auxiliaries. Forms derived from a verb (*verbals*) cannot serve as the main verb of a clause; such forms are an *-ing* form, a past participle (ending in *-ed* for a regular verb), or an infinitive (*to* + base form). Because readers get so much information from verbs, they have a relatively low level of tolerance for error, so make sure you edit with care and use auxiliary verbs whenever necessary.

59a The *be* auxiliary

Inclusion The *be* auxiliary must be included in a verb phrase in English, though in languages such as Chinese, Russian, and Arabic it can be omitted (see also 39c).

are
▶ They studying this evening.

been
▶ They have studying since dinner.

Sequence   What comes after a *be* auxiliary? (see also 39c)

- The *-ing* form follows a verb in the active voice: He *is sweeping* the floor.
- The past participle follows a verb in the passive voice: The floor *was swept* yesterday.

59b Modal auxiliary verbs: Form and meaning

The nine modal auxiliary verbs are *will, would, can, could, shall, should, may, might,* and *must.* Note the following three important points.

1. The modals do not change form.
2. The modals never add an *-s* ending.
3. The form immediately following a modal is always a base form of a verb without *to: could go, should ask, must arrive, might have* seen, *would be* sleeping.

▸ The committee must t̶o̶ vote tomorrow.

▸ The proposal might improve̶s̶ the city.

▸ The residents could disapprove̶d̶.

Meanings of Modal Verbs

Meaning	Present and Future	Past
1. Intention	*will, shall*	*Would*
	She *will* explain. [*Shall* is used mostly in questions: *Shall I buy that big green ceramic horse?*]	She said that she *would* explain.
2. Ability	*can (am/is/are able to)*	*could (was/were able to)*
	He *can* cook well. [Do not use *can* and *able to* together: *He is able to cook well.*]	He *could* not read until he was eight. [He was not able to read until he was eight.]
3. Permission	*may, might, can, could*	*might, could*
	May I refer to Auden again? [*Might* or *could* is more tentative.]	Her instructor said she *could* use a dictionary.

(Continued)

(Continued)

Meaning	Present and Future	Past
4. Polite question	*would, could* *Would* readers please indulge me for a moment? *Could* you try not to read ahead?	
5. Speculation	*would, could, might* If he had more talent, he *could* become a professional pianist. [See also 39j.]	*would* or *could* or *might* + *have* + past participle If I had studied, I *might have* passed the test.
6. Advisability	*should* You *should* go home and rest.	*should* + *have* + past participle You *should have* taken your medication. [Implied here is "but you did not."]
7. Necessity (stronger than *should*)	*must* (or *have to*) Applicants *must* apply for a mortgage.	*had to* + base form Theo van Gogh *had to* support his brother.
8. Prohibition	*must* + *not* Participants *must not* leave until all the questions have been answered.	
9. Expectation	*should* The author *should* receive a check soon.	*should* + *have* + past participle You *should have* received your check a week ago.

Meaning	Present and Future	Past
10. Possibility	*may, might*	*might* + *have* + past participle
	The technician *may* be working on the problem now.	She *might* already *have* revised the ending.
11. Logical assumption	*must*	*must* + *have* + past participle
	She's late; she *must* be stuck in traffic.	She *must have* taken the wrong route.
12. Repeated past action		*would* (or *used to*) + base form
		When I was a child, I *would* spend hours drawing.

59c Infinitive after verbs and adjectives

Some verbs are followed by an infinitive (*to* + base form) or a base form alone. Some adjectives also occur with an infinitive. Such combinations are highly idiomatic. You need to learn each one individually as you come across it in your reading.

Verb + infinitive   These verbs are commonly followed by an infinitive (*to* + base form):

agree	choose	fail	offer	refuse
ask	claim	hope	plan	venture
beg	decide	manage	pretend	want
bother	expect	need	promise	wish

Note any differences between English and your native language. For example, in Spanish, the word for *refuse* is followed by the equivalent of an *-ing* form. In English, you need *to* + the base form.

▸ He refused ~~criticizing~~ the system.
        to criticize

Position of a negative   In a verb + infinitive pattern, the position of the negative affects meaning. Note the difference in meaning that the position of a negative (*not, never*) can create.

▶ He did *not* decide to buy a new car. His wife did.

▶ He decided *not* to buy a new car. His wife was disappointed.

Verb + noun or pronoun + infinitive   Some verbs are followed by a noun or pronoun and then an infinitive. See also 42a (p. 475) for a pronoun used before an infinitive.

V   pron.   ⌐inf.⌐

▶ The librarian *advised them to use* a better database.

Verbs that follow this pattern are *advise, allow, ask, cause, command, convince, encourage, expect, force, help, need, order, persuade, remind, require, tell, urge, want, warn*.

   Spanish and Russian use a *that* clause after verbs like *want*. In English, however, *want* is followed by an infinitive.

to

▶ Rose wanted ~~that~~ her son ~~would~~ become a doctor.

Make, let, and have   After these verbs, use a noun or pronoun and a base form of the verb (without *to*).

▶ He *made his son practice* for an hour.

▶ They *let us leave* early.

▶ The editor *had her secretary write* the rejection letter.

Note the corresponding passive voice structure with *have:*

▶ She usually *has the car washed* once a month.

Adjective + infinitive   Some adjectives are followed by an infinitive. The filler subject *it* often occurs with this structure.

infinitive

▶ It is dangerous to hike alone in the woods.

These are some of the adjectives that can be followed by an infinitive: *anxious, correct, dangerous, eager, essential, foolish, happy, (im)possible, (in)advisable, likely, lucky, powerless, proud, right, silly, sorry, (un)fair, (un)just, (un)kind, (un)necessary, wrong*.

▶ They were foolish to think they could climb to the top of the mountain.

59d Verbs followed by an -*ing* verb form used as a noun

▶ I can't help *laughing* at Jon Stewart.

The verbs that are systematically followed by an -*ing* form (known as a *gerund*) make up a relatively short and learnable list.

admit	consider	enjoy	miss	resist
appreciate	delay	finish	postpone	risk
avoid	deny	imagine	practice	suggest
be worth	discuss	keep	recall	tolerate
can't help	dislike			

           inviting
▶ We considered ~~to invite~~ his parents.

           hearing
▶ Most people dislike ~~to hear~~ cell phones at concerts.

Place a negation between the verb and the -*ing* form:

▶ On weekends, drivers enjoy *not* sitting in traffic jams.

Note: An -*ing* form can also be used as a noun in the subject position of a sentence:

▶ *Swimming* helps people maintain their weight.

59e Verbs followed by an infinitive or an -*ing* verb form

Some verbs can be followed by either an infinitive or an -*ing* verb form (a gerund) with almost no discernible difference in meaning: *begin, continue, hate, like, love, start*.

▶ She loves *cooking*.

▶ She loves *to cook*.

The infinitive and the -*ing* form of a few verbs (*forget, remember, try, stop*), however, signal different meanings:

▶ He remembered *to mail* the letter. [an intention]

▶ He remembered *mailing* the letter. [a past act]

59f *-ing* and *-ed* forms used as adjectives

Both the present participle (*-ing* verb form) and the past participle (ending in *-ed* in regular verbs) can function as adjectives (see 39a and 39g). Each form has a different meaning: The *-ing* adjective indicates that the word modified produces an effect; the past participle adjective indicates that the word modified has an effect produced on it.

▶ The *boring* cook served baked beans yet again. [The cook produces boredom. Everyone is tired of baked beans.]

▶ The *bored* cook yawned as she scrambled eggs. [The cook felt the emotion of boredom as she did the cooking, but the eggs could still be appreciated.]

Produces an Effect	Has an Effect Produced on It
amazing	amazed
amusing	amused
annoying	annoyed
confusing	confused
depressing	depressed
disappointing	disappointed
embarrassing	embarrassed
exciting	excited
interesting	interested
satisfying	satisfied
shocking	shocked
surprising	surprised
worrying	worried

Note: Do not drop the *-ed* ending from a past participle. Sometimes in speech, it blends with a following *t* or *d* sound, but in writing, the *-ed* ending must be included.

▶ I was surprise to see her wild outfit.
                   ^d

▶ The researchers were ~~worry~~ that the results were contaminated.
                                 worried

Sentence Structure and Word Order

60a A subject in every clause

In some languages, a subject can be omitted. In English, you must include a subject in every clause, even just a filler subject such as *there* or *it*.

▶ When the director's business partners lost money, ^there^ were immediate effects on the share prices.

▶ The critics hated the movie because ^it^ was too sentimental.

Do not use *it* to point to a long subject that follows. Put the long subject in the subject position before the verb.

▶ We can say that ~~it~~ does not matter the historical period of the society.

The editing mark here points to reversing the order: We can say that the historical period of the society does not matter.

60b Order of sentence elements

Subject, verb, object Languages vary in their basic word order for the sentence elements of subject (S), verb (V), and direct object (DO). In English, the most commonly occurring sentence pattern is S + V + DO ("Children like candy") (see also 35d).

▶ ~~Good grades received~~ Every ~~every~~ student in the class received good grades.

Expressions of time and place Do not put an adverb or a phrase between the verb and its direct object.

▶ The quiz show host congratulated ~~many times~~ the winner many times.

Descriptive adjective phrases Put a descriptive adjective phrase after, not before, the noun it modifies.

▶ I would go to known only to me places.

60c Direct and indirect objects

Some verbs—such as *give, send, show, tell, teach, find, sell, ask, offer, pay, pass,* and *hand*—can be followed by both a direct object (DO) and an indirect object (IO). The indirect object is the person or thing to whom or to which, or for whom or for which, something is done. It follows the verb and precedes the direct object (35d).

▶ He gave his mother some flowers.

IO — DO

▶ He gave her some flowers.

An indirect object can be replaced with a prepositional phrase that *follows* the direct object:

DO — prepositional phrase

▶ He gave some flowers to his mother.

Some verbs—such as *explain, describe, say, mention,* and *open*—are never followed by an indirect object. Rather, they are followed by a direct object and a prepositional phrase with *to* or *for*:

to me.

▶ She explained ~~me~~ the election process.

Note that *tell*, but not *say*, can take an indirect object.

told

▶ She ~~said~~ him the secret.

60d Direct and indirect quotations and questions

The sentence structure and word order you use relates directly to whether your quotations and questions are direct or indirect.

In a direct quotation or direct question, the exact words used by the speaker are enclosed in quotation marks. In an indirect quotation or indirect question, commonly used in expository writing, the writer reports what the speaker said, and quotation marks are not used. Changes also occur in pronouns, time expressions, and verb tenses. See also 38d and 39i for problems to avoid with shifts and with the use of tenses.

direct quotation

▶ He said, "I have forgotten my password."

indirect quotation

▶ He said that he had forgotten his password.

▸ He asked, "Do you know it?"

<small>┌— direct question —┐</small>

▸ He asked if anyone knew it.

<small>┌— indirect question —┐</small>

Direct and indirect quotations Usually, you must make several changes when you report a direct quotation as an indirect quotation. You will do this often when you write college papers and report the views of others.

Note: Style guides vary in the tenses they recommend for reporting the words of others, so in formal research papers, always follow the style of the discipline (chapter 5) for reporting authors' words.

Be careful to avoid shifting randomly between direct and indirect quotations (38d). For expository writing in college essays, as a general rule use indirect rather than direct quotation. However, to make a significant point, a direct quotation can pack a punch.

Direct and Indirect Quotations

Change	Direct/ Indirect Quotation	Example	Explanation
Punctuation and tense	Direct	Oscar Wilde said of his era, "Whatever *is* popular *is* wrong."	Exact words within quotation marks
	Indirect	Oscar Wilde said of his era that whatever *was* popular *was* wrong.	No quotation marks; tense change (39i)
Pronoun and tense	Direct	He insisted, "*I understand* the figures."	First person pronoun and present tense
	Indirect	He insisted that *he understood* the figures.	Change to third person pronoun; tense change

(Continued)

(Continued)

Change	Direct/ Indirect Quotation	Example	Explanation
Command to statement	Direct	"Cancel the payment," her lawyer said.	
	Indirect	Her lawyer *advised* her *to* cancel the payment.	Verb (*tell, instruct*) + *to*
Expressions of time, place, and tense	Direct	The bankers promised, "We *will* work on *this* deal *tomorrow.*"	
	Indirect	The bankers promised *they would* work on *that* deal *the next day.*	Expressions of time and place not related to speaker's perspective; tense change (39i); change to third person pronoun
Colloquial to formal	Direct	The clients said, "Well, no thanks; *we won't* wait."	
	Indirect	The clients thanked the bankers but said *they would not* wait.	Spoken words and phrases omitted or rephrased; also a tense change

The sample essays in this book in parts 1, 3, and 4, show examples of direct and reported quotation from sources.

Direct and indirect questions When a direct question is reported indirectly in writing, it loses the word order of a question (V + S) and the question mark. Sometimes, changes in tense are necessary too (see also 39i).

Direct question

                   V   S

The buyer asked, "*Are* the goods ready to be shipped?"

Indirect question

                          S   V
The buyer asked if the goods *were* ready to be shipped.

Direct question

                            V   S
The boss asked, "What *are* they doing?"

Indirect question

                              S   V
The boss asked what they *were* doing.

Direct question

                      V   S   V
"Why *did* they *send* a letter instead of an e-mail?" her secretary asked.

Indirect question

                              S   V   V
Her secretary asked why they [*had*] *sent* a letter instead of an e-mail.

Use only a question word such as *why* or the word *if* or *whether* to introduce an indirect question. Do not use *that* as well.

▶ Her secretary asked ~~that~~ why they had sent a letter instead of an e-mail.

Direct and Indirect Questions

	Introductory Words	Auxiliary Verb	Subject	Auxiliary Verb(s)	Main Verb and Rest of Clause
Direct	What	are	they		thinking?
Indirect	Nobody knows what		they	are	thinking.
Direct	Where	does	he		work?
Indirect	I can't remember where		he		works.
Direct	Why	did	she		write that poem?
Indirect	The poet does not reveal why		she		wrote that poem.

(Continued)

(Continued)

	Introductory Words	Auxiliary Verb	Subject	Auxiliary Verb(s)	Main Verb and Rest of Clause
Direct		Have	the diaries	been	published yet?
Indirect	The Web site does not say if (whether)		the diaries	have been	published yet.
Direct		Did	the space program		succeed?
Indirect	It is not clear if		the space program		succeeded.

60e Clauses beginning with *although* and *because*

In some languages, a subordinating conjunction (such as *although* or *because*) can be used along with a coordinating conjunction (*but, so*) or a transitional expression (*however, therefore*) in the same sentence. In English, only one is used.

No   *Although* he loved his father, *but* he did not have much opportunity to spend time with him.

Possible revisions   *Although* he loved his father, he did not have much opportunity to spend time with him.

He loved his father, *but* he did not have much opportunity to spend time with him.

No   *Because* she had been trained in the church, *therefore* she was sensitive to the idea of audience.

Possible revisions   *Because* she had been trained in the church, she was sensitive to the idea of audience.

She had been trained in the church, *so* she was sensitive to the idea of audience.

She had been trained in the church; *therefore*, she was sensitive to the idea of audience.

See 45e for punctuation with transitional expressions.

60f Unnecessary pronouns

Do not restate the simple subject of a sentence as a pronoun (see also 38i).

▸ Visitors to the Statue of Liberty ~~they~~ have worn the steps down.

▸ The counselor who told me about dyslexia ~~he~~ is a man I will never forget.

In a relative clause introduced by *whom, which*, or *that*, do not include a pronoun that the relative pronoun has replaced (see also 44d).

▸ The house that I lived in ~~it~~ for ten years has been sold.

60g Order of adjectives

Put adjectives after an article (*a, an, the*), a numeral (such as *four*), or a possessive (such as *my, his*). Cumulative adjectives cannot have the word *and* inserted between them as each modifies the whole noun phrase that follows it. With cumulative adjectives, follow the conventional sequence before the head noun: (1) size, (2) shape, (3) age, (4) color, (5) region or geographical origin, (6) architectural style or religion, (7) material, (8) noun used as adjective to modify the head noun.

      1   3   5   7   head noun

▸ the big old Italian stone house

        2   4   6   8   head noun

▸ our rectangular green Art Deco storage chest

Do not use commas between cumulative adjectives. For punctuation with other types of adjectives (coordinate adjectives), see 45g.

61 Prepositions and Idioms

Prepositions appear in phrases with nouns and pronouns, and they also combine with adjectives and verbs in specific and set ways, as illustrated in 61a–61e. An idiom is a group of words that takes on a special, not necessarily literal, meaning, such as "kick the bucket" (die) and "smell a rat" (suspect). Learn idioms like these one by one as you come across them, and keep your own list.

61a Expressions with three common prepositions

Learn the uses of prepositions by writing them in lists when you come across them in your reading. Here is a start:

IN + YEAR, MONTH, PART OF DAY, STATE, COUNTRY, CITY, LANGUAGE, ETC.

in 2009, in July, in the morning, in Ohio, in the United States, in Milwaukee, in Spanish, in the drawer, in the closet, in the cookie jar, in the library stacks, in a book, in the rain, in his pocket, in bed, in school, in class, in time (to participate in an activity), in the envelope, in the newspaper, in love

ON + DAY, DATE, STREET NAME, ETC.

on Saturday, on 9 September, on Union Street, on the weekend, on the moon, on Earth, on the menu, on the library shelf, on the roof, a ring on her finger, an article on education, on occasion, on time (punctual), on foot, on the couch, knock on the door, the address on the envelope

AT + TIME, ETC.

at eight o'clock, at home, at a party, at night, at work

61b Adjective + preposition

When you are writing, use a dictionary to check the specific prepositions used with an adjective.

▶ The botanist is *afraid of* spiders.

▶ E. O. Wilson was *interested in* ants.

Some adjective + preposition combinations are *afraid of, ashamed of, aware of, fond of, full of, jealous of, proud of, suspicious of, tired of, interested in, grateful to* (someone), *grateful for* (something), *responsible to* (someone), *responsible for* (something), *anxious about, content with,* and *satisfied with.*

61c Verb + preposition

Some idiomatic verb + preposition combinations are *apologize to* (someone), *apologize for* (an offense or error), *arrive in* (a country or city), *arrive at* (a building or an event), *blame* (someone) *for* (an offense or error), *complain about, concentrate on, congratulate* (someone) *on* (success or good fortune), *consist of, depend on, explain* (facts) *to* (someone), *insist on, laugh at, rely on, smile at, take care of, thank* (someone) *for* (a gift or favor), *throw* (an object) *to* (someone waiting to catch it), *throw* (an object) *at* (someone not expecting it), and *worry about.* Keep a list of others you notice.

61d Phrasal verbs

Prepositions and a few adverbs (such as *away* and *forward*) can combine with verbs in such a way that they no longer function as prepositions or ordinary adverbs. They are then known as *particles.* Only a few languages other than English—Dutch, German, and Swedish, for example—have this verb + particle (preposition or adverb) combination, which is called a *phrasal verb.*

The meaning of a phrasal verb is entirely different from the meaning of the verb alone. Note the idiomatic meanings of some common phrasal verbs.

break down [stop functioning]	get over [recover from]
	put up with [tolerate, endure]
put off [postpone]	run across [meet unexpectedly]
run out [become used up]	take after [resemble]
look into [examine]	

Always check the meanings of such verbs in a specialized dictionary such as *The American Heritage English as a Second Language Dictionary.*

A particle can be followed by a preposition to make a three-word combination:

▶ She *gets along with* everybody. [She is friendly toward everybody.]

Other three-word verb combinations are

catch up with [draw level with]	look up to [admire]
look down on [despise]	put up with [endure]
look forward to [anticipate]	stand up for [defend]

Position of direct objects with two-word phrasal verbs   Some two-word transitive phrasal verbs are separable. The direct object of these verbs can come between the verb and the accompanying particle.

▶ She *put off* her dinner party. [She postponed her dinner party.]

▶ She *put* her dinner party *off.*

When the direct object is a pronoun, however, always place the pronoun between the verb and the particle.

▶ **She *put* it *off*.**

Some commonly used phrasal verbs that follow that principle are listed here. They *can* be separated by a noun as a direct object, but they *must* be separated when the direct object is a pronoun.

call off [cancel]	give up [surrender]	make up [invent]
fill out [complete]	leave out [omit]	turn down [reject]
find out [discover]	look up [locate]	turn off [stop]

Most dictionaries list phrasal verbs that are associated with a particular verb along with their meanings and examples. Develop your own list of such verbs from your reading.

61e Preposition + -*ing* verb form used as a noun

The -*ing* verb form that functions as a noun (the *gerund*) frequently occurs after a preposition.

▶ **They congratulated him *on winning* the prize.**

▶ **The school principal expressed interest *in participating* in the fundraiser.**

▶ **He ran three miles *without stopping*.**

▶ **The cheese is the right consistency *for spreading*.**

Note: Take care not to confuse *to* when used as a preposition with *to* used in an infinitive. When *to* is a preposition, it is followed by an object—a noun, a pronoun, a noun phrase, or an -*ing* verb form, not by the base form of a verb.

┌ infinitive ┐
▶ **They want *to adopt* a child.**

preposition + -*ing* form (gerund)
▶ **They are looking forward *to adopting* a child.**

Determine which to use by testing whether a noun replacement fits the sentence:

▶ **They are looking forward to *parenthood*.**

Note also *be devoted to, be/get used to* (see 62h).

62 Language Learners' FAQs

These are commonly asked questions. For more on sentence-level topics, see parts 7 and 8.

62a When do I use *no* and *not*?

Not is an adverb that negates a verb, an adjective, or another adverb. *No* is an adjective and therefore modifies a noun.

▶ She is *not* wealthy.

▶ She is *not* really poor.

▶ The author does *not* intend to deceive the reader.

▶ The author has *no* intention of deceiving the reader.

62b What is the difference between *too* and *very*?

Both *too* and *very* intensify an adjective or adverb, but they are not interchangeable. *Too* indicates excess. *Very* indicates degree and means "extremely."

▶ It was *very* hot.

▶ It was *too* hot to sit outside. [*Too* occurs frequently in the pattern *too* + adjective or adverb + *to* + base form of verb.]

▶ The Volvo was *very* expensive, but he bought it anyway.

▶ The Volvo was *too* expensive, so he bought a Ford instead.

62c Does *few* mean the same as *a few*?

A few is the equivalent of *some*. *Few* is the equivalent of *hardly any*; it has more negative connotations than *a few*. Both expressions are used with countable plural nouns. Although *a* is not generally used with plural nouns, the expression *a few* is an exception.

some
▶ She feels fortunate because she has *a few* helpful colleagues.

hardly any
▶ She feels depressed because she has few helpful colleagues.

You might prefer to use only the more common *a few* and use *hardly any* in sentences where the context demands *few*. Similar expressions used with uncountable nouns are *little* and *a little*.

> ⌐ some ¬
> ▶ She has *a little* time to spend on work-related projects.

> hardly any
> ▶ She has *little* time to spend on recreation.

62d How do I distinguish *most*, *most of*, and *the most*?

Most expresses a generalization, meaning "nearly all."

> ▶ *Most* young children like ice cream.

When a word like *the, this, these, that*, or *those* or a possessive pronoun (such as *my, their*) precedes the noun to make it specific, *most of* is used. The meaning is "nearly all of."

> ▶ Her secretary wrote *most of* the report.

> ▶ *Most of his colleagues* work long hours.

The most is used to compare more than two people or items.

> ▶ Bill is *the most* efficient of all the technicians.

62e What structures are used with *easy*, *hard*, and *difficult*?

The adjectives *easy*, *hard*, and *difficult* cause problems for speakers of Japanese and Chinese. All of the following patterns are acceptable in English.

> ▶ It is *difficult* for some people to learn a new language.

> ▶ It is *difficult* to learn a new language.

> ▶ To learn a new language isn't *easy*.

> ▶ Learning a new language is *hard* for some people.

> ▶ Learning a language can be *difficult*.

> ▶ Her students find it *difficult* to learn Chinese.

However, a sentence like the following needs to be edited in English into one of the patterns listed above or as follows:

> think it is
> ▶ I ~~am~~ *easy* to learn a new language.
> ⌃

62f How do I use *it* and *there* to begin a sentence?

Use *there* to indicate that something exists (or existed) or happens (or happened) (see also 29b).

> There
> ► ~~It~~ was a royal wedding in London in April, 2011.

> There
> ► ~~It~~ is a tree on the corner of my block.

Use *it* for weather, distance, time, and surroundings.

> ► It is a long way to Tipperary.

> ► It is hot.

Use *it* also in expressions such as *it is important, it is necessary,* and *it is obvious*, emphasizing the details that come next (see also 29b).

> ► It is essential for all of you to sign your application forms.

It or *there* cannot be omitted as a filler subject.

> it
> ► As you can see, is dark out already.

62g Which possessive adjective do I use: *His* or *her*?

In English and some other languages, the form of the adjective used to indicate possession changes according to the gender of the noun that precedes it.

> ► Mary and *her* mother

> ► Peter and *his* mother

> ► Peter and *his* father

Note that Spanish uses one possessive adjective (*su*) for both *his* and *her*, with the gender inferred from the antecedent:

> ► Maria y su madre.

> ► Pedro y su madre.

> ► Pedro y su padre.

In French, however, *son* or *sa* can both mean "his" or "her," with the gender determined not by the noun that *son* or *sa* refers back to but by the word that follows the possessive adjective:

▶ **Marie et sa mère** [Marie and her mother]

▶ **Pierre et sa mère** [Pierre and his mother]

▶ **Pierre et son père** [Pierre and his father]

With all this variability across languages, if English is not your native language, always check your writing for the accurate use of *his* and *her*.

62h What is the difference between *be/get used to* and *used to*?

For multilingual writers of English, understanding the distinction between *used to* + base form and *be/get used to* + *-ing* (gerund) is difficult.

▶ **The bankers *used to eat* lunch at a fancy restaurant.** [They don't any more.]

▶ **Now they are *getting used to eating* lunch in the cafeteria.** [They are getting accustomed to it.]

Exercises on Writing across Languages and Cultures

EXERCISE 1   Identify transfer errors.   `57d`

From samples of your writing marked by instructors, gather examples of transfer errors that you know you need to be aware of. Use a language notebook or blog to keep a list of transfer errors that you make, with an edited version (see p. XX).

EXERCISE 2   Use proper and common nouns.   `58a`

Decide which nouns are proper and which are common. Then edit these sentences so that all the proper nouns are capitalized and the common nouns are lowercased.

> Example   The store on ~~hudson street~~ has slashed its prices on ~~Clothing,~~
>
> Hudson Street   clothing,
>
> ~~Sunglasses,~~ and French perfume.
>
> sunglasses,

1. Have you seen Stores with Signs saying "Going out of business" and "Everything must go"? According to the magazine *consumer reports,* some of these Stores may not offer real Bargains.
2. Many stores bring in a Company that specializes in selling off Stock, says *the washington Post.* This second company, known as a *liquidator,* may jack up the prices in order to make a Profit.
3. When the circuit city chain went bankrupt, liquidators charged up to 100 Percent more than the store's Regular Prices.
4. *Time* magazine reporter brad tuttle writes that Investigators who visited a closing sale at a Borders store in new york city found Prices higher than they were before the Sale.
5. Usually, a Customer cannot return anything bought at a Liquidation Sale. Be sure you really want the Item and are not just reacting to the false promise of a Bargain.

EXERCISE 3   Use uncountable nouns correctly.   `58b`

Correct any errors in the use of countable and uncountable nouns. Remember to check for subject-verb agreement when correcting errors.

>   paper   pieces   was
>
> Example   Until about 1810, ~~papers~~ made from ~~piece~~ of cloth ~~were~~ used
>
> for printing books.

1. In most cases, the page of books made before 1840 is still flexible and well preserved.
2. Between 1840 and 1950, however, publishers began to use less expensive paper that was made from wood pulps instead of from cloth.

EXERCISES

3. To turn wood into paper, manufacturers added acidic chemicals that could break down and soften the wood. The pages created from these paper still contained some of the acid.
4. The pages of many books printed between 1840 and 1950 are beginning to crumble into dusts because acid is eating away the wood fiber in the pages.
5. The Library of Congress, which owns a huge collection of books, has begun to soak books made with acid paper in chemical bath to remove any remaining acid from the pages; books treated in this way can last for another several hundred years.

EXERCISE 4 Use articles, including *the*, correctly. `58c, 58d`

In each of the following sentences, correct any errors in article use.

Example   Many inactive people suffer from ~~the~~ depression.

1. Many scientific studies have proved that exercise helps the people sleep better and lose a weight.
2. A active lifestyle seems to improve not only a person's health but also his or her mood.
3. Endorphins, which are chemicals in human brain that are linked to feelings of well-being, increase when people get the enough exercise.
4. People who do not exercise are twice as likely as active people to suffer a symptoms of depression.
5. However, the scientists are not certain whether people do not exercise because they are depressed or whether they are depressed because they do not exercise.

EXERCISE 5 Use nouns and articles correctly. `58f`

In the following passage, correct any errors in article use.

Name of Emmanual "Toto" Constant may not be familiar to everyone in United States, but to Haitian immigrants in this country, he is familiar and controversial figure. Constant, the son of an powerful Haitian military leader, was raised as a aristocrat in the impoverished Caribbean nation. In 1991, he formed political party known as FRAPH. Purpose of FRAPH was to fight against return of exiled president Jean-Bertrande Aristide, whom most poor Haitians supported as a their leader. FRAPH men, armed with the machine guns and machetes, roamed country, terrorizing Aristide supporters with torture, rape, and murder. Constant encouraged Haitians to fear him, claiming that he had the voodoo powers. Observers from United Nations said that FRAPH had been "linked to assassinations and rapes," and a American military official in Haiti warned that FRAPH was turning into "a sort of Mafia."

Even after a American peacekeeping force helped Aristide return to power in the 1994, Toto Constant remained the powerful man in Haiti. He apparently cooperated with an American intelligence officers, revealing details about his group's terrorist activities. Somehow, Toto Constant got out of Haiti and migrated to the New York, where he lived in an Haitian immigrant neighborhood and became real estate broker. Many of his neighbors recognized a face of Toto Constant.

In 2000, the most Haitian immigrants in New York wanted Toto Constant deported to Haiti. A trials were being held there to determine if he and other FRAPH members were guilty of the murder and torture. Although Constant did not return to Haiti, the Haitian court convicted him of murder and sentenced him to the life imprisonment. However, Constant remained free, and United States Immigration and Naturalization Service did not deport him. In 2001, after terror attacks on New York City, Haitians in a city demanded that the United States stop sheltering man who had terrorized his own people. As 2011 began, Constant was serving prison term of twelve to thirty-seven years in United States for the mortgage fraud, and he had still not returned to Haiti.

EXERCISE 6 Use the *be* auxiliary and modal auxiliary verbs correctly. `59a, 59b`

Correct any errors in the use of the *be* auxiliary and modal auxiliaries.

Example   Young people who ~~are~~ learning to play an instrument ~~would~~ *should*

practice if they want to improve.

Most people believe that musicians must to have talent in order to succeed. However, a 1998 study by British psychologist John Sloboda may indicates that the number of hours spent practicing affects musical ability more than inborn talent does. The study included musicians aged ten to sixteen years, from both public and private schools. Sloboda investigated how much each young musician practiced, whether parents and teachers involved in helping each musician improve, and how well each student scored on the British national music examination. Young musicians who had practicing most frequently were most successful on the exam; students whose parents and teachers working closely with them also received high scores. After looking at the exam results, Sloboda cannot help noticing that the students with the highest scores practiced eight hundred times more than the students with the lowest scores. Sloboda believes that individual differences in musical ability would be related to the amount students practice and the amount of support they get from teachers and parents. According to Sloboda's research, even people who do not believe they have musical talent became excellent musicians if they practiced hard enough.

EXERCISE 7 Use verbs and adjectives followed by infinitives and *-ing* or *-ed* forms. `59c–59f`

Example   A ~~respecting~~ *respected* pop singer was ~~sentence~~ *sentenced* to twenty days of

community service.

1. The United States Constitution prohibits force someone to work, except as punishment for a crime. Therefore, the corrections system can make criminals to provide labor without pay.

2. True, some convicted criminals may dislike performing their required tasks. Others may be relieve to have an occupation.

3. Prisoners at the Washington State Corrections Center for Women practice to groom dogs and to train them as service animals. Teams of male prisoners enjoy rehabilitate troubling dogs so that the dogs can be adopted.

4. In California, about 4,300 inmates risk to be injured at their jobs fighting wildfires. Women and juvenile offenders live in fire camps so they can remove brush from the perimeter of a blazed fire to prevent the fire from spread.

5. It is common for celebrities choose work when they wish shortening a jail term. Actor Lindsay Lohan chose working ten days for the American Red Cross to avoid spend more than two days in jail.

EXERCISE 8 Use correct verbs and verb forms. `59 and 39`

In the following passage, correct any errors in verbs and verb forms.

Can money makes people happy? A well-known proverb says, "Money can't buy happiness," but some people probably would to agree that money is important for a happy life. Andrew Oswald and Jonathan Gardner of the University of Warwick in England has investigating the connection between money and happiness over eight years. The results are not surprised. If people suddenly get money that they not expecting—from the lottery, for example—they generally feel more satisfying with their lives.

In general, according to the study, receiving about $75,000 must mean the difference between being fairly happy and being very happy. However, people who admitted to be miserable before they had money needed to get $1.5 million before they considered themselves happy. But Oswald and Gardner advise to recognize that the study is not finished. They not admit knowing whether the happiness from receiving unexpected money lasts for a long time.

People who do not expect getting a large amount of money can find other reasons not to despair. The researchers say that money is not the most important factor in whether a person is happy or not. People who married are happier than those who are not: the researchers estimate that a lasting marriage makes the partners as happy as an extra $100,000 a year can. Perhaps looking for love is as important as trying to make—or win—a large amount of money.

EXERCISE 9 Correct errors in inclusion of a subject, order of elements, direct and indirect objects. `60a–60c`

Correct any errors in the inclusion of a subject, in the order of elements, and in the use of direct and indirect objects. Some sentences may be correct.

Example   In the United States, more people are having ~~every year~~ plastic surgery *every year*

even though are sometimes side effects from the surgery.
            there

1. Cosmetic surgery had in the past a stigma, but now many people consider changing their appearance surgically.

2. In addition, the price of such surgery was once high, but it has declined in recent years.

3. In 2009, cosmetic surgeons 10 million procedures of one kind or other performed.

4. Six percent of those procedures were performed on African Americans, and African Americans represent a growing percentage of wanting plastic surgery people.

5. Cosmetic surgery gives to some people an improved self-image.

6. However, can be drawbacks to changing one's appearance.

7. Psychologists are concerned that some African American women reject their African features because they accept the most commonly seen in magazines standards of beauty.

8. Such women might say, for example, that it is a universal standard of beauty a narrow nose.

9. Some middle-class African Americans may also consider plastic surgery when they see that certain African American celebrities have changed their features.

10. Many psychologists say a patient considering cosmetic surgery that beauty comes from inside.

EXERCISE 10 Rewrite direct quotation as indirect (reported) quotation. 60d

Rewrite the following sentences as indirect (reported) quotation, making any necessary changes. In each case, use the given tag followed by *that, if,* or a question word.

Example "The soup is too spicy." (She complained)
She complained that the soup was too spicy.

1. "I cannot abide such pretentious prose." (The critic announced)
2. "Who is in charge?" (The mayor wanted to know)
3. "What is the square root of 2209?" (The contestant cannot work out)
4. "The economy will rebound." (The broker predicted)
5. "Will I lose all my savings?" (Investors constantly wonder)
6. "I understand the problems." (The candidate assured everyone)
7. "Who knows the answer?" (The game-show host asked)
8. "We will leave early tomorrow." (The guests hinted)
9. "Did my sweater shrink in the wash?" (Her son asked)
10. "We are going to a new French restaurant this evening." (The committee members said)

EXERCISE 11 Use adjectives in the correct order. 60g

In each of the following sentences, make any necessary changes in the order of adjectives and use of commas. Some sentences may be correct.

Example ~~Dark, winter, short~~ days can cause some people to become depressed.
Short, dark winter

1. In northern states in wintertime, many office workers spend most of the daylight hours indoors.

2. Architects are beginning to design some new big buildings to admit as much natural light as possible.

3. A building with features such as skylights, large windows, or an atrium reduces the need for artificial light, but the most one money-saving benefit of outside light is its effect on many workers.

4. A recent architectural study demonstrated that workers in buildings with natural light were happier, more productive employees than workers in dark or artificially lighted offices.

5. Concerned employers can help their office workers maintain a positive outlook through winter dreary months by ensuring that workplaces are brightly lit, preferably with natural light.

EXERCISE 12 Use correct word order and sentence structure. 60a, 60b

Correct any errors in word order, missing words, or sentence structure in the following passage.

Many people fear in China and Japan the number *four*. Is a good reason for this fear: in Japanese, Mandarin, and Cantonese, the word for *four* and the word for *death* are nearly identical. A study in the *British Medical Journal* suggests that cardiac patients from Chinese and Japanese backgrounds they may literally die of fear of the number four. According to the study, which looked at U.S. mortality statistics over a twenty-five-year period, Chinese and Japanese hospitalized for heart disease patients were more likely to die on the fourth day of the month. Although Chinese and Japanese cardiac patients across the country were all statistically more likely to die on that day, but the effect was strongest among Californian Chinese and Japanese patients. Is not clear why Californians are more at risk. However, one researcher suggested that because California's large Asian population includes many older people, the older generation may therefore teach to younger generations traditional beliefs.

Chinese and Japanese patients with other diseases they were no more likely to die on the fourth of the month than at any other time. White patients, whether they had heart disease or any other illness, they were no more likely to die on the supposedly unlucky thirteenth of the month than on any other day. Psychiatrist Jiang Wei of Duke University Medical School said, "She still didn't know the biological reason for the statistical effect" on Chinese and Japanese cardiac patients. David P. Phillips, the sociologist who conducted the study, said that the only explanation that makes sense is that the number four causes extra stress in Chinese and Japanese heart patients. More research may someday prove whether or not the stress on the fourth of the month it can be enough to kill.

EXERCISE 13 Use adjective + preposition, verb + preposition. `61b`, `61c`

In each of the following sentences, correct any errors in the choice of prepositions.

about
Example   Many Americans have been worried ~~from~~ the possibility of biological
                                                              ^

of
terrorism, but some doctors are more afraid ~~from~~ the naturally
                                                                      ^

caused influenza than any biological agent.

1. Although some Americans wanted to take antibiotics as a precaution against anthrax in the fall of 2001, the percentage of people who asked their doctors of flu shots at that time was no higher than normal.
2. Influenza has been responsible to the deaths of many healthy people in the past century, and doctors do not know when a dangerous strain of flu may appear.
3. Doctors in 1918 were unable to prevent the flu epidemic to killing millions of people around the world; more people died of the flu than as a result of World War I that year.
4. Many people may not be aware to the dangers of influenza.
5. Medical specialists are studying genetic samples from people who died with influenza in 1918 to try to find ways to prevent such a deadly flu from reoccurring.

EXERCISE 14 Use prepositions in phrasal verbs. `61d`

Correct the preposition in each phrasal verb. A clue to the verb's meaning appears in brackets.

down   *off*
Example   My car broke ~~off~~ but I kept putting ~~down~~ the repairs.
                                ^   ^

1. When Fran needed to move out from [vacate] her apartment early, she looked onto [researched] subletting the apartment to another student. She checked the details on the application she filled over [completed] when she had moved along [inhabited].
2. Fran looked forward at [anticipated] leaving town without giving in [sacrificing] another month's rent. Luckily, she ran over [met unexpectedly] a classmate who had just found on [discovered] that he was losing his apartment.
3. Unfortunately, the landlord turned around [rejected] the new tenant and called out [cancelled] the deal. Fran gave away [surrendered] trying to sublet the place; she would allow her lease to run away [expire].
4. Because she had put across [delayed] making her arrangements for so long, she would have to put on with [endure] the extra expense.
5. It pained Fran to make down [compensate for] the several hundred dollars she was wasting, but she told herself to get under [recover from] it.

EXERCISE 15 Use preposition + -*ing* form as a noun (gerund). 61e

Edit these sentences so that prepositions are followed by gerunds when appropriate. Do not use the –*ing* form with infinitives.

>   participate   accepting
>
> Example   Many states have decided to ~~participating~~ in a program for ~~accept~~
>
>   tolls electronically.

1. The E-ZPass can save time for U.S. motorists who do a great deal of drive. The pass allows drivers to paying at a toll booth without stop.
2. Upon enroll in E-ZPass, drivers attach an electronic tag to their windshield. Then they set up a prepaid account for cover their toll expenses.
3. After detect the tag, an antenna at the toll station debits the driver's account. If widely used, the pass can prevent long lines from form at the entrance to major highways.
4. The Interagency Group, which oversees E-ZPass, plans on expand the system through the entire I-95 corridor of the eastern U.S.
5. Some states are not averse to implement E-ZPass, but they need time to integrating it with their own toll systems.

EXERCISE 16 Use *no* and *not*, *too* and *very*, *few* and *a few* correctly. 62a–62c

Correct any errors in the use of *no* and *not*, *too* and *very*, or *few* and *a few*.

>   not
>
> Example   A wildfire in a wilderness area is ~~no~~ necessarily a disaster.

1. Natural disasters such as fires, floods, and storms are usually seen as terrible events, but sometimes they have few positive results.
2. For example, a forest with many tall trees may be very dark for new plant growth, but fires can change the situation to allow sunlight to reach the ground.
3. A river that has no flooded for many years collects silt, which often means that a few fish can spawn.
4. Few human attempts to control disasters have been successful, and trying to ensure that not fire or flood can occur often means that fires and floods are more damaging when they do happen.
5. Although many ecologists have found it too difficult to stop trying to prevent natural disasters, they are now working instead to keep disasters from being too devastating.

EXERCISE 17 Use *most*, *most of*, and *the most*. 62d

Correct the phrases that use *most*, *most of*, and *the most* incorrectly.

Example   Obesity is becoming one of ^the^ most dangerous health problems
in the world.

1. Most of Americans would be better off if they lost a little weight. But most the world is now in the same boat.
2. Developing nations such as China and India are seeing most rapid rise in obesity. Most of this increase occurs when people move to cities.
3. Rural lifestyles are often healthier, because people are more active and the most of their food is locally grown.
4. City life means less exercise and more exposure to processed foods, which can be the most of unhealthy.
5. The countries with most obese people are in the South Pacific. Some health experts believe that most that problem is due to an influx of Western-style junk food.

EXERCISE 18 Use *easy*, *hard*, and *difficult*. 62e

Correct the following sentences that use the patterns for *easy, hard,* and *difficult*.

Example   ^It is easy^ ~~Easy~~ for many people with Asperger's to talk at length about a
favorite subject.

1. People with Asperger's syndrome are hard to know what another person is feeling. Reading body language and tone of voice difficult for people with this disorder.
2. Maintaining eye contact during a conversation can also difficult. Easy for people with AS to simply avoid looking at others while they are speaking.
3. While talking about their favorite subjects is often easy, they may be hard for them to join a conversation initiated by someone else.
4. Because of an upcoming change in the way this disorder is defined, people with AS may be more difficult to get the support they need.
5. To raise a child not easy for any parent. To find adequate services for a child with Asperger's a challenge for parents in the next few years.

EXERCISE 19 Use *it* and *there* appropriately. 62f

Correct the use of *there* and *it* in these sentences. Make sure every sentence has a subject.

Example   In my opinion, ^there^ was not enough food at the banquet.

1. It dry and dusty in parts of Oklahoma.
2. Is about five hundred miles from here to Houston.
3. It was a religious festival in my town last weekend.
4. Necessary to bring your passport when you sign up for insurance.
5. If you don't like the movie, is no point in staying to the end.

EXERCISE 20 Use the possessive pronouns *his* and *her*. `62g`

Make sure the gender of each possessive pronoun matches the antecedent elsewhere in the sentence.

Example   Rosa is always losing things in ~~its~~ desk.

                                            her

1. Tomas wants to visit her mother.
2. Adèle needs to call his husband this afternoon.
3. Did Raul show you her aunt's military medals?
4. Sarah drove his daughter's car back home.
5. Gabrielle and his sister are both pregnant.

EXERCISE 21 Use phrasal verbs, preposition + *-ing*, *get used to*,
              and *used to* correctly. `61d–61e, 62h`

Correct any errors in the use of phrasal verbs, gerunds after prepositions, and the phrases *get used to* and *used to*.

Example   AIDS ~~is used to being~~ a death sentence, but more people now

                         used to be

survive for years with the disease.

      Since scientists began to learn about AIDS more than thirty years ago, many people have been counting up a cure for the disease. The cure has not yet been found, but today many people with AIDS in this country used to live with the medications and other treatments that allow them to having a reasonably healthy life. In poorer countries, unfortunately, fewer people can look forward on living with AIDS, but AIDS researchers are excited about a recent discovery in the central African country of Rwanda. In Kigali, Rwanda's capital, a study followed a group of sixteen people who tested positive for HIV more than ten years ago but have neither taken medicine to treating the illness nor gotten sick. In most AIDS patients, the virus breaks out the immune system; in many patients in the Rwandan study, however, the virus shows an unusual mutation that seems to allow the body to put the virus up with. Researchers do not yet know whether this discovery will assist them in find a cure for the AIDS virus, but every new piece of information in this puzzle may be helpful in fight the disease.

10 Glossaries

Check

To obtain study resources for this section, visit the English CourseMate for this text at **www.cengagebrain.com**

PART 10 Glossaries

10 Glossaries

63 Words to Watch For: Glossary of Usage

Listed in this glossary are words that are often confused (*affect/effect*, *elicit/illicit*) or misspelled (*it's/its*). Also listed are nonstandard words (*irregardless*, *theirself*) and colloquial expressions (*OK*) that should be avoided in formal writing.

a, an Use *an* before words that begin with a vowel sound (the vowels are *a, e, i, o,* and *u*): *an apple, an hour* (*h* silent). Use *a* before words that begin with a consonant sound: *a planet, a yam, a ukulele, a house* (*h* pronounced).

accept, except, expect *Accept* is a verb: *She accepted the salary offer.* *Except* is usually a preposition: *Everyone has gone home except my boss.* *Expect* is a verb: *They expect to visit New Mexico on vacation.*

adapt, adopt *Adapt* means "to adjust" and is used with the preposition *to:* *It takes people some time to adapt to the work routine after college. Adopt* means "to take into a family" or "to take up and follow": *The couple adopted a three-year-old child. The company adopted a more aggressive policy.*

adverse, averse *Adverse* is an adjective describing something as hostile, unfavorable, or difficult. *Averse* indicates opposition to something and usually takes the preposition *to: The bus driver was averse to driving in the adverse traffic conditions.*

advice, advise *Advice* is a noun: *Take my advice and don't start smoking. Advise* is a verb: *He advised his brother to stop smoking.*

affect, effect In their most common uses, *affect* is a verb, and *effect* is a noun. To *affect* is to have an *effect* on something: *Pesticides can affect health. Pesticides have a bad effect on health. Effect,* however, can be used as a verb meaning "to bring about": *The administration hopes to effect new health care legislation. Affect* can also be used as a noun in psychology, meaning "a feeling or emotion."

aisle, isle You'll walk down an *aisle* in a supermarket or a church. An *isle* is an island.

all ready, already *All ready* means "totally prepared": *The students were all ready for their final examination. Already* is an adverb meaning "by this time": *He has already written the report.*

all right, alright   *All right* (meaning "satisfactory") is standard. *Alright* is nonstandard. However, *alright* is used in popular culture to mean "wonderful."

all together, altogether   *All together* is used to describe acting simultaneously: *As soon as the boss had presented the plan, the managers spoke up all together.* *Altogether* is an adverb meaning "totally," often used before an adjective: *His presentation was altogether impressive.*

allude, elude   *Allude* means "to refer to": *She alluded to his height. Elude* means "to avoid": *He eluded her criticism by leaving the room.*

allusion, illusion   The noun *allusion* means "reference to": *Her allusion to his height made him uncomfortable.* The noun *illusion* means "false idea": *He had no illusions about being Mr. Universe.*

almost, most   Do not use *most* to mean a*lmost: Almost* [not *Most*] *all my friends are computer literate.*

alot, a lot of, lots of   *Alot* is nonstandard. *A lot of* and *lots of* are regarded by some as informal for *many* or *a great deal of: Students send lots of text messages.*

aloud, allowed   *Aloud* is an adverb meaning "out loud": *She read her critique aloud. Allowed* is a form of the verb *allow: Employees are not allowed to participate in the competition.*

ambiguous, ambivalent   *Ambiguous* is used to describe a phrase or act with more than one meaning: *The ending of the movie is ambiguous; we don't know if the butler really committed the murder. Ambivalent* describes uncertainty and the coexistence of opposing attitudes and feelings: *The committee is ambivalent about the proposal for restructuring the company.*

among, between   Use *between* for two items, *among* for three or more: *I couldn't decide between red or blue. I couldn't decide among red, blue, or green.*

amoral, immoral   *Amoral* can mean "neither moral nor immoral" or "not caring about right or wrong," whereas *immoral* means "morally wrong": *Some consider vegetarianism an amoral issue, but others believe eating meat is immoral.*

amount, number   *Amount* is used with uncountable expressions: *a large amount of money, work, or effort. Number* is used with countable plural expressions: *a large number of people, a number of attempts.* See 58b.

an   See *a.*

ante-, anti- *Ante-* is a prefix meaning "before," as in *anteroom*. *Anti-* means "against" or "opposite," as in *antiseptic* or *antifreeze*.

anyone, any one *Anyone* is a singular indefinite pronoun meaning "anybody": *Can anyone help me? Any one* refers to one from a group and is usually followed by *of* + plural noun: *Any one* [as opposed to any two] *of the suggestions will be acceptable.*

anyplace The standard *anywhere* is preferable.

anyway, anywhere, nowhere; anyways, anywheres, nowheres *Anyway, anywhere,* and *nowhere* are standard forms. The others, ending in *-s,* are not.

apart, a part *Apart* is an adverb: *The old book fell apart. A part* is a noun phrase: *I'd like to be a part of that project.*

as, as if, like See *like.*

as regards See *in regard to.*

assure, ensure, insure All three words mean "to make secure or certain," but only *assure* is used in the sense of making a promise: *He assured us everything would be fine. Ensure* and *insure* are interchangeable, but only *insure* is commonly used in the commercial or financial sense: *We wanted to ensure that the rate we paid to insure our car against theft would not change.*

awful Avoid using *awful* to mean "bad" or "extremely": not *He's awful late,* but *He's extremely late.*

a while, awhile *A while* is a noun phrase: *a while ago; for a while. Awhile* is an adverb meaning "for some time": *They lived awhile in the wilderness.*

bad, badly *Bad* is an adjective, *badly* an adverb. Use *bad* after linking verbs (such as *am, is, become, seem*): *They felt bad after losing the match.* Use *badly* to modify a verb: *They played badly.*

bare, bear *Bare* is an adjective meaning "naked": the *bare* facts, a *bare*-faced lie. *Bear* is a noun (the animal) or a verb meaning "to carry" or "to endure": *He could not bear the pressure of losing.*

barely Avoid creating a double negative (such as *can't barely type*). *Barely* should always take a positive verb: *She can barely type. They could barely keep their eyes open.* See *hardly.*

because, because of *Because* is a subordinating conjunction used to introduce a dependent clause: *Because it was raining, we left early. Because of* is a two-word preposition: *We left early because of the rain.*

being as, being that   Avoid. Use *because* instead: *Because* [not *Being as*] *I was tired, I didn't go to class.*

belief, believe   *Belief* is a noun: *She has radical beliefs. Believe* is a verb: *He believes in an afterlife.*

beside, besides   *Beside* is a preposition meaning "next to": *Sit beside me. Besides* is a preposition meaning "except for": *He has no assistants besides us. Besides* is also an adverb meaning "in addition": *I hate horror movies. Besides, there's a long line.*

better   See *had better.*

between   See *among.*

brake, break   To slow down, we *brake* by applying the *brake(s)* in a car. We can *break* a window or even get a bad *break.*

breath, breathe   *Breath* is a noun, *breathe* a verb: *Take three deep breaths. Breathe in deeply.*

bring, take   Use *bring* to suggest carrying something from a farther place to a nearer one and *take* for any other transportation: *First bring me a cake from the store, and then we can take it to the party.*

can't hardly   This expression is nonstandard. See *hardly.*

censor, censure   The verb *censor* refers to editing or removing from public view. *Censure* means to criticize harshly. *The new film was censored for graphic content, and the director was censured by critics for his irresponsibility.*

cite, site, sight   *Cite* means "to quote or mention"; *site* is a noun meaning "location"; *sight* is a noun meaning "view": *She cited the page number in her paper. They visited the original site of the abbey. The sight of the skyline from the plane produced applause from the passengers.*

compare to, compare with   Use *compare to* when implying similarity: *They compared the director to Alfred Hitchcock.* Use *compare with* when examining similarities or differences: *She wrote an essay comparing Hitchcock with Orson Welles.*

complement, compliment   As verbs, *complement* means "to complete or add to something," and *compliment* means "to make a flattering comment about someone or something": *The wine complemented the meal. The guests complimented the hostess on the fine dinner.* As nouns, the words have meanings associated with the verbs: *The wine was a fine complement to the meal. The guests paid the hostess a compliment.*

compose, comprise   *Compose* means "to make up"; *comprise* means "to include." *The conference center is composed of twenty-five rooms. The conference center comprises twenty-five rooms.*

conscience, conscious   *Conscience* is a noun meaning "awareness of right and wrong": *Conscious* is an adjective meaning "awake" or "aware." *Her conscience troubled her after the accident. The victim was still not conscious.*

continual, continuous   *Continual* implies repetition; *continuous* implies lack of a pause: *The continual interruptions made the lecturer angry. Continuous rain for two hours stopped play.*

could care less   This expression is often used but is regarded by some as nonstandard. In formal English, use it only with a negative: *They could not care less about their work.*

council, counsel   A *council* is a group formed to consult, deliberate, or make decisions. *Counsel* is advice or guidance. *The council was called together to help give counsel to the people. Counsel* can also be a verb: *We counseled the students to withdraw from the course.*

credible, creditable, credulous   *Credible* means "believable": *The jury found the accused's alibi to be credible and so acquitted her. Creditable* means "deserving of credit": *A B+ grade attests to a creditable performance. Credulous* means "easily taken in or deceived": *Only a child would be so credulous as to believe that the streets are paved with gold.* See also *incredible, incredulous.*

criteria, criterion   *Criteria* is the plural form of the singular noun *criterion*: *There are many criteria for a successful essay. One criterion is sentence clarity.*

curricula, curriculum   *Curricula* is the plural form of *curriculum. All the departments have well-thought-out curricula, but the English Department has the best curriculum.*

custom, customs, costume   All three words are nouns. *Custom* means "habitual practice or tradition": *a family custom. Customs* refers to taxes on imports or to the procedures for inspecting items entering a country: *go through customs at the airport.* A *costume* is "a style of dress": *a Halloween costume.*

dairy, diary   *Dairy* is associated with cows and milk, *diary* with a daily journal.

decease, disease   *Decease* is a verb or noun meaning "die" or "death." *Disease* is an illness: *The disease caused an early decease.*

decent, descent, dissent *Decent* is an adjective meaning "good" or "respectable": *decent clothes, a decent salary. Descent* is a noun meaning "way down" or "lineage": *She is of Scottish descent. Dissent,* used both as a noun and a verb, refers to disagreement: *The dissent about freedom led to civil war.*

desert, dessert *Desert* can be pronounced two ways. It can be a noun with the stress on the first syllable (*the Mojave Desert*) or on the second syllable as in the expression derived from the verb "to deserve": *They got their just deserts.* It can also be a verb with the stress on the second syllable meaning "to abandon": *When did he desert his family? Dessert* (with stress on the second syllable) is the sweet course at the end of a meal.

device, devise *Device* is a noun: *He said they needed a device that could lift a car. Devise* is a verb: *She began to devise a solution to the problem.*

different from, different than Standard usage is *different from*: *She looks different from her sister.* However, *different than* appears frequently in speech and informal writing, particularly when *different from* would require more words: *My writing is different than* [in place of *different from what*] *it was last semester.*

differ from, differ with To *differ from* means "to be unlike": *Lions differ from tigers in several ways, despite being closely related.* To *differ with* means to "disagree with": *They differ with each other on many topics but are still good friends.*

discreet, discrete *Discreet* means "tactful": *Be discreet when you talk about your boss. Discrete* means "separate": *He writes on five discrete topics.*

disease See *decease.*

disinterested, uninterested *Disinterested* means "impartial or unbiased": *The mediator was hired to make a disinterested settlement. Uninterested* means "lacking in interest": *He seemed uninterested in his job.*

dissent See *decent.*

do, due *Do* is a verb. Do not write "*Do* to his absences, he lost his job"; instead use the two-word preposition *due to* or *because of. Due* is also an adjective meaning "expected at a certain time": *When will the final payment be due?*

drag, dragged Use *dragged* for the past tense of the verb *drag. Drug* is nonstandard.

drown, drowned The past tense of the verb *drown* is *drowned; drownded* is not a word: *He almost drowned yesterday.*

due to the fact that, owing to the fact that   Wordy. Use *because* instead: *They stopped the game because* [not *due to the fact that*] *it was raining.*

each, every   These are singular pronouns; use them with a singular verb. See also 41h and 42d.

each other, one another   Use *each other* with two; use *one another* with more than two: *The twins love each other. The triplets all love one another.*

effect   See *affect.*

e.g.   Use *for example* or *for instance* in place of this Latin abbreviation.

elicit, illicit   *Elicit* means "to get or draw out": *The police tried in vain to elicit information from the suspect's accomplice. Illicit* is an adjective meaning "illegal": *Their illicit deals landed them in prison.*

elude   See *allude.*

emigrate, immigrate   *Emigrate from* means "to leave a country"; *immigrate to* means "to move to another country": *They emigrated from Ukraine and immigrated to the United States.* The noun forms *emigrant* and *immigrant* are derived from the verbs.

eminent, imminent   *Eminent* means "well known and noteworthy": *an eminent lawyer. Imminent* means "about to happen": *an imminent disaster.*

ensure   See *assure.*

etc.   This abbreviation for the Latin *et cetera* means "and so on." Do not let a list trail off with *etc.* Rather than *They took a tent, a sleeping bag, etc.,* write *They took a tent, a sleeping bag, cooking utensils, and a stove.*

every, each   See *each.*

everyday, every day   *Everyday* (one word) is an adjective meaning "usual": *Their everyday routine is to break for lunch at 12:30. Every day* (two words) is an adverbial expression of frequency: *I get up early every day.*

except, expect   See *accept.*

explicit, implicit   *Explicit* means "direct": *She gave explicit instructions. Implicit* means "implied": *A tax increase is implicit in the proposal.*

farther, further   Both words can refer to distance: *She lives farther (further) from the campus than I do. Further* also means "additional" or "additionally": *The management offered further incentives. Further, the union proposed new work rules.*

female, male   Use these words as adjectives, not as nouns in place of *man* and *woman: There are only three women* [not *females*] *in my class. We are discussing female conversational traits.*

few, a few   *Few* means "hardly any": *She feels depressed because she has few helpful colleagues. A few* means "some"; it has more positive connotations than *few: She feels fortunate because she has a few helpful colleagues.* See 62c.

fewer, less   Formal usage demands *fewer* with plural countable nouns (*fewer holidays*), *less* with uncountable nouns (*less sunshine*). However, in informal usage, *less* with plural nouns commonly occurs, especially with *than: less than six items, less than ten miles, fifty words or less.* In formal usage, *fewer* is preferred.

first, firstly   Avoid *firstly, secondly,* and so on, when listing reasons or examples. Instead, use *first, second.*

flammable, inflammable, nonflammable   Both *flammable* and *inflammable* mean the same thing: able to be ignited easily. *Nonflammable* means "unable to be ignited easily." *Dry wood is flammable,* or *Dry wood is inflammable. Asbestos is nonflammable.*

flaunt, flout   *Flaunt* means "to show [something] off" or "to display in a proud or boastful manner." *Flout* means "to defy or to show scorn for." *When she flaunted her jewels, she flouted good taste.*

former, latter   These terms should be used only in reference to a list of two people or things: *We bought lasagna and rhubarb, the former for dinner and the latter for dessert.* For more than two items, use *first* and *last: I had some pasta, a salad, and rhubarb; though the first was very filling, I still had room for the last.*

get married to, marry   These expressions can be used interchangeably: *He will get married to his fiancée next week. She will marry her childhood friend next month.* The noun form is *marriage: Their marriage has lasted thirty years.*

go, say   Avoid replacing the verb *say* with *go,* as this is nonstandard usage: *Jane says* [not *goes*], *"I'm tired of this game."*

good, well   *Good* is an adjective; *well* is an adverb: *If you want to write well, you must use good grammar.* See 43a.

had better   Include *had* in Standard English, although it is often omitted in advertising and in speech: *You had better* [not *You better*] *try harder.*

hardly   This is a negative word. Do not use it with another negative: not *He couldn't hardly walk,* but *He could hardly walk.*

have, of   Use *have,* not *of,* after *should, could, might,* and *must: They should have* [not *should of*] *appealed.*

height   Note the spelling and pronunciation: not *heighth.*

heroin, heroine   Do not confuse these words. *Heroin* is a drug; *heroine* is a brave woman. *Hero* may be used for an admirable person of either sex.

hisself   Nonstandard; instead, use *himself.*

hopefully   This word is an adverb meaning "in a hopeful manner" or "with a hopeful attitude": *Hopefully, she e-mailed her résumé.* Avoid using *hopefully* in place of *I hope that:* not *Hopefully, she will get the job,* but *I hope that she will get the job.* The former usage is, however, quite common.

I, me   Do not confuse *I* and *me.* Use *I* only in the subject position, and use *me* only in the object position. To check subjects and objects using *and,* simply drop any additional subject or object so that only the pronoun remains: not *The CFO and me were sent to the conference,* but *The CFO and I were sent* (I was sent); not *Please send copies to my secretary and I,* but *Please send copies to my secretary and me* (send copies to me). See 42a.

illicit   See *elicit.*

illusion   See *allusion.*

immigrate   See *emigrate.*

imminent   See *eminent.*

implicit   See *explicit.*

imply, infer   *Imply* means "to suggest in an indirect way": *He implied that further layoffs were unlikely. Infer* means "to guess" or "to draw a conclusion": *I inferred that the company was doing well.*

incredible, incredulous   *Incredible* means "difficult to believe": *The violence of the storm was incredible. Incredulous* means "skeptical, unable to believe": *They were incredulous when he told them about his daring exploits in the whitewater rapids.*

infamous   *Infamous* is an adjective meaning "notorious": *Blackbeard's many exploits as a pirate made him infamous along the American coast.* Avoid using it as a synonym for "not famous."

inflammable   See *flammable.*

in regard to, as regards   Use one or the other. Do not use the nonstandard *in regards to.*

insure   See *assure.*

irregardless   Nonstandard; instead, use *regardless: He selected a major regardless of the preparation it would give him for a career.*

it's, its   The apostrophe in *it's* signals not a possessive but a contraction of *it is* or *it has. Its* is the possessive form of the pronoun *it: The city government agency has produced its final report. It's available upon request.* See also 46f.

kind, sort, type   In the singular, use each of these nouns with *this* and a singular noun: *this type of book.* Use in the plural with *these* and a plural noun: *these kinds of books.*

kind of, sort of   Do not use these to mean "somewhat" or "a little." *The pace of the baseball game was somewhat* [not *kind of*] *slow.*

knew, new   *Knew* is the past tense of the verb *know. New* is an adjective meaning "not old": *He knew that the book was new.*

lend, loan   *Lend* is a verb, and *loan* is ordinarily used as a noun: *Our cousins offered to lend us some money, but we refused the loan.*

less   See *fewer.*

lie, lay   Be sure not to confuse these verbs. *Lie* does not take a direct object; *lay* does. See 39b.

like, as, as if   In formal usage, *as* and *as if* are subordinating conjunctions and introduce dependent clauses: *She walks as her father does. She looks as if she could win the contest. Like* is a preposition and is followed by a noun or pronoun, not by a clause: *She looks like her father.* In speech, however, and increasingly in writing, *like* is often used where formal usage dictates *as* or *as if: She walks like her father does. He looks like he needs a new suit.* Know your audience's expectations.

likely, liable   *Likely* means "probably going to," while *liable* means "at risk of" and is generally used to describe something negative: *Eddie plays the guitar so well he's likely to start a band. If he keeps playing that way, he's liable to break a string. Liable* also means "responsible": *The guitar manufacturer cannot be held liable.*

literally   Avoid overuse: *literally* is an adverb meaning "actually" or "word for word" and should not be used in conjunction with figurative expressions such as *my jaw literally hit the floor* or *he was literally bouncing off the walls. Literally* should be used only when the words describe exactly what is happening: *He was so scared his face literally went white.*

loan   See *lend*.

loose, lose   *Loose* is an adjective meaning "not tight": *This jacket is comfortable because it is so loose. Lose* is a verb (the past tense form and past participle are *lost*): *Many people lose their jobs in a recession.*

lots of   See *alot*.

man, mankind   Avoid using these terms, as they are gender specific. Instead, use *people, human beings, humankind, humanity,* or *men and women.*

marital, martial   *Marital* is associated with marriage, *martial* with war: *Their marital relationship was sometimes martial.*

may be, maybe   *May be* consists of a modal verb followed by the base form of the verb *be; maybe* is an adverb meaning "perhaps." If you can replace the expression with *perhaps,* make it one word: *They may be there already, or maybe they got caught in traffic.*

me, I   See *I*.

media, medium   *Media* is the plural form of *medium: Television and radio are both useful communication media, but his favorite medium is the written word.*

most   See *almost*.

myself   Use only as a reflexive pronoun (*I told them myself*) or as an intensive pronoun (*I myself told them*). Do not use *myself* as a subject pronoun: not *My sister and myself won,* but *My sister and I won.*

no, not   *No* modifies a noun: *The author has no intention of deceiving the reader. Not* modifies a verb, adjective, or adverb: *She is not wealthy. He does not intend to deceive.*

nonflammable   See *flammable*.

nowadays   All one word. Be sure to include the final *-s.*

nowhere, nowheres   See *anyway*.

number   See *amount*.

off, off of   Use only *off,* not *off of: She drove the car off* [not *off of*] *the road.*

oftentimes   Do not use. Prefer *often.*

OK, O.K., okay   Reserve these forms for informal speech and writing. Choose another word in a formal context: not *Her performance was OK,* but *Her performance was satisfactory.*

one another   See *each other.*

owing to the fact that   See *due to the fact that.*

passed, past   *Passed* is a past tense verb form: *They passed the deli on the way to work. He passed his exam. Past* can be a noun (*in the past*), an adjective (*in past years*), or a preposition (*She walked past the bakery*).

peak, peek, pique   *Peak* is the top of a summit: *She has reached the peak of her performance. Peek* (noun or verb) means "glance": *A peek through the window is enough. Pique* (also a noun or a verb) has to do with being indignant: *Feeling insulted, he stormed out in a fit of pique.*

personal, personnel   *Personal* is an adjective meaning "individual," while *personnel* is a noun referring to employees or staff: *It is my personal belief that a company's personnel should be treated like family.*

phenomena, phenomenon   *Phenomena* is the plural form of the noun *phenomenon: Outer space is full of celestial phenomena, one spectacular phenomenon being the Milky Way.*

plus   Do not use *plus* as a coordinating conjunction or a transitional expression. Use *and* or *moreover* instead: *He was promoted, and* [not *plus*] *he received a bonus.* Use *plus* as a preposition meaning "in addition to": *His salary plus his dividends placed him in a high tax bracket.*

pore, pour   To *pore* is to read carefully or to ponder: *I saw him poring over the want ads before he poured himself a drink.*

precede, proceed   *Precede* means "to go or occur before": *The Roaring Twenties preceded the Great Depression. Proceed* means "to go ahead": *After you pay the fee, proceed to the examination room.*

prejudice, prejudiced   *Prejudice* can be a noun (*Prejudice is harmful to society*) or a verb, with *prejudiced* as its past participle: *He is prejudiced against ethnic minorities.*

pretty   Avoid using *pretty* as an intensifying adverb. Use *really, very, rather,* or *quite: The stew tastes very* [not *pretty*] *good.*

principal, principle   *Principal* is a noun (*the principal of a school*) or an adjective meaning "main" or "most important": *His principal motive was monetary gain. Principle* is a noun meaning "standard or rule": *He always acts on his principles.*

quite, quiet   Do not confuse the adverb *quite,* meaning "very," with the adjective *quiet* ("still" or "silent"): *We were all quite relieved when the audience became quiet.*

quote, quotation   *Quote* is a verb. Do not use it as a noun; use *quotation: The quotation* [not *quote*] *from Walker tells the reader a great deal.*

real, really   *Real* is an adjective; *really* is an adverb. Do not use *real* as an intensifying adverb: *She acted really* [not *real*] *well.*

reason is because   Avoid *the reason is because.* Instead, use *the reason is that* or rewrite the sentence. See 38f.

regardless   Use this to mean "in spite" or "anyway": *They finished the game regardless of the weather. It rained, but they finished the game regardless.* See also the nonstandard *irregardless.*

respectable, respectful, respective   *Respectable* means "presentable, worthy of respect": *Wear some respectable shoes to your interview. Respectful* means "polite or deferential": *Parents want their children to be respectful to adults. Respective* means "particular" or "individual": *The friends of the bride and the groom sat in their respective seats in the church.*

respectfully, respectively   *Respectfully* means "showing respect": *He bowed respectfully when the queen entered. Respectively* refers to items in a list and means "in the order mentioned": *Horses and birds gallop and fly, respectively.*

rise, raise   *Rise* is an intransitive verb: *She rises early every day. Raise* is a transitive verb: *We raised alfalfa last summer.* See 39b.

sale, sell   *Sale* is a noun: *The sale of the house has been postponed. Sell* is a verb: *They are still trying to sell their house.*

should (could, might) of   Nonstandard; instead use *should have: You should have paid.* See 39c.

since   Use this subordinating conjunction only when time or reason is clear: *Since you insist on helping, I'll let you paint this bookcase.* Unclear: *Since he got a new job, he has been happy. Since* here may refer to time or to reason (*because*).

site, sight   See *cite.*

sometimes, sometime, some time   The adverb *sometimes* means "occasionally": *He sometimes prefers to eat lunch at his desk.* The adverb *sometime* means "at an indefinite time": *I read that book sometime last year.* The noun phrase *some time* consists of the noun *time* modified by the quantity word *some: After working for Honda, I spent some time in Brazil.*

sort, type   See *kind.*

sort of   See *kind of.*

stationary, stationery   *Stationary* is an adjective meaning "not moving" (*a stationary vehicle*); *stationery* is a noun referring to writing paper.

supposedly   Use this, not *supposably*: *She is supposedly a great athlete.*

taught, thought   Do not confuse these verb forms. *Taught* is the past tense and past participle form of *teach*; *thought* is the past tense and past participle form of *think*: *The students thought that their professor had not taught essay organization.*

than, then   *Then* is a time word; *than* must be preceded by a comparative form: *bigger than, more interesting than.*

their, there, they're   *Their* is a pronoun indicating possession; *there* indicates place or is used as a filler in the subject position in a sentence; *they're* is the contracted form of *they are*: *They're over there, guarding their luggage.*

theirself, theirselves, themself   Nonstandard; instead, use *themselves.*

threat, treat   A *threat* is a "possible danger": *The threat of an earthquake was alarming.* A *treat* is a "source of pleasure": *She gave the children some cookies as a treat.*

thusly   Incorrect form of *thus.*

to, too, two   Do not confuse these words. *To* is a sign of the infinitive and a common preposition; *too* is an adverb meaning *also*; *two* is the number: *She is too smart to agree to report to two bosses.*

undoubtedly   This is the correct word, not *undoubtably.*

uninterested   See *disinterested.*

unique   The adjective *unique* means "the only one of its kind" and therefore should not be used with qualifying adjectives like *very* or *most*: *His recipe for chowder is unique* [not *most unique* or *quite unique*]. See 43h.

used to, get (become) used to   These expressions share the common form *used to*. But the first, expressing a past habit that no longer exists, is followed by the base form of a verb: *He used to wear his hair long.* (Note that after *not*, the form is *use to*: *He did not use to have a beard.*) In the expression *get (become) used to, used to* means "accustomed to" and is followed by a noun or an *-ing* verb form: *She couldn't get used to driving on the left when she was in England.* See also 62h.

way, ways   Use *way* to mean "distance": *He has a way to go. Ways* in this context is nonstandard.

wear, were, we're   *Wear* is a verb meaning "to have on as covering adornment or protection" (*wearing a helmet*); *were* is a past tense form of *be*; *we're* is a contraction for *we are.*

weather, whether   *Weather* is a noun; *whether* is a conjunction: *The weather will determine whether we go on the picnic.*

whose, who's   *Whose* is a possessive pronoun: *Whose goal was that? Who's* is a contraction of *who is* or *who has: Who's the player whose pass was caught? Who's got the ball?*

your, you're   *Your* is a pronoun used to show possession. *You're* is a contraction for *you are: You're wearing your new shoes today, aren't you?*

64 Glossary of Grammatical Terms

absolute phrase   A phrase consisting of a noun phrase followed by a verbal or a prepositional phrase and modifying an entire sentence: *Flags flapping in the wind,* the stadium looked bleak. 45i.

acronym   A pronounceable word formed from the initials of an abbreviation: *NATO, MADD, NOW.* 49a.

active voice   The attribute of a verb when its grammatical subject performs the action: The dog *ate* the cake. See also 40a on the passive voice.

adjective   The part of speech that modifies a noun or pronoun: She wears *flamboyant* clothes. His cap is *orange.* 35d, 43a, 60g. See also *comparative; coordinate adjective; cumulative adjective; superlative; parts of speech.*

adjective clause   A dependent clause beginning with a relative pronoun (*who, whom, whose, which,* or *that*) and modifying a noun or pronoun: The writer *who won the prize* was elated. Also called a *relative clause.* 35d, 44a.

adverb   The part of speech that modifies a verb, an adjective, another adverb, or a clause: She ran *quickly.* He will *inevitably* become a success. The children were *well* liked. Many adverbs end in *-ly.* 35d, 43a, 43b. See also *comparative; conjunctive adverb; frequency adverb; parts of speech; superlative.*

adverbial clause   A dependent clause that modifies a verb, an adjective, or an adverb and begins with a subordinating conjunction: He left early *because he was tired.* 35d.

agent The person or thing doing the action described by a verb: *His sister* won the marathon. The marathon was won by *his sister.* 40b.

agreement The grammatical match in person, number, and gender between a verb and its subject or between a pronoun and its antecedent (the word the pronoun refers to): The *benefits continue; they are* pleasing. The *benefit continues; it is* pleasing. 41a, 42d.

antecedent The noun that a pronoun refers to: My son who lives nearby found a *kitten. It* was black and white. 42c, 42d, 44a.

appositive phrase A phrase occurring next to a noun and used to describe it: His father, *a factory worker,* is running for office. 45d.

article *A, an* (indefinite articles), or *the* (definite article). Also called a *determiner.* 58c–58e.

auxiliary verb A verb that joins with another verb to form a complete verb. Auxiliary verbs are forms of *do, be,* and *have,* as well as the modal auxiliary verbs. 35d, 39c. See also *modal auxiliary verb.*

base form The dictionary form of a verb, used in an infinitive after *to: see, eat, go, be.* 39, 39a.

clause A group of words that includes a subject and a verb. 35d. See also *dependent clause; independent clause.*

cliché An overused, predictable expression: *as cool as a cucumber.* 32g.

collective noun A noun naming a collection of people or things that are regarded as a unit: *team, jury, family.* For agreement with collective nouns, see 41f, 42d.

comma splice The error that results when two independent clauses are incorrectly joined with only a comma. 37a–37c.

common noun A noun that does not name a unique person, place, or thing. 58a, 58b. See also *proper noun.*

comparative The form of an adjective or adverb used to compare two people or things: *bigger, more interesting.* 43h. See also *superlative.*

complement A *subject complement* is a word or group of words used after a linking verb to refer to and describe the subject: Harry looks *happy.* An *object complement* is a word or group of words used after a direct object to complete its meaning: They call him a *liar.* 35d, 41c.

complete verb A verb that shows tense. Some verb forms, such as *-ing* (present) participles and past participles, require auxiliary verbs to make them complete verbs. *Going* and *seen* are not complete verbs; *are going* and *has been seen* are complete. 36a, 39c.

complex sentence   A sentence that has one independent clause and one or more dependent clauses: *He wept when he won the marathon.* 31d.

compound adjective   An adjective formed of two or more words often connected with hyphens: a *well-constructed* house. 43d, 54b.

compound-complex sentence   A sentence that has at least two independent clauses and one or more dependent clauses: *She works in Los Angeles, but her husband works in San Diego, where they both live.* 31d.

compound noun   A noun formed of two or more words: *toothbrush, merry-go-round.* 54b.

compound predicate   A predicate consisting of two or more verbs and their objects, complements, and modifiers: He *whistles and sings in the morning.* 36d, 38h.

compound sentence   A sentence that has two or more independent clauses: *She works in Los Angeles, but her husband works in San Diego.* 31d.

compound subject   A subject consisting of two or more nouns or pronouns and their modifiers: *My uncle and my aunt* are leaving soon. 41g, 42a.

conditional clause   A clause introduced by *if* or *unless,* expressing conditions of fact, prediction, or speculation: *If we earned more,* we would spend more. 39j.

conjunction   The part of speech used to link words, phrases, or clauses. 35d, 36c. See also *coordinating conjunction; correlative conjunctions; parts of speech; subordinating conjunction.*

conjunctive adverb   A transitional expression used to link two independent clauses. Some common conjunctive adverbs are *moreover, however,* and *furthermore.* 2f, 35d.

connotation   The meanings and associations suggested by a word, as distinct from the word's denotation, or dictionary meaning. 32c.

contraction   The shortened form that results when an apostrophe replaces one or more letters: *can't* (for *cannot*), *he's* (for *he is* or *he has*), *they're* (for *they are*). 46d.

coordinate adjective   An evaluative adjective modifying a noun. When coordinate adjectives appear in a series, their order can be reversed, and they can be separated by *and.* Commas are used between coordinate adjectives: the *comfortable, expensive car.* 45g.

coordinating conjunction   The seven coordinating conjunctions are *and, but, or, nor, so, for,* and *yet.* They connect sentence elements that are parallel in structure: He couldn't call, *but* he sent an e-mail. 30b, 35d, 45b.

coordination   The connection of two or more ideas to give each one equal emphasis: *Sue worked after school, so she didn't have time to jog.* 30b.

correlative conjunctions   A pair of conjunctions joining equivalent elements. The most common correlative conjunctions are *either . . . or, neither . . . nor, both . . . and,* and *not only . . . but also: Neither* my sister *nor* I could find the concert hall. 38j.

countable noun   A common noun that has a plural form and can be used after a plural quantity word (such as *many* or *three*): one *book,* three *stores,* many *children.* 58a, 58e.

cumulative adjective   An adjective that modifies a noun and occurs in a conventional order with no comma between adjectives: a *new red plastic* bench. 60g.

cumulative sentence   A sentence that adds elements after the independent clause. 31d.

dangling modifier   A modifier that fails to modify the noun or pronoun it is intended to modify: not *Turning the corner,* the lights went out, but *Turning the corner, we* saw the lights go out. 38c.

demonstrative pronoun   The four demonstrative pronouns are *this, that, these,* and *those: That* is my glass. 41j.

denotation   A word's dictionary meaning. See also *connotation.* 32b, 32c.

dependent clause   A clause that cannot stand alone as a complete sentence and needs to be attached to an independent clause. A dependent clause begins with a subordinating word such as *because, if, when, although, who, which,* or *that: When it rains,* we can't take the children outside. 35d, 36c.

diction   The choice of appropriate words and tone. 32a–32g.

direct object   The person or thing that receives the action of a verb: They ate *cake* and *ice cream.* 35d, 60c.

direct quotation   A person's words reproduced exactly and placed in quotation marks: *"I won't be home until noon,"* she said. 10c, 38d, 60d.

double negative   The use of two negative words in the same sentence: He does *not* know *nothing.* This usage is nonstandard and needs to be avoided: *He does not know anything. He knows nothing.* 43g.

Edited American English   The variety of English to use in formal academic writing. 35c, 57a.

ellipsis   The omission of words from a quotation, indicated by three dots: "I pledge allegiance to the flag…and to the republic for which it stands…" 49g.

etymology   The origin of a word. 32b.

euphemism   A word or phrase used to disguise literal meaning: She *is in the family way* [meaning "pregnant"]. 32g.

faulty predication   The error that results when subject and verb do not match logically: not The *decrease* in stolen cars *has diminished* in the past year, but The *number* of stolen cars *has decreased* in the past year. 38e.

figurative language   The use of unusual comparisons or other devices to draw attention to a specific meaning. See *metaphor; simile.* 5e, 32e.

filler subject   *It* or *there* used in the subject position of a clause, followed by a form of *be: There are* two elm trees on the corner. 29b, 41d, 62f.

first person   The person speaking or writing: *I* or *we.* 42a.

fragment   A group of words that is punctuated as if it were a sentence but is grammatically incomplete because it lacks a subject or a predicate or begins with a subordinating word: *Because it was a sunny day.* 36a–36e.

frequency adverb   An adverb that expresses time (such as *often, always,* or *sometimes*). It can be the first word in a sentence or placed between the subject and the main verb, after an auxiliary verb, or as the last word in a sentence. 43e.

fused sentence   See *run-on sentence.*

gender   The classification of a noun or pronoun as masculine (*Uncle John, he*), feminine (*Ms. Torez, she*), or neuter (*book, it*). 42e, 62g.

generic noun   A noun referring to a general class or type of person or object: A *student* has to write many papers. 42d.

gerund   The *-ing* verb form used as a noun: *Walking* is good for your health. 41e, 59d, 59e, 61e. See also *verbal.*

helping verb   See *auxiliary verb.*

imperative mood   The verb mood used to give a command: *Follow* me. 31d.

indefinite pronoun　A pronoun that refers to a nonspecific person or thing: *anybody, something.* 41h, 42d.

independent clause　A clause that has a subject and predicate and is not introduced by a subordinating word. An independent clause can function as a complete sentence. *Birds sing. The old man was singing a song.* Hailing a cab, *the woman used a silver whistle.* 30b, 35d.

indicative mood　The verb mood used to ask questions or make statements. It is the most common mood, used for declarative statements and questions. See also *subjunctive mood.*

indirect object　The person or thing to whom or to which, or for whom or for which, an action is performed. It comes between the verb and the direct object: He gave his *sister* some flowers. 35d, 60c.

indirect question　A question reported by a speaker or writer, not enclosed in quotation marks: They asked *if we would help them.* 60d.

indirect quotation　A description or paraphrase of the words of another speaker or writer, integrated into a writer's own sentence and not enclosed in quotation marks: He said *that they were making money.* 38d, 60d.

infinitive　The base form, or dictionary form, of a verb, preceded by *to: to see, to smile.* 39a, 59c, 59e.

infinitive phrase　An infinitive with its objects, complements, or modifiers: *To wait for hours* is unpleasant. He tries hard *to be punctual.* 36b, 41e.

intensive pronoun　A pronoun ending in *-self* or *-selves* and used to emphasize its antecedent: They *themselves* will not attend. 42h.

interjection　The part of speech that expresses emotion and is able to stand alone: *Aha! Wow!* Interjections are seldom appropriate in academic writing. 35d.

interrogative pronoun　A pronoun that introduces a direct or indirect question: *Who* is that? I don't know *what* you want. 42i.

intransitive verb　A verb that does not take a direct object: Exciting events *have occurred.* He *fell.* 35d, 40b. See also *transitive verb.*

inverted word order　The presence of the verb before the subject in a sentence; used in questions or for emphasis: *Do you expect* an award? Not only *does she do* gymnastics, she also wins awards. 29b, 41d.

irregular verb　A verb that does not form its past tense and past participle with *-ed: sing, sang, sung; grow, grew, grown.* 39a.

linking verb A verb connecting a subject to its complement. Typical linking verbs are *be, become, seem,* and *appear:* He *seems* angry. A linking verb is intransitive; it does not take a direct object. 35d, 39c, 42a, 43c.

mental activity verb A verb not used in a tense showing progressive aspect: *prefer, want, understand:* not He *is wanting to leave,* but He *wants* to leave. 39d.

metaphor A figure of speech implying a comparison but not stating it directly: a *gale* of laughter. 5e, 32e.

misplaced modifier An adverb (particularly *only* and *even*) or a descriptive phrase or clause positioned in such a way that it modifies the wrong word or words: She showed the ring to her sister *that her aunt gave her.* 38b.

mixed construction A sentence with two or more types of structures that clash grammatically: *By doing* her homework at the last minute *caused* Meg to make many mistakes. 38a, 38e, 38f.

modal auxiliary verb The nine modal auxiliaries are *will, would, can, could, shall, should, may, might,* and *must.* They are followed by the base form of a verb: *will go, would believe.* Modal auxiliaries do not change form. 39c, 59b.

modifier A word or words that describe another noun, adverb, verb, phrase, or clause: He is a *happy* man. He is smiling *happily.* 43a–43e.

mood The mood of a verb tells whether the verb states a fact (*indicative:* She *goes* to school); gives a command (*imperative: Come* back soon); or expresses a condition, wish, or request (*subjunctive:* I wish you *were* not leaving). 39j. See also *imperative mood; indicative mood; subjunctive mood.*

nonrestrictive phrase or clause A phrase or clause that adds extra or nonessential information to a sentence and is set off with commas: His report, *which he gave to his boss yesterday,* received enthusiastic praise. 44b, 45d.

noun The part of speech that names a person, place, thing, or idea. Nouns are proper or common and, if common, countable or uncountable. 35d, 58a, 58b. See also *collective noun; common noun; compound noun; countable noun; generic noun; noun clause; parts of speech; proper noun; uncountable noun.*

noun clause A dependent clause that functions as a noun: I like *what you do. Whoever scores a goal* will be a hero. 35d.

noun phrase A noun with its accompanying modifiers and articles: *a brilliant, hard-working student.* 35d.

number   The indication of a noun or pronoun as singular (one person, place, thing, or idea) or plural (more than one). 41a, 42d.

object of preposition   The noun or pronoun (along with its modifiers) that follows a preposition: on *the beach.* 35d.

paragraph   A group of sentences set off in a text, usually on one topic. 2e, 2g.

parallelism   The use of coordinate structures that have the same grammatical form: She likes *swimming* and *playing* tennis. 38j.

participle phrase   A phrase beginning with an *-ing* verb form or a past participle: The woman *wearing a green skirt* is my sister. *Baffled by the puzzle,* he gave up. 31d. See also *verbal.*

particle   A word (frequently a preposition or adverb) that combines with a verb to form a phrasal verb, a verb with an idiomatic meaning: get *over,* take *after.* 61d.

parts of speech   Eight traditional categories of words used to form sentences: noun, pronoun, verb, adjective, adverb, conjunction, preposition, and interjection. See 35d and the entry for each in this glossary.

passive voice   The attribute of a verb when its grammatical subject is the receiver of the action that the verb describes: The book *was written* by my professor. 29c, 40a–40d. See also *active voice.*

past participle   A verb form that in regular verbs ends with *-ed.* The past participle needs an auxiliary verb to function as the complete verb of a clause: *has chosen, was cleaned, might have been told.* The past participle can function alone as an adjective. 39a, 39c, 39d, 39g, 59f.

perfect progressive tense forms   The verb tenses that show actions in progress up to a specific point in present, past, or future time. For active voice verbs, use forms of the auxiliary *have been* followed by the *-ing* form of the verb: *has/have been living, had been living, will have been living.* 39d.

perfect tense forms   The verb tenses that show actions completed by present, past, or future time. For active voice verbs, use forms of the auxiliary *have* followed by the past participle of the verb: *has/have arrived, had arrived, will have arrived.* 39d.

periodic sentence   A sentence that uses words and phrases to build up to the independent clause. 31d.

person   The form of a pronoun or verb that indicates whether the subject is doing the speaking (first person, *I* or *we*), is spoken to (second person, *you*), or is spoken about (third person, *he, she, it,* or *they*). 41a, 42a.

phrasal verb   An idiomatic verb phrase consisting of a verb and a preposition or adverb called a *particle: put off, put on.* 61d.

phrase   A group of words that lacks a subject or predicate and functions as a noun, verb, adjective, or adverb: *under the tree, has been singing, amazingly simple.* 35d. See also *absolute phrase; appositive phrase; infinitive phrase; participle phrase; prepositional phrase.*

possessive   The form of a noun or pronoun that indicates ownership. Possessive pronouns include *my, his, her, their, theirs,* and *whose: my* boat, *your* socks. The possessive form of a noun is indicated by an apostrophe or an apostrophe and *-s: Mario's* car, the *children's* nanny, the *birds'* nests. 41j, 42b, 46a, 46b, 46c.

predicate   The part of a sentence that contains the verb and its modifiers and that comments on or makes an assertion about the subject. To be complete, a sentence needs a subject and a predicate. 35d.

prefix   The letters attached to the beginning of a word that change the word's meaning: *un*necessary, *re*organize, *non*stop. 54a.

preposition   The part of speech used with a noun or pronoun in a phrase to indicate time, space, or some other relationship. 35d, 44d, 61a–61e. The noun or pronoun is the object of the preposition: *on the table, after dinner, to her.*

prepositional phrase   A phrase beginning with a preposition and including the object of the preposition and its modifiers: The head *of the electronics company* was waiting *for an hour.* 31d, 35d, 44d.

present participle   The *-ing* form of a verb, showing an action as being in progress or continuous: They are *sleeping.* Without an auxiliary, the *-ing* form cannot function as a complete verb but can be used as an adjective: *searing* heat. When the *-ing* form is used as a noun, it is called a *gerund: Skiing* can be dangerous. 39a, 41e, 59d, 59f. See also *verbal.*

progressive tense forms   The verb tenses that show actions in progress at a point or over a period of time in past, present, or future time. They use a form of *be* + the *-ing* form of the verb: They *are working;* he *will be writing.* 39d–39f.

pronoun   The part of speech that takes the place of a noun, a noun phrase, or another pronoun. 35d, 41h, 42a, 42b. See *parts of speech.*

pronoun reference   The connection between a pronoun and its antecedent. Reference should be clear and unambiguous: Mr. Estern picked up *his* hat and left. 42c.

proper noun   The capitalized name of a specific person, place, or thing: *Golden Gate Park, University of Kansas.* 35d, 51b, 58f. See also *common noun.*

quantity word   A word expressing the idea of quantity, such as *each, every, several, many,* and *much.* Subject-verb agreement is tricky with quantity words: *Each* of the students *has* a different assignment. 41i. See also *agreement.*

reflexive pronoun   A pronoun ending in *-self* or *-selves* and referring to the subject of a clause: They incriminated *themselves.* 42h.

regular verb   A verb that ends with *-ed* in its past tense and past participle forms. 39a.

relative clause   See *adjective clause.*

relative pronoun   A pronoun that introduces a relative clause: *who, whom, whose, which, that.* 44a.

restrictive phrase or clause   A phrase or clause that provides information essential for identifying the word or phrase it modifies. A restrictive phrase or clause is not set off with commas: The book *that is first on the bestseller list* is a memoir. 44b, 45d.

run-on sentence   The error that results when two independent clauses are not separated by a conjunction or by any punctuation: not *The dog ate the meat the cat ate the fish,* but *The dog ate the meat; the cat ate the fish.* Also called a *fused sentence.* 37a–37c.

second person   The person addressed: *you.* 42a, 42g.

shifts   The inappropriate switches in grammatical structure such as from one tense to another or from statement to command or from indirect to direct quotation: not *Joan asked whether I was warm enough and did I sleep well,* but *Joan asked whether I was warm enough and had slept well.* 38d, 39h.

simile   A figure of speech that makes a direct comparison: She has a laugh *like a fire siren.* 5e, 32e.

simple tense forms   The verb tenses that show present, past, or future time with no perfect or progressive aspects: they *work,* we *worked,* she *will work.* 39d–39g.

split infinitive   An infinitive with a word or words separating *to* from the base verb form: *to successfully complete.* This structure has become acceptable. 38b.

Standard English "The variety of English that is generally acknowledged as the model for the speech and writing of educated speakers." This *American Heritage Dictionary,* 4th edition, definition warns that the use of the term is "highly elastic and variable" and confers no "absolute positive evaluation." 32d, 35c, 57a. See also *Edited American English.*

subject The noun or pronoun that performs the action of the verb in an active voice sentence or receives the action of the verb in a passive voice sentence. To be complete, a sentence needs a subject and a verb. 35d, 36d, 38i, 60a.

subjunctive mood The verb mood used in conditions and in wishes, requests, and demands: I wish he *were* here. She demanded that he *be* present. 39j.

subordinate clause See *dependent clause.*

subordinating conjunction A conjunction used to introduce a dependent adverb clause: *because, if, when, although, since, while.* 30b, 35d, 36c.

suffix The letters attached to the end of a word that change the word's function or meaning: gentle*ness,* humor*ist,* slow*er,* sing*ing.* 56e.

superlative The form of an adjective or adverb used to compare three or more people or things: *biggest; most unusual; least effectively.* 43h, 58d. See also *comparative.*

synonym A word that has the same or nearly the same meaning as another word.

tense The form of a verb that indicates time. Verbs change form to distinguish present and past time: he *goes;* he *went.* Various structures are used to express future time, mainly *will* + the base form, or *going to* + the base form. 39d. See also *perfect progressive tense forms; perfect tense forms; progressive tense forms; simple tense forms.*

third person The person or thing spoken about: *he, she, it, they,* or nouns. 41a, 42a.

topic chain The repetition of key words or related words throughout a passage to aid cohesion. 30a, 40c.

transitional expression A word or phrase used to connect two independent clauses, such as *for example, however,* and *similarly.* 2f, 45e, 48a.

transitive verb A verb that takes an object—the person or thing that receives the action (in the active voice): Dogs *chase* cats. When transitive verbs are used in the passive voice, the subject receives the action of the verb: Cats *are chased* by dogs. 35d, 39b, 40b. See also *intransitive verb.*

uncountable noun   A common noun that cannot follow a plural quantity word (such as *several* or *many*) is never used with *a* or *an,* is used with a singular third person verb, and has no plural form: *furniture, happiness, information.* 41e, 58b.

verb   The part of speech that expresses action or being and tells (in the active voice) what the subject of the clause is or does. The complete verb in a clause might require auxiliary or modal auxiliary verbs to complete its meaning. 35d, 39a–39j, 59a–59f.

verbal   A form, derived from a verb, that cannot function as the main verb of a clause. The three types of verbals are the infinitive, the *-ing* participle, and the past participle (for example, *to try, singing, stolen*). A verbal can function in a phrase as a noun, adjective, or adverb. 59c–59f, 61e.

verb chain   The combination of an auxiliary verb, a main verb, and verbals: She *might have promised to leave;* they *should deny having helped* him. 59a–59e.

verb phrase   A complete verb formed by auxiliaries and the main verb: *should have waited.* 35d.

voice   The transitive verbs (verbs that take an object) can be used in the active voice (*He is painting the door*) or the passive voice (*The door is being painted*). 40a, 40b.

zero article   The lack of an article (*a, an,* or *the*) before a noun. Uncountable nouns are used with the zero article when they make no specific reference. 58b, 58d, 58e.

Index

Note: An asterisk (*) refers to a page number in the Glossary of Grammatical Terms.

Documentation

Grammar and Punctuation

For Multilingual Writers

Design and Media

Common Editing and Proofreading Marks

SYMBOL	EXAMPLE (CHANGE MARKED)	EXAMPLE (CHANGE MADE)
⌒○	Correct a typu.	Correct a typo.
⌒r⌒/m⌒/⌒○	Corriect more than one typu.	Correct more than one typo.
⌵	Insert a leter.	Insert a letter.
or words	Insert a word.	Insert a word or words.
⌿	Make a a deletion.	Make a deletion.
⌿	Delelte and close up space.	Delete and close up space.
⌒	Close up ex tra space.	Close up extra space.
#	Insertproper spacing.	Insert proper spacing.
#/⌒	Inserts pace and close up.	Insert space and close up.
tr	Transpose letters inidcated.	Transpose letters indicated.
tr	Transpose as words indicated.	Transpose words as indicated.
tr	Reorder shown as words several.	Reorder several words as shown.
⊏	⊏ Move text to left.	Move text to left.
⊐	⊐ Move text to right.	Move text to right.
⁋	Indent for paragraph.	Indent for paragraph.
no ⁋	No paragraph indent.	No paragraph indent.
run in	Run back turnover lines.	Run back turnover lines.
⌐	Break line when it runs far too long.	Break line when it runs far too long.
⊙	Insert period here.	Insert period here.
⌃	Commas commas everywhere.	Commas, commas everywhere.
⌄	Its in need of an apostrophe.	It's in need of an apostrophe.
⌄/⌄	Add quotation marks he begged.	"Add quotation marks," he begged.
;	Add a semicolon don't hesitate.	Add a semicolon; don't hesitate.
:	She advised "You need a colon."	She advised: "You need a colon."
?	How about a question mark	How about a question mark?
⌐=⌐	Add a hyphen to a bill like receipt.	Add a hyphen to a bill-like receipt.
⟨/⟩	Add parentheses as they say.	Add parentheses (as they say).
lc	Sometimes you want Lowercase.	Sometimes you want lowercase.
caps	Sometimes you want upperCASE.	Sometimes you want UPPERCASE.
ital	Add italics instantly.	Add italics *instantly*.
rom	But use *roman* in the main.	But use roman in the main.
bf	Add boldface if necessary.	Add **boldface** if necessary.
sp	Spell out all 3 terms.	Spell out all three terms.
stet	Let stand as is.	Let stand as is. (This retracts a change already marked.)

...nbers refer to chapters and sections in the book.